"David Peterson has composed a great volume on Romans that is both a terrific survey of its themes and an able commentary on its text. Careful, learned, and judicious."

Michael F. Bird, *lecturer in Theology, Ridley College, Melbourne*

"It is a pleasure to commend this fine commentary on the apostle Paul's letter to the Romans. Among the plethora of commentaries on this letter, Peterson's stands out with its blend of carefully nuanced exegesis, overarching biblical theology, sensible interaction with contemporary scholarship, and pleasing concision and clarity. Highly recommended."

Constantine Campbell, *associate professor of New Testament, Trinity International University*

"The last few years have seen an explosion in technical commentaries on Romans appearing on the market. A capable translator of the ancient text, David Peterson has also translated the best of those discussions and placed them into a single, accessible volume for pastors and students of Scripture. This is the first book they will reach for on Romans."

A. Andrew Das, *professor of Religious Studies, Elmhurst College*

"A career of research involving both fine-grained New Testament exegesis and biblical-theological integration makes David Peterson an ideal person to write this exposition of Romans. The verse-by-verse commentary is brimming with insightful exegesis, and the elucidation of the biblical-theological themes of Romans contains a careful and powerful articulation of the gospel. I think Paul would like this commentary!"

Simon Gathercole, *reader in New Testament, University of Cambridge; fellow and director of studies in Theology, Fitzwilliam College*

"David Peterson has written a concise but thorough commentary on Paul's most important letter. He interacts with the biblical text, biblical theology, and biblical scholarship on Romans and so adds a significant volume to the Biblical Theology for Christian Proclamation series. In keeping with the goal of that series, Peterson's work is based on an analysis of the Greek text but is still accessible to individuals who are actively engaged in ministries of preaching and teaching Scripture. They should find this volume a helpful addition to their libraries."

John D. Harvey, *dean and professor of New Testament, Columbia Biblical Seminary of Columbia International University*

"In the Bible, as one pundit put it, all roads lead to Romans. Indeed no book in the New Testament has more connections with the Old Testament than Romans. Understanding those connections, reading Romans in the light of the storyline of the whole Bible is vital both for accurate interpretation and responsible preaching of the book. David Peterson's commentary does an outstanding job of equipping preachers of the letter to do just that. Highly recommended."

Brian Rosner, *principal, Ridley College, Melbourne*

"David Peterson's contribution to this important new series of commentaries is both impressive in its scholarship and admirable in its accessibility. David's long immersion in this magnificent epistle gives strength and maturity to his judgments and repeatedly yields fresh insights, while his pastoral heart has ensured that the significance of Paul's message for Christians, the church, and the world is made abundantly clear. Placing Romans firmly in its biblical theological framework is richly rewarding. Scholars and preachers alike will benefit from this commentary."

Mark D Thompson, *principal, Moore Theological College, Sydney*

BIBLICAL THEOLOGY FOR CHRISTIAN PROCLAMATION

COMMENTARY ON

ROMANS

GENERAL EDITORS: T. DESMOND ALEXANDER, ANDREAS J. KÖSTENBERGER, AND THOMAS R. SCHREINER

BIBLICAL THEOLOGY FOR CHRISTIAN PROCLAMATION

COMMENTARY ON ROMANS

DAVID G. PETERSON

NASHVILLE, TENNESSEE

Published by B&H Publishing Group
Nashville, Tennessee

ISBN: 978–0–8054–9622–2

Dewey Decimal Classification: 227.1

Subject Heading: BIBLE. N.T. ROMANS \ THEOLOGY \ CHRISTIANITY

Printed in the United States of America
21 20 19 18 17 • 8 7 6 5 4 3 2 1
BP

Contents

General Editors' Preface

In recent years biblical theology has seen a remarkable resurgence. Whereas, in 1970, Brevard Childs wrote *Biblical Theology in Crisis*, the quest for the Bible's own theology has witnessed increasing vitality since Childs prematurely decried the demise of the movement. Nowhere has this been truer than in evangelical circles. It could be argued that evangelicals, with their commitment to biblical inerrancy and inspiration, are perfectly positioned to explore the Bible's unified message. At the same time, as D. A. Carson has aptly noted, perhaps the greatest challenge faced by biblical theologians is how to handle the Bible's manifest diversity and how to navigate the tension between its unity and diversity in a way that does justice to both.[1]

What is biblical theology? And how is biblical theology different from related disciplines such as systematic theology? These two exceedingly important questions must be answered by anyone who would make a significant contribution to the discipline. Regarding the first question, the most basic answer might assert that biblical theology, in essence, is *the theology of the Bible*, that is, the theology expressed by the respective writers of the various biblical books *on their own terms* and *in their own historical contexts*. Biblical theology is the attempt to understand and embrace *the interpretive perspective of the biblical authors*. What is more, biblical theology is the theology of the *entire* Bible, an exercise in *whole-Bible theology*. For this reason biblical theology is not just a modern academic discipline; its roots are found already in the use of earlier Old

[1] D. A. Carson, "New Testament Theology," in *DLNT* 810.

Testament portions in later Old Testament writings and in the use of the Old Testament in the New.

Biblical theology thus involves a close study of *the use of the Old Testament in the Old Testament* (that is, the use of, say, Deuteronomy by Jeremiah, or of the Pentateuch by Isaiah). Biblical theology also entails the investigation of *the use of the Old Testament in the New*, both in terms of individual passages and in terms of larger Christological or soteriological themes. Biblical theology may proceed *book by book*, trace *central themes* in Scripture, or seek to place the contributions of individual biblical writers within the framework of the Bible's larger overarching *metanarrative*, that is, the Bible's developing story from Genesis through Revelation at whose core is *salvation* or *redemptive history*, the account of God's dealings with humanity and his people Israel and the church from creation to new creation.

In this quest for the Bible's own theology, we will be helped by the inquiries of those who have gone before us in the *history of the church*. While we can profitably study the efforts of interpreters over the entire sweep of the history of biblical interpretation since patristic times, we can also benefit from the labors of scholars since J. P. Gabler, whose programmatic inaugural address at the University of Altdorf, Germany, in 1787 marks the inception of the discipline in modern times. Gabler's address bore the title "On the Correct Distinction between Dogmatic and Biblical Theology and the Right Definition of Their Goals."[2] While few (if any) within evangelicalism would fully identify with Gabler's program, the proper distinction between dogmatic and biblical theology (that is, between biblical and systematic theology) continues to be an important issue to be adjudicated by practitioners of both disciplines, and especially biblical theology. We have already defined biblical theology as whole-Bible theology, describing the theology of the various biblical books *on their own terms* and *in their own historical contexts*. Systematic theology, by contrast, is more topically oriented and focused on contemporary contextualization. While there are different ways in which the relationship between biblical and systematic theology can be construed, maintaining a proper distinction

[2] The original Latin title was *Oratio de iusto discrimine theologiae biblicae et dogmaticae regundisque recte utriusque finibus*.

between the two disciplines arguably continues to be vital if both are to achieve their objectives.

The present set of volumes constitutes an ambitious project, seeking to explore the theology of the Bible in considerable depth, spanning both Testaments. Authors come from a variety of backgrounds and perspectives, though all affirm the inerrancy and inspiration of Scripture. United in their high view of Scripture and in their belief in the underlying unity of Scripture, which is ultimately grounded in the unity of God himself, each author explores the contribution of a given book or group of books to the theology of Scripture as a whole. While conceived as stand-alone volumes, each volume thus also makes a contribution to the larger whole. All volumes provide a discussion of introductory matters, including the historical setting and the literary structure of a given book of Scripture. Also included is an exegetical treatment of all the relevant passages in succinct commentary-style format. The biblical theology approach of the series will also inform and play a role in the commentary proper. The commentator permits a discussion between the commentary proper and the biblical theology it reflects by a series of cross-references.

The major contribution of each volume, however, is a thorough discussion of the most important themes of the biblical book in relation to the canon as a whole. This format allows each contributor to ground biblical theology, as is proper, in an appropriate appraisal of the relevant historical and literary features of a particular book in Scripture while at the same time focusing on its major theological contribution to the entire Christian canon in the context of the larger salvation-historical metanarrative of Scripture. Within this overall format, there will be room for each individual contributor to explore the major themes of his or her particular corpus in the way he or she sees most appropriate for the material under consideration. For some books of the Bible, it may be best to have these theological themes set out in advance of the exegetical commentary. For other books it may be better to explain the theological themes after the commentary. Consequently, each contributor has the freedom to order these sections as best suits the biblical material under consideration so that the discussion of biblical-theological themes may precede or follow the exegetical commentary.

This format, in itself, would already be a valuable contribution to biblical theology. But other series try to accomplish a survey of the Bible's theology as well. What distinguishes the present series is its orientation toward Christian proclamation. This is the Biblical Theology *for Christian Proclamation* commentary series! As a result, the ultimate purpose of this set of volumes is not exclusively, or even primarily, academic. Rather, we seek to relate biblical theology to our own lives and to the life of the church. Our desire is to equip those in Christian ministry who are called by God to preach and teach the precious truths of Scripture to their congregations, both in North America and in a global context.

The base translation for the Biblical Theology for Christian Proclamation commentary series is the Christian Standard Bible (CSB). The CSB places equal value on faithfulness to the original languages and readability for a modern audience. The contributors, however, have the liberty to differ with the CSB as they comment on the biblical text. Note that, in the CSB, OT passages that are quoted in the NT are set in boldface type.

We hope and pray that the forty volumes of this series, once completed, will bear witness to the unity in diversity of the canon of Scripture as they probe the individual contributions of each of its sixty-six books. The authors and editors are united in their desire that in so doing the series will magnify the name of Christ and bring glory to the triune God who revealed himself in Scripture so that everyone who calls on the name of the Lord will be saved—to the glory of God the Father and his Son, the Lord Jesus Christ, under the illumination of the Holy Spirit, and for the good of his church. To God alone be the glory: *soli Deo gloria*.

Dedication

To my wife Lesley,
who has accompanied me
in the writing of this book
with her continuing love, insight, and support

Acknowledgments

It has been an extraordinary privilege and responsibility to write a commentary on Paul's letter to the Romans. I am grateful to the editors of this series for initiating the project and for inviting me to contribute to its outcome. The format they have proposed allows for detailed analysis of the text, theological reflection within the context of the Bible's whole story line, and regular attempts to provide a bridge to contemporary application. I was glad to be able to use the most recent edition of the Christian Standard Bible (CSB) and evaluate it in the light of my study of the Greek text. Technical discussions are mostly confined to the footnotes.

After a lifetime of teaching and preaching from Romans, I have had the opportunity to work again through Paul's most elaborate letter, conversing with a representative range of contemporary commentators and other scholars, moving from Greek exegesis, through theological analysis, to suggestions for exposition. The literature on Romans and the theological issues it addresses are so extensive that no commentator can read and interact with everything involved. Difficult decisions have to be made about what to include and what to exclude. Unfortunately, Richard Longenecker's commentary was not available to be consulted until I had finished my work, though I did benefit from reading his introductory volume. My focus has ultimately been on the text rather than on scholarly debates about the text, and I have spent many hours reflecting on the theological significance and contemporary relevance of Paul's arguments.

Since most of my life has been spent living and working in Australia, this commentary reflects the influence of numerous fellow Australians on my thinking about Paul and the wider issues of biblical theology. Teachers and colleagues have influenced my understanding of current issues in the study of New Testament Greek, discourse analysis, and Pauline theology. In particular, I want to acknowledge my debt to Richard Gibson, whose groundbreaking work with Grant Nichols on the structure of Romans has contributed to the shape of this commentary. I am also thankful to Con Campbell for regular discussions about the significance of particular Greek constructions and to Peter Jensen who read through much of my work and made helpful comments about my argument and conclusions. Tim Escott provided valuable reflections on the Bridge sections. I would also like to thank Chris Cowan for his helpful supervision of the publication process.

List of Abbreviations

General

AB	Anchor Bible
ABR	*Australian Biblical Review*
AGJU	Arbeiten zur Geschichte des antiken Judentums und des Urchristentums
AnBib	Analecta Biblica
BDAG	*A Greek-English Lexicon of the New Testament and Other Early Christian Literature*, ed. Walter Bauer, Frederick W. Danker, William F. Arndt, and F. Wilbur Gingrich, 3rd ed. (Chicago: University of Chicago, 2000)
BDB	*A Hebrew and English Lexicon of the Old Testament*, ed. Francis Brown, S. R. Driver and Charles A. Briggs (Oxford: Clarendon, 1907)
BDF	*A Greek Grammar of the New Testament and Other Early Christian Literature*, ed. F. Blass and A. Debrunner (trans. R. W. Funk; Chicago: University of Chicago, 1961)
BECNT	Baker Exegetical Commentary on the New Testament
BETL	Bibliotheca Ephemeridum Theologicarum Lovaniensium

BJRL	*Bulletin of the John Rylands University Library of Manchester*
BNTC	Black's New Testament Commentaries
BSac	*Bibliotheca Sacra*
BTB	*Biblical Theology Bulletin*
BZNW	Beihefte zur Zeitschrift für die neutestamentliche Wissenschaft
CBET	Contributions to Biblical Exegesis and Theology
CBQ	*Catholic Biblical Quarterly*
CurTM	*Currents in Theology and Mission*
CSB	Christian Standard Bible (2016)
DPL	*Dictionary of Paul and His Letters*, ed. Gerald F. Hawthorne, Ralph P. Martin, and Daniel G. Reid (Downers Grove: InterVarsity, 1993)
ed(s).	editor(s)
EDNT	*Exegetical Dictionary of the New Testament*, 3 vols., ed. Horst R. Balz and Gerhard Schneider (Grand Rapids: Eerdmans, 1990–93)
ESV	English Standard Version (2001)
ET	English Translation
ETL	*Ephemerides theologicae lovanienses*
ETS	Erfurter theologische Studien
EvQ	*Evangelical Quarterly*
ExpTim	*Expository Times*
FilN	*Filología neotestamentaria*
GNT	Greek New Testament
ICC	International Critical Commentary
Int	*Interpretation: A Journal of Bible and Theology*
JBL	*Journal of Biblical Literature*
JETS	*Journal of the Evangelical Theological Society*
JSNT	*Journal for the Study of the New Testament*
JSNTSup	Journal for the Study of the New Testament Supplement Series
JSOT	*Journal for the Study of the Old Testament*

JTS	*Journal of Theological Studies*
KJV	King James Version (1611)
lit.	literally
LNTS	Library of New Testament Studies
LSJM	*A Greek-English Lexicon*, ed. G. G. Liddell and R. Scott, rev. H. S Jones and R. McKenzie (Oxford: Clarendon, 1968)
LTPM	Louvain Theological and Pastoral Monographs
LXX	Septuagint (Greek) Text of the OT
ms(s)	manuscript(s)
MT	Masoretic (Hebrew) Text of the OT
NAB	New American Bible (2002)
NASB	New American Standard Bible
NEB	New English Bible (1970)
New Docs	*New Documents Illustrating Early Christianity*, ed. G. H. R. Horsley and S. Llewelyn (North Ryde, NSW: Ancient History Documentary Research Centre, 1976–)
NICNT	New International Commentary on the New Testament
NICOT	New International Commentary on the Old Testament
NIDNTT	*New International Dictionary of New Testament Theology*, 4 vols., ed. Colin Brown (Exeter: Paternoster/Grand Rapids: Zondervan, 1975–78)
NIDOTTE	*New International Dictionary of Old Testament Theology and Exegesis*, 5 vols., ed. Willem A. VanGemeren (Carlisle: Paternoster, 1997)
NIGTC	New International Greek Testament Commentary
NIV	New International Version (2011)
NKJV	New King James Version (1982)
NovT	*Novum Testamentum*
NovTSup	Supplements to Novum Testamentum

NRSV	New Revised Standard Version with Apocrypha (1995)
ns	new series
NSBT	New Studies in Biblical Theology
NTG	New Testament Guides
NTS	*New Testament Studies*
NTTS	New Testament Tools and Studies
par.	and parallels
PNTC	Pillar New Testament Commentary
repr.	reprint
rev.	revised
RB	*Revue biblique*
RTR	*Reformed Theological Review*
SBLDS	Society for Biblical Literature Dissertation Series
SBLMS	Society for Biblical Literature Monograph Series
SBT	Studies in Biblical Theology
SD	Studies and Documents
SJLA	Studies in Judaism in Late Antiquity
SJT	*Scottish Journal of Theology*
SNTSMS	Society for New Testament Studies Monograph Series
SNTSU	Studien zum Neuen Testament undseiner Umwelt
SP	Sacra Pagina
Str-B	*Kommentar zum Neuen Testament aus Talmud und Midrasch*, 6 vols., ed. H. L. Strack and P. Billerbeck (Munich: Beck, 1922–61)
TDNT	*Theological Dictionary of the New Testament*, 10 vols., ed. Gerhard Kittel and Gerhard Friedrich, trans. Geoffrey W. Bromiley (Grand Rapids: Eerdmans, 1964–76)
TJ	*Trinity Journal*
TR	Textus Receptus (Received Text)
trans.	translator(s)
TynBul	*Tyndale Bulletin*

TZ	*Theologische Zeitschrift*
UBS	United Bible Societies
VE	*Vox Evangelica*
vol(s).	volume(s)
WBC	Word Biblical Commentary
WTJ	*Westminster Theological Journal*
WUNT	Wisenschaftliche Untersuchungen zum Neuen Testament
ZNW	*Zeitschrift für die neutestamenthiche Wissenschaft und die Kunde der älteren Kirche*

Early Jewish and Christian Sources

'Abot. R. Nat.	'Abot of Rabbi Nathan
Apoc. Ab.	Apocalypse of Abraham
Apoc. Mos.	Apocalypse of Moses
b. Sanh.	Sanhedrin (Babylonian Talmud)
Bar	Baruch
2 Bar.	2 Baruch (Syriac Apocalypse)
3 Bar.	3 Baruch (Greek Apocalypse)
CD	Damascus document
Did.	Didache
1 En.	1 Enoch (Ethiopic Apocalypse)
2 En.	2 Enoch (Slavonic Apocalypse)
1–2 Esd	1–2 Esdras
Exod. Rab.	Exodus Rabbah
4 Ezra	4 Ezra (= 2 Esdras 3–14)
Gen. Rab.	Genesis Rabbah
Herm. Sim.	Shepherd of Hermas, Similitudes
Herm. Vis.	Shepherd of Hermas, Vision
Ign.	Ignatius
Eph.	*To the Ephesians*
Magn.	*To the Magnesians*
Pol.	*To Polycarp*
Jdt	Judith

Josephus	
Ag. Ap.	*Against Apion*
Ant.	*Jewish Antiquities*
War	*Jewish War*
Jos. Asen.	Joseph and Aseneth
Jub.	Jubilees
Let. Aris.	Letter of Aristeas
1–4 Macc	1–4 Maccabees
m. Sanh.	Mishnah Sanhedrin
Midr. Cant.	Midrash Canticles (Song of Songs)
Mart. Pol.	Martyrdom of Polycarp
Odes Sol.	Odes of Solomon
Philo	
Abr.	*De Abrahamo (On the Life of Abraham)*
Cher.	*De cherubim (On Cherubim)*
Her.	*Quis rerum divinarum heres sit (Who is the Heir?)*
Migr.	*De migratione Abrahami (On Abraham's Migration)*
Mos.	*De vita Mosis (On the Life of Moses)*
Mut.	*De mutatione nominum (On the Change of Names)*
Post.	*De posteritate Caini (On the Posterity of Cain)*
Praem.	*De praemiis et poenis (On Rewards and Punishments)*
Spec.	*De Specialibus legibus (On Special Laws)*
Virt.	*De vertutibus (On Virtues)*
Pss. Sol.	Psalms of Solomon
Qumran documents	
1QH	Hodayot (Thanksgiving Hymns)
1QpHab	Pesher Habakkuk
1QM	Milhamah (War scroll)
1 QS	Serek Hayahad (Rule of the Community)
1 QSb	Appendix b to the Rule of the Community
4QFlor	Florilegium
4QMMT	Halakhic letter
11QMelch	Melchizedek scroll
4QPat	Patriarchal blessings

4QpIsa	Isaiah pesher
4QpPs[a]	Psalm pesher
Pesiqt. Rab.	Pesiqta Rabbati
Sib. Or.	Sibylline Oracles
Sir	Sirach/Ecclesiasticus
T. Ash.	Testament of Asher
T. Benj.	Testament of Benjamin
T. Job	Testament of Job
T. Jos.	Testament of Joseph
T. Jud.	Testament of Judah
T. Levi.	Testament of Levi
T. Naph.	Testament of Naphtali
T. Reu.	Testament of Reuben
T. Sim.	Testament of Simeon
Tg. Neof.	Targum Neofiti
Tob	Tobit
Wis	Wisdom of Solomon

Greco-Roman Sources

Diatr.	Epictetus, *Diatribai (Dissertationes)*
Did. Sic., *Hist.*	Diodorus Siculus, *Bibliotheca historica*
Hor., *Sat.*	Horace, *Satires*
Plato, *Apol.*	Plato, *Apology*
Plut., *Cohib. ira*	Plutarch, *De cohibenda ira*
Quint., *Inst.*	Quintilian, *Institio oratoria*
Tacitus, *Ann.*	Tacitus, *Annales*

INTRODUCTION

Paul wrote Romans toward the end of his extensive ministry in the eastern part of the Roman Empire, from Jerusalem and Syria to the province of Illyricum (cf. 15:19). Most likely, he composed the letter during his three-month winter stay in Corinth (cf. 16:1, 21–23; Acts 20:1–3 ["Greece"]; 1 Cor 16:6) before returning to Jerusalem. From there he hoped to visit Rome to begin a new sphere of ministry in the western part of the Empire, journeying as far as Spain (Rom 15:25–28). Various dates have been proposed, but all of them fall within the range AD 55–59, with the majority of scholars arguing for the winter of 57–58.[1] There is much agreement with regard to these introductory matters but considerable disagreement about the character, structure, and purpose of Romans.

I. Character

Romans is sometimes treated as a compendium of Pauline theology or as a theological treatise on a particular theme or selection of topics. However, although it is the longest and theologically most dense Pauline writing we have, it begins and ends as a letter addressed to first-century Christians in the capital of the Roman Empire (1:1–15; 15:14–16:27).

Some scholars have argued that all or part of chapters 15 and 16 were later additions to Paul's work. Most obviously, the doxology

[1] Cf. Richard N. Longenecker, *Introducing Romans: Critical Issues in Paul's Most Famous Letter* (Grand Rapids: Eerdmans, 2011), 43–50. Robert Jewett (*Romans: A Commentary*, Hermeneia [Minneapolis: Fortress, 2007], 18–22) argues for 56–57 as the date of composition and 60 as the year of Paul's arrival in Rome.

found at 16:25–27 in some of the best and earliest witnesses is either missing or placed after 14:23 or 15:33. Textual and literary issues combine to raise serious questions about the transmission history of these concluding chapters.[2] However, Gamble has convincingly argued that the sixteen-chapter version was original and that the final chapter exhibits the epistolary features and conventions of a typical Pauline letter. Gamble accounts for the existence of shorter forms of Romans in some manuscripts as evidence of later attempts "to convert the letter from a specific communication to a particular community into a document suitable for a wider and general audience."[3]

Many believers in Rome are mentioned by name in 16:3–15, even though the apostle had not yet visited that city. Most were known to him from previous ministry contexts. Some could have sent him details about theological and pastoral issues that needed to be addressed in the Roman situation. Whatever the source of his local knowledge, it is important to identify the aspects of Paul's argument that may have been specifically included in the letter for the benefit of the original recipients.

A. The Epistolary Framework

In his opening salutation (1:1–7), the apostle does not address the recipients as "the church of God at Rome" (cf. 1 Cor 1:1; 2 Cor 1:1; 1 Thess 1:1; 2 Thess 1:1) or as "the churches of Rome" (cf. Gal 1:2) but as those "who are also called by Jesus Christ" and as those who are "in Rome, loved by God, called as saints" (1:6–7; cf. Phil 1:1; Col 1:2).[4] Right from the start, he is concerned to portray them as part of the wider movement among the nations that God is estab-

[2] The different text forms are conveniently listed and discussed by Douglas J. Moo, *The Epistle to the Romans*, NICNT (Grand Rapids: Eerdmans: 1996), 6–9. Jewett (*Romans*, 4–18) takes a more radical approach, concluding that Paul's original letter consisted of 1:1–16:16 + 16:21–23 + 16:24. Text-critical issues are considered in my commentary at appropriate points in the exegesis.

[3] Harry Y. Gamble Jr., *The Textual History of the Letter to the Romans: A Study in Textual and Literary Criticism*, SD 42 (Grand Rapids: Eerdmans, 1977), 115–16. Longenecker (*Introducing Romans*, 28–30) endorses Gamble's study and particularly notes how it explains the absence of references to Rome in 1:7, 15 in some later manuscripts.

[4] We only read of a church in the home of Prisca and Aquila (16:5a) and of churches in places outside of Rome (16:1, 4, 16, 23). Other household gatherings in Rome are not called churches (vv. 10b, 11b, 15d) but may have functioned as such. See §2.5.

lishing through the preaching of the gospel about his Son. Paul's own calling to be an apostle is clearly linked to the progress of this gospel, as he works "to bring about the obedience of faith for the sake of his name among all the Gentiles" (1:5).

Three critical issues are raised in this greeting and then developed in the body of the letter: the centrality of the gospel to what God is doing in the world, Jesus Christ and what God has accomplished through him as the focus of the gospel, and Paul's God-given role in the exposition and propagation of this gospel.

In the introductory thanksgiving (1:8–12) Paul identifies the particular significance of the Roman Christians within this wider movement when he records his gratitude to God that news of their faith is impacting people "in all the world" (1:8). Then he reveals how he regularly prays for them and asks that God would make it possible for him to visit them (1:9–10). His immediate concern is, "so I may impart to you some spiritual gift to strengthen you, that is, to be mutually encouraged by each other's faith, both yours and mine" (1:11–12).[5]

Fee observes that a letter in antiquity was meant to serve as "a second-best substitute for a personal visit."[6] The "spiritual gift" (χάρισμα πνευματικόν) Paul has in mind is not some "gifting" by the Spirit, as in 1 Cor 12:8–10 and Rom 12:6–8, but

> his understanding of the gospel that in Christ Jesus God has created from Jews and Gentiles one people for himself, apart from Torah. This is the way they are to be "strengthened" by Paul's coming, and this surely is the "fruit" he wants to have among them when he comes (v. 13). If so, then in effect our present letter functions as his "Spirit gifting" for them. This is what he would impart if he were

---

[5] Longenecker (*Introducing Romans*, 138–41) observes that the thanksgiving sections of Paul's letters mostly speak about the issues and concerns of his addressees, but in Rom 1:8–12 his own desires and concerns dominate. This could suggest that Paul's interests, desires, and concerns should be given highest priority in evaluating the purpose of Romans, but see III below.

[6] Gordon D. Fee, *God's Empowering Presence: The Holy Spirit in the Letters of Paul* (Peabody: Hendrickson, 1994), 486.

there in person: this is what he now "shares" since he cannot presently come to Rome.[7]

In the formal beginning to the argument of the letter (1:13–17), Paul reiterates his desire to visit the Romans and to have "a fruitful ministry" among them.[8] His plan is once again set within the context of his wider commitment: "I am obligated both to Greeks and barbarians, both to the wise and the foolish. So I am eager to preach the gospel to you also who are in Rome" (1:14–15). In what turns out to be a theme sentence introducing the argument to follow, Paul goes on to describe the gospel as "the power of God for salvation to everyone who believes, first to the Jew, and also to the Greek," and summarizes its message in terms of the revelation of the righteousness of God "from faith to faith" (1:16–17).

In the closing sections of the letter, the apostle returns to the theme of his commission to preach the gospel to the nations. He first attributes his writing to the Romans to the grace given to him by God "to be a minister of Christ Jesus to the Gentiles, serving as a priest of the gospel of God" (15:14–16). This last expression is explained by saying that the aim of his ministry is "that the Gentiles may be an acceptable offering, sanctified by the Holy Spirit." Paul acts as a "priest" with the gospel when he enables people everywhere to present their bodies "as a living sacrifice, holy and pleasing to God," which he describes as (lit.) "your understanding service" (12:1, τὴν λογικὴν λατρείαν ὑμῶν). His ministry makes possible "the obedience of faith" (1:5; 16:26), which involves obeying the call to believe in Christ (10:8–13, 16) and offering the obedient service that is the appropriate outcome of this faith.

When Paul speaks again of his long-standing desire to visit the Romans, he announces his intention to see them before moving on to Spain (15:22–24). But he first wants to visit Jerusalem

[7] Ibid., 488–89. Longenecker (*Introducing Romans*, 158, 353–55) agrees that the "spiritual gift" Paul is uniquely able to give the Romans is his understanding of the gospel and its implications, as expressed in his letter (cf. 2:16; 16:25, "my gospel"). However, Longenecker disagrees with Fee about the heart of Paul's message.

[8] Although some commentators would see the thanksgiving section of the letter extending to 1:15, Longenecker (*Introducing Romans*, 387) rightly observes that the beginning of the body opening of Romans is signaled by a disclosure formula that appears at the start of 1:13, οὐ θέλω δὲ ὑμᾶς ἀγνοεῖν ("I do not want you to be unaware"), coupled with the vocative ἀδελφοί ("brothers [and sisters]").

to deliver the collection from the Gentile churches he founded for "the poor among the saints" in that city (15:25–29). So he appeals to the Roman Christians to pray with him, "that I may be rescued from the unbelievers in Judea, that my ministry to Jerusalem may be acceptable to the saints, and that, by God's will, I may come to you with joy and be refreshed together with you" (15:31–32).

There is a degree of symmetry in the epistolary framework, as Paul seeks to inform his readers about his plans and involve them in the task given to him by God:

Paul's apostleship to the nations (1:1–7)	⟶	Paul's apostleship to the nations (15:14–21)
Paul's longing to visit the Romans (1:8–15)	⟶	Paul's longing to visit the Romans (15:22–33)

In the final chapter Paul commends Phoebe as the bearer of the letter (16:1–2), greets various acquaintances at Rome (16:3–16), warns his readers about "those who create divisions and obstacles contrary to the teaching that you learned" (16:17–19), and concludes with a grace benediction, further greetings, and a doxology (16:20–27).[9] The greetings in vv. 3–16 reveal important details about the background and present situation of twenty-six Christians in the city and identify two particular households (vv. 10b, 11b) and various other groups of unnamed believers (vv. 14b, 15d). Far from being incidental to Paul's purpose, this chapter raises important questions about the nature of his argument in the body of the letter and its relevance to the situation of the original recipients.[10]

B. The Body of the Letter

Within the body of the letter, there is a lengthy and sustained theological argument (1:16–11:36) before Paul turns to exhortation

[9] Jewett (*Romans*, 23) proposes that Tertius as scribe and Phoebe as patron were both involved "in the creation, the delivery, the public reading, and the explanation of the letter in the course of 57 CE."

[10] Paul S. Minear (*The Obedience of Faith: The Purpose of Paul in the Epistle to the Romans*, SBT 2nd Series 19 [London: SCM, 1970]) works backwards from the situation reflected in 14:1–16:27 through the earlier chapters to determine Paul's purpose. But he is too precise in linking supposed groups in Rome with sections of the preceding argument.

(12:1–15:13). Moo observes that the argument develops according to the inner logic of Paul's own teaching: "even the questions and objections that periodically interrupt the argument arise naturally from the flow of Paul's presentation."[11] Moo concludes that the issues addressed here are so general as to be applicable to any group of Christians, but this view will be challenged below.

Most obviously Paul expounds the gospel he outlines in 1:3–4, 16–17, drawing out the implications for believers (1:18–32; 3:21–26; 5:1–11; 6:1–23; 8:1–39; 12:1–13:14). He wants all his readers to enjoy all the life-changing benefits of Christ's saving work. Alternating with his exposition of the gospel and its implications, there are reflections on matters relating to the law and God's purpose for Israel: circumcision and the written code, faith and works, the covenant with Abraham and his offspring, the process of election and the blessing of the nations, food and Sabbath laws (2:1–3:20; 3:37–4:25; 5:12–21; 7:1–25; 9–11; 14:1–15:7). More will be said about this in the discussion of the letter's structure below. At this point, it is sufficient to note that Paul regularly pauses in his exposition of the gospel to address specifically Jewish concerns using a more defensive, argumentative style.

Among Paul's extant letters, only in Galatians is there comparable attention to such matters. Galatians is widely considered to be challenging the teaching and influence of Judaizers in the churches founded on Paul's first missionary journey. The larger-scale development of similar issues in Romans, sometimes using the rhetorical device of arguing with a Jewish opponent, is not simply a logical development of Paul's gospel. Romans was not written for the same reason as Galatians, but Paul clearly considered a treatment of these questions important for the recipients of this letter.

The hortatory section begins in a general way (12:1–13:14) but moves to issues more specifically related to the situation of the Roman Christians (14:1–15:13). Some have denied this,[12] but I will develop this point below. The climax of the section is the challenge to live in harmony with one another, each one seeking to "please his neighbor for his good, to build him up" (15:1–2). Christ himself

[11] Moo, *Romans*, 14.

[12] See, for example, Robert J. Karris, "Romans 14:1–15:13 and the Occasion of Romans," in *The Romans Debate*, ed. Karl P. Donfried, rev. and exp. (Peabody: Hendrickson, 1991), 65–84.

is the inspiration for this pattern of behavior since he became "a servant of the circumcised on behalf of God's truth, to confirm the promises to the fathers, and so that Gentiles may glorify God for his mercy" (15:8–9). The salvation-historical nature of Paul's argument in this section specifically recalls the long section in chapters 9–11 about Jews and Gentiles being blessed together in the purpose of God. This in turn is a development of certain arguments in chapters 1–8. So Jew-Gentile questions are significant for a consideration of Paul's purpose in writing both the doctrinal and hortatory sections of this letter.

A further observation is significant for understanding Paul's rhetorical strategy in this letter. In 1:2 he announces that the gospel was promised long ago by God "through his prophets in the Holy Scriptures." Although there are biblical allusions throughout Romans, Paul mostly cites only biblical texts in the defensive sections.[13] He assumes readers will recognize the authority of these texts and the significance of his references. His aim is to ground his gospel in God's revelation given to Israel and to convince his Christian readers that "whatever was written in the past was written for our instruction, so that we may have hope through endurance and through the encouragement from the Scriptures" (15:4).

The doxology in 16:25–26 relates Paul's proclamation of Jesus Christ to "the revelation of the mystery kept silent for long ages, but now revealed and made known through the prophetic Scriptures, according to the command of the eternal God to advance the obedience of faith among all the Gentiles." The gospel fulfills what the prophets foretold, but there was an element of mystery about what was promised in the OT that Paul needed to disclose and explain in his preaching and writing (cf. Eph 3:1–13; Col 1:24–28).

[13] Cf. Ben Witherington III with Darlene Hyatt, *Paul's Letter to the Romans: A Socio-Rhetorical Commentary* (Grand Rapids: Eerdmans, 2004), 20. In the sections where Paul expounds or applies the gospel, there are possibly six quotations (one in 1:16–17; one in 8:1–39; four in 12:1–13:14), but in the defensive sections there are at least fifty-five (eight in 2:1–3:20; seven in 3:27–4:25; two in 7:1–25; possibly thirty-two in 9:1–11:36; six in 14:1–15:13). See §2.2 for more detail.

II. Structure and Argument

How may we discern the structure of Romans? Are the sections and subsections of the letter to be determined "by subject matter, by the epistolary and rhetorical conventions reflected in the materials, or by some combination of these two approaches?"[14]

A. Thematic Approaches

Many modern commentators pursue a broadly thematic approach and see four main divisions in the argument.[15] For example, Moo rightly separates the epistolary framework from the body of the letter and views it as essentially an exposition of the gospel and its implications.[16] Schreiner's headings more closely associate the opening and closing sections with the body of the letter and highlight God's righteousness as the main theme throughout. Inside the epistolary framework he identifies five major divisions:[17]

1:1–17	The gospel as the revelation of God's righteousness
1:18–3:20	God's righteousness in his wrath against sinners
3:21–4:25	The saving righteousness of God
5:1–8:39	Hope as a result of righteousness by faith
9:1–11:36	God's righteousness to Israel and the Gentiles
12:1–15:13	God's righteousness in everyday life
15:14–16:23	The extension of God's righteousness through the Pauline mission
16:25–27	Final summary of the gospel of God's righteousness

[14] Longenecker, *Introducing Romans*, 378.

[15] E.g., N. T. Wright, "The Letter to the Romans: Introduction, Commentary, and Reflections," in *The New Interpreter's Bible*, ed. Leander E. Keck, 13 vols (Nashville: Abingdon, 1994–2004), 10:410–11.

[16] Cf. Moo, *Romans*, 33–35.

[17] Thomas R. Schreiner, *Romans*, BECNT (Grand Rapids: Baker Academic, 1998), vii–viii. Compare Colin G. Kruse, *Paul's Letter to the Romans*, PNTC (Grand Rapids: Eerdmans, 2012), viii–xiii.

B. Rhetorical and Epistolary Studies

Another approach involves comparing the letter with patterns of Greco-Roman oral, rhetorical, and epistolary conventions, which would have been familiar to Paul and his first-century addressees. For example, Longenecker examines oral patterning in Romans, and evaluates various forms of rhetorical analysis that have been applied to the letter. He follows Aune in arguing that the central section of Romans is an example of "protreptic speech," which was the primary rhetorical tool used by philosophic writers "to attract adherents by exposing the errors of alternate ways of living and demonstrating the truth claims of a particular philosophical tradition over its competitors."[18]

Some have classified Romans as "a letter of introduction," even as an "ambassadorial letter of self-introduction," though Longenecker disputes the adequacy of this approach.[19] He argues that it is much more like an ancient "letter essay," that is, "instructional material set within an epistolary frame."[20] Epistolary conventions appear in the opening and closing sections but only occasionally in the body of the letter.[21]

Longenecker provides important insights into the way the opening and closing sections of the letter function, and about the way the body of the letter is introduced. But there is more to be revealed about the structure and flow of the argument here and in the "protreptic" heart of the letter. In particular, I do not think he has justified his claim that the material in 1:16–4:25 represents matters on which Paul and the Roman Christians were in agreement or that "the material of 5–8 should be viewed as expressing the focus of what Paul writes in Romans."[22]

---

[18] David E. Aune, *Westminster Dictionary of New Testament and Early Christian Literature and Rhetoric* (Louisville: Westminster/John Knox, 2003): 383. Cf. David E. Aune, "Romans as a *Logos Protreptikos*," in *The Romans Debate*: 278–96; Longenecker, *Introducing Romans*, 193–200. Witherington (*Romans*, 20) contends that "Romans is a deliberative discourse which uses an epistolary framework, and in some ways comports with a protreptic letter."

[19] Longenecker, *Introducing Romans*, 215–16; cf. Robert Jewett, "Romans as an Ambassadorial Letter," *Int* 36 (1982): 5–20; Jewett, *Romans*, 43–46.

[20] Longenecker, *Introducing Romans*, 217.

[21] Ibid., 220–25.

[22] Ibid., 373.

C. A New Approach

I want to propose a different structure, drawing on insights from a variety of studies and majoring on four important literary factors: alternation, refrain, progression/digression, and recursion.[23]

1. Alternation

In the body of the letter, Paul systematically alternates between two distinct types of material. In one strand he *confirms* or establishes his gospel and its implications for salvation and the transformation of believers. He focuses on Jesus's death and resurrection and the need for "the obedience of faith" without distinguishing between Jews and Gentiles. In the other strand he *defends* his gospel in the face of objections arising from the priority of Israel in God's plan, addressing the particular concerns of first-century Jews: their Scriptures, their pattern of interpretation, their self-understanding, and their traditions.[24]

Tobin similarly distinguishes the sections of Romans that read like expositions or explanations from those that are marked by "various rhetorical devices that create a much livelier, more engaged, and argumentative tone."[25] Apart from style and tone, Tobin notes that the expository sections characteristically "draw on and develop traditional cultic language and imagery about Christ's death as sacrifice" (3:25; 5:8–9; 8:3) but mostly do not quote from the Jewish Scriptures.[26] In contrast the argumentative sections are marked by extensive use of Scripture.

---

[23] I am indebted to Grant S. Nichols and Richard J. Gibson ("Four Keys to the Literary Structure of Romans" [unpublished]) for these insights. They agree with Thomas H. Tobin (*Paul's Rhetoric in Its Contexts: the Argument of Romans* [Peabody: Hendricksen, 2004], 3) that "literary cues are surer guides to the structure of Romans than the theologically oriented 'topics' are." Literary and topical factors must be taken together.

[24] Junji Kinoshita ("Romans—Two Writings Combined: A New Interpretation of the Body of Romans," *NovT* 7 [1964]: 262) outlines "two strata of argument" and proposes that we have an original letter to the Romans combined with a "manual of instruction on Jewish problems." But the two strands do not necessarily point to two different sources.

[25] Tobin, *Paul's Rhetoric*, 3.

[26] Ibid., 85. Witherington (*Romans*, 20) similarly observes "the alternation between sections with many allusions, quotes, and echoes of the OT, and sections with virtually none."

Using the language of Phil 1:7, we may say that Paul is engaged in "the defense (ἀπολογία) and confirmation (βεβαίωσις) of the gospel." The second noun refers to the "process of establishing or confirming something, *confirmation, validation*" (BDAG). Paul uses the cognate verb in Rom 15:8 for Jesus's validation of promises made to the patriarchs of Israel. In the sections of the letter where the gospel is expounded, he confirms or establishes it by demonstrating its coherence and efficacy. In the apologetic sections he responds to charges made against his gospel and shows how his message is consistent with the Scriptures of Israel.

2. Refrain

Harvey notes that in Romans 5–8 Paul employs "a repeated refrain that gives unity to the section and is suggestive for identifying divisions within the text."[27] In 5:1, 11, 21; 7:25 the phrase "through our Lord Jesus Christ" is used, and in 6:23; 8:39 there is a variation ("in Christ Jesus our Lord").[28] But if the simpler, preposition-less expression "the Lord Jesus Christ" and variations are treated as the refrain, a broader pattern emerges. This phrase is found in the epistolary framework three times (1:3, 7; 15:30) and in the body of the letter eight times (5:1, 11, 21, 6:23; 7:25; 8:39; 13:14; 15:6; cf. 4:24, "Jesus our Lord").

The confession of Jesus as Lord and Christ is fundamental to Paul's gospel, and each of these declarations seems to mark a significant development in the argument. "The Lord Jesus Christ" serves as a formal boundary marker for all the literary units from 5:1 to 15:6, with the exception of 11:36, where a doxology ends the section. Use of this formula in 13:14 and 15:6 raises the possibility that the alternation between gospel exposition and defense against Jewish issues continues in 12:1–15:7. Paul first expounds the lifestyle made possible by God's merciful provisions in Christ, enabling believers to fulfill the law by acting in love (12:1–13:14). Then he addresses alternative ways of honoring God that potentially threatened the unity of the Roman Christians: matters of diet and the observance

[27] John D. Harvey, *Listening to the Text: Oral Patterning in Paul's Letters*, ETS (Grand Rapids: Baker, 1998), 104.

[28] Harvey, *Listening*, 125. Harvey says the expressions in 5:1 and 8:39 are "probably best seen as an instance of ring composition."

of certain days in honor of the Lord (14:1–15:7). A celebratory coda in 15:8–13 forms a conclusion to this section and a transition to the next stage of the argument, where Paul becomes more explicit about his role in God's plan for the nations (cf. 11:13–15).[29]

Observing Paul's pattern of alternation in the light of his repeated refrain, the following structure emerges from the body of the letter:

Confirmation of the gospel	Defense against Jewish objections
1:18–32	2:1–3:20
3:21–26	3:27–4:25
5:1*–11*	5:12–21*
6:1–23*	7:1–25*
8:1–39*	9:1–11:36
12:1–13:14*	14:1–15:(6*)7
*Instances of the refrain	

3. Progression/Digression

Tobin argues that the expository and argumentative sections of Romans are "interrelated to one another in four fairly complex ways."[30]

a. The expository material develops in a linear fashion to give a coherent account of Paul's gospel and its implications for Christian living. In these passages, "Paul consistently moves beyond the previous argumentative section to a new stage in the argument."[31]

b. Each of the argumentative sections takes off from some aspect of the preceding expository section. So, for example, 2:1–3:20 picks up the theme of God's wrath against human sin from 1:18–32 and

[29] Richard J. Gibson ("Paul the Missionary, in Priestly Service of the Servant-Christ [Romans 15.16]," in *Paul as Missionary: Identity, Activity, Theology and Practice*, ed. Trevor J. Burke and Brian S. Rosner, LNTS [London: T&T Clark, 2011], 57–62) argues for 15:8–21 as a distinct literary unit with a chiastic structure. But the thematic links between 15:8–13 and 15:1–7 are sufficient to classify this as a conclusion to the latter and a transition to the next stage of the argument.

[30] Tobin, *Paul's Rhetoric*, 85.

[31] Ibid., 86.

establishes that Jews and Gentiles are all under God's righteous judgment; 3:27–4:25 picks up the theme of faith from 3:21–26 and argues that justification by faith apart from works of the law is the scriptural pattern laid down for Abraham and his offspring.[32]

c. Tobin designates four "larger arguments" (1:18–3:20; 3:21–4:25; 5:1–7:25; 8:1–11:36) and says they are clearly intended as an articulated whole. They are "linear in the sense of being sequential and interlocking." The equal sinfulness of Jew and Gentile (1:18–3:20) gives way to the righteousness of God available equally to Jews and Gentiles (3:21–4:25), which is shown to be incompatible with sin (5:1–7:25). Then 8:1–11:36 struggles with issues related to the interlocking eschatological fate of Jews and Gentiles, which have arisen from the arguments in 1:18–7:25.[33]

d. These larger arguments are also linear in the sense that Paul places them in a temporal sequence. The framework "is intentionally and essentially temporal or historical in character," progressing from all humanity under sin (1:18–3:20), to the new situation established by Jesus (3:21–4:25), to the ethical implications of Jesus's death (5:1–7:25), to Paul's eschatological vision (8:1–11:36).

However, given Paul's careful use of the refrain "Jesus Christ our Lord" and the possible inclusion of 12:1–15:7 as a further large section containing both exhortation and argumentation, I suggest six basic units rather than Tobin's four: 1:18–3:20; 3:21–4:25; 5:1–21; 6:1–7:25; 8:1–11:36; 12:1–15:7 (with 15:8–13 being a coda to this final unit).

4. Recursion

In an essentially oral culture, certain devices provided clues to the organization, emphases, and development of a work for the listener. Among the elements of oral patterning available to Paul were recursive patterns often described as "chiasms." Such patterns

---

[32] Tobin (ibid., 88) notes the disproportionate length of the argumentative sections and infers the need to understand Paul's message "not primarily in terms of themes or subject matter but in terms of issues between himself and the Roman Christian audience he was addressing."

[33] Tobin does not include 12:1–15:7 in this material and thus concludes that Paul's argument moves in the direction of "a universalizing eschatology, which is explicitly the subject of 8:18–30 and 8:31–11:36." But this is a limited view of Paul's purpose.

may be discerned within and between the units of Romans outlined above.

Numerous examples of chiasm, inversion, ring composition, and concentric symmetry have been observed in single verses and larger segments of the letter.[34] For example, a concentric structure of Romans 5–8 is proposed by Moo. He treats 5:1 as "a transition in topic" and 5–8 as a unit, observing the density of verbal parallels between 5:1–11 and 8:18–39.

However, the parallels noticed by Moo can also be accounted for by recognizing a broader, recursive structure in the expository sections of Romans, where there is an overarching concentric symmetry (ABCDC´B´A´):[35]

A Idolatrous worship, 1:18–32
  B Standing in grace, 3:21–26; 5:1–11
    C Transfer from death to life, 6:1–11
      D As those made alive, present yourselves to God, 6:12–14
    C´ Transfer from sin to righteousness, 6:15–23
  B´ Walking in the Spirit, 8:1–39
A´ Acceptable worship, 12:1–13:14

This structure observes significant linguistic parallels between 1:18–32 and 12:1–2, where true worship is contrasted with the various forms of false worship that characterize human life.[36] The exhortations in 12:3–13:14 bring Paul's exposition of the gospel and its fruit to a practical end by illustrating what acceptable worship entails. Believers are rescued by Christ from the consequences of sin and are set free to serve God in love, thus fulfilling the law. The tragic predicament of 1:18–32 has been reversed by "the mercies of God," particularly expressed in the sacrifice of Jesus. Cultic

[34] Harvey (*Listening*, 97–109, 119–54) carefully distinguishes these terms, evaluates criteria, and illustrates from the literature on Romans.

[35] There are verbal and thematic parallels between 3:21–26 and 8:1–4 in addition to the parallels between 5:1–11 and 8:18–39 noted by Moo. I acknowledge my dependence on Nichols and Gibson ("Four Keys," 15–27) in this connection and in the following observations about the letter's structure.

[36] Cf. David G. Peterson, *Engaging with God: A Biblical Theology of Worship* (Downers Grove: InterVarsity, 1992), 169–79.

language is significantly applied both to the death of Jesus (3:25; 5:8–9; 8:3) and to the response of those united with him (6:13; 12:1).

In this recursive structure Romans 6 has a pivotal role. There is symmetry between 6:1–11 and 6:15–23 in the style of Paul's argument, using different terms. The first passage explains how those united with Christ in his death and resurrection have been transferred from death to life. The second speaks of their release from sin's dominion and a new slavery to righteousness. The first passage summarizes the message of 1:18–32; 3:21–26; 5:1–11 about the new life made possible for those who put their faith in Jesus. The second prefaces the argument developed in 8:1–39; 12:1–13:14 about believers offering themselves to God, using language revisited in 12:1 (cf. 6:13, 16, 19).

The two halves of Rom 6 are woven together in 6:12–14. In an unmistakable chiasm, Paul provides a succinct summary of his gospel and emphasizes the obligation laid on believers to live as those who have been brought by Christ from death to life:

A Therefore do not let sin reign in your mortal body, so that you obey its desires.
  B And do not offer any parts of it to sin as weapons for unrighteousness.
    C But as those who are alive from the dead, offer yourselves to God,
  B´ and all the parts of yourselves to God as weapons for righteousness.
A´ For sin will not rule over you, because you are not under law but under grace.

Chapter 6 is the fulcrum for Paul's movement from the justification and salvation of sinners by the death of Jesus to the inherent obligation to offer their justified and renewed selves to God. This movement facilitates the restoration of true worship and righteousness among the nations.[37]

[37] Against Moo (*Romans*, 294), Rom 6:1–7:25 is not "parenthetical to the main point of the section" but a pivotal point in Paul's exposition of the gospel and its implications.

There is also evidence of a recursive relationship in the defensive material. Here the symmetry takes the form of a ring composition (ABCC´B´A´).

A Judgment and identity: revealing the true children of God, 2:1–3:20
  B Faith, not law, as the defining characteristic of God's people, 3:27–4:25
    C Law not a source of life: Adam's sin, 5:21–21
    C´ Law not a source of life: human experience, 7:1–25
  B´ Faith in Christ, not law, as the way of salvation for Jews and Gentiles, 9:1–11:36
A´ Judgment and identity: resolving conflicts in the Christian community, 14:1–15:13

Judgment and identity are key themes in the outer ring of Paul's argument (2:1–3:20 and 14:1–15:13). In the first passage the propensity of self-righteous Jews to pass judgment on others is highlighted, and external circumcision is contrasted with that which is inward and real (2:25–29). In the concluding passage weak Christians, whose consciences are constrained by Jewish convictions regarding food and festivals, are warned not to pass judgment on the "strong," and the strong are warned not to despise the "weak." Circumcision, food, and Sabbath were three particular concerns that "marked off Israel most clearly from the other nations."[38] So the outer ring of Paul's defensive argument brings these identity issues together in relation to the new people of God in Christ. An inclusion is formed by the charge to welcome or accept one another at the beginning and end of this section (14:1; 15:7), particularly since "Christ also accepted you." However, as previously argued, the transitional passage 15:8–13 is a coda that forms an impressive conclusion to the exhortation in 14:1–15:7, while summarizing the argument about God's purpose for Jews and Gentiles outlined earlier in the letter.

An inner ring of Paul's argument in 3:27–4:25 and 9:1–11:36 is concerned to establish the relationship of the people of God in Christ to Abraham and the patriarchs. God's people are now defined by faith in Christ and not racial descent or obedience to the law. In the first passage the apostle is forced to explain how Abraham

[38] James D. G. Dunn, *Romans 1–8*, WBC 38A (Dallas: Word, 1988), lxxi.

can be the father of both Jew and Gentile. In 9–11 Paul surveys the history of Abraham's descendants to expose the way God's election and mercy have been at work to establish a remnant chosen by grace from among the physical descendants of Abraham. At the same time, salvation has come to the Gentiles. Paul pursues his ministry to the nations in the hope that he may somehow arouse his own people to jealousy and save some of them.

The core of Paul's engagement with Jewish issues is in 5:12–21 and 7:1–25. Here he addresses the expectation that through the law Israel would undo Adam's sin and death as its penalty: the law would expel sin, guarantee righteousness, and bring life. Paul confronts this belief with the failure of the law to achieve these things and reiterates the need for Jesus's death. The vocabulary of sin, law, death, and life saturates both contexts. Paul first exposes the failure of the law in salvation-historical terms (5:12–21). Rather than alleviating the problems of sin and death, the introduction of the law only ensured the multiplication of Adam's transgression and the increase of sin (5:20). In 7:1–25 the personal and experiential dimension of this crisis is explored.[39]

D. Conclusions about Structure

The following thematic headings show how the two major strands of argument in the body of the letter are related and progress. These strands are set within the epistolary framework, which expresses Paul's purpose in writing to the Romans in this way.

[39] In addition to various parallels tying 5:12–21 and 7:1–25 together, an underlying symmetry is provided by explicit and implicit allusions to Adam's sin.

1:1–17 Paul's desire to minister to the Romans: the epistolary introduction

1:18–32 God's righteous judgment against sin revealed

2:1–3:20 Judgment and identity: revealing the true children of God

3:21–26 God's saving righteousness revealed: the redemptive sacrifice that makes justification possible

3:27–4:25 God's saving righteousness revealed: faith, not law, the defining characteristic of God's people

5:1–11 The fruit of justification: present and future

5:12–21 Adam's transgression and Christ's gift: grace, not law, the source of life

6:1–23 Dying and rising with Christ: freed from sin's penalty to be slaves to God and to righteousness

7:1–25 Released from the law to serve God in the new way of the Spirit

8:1–39 The new way of the Spirit: life and adoption, perseverance and hope

9:1–11:36 The way of salvation for Jews and Gentiles: the righteousness that comes from faith in Christ

12:1–13:14 True and proper worship: love and obedience to God's will

14:1–15:13 Judgment and identity: resolving conflicts in the Christian community

15:14–16:27 Paul's mission plans and final messages: the epistolary conclusion

These broad divisions will be followed in the commentary, though further subdivisions in the larger units will be observed. Since this commentary series aims to provide guidelines for exposition, it will be necessary to consider how much of Paul's argument can reasonably be conveyed on a given occasion. In addition to the structural factors already considered, when segments for exposition are suggested, issues such as the thematic unity and length of passages will be taken into account.

III. Purpose

There are three major contemporary approaches to the purpose of Romans. Some would argue that, as in his other letters to churches, Paul is primarily occupied with the concerns of the community he addresses. He expounds his gospel in a way that will unite Jewish and Gentile believers in Rome. Others would argue that, right from the start, the apostle is focused on winning the support of the Roman Christians for the next phase of his missionary work and does not specifically address problems in their community. A third position involves some combination of these alternatives.[40]

I have noted the alternation between gospel exposition and intensive engagement with Jewish issues in Romans. This mirrors the pattern of Paul's missionary activity recorded in the latter half of the Acts of the Apostles. Luke regularly portrays Paul preaching to Jews first and then to Gentiles, often needing to dialogue with Jewish audiences about their objections to his message and responding to challenges about its consistency with Scripture. In these apologetic situations Paul speaks with particular boldness (Acts 9:27–28; 13:46; 14:3; 18:26; 19:8) and engages in reasoning (17:2, 17; 18:4, 19), sharp dispute, or persuasion (9:29; 15:2; 18:13; 28:23).

In the body of Romans, Paul expounds his law-free gospel and its implications while dealing with specifically Jewish issues concerning their heritage as God's covenant people. This is consistent with the portrayal of Paul's ministry in Acts, but how was it relevant for the Christians in Rome? The epistolary framework indicates his desire to minister to them in person and by letter and to win their support for the next stage of his ministry. How does the argument in the body of the letter relate to these expressed intentions?[41]

---

[40] Kruse (*Romans*, 8–11) summarizes a range of theories in connection with these three major approaches. Longenecker (*Introducing Romans*, 92–160) offers a more comprehensive discussion of alternatives. Donfried (*Romans Debate*) offers a range of essays on the topic, arguing for a variety of positions.

[41] Nichols and Gibson ("Four Keys") conclude that the dual character of the letter "correlates to two audiences, not necessarily within the Roman church to which he is writing, but which characterized his experience of preaching on his missionary

A. Jews in First-Century Rome

By the year 60, when Paul visited Rome, the Jewish community had grown to between twenty thousand and fifty thousand members.[42] They mostly lived together in the area across the Tiber known as Trastevere (Philo, *Embassy to Gaius*, 155–57) and belonged to at least eleven different synagogues. Since there was apparently no central organization overseeing these gatherings, the Jews must have been a difficult community to reach in any unified way.[43] Indeed, evidence from the Mishnah suggests that "relations between the early groups or congregations of Jews living at Rome and the Jewish religious leadership at Jerusalem were stronger than they were between the various 'synagogues' in the city of Rome itself."[44] Contemporary records show that some Gentile inhabitants of the capital were sympathetic to Jewish beliefs and practices, especially monotheism, Sabbath observance, abstention from certain foods, and the Jewish ethic.[45]

Luke's record of Paul's visit to Rome only briefly mentions a meeting with Christians (Acts 28:15) and focuses instead on two significant encounters with Jews (28:17–28).[46] In the first scene Paul tells the Jewish leaders, "It is for the hope of Israel that I'm wearing this chain" (28:20). They acknowledge they have received no bad report about Paul from Judea, but they want to hear more of his teaching since "people everywhere are speaking against this

---

journeys." However, I think more can be said about the specific relevance to the Roman situation.

[42] Andrew D. Clarke ("Rome and Italy," in *The Book of Acts in Its First Century Setting*, vol. 2: *Graeco-Roman Setting*, ed. David W. J. Gill and Conrad Gempf [Grand Rapids: Eerdmans, 1994], 466) argues for forty thousand to fifty thousand. Cf. Tobin, *Paul's Rhetoric*, 22–25.

[43] Longenecker, *Introducing Romans*, 60–66. Cf. Clarke, "Rome and Italy": 466; Brian Rapske, *The Book of Acts in Its First Century Setting*, vol. 3: *The Book of Acts and Paul in Roman Custody* (Grand Rapids: Eerdmans, 1994), 180.

[44] Longenecker, *Introducing Romans*, 67. Jewett (*Romans*, 55–59) provides a helpful description of the situation faced by Jews in Rome at the time of Paul's visit.

[45] Cf. Tobin, *Paul's Rhetoric*, 25–34.

[46] Cf. David G. Peterson, *The Acts of the Apostles*, PNTC (Grand Rapids: Eerdmans; Nottingham: Apollos, 2009), 706–23. Paul took the initiative with the Jewish leaders because he wanted to forestall any opposition or antagonism that might have followed him from other places. But it is also clear from Acts 28:20, 23 that he wanted to preach the gospel to the Jewish community before embarking on a wider ministry.

sect" (28:21–22). The second scene involves explaining to a larger group of Jews about the kingdom of God and persuading them about Jesus "from both the Law of Moses and the Prophets" (28:23). Their mixed response is reminiscent of earlier encounters with Jews in Acts. Although Luke does not indicate any theological interaction between Jews and Christians in Rome before Paul's arrival, the argument of Romans suggests otherwise.[47]

At the very least Paul must have thought it important to equip the Roman Christians for debates with Jews in their city. Such a large Jewish population made it necessary for Christians to have an informed, biblical apologetic. Moreover, his readers could hardly have supported Paul's missionary endeavors without being convinced of his stand on the sort of critical issues addressed in the defensive passages in Romans. They too must have heard of the controversy created by Paul's preaching in other places.

B. Roman Christianity

Given the traffic between Rome and the eastern part of the empire, it is likely that Christian converts brought the gospel to Rome at an early date. Tajra argues that Christianity reached Rome through the agency of the Jewish Dispersion toward the end of Tiberius's reign in 37.[48] Although some later Christian writers attributed the foundation of the Roman church to the apostle Peter, the fourth-century commentator known as Ambrosiaster testifies that the Romans "came to embrace faith in Christ without seeing any sign of miracles and without any of the apostles, though according to the Jewish rite."[49]

If itinerant Jewish believers brought a distinctly Jewish-flavored Christianity to Rome in those early days, the existence of "newly

---

[47] It is likely that "everywhere" in Acts 28:22 includes the city of Rome and indicates that these Jewish leaders had some knowledge of what local groups of Christians were teaching. Cf. Jewett, *Romans*, 59–61.

[48] Harry W. Tajra, *The Martyrdom of St. Paul: Historical and Judicial Contexts, Traditions and Legends*, WUNT 2.67 (Tübingen: Mohr, 1994), 76–77. Cf. Cf. Tobin, *Paul's Rhetoric*, 34–36.

[49] Cited by Longenecker (*Introducing Romans*, 69–72), who evaluates the conflicting historical evidence and observes that "neither Paul in Romans nor Luke in Acts says anything about Peter, or any other apostle, as having founded the church at Rome, which would have been an almost intolerable omission on the part of either of them had Peter or another apostle been so involved."

converted Christians alongside the traditional members of the synagogues may have led to increased factions and even to tumultuous disputes."[50] By the time Paul wrote his letter, most Jewish Christians are likely to have moved out of the synagogues to join the house churches he addresses.[51]

Conflict between Jewish groups in the capital apparently necessitated the publication of an edict by Emperor Claudius in 49, expelling from Rome "Jews who were making constant disturbances at the instigation of Chrestus" (Suetonius, *Divus Claudius*, 25.4; cf. Acts 18:2). The Roman historian may simply have identified Jewish infighting caused by someone "whose fame was sufficiently ephemeral for his precise identity to have been lost."[52] However, most scholars understand him to be referring to trouble created by Christian claims about Jesus being the Christ (misrepresented as "Chrestus"). On this reading Jewish Christians are likely to have been included in the expulsion from the city with some traditional Jews. According to the evidence of Acts and Romans, if the expulsion in 49 was the result of Jews fighting with Christians, their return to the city when Claudius died in 54 did not lead to outright hostility again.

Although many of the names mentioned in Rom 16 suggest Gentile origins, a number of Jewish Christians are identified among Paul's contacts in the city. As in other first-century contexts, even with a significant number of Jewish Christians in their midst, the house churches in Rome must soon have become predominantly Gentile in character and are addressed by Paul in this way (cf. Rom 1:5–6, 13–15; 11:13–32, 15:15–16).[53] But some of the Roman Christians may still have seen themselves as "rooted in, and still part

[50] Wolfgang Wiefel, "The Jewish Community in Ancient Rome and the Origins of the Roman Church," in *The Romans Debate*, 92.

[51] The argument of Mark D. Nanos ("To the Churches within the Synagogues of Rome," in *Reading Paul's Letter to the Romans*, ed. Jerry L. Sumney [Atlanta: SBL, 2012], 11–28) that Paul's audience met together as subgroups of the larger Jewish community of Rome does not adequately deal with the evidence of the letter. Cf. Witherington, *Romans*, 11–16; Tobin, *Paul's Rhetoric*, 34–40.

[52] E. A. Judge and G. S. R. Thomas, "The Origin of the Church at Rome: A New Solution," *RTR* 25 (1966): 87. Longenecker (*Introducing Romans*, 73) argues that Suetonius assumed Chrestus to be "a local Gentile troublemaker rather than the Jew from Nazareth who was revered by Christians as the Jewish Messiah."

[53] On the mixed, though predominantly Gentile character of the Roman churches, see Joseph A. Fitzmyer, *Romans: A New Translation with Introduction and*

of, the Jewish way of life, even though the Roman Jewish community saw it otherwise."[54]

C. The Issue in 14:1–15:13

Paul's approach in the heritage or defensive passages is passionate and pointed, often employing a diatribal style familiar from antiquity. He regularly seems to dialogue with an imaginary Jewish discussion partner to advance his argument. By this means, "the Gentiles would overhear the 'Jew' addressed by Paul and would be forced to revise their understanding of their relationship to the Jewish faith."[55]

However, when Paul addresses a specific division that he knows to exist in the Roman churches (14:1–15:7), his approach is different. Some hostility and suspicion over questions of law was evident, especially regarding food and the observance of holy days.[56] But his address to the "weak" and the "strong" suggests that there could have been Jewish and Gentile believers on both sides of the argument. Specific groups meeting in various places in the city may have been more Jewish in origin and character, and others more Gentile.[57] But in broad terms the question of continuity between Judaism and Christianity was a continuing issue for the Christians in Rome.

Significantly, in 15:8–13 Paul quotes passages from the Law, the Prophets, and the Writings to support his appeal for Jewish and Gentile believers to "accept one another, just as Christ also accepted you, to the glory of God" (15:7). If the chiastic pattern of the letter

---

Commentary, AB 33 (New York: Doubleday, 1993), 33–34; Moo, *Romans*, 9–13; Longenecker, *Introducing Romans*, 76–84. Cf. Witherington, *Romans*, 7–11.

[54] Tobin, *Paul's Rhetoric*, 38.

[55] A. Andrew Das, "The Gentile-Encoded Audience of Romans: The Church outside the Synagogue," in Sumney, ed., *Reading Paul's Letter*, 34. Cf. Stanley Stowers, *The Diatribe and Paul's Letter to the Romans*, SBLDS 57 (Chico: Scholars Press, 1981).

[56] Cf. Tobin, *Paul's Rhetoric*, 41–44; Jewett, *Romans*, 62–74.

[57] Minear (*The Obedience of Faith*) proposed five Christian groups derived from different social and religious backgrounds. Francis Watson ("Two Roman Congregations," in *The Romans Debate*, 203–15) argued for a Jewish Christian and a Gentile Christian congregation in conflict with each other over the matters addressed by Paul. Compare William S. Campbell, "The Rule of Faith in Romans 12:1–15:13"; and Mark Reasoner, "The Theology of Romans 12:1–15:13," in *Pauline Theology, Volume III: Romans*, ed. David M. Hay and E. Elizabeth (Minneapolis: Fortress, 1995), 259–99.

is recognized, the particular relevance of the first defensive section (2:1–3:20) to the argument in 14:1–15:7 emerges. To some extent Paul prepares for his exhortation to abstain from judging one another by addressing such attitudes in that earlier section.

Longenecker argues that the admonition in 16:17–19 may also refer to the divisions noted in 14:1–15:7.[58] But here Paul addresses his readers collectively rather than as the strong and the weak. He urges them to "watch out for those who create divisions and obstacles contrary to the teaching that you learned" and to avoid those who "do not serve our Lord Christ but their own appetites. They deceive the hearts of the unsuspecting with smooth talk and flattering words." When Paul says, "The report of your obedience has reached everyone" and reveals that he rejoices over them, the implication is that they have not succumbed to such teaching. So he concludes by saying, "I want you to be wise about what is good, and yet innocent about what is evil." In short, this is a more general warning arising from Paul's previous experience and now applied to the believers in Rome in a collection of final greetings.

D. Paul's Future Mission

Paul wrote this letter to give and receive in ministry. His *gift* to strengthen and encourage the Romans (1:11–12; cf. 15:14–16; 16:25–27) was the exposition of his gospel and its implications for Christian living. This was interwoven with a defense against Jewish objections and a focus on particular Jewish concerns. To some extent his letter anticipated the ministry he hoped to have among them when he visited them (1:13–15; cf. 15:23–28). In return he hoped to *receive* their prayers and support for his impending visit to Jerusalem and his proposed mission to Spain (15:29–33). Just as Christians in Antioch had partnered with him in his missionary campaigns in the East (Acts 13:1–3; 14:26–28), so he sought the partnership of the Roman Christians for the next sphere of his ministry in the western part of the empire.

Rome took over Spain and subjugated the population in a series of military campaigns throughout the two hundred years before Christ. Most of the people spoke their own languages, rather than

[58] Longenecker, *Introducing Romans*, 455–56. Contrast Kruse (*Romans*, 576–80), who takes this passage as a reference to false teachers who cannot now be identified.

Greek or Latin, and would have been regarded by the Romans as barbarians. Paul's proposed mission to Spain presented cultural, political, linguistic, and religious challenges. He could not simply proceed by preaching in synagogues or relying on Jewish hospitality, as previously, since evidence is lacking for a substantial Jewish population before the third and fourth centuries AD. Spiritually and practically, Paul needed the support of the Roman Christians for this venture.[59]

The unusual character of this letter, interweaving gospel exposition and defense against Jewish arguments, was partly driven by the nature of Paul's own apostolic ministry and previous experience and partly by his knowledge of Rome. A number of his rhetorical questions allude to criticisms and challenges that were probably often faced in the course of his ministry (e.g. 3:8, 31; 4:1; 6:1, 15; 7:7, 13, 14). Refuting such criticisms and answering such challenges was a natural way of developing his exposition of the gospel in this letter. But this approach was particularly relevant for the Roman Christians, who were living in a city with a large Jewish population. They had a history that tied them to Jewish perspectives and concerns. The specific application of Paul's message to their ecclesial situation becomes clearer in 14:1–15:13. His call for mutual respect and loving service to one another is echoed in the pattern of greeting that he encourages in 16:3–16.

Paul was not confronting Judaizers in the same way he did in his earlier letter to the Galatians. But Roman Christianity appears to have been confused about Jewish heritage issues, both theologically and practically. There may have been different Christian gatherings in the city with different perspectives on these matters, but we have no way of being certain about this. The "weak" and the "strong" cannot simply be identified with Jewish and Gentile believers since Paul the Jew counts himself among the strong, and some Gentile converts may have identified with the concerns of the weak.[60]

---

[59] Jewett (*Romans*, 74–79) gives details about Spain and the implications for Paul's missionary strategy. Jewett (84–91) discusses five ways the purpose of Romans has been understood with reference to Paul's missionary plans. But see J. Paul Sampley, "Romans in a Different Light: A Response to Robert Jewett," in *Pauline Theology, Volume III: Romans*, 109–29.

[60] Alexander J. M. Wedderburn (*The Reasons for Romans* [Edinburgh: T&T Clark, 1988] 64–65) argues that the conflict was simply between law-observant Christian

Theologically, Romans is an explanation of how the new covenant inaugurated by Jesus in his sacrificial death and heavenly exaltation fulfills the promises of Scripture (cf. Jer 31:31–34; Ezek 36:25–27) and brings a transformation of life and hope for Jews and Gentiles together in Christ. The new covenant surpasses the provisions of the Sinai covenant, challenging any adherence to the law for salvation, holiness of life, or fruitfulness in God's service. It makes possible the fulfillment of promises made to Abraham and the patriarchs about the ultimate blessing of the nations (4:9–25; cf. Gen 12:1–3; 17:4–6; 22:17–18).

Paul's own ministry was itself an exercise in Jew-Gentile relationships. He proclaimed a gospel that was promised in the Jewish Scriptures about a Jewish Messiah who sent him to the Gentiles. Paul is both an Israelite and an apostle to the Gentiles. It is not surprising, therefore, "in a letter in which Paul calls his addressees to be partners in his gospel-preaching, to find him frequently addressing issues pertaining to Jew-Gentile interaction."[61]

If Paul's primary aim was to secure the support of the Roman Christians for his proposed mission to Spain, it was necessary that "the gospel of impartial, divine righteousness revealed in Christ be clarified to rid it of prejudicial elements that [were] currently dividing the congregations in Rome."[62] In this way Paul's theological, pastoral, and missional agendas were brought together in the writing of this extraordinary letter.

IV. Continuing Relevance

History bears witness to the continuing significance of Paul's letter to the Romans for Christians in different eras and situations. Most obviously its impact on individuals such as Martin Luther,

---

Jews and law-free Gentile Christians. Jewett (*Romans*, 71) contends that "the profile of the weak and the strong in 14:1–15:13 is abstractly drawn so as to depict extreme positions in opposite directions, within which a range of congregational viewpoints can be encompassed." See n. 57 above for a variety of responses to this issue.

[61] Lionel J. Windsor, *Paul and the Vocation of Israel: How Paul's Jewish Identity Informs His Apostolic Ministry, with Special Reference to Romans*, BZNW 205 (Berlin/Boston: de Gruyter, 2014), 17.

[62] Jewett, *Romans*, 1. Given the limited evidence in the letter itself, Jewett is somewhat overconfident in his reconstruction of the problems in the Roman Christian community. See n. 59 above.

John Wesley, and Karl Barth led them to preach and to write in ways that transformed others, reformed churches, and profoundly influenced the cultures in which they lived.

Contemporary readers may struggle with the close argument of Romans and wonder about its immediate application, especially when specifically Jewish issues are addressed. But Paul's great gift in this letter is his exposition of the gospel and its implications in a biblical-theological framework—from Adam to Christ, and from creation to new creation. Like Hebrews, which may also have been written to believers in Rome, this letter unfolds salvation history and points to its consummation in glory.[63] It provides Christians in every generation with the big picture for understanding themselves and their world in relation to God and his purpose for humanity.

Romans shows us how to read the Scriptures appropriately, revealing how the Old Testament is fulfilled in the New and demonstrating that the gospel cannot be adequately grasped and related to our world unless it is understood in the light of its Old Testament roots. The great doctrines of salvation——justification, redemption, atonement, reconciliation, God's electing grace, new life in Christ, the gift of the Holy Spirit, sanctification, and glorification—should all be explained against this background. Faith as the essential response to God's promises and saving actions should also be explained with reference to Old Testament teaching.

God has dealt definitively with the effects of human rebellion by the sacrificial death of his Son, his resurrection from the dead, and his exaltation to heavenly rule. The preaching of this gospel about Christ's saving work draws people from every nation to faith in a glorified Savior. It unites people from different social, cultural, and religious backgrounds as children of God under the new covenant. This letter provides a profound theology of church, even though the term itself is not much used.[64]

A surprising amount of Romans is also devoted to explaining the practical consequences of our new life in Christ. As we learn to

[63] Cf. Peter T. O'Brien, *The Letter to the Hebrews*, PNTC (Grand Rapids: Eerdmans, 2010), 14–15.

[64] Cf. §2.5; Mark A. Seifrid, "Paul's Message Yesterday, Today, and Tomorrow: For Doug Moo in Gratitude," in *Studies in the Pauline Epistles: Essays in Honor of Douglass J. Moo*, ed. Matthew S. Harmon and Jay E. Smith (Grand Rapids: Zondervan, 2014), 274–86.

praise and serve him together through the enabling presence of the Holy Spirit, we experience God's transforming grace in advance of resurrection to eternal life, and we learn to live in the hope the gospel gives. Paul has much to teach us about the worship that pleases God, the love and support we owe to other believers, living as Christians in a hostile environment, and enduring suffering. The ultimate challenge of the letter is to unite with the apostle in a commitment to advance "the obedience of faith" in every nation and thus to glorify God (16:26–27).

V. Outline

I. Paul's Desire to Minister to the Romans (1:1–17)
   A. Introduction and Greeting (1:1–7)
   B. Thanksgiving, Prayer, and Thematic Introduction (1:8–17)

II. God's Righteous Judgment Against Sin Revealed (1:18–32)

III. Judgment and Identity: Revealing the True Children of God (2:1–3:20)
   A. God's Impartiality in Judgment (2:1–16)
   B. Misplaced Confidence (2:17–29)
   C. God's Righteousness in Judgment (3:1–20)

IV. God's Saving Righteousness Revealed: The Redemptive Sacrifice That Makes Justification Possible (3:21–26)

V. God's Saving Righteousness Revealed: Faith, Not Law, the Defining Characteristic of God's People (3:27–4:25)

VI. The Fruit of Justification: Present and Future (5:1–11)

VII. Adam's Transgression and Christ's Gift: Grace, Not Law, the Source of Life (5:12–21)

VIII. Dying and Rising with Christ: Freed from Sin's Penalty to Be Slaves to God and to Righteousness (6:1–23)

IX. Released from the Law to Serve God in the New Way of the Spirit (7:1–25)

X. The New Way of the Spirit: Life and Adoption, Perseverance and Hope (8:1–39)

A. Life and Adoption through the Spirit (8:1–17)
B. Perseverance and Hope (8:18–39)

XI. The Way of Salvation for Jews and Gentiles: The Righteousness that Comes from Faith in Christ (9:1–11:36)
A. Israel's Failure and God's Electing Grace (9:1–29)
B. Israel's Failure to Pursue Righteousness by Faith (9:30–10:4)
C. Israel's Failure to Understand the Law and the Prophets (10:5–21)
D. Hope in the Face of Judgment (11:1–10)
E. Hope in the Conversion of the Nations (11:11–24)
F. Hope in the Mercy of God (11:25–36)

XII. True and Proper Worship: Love and Obedience to God's Will (12:1–13:14)
A. Living in the Light of God's Mercies (12:1–2)
B. Serving One Another with Gifts and Ministries (12:3–8)
C. Love toward Believers and Unbelievers (12:9–21)
D. Living as Responsible Citizens (13:1–7)
E. Love in the End-time (13:8–14)

XIII. Judgment and Identity: Resolving Conflicts in the Christian Community (14:1–15:13)
A. Leaving Judgment to God (14:1–12)
B. Loving Those Who Think Differently (14:13–23)
C. Living to Glorify God (15:1–13)

XIV. Paul's Mission Plans and Final Messages (15:14–16:27)
A. Three Significant Destinations (15:14–33)
B. Commendation, Greetings, Warnings, and Blessings (16:1–27)

Biblical and Theological Themes

§1 Romans and the Story Line of the Bible

More than any other Pauline letter, Romans alludes to key events in the biblical narrative of God's dealings with the world and its inhabitants and records prophetic perspectives on those events. Paul is concerned with the pattern of God's historic interventions and how they relate to one another. Most importantly, he reflects on what they reveal about the character and purpose of God and how they prepare for and illuminate the work of Christ. Paul has a way of understanding OT Scripture that is critical for understanding the gospel and its implications. He wants to situate his readers within the unfolding story of God's engagement with humanity, which has past, present, and future significance for them.[1]

§1.1 Creation, Sin, and Judgment

God is introduced as Creator of all that exists, as Paul draws attention to what can be known about him from the natural world (1:18–23). People across time have clearly seen God's eternal power and divine nature, "being understood through what he has made " (1:20). But this knowledge has left them without excuse because they did not glorify him as God or show gratitude. "Instead, their

[1] There are different ways of understanding the theology of Romans. A helpful consideration of two divergent methodologies is provided by Richard B. Hays, "Adam, Christ, Israel—the Question of Covenant in the Theology of Romans: A Response to Leander E. Keck and N. T. Wright," in *Pauline Theology, Volume III: Romans*, ed. David M. Hay and E. Elizabeth Johnson (Minneapolis: Fortress, 1995), 68–86.

thinking became worthless, and their senseless hearts were darkened. Claiming to be wise, they became fools and exchanged the glory of the immortal God for images resembling mortal man, birds, four-footed animals, and reptiles" (1:21–23).

This portrait of humanity in rebellion against God is not yet specifically linked to Adam's sin or to death as its penalty (though see 1:32). Rather, Paul gives an account of what has characterized human life since Adam's fall, reflecting some of the perspectives of Genesis 3–11. Paul mentions people being handed over by God "in the desires of their hearts to sexual impurity, so that their bodies were degraded among themselves" (1:24). Such is the outcome for those who "exchanged the truth of God for a lie, and worshiped and served what has been created instead of the Creator" (1:25).[2] Paul further describes people being handed over to "disgraceful passions," resulting in unnatural sexual relationships (1:26–27), and being handed over to attitudes and practices that hinder authentic human relationships (1:28–32).

Paul identifies these consequences of humanity's rebellion against God as a present manifestation of God's wrath (1:18). Echoing the predictions of the eschatological prophets, Paul asserts that the wrath of God is soon to be fully and finally expressed in a day of universal judgment (2:5; cf. Isa 2:12–22; Amos 5:18–20; Zeph 1:14–18). The effect of sin in human life continues to be exposed in Rom 2:1–3:20, where the focus is specifically on Israel's failure to be God's holy people.

When Paul concludes that "all have sinned and fall short of the glory of God" (3:23), he echoes the Jewish tradition that when Adam sinned he lost the glory that was his when he was created in the image of God (Gen 1:26–27; Ps 8:5).[3] The gospel hope is that believers will encounter the glory of God at the end of the age through physical resurrection and be fully transformed into the likeness of God's Son (5:2; 8:18–21, 29–30). Those who suffer with Christ will be glorified with him (8:17), making him "the firstborn among many brothers and sisters" (8:29). However, Paul's claim

---

[2] Alluding to Ps 106:20 in Rom 1:25 (see also Deut 4:15–19; Jer 2:11), Paul includes Israel's idolatry in his analysis of humanity's failure to respond appropriately to God as Creator.

[3] Cf. Apoc. Mos. 20:2–3; 21.6; 3 Bar. 4.16; Gen. Rab. 12:6; 1QS 4:22–23; CD 3:19–20; 4QpPs[a] 3.1–2.

that believers "will . . . reign in life through the one man, Jesus Christ" (5:17) has a present application. Even now, those who have died with Christ begin to reign over sin and death and reflect something of the likeness of Christ in anticipation of that final encounter with him through resurrection (6:1–14).[4]

Paul's specific explanation of how sin and death came into the world through Adam's transgression (5:12–21) brings the teaching of Genesis 3 more precisely to the fore. Here the focus is on Adam's disobedience to a specific command of God, which the apostle links with Israel's subsequent disobedience to the law given through Moses (5:13–14). This prepares for the argument in 7:7–13 about the fatal effect of the law in revealing, provoking, and condemning sin in Israel (see §1.4).[5]

Paul's typological comparison of Adam and Christ presents them as epochal figures. Adam's sin determines the character of the present age, and Christ's obedience determines the character of the coming age (5:15–21; cf. 1 Cor 15:22). Adam's sin is "the bridgehead that paves the way for 'sinning' as a condition of humanity."[6] Human beings became sinners not merely by imitating Adam's transgression, but "they were constituted sinners by him and his act of disobedience."[7] As already noted, the analysis of the human situation in 1:18–32 describes the historic outworking of Adam's sin and its consequences, showing how "death spread to all people, because all sinned" (5:12).

---

[4] Cf. Ardel B. Caneday, "Already Reigning in Life through One Man: Recovery of Adam's Abandoned Dominion (Romans 5:12–21)," in *Studies in the Pauline Epistles: Essays in Honor of Douglass J. Moo*, ed. Matthew S. Harmon and Jay E. Smith (Grand Rapids: Zondervan, 2014), 27–43.

[5] Cf. Chris A. Vlachos, "The Catalytic Operation of the Law and Moral Transformation in Romans 6–7," in Harmon and Smith, eds., *Studies in the Pauline Epistles*, 44–56.

[6] Douglas J. Moo, *The Epistle to the Romans*, NICNT (Grand Rapids: Eerdmans: 1996), 319. Cf. James D. G. Dunn, "Adam and Christ," in *Reading Paul's Letter to the Romans*, ed. Jerry L. Sumney, SBL Resources for Biblical Study 73 (Atlanta: SBL, 2012), 125–38.

[7] Joseph A. Fitzmyer, *Romans: A New Translation with Introduction and Commentary*, AB 33 (New York: Doubleday, 1993), 421 (commenting on 5:19). Cf. Charles E. B. Cranfield, *Introduction and Commentary on Romans I–VIII*, vol. 1 of *A Critical and Exegetical Commentary on the Epistle to the Romans*, ICC (Edinburgh: T&T Clark, 1975), 277–79.

An allusion to Gen 3:17–19 is implicit in Paul's consideration of "the sufferings of this present time" (8:18–25). A futility about the created order makes it a suitable environment for those who have sinned and fall short of the glory of God (3:23; cf. Eccl 1–12). The creation was "subjected to futility—not willingly, but because of him who subjected it" (8:20). It is now in "the bondage to decay," which makes it captive to corruption and death (8:21). Indeed, "the whole creation has been groaning together with labor pains until now" (8:22). This personification of a suffering creation picks up the notion of God's subjecting it to futility "in hope" (8:20; cf. Gen 3:15; Rom 16:20). Echoing the prophetic expectation of a new creation (e.g., Isa 11:6–9; 65:17, 25; 66:22; Ezek 34:25–31), Paul claims that the creation itself will be set free "from the bondage to decay into the glorious freedom of God's children" (8:21). This explains his previous claim that "the creation eagerly waits with anticipation for God's sons to be revealed" (8:19). Creation shares in the consequences of human sin, but it will be transformed when believers are resurrected from the dead (8:23; see §1.6).

A climactic expression of Paul's creation theology occurs in a summary statement at the end of the hymn of praise in 11:33–36. God is the source of all that exists, the sustainer of all things, and the goal of everything. His redemptive plan embraces people from every nation (11:25–32), and he will bring every aspect of our disordered world into conformity with his own will and purpose. The gospel promises will be fulfilled because God as Creator has a plan for humanity that cannot ultimately be frustrated by human sin (8:28–39; 16:25–27).

§1.2 God's Promises to Abraham and His Offspring

God's creative power is specifically linked to redemption in Paul's treatment of Abraham: he believed in "the God who gives life to the dead and calls things into existence that do not exist" (4:17). The apostle explains how each of the foundational promises made by God to Abraham in Gen 12:1–3, and confirmed in subsequent revelations, is fulfilled in Christ.[8] In the process he focuses

[8] Paul R. Williamson (*Sealed with an Oath: Covenant in God's Unfolding Purpose*, NSBT 23 (Downers Grove: InterVarsity, 2007], 77–91) examines the relationship between the programmatic agenda of Gen 12:1–3 and the covenants of Gen 15 and 17. Williamson (186–92) discusses the covenant theology in Romans briefly.

on Abraham's faith, which was "credited to him for righteousness" (4:1–3, 18–22; cf. Gen 15:6), and which functions as a model for faith in the crucified and resurrected Lord Jesus (4:23–25).

The relationship between Abraham's faith and Christian faith is first indicated by insisting that Abraham was not justified by works but by believing "on him who declares the ungodly to be righteous" (4:5). This language links Abraham with the portrait of humanity in Rom 1:18–3:20 in need of God's forgiveness and release from the consequences of sin (see also 3:22–24, 28–30). A citation from Ps 32:1–2 suggests that the essential blessing God gave to Abraham was to "cover" his sins and credit him with "righteousness apart from works" (4:6–8; cf. Gen 12:2; 15:6).

Paul stresses the wider implications of this blessing when he observes that Abraham was declared righteous by faith *before* he received the covenant sign of circumcision. This made him the father of Gentiles who believe but are not circumcised as well as the father of Jews, who "follow in the footsteps of the faith our father Abraham had while he was still uncircumcised" (4:9–12). Paul alludes to the blessing of Gen 12:3 ("and all the peoples on earth will be blessed through you") when he talks about Gentiles and Jews being similarly justified by faith. This is articulated in Rom 4:16–18 with reference to Abraham's God-given role as "father of many nations" (Gen 17:5). As Creator, God is concerned to bless the whole human race, but he chooses to do this by first blessing Abraham and his physical offspring. Ultimately, salvation through faith in Christ is available for Abraham's spiritual offspring—those in Israel and those among the nations—bringing deliverance from God's judgment and new life (4:22–25; cf. 10:9–13; Gal 3:6–14).

Paul takes the promise to Abraham about the land that God would show him (Gen 12:1) to mean that his offspring would inherit "the world" (4:13). This is in line with Jewish thinking, which came to identify the inheritance of God's people with "the world to come."[9] Paul argues that believing Jews and Gentiles may glorify God together for the Messianic salvation that unites them and gives them the hope of sharing together in God's new creation (3:29–30; 4:9–17; 11:25–32; 15:8–13).

[9] Cf. Sir 44:21; Jub. 19:21; Philo, *Mos.* 1.155; Pss. Sol. 12:6; Josephus, *Ant.* 32:3; Sib. Or. 3:768–69; 4 Ezra 6:59; 7:9; 2 Bar. 14:13; 44:13; 51:3.

Paul's final focus is on the promise that the patriarch would have numerous offspring (Gen 12:2; 13:16; 15:4–5).[10] When Abraham and Sarah were too old to conceive a child, God began to fulfill his promise by enabling the birth of Isaac (4:17b–21; cf. Gen 21:1–7). This exercise of God's power anticipated the raising of Jesus from death, making it possible for believers from every nation to be justified and receive new life through him (4:22–25; cf. 6:4–11; 7:4–6; 8:10–11; 10:9–13). As already noted, Abraham's spiritual offspring are Jews and Gentiles who manifest the same faith in God for acceptance and eschatological blessing in Christ.

The climactic expression of this teaching is in Rom 15:8–13. There Paul insists that "Christ became a servant of the circumcised on behalf of God's truth, to confirm the promises to the fathers, *and* so that Gentiles may glorify God for his mercy" (15:8–9). This claim is supported by citations from each section of the biblical canon: one from the Law (Deut 32:43 in 15:10), two from the Psalms (Ps 18:49 in 15:9; Ps 117:1 in 15:11), and one from the Prophets (Isa 11:10 in 15:12). For Paul this is a consistent biblical theme, which must be articulated and lived out by believers in ways that demonstrate its fulfillment in the Lord Jesus Christ.

§1.3 Israel and God's Electing Grace

"The covenants" and "the ancestors" (the patriarchs) are mentioned in 9:4–5 among the foundational gifts of God to Israel.[11] But Paul questions whether God's word has failed (9:6) because so many Israelites have stumbled in unbelief over "the stumbling stone" of the Messiah (9:32; cf. Isa 8:14; 28:16). He responds by outlining the biblical evidence for a process of divine election taking place among the offspring of Abraham. Ultimately, he intends to show that "not all who are descended from Israel are Israel" (9:6; cf.

[10] With a restatement of the promises previously given and a ritual confirming the relationship established with Abraham, Gen 15:18 declares that, "on that day the Lord made a covenant with Abram." Paul uses the word "covenant" to describe God's commitment to Abraham in Gal 3:16–18 but not in Romans.

[11] "The covenants" will be the various expressions of God's commitment to Israel given throughout her history (e.g., Gen 15:18; 17:1–14; Exod 19:5; 24:7–8; 34:27; Deut 29:1; 2 Sam 23:5; Jer 31:31–24). Hellenistic and Rabbinic Jewish texts similarly refer to covenants in the plural (e.g., Wis 18:22; Sir 44:12, 18; 2 Macc 8:15; 4 Ezra 3:22; Str-B 3:262). Cf. Williamson, *Sealed with an Oath*, 94–181.

9:27–29, 31–33). Biblical history indicates that God has narrowed "the apparent boundaries of election by choosing only some Jews to be saved."[12]

The first example of divine choice is Isaac, rather than Ishmael, as the inheritor of the blessings promised to Abraham (9:7–9; cf. Gen 21:1–13). Israel's election is then portrayed with reference to the extraordinary choice of Jacob over Esau (9:10–13; cf. Gen 25:19–34). God's sovereign grace is revealed in the promise about the older serving the younger, which was given before they were born and before they had a chance to do good or evil (cf. Gen 25:27–34; 27:1–40). The pattern of unconditional election illustrated in the call of Abraham continues with his offspring. God's choice of Israel as a nation is confirmed with the retrospective declaration "I loved Jacob, but I hated Esau" (Mal 1:2–3).

A series of citations covering the period of the exodus highlight God's intention to display his power and make his "name" or character known in all the earth (9:14–18; cf. Exod 9:16). Israel's rescue from Egypt was designed to disclose God's character to the nations and so bless them in line with his promise to Abraham (Gen 12:3). God showed mercy and compassion to his people by powerfully delivering them from Pharaoh's control (cf. Exod 33:19). Until the moment of release, God hardened Pharaoh's heart against him so that he might multiply his wonders in the land of Egypt (cf. Exod 11:9–10). As with Jacob and Esau (Rom 9:11–12), God's choice of Israel over Pharaoh did not depend on "human will or effort but on God who shows mercy" (9:16). Yet in both cases God's choice was reflected or demonstrated in subsequent human behavior. Moses as God's agent encouraged Israel to "stand firm and see the LORD's salvation" (Exod 14:13) so that "when Israel saw the great power that the LORD used against the Egyptians, the people feared the LORD and believed in him and in his servant Moses" (14:31). God's promise and its fulfillment enabled the obedience of faith.

In response to his teaching about God's hardening whom he wills, Paul has an imaginary opponent ask, "Why then does [God] still find fault? For who can resist his will?" (9:19) Drawing on familiar biblical imagery, Paul warns against any arrogant challenge to God's justice and asserts that a potter has the right over his clay

---

[12] Moo, *Romans*, 569.

"to make from the same lump one piece of pottery for honor and another for dishonor" (9:20–21; cf. Isa 29:16; 45:9; 64:8; Jer 18:1–11). "God's right to choose is grounded in his role as Creator. What is molded has no right to challenge him who does the molding."[13] Paul then moves from the exodus situation to the gospel era, using linked citations from the prophetic literature to explain the relationship between Israel and God in the intervening period (9:22–29).

Picking up some of the language of the preceding verses, Paul begins to apply his argument to the situation of Jews and Gentiles faced with the gospel of Christ. His first question is, "And what if God, wanting to display his wrath and to make his power known, endured with much patience objects of wrath prepared for destruction?" (9:22). His second question is, "And what if he did this to make known the riches of his glory on objects of mercy that he prepared beforehand for glory—on us, the ones he also called, not only from the Jews but also from the Gentiles?" (9:23–24).

Paul uses Scripture to highlight both Israel's historic failure to serve God and God's response. Hosea predicted the Assyrian invasion and exile of the northern tribes but also anticipated a comprehensive restoration of God's covenant people (Hos 2:23; 1:10 in 9:25–26). This combination of texts illustrates that God's call "can completely transform what had appeared to be a clear-cut case of divine rejection."[14] Nevertheless, Isaiah predicted that only a remnant would be saved from enemy attack and invasion (9:27–29; cf. Isa 10:22–23; 28:22; 1:9). Many in Israel were "objects of wrath prepared for destruction," while some were "objects of mercy that he prepared beforehand for glory" (Rom 9:22–23).

Paul turns to the eschatological application of this teaching by relating it to the failure of many Israelites to pursue the righteousness that is by faith (9:30–10:4). In effect he accuses unbelieving

---

[13] Craig A Evans, "Paul and the Prophets: Prophetic Criticism in the Epistle to the Romans (with Special Reference to Romans 9–11)," in *Romans and the People of God*, ed. Sven K. Soderlund and N. T. Wright (Grand Rapids: Eerdmans, 1999), 124. Theocentrism lies at the heart of Paul's "prophetic criticism" of Israel.

[14] James D. G. Dunn, *Romans 9–16*, WBC 38B (Dallas: Word, 1988), 575. Paul sees in these words of Hosea a promise of Israel's restoration. But Dunn also concludes that, "the privilege of sonship with which Israel had been favored (vv. 4, 8) has been extended to all who respond to God's call now through the gospel." See my comments on 9:25.

Israelites of failing to "follow in the footsteps of the faith our father Abraham had" (4:12). A combination of Isa 28:16 and 8:14 is used to highlight Israel's stumbling over the Messiah rather than believing in him and not being put to shame at the approaching judgment (9:32–33). Paradoxically, however, "Gentiles, who did not pursue righteousness, have obtained righteousness—namely the righteousness that comes from faith" (9:30; see §2.5). By implication this happened because of their believing response to Israel's Messiah (cf. 3:27–31; 4:9–12).

Although Paul concedes that "a partial hardening has come upon Israel" (11:25), he insists that this is part of God's saving plan to bring riches to the Gentiles and reconciliation to the world (11:7–15). Paul's optimism about "all Israel" being saved and "the fullness of the Gentiles" coming to faith is based on his understanding of the kindness and mercy of God (11:22–32). These expressions refer to the full number of the elect in Israel and the nations. The covenantal basis of this assurance is indicated by the image of "the root" being holy and sanctifying the original branches of "the olive tree," which signifies the people of God (11:16–21).[15] The divine covenants are also the basis of Paul's optimism when he claims that Israelites are loved "because of the patriarchs" and concludes that "God's gracious gifts and calling are irrevocable" (11:28–29).[16]

§1.4 Israel and the Law

The word νόμος ("law") occurs seventy-two times in Romans, mostly with reference to the law of God.[17] Paul lists "the giving of the law" (9:4, ἡ νομοθεσία) as one of the privileges of Israel, referring to what happened when God brought his people to Sinai/Horeb in fulfillment of his covenants with Abraham, Isaac, and Jacob (Exod 2:23–25; 3:6–10, 14–18; 6:2–9). Israel was challenged to listen to God and carefully keep the covenant he was making with them. God's promise was: "You will be my own possession out of all the

[15] Israel is portrayed as God's "olive tree" in Jer 11:16 and Hos 14:6 and as God's "planting" in later Jewish literature (e.g., 2 Macc 1:29; Jub. 1:16; 1 En. 10:16; 26:1). But the olive tree here is more broadly the people of God, comprising believing Jews and Gentiles.

[16] Cf. William S. Campbell, "Israel," *DPL* 441–46.

[17] Cf. Thomas R. Schreiner, *The Law and Its Fulfillment: A Pauline Theology of Law* (Grand Rapids: Baker, 1993), 33–40.

peoples, although the whole earth is mine, and you will be my kingdom of priests and my holy nation" (Exod 19:5–6; cf. Deut 5–6). The covenant with Israel was a development of the covenants made with the forefathers, spelling out the kind of nation God intended them to be.[18]

A complex set of moral, social, and cultic obligations established how this people could respond to God's gracious initiative in choosing and saving them. Israel was singularly blessed by the giving of the law, and the ultimate aim was that all the people on earth would be blessed through Israel's obedience to this law (cf. Gen 18:18–19; 19:5–6; Isa 2:2–3).[19] The covenantal relationship between God and Israel was confirmed by a sacrificial ceremony in Exod 24:3–8 when Moses read out the commandments and ordinances of the Lord and the people expressed their intention to obey.

Paul has many positive things to say about the law in Romans. It reveals the will of God and enables right decisions about what really matters in life (2:18). It was given for Israel to be "a guide for the blind, a light to those in darkness" (2:19; cf. Isa 42:6–7). Jews could teach and model God's values to people of other nations, "having the embodiment of knowledge and truth in the law" (2:20). But Paul points to the hypocrisy of Jews who preached the law to Gentiles but who dishonored God by breaking it themselves (2:21–23). This behavior caused the blaspheming of God's name among the nations (2:24; cf. Isa 52:5).

Paul echoes the teaching of passages such as Lev 18:5; Deut 5:32–33; 30:11–20 when he says the commandment was meant "for life" (7:10). Indeed, "the law is holy, and the commandment is holy and just and good" (7:12). But the problem is that sin "was producing death in me through what is good, so that through the commandment, sin might become sinful beyond measure" (7:13). This

[18] "The giving of the law was not intended to set aside the promise (cf. Gal 3:17); rather, it was the means by which the goal of the promise would be advanced in and through Abraham's national descendants (Gen 12:2; cf. 18:18–19)" (Williamson, *Sealed with an Oath*, 94).

[19] Exodus 19:5–6 suggests that the whole nation had inherited the responsibility formerly conferred on Abraham, "that of mediating God's blessing to the nations of the earth" (ibid., 97). Given this role, it was vital that the nation remained distinct from other nations. Indeed, retention of the land depended on maintaining their distinctiveness (cf. Exod 23:20–33; Lev 18:24–30; Deut 29:16–29).

problem is illustrated in many of the biblical narratives, beginning with Exod 32:1–6, and it is picked up in numerous prophetic oracles about Israel's failure to obey God (e.g., Isa 1:1–23; Jer 7:1–34; Hos 12–13).

An important function of the law was to reveal human sin and make the whole world subject to God's judgment (3:19–20; cf. 7:7c–d).[20] The claim that "both Jews and Gentiles are all under sin" (3:9) is supported by a catena of biblical texts from Ecclesiastes, Psalms, and Isaiah (3:10–18). Paul concludes this sequence (3:19) using ὁ νόμος with reference to the three sections of the Hebrew canon (the Law, the Prophets, and the Writings).[21] But he mostly employs this noun narrowly. So "where there is no law, there is no transgression" (4:15b) means that "sin is not charged to a person's account" when there is no possibility of breaking an explicit command of God (5:13b). Paul goes a step further in 7:9–11, arguing that, "when the commandment came, sin sprang to life again and I died. The commandment that was meant for life resulted in death for me. For sin, seizing an opportunity through the commandment, deceived me, and through it killed me." This unpacks his previous claim that "the law came along to multiply the trespass" (5:20a).

Various features of the fall narrative in Gen 3:1–7 are echoed in Rom 7:7–11. But Paul also seems to allude to Israel's rebellion in Exod 32:1–6, when the people turned to idolatry and immorality immediately after receiving the covenant law at Sinai. The law turned sin into transgression, increased the trespass, and produced wrath (cf. Exod 32:7–29).[22] The serpent used God's good law in Eden to bring death into the world, and sin used the law given at

---

[20] Schreiner (*The Law and Its Fulfillment*, 91) argues that "for Paul, God's transcendent purpose in giving the law was to increase sin, for the multiplication of transgressions would demonstrate that no one could be righteous through obeying the law."

[21] Compare the use of νόμος with reference to Scripture other than the Pentateuch in John 10:34; 15:25; 1 Cor 14:21. This reflects wider Jewish usage of the term (cf. Str-B 3:159, 463).

[22] Cf. Moo, *Romans*, 428–31. N. T. Wright ("The Letter to the Romans: Introduction, Commentary, and Reflections," in *The New Interpreter's Bible*, ed. Leander E. Keck, 13 vols. [Nashville: Abingdon, 1994–2004], 10:563) similarly contends that "what happened on Sinai recapitulated what had happened in Eden." He notes the link between covetousness and the sin of Adam in Jewish literature (*b. Sanh.* 38b; 102a; Exod. Rab. 21:1; 30:7; 32:1, 7, 11). Cf. James D. G. Dunn, *Romans 1–8*, WBC 38A (Dallas: Word, 1988), 379.

Sinai to bring condemnation and death to the covenant people. This composite biblical picture is expressed in the first-person singular not just for rhetorical vividness but because of Paul's "deep sense of personal involvement, his consciousness that in drawing out the general truth he is disclosing the truth about himself."[23]

Paul's extraordinary conclusion is that sin "was producing death in me through what is good, so that through the commandment, sin might become sinful beyond measure" (7:13). Sin's sinfulness was enhanced by its use of God's law. But the broader argument of Romans suggests that this was part of a wider divine purpose. "God gave the law (to Israel) precisely to bring sin to a point of maximum concentration so that right there (Israel) 'where sin increased, grace might abound' (5:20b), for the benefit of the entire world, in the person of Israel's Messiah (cf. 8:3–4)."[24]

As Paul defends the goodness of the law of God in 7:7–25, he warns about the impossibility of bearing fruit for God by attempting to keep the written code. This is because of the captivating power of sin and the flesh. The apostle's approach highlights the need for the new way of the Spirit announced in 7:4–6 and expounded in 8:1–14. God's Spirit sets believers free from "the law of sin and death" by convincing them about freedom from condemnation through Christ's atoning sacrifice (8:1–3; cf. 5:5–8; 7:4–5).[25]

The gift of the Spirit also makes it possible for "the law's requirement" to be fulfilled in those who "do not walk according to the flesh but according to the Spirit" (8:4; cf. 7:6; 13:8–10). This promise echoes Jeremiah's prediction that God would place his law within his people and write it "on their hearts" (Jer 31:33), enabling them to know his will and be moved to do it. Such renewal would flow from the definitive forgiveness of their sins (31:34). In a parallel

[23] Cranfield, *Romans*, 1.344. Cranfield (1.342) thinks Paul is speaking "in a generalizing way without intending a specific reference to any particular individual or clearly defined group," but his comment about the significance of the first person singular is applicable to the Adam-Israel view.

[24] Brendan Byrne, *Romans*, SP (Collegeville: Liturgical Press, 1996), 221. This salvation-historical perspective fits with Paul's argument in 9:30–11:24 and Gal 3:19–26. Cf. n. 19 above.

[25] Although some have argued otherwise, the word νόμος ("law") is most naturally understood figuratively in 8:2 ("the law of the Spirit of life," "the law of sin and death"), as in 7:21 ("this law"); 7:23 ("a different law," "the law of my mind," "the law of sin"); 7:25 ("the law of sin"). Cf. 3:27 ("[the law] of works," "a law of faith").

passage, Ezekiel promised that God would cleanse and renew his people, giving them a new heart and placing his Spirit within them to enable them to keep his law (Ezek 36:25–27).[26]

There are also allusions to new covenant expectations in 2:14–15, 26–29. Preparing for his denunciation of the disobedient Jew in 2:17–24, Paul makes clear that "the hearers of the law are not righteous before God, but the doers of the law will be justified" (2:13).[27] As a challenge to those who are not genuinely doers of the law, he points to Gentile Christians who "do not by nature (φύσει) have the law" but who "do what the law demands" (2:14).[28] These people "show that the work of the law is written on their hearts," and "their consciences confirm this" (2:15). Later in Romans Paul negatively uses the plural expression "the works of the law" (3:20, 28; Gal 2:16; 3:2, 5, 10), but the singular expression "the work of the law" (τὸ ἔργον τοῦ νόμου) has a positive meaning in 2:15. It signifies "the essential unity of the law's requirements,"[29] which God writes on the hearts of his new covenant people.

In 2:25–29 Paul asserts that a true Jew will have a circumcised heart. 2:26–27 echoes 2:14–15 with the claim that Gentiles who are physically uncircumcised, yet fulfill the law's demands, expose the

---

[26] Cf. David G. Peterson, *Transformed by God: New Covenant Life and Ministry* (Downers Grove: InterVarsity, 2012), 29–43, 136–55; Schreiner, *The Law and Its Fulfillment*, 145–78; Brian S. Rosner, *Paul and the Law: Keeping the Commandments of God*, NSBT 31 (Nottingham: Apollos; Downers Grove: InterVarsity, 2013), 158–222.

[27] Although this appears to contradict Paul's later insistence that no one will be justified by "works of the law" (3:20), he is arguing in 2:13 "with imagined Jews on their own ground, exploiting the tension he sees between the claim to privileged status and divine impartiality" (Francis Watson, "The Law in Romans," in Sumney, ed., *Reading Paul's Letter*, 97).

[28] Since φύσει is more likely to modify the verb that immediately precedes it, rather than the verb that follows it, the meaning is "they do not have the law *by virtue of their birth*."

[29] Cranfield, *Romans*, 1:158. Simon J. Gathercole ("A Law unto Themselves: The Gentiles in Romans 2:14–15 Revisited," *JSNT* 85 [2002]: 41–43) addresses objections to the view that 2:15 proclaims the fulfillment of Jer 31:33. Others who argue that the passage is about Gentile Christians include Cranfield, *Romans*, 1:155–59; N. T. Wright, "The Law in Romans 2", in *Paul and the Mosaic Law*, ed. James D. G. Dunn, WUNT 89 (Tübingen: Mohr, 1996; Grand Rapids: Eerdmans, 2000), 131–50; Robert Jewett, *Romans: A Commentary*, Hermeneia (Minneapolis: Fortress, 2007), 213–17; Colin G. Kruse, *Paul's Letter to the Romans*, PNTC (Grand Rapids: Eerdmans, 2012), 130–40.

failure of those who have "the letter of the law and circumcision" but are lawbreakers.[30] But then Paul claims that "a person is a Jew who is one inwardly, and circumcision is of the heart—by the Spirit, not the letter" (2:29). This recalls the command of Deut 10:16 ("circumcise your hearts"; cf. Lev 26:41) and the promise in Deut 30:6 ("The LORD your God will circumcise your heart and the hearts of your descendants"). Israel's historic failure to respond to God's demand is picked up by Jeremiah (4:4; 9:26), who announces God's intention to transform the hearts of his people by the provision of a new covenant (Jer 31:33; cf. 24:7; 32:40). Ezekiel 36:26–27 clarifies that this will be accomplished when God puts his Spirit within his people, causing them to follow his statutes and carefully observe his ordinances.

§1.5 Israel's Failure and God's Judgment

When Paul links God's promises to Abraham and the salvation made possible through the death and resurrection of Jesus, he makes plain that "the promise to Abraham or to his descendants that he would inherit the world was not through the law, but through the righteousness that comes by faith" (4:13). Recalling his previous argument about faith being credited to Abraham before he was circumcised (4:9–12), Paul asserts, "If those who are of the law are heirs, faith is made empty and the promise nullified" (4:14). It was always God's intention that salvation for Jews and Gentiles would depend on faith in God and his promises, not on obedience to his commands.

This focus on "the righteousness that comes by faith" reflects what Gen 15:6 says about Abraham's relationship with God. It is another way of speaking about divine justification, which Paul has asserted is not "by the works of the law" (3:20, ἐξ ἔργων νόμου), but "by faith apart from the works of the law" (3:28, πίστει . . . χωρὶς ἔργων νόμου; cf. Gal 2:16; 3:2, 5, 10). "The works of the law" have been understood narrowly by some scholars to refer to boundary

[30] In view of Gen 17:12–14, Paul's fellow Jews would have denied that a Gentile's "uncircumcision" could be "counted as circumcision." But he explains in 3:21–4:25 that Gentiles can be justified by faith together with Jews who trust in Jesus, and thus be reckoned as one of Abraham's true descendants. The outcome is a life of faithful obedience to the will of God, directed and empowered by his Spirit (e.g., 7:4–6; 8:1–5).

markers, such as Sabbath keeping, circumcision, and food laws, which clearly distinguished Jews from Gentiles.[31] But Paul's condemnation of his fellow Israelites does not simply focus on their failure to observe these requirements.

The benefit of circumcision without obedience to the law's other requirements is certainly challenged (2:25–29). More broadly, however, Paul exposes the false confidence of Jews who know the will of God from the law and believe they are in a position to teach others but dishonor God by breaking the law comprehensively (2:17–24; cf. 3:9–18). "The works of the law" are simply "things done in obedience to the law."[32] The term "works" is apparently used as a substitute for "works of the law" in 4:2, 6; 9:11–12, 32; 11:6. Justification in God's sight cannot be based on "the works of the law" because "the knowledge of sin comes through the law" and the law makes everyone "subject to God's judgment" (3:19–20; cf. 4:15; 5:13; 7:13).

In 9:30–31 Paul resumes his teaching about the righteousness that comes from faith and is the outcome of God's justifying work in Christ (3:21–4:25). Righteousness by faith has been "obtained" by Gentiles, who did not pursue it. But Israel as a people pursued the law for righteousness, as if it were by works. This caused them to stumble over the Messiah and reject the gospel proclaiming the righteousness that is through faith in him (9:32–33). Disregarding "the righteousness of God" and attempting to establish their own righteousness, "they have not submitted to God's righteousness" (10:3), "for Christ is the end of the law for righteousness to everyone who believes" (10:4). Now that the Messiah has come, the law has completed its task of revealing God's righteousness to everyone who believes.[33] The law itself showed that righteousness could only be by

---

[31] Cf. Dunn, *Romans 1–8*, lxiii–lxxii, 158–59; Wright, "Romans," 459–61. Simon J. Gathercole (*Where Is Boasting? Early Jewish Soteriology and Paul's Response in Romans 1–5* [Grand Rapids: Eerdmans, 2001]: 218–22, 248–49) critiques this argument, as does Moo, *Romans*, 206–17; Fitzmyer, *Romans*, 338; Byrne, *Romans*, 120–21; Schreiner, *Romans*, 169–73.

[32] Moo, *Romans*, 209. Watson ("The Law in Romans," 93) similarly argues that "works of the law" includes "those practices that together constitute the distinctive Jewish way of life."

[33] Robert Badenas (*Christ the End of the Law: Romans 10:4 in Pauline Perspective*, JSNTSup 10 [Sheffield: JSOT, 1985], 118) argues that "Christ embodies that righteousness which the law promised." Moo (*Romans*, 641) concludes that Christ is the

faith (10:6–8, reflecting on Deut 30:12–14), namely, by relying on the grace of God for the gift of righteousness and deliverance from judgment. In Christ and the gospel, these gifts are now available for "everyone who calls on the name of the Lord" (10:9–13, citing Isa 28:16; Joel 2:32).

Not much attention is given in Romans to biblical history between the exodus and the coming of the Christ. But Elijah's struggle with Ahab, Jezebel, and the prophets of Baal lies behind the use of 1 Kgs 19:10, 14, 18 in 11:2–4. Paul also refers to prophecies concerning the Assyrian invasions in the eighth century BC (Hos 2:23; 1:10 in 9:25–26) and cites predictions that only a remnant of Israel would be saved from divine judgment (Isa 10:22–23; 28:22; 1:9 in 9:27–29). Such passages highlight Israel's idolatry and disloyalty to God in every sphere of life. Paul's use of Deut 32:21 in 10:19; 11:11, 14 concerns God's use of unspecified foreigners to punish Israel for her disobedience and make her jealous. Other prophetic texts also come from contexts where judgment for Israel is either predicted or in train (e.g. Deut 30:12–14, and Joel 2:32 in 10:6–13; Hab 2:4 in 1:17).

These passages in their original context point to the need for God to intervene and save his people in a new way. They also highlight the need for Israel to trust God and live in the light of his promises. Using key terms from the prophetic literature and drawing upon significant texts, Paul points to Jesus as the anticipated messianic deliverer who comes to rescue Israel from her failure and apostasy and fulfill God's promise to bring eschatological blessing to the nations (e.g., Isa 59:20–21 in 11:26–27 and a catena of texts in 15:8–12).

§1.6 Promises of Ultimate Deliverance

Much of the argument of Romans concerns the fulfillment of prophetic predictions about the future of Israel and the nations. Paul claims that his gospel comes from God and was "promised beforehand through his prophets in the Holy Scriptures" (1:2). The focus of this gospel is God's Son, whom Paul immediately describes in

"end" of the law in the sense that he brings its era to a close and its "goal" in the sense that "he is what the law anticipated and pointed towards."

two related confessional statements (1:3–4; cf. 1:9; 5:10; 8:3, 29, 32).

God's Son is first proclaimed as "a descendant of David according to the flesh" (1:3).[34] God's promise to King David that he would establish the throne of his descendant forever (2 Sam 7:12–16) became the basis of messianic expectation before, during, and after the period of Israel's Babylonian exile (e.g., Isa 9:6–7; 11:1–10; Jer 23:5–6; Ezek 34:23–24; Zech 9:9–10; 12:7–13:1). This hope is also evidenced in later Jewish writings (e.g., Pss. Sol. 17:21 ["the Son of David"]; 18:5 ["his anointed"]; 4QFlor 1:1–19; 1 En. 48:10; 52:4). God's rule over his people would be renewed by the provision of a king who perfectly reflected God's values and intentions for his people. The broader context of these prophecies acknowledges the failure of Davidic kings to lead in a way that could deliver Israel from apostasy and the consequent judgment of God.[35]

The messiahship of Jesus is foundational to the gospel Paul preaches (e.g., 1:3–4; 15:7–12; 16:25–27; 1 Cor 15:3–8; 2 Tim 2:8), though he amplifies, transforms, and transcends early Jewish ideas about the Messiah.[36] Echoing 1:3, he declares that from the Israelites, "by physical descent, came the Christ, who is God over all, praised forever" (9:5). God's salvific purpose was achieved through the incarnation and death of his Son. God "condemned sin in the flesh by sending his own Son in the likeness of sinful flesh as a sin offering" (8:3; cf. 5:10; 8:32; 1 Cor 15:3). Moreover, Jesus's resurrection enabled him to fulfill the promise of an eternal rule for David's Son: he "was appointed to be the powerful Son of God according to the Spirit of holiness by the resurrection of the dead" (1:4; cf. 4:25 ["raised for our justification"]). Indeed, as the one who

---

[34] Moo (*Romans*, 46) rightly argues that several key texts in Paul's writings presume the preexistence of the Son, which is the implication of 1:3. Cf. Schreiner, *Romans*, 38–39.

[35] Cf. Philip E. Satterthwaite, Richard S. Hess, Gordon J. Wenham, eds., *The Lord's Anointed: Interpretation of Old Testament Messianic Texts* (Carlisle: Paternoster; Grand Rapids: Baker, 1995).

[36] Ben Witherington III ("Christ," *DPL* 98) argues that three elements in Paul's preaching about Christ are without known precedent in early Judaism: "(1) Messiah is called God; (2) Messiah is said to have been crucified, and his death is seen as redemptive; (3) Messiah is expected to come to earth again." Paul's use of the term Χριστός was "mainly derived from the Christ event and his experience of that event."

died and was raised, "he also is at the right hand of God and intercedes for us" (8:34; cf. Ps 110:1).

Various combinations of the titles Christ and Lord appear with the name Jesus at critical points throughout Romans (1:4, 7; 4:24; 5:1, 11, 21; 6:23; 7:25; 8:39; 13:14; 14:14; 15:6, 30; 16:18, 20; cf. 10:9–13). This combination of terms mostly occurs at a climax or turning point in the argument and highlights the focus of Paul's gospel on the person and work of the divine Messiah. With this Christological focus, Paul proclaims the fulfillment of biblical predictions about the renewal of Israel's relationship with God, the blessing of the nations, and the hope of being glorified with Christ in a renewed creation.

Prophetic eschatology focused on the return of a remnant of Israel from exile and the restoration of the nation in the promised land. Critically, "the prophetic perspectives of the future restoration and ultimate salvation are based on, and follow the pattern of, the salvation history of the past."[37] As they proclaim the return from exile and its consequences, the writing prophets convey "the more distant view of the Day of the Lord when God finally acts in a way that has ultimate significance for the coming of the kingdom of God."[38] In association with promises about a new David, these prophets speak about a new creation (e.g., Isa 11:1–9; 65:17–21; Ezek 36:33–36), a new covenant (e.g., Isa 49:5–9; Jer 31:31–34; 33:25–26; Ezek 34:25–31), a new exodus (e.g., Isa 40:1–5; 43:1–7; Jer 23:5–8), a new entry and possession of the land (e.g., Ezek 34:11–16), a new Jerusalem (e.g., Isa 44:24–28; 49:14–21; 62:1–12), and a new temple (e.g., Isa 2:2–3; Ezek 40–47; Hag 2:6–9).

Paul reflects these perspectives in various ways throughout his letters. We have already noted his focus in Romans on the hope of glory and resurrection to new life with Christ in a new creation (e.g., 5:1–2; 8:17–25; cf. §1.1). The exodus and the promised return of the exiles form the basis of Paul's explanation of how God is

[37] Graeme Goldsworthy, *Christ-Centered Biblical Theology: Hermeneutical Foundations and Principles* (Nottingham: Apollos, 2012), 133. Goldsworthy observes that, "each prophet responds in his own way to the contemporary events and situation so as to reflect the nation's condition as a covenant breaker. From a canonical point of view the overall message is the renewal of all things against the background of judgment and cleansing."

[38] Ibid., 135.

dealing with Israel in the gospel era (e.g., 9:14–33; cf. §1.3; 1.5). The fulfillment of new covenant expectations through the death of Christ and the eschatological gift of the Spirit is implied in various contexts (e.g., 2:14–16, 26–29; 5:5; 6:17–18; 7:4–6; 8:4; 11:25–27; cf. §1.4). The new Jerusalem and new temple themes are reflected in Paul's use of cultic terms to describe his gospel ministry and the resulting establishment of believing communities everywhere (1:9; 15:15–19). God's mercy toward Jews and Gentiles in the sending of his Son makes it possible for them to be united in calling upon the Lord Jesus for salvation (10:10–12) and to offer to God the service and praise that is due to him (12:1; 15:8–12).

Many other theological themes, such as Christology, pneumatology, ecclesiology, soteriology, ethics, and anthropology are "built upon the eschatological foundation of Paul's thought."[39] This will be illustrated in the examination of selected themes in the next section of this chapter. One of the features of Jewish apocalyptic is the division of time into two ages (e.g., 4 Ezra 7:50). Paul reflects this view when he warns about being conformed to "this age" in 12:2 (cf. 1 Cor 1:20; 2:6–8; 3:18; 2 Cor 4:4; Gal 1:4 ["this present evil age"]). But he also implies that "the age to come" has impinged on the present with the death and resurrection of Jesus (3:21–26; 5:1–11, 17; 6:3–11; 7:4–6; 8:1–11; 14:17; cf. Eph 1:21). Christians are to live as those who are still in "this age" but belong to the coming "day" (13:11–14; cf. 1 Thess 5:1–11).[40]

§2 Other Significant Themes

Some of the themes mentioned in the preceding biblical-theological overview will be considered again under different headings and in relation to other themes. New topics are introduced here because of their obvious significance in the argument of Romans,

[39] Larry J. Kreitzer, "Eschatology," *DPL* 253. Kreitzer demonstrates this in his exposition of Pauline eschatology. Cf. James D. G. Dunn, *The Theology of Paul the Apostle* (Grand Rapids: Eerdmans, 1998), 177–81.

[40] Kreitzer ("Eschatology," *DPL* 259–60) shows how Paul develops the prophetic view of an eschatological day of the Lord in the light of his Christology so that it becomes "the day when God judges what people have kept secret, according to my gospel *through Christ Jesus*" (2:16; cf. 2 Cor 5:10). Although Romans does not explicitly mention the parousia or second coming of Christ, it is the assumption behind 13:11–14 (cf. 1 Cor 1:7–8; 4:5; 11:26; 15:23; 1 Thess 2:19; 3:13; 4:15; 5:23).

but these may not be fully treated in terms of redemptive-historical progression. The discipline of biblical theology involves more than a salvation-historical analysis of major themes or the situating of a book in its canonical context. Biblical theology may include an examination of how a particular topic is developed and relates to other themes in a given book or in the body of writings attributed to a specific biblical author.

§2.1 The Gospel

The noun εὐαγγέλιον ("gospel") occurs nine times in Romans (1:1, 9, 16; 2:16; 10:16; 11:28; 15:16, 19; 16:25) and the verb εὐαγγελίζομαι ("evangelize, proclaim the gospel") three times (1:15; 10:15; 15:20). Most of these references are in the opening and closing chapters of the letter, where Paul describes his own ministry and travel plans. Given the programmatic significance of 1:16–17, it could be concluded that Romans is an exposition of the gospel and its many implications, with specific reference to Paul's role in propagating that message.

Since the LXX never employs the singular εὐαγγέλιον with any theological significance, some have argued that Paul was influenced by the use of the plural εὐαγγέλια in the Greco-Roman world for announcements of events such as the birth of an heir to the emperor, his coming of age, and his accession to the throne.[41] However, although the plural noun had such popular connotations, it is unlikely that Paul simply derived his use of the singular from that source. There is a significant biblical background to his use of the related verb.

In 10:15 Paul cites Isa 52:7 (lit., "how welcome are the feet of those who announce the gospel of good things" [τῶν εὐαγγελιζομένων [τὰ] ἀγαθά]),[42] identifying himself with those sent by God to proclaim "the message of faith" (10:8) to Israel and the nations. There are similar uses of the verb in Isa 40:9 (ὁ εὐαγγελιζόμενος Σιων, "Zion, herald of good news"), 60:6 (τὸ σωτήριον κυρίου εὐαγγελιοῦνται,

[41] Cf. Gerhard Friedrich, "εὐαγγελίζομαι, εὐαγγέλιον, κτλ.," *TDNT* 2:721–25.

[42] In LXX Isa 52:7 the participle is singular (εὐαγγελιζόμενος), as is the Hebrew (מְבַשֵּׂר). There is a parallel expression in Nah 1:15 (MT and LXX 2:1). The noun derived from the same Hebrew root has the sense of "good news" in 2 Sam 18:20, 25, 27; 2 Kgs 7:9, and "reward for good news" in 2 Sam 4:10; 18:22. But the news is not "religious" in these contexts. Cf. Friedrich, "εὐαγγελίζομαι," *TDNT* 2:721.

"they will proclaim [the good news of] the Lord's salvation"), and 61:1 (εὐαγγελίσασθαι πτωχοῖς, "to proclaim good news to the poor").[43] The last reference is particularly important because Jesus applied it to himself (Luke 4:18; cf. Matt 11:5; Luke 7:22). John the Baptist was the preparatory preacher (Luke 3:18, εὐηγγελίζετο τὸν λαόν, "he proclaimed good news to the people"), but Jesus was the epoch-changing preacher who made available the things promised long ago. In essence this meant proclaiming the good news about the advent of "the kingdom of God" and its consequences (Luke 4:43; 8:1; cf. Matt 4:23; 9:35; Mark 1:14 [κηρύσσων τὸ εὐαγγέλιον τοῦ θεοῦ, "preaching the good news of God"]).

So εὐαγγέλιον may have been drawn into play in early Christian circles as the appropriate noun to match the use of the verb in the Isaianic texts. Jesus himself is likely to have been the inspiration for this development.[44] The content of the message was derived from Jesus's own teaching and from an understanding of what the Scriptures reveal about the significance of his life, death, resurrection, and heavenly exaltation (1:3; cf. Luke 24:44–49; Acts 1:3). In some contexts Paul uses the noun in a dynamic way to refer to the *activity* of "telling the good news" (e.g., 1:1, 9; 15:19), effectively employing it as an alternative to the cognate verb. Fundamentally, however, the term refers to a specific message that needs to be proclaimed.

Paul first asserts the divine origin of his gospel (1:1, θεοῦ, "from God"), claiming that God promised it long ago "through his prophets in the Holy Scriptures" (1:2; cf. §2.2). He then identifies it as essentially a message "concerning his Son" (1:3, περὶ τοῦ υἱοῦ αὐτοῦ; cf. 1:9). The Christological focus of his gospel was discussed in §1.6, where we noted that this emphasis comes to the fore at critical points in the letter with various declarations about Jesus's

---

[43] In these passages the messenger of God proclaims the royal dominion of God and "with his effective word ushers in the eschatological period" (Friedrich, "εὐαγγελίζομαι," *TDNT* 2:709). The Isaianic theme is echoed in Pss. Sol. 11:1; 11QMelch 2:15–24. Other significant uses of the verb in the LXX include Pss 39:10; 67:12; 95:2 (English Bible: 40:9; 68:11; 96:2).

[44] Dunn (*Theology of Paul*, 168) argues that Paul himself "coined the usage as a new technical term for his own proclamation," though he acknowledges that in Rom 1:16 the apostle may be echoing the words of Jesus preserved in Mark 8:38/ Luke 9:26.

being "Christ" and "Lord" (1:4, 7; 4:24; 5:1, 11, 21; 6:23; 7:25; 8:39; 13:14; 14:14; 15:6, 30; 16:18, 20; cf. 10:9–13).[45]

In 1:16–17, however, Paul marries his Christological focus with a soteriological one: the gospel is "the power of God for salvation to everyone who believes, first to the Jew, and also to the Greek. For in it the righteousness of God is revealed from faith to faith, just as it is written: 'The righteous will live by faith.'"[46] The exposition of this soteriological message begins in 3:21–26, where it is clarified that faith in Christ and his redemptive achievement is the required response to the gospel about the eschatological manifestation of God's righteousness. The reason for Paul's exposition of the gospel in terms of righteousness, justification, and faith will be considered in §2.4.

The Christological and soteriological dimensions of Paul's gospel must be understood together. Where there is a Christological focus, the soteriological implications must be kept in mind, and when the soteriology of the gospel is being expounded, the Christological foundation must be considered. As Paul raises questions about "faith" and "works," and asks how the gospel can benefit Jews and Gentiles together (3:27–4:25), he reflects on what the Scripture says about Abraham. An integrated Christological and soteriological statement concludes this reflection, establishing a pattern that is developed in 5:1–11. Righteousness will be "credited to us who believe in him who raised Jesus our Lord from the dead. He was delivered up for our trespasses and raised for our justification" (4:24–25).

Paul returns to this sort of integrated confession in 10:9–13, where faith in the resurrected Lord Jesus results in righteousness and salvation. The argument in previous chapters demands that we

---

[45] Richard N. Longenecker (*Biblical Exegesis in the Apostolic Period* [Grand Rapids: Eerdmans, 1975], 104]) contends that Paul worked from two fixed points: "the Messiahship and Lordship of Jesus, as validated by the resurrection and as witnessed to by the Spirit," and "the revelation of God in the Scriptures of the Old Testament." But, although in Paul's own experience "a true understanding of Christ preceded a proper understanding of Scripture, in his exegetical endeavors he habitually began with Scripture and moved on to Christ."

[46] Watson ("The Law in Romans," 95) observes that Paul's "Christological reticence" in 1:16–17 has led many to suppose that the theme of his gospel is "*not* Jesus per se but 'justification by faith.'" Watson shows how this view has been critiqued and defended.

view Jesus's atoning death and his bodily resurrection as the combined means by which those eschatological benefits are secured for believers (5:1–11; 6:1–11; 8:1–11). When the apostle mentions one, the other must be related to what he says.

Paul's teaching about the saving outcome for believing Jews and Gentiles is developed in 9:1–11:36, and the practical implications are explored in 12:1–15:13. The apostle is not simply concerned about the way individuals may be justified by faith and escape final judgment. Rather, his aim is to explain how God's saving plan is to restore people from every nation to a right relationship with their Creator and with one another, ultimately to share in the glory of a redeemed creation (8:18–39).

§2.2 The Scriptures

> The gospel of which Paul is not ashamed, in which the righteousness of God is revealed as by and for faith, corresponds precisely to the prophetic assertion that "the person who is righteous by faith will live" (1:16–17, citing Hab 2:4). The divine mystery is disclosed not only in "the *kerygma* (preaching or proclamation) of Jesus Christ" but also "through the prophetic writings" (16:26).[47]

Biblical citations abound in this letter, mostly in Rom 2:1–3:20; 4:1–25; 9:1–11:36; and 15:7–13.[48] Specifically in line with the claim in 1:2, some texts ground *an aspect of the gospel* in the revelation previously given by God to his people (Hab 2:4 in 1:17; Gen 15:6 in 4:3, 9, 22; Ps 32:1–2 [LXX 31:1–2] in 4:7–8; Gen 17:5 in 4:17; Gen 15:5 in 4:18; Isa 28:16 in 10:11; Joel 2:32 [MT and LXX 3:5] in 10:13).[49]

---

[47] Ibid., 102. Paul uses Scripture to show that "this gospel was not a *novum* or unexpected turn in God's purposes" (Dunn, *Theology of Paul*, 169). Cf. 3:21 ("attested by the Law and the Prophets"); 1 Cor 15:3–4; Gal 3:8.

[48] There are also numerous allusions to biblical texts and echoes of biblical passages and themes in Romans, ranging from the obvious (Adam in Rom 5:12–21), to the subtle (Ps 106:20 in 1:25), to the possible (Exod 32:1–6 in 7:7–11). Cf. Richard B. Hays, *Echoes of Scripture in the Letters of Paul* (New Haven: Yale University, 1989).

[49] Two of these texts stand at the heart of his exposition of the gospel in Galatians (Gen 15:6 in Gal 3:6–9; Hab 2:4 in Gal 3:11), showing a pattern of argument in relation to Jewish objections. See also Gen 12:3 in Gal 3:8 and Lev 18:5 in Gal 3:12.

The need for the gospel is demonstrated by other texts, which identify the culpability of Israel (Isa 52:5 in 2:24; Exod 20:17 in 7:7), or of Jews and Gentiles together (Eccl 7:20; Pss 14:2–3 [LXX 13:2–3; 5:9 [LXX 5:10]; 140:3 [MT 140:4; LXX 139:4]; 10:7 [LXX 9:28]; Isa 59:7–8; Ps 36:1 [MT 36:2; LXX 35:2] in 3:10–18). The *judgment of God* in response to human sin is the theme of a further set of texts (Prov 24:12 with Ps 62:12 [LXX 61:13] in 2:6; Ps 51:4 [MT 51:6; LXX 50:6] in 3:4).

Scripture is extensively used to establish the pattern of God's relationship with *Abraham's immediate descendants* (Gen 21:12 in 9:7; Gen 18:10, 14 in 9:9; Gen 25:23 in 9:12), and then with *national Israel* (Mal 1:2–5 in 9:13; Exod 33:19 in 9:15; Exod 9:16 in 9:17; Hos 2:23 [MT 2:25] and 1:10 [MT 2:1] in 9:25–26; Isa 10:22–23 in 9:27–28; Isa 1:9 in 9:29; Isa 28:16 with 8:14 in 9:33; Lev 18:5 in 10:5; Deut 30:12–14 in 10:6–8; 1 Kgs 19:14 in 11:3; 1 Kgs 19:18 in 11:4; Isa 29:10 with Deut 29:4 [MT 29:3]; Ps 69:22–23 [MT 69:23-24; LXX 68:23).[50]

God's saving plan for rebellious Israel is encapsulated in a quotation from Isa 59:20–21 (combined with words from Isa 27:9) in 11:26–27. Paul is optimistic about God's mercy being shown to Israelites who are hardened against the gospel (11:28–32), and he invites his readers to join him in praising God for the inexhaustible depths of his riches, wisdom, and knowledge (11:33–36). Questions from LXX Isa 40:13 and Job 41:11a (LXX 41:3a, possibly influenced by LXX Job 35:7) function doxologically in this context.

Meanwhile Paul uses Isa 52:15 in 15:21 to reveal *a motivation for his ministry*. He keeps preaching the gospel and establishing churches, where Christ has not been named, encouraged by the expectation that people everywhere will see and understand his message about the heavenly exaltation of the Suffering Servant. A series of texts in 10:15–21 explain that, although God has sent gospel

[50] Christopher D. Stanley (*Arguing with Scripture: The Rhetoric of Quotations in the Letters of Paul*, New Testament Series [New York/London: T&T Clark, 2004], 139–40) lists the things Paul expected his Roman readers to know from Scripture and argues that he "frames the majority of his quotations in a way that a person with little or no specific knowledge of the Jewish Scriptures could grasp his essential point." Although there is some wisdom in this conclusion, I think Paul's defense against Jewish objections often shows the need for a more sophisticated grasp of key passages in their biblical context.

preachers to Israel and the nations, Israel has largely remained *unbelieving and disobedient* (Isa 52:7 in 10:15; Isa 53:1 in 10:16; Ps 19:4 [MT 19:5; LXX 18:5] in 10:18; Deut 32:21 in 10:19; Isa 65:1–2 in 10:20–21).[51] But an echo of Deut 32:21 in 11:11–15 forms the basis for Paul's hope that more *Jews will come to faith as a result of his preaching to Gentiles*.

Another group of biblical texts is employed with reference to *Christian life and ministry*. In 8:36 Paul cites Ps 44:22 (MT 44:23; LXX 43:23) to show that suffering has always been the lot of God's people. But for the Christian the expression "because of you" specifically means "because of Christ." In 12:19–20 he combines Deut 32:35 with Prov 25:21–22 to encourage his readers not to seek vengeance against those who oppress them. In 13:9 he cites four of the Ten Commandments (Exod 20:13–17; Deut 5:17–21) before concluding that every commandment is summed up by the love commandment (Lev 19:18). In 14:11 he uses Isa 45:23 to support his claim that "we will all stand before the judgment seat of God." In 15:3 he reads Ps 69:9 (MT 69:10; LXX 68:10) as a prophecy about the Messiah's not pleasing himself and makes this the basis for exhorting the Romans to act in the same way toward one another.

A catena of texts in 15:9–12 explains why Paul has been so concerned for Christians to *welcome and support one another* in the Roman context. Linked quotations from the Law, the Prophets, and the Psalms (Ps 18:49 [MT 18:50; LXX 17:50]; Deut 32:43; Ps 117:1 [LXX 116:1]; Isa 11:10) justify the assertion that "Christ became a servant of the circumcised on behalf of God's truth, to confirm the promises to the fathers, and so that Gentiles may glorify God for his mercy" (15:8–9a). Paul's *missionary activity* is governed by this perspective, and his efforts to strengthen and mature churches through teaching, prayer, and the writing of letters have in view the glorification of God for his mercy (1:8–14; 15:14–19). So doxology and missiology overlap here.

In summary Scripture is used *didactically* in relation to God's character, his response to human sin, and his covenantal commitment to Abraham and his offspring. It is viewed *prophetically* in relation to the Messiah, Israel, and the nations, particularly in view

[51] Cf. J. Ross Wagner, *Heralds of the Good News: Paul and Isaiah "in Concert" in the Letter to the Romans*, NovTSup 101 (Leiden: Brill, 2002).

of the coming judgment of God. It is employed in a *hortatory* way to encourage Christians to make certain responses to God and other people, arising from their knowledge of God and his saving plan. It functions *missiologically* to explain Paul's ministry agenda and *doxologically* to celebrate its expected outcome.

The divine authority of these texts is indicated in various ways. Many are introduced with the formula καθὼς γέγραπται ("just as it is written" [1:17; 2:24; 3:4, 10; 4:17; 8:36; 9:13, 33; 10:15; 11:8, 26; 12:19 (without καθὼς); 15:3, 9, 21]). A parallel expression is ἡ γραφὴ λέγει ("Scripture says," 4:3; 10:11; 11:2). Biblical texts convey τὰ λόγια τοῦ θεοῦ (3:2, "the very words of God" [lit. "the oracles of God"]).[52] Although the human authors are acknowledged (David in 4:6–8; 11:9–10; Hosea in 9:25–26; Isaiah in 9:27–28, 29; 10:16, 20–21; 15:12; Moses in 10:5, 19), God speaks through their writings (9:25–26, God speaks to Israel "in [the book of] Hosea" [ἐν τῷ Ὡσηὲ λέγει]; 11:2–4, God speaks to Elijah "in [the passage about] Elijah" [ἐν Ἠλίᾳ]). In the book of Exodus God tells Moses what to say (9:15), and God speaks to Pharaoh through him (9:17).

Given this conviction about Scripture as the means by which God speaks to people, it may seem strange to modern readers that Paul's rendering of OT texts sometimes differs from the version printed in our English Bibles or that he gives verses novel interpretations. His primary source was the Septuagint (LXX), which was a Greek translation of the Hebrew original. Some of the variations in this text are particularly suitable for Paul's purpose. For example, the promise of LXX Isa 28:16 ("yet the one who believes *on him* will not be put to shame") is cited in 9:33 (conflated with Isa 8:14) and 10:11. This contains the important words ἐπ' αὐτῷ ("on him"), which are not found in the Hebrew but allow for the development of a Christological interpretation.

Most of the modifications Paul makes to LXX citations are simply "adaptations in grammar or syntax or wording to fit the text most appropriately to the syntax and rhetoric of the letter."[53] But some have a theological aim. For example, Paul cites Hab 2:4 in

---

[52] Dunn (*Theology of Paul*, 170) points out that Paul echoes earlier LXX usage here (e.g., Num 24:16; Deut 33:9; Pss 12:6 [LXX 11:7]; 18:30 [LXX 17:31]; Wis 16:11). Paul took for granted the claim that there were God-given oracles in a written form.

[53] Ibid., 171. Although it is possible in some contexts that Paul is using a different version of the LXX from the ones now extant or is translating freely from the

1:17 without a possessive pronoun so that the emphasis falls on faith generically as trust or reliance on God ("The righteous will live by faith").[54] In 10:6–8 "the righteousness that comes from faith" is said to "speak" through a Christological reading of Deut 30:12–14. In 11:26–27 a citation from Isa 59:20–21 mostly follows the LXX, with words from Isa 27:9 added ("when I take away their sins"). This brings the former more closely in line with the new covenant expectations of Jer 31:34 (cf. Ezek 36:25).

Both Greco-Roman and Jewish literature provide "strong evidence for a general cultural and literary ethos in which incorporating interpretive elements into the wording of a quotation was considered a normal and acceptable means of advancing one's argument."[55] In Paul's case a conviction that God's long-standing plan of salvation has been fulfilled in Jesus Christ gives him a hermeneutical principle by which to read and explain the Scriptures.

§2.3 God as Trinity

The word "God" occurs fewer than 153 times in this letter and is related in different ways to all its major themes. A comparison with the use of other terms shows that "Paul speaks of God so often that no other subject comes even remotely near it."[56] Fundamentally, Romans is about God!

Paul identifies God's invisible attributes as "his eternal power and divine nature" (1:20) but also draws attention to "the glory of the immortal God" revealed in his creation (1:23). In line with biblical prophecy, he warns about "the day of wrath, when God's righteous judgment is revealed" (2:5). Nevertheless, God has shown himself to be rich in "kindness, restraint, and patience" (2:4), desiring that

---

Hebrew himself, mostly it seems that he modifies the LXX for rhetorical and theological reasons.

[54] The MT reads "the righteous by *his* faith(fullness) shall live," and the LXX reads "the righteous by *my* faith(fullness) shall live."

[55] Christopher D. Stanley, *Paul and the Language of Scripture: Citation Technique in the Pauline Epistles and Contemporary Literature*, SNTSMS 74 (Cambridge: Cambridge University, 1992), 337.

[56] Leon L. Morris, "The Theme of Romans," in *Apostolic History and the Gospel: Biblical and Historical Essays Presented to F. F. Bruce on His 60th Birthday*, ed. W. Ward Gasque and Ralph P. Martin (Exeter: Paternoster, 1970), 250. Morris (251) concludes his statistical analysis by saying that "no other book in the New Testament has this same concentration on the God-theme."

all should repent and seek the salvation he promises (2:5–10). God revealed his character and will in spoken words to Israel (3:2), and even their unbelief could not "nullify God's faithfulness" (3:3). God must be true even though human beings prove to be false (3:4). God is righteous, and his righteousness is expressed in judgment and wrath (1:32; 2:5; 3:5–6; 9:22) but also in salvation, even in the justification of sinners (1:16–17; 3:21–26, 28; 4:5).[57]

God's plan of salvation involves showing love toward those who oppose him (5:6–10) and mercy toward the disobedient (9:14–15; 11:28–32). His wisdom, knowledge, and judgments surpass human understanding. Believers should acknowledge that "from him and through him and to him are all things" and glorify him forever (11:33–36). Jews and Gentiles who have already experienced his mercy in the Messiah Jesus are to glorify God with one mind and one voice (15:5–12).[58] He is the God of endurance and encouragement (15:5), the God of hope (15:13), the God of peace (15:33; 16:20), the eternal God (16:26), and the only wise God (16:27). Most importantly, he is "the God and Father of our Lord Jesus Christ" (15:6) and "God our Father" (1:7; cf. 6:4, "the Father"; 8:15, "*Abba*, Father").[59]

"Christ" is mentioned sixty-five times in Romans, mostly as a personal reference combined with the name Jesus, and often associated with the title Lord. The Davidic or messianic significance of Χριστός is indicated in 1:3–4 (cf. §1.6), and sometimes when the definite article is used, it would be appropriate to translate "the Messiah" (e.g., 9:5; 14:18; 15:3, 7). First and foremost, however, he is God's Son (1:3, 4, 9; 5:10; 8:29), whom God sent "in the likeness of sinful flesh as a sin offering" (8:3).[60]

---

[57] Cf. ibid., 255–58; Dunn, *Theology of Paul*, 27–50.

[58] Morris ("Theme of Romans," 260–62) explores more fully what Romans teaches about having God at the center of one's life.

[59] Marianne Meye Thompson ("'Mercy upon All': God as Father in the Epistle to the Romans," in Soderlund and Wright, eds., *Romans and the People of God*, 207) argues that "Paul's understanding of God as Father has less to do with certain attributes or characteristics that might be assigned to God, and much more to do with the way in which God's mercy and faithfulness persistently seek out a people as heirs of the divine promises." But the relational implications of calling God "Father" are significant in these references.

[60] Cf. Dunn, *Theology of Paul*, 202–6, 216–23.

The designation "his own Son" (8:32, τοῦ ἰδίου υἱοῦ) stresses the uniqueness of Christ's relationship to God as Father, compared with those who are adopted as "God's sons" through faith in him and reception of God's Spirit (8:14–17, 19; cf. 9:26).[61] Paul does not give much attention in Romans to the ontological aspect of this Father-Son relationship, but I argue in the commentary that the Messiah's divinity is affirmed in 9:5 (cf. Phil 2:6; Col 1:15–20; Titus 2:13). In 10:9–13 Paul identifies Christ with "the Lord" of Joel 2:32, upon whom everyone must call for salvation. In its original context this text refers to the Creator God, who is Israel's Lord. Moreover, when the day of the Lord comes, Christ Jesus will be the agent of God's judgment (2:16).[62]

God's Spirit is first mentioned in connection with the resurrection of Jesus from the dead (1:4). "The Spirit of holiness" is a Semitic way of speaking about the Holy Spirit, modeled on the Hebrew of Ps 51:11 and Isa 63:10–11.[63] The sense could be that the establishment of Jesus as Son-of-God-in-power was by the operation of God's Spirit or that his resurrection was by means of the Spirit. Alternatively, the sense is that the gift of the Spirit is the manifestation of his power as the exalted Christ and so "the guarantee of his having been appointed Son of God in might."[64]

The promised eschatological gift of God's Spirit to his people (cf. Isa 32:15–17; Ezek 36:26–27; Joel 2:28–29) is first marked by Paul's reference to circumcision "by the Spirit" (2:29) and the fact that "God's love has been poured out in our hearts through the

---

[61] Larry W. Hurtado ("Jesus' Divine Sonship in Paul's Epistle to the Romans," in *Romans and the People of God*, 223) argues that divine sonship language rhetoric is "clearly intended, at least in part, as honorific of Jesus," it carries "a strongly *theocentric* force that emphasizes God's involvement in Jesus," and it is also used "to link the salvation of the elect with the status of Jesus."

[62] Dunn (*Theology of Paul*, 234–60) argues that Jesus's lordship is "a status granted by God, a sharing in his authority" (254) but does not consider that Paul equates the exalted Christ with God in 9:5. Cf. Murray J. Harris, *Jesus as God: The New Testament Use of* Theos *in Reference to Jesus* (Grand Rapids: Baker, 1992), 154–65.

[63] Cf. Dunn, *Romans 1–8*, 15.

[64] Cranfield, *Romans*, 1:64. Gordon D. Fee (*God's Empowering Presence: The Holy Spirit in the Letters of Paul* [Peabody: Hendrickson, 1994], 483) argues that the expression is best understood as meaning "the Spirit who gives/supplies holiness" and that it anticipates much of the argument to come about the Spirit's work in believers. Fee denies that here or in 8:11 Paul means that the Spirit is God's agent in raising the dead.

Holy Spirit who was given to us" (5:5). Now it is possible to serve God "in the newness of the Spirit" (7:6), who sets believers free from "the law of sin and death" (8:2) and makes it possible for "the law's requirement" to be "fulfilled in us who do not walk according to the flesh but according to the Spirit" (8:4). The Spirit brings a life-changing "mind-set" and freedom to serve God in the present (8:5–8, 12–14; 9:1; 12:11). The Spirit's presence also assures us about our future bodily resurrection with Christ (8:10–11; cf. 1:4).

The Spirit of God is also called "the Spirit of Christ" (8:9; cf. Gal 4:6; Phil 1:19), and the indwelling Spirit is equated with Christ being "in you" (8:10).[65] These verses, together with those that speak of the relationship of Christ to God or the Son to the Father, point to an implicit Trinitarianism. This is not formally argued, but Paul clearly distinguishes between the three "in terms of the distinctive role of each in salvation."[66] At the same time, Paul makes close links between the risen Christ and the Holy Spirit, and the Father and the Son, making it clear that he is speaking about the way we encounter the one divine being (cf. 2 Cor 13:13).

The Spirit enables God's children to cry "*Abba*, Father" and to be assured thereby of adoption as "God's sons." As such, they are "coheirs with Christ" of the glory to come (8:15–17). As "the firstfruits" of redemption, the Spirit enables believers to wait eagerly for the full experience of adoption in "the redemption of our bodies" (8:23). Meanwhile, "the Spirit also helps us in our weakness," interceding for us with "unspoken groanings" (8:26–27). The Spirit enables joy (14:17), the overflowing of hope (15:13), sanctification through faith in Christ (15:16), and love (15:30).[67]

---

[65] "The Spirit is none other than the way the eternal God and his Christ have come to us in the present, as a personal presence taking up residence within the life of the believer" (Fee, *God's Empowering Presence*, 554). Constantine R. Campbell (*Paul and Union with Christ: An Exegetical and Theological Study* [Grand Rapids: Zondervan, 2012], 353–68) observes how the theme of union with Christ in Paul's writings exposes his implicit Trinitarianism.

[66] Fee, *God's Empowering Presence*, 554. "God is the ground of all things and the one who raises the dead; Christ is the one who has brought righteousness; and the Spirit is the presence of both God and Christ in the present, thus giving life now and guaranteeing life for the future" (554).

[67] Contextually, "the power of God's Spirit" in 15:19 relates to Paul's ministry of the word, and "the power of miraculous signs and wonders" relates to the "deeds" that were part of his apostolic ministry. "The power of God's Spirit" refers to what was

§2.4 Righteousness and Justification

Righteousness and justification are related themes in the argument of Romans, but readers of the English text may not immediately discern the connection. The Greek words Paul uses have the same root, as do the relevant Hebrew terms, but "righteousness" and "justification" are not so linked in English. Linguistic, contextual, and theological factors must be considered together in exploring the way Paul blends various strands of biblical thought when he uses this terminology.[68]

"The righteousness of God" (δικαιοσύνη θεοῦ) is central to Paul's presentation of the gospel in 1:17; 3:5, 21, 22; 10:3, and "his righteousness" (τῆς δικαιοσύνης αὐτοῦ) is mentioned in 3:25, 26.[69] God's righteousness is set against human unrighteousness (1:18, 29; 2:8; 3:5; 6:13[ἀδικία]). But Paul's gospel also proclaims a righteousness God attributes to human beings "by faith" (4:3, 5–6, 9, 11, 13, 22; 9:30; 10:6, 10). This is called "the gift of righteousness" (5:17; cf. 5:21; 8:10; 14:17). It is contrasted with "the righteousness of the law" (9:31; 10:4) and any attempt to establish one's own righteousness before God (10:3).

Paul's teaching about attributed righteousness parallels his extensive discussion of justification by faith and the impossibility of being "justified" or "declared righteous" (using the verb δικαιόω) by "works" or "works of the law" (3:20, 24, 26, 28, 30; 4:2, 5; 5:1, 9; 8:30, 33). Justification by faith brings people into a relationship with God that enables them to exhibit righteous behavior (6:12-14) and to be "enslaved to righteousness" (6:18–19).

Some would explain God's righteousness it terms of his covenant faithfulness.[70] However, "if a special notion like covenant is assumed,

---

highlighted in 15:16, namely, the drawing of Gentiles into a sanctified relationship with God through faith in Christ. Paul teaches that the Spirit enables faith through the preaching of the gospel (cf. 5:5; 2 Cor 3:3, 16–17; 2 Thess 2:13–14).

[68] For a simple introduction to the "old perspective"-"new perspective" debate on these issues, see James D. G. Dunn, "What's Right about the Old Perspective on Paul," and Stephen Westerholm, "What's Right about the New Perspective on Paul," in Harmon and Smith, eds., *Studies in the Pauline Epistles*, 214–42.

[69] In the LXX, words with δικ- as their root are consistently used to render Hebrew words in the צדק group. These terms deal with behavior that accords with some benchmark or norm, often God's revealed will or his character.

[70] Cf. John A. Zeisler, *The Meaning of Righteousness in Paul: A Linguistic and Theological Investigation*, SNTSMS 20 (Cambridge: Cambridge University 1972),

it remains firmly in the background."[71] When the noun δικαιοσύνη is used in the LXX with reference to human righteousness, right behavior is overwhelmingly in view. In some contexts the covenant with Israel defines what is righteous (e.g., Deut 6:25; Ezek 18:5–9), but in other contexts the covenant is not in view (e.g., Gen 20:4). God's righteousness moves him to act in ways that are consistent with his righteous character, and there is no injustice with God (Rom 9:14).

The actual phrase δικαιοσύνη θεοῦ ("the righteousness of God") never occurs in the LXX, though δικαιοσύνη κυρίου is used with reference to the Lord's righteous acts (1 Sam 12:7; Mic 6:5). Regularly in the Psalms and Isaiah, however, δικαιοσύνη is modified by a personal pronoun referring to God. In these verses righteousness is ascribed to God, or God is said to do or speak righteousness (e.g., Ps 22:31; 35:28; 40:10; 51:14; Isa 51:5–6; Mic 7:9). Sometimes God's righteousness is understood with reference to the judgment or vengeance he brings upon the wicked (e.g., Pss 7:17; 9:8; 50:6; 97:2; Isa 59:17). Sometimes the context indicates that God's righteousness is an activity equivalent to his saving intervention on behalf of his people (e.g., Pss 51:14 [LXX 50:16]; 71:15–16; Isa 46:13).[72] Many of these texts predict the arrival of God's righteousness in some ultimate, transforming way at the time of his eschatological deliverance. For example, when God acts to vindicate and save his people, he will wrap them "in a robe of righteousness" (Isa 61:10 [MT]; cf. Zech 3:3–5).

In a number of passages, God's righteousness is more the basis, or the motivation, for his saving activity rather than a way of describing the activity itself (e.g., Pss 31:1; 35:24; 36:6, 10; 103:17; 143:1). It identifies an aspect of God's character that is revealed in judging or saving.[73] Despite the fact that God's righteousness is often par-

36–39; Wright, "Romans," 397–406.

[71] David J. Reimer, "צדק," *NIDOTTE* 3:750.

[72] While some texts point to the way believers benefit from God's righteousness when it is manifested, others may not (e.g., Pss 35:24, 27–28; 51:14; 69:27; Isa 46:12–13; 62:1–2; Mic 7:9). Moo (*Romans*, 82) reads too much into the evidence when he argues that, in certain contexts, "God's righteousness clearly includes the aspect of gift or status enjoyed by the recipient." It may be better to say that vindication and transformation of the situation of individuals or nation is suggested by such passages.

[73] Reimer ("צדק," 3:752) examines how "the declarations concerning Yahweh's actions using *tsdq* shade naturally towards reflections on his being or character."

alleled with his love or his faithfulness toward his people (e.g., Pss 33:4–5; 36:5–7; Isa 51:1–6; Dan 9:7–9; Rom 3:2–5), these terms should not be merged or confused.

Righteousness language in the Hebrew Scriptures is sometimes used in connection with creation theology. This particularly applies to passages that have to do with the divine administration of justice, where God appears as the king who effects justice or righteousness in and for the world he has made.[74] The fact "*that* God acts first on behalf of Israel (and against Israel) may be said to arise from his covenantal relationship with the nation. *What* he enacts, however, is that right order between himself and the *world* which constitutes its salvation."[75] God acts in this way because he is righteous.

In judicial settings where God is a party to the dispute, verdicts are sometimes expressed in vindicating or justifying acts. So, "righteousness" can refer to "an act of judgment or state of affairs which results from it, signifying it as the triumphant outcome of a struggle over justice."[76] "Precisely in its forensic sense, therefore, 'justification' entails deliverance and salvation."[77] The triumph of one party brings defeat to another, and so the "justification of God" has the condemnation of his enemies as its counterpart (cf. Exod 9:27; 2 Chr 12:1–6; Neh 9:33; Lam 1:18; Dan 9:7; Rom 3:4, citing Ps 51:4). Even in contexts where God is said to act punitively, "terms for righteousness express the divine victory that emerges from judgment."[78]

In 1:17 "the righteousness of God" revealed in the gospel is said to be attested by Hab 2:4 ("the righteous will live by faith"), which speaks of deliverance through judgment. This theme is developed

---

[74] Mark A. Seifrid, "Righteousness Language in the Hebrew Scriptures and Early Judaism," in *Justification and Variegated Nomism*: Volume 1, *The Complexities of Second Temple Judaism*, ed. Donald A. Carson, Peter T. O'Brien, Mark A. Seifrid, WUNT 2.140 (Mohr Siebeck: Tübingen, 2001): 415–42.

[75] Mark A. Seifrid, "Paul's Use of Righteousness Language Against Its Hellenistic Background," in *Justification and Variegated Nomism*: Volume 2—*The Paradoxes of Paul*, ed. Donald A. Carson, Peter T. O'Brien, Mark A. Seifrid, WUNT 2.181 (Mohr Siebeck: Tübingen, 2004), 40. See also his comments on pp. 41–43 regarding the relationship between righteousness and salvation in biblical thought.

[76] Ibid., 41 (emphasis removed). E.g., 1 Sam 26:23; 2 Sam 22:21; Isa 58:2; Ezek 3:20; Ps 18:21–25; 2 Chr 6:24. Seifrid includes Gen 15:6 and Ps 106:31 here.

[77] Ibid. (emphasis removed).

[78] Ibid., 44. Cf. Pss 11:1–7; 50:6; Isa 1:27–28; 5:14–17; 10:20–23; 28:17.

in 1:18–3:20, climaxing in Paul's exposition of the way God's righteousness has been revealed in the saving work of Christ (3:21–26).[79]

The noun "righteousness" (δικαιοσύνη) is then used with reference to believers in Rom 4:3, 5–6, 9, 11, 13, 22, echoing the claim in Gen 15:6 that "Abraham believed the LORD, and he credited it to him as righteousness." The crediting on view here is a reckoning of something that is not inherent to that person, in this case righteousness before God. Paul relates the reckoning of righteousness to the nonreckoning of sin (4:8; cf. Ps 32:2), suggesting "a creative act, whereby the believer is given a new 'status.'"[80] The chapter concludes by saying that righteousness will be "credited to us who believe in him who raised Jesus our Lord from the dead. He was delivered up for our trespasses and raised for our justification (δικαίωσις)" (4:24–25). As previously noted, Paul uses the language of righteousness to express in a different way what he means by justification by faith.

The verb "justify" (δικαιόω) occurs with different applications in Rom 2:13; 3:4, 20, 24, 26, 28, 30; 4:2, 5; 5:1, 9; 6:7; 8:30, 33. This verb is used in the LXX to translate the hiphil form of the Hebrew צָדַק, which almost always has a judicial or forensic meaning, having to do with "the adjudication or declaration of right behavior or status."[81] Sometimes the judge who pronounces people righteous or acquits is human (e.g., Deut 25:1; Isa 5:23), while at other times the judge is God (e.g., Exod 23:7; 1 Kgs 8:32; Ps 82:3; Isa 50:8). The obligation for kings to dispense justice is highlighted in various ways (e.g., 2 Sam 8:15; 1 Kgs 10:9; Jer 22:15) and becomes a feature in prophecies about the rule of the Messiah (e.g., Isa 9:7; 11:1–5; 32:1, 16; Jer 23:5).

In Paul's letters the verb δικαιόω is consistently forensic and positive in meaning: "to 'justify' someone is to vindicate them, not

[79] A. Katherine Grieb ("The Righteousness of God in Romans," in Sumney, ed. *Reading Paul's Letter*, 65–78) argues that the "moral integrity of God" is expressed by this term and lies at the heart of Paul's argument in Romans.

[80] Moo, *Romans*, 264. D. A. Carson ("The Vindication of Imputation: On Fields of Discourse and Semantic Fields," in *Justification: What's at Stake in the Current Debates*, ed. Mark Husbands and Daniel J. Treier [Downers Grove: InterVarsity, 2004], 56–68) considers the extent to which this may be described as an imputation of righteousness. Campbell (*Paul and Union with Christ*, 388–405) explores the relationship between union with Christ and justification in Paul's letters.

[81] Reimer, "צדק," 3:746.

to punish them."[82] Sinners are justified freely "through the redemption that is in Christ Jesus," whom God put forward as "an atoning sacrifice in his blood, received through faith" (3:23–25a; cf. 8:3, "a sin offering"). God is able to declare "the ungodly to be righteous" (4:5), and remain righteous himself (3:26), because of his penal and substitutionary provision in the sacrificial death of his Son. Justification and the righteous status it achieves are bound up with the death and resurrection of the Messiah (4:25). We are "declared righteous by his blood" (5:9) and "saved by his life" (5:10). Indeed, the gift of righteousness to believers makes it possible for them to "reign in life through the one man, Jesus Christ" (5:17, 21). Victory over sin and death is achieved for us by the one "righteous act" of Christ (5:18, δικαίωμα).[83]

In 6:7 Paul speaks in a novel way about being (lit.) "justified from sin" (δεδικαίωται ἀπὸ τῆς ἁμαρτίας).[84] He goes on to imply that freedom from the penalty for sin through justification by faith enables resistance to the power of sin (6:11–23). Attributed righteousness is a power for moral transformation, issuing in the practical righteousness that is consistent with God's character and will (6:13, 16, 18–20; cf. 14:17). This passage picks up and applies the claim in 5:21: "Just as sin reigned in death, so also grace will reign through righteousness, resulting in eternal life through Jesus Christ our Lord." God's justification of his elect in 8:30–31 enables them to triumph over everything that may "separate us from the love of God in Christ Jesus our Lord" (8:39). In short, Paul uses this verb with reference to eschatological vindication, which is experienced in advance of final salvation through faith in Christ and his finished work.

The language of righteousness and justification in Romans embraces much the apostle wants to say about God and the gospel. Primarily he wants to show how God has acted in fulfillment

[82] Seifrid, "Paul's Use of Righteousness Language," 52.

[83] The noun δικαίωμα means "righteous requirement" or "righteous action" in 1:32; 2:26; 5:18; 8:4. In 5:16 it is used as a substitute for δικαίωσις (4:25; 5:18, "justification"), where Paul appears to have chosen it to function as a rhetorical counterpart to κατάκριμα ("condemnation").

[84] CSB "freed from sin" should be understood to mean "declared free from (responsibility in relation to) sin" (Dunn, *Romans 1–8*, 320). Byrne (*Romans*, 197) suggests the translation "legally free from sin."

of his ancient promises to put things right for those who believe, "first to the Jew, and also to the Greek" (1:16). This claim anticipates the salvation-historical perspective that is developed in 9:1–11:36. Although the messianic salvation has been proclaimed to Jews everywhere, many remain "disobedient and defiant" (10:21). Paradoxically, Paul magnifies his ministry to the Gentiles so as to make unbelieving Israelites jealous (11:11–15; cf. §2.5; 2.7). Israel's unbelief is related to their pursuit of righteousness "by the works of the law" (3:20, 27–28; 4:1–5, 13–15; 9:30–10:12). But the gospel is the power of God for salvation to everyone who *believes* because "in it the righteousness of God is revealed from faith to faith" (1:17).

God has acted decisively in the death and resurrection of Israel's Messiah to put Jews and Gentiles right with himself through faith (3:21–26; 4:23–25). The resurrection of Jesus is essential for justification because it is the divine vindication of the one who was "delivered up for our trespasses" (4:25). We are "saved by his life" (5:10) in the sense that we are brought through resurrection ourselves into the glory of a renewed creation with him (5:1–2; 8:17–30).

The righteousness of God continues to be powerfully revealed in the preaching of the gospel of grace. God acts to justify people by faith through the proclamation of his justifying work in the death and resurrection of Jesus. Righteousness in the sense of a right standing with God becomes a power at work in believers, enabling righteous living in the present and perseverance in hope (5:1–5). In his comprehensive provision of redemption for the whole created order, God has fulfilled the covenant made with Abraham and his spiritual offspring by bringing eschatological blessing to Israel and the nations.

§2.5 Israel and the Church

The word ἐκκλησία ("gathering, assembly, church"), which is much used in Paul's other letters, can only be found in the final chapter of Romans. It is used in the plural to describe the many gatherings that belong to Christ (16:16), which are dispersed throughout the nations (16:4), and in the singular to identify a Christian congregation in a particular town or city (16:1, 23). More narrowly, it is applied to a gathering in the home of Prisca and Aquila (16:5), who were patrons or hosts of that church. House churches may be indicated by different terminology in 16:10, 11, 14–15.[85]

When Paul first addresses his Roman readers, no leaders are mentioned, and he does not describe them as a church.[86] They are simply those who are "called by Jesus Christ" (1:6). As such, they are "brothers and sisters" in Christ (1:13; 7:1, 4; 8:12; 10:1; 11:25; 12:1; 15:14, 30; 16:17). God's love for them and his calling of them to be "saints" sets them apart from the other citizens of Rome (1:7; cf. 8:27; 12:13; 16:2, 15). This designation raises the question of their relationship with Israel, which was called to be a "holy nation" (Exod 19:6), set apart to God as his special possession.[87] Paul begins to answer this question in Romans 2–4 and explores it more fully in 9–11.

Before dealing with that issue, Paul uses the image of the body in 12:4–5 as a foundation for exhorting the Romans collectively about the exercise of gifts and ministries for one another's benefit (cf. 1 Cor 12:1–31; Eph 4:4, 11–16). He then encourages them to express love in ways that demonstrate affectionate, familial relationships (12:9–16) and challenges them to have a united approach to opponents and civic authorities (12:17–13:10). Paul's extended exhortation in 14:1–15:7 calls them to recognize the need to walk in love toward one another and serve Christ by pursuing what promotes peace and builds up one another. Such language is used in 1 Cor 12–14 for gatherings of the whole church in that city. So, even if Paul does not call the Christians in Rome "the church in Rome," and even if they never meet in one place together, he expects them to act as "one body in Christ" (12:5).[88]

---

[85] Cf. Jewett, *Romans*, 53–55, 62–69. Four of the five groups mentioned in Rom 16 lack patrons and could simply have met in crowded tenement buildings, where the leadership pattern may have been more collective and egalitarian.

[86] Moo (*Romans*, 54) does not think much should be made of this since Paul does not consistently use the word in his letter openings (cf. Eph 1:1; Phil 1:1; Col 1:1). So also Schreiner, *Romans*, 37. But Paul's failure to use the term collectively in Romans raises questions about the nature of their gatherings, how they related to one another, and how he would consider them as a unity.

[87] The term ἁγίοι ("saints" or "holy ones") is generally used by Paul to describe God's new covenant people, set apart through faith in Christ to belong to God and to one another (cf. 1 Cor 1:2, 30; 6:11; 2 Thess 2:13). In Rom 15:25, 26, 31 the saints in Jerusalem are Jewish Christians. Cf. Otto Procksch, "ἅγιος, κτλ.," *TDNT* 1:105–7.

[88] Peter T. O'Brien (*The Letter to the Ephesians*, PNTC [Grand Rapids: Eerdmans, 1999], 146–47) observes that the word "church" has a wider meaning in Eph 1:22;

The apostle builds toward a new definition of the people of God when he focuses on the Jew who is one inwardly, whose circumcision is "of the heart—by the Spirit, not the letter" (2:29). This is in the context of exposing Israel's historic failure (2:17–3:19), enabling Paul to conclude that no human being will be justified in God's sight by "the works of the law, because the knowledge of sin comes through the law" (3:20). Paul returns to the problem of Israel's failure and God's response in 9–11.

Meanwhile, Paul celebrates that believing Gentiles can share with believing Jews in the messianic salvation (3:21–31). The biblical foundation for this community of faith is located in the promises made to Abraham (4:9–18; cf. §1.2). Most importantly, Scripture teaches that Abraham was declared righteous by faith before he received the covenant sign of circumcision. This made him the father of Gentiles who believe but are not circumcised, as well as the father of Jews who "follow in the footsteps of the faith our father Abraham had while still uncircumcised" (4:11–12).

Paul alludes to the blessing of Gen 12:3 ("and all the peoples on earth will be blessed through you") when he talks about Gentiles and Jews being equally justified by faith. This is articulated in Rom 4:16–18 with reference to Abraham's God-given role as "father of many nations" (Gen 17:5). God is concerned to bless the whole human race, but he chose to do this by first blessing Israel as a nation, in line with his ancient promises. Salvation through faith in Christ is now available for Abraham's spiritual offspring in Israel *and* among the nations, bringing deliverance from God's judgment and new life (4:22–25; cf. 10:9–13). The renewing Spirit of God is one of the gifts flowing from justification by faith (5:1–6; 7:4–6; 8:1–17; cf. Gal 3:6–14).

In 9–11 Paul seeks to answer certain questions posed by the failure of many Jews to believe the gospel. Have the promises of God failed? Why have only a remnant of Jews acknowledged Jesus as the promised Savior while many Gentiles believe? Is there any hope for the unbelieving majority of Israel? Why are the Jews so

3:10, 21; 5:23–24, 27, 29, 32; Col 1:18, 24. He understands this metaphorically in terms of a heavenly gathering of believers around Christ (cf. Heb 12:22–24), which finds concrete, visible expression in local congregational or house-church gatherings.

hardened if they are God's elect nation? Can there be salvation for ethnic Israel apart from faith in Christ?

Faced with the prospect of God's inevitable judgment for Israel's sin, the prophets predicted invasion and exile, out of which only a remnant would be saved (9:25–29, citing Hos 2:23 with 1:10; Isa 10:22–23 with 1:9). Paul sees this process of election within Israel continuing in the gospel era. Pursuing the law for righteousness, Israel as a whole "has not achieved the righteousness of the law" because "they did not pursue it by faith, but as if it were by works" (9:31–32). They have "stumbled over the stumbling stone," which is their Messiah (9:33, citing Isa 28:16 with 8:14). They have refused to submit to God's righteousness and to acknowledge that "Christ is the end of the law for righteousness to everyone who believes" (10:4).

Gentiles, who have turned to Christ in great numbers, have obtained "the righteousness that comes from faith" (9:30). The message that righteousness and salvation are available through faith in Christ has gone out "to the whole earth" (10:9–18), but Israel as a people remains disobedient and defiant (10:20–21, citing Isa 65:1–2). Some Israelites have believed, including Paul himself—whom he calls "a remnant chosen by grace" (11:5) and "the elect" (11:7)—but "the rest were hardened" (11:7–10, citing Isa 29:10 with Deut 29:4 and Ps 69:22–23).

As Paul turns to address his Gentile readers directly about this situation, he insists that some Israelites who are hardened may not have stumbled irreparably. "On the contrary, by their transgression, salvation has come to the Gentiles to make Israel jealous" (11:11, alluding to Deut 32:21, as cited in 10:19). God's ultimate plan is to bring "their fullness" (11:12, τὸ πλήρωμα αὐτῶν) to share in the promised eschatological salvation. Use of the same noun in the expression τὸ πλήρωμα τῶν ἐθνῶν (11:25, "the fullness of the Gentiles") suggests that the reference in 11:12 is to the full number of the elect in Israel.[89] This is also what Paul means by "all Israel will be saved" (11:26).

Pursuing his ministry as apostle to the Gentiles (11:13), Paul preached in a broad sweep from Jerusalem to Illyricum, establishing

[89] Jewett (*Romans*, 678) observes that, like 4 Ezra 4:35–37; 2 Bar. 23:4–5, Paul has in mind "the predestined number of the saved." Cf. Moo, *Romans*, 689–90.

people from different nations as disciples of Christ (cf. 1:8–15; 15:14–32). By this means he also hoped to make some of his own nation jealous and thus save some of them (11:14, alluding to Deut 32:21 again). God's setting apart a portion of Israel as "the first-fruits" of eschatological salvation through faith in the Messiah guarantees the consecration of "the whole batch" (11:16). Changing the metaphor, Paul insists that "if the root is holy, so are the branches." This anticipates the argument to come, where the patriarchs are most likely "the root" (11:17–18; cf. 9:5; 11:28).[90]

In a passage that is vital for determining the relationship between Israel and the church, the people of God are likened to an olive tree that has both wild and natural branches (11:17–24).[91] This figure is used to explain how Jews and Gentiles can be one people, united in Jesus the Messiah, and fulfilling God's covenant promises to the patriarchs. The historic "breaking off" of some of the branches refers to the hardening of unbelieving Israelites against the gospel (10:16–21; 11:7–10), which Paul also describes as "their rejection" (11:15). In Jer 11:16 and Hos 14:6 Israel is portrayed as God's "olive tree" and in later Jewish literature as God's "planting" (e.g., 2 Macc 1:29; Jub. 1:16; 1 En. 10:16; 26:1). However, the olive tree in Rom 11:17–24 is more broadly "the people of God, which is composed of both Jews and Gentiles."[92]

Every individual Gentile who has been grafted in with the believing remnant of Israel is identified as being "a wild olive branch." God's grafting makes it possible for each one to share together with

[90] Abraham and the patriarchs are described this way in Jewish texts such as 1 En 93:5, 8; Philo, *Her.* 279; Jub. 21:24. Schreiner (*Romans*, 600) argues that both images in Rom 11:16 relate to the consecration of "all Israel" to God by his choice of the patriarchs. Kruse (*Romans*, 433–34) concludes that they relate to the consecration of true Jews by the faith of Abraham (cf. 4:12).

[91] In this case I am using "the church" as a theological description of the new covenant people of God in a way that Paul does not use it in Romans. However, see n. 88 above concerning the wider application of this term in other Pauline letters.

[92] Schreiner, *Romans*, 805. Donald W. B. Robinson ("The Salvation of Israel in Romans 9–11," in *Assembling God's People*, vol. 1 of *Donald Robinson Selected Works*, ed. Peter G. Bolt and Mark D. Thompson [Sydney: Australian Church Record/Moore College, 2008], 57–58) observes that unbelieving Jews are "still 'holy,' having an inalienable title to the privileges of Israel, and though God's severity has fallen on them for their present unbelief, the olive tree to which God is well able to restore them is 'their own olive tree.'"

believing Israelites in "the rich root of the cultivated olive tree" (11:17). Despite the hardness of many, God has not finished with Israel as an elect nation, and he still intends to be merciful to their full number (11:12; cf. 11:25–32). "All Israel" will be saved by "the Deliverer," who will "turn godlessness away from Jacob" and "take away their sins" (11:26–27, citing Isa 59:20–21 with a portion of Isa 27), thus fulfilling the promise of a new covenant with the house of Israel and the house of Judah (Jer 31:31–34; cf. Ezek 36:25–27).[93]

Salvation comes to Israel and the nations by different routes, although the death and resurrection of the Messiah is the only *means* of rescue for both. Israelites come to Christ from the privileged position of being members of an elect nation, possessing "the very words of God" (3:2) and having all the provisions of the law of God (9:4–5). Gentiles become partners in the messianic salvation by hearing and believing the gospel, not by becoming Israelites. Gentile believers share with believing Israelites the same benefits of "the root," but they can never become "natural branches" (11:17–24).

Jews and Gentiles lose their distinctive identity in the body of Christ (cf. Gal 3:28–29; Eph 2:11–22; Col 3:11), which is "not a new Israel, but a new mankind, the church in its spiritual and heavenly reality."[94] The church has not simply replaced Israel. "As a national entity, as Paul has made clear (11:1–2), Israel continues to exist as the object of God's care and attention."[95] But the church is both the continuation of spiritual Israel into the new age and a new creation including many Gentiles who have put their trust in the Lord Jesus Christ (cf. Rev 7). This eschatological fellowship is the intended outcome of God's plan of salvation for Israel and the nations (e.g., Isa 2:1–5; 49:5–6; Jer 3:16–18). Indeed, "the church, not Israel, is now the locus of God's work in the world."[96]

---

[93] The blessings of the new covenant come to Gentiles through faith in Israel's Messiah. He makes possible the promised moral and spiritual renewal because of the definitive forgiveness of sins.

[94] Donald W. B. Robinson, "Jew and Greek: Unity and Division in the Early Church," in Bolt and Thompson, eds., *Assembling God's People*, 85.

[95] Moo, *Romans*, 709. As in the first century, national or ethnic Israel must include Jews scattered across the world, not simply those living in the land.

[96] Moo, *Romans*, 709. According to Matt 16:17–19, Jesus spoke of the eschatological community of believers as "my church." This was in contrast to the "assembly" of Israel, gathered by God at Sinai (Exod 19:1–6) and then established in the land with a physical sanctuary at the center. Jesus gathered disciples into his eschatological

Paul uses the allegory in 11:13–24 to warn Gentile Christians not to be arrogant about unbelieving Jews or to retreat into unbelief themselves. At the same time, he highlights the possibility that God might graft many "natural branches" from Israel back into "their own olive tree." His wider concern is to show how the word of God has not failed (9:6) and to expose how God may act to make Israel jealous and to save their full number (11:11–12, 25–32). Paul draws attention to the significance of his own ministry in this context and prepares for his appeal to the Romans Christians to support his mission to Spain (15:22–32).

The argument that the word of God has not failed assures us that God's promises about the future are trustworthy. Christians should be prayerful about the salvation of "all Israel," as Paul was (10:1), and not dismiss the possibility that God could soften hard hearts and bring many more Jews to faith in Jesus Christ. There is no justification for anti-Semitism in Paul's writings, but neither will he allow us to think that Jews may experience salvation in some other way. Paul's warning about the kindness and severity of God is an encouragement to persevere in faith and remain part of the community that is rooted in the promises of God to the patriarchs of Israel.

§2.6 Worship, Sanctification, and Holy Living

In 12:1–15:13 Paul urges his readers to adopt patterns of thinking and behavior impelled by the gospel. As recipients together of the eschatological mercies of God, they are to use their gifts for the benefit of others in the body of Christ (12:3–8), to love one another with family affection (12:9–13), to respond in a Christlike way to persecutors (12:14–21), and to submit to the governing authorities, especially in the payment of financial obligations (13:1–7). The command to "love your neighbor as yourself" is fulfilled by doing no wrong to a neighbor (13:8–10, citing Lev 19:18). Christians are

community as they expressed their faith in him (Matt 16:13–16). This process continued after his death and resurrection as the gospel was preached to Jewish audiences (Acts 2:36–47). In its infancy the church was essentially the new or reconstituted Israel of biblical prophecy. With the influx of people from many nations, it became the new humanity, uniting believing Jews and Gentiles as "a holy temple in the Lord," indwelt by the Spirit of God (Eph 2:13–22). Cf. David G. Peterson, *The Acts of the Apostles*, PNTC (Grand Rapids: Eerdmans, 2009), 92–97.

not called to live under the law of Moses[97] but to conduct their lives in a way that shows they have "put on the Lord Jesus Christ" and are waiting expectantly for the experience of final salvation (13:11–14; cf. 8:23–30).[98]

Paul's exhortation in 14:1–15:13 focuses more specifically on the way love, rather than a judgmental attitude, should be reflected among the Roman believers. References to disputes about food and the observance of certain days in honor of the Lord suggest that some were concerned to keep aspects of the Jewish ceremonial law while others believed themselves to be free from these obligations. An inclusion is formed between the opening challenge to welcome one another (14:1) and the charge to welcome one another (lit.) "just as the Messiah also welcomed you, to the glory of God" (15:7).[99] The Christological focus of this passage climaxes with a statement about God's purpose in bringing Jews and Gentiles together in Christ to "glorify God for his mercy," which is supported by a series of biblical citations (15:8–13).

The exhortation to "present your bodies as a living sacrifice, holy and pleasing to God" (12:1) introduces the letter's hortatory section.[100] Paul's language recalls the pivotal challenge in 6:13 to "offer yourselves to God, and all the parts of yourselves to God as weapons for righteousness." This is now identified as (lit.) "your reasonable service" or "your understanding service" (τὴν λογικὴν λατρείαν ὑμῶν).[101] A parallel exhortation about not being conformed to this age but being "transformed by the renewing of your mind"

[97] Cf. §1.4; Schreiner, *The Law and Its Fulfillment*, 145–78; Rosner, *Paul and the Law*, 158–222.

[98] As well as suggesting a personal devotion to Christ, "put on the Lord Jesus Christ" (13:14) should be understood in terms of obeying from the heart "that pattern of teaching to which you were handed over" (6:17).

[99] "Welcome" (BDAG, NRSV, ESV), rather than simply "accept" (CSB, NIV), is a better rendering of προσλαμβάνω in both verses. The meaning could be "welcome into your homes" or "welcome into the fellowship of the church in your homes" (cf. Jewett, *Romans*, 835–36).

[100] Victor P. Furnish ("Living to God, Walking in Love: Theology and Ethics in Romans," in Sumney, ed., *Reading Paul's Letter*, 187–202) outlines the way Rom 1–11 provides the theological foundation and "shapes the actual content of the ethical appeals that follow" (187).

[101] Cf. David G. Peterson, *Engaging with God: A Biblical Theology of Worship* (Downers Grove: InterVarsity, 1992), 64–70. Paul is talking about the service rendered by those who truly understand the gospel and its implications for everyday life.

(12:2) offers the possibility of discerning and doing the will of God in everyday life. Paul is not advocating the interiorizing or moralization of worship but indicating that God is to be served by regularly presenting ourselves to him on the basis of his merciful provisions in the Lord Jesus Christ. This is the service that is "consonant with the truth of the gospel."[102]

In Romans 12–15 worship, ministry, and a gospel-based ethic are closely linked together. Various terms in 12:1–2 and 15:5–12 recall 1:18–32 but signal a reversal of the downward spiral of humanity's rebellion against God.[103] Human beings characteristically refuse to glorify God as God and show gratitude to him (1:21), but those who have come under the Messiah's rule can glorify God "with one mind and one voice" (15:6).[104] Humanity's exchange of the truth of God for a lie resulted in the fact that they "worshiped and served (ἐλάτρευσαν) what has been created instead of the Creator, who is praised forever" (1:25). Using the cognate noun, Paul proclaims the possibility of a new kind of "service" (λατρεία) to God because of the sacrificial death of Jesus and its transforming implications (3:24–26; 8:1–4).

The renewal of worship is linked to "the renewing of your mind" (12:2). Senseless, darkened minds (1:21) are transformed when people turn to God in Christ and are led by God's Spirit. Transformed thinking leads to changed behavior (8:5–14; cf. Titus 3:5).[105] Bodies degraded through unnatural sexual indulgence (1:24, 26–27) can be presented "as a living sacrifice, holy and pleasing to God" (12:1).

---

[102] Charles E. B. Cranfield, *Introduction and Commentary on Romans IX–XVI and Essays*, vol. 2 of *A Critical and Exegetical Commentary on the Epistle to the Romans*, ICC (Edinburgh: T&T Clark, 1979), 2:605.

[103] Cf. Michael Thompson, *Clothed with Christ: The Example and Teaching of Jesus in Romans 12.1–15.13*, JSNTSup 59 (Sheffield: JSOT, 1991), 82; David G. Peterson, "Worship and Ethics in Romans 12," *TynBul* 44 (1993): 271–88.

[104] In the catena of texts listed in 15:9–12, glorifying God involves praise, singing, rejoicing, and confessing God's name together. Note also the extent to which praise and thanksgiving naturally flow from Paul's own reflections on the character and will of God (1:25 [the Creator is to be "praised forever"]; 6:17; 7:25 [the gospel elicits thanksgiving to God]; 11:33–36; 16:25–27 [God is to be praised for who he is and what he has done]).

[105] This is the first use of the term ἀνακαίνωσις ("renewal") in Greek literature. The corresponding verb is used in 2 Cor 4:16; Col 3:10. Paul also expresses the notion of renewal with terms such as καινότης ("newness") in 6:4; 7:6 and καινὴ κτίσις ("new creation") in Gal 6:15; 2 Cor 5:17.

Every form of moral corruption worthy of God's condemnation (1:28–32) can be forgiven and replaced by behavior pleasing to God (12:3–13:14).

In biblical thought, what is offered to God is holy (12:1, ἁγίαν), set apart for God.[106] Christian believers are "sanctified [ἡγιασμένοις] in Christ Jesus, called as saints [ἁγίοις]" (1 Cor 1:2; cf. Rom 1:7). The crucified and glorified Messiah has become for us "righteousness, sanctification [ἁγιασμός], and redemption" (1 Cor 1:30). So Paul could say to the Corinthians: "You were washed, you were sanctified [ἡγιάσθητε], you were justified in the name of the Lord Jesus Christ and by the Spirit of our God" (1 Cor 6:11; cf. Eph 5:26). The Spirit's role in this definitive work is to enable faith in Christ or "belief in the truth" (2 Thess 2:13–14; cf. Rom 15:16).[107] Those who are established as God's people are called to express their holiness in obedient service, empowered and led by the Holy Spirit (2 Cor 6:14–7:1; 1 Thess 4:1–8; cf. 1 Pet 1:2, 14–16).[108]

In 6:17–19 Paul talks about becoming slaves to righteousness "for sanctification" (εἰς ἁγιασμόν). There has been debate about whether the noun here and in 6:22 describes a process of moral renewal or a state of holiness resulting from consecration to God and his service.[109] As noted already, Paul uses this noun in parallel with "righteousness" and "redemption" to describe the "sanctification" or "consecration" available for those who call on Jesus Christ as Lord (1 Cor 1:30, supplying the ground for 1 Cor 1:2; 6:11). In 1 Thess 4:3–7 "sanctification" is contrasted with uncleanness and

[106] The sacrifice of those who present their bodies to God in Christ is "living" (ζῶσαν) because it is offered by those who have been brought from death to life through faith-union with Christ (12:1; cf. 6:4, 11, 13; 8:13). It is "pleasing to God" (εὐάρεστον τῷ θεῷ) because it fulfills the ideal of sacrifice, which is obedient service to God (cf. Heb 10:5–10).

[107] The clause "sanctified by the Holy Spirit" in 15:16 stands in apposition to "acceptable," suggesting that the work of the Spirit in drawing Gentiles into a faith relationship through Jesus Christ is what makes them acceptable to God.

[108] Cf. David G. Peterson, *Possessed by God: A New Testament Theology of Sanctification and Holiness*, NSBT 1 (Downers Grove: InterVarsity, 1995), 69–92. As the holy people of the new covenant, Christians inherit the responsibility of mediating God's character and will to the nations of the earth.

[109] Cranfield (*Romans*, 1:327–29) opts for the former, whereas Dunn (*Romans 1–8*, 346–49) argues that "consecration" or "a dedicated state" is more consistent with the biblical use of this term. Cf. Peterson, *Possessed by God*, 139–42.

lawlessness as a condition to be maintained and preserved. So also in Rom 6:19, the most likely meaning is that sanctification is a dedicated state arising from being set free from the penalty for sin and becoming slaves to righteousness. Changing the metaphor in 6:22, Paul talks about being "set free from sin" and becoming "enslaved to God." The immediate "fruit" of this change of ownership is "sanctification," and the ultimate outcome is eternal life.

§2.7 Apostolic Ministry

Paul frequently describes himself as "an apostle of Christ Jesus by God's will" (1 Cor 1:1; 2 Cor 1:1; Eph 1:1; Col 1:1; 2 Tim 1:1). More fully, he says he is "an apostle—not from men or by man, but by Jesus Christ and God the Father who raised him from the dead" (Gal 1:1; cf. 1 Tim 1:1; 2 Tim 1:1). Elsewhere he associates his claim to be an apostle with having "seen Jesus our Lord" (1 Cor 9:1) and asserts that he performed "the signs of an apostle" among the Corinthians "with unfailing endurance . . . including signs and wonders and miracles" (2 Cor 12:12; cf. Rom 15:18–19).[110]

Paul introduces himself to the Romans as "a servant of Christ Jesus, called as an apostle and set apart for the gospel of God" (1:1). The emphasis on divine calling parallels the opening of most of his other letters, without any mention of coworkers here.[111] As a "servant of Christ Jesus," Paul's ministry is "an extension or participation in the ministry of Christ to Israel, and through Israel to the world."[112]

[110] Sometimes Paul uses ἀπόστολος with the nontechnical sense of "messenger" (2 Cor 8:23; Phil 2:25; cf. John 13:16). In a technical sense it is used of the Twelve (Gal 1:17) and of a wider group to whom the risen Lord appeared (1 Cor 15:7). Although Paul occasionally includes an even wider group of coworkers in the category of "apostles" (Rom 16:7; 1 Cor 4:9; 9:5–6; Gal 1:19), Paul W. Barnett ("Apostle," *DPL* 48) argues that, as the "last of all" to whom the Lord appeared (1 Cor 15:8), Paul was the last who was strictly an apostle commissioned by Christ. Note the treatment of "super-apostles" in 2 Cor 11–12.

[111] Coworkers, benefactors, and associates are identified at some length in 16:1–15, 21–23. Cranfield (*Romans*, 1:52) observes that Paul's self-description in 1:1 points away from his person to the one whose apostle he is: "It is thus both a very humble word and also at the same time expressive of the most august authority."

[112] Lionel J. Windsor, *Paul and the Vocation of Israel: How Paul's Jewish Identity Informs His Apostolic Ministry, with Special Reference to Romans*, BZNW 205 (Berlin/Boston: de Gruyter, 2014), 103. Windsor argues that Paul may be linking his vocation to that of the Servant of the Lord in Isaiah 40–55 (esp. 49:1–7, where δοῦλος is used three times in the LXX).

Uniquely in Romans, Paul's calling is described in terms of being "set apart for the gospel of God." This is related to the resurrection of Jesus from the dead, through whom he claims to have received "grace and apostleship [χάριν καὶ ἀποστολήν] to bring about the obedience of faith for the sake of his name among all the Gentiles" (1:5). As the commissioned servant and witness of the risen Lord, the task of this Jewish apostle was to expound and apply the gospel he received for the benefit of the nations (cf. 1 Cor 15:1–11).

Paul's apostolic ministry is explicated in 1:9–15, where he talks about serving God with his spirit "in telling the good news about his Son." This involved primary evangelism, praying for opportunities to visit believing communities so as to minister to them and be encouraged by them, and writing letters to strengthen them. His particular calling as "apostle to the Gentiles" is mentioned again in 11:13 (ἐθνῶν ἀπόστολος; cf. Gal 2:7–9), though this is in the context of expressing his grief about the unbelief of so many fellow Israelites. Paul magnifies his ministry to the nations so as to make his own people jealous and "save some of them" (11:13–14; cf. §2.5). More broadly he counts himself among those who have proclaimed "the message of faith" to Jews and Greeks (10:8–13), having been "sent" (ἀποσταλῶσιν) by God to "bring good news" (10:15).

In 15:15–21 Paul returns to the theme of the grace given to him by God to minister the gospel to the Gentiles. On this basis he has presumed to write somewhat boldly to the Romans even though he was not involved in bringing the gospel to them in the first place. Here he portrays his calling in terms of being (lit.) "a minister of Christ Jesus to the Gentiles, serving as a priest of the gospel of God, so that the offering of the Gentiles may be acceptable, sanctified by the Holy Spirit" (v. 16; cf. 12:1; 15:8–13).[113]

As in 1:1, 5–6, and 9–15, Paul views himself as a special agent of God, whose role is to be a minister or "servant" (λειτουργός) of Christ Jesus. This is explained with a sacrificial metaphor (ἱερουργοῦντα τὸ εὐαγγέλιον τοῦ θεοῦ, [lit.] "serving as a priest with the gospel of God"). The reason for this is revealed in the purpose clause that follows. Paul is not a priestly mediator between his converts and God, and he has no material sacrifice to offer. But he preaches the gospel

[113] CSB takes the purpose clause to refer to Paul's purpose ("my purpose"), but the reference is more likely to God's purpose.

so that Gentiles can offer their praise (15:9) and obedience (15:18) to God (cf. 1:5; 16:26 ["the obedience of faith"]). Paul's ministry enables the self-offering of people from every nation to God. They present themselves "as a living sacrifice, holy and pleasing to God," which is their (lit.) "understanding service" (12:1; cf. §2.6). In other words, Paul's preaching facilitates the worship made possible by the death and resurrection of the Lord Jesus Christ.

Paul claims to have "fully proclaimed the gospel of Christ from Jerusalem all the way around to Illyricum" (15:19), meaning that he has faithfully fulfilled his commission to proclaim and establish the gospel in that region (cf. Col 1:25). This involved founding and nurturing churches, teaching believers, and grounding them firmly in the faith. Paul keeps preaching the gospel where Christ has not been named, encouraged by the expectation that people everywhere will see and understand his message about the Lord Jesus Christ (15:20–21). For this reason he plans to begin another arc of gospel work, beginning from Rome and terminating in Spain, and seeks the support and encouragement of the Roman believers for this new venture (15:22–32).

Many have compared Paul's strong sense of divine calling with the calling of the OT prophets (e.g., Isa 6; Jer 1).[114] The language he uses concerning the representative character of his apostolate has also suggested to some scholars that he understood it "in terms not unlike those used in relation to the Jewish *šālîah* concept—as an agent representing his principal, and functioning with the authority of the principal insofar as he was carrying out his principal's commission."[115]

Paul identifies numerous coworkers who shared with him in gospel ministry (16:1–4, 6–9, 21) and points to ways in which Christians generally could be involved in supporting his endeavors (15:23–32). But his concluding doxology picks up several themes expounded earlier in the letter, drawing attention to his own special

[114] Cf. Karl O. Sandnes, *Paul—One of the Prophets? A Contribution to the Apostle's Self-Understanding*, WUNT 2/43 (Tübingen: Mohr, 1991).

[115] Kruse, *Romans*, 57. See, more fully, Colin G. Kruse, *New Testament Models for Ministry: Jesus and Paul* (Nashville: Thomas Nelson, 1983), 78–82, 90–93, 106–11, 126–28, 136–40, 145–51, 160–69, 177–79.

role in the plan and purpose of God (16:25–27).[116] The apostle's preaching about Jesus Christ assures believers of God's power to strengthen and sustain his people to the end. In fact, he regards it as the means by which God achieves that goal. As expounded in this letter, his gospel becomes a resource for others also to have an effective ministry.

In particular, Paul's task has been to show how "the mystery kept silent for long ages" is now "revealed and made known through the prophetic Scriptures" (16:25–26; cf. 1:2; §2.2). The revelation of "the mystery" is for the purpose of bringing the nations to faith in Israel's Messiah, which has been Paul's God-given responsibility ("according to the command of the eternal God to advance the obedience of faith among all the Gentiles," 16:26). Paul has explained how Scripture has been fulfilled in the person and work of Christ and continues to be fulfilled in the proclamation and application of his biblically shaped gospel. In this respect he functions both as a uniquely authorized agent of God and as a model for other preachers and teachers of the gospel.

[116] On the strength of impressive manuscript evidence (𝔓[61] א B C D 81 1739 and others), these verses should be regarded as part of the original form of the letter, though important questions remain about the placement of the doxology in different positions by different manuscript traditions.

Exposition

I. Paul's Desire to Minister to the Romans (1:1–17)

A. Introduction and Greeting (1:1–7)

[1]Paul, a servant of Christ Jesus, called as an apostle and set
apart for the gospel of God—[2]which he promised beforehand
through his prophets in the Holy Scriptures—[3]concerning his
Son, Jesus Christ our Lord, who was a descendant of David according to the flesh [4]and was appointed to be the powerful Son
of God according to the Spirit of holiness by the resurrection of
the dead. [5]Through him we have received grace and apostleship
to bring about the obedience of faith for the sake of his name
among all the Gentiles, [6]including you who are also called by
Jesus Christ.

[7]To all who are in Rome, loved by God, called as saints.

Grace to you and peace from God our Father and the Lord Jesus Christ.

Context

These opening verses introduce key aspects of the message that will be developed in the body of the letter and expose something of Paul's motivation for gospel ministry. The apostle first raises the subject of his calling and the Christ-centered nature of the message he proclaims (vv. 1–7). In the thanksgiving and prayer report that follows (vv. 8–15), he relates how his desire to visit the Romans and minister to them is a specific outworking of his calling. In a theme statement about the gospel (vv. 16–17), he reveals why he is convinced about its universal relevance and significance.

Structure

Paul introduces himself as "a servant of Christ Jesus, called as an apostle and set apart for the gospel of God" (v. 1) before outlining the message he has been commissioned to proclaim (vv. 2–4). The gospel is first described as the message "which (God) promised beforehand through his prophets in the Holy Scriptures—concerning his Son" (vv. 2–3a). The Son, who is the focus of the gospel, is then described in two confessional statements (vv. 3b–4) before his name and titles are revealed. Paul returns to the subject of his own calling in v. 5, when he indicates that through the risen Lord Jesus he received grace and apostleship "to bring about the obedience of faith for the sake of his name among all the Gentiles." The Roman Christians are identified as those "who are also called by Jesus Christ" (v. 6). They are formally addressed as those who are "loved by God, called as saints" and are greeted with a wish-prayer for God's grace and peace (v. 7).

Outline:

1. Paul's authority as an apostle of Christ (v. 1)
2. The Christ-centered character of Paul's gospel (vv. 2–4)
3. Paul's commission and its implications (vv. 5–7)

1:1. Greek letters typically began with a one-sentence identification of sender and recipients, and a greeting (A to B "greetings," as in Acts 15:23; 23:26; Jas 1:1). Paul expands this formula in Romans to describe his divine calling and the gospel he preached. This was apparently necessary because he had not previously visited Rome and was personally known to only some of the believers (16:3–16). Perhaps he knew that his authority was questioned by some (cf. 1:9–10 comment). Three phrases in apposition to "Paul" identify the author with respect to "his master, his office, and his purpose."[1]

All Christians are meant to be "slaves" of Christ, which is the literal meaning of the term here (cf. BDAG, δοῦλος), and Paul may be simply identifying himself as a faithful disciple, completely at the disposal of his master, "Christ Jesus" (cf. 2 Cor 4:5; Gal 1:10;

---

[1] Douglas J. Moo, *The Epistle to the Romans*, NICNT (Grand Rapids: Eerdmans, 1996), 40. Paul normally includes others in his opening greetings (e.g., 1 Cor 1:1; 2 Cor 1:1–2; Gal 1:1–2) but not here, even though Timothy was with him (16:21). Perhaps the reason for this was to highlight his distinctive role as apostle to the Gentiles and so his authority to address the Romans.

Phil 1:1; Titus 1:1).[2] However, in association with the other terms in this verse, it is more likely that Paul uses δοῦλος to identify himself as a special agent of God's purpose. In particular, he may be linking his vocation to that of the Servant of the Lord in Isaiah 40–55 (esp. 49:1–7, where δοῦλος is used three times in the LXX). As "a servant of Christ Jesus," Paul's ministry is "an extension or participation in the ministry of Christ to Israel, and through Israel to the world."[3]

Paul's second self-designation indicates that he is literally "a called apostle" (κλητὸς ἀπόστολος). All Christians are "called" by God to belong to Jesus Christ and to serve him (1:6–7; 8:28), but the verbal adjective in 1:1 is linked to Paul's special role as an apostle of Christ (1:5–6; cf. Gal 1:1, 15). His Christian conversion coincided with his calling to be Christ's apostle to the nations (11:13; cf. Acts 9:1–16; 22:6–16; 26:12–18). Paul sometimes uses the term "apostle" generally to mean "commissioned missionary" or "messenger" (16:7 comment; cf. Phil 2:25; 2 Cor 8:23). However, the context here makes clear that he regarded himself as "one among that unique group appointed by Christ himself to have the salvation-historical role as the 'foundation' of the church (Eph 2:10)"[4] (see §2.7).

Paul indicates the purpose of his calling by the final expression in the verse, "set apart for the gospel of God." In the LXX the verb ἀφορίζειν is used with reference to God's separation of Israel from the nations as his holy people (Lev 20:26) and for various forms of

---

[2] The word order suggests that Jesus is identified from the beginning of the letter by his *title* as the promised Messiah. Some manuscripts read Ἰησοῦ Χριστοῦ ("Jesus Christ") and others Χριστοῦ Ἰησοῦ ("Christ Jesus"). The weight of witnesses supporting each reading is evenly balanced, but the latter is more commonly the pattern in the later Pauline letters and is more likely to have been what Paul wrote here. Cf. Robert K. Jewett, *Romans: A Commentary*, Hermeneia (Minneapolis: Fortress, 2007), 95.

[3] Lionel J. Windsor, *Paul and the Vocation of Israel: How Paul's Jewish Identity Informs His Apostolic Ministry, with Special Reference to Romans*, BZNW 205 (Berlin/Boston: de Gruyter, 2014), 103. Windsor points to Paul's use of Isa 52:5 in 2:24; Isa 52:7 in 10:15; Isa 53:1 in 10:16; and Isa 52:15 in 15:21 to show how his vocation is related to that of Israel and the Servant of the Lord. Moses, Joshua, the prophets, and David are called servants of the Lord in Josh 14:7; 24:29; 2 Kgs 17:23; Ps 89:3.

[4] Moo, *Romans*, 41. Jewett (*Romans*, 101) argues that the sending convention of the OT provides the most likely source of the NT concept of apostle (e.g., Isa 6:8). An extensive discussion of the concept of apostleship in Paul's writings is provided by Anthony C. Thiselton, *The First Epistle to the Corinthians: A Commentary on the Greek Text*, NIGTC (Grand Rapids: Eerdmans, 2000), 64–68, 666–74.

consecration to God and his service (Exod 13:12; Num 8:11; 15:20). Acts 13:2 records the "setting apart" of Saul and Barnabas by the leaders of the church in Antioch for their mission to the nations. Here the setting apart of Paul "for the gospel of God" (εἰς εὐαγγέλιον θεοῦ) refers to his Damascus-road commissioning by the risen Lord Jesus (cf. Acts 9:15).[5] It is clear from 1:2–4 that the gospel is essentially a message about the fulfilment of God's promises in Jesus Christ (see §2.1). However, in 1:9 Paul uses the expression ἐν τῷ εὐαγγελίῳ in a dynamic way to refer to the *activity* of "telling the good news about his Son." So it is possible to understand the expression "set apart for the gospel of God" broadly to mean "a dedication that involves both his own belief in, and obedience to, that message as well as his apostolic proclamation of it."[6] The genitive θεοῦ most likely indicates the origin of the gospel: it is *from* God, having been promised by him in the Holy Scriptures.[7]

1:2. Before he expands on the implications of his calling (vv. 5–6), Paul makes some important claims about the gospel he has been commissioned to preach (vv. 2–4). A relative clause first defines the gospel as the fulfillment of what God "promised beforehand through his prophets in the Holy Scriptures" (compare 3:21; 16:25–26; 1 Cor 15:3–4).[8] The OT foreshadowed and articulated the gospel as God's prophets revealed his character and will (cf. 1:17; 4:3, 6–8, 9, 16–17, 22; 9:25–26; 10:6–8, 11–13, 11:26–27; 15:9–12). God was the source of the revelation, the prophets were "the human medium of initial delivery," and the Scriptures are "its

[5] Both "separation" (ἀφορίζειν) and "calling" (καλεῖν) are mentioned in Gal 1:15, where Paul says God set him apart from his mother's womb and then called him by his grace. This language particularly recalls Isa 49:1.

[6] Moo, *Romans*, 43. Cf. Thiselton, *Corinthians*, 673. Note that εἰς ὑπακοὴν πίστεως (1:5) is rendered in a dynamic way by CSB ("to bring about the obedience of faith").

[7] Thomas R. Schreiner (*Romans*, BECNT [Grand Rapids: Baker Academic, 1998], 37) contends that θεοῦ should be understood both as a genitive of source ("the gospel from God") and as an objective genitive ("the gospel about God"). However, apart from the awkwardness of this reading, 1:3–4 indicates that the gospel is specifically about God's Son. Paul's term "the gospel of God" is used to distinguish it from "all other 'gospels,' in particular those of Roman emperors" (Colin G. Kruse, *Paul's Letter to the Romans*, PNTC [Grand Rapids: Eerdmans, 2012], 40).

[8] The verb προεπαγγέλλομαι ([lit.] "promised beforehand") is also used in 2 Cor 9:5. The expression "the Holy Scriptures" is only found here in Paul's writings, but the simplified plural form "the Scriptures" occurs in Rom 15:4; 16:26; 1 Cor 15:3–4.

medium of preservation and universal dissemination."[9] A major concern in the defensive sections of Romans is the interpretation of Scripture in the light of its fulfilment in Christ. But Paul's aim is not simply to argue against Jewish objections or alternative interpretations. Gentile readers need to understand that God's message to them is none other than the good news of the fulfilment of his promises to *Israel* (cf. Mark 1:14–15). The gospel for the nations cannot be severed from its OT roots (see §2.2).

1:3–4. The focus of the gospel is what God proclaimed in advance "concerning his Son." Two important claims about the Son are made, leading to the climactic declaration that he is "Jesus Christ our Lord." Given the structure and content of these verses, many commentators argue that the apostle quotes or adapts a confessional formula known to the Romans, as a way of underlining his agreement with them in these essential matters. However, there can be no certainty about the original form of this confession or about the significance of any modifications to it by Paul.[10] A literal rendering of the Greek text exhibits this pattern:

concerning his Son
    who was a descendant of David
        according to the flesh
    who was appointed Son of God in power
        according to the Spirit of holiness
        by resurrection from the dead
Jesus Christ our Lord

"Concerning his Son" (περὶ τοῦ ὑιοῦ αὐτοῦ) is the primary phrase, and the two participial clauses that follow must be understood in the light of this. These express two antitheses: "was"—"appointed"

---

[9] Robert M. Calhoun, *Paul's Definition of the Gospel in Romans I*, WUNT 2.316 (Tübingen: Mohr Siebeck, 2015), 90.

[10] Jewett (*Romans*, 103–8) proposes different levels of redaction, culminating in Paul's insertion of certain lines. However, Calhoun (*Paul's Definition*, 92–123) argues that none of Jewett's observations *necessarily* point to Paul's appropriation of a traditional formula. N. T. Wright ("The Letter to the Romans: Introduction, Commentary, and Reflections," in *The New Interpreter's Bible*, ed. Leander E. Keck, 13 vols. [Nashville: Abingdon, 1994–2004]: 416–17) observes that "the reason why Paul quoted things, if he did, was that they expressed exactly what he intended to say at the time."

and "according to the flesh"—"according to the Spirit of holiness."[11] God's Son is first described here as "a descendant of David according to the flesh," the sequence suggesting the incarnation of the preexistent Son (cf. 8:3 comment).[12] The participle γενομένου (CSB "was") can be rendered "born," although that is not the usual meaning of the verb (cf. Gal 4:4; Phil 2:7; BDAG, γίνομαι). Following the primary phrase, however, this clause could imply that at a particular point in time the Son of God "became" a descendant of David. God's promise to King David that he would establish the throne of his descendant forever (2 Sam 7:12–16) became the basis of messianic expectation in the OT (e.g., Isa 9:6–7; 11:1–10; Jer 23:5–6; Ezek 34:23–24; Zech 9:9–10; 12:7–13:1) and in later Jewish writings (e.g., Pss. Sol. 17:21; 18:5; 4QFlor 1:1–19; 1 En. 48:10; 52:4). The fulfilment of that hope in Jesus was foundational to the gospel Paul preached (cf. 9:5; 15:7–12; 2 Tim 2:8; §1.6). The qualifying phrase "according to the flesh" (κατὰ σάρκα) could be rendered "so far as his human nature is concerned" or "as to his earthly life" (compare 9:5).[13] This phrase implies that the title Son of David is "a valid description of him so far as it is applicable, but the reach of its applicability is not coterminous with the fullness of his person (cf. Mark 12:35–37)."[14]

---

[11] Calhoun (*Paul's Definition*, 123) observes that "the accent falls primarily upon (Christ's) birth and appointment on the one hand, and his flesh and spirit on the other: these two pairs represent the points at which God's pre-proclamation and promise in the scriptures intersect with comprehensive fulfilments in the Son."

[12] Moo (*Romans*, 46) rightly argues that several key texts in Paul's writings presume the preexistence of the Son. Wright ("Romans," 416) unnecessarily restricts the meaning of "his Son" to the messianic dimensions of the title. Yet he acknowledges that in Gal 4:1–7 Paul had already moved beyond the Jewish tradition of Israel/kingship to make the point that the Son is "one sent into the world not only as a messenger but also as the personal expression of God's love and purpose." Cf. Schreiner, *Romans*, 38–39.

[13] Moo (*Romans*, 47) notes that Paul's more neutral use of the term "flesh" (σάρξ) points to "human existence, with emphasis on the transitory, weak, frail nature of that existence" (e.g., 4:1; 9:3, 5, 8; Gal 2:20). Paul's more negative or ethical use of the term emerges in passages such as 7:5; 8:8; 13:14 (cf. Gal 5:13–18). Cf. Calhoun, *Paul's Definition*, 136.

[14] Charles E. B. Cranfield, *Introduction and Commentary on Romans I–VIII*, vol. 1 of *A Critical and Exegetical Commentary on the Epistle to the Romans*, ICC (Edinburgh: Clark, 1975), 1.60. Cranfield also makes the point that the expression

The next clause characterizes the Son of God by reference to another important event: "[who] was appointed to be the powerful Son of God according to the Spirit of holiness by the resurrection of the dead." The natural meaning of the participle ὁρισθέντος is "defined" or "appointed" (BDAG, ὁρίζω). Some English versions translate "declared" (NRSV, ESV), even though there are no first-century parallels to this usage.[15] Such a reading avoids any suggestion that the human Jesus *became* the divine Son at the resurrection. However, the nature of Christ's appointment or installation is clarified when the expression "in power" (ἐν δυνάμει) is read as qualifying "Son of God," rather than the preceding verb, so that the sense is "Son-of-God-in-power" (CSB, "the powerful Son of God"). The transition from v. 3 to v. 4 is not "from a human messiah to a divine Son of God (adoptionism), but from the Son as Messiah to the Son as both Messiah *and* powerful, reigning Lord."[16]

The expression ἐξ ἀναστάσεως νεκρῶν may be understood instrumentally ("by the resurrection of the dead"), or as a time reference ("from [the time of] his resurrection from the dead"). Either way, the resurrection of the human Jesus is presented as the event that was "the beginning of his exalted life."[17] Some commentators take "according to the spirit of holiness" in parallel with "according to the flesh" to refer to Christ's divine nature in contrast with his humanity. However, the former most likely refers to the Holy Spirit, indicating a trinitarian view of God (see §2.3). The Holy Spirit is not described in this way elsewhere in the NT, though "the term is clearly Semitic in character, modelled on the Hebraic form (not the

---

does not limit Christ's kinship with David to his earthly, historical life. Cf. Ben Witherington III, "Christ," *DPL* 98.

[15] In its seven other NT occurrences, this verb means "determine, appoint, fix" (Luke 22:22; Acts 2:23; 10:42; 11:29; 17:26, 31; Heb 4:7). Kruse (*Romans*, 45n31) argues that the background to Paul's statement is the promise to David in 2 Sam 7:5–16 and the divine decree in Ps 2:7. Cf. Cranfield, *Romans*, 1.61–64.

[16] Moo, *Romans*, 49. Moo rightly argues that the need to demarcate the second occurrence of "Son of God" in v. 4 from the first occurrence in v. 3 strongly favors reading the second as "Son-of-God-in-power."

[17] Cranfield, *Romans*, 1:62. CSB "the resurrection of the dead" implies that the general resurrection began with the resurrection of Jesus. Cf. 1 Cor 15:20–22; Wright, "Romans," 419.

LXX) of Ps 51:11 and Isa 63:10–11."[18] The sense could be that the establishment of Jesus as Son-of-God-in-power was by the operation of God's Spirit or that his resurrection was by means of the Spirit. Alternatively, the sense is that the gift of the Spirit is the manifestation of his power as the exalted Christ and so "the guarantee of his having been appointed Son of God in might."[19]

Like the preceding clauses, "Jesus Christ our Lord" stands in apposition to "his Son" in v. 3 and provides a further description of the one who is the content of the gospel. Jesus's messiahship is affirmed by the title "Christ," while the designation "our Lord" expresses both his "cosmic majesty and his status as master of the believer."[20] Various combinations of these titles appear with the name Jesus at critical points throughout Romans (1:4, 7; 4:24; 5:1, 11, 21; 6:23; 7:25; 8:39; 13:14; 14:14; 15:6, 30; 16:18, 20), mostly indicating a climax or turning point in the argument. Paul's gospel outline in 1:3–4 is Jewish in character, but its applicability to a Gentile audience becomes clear as the letter proceeds, climaxing in the challenge of 15:7–13.

1:5. Returning to the subject of his divine calling (v. 1), Paul claims to have received "grace and apostleship" through the mediation of the risen Lord Jesus ("through him"). The expression χάριν καὶ ἀποστολήν could be read as a hendiadys, with the second term defining the particular application of the first term ("the grace of apostleship").[21] On the road to Damascus, the grace of God was manifested in bringing the great persecutor of Christians to faith and

---

[18] James D. G. Dunn, *Romans 1–8*, WBC 38A (Dallas: Word, 1988), 15. Less likely is the view of Calhoun (*Paul's Definition*, 136) that "the spirit of holiness" refers to "the part of (Christ) that continues to exist in his exalted state, the main ingredient of his resurrected body."

[19] Cranfield, *Romans*, 1:64. In Acts 2:32–36, resurrection, ascension, and pouring out the Spirit are linked. Brendan Byrne (*Romans*, SP [Collegeville: The Liturgical Press, 1996], 39) says that at his resurrection Jesus entered into "the new age marked by the Spirit ('the Spirit of holiness')." Cf. Wright, "Romans," 418–19; Gordon D. Fee, *God's Empowering Presence: The Holy Spirit in the Letters of Paul* (Peabody: Hendrickson, 1994), 482–84.

[20] Moo, *Romans*, 50. Kruse (*Romans*, 47) points out that in the city of Rome, where Caesar claimed to be lord, this Christian confession would have been a bold acknowledgment of Jesus as a greater power with heavenly authority.

[21] Moo (*Romans*, 51) compares the use of χάρις with reference to gifts and ministry in 12:3; 15:15 (cf. 1 Cor 3:10; 15:10; Eph 4:7, 10). See comment at 3:24 about the grace of God in salvation.

giving him a distinct ministry to fulfil (cf. Acts 9:1–19; Gal 1:15–16). The authorial plural "we have received" is best understood as a way of speaking about this unique experience.[22] The purpose of Paul's calling is outlined in the three expressions that follow.

First, his *essential task* was "to bring about the obedience of faith" (εἰς ὑπακοὴν πίστεως [lit. "for the obedience of faith"]; cf. 16:26). This pregnant expression has been understood in a variety of ways. Most commonly, the genitive πίστεως ("of faith") is either taken to refer to the source of obedience ("the obedience that comes from faith") or it is taken as a genitive of definition ("the obedience that consists in faith").[23] Both approaches are supported by parallels elsewhere in Paul's writings, but the critical question is how to interpret the phrase in this particular context. Linked with Paul's claim to be an apostle set apart to proclaim the gospel of God, "the obedience of faith" means "obedience to the gospel's call to believe in God's Son, that is, the obedience that consists in faith."[24] However, Paul later asserts that a genuine faith in Christ will lead to a life of obedience (6:15–23), then he spells out what that involves in practical, everyday terms (12:1–15:13). Romans concludes with another allusion to Paul's role in God's plan to "advance the obedience of faith among all the Gentiles" (16:26). As well as engaging in primary evangelism (15:18–21), he expounds the gospel to Christians in the light of what the Scriptures reveal (15:14–17). So neither "the obedience that consists in faith" nor "the obedience that comes from faith" may be sufficient to convey the meaning of Paul's deliberately ambiguous expression (CSB maintains the ambiguity by translating

---

[22] Dunn (*Romans 1–8*, 16) and Jewett (*Romans*, 109) suggest that Paul could have included others in this category, but this flies in the face of his distinctive appeal to the Romans about his God-given role in 1:1–15 and 15:15–32, his argument in Gal 1:1–2:10, and Luke's various representations of Paul's calling in Acts.

[23] Cranfield (*Romans*, 1:66) lists seven alternative renderings of the expression and concludes that it means "the faith which consists in obedience." Glenn N. Davies (*Faith and Obedience in Romans: A Study of Romans 1–4*, JSNTSup 39 [Sheffield: Sheffield Academic, 1990], 28–30) argues for "an obedience motivated by and dependent upon faith."

[24] Kruse, *Romans*, 51. Paul immediately goes on to give thanks for the fact that the *faith* of the Roman Christians is being reported "in all the world" (1:8), but in 16:19 he says, "The report of your *obedience* has reached everyone." Paul's gospel preaching is designed to bring about the obedience of Israel and the nations, according to 10:16; 15:18.

it literally). Both meanings must be held together, suggesting the translation "faith's obedience" or "believing obedience."[25]

Second, Paul's *sphere of ministry* is identified by the expression "among all the Gentiles" (ἐν πᾶσιν τοῖς ἔθνεσιν), which is found again in 16:26. The word "all" is significant here and suggests that the sociopolitical rendering "nations" rather than "Gentiles" might be better.[26] The apostle had a significant role in bringing the blessing promised to Abraham to "all the peoples on earth" (cf. Gen 12:3; 17:4–6; 22:17–18; Rom 4:13–25; Gal 3:6–29). Paul did this by preaching the gospel to Gentiles everywhere but also to Jews who were dispersed among the nations, calling them to acknowledge their Messiah and enjoy the benefits of the new covenant inaugurated by the death of Jesus (cf. 1 Cor 11:25; 2 Cor 3:1–18) (see §2.7).

Third, the *ultimate aim* of this international ministry is revealed by the expression "for the sake of his name." Paul's commission was to represent the Lord Jesus and make his character and will known among the nations. He viewed himself as the personal envoy of the risen Christ.

1:6. As a bridge to the formal address and greeting in v. 7, Paul uses the emphatic expression "including you who are also" (ἐν οἷς ἐστε καὶ ὑμεῖς). This identifies the readers as being "among the nations" and therefore falling within the sphere of his apostolic ministry. They are marked out from the nations as those who are "called by Jesus Christ" (κλητοὶ Ἰησοῦ Χριστοῦ, cf. 8:30; 9:24). This refers to "the powerful and irresistible reaching out of God in grace to bring people into his kingdom."[27] Paul may not have played a direct part in God's calling of the Roman believers to faith in Christ, but

[25] Cf. Don B. Garlington, "The Obedience of Faith in the Letter to the Romans Part 1: The Meaning of *hypakoē pisteōs* (Rom 1:5; 16:26)," *WTJ* 52 (1990): 224. Several recent commentators argue similarly for a "both/and" understanding of Paul's expression: e.g., Dunn, *Romans 1–8*, 17; Moo, *Romans*, 51–53; Schreiner, *Romans*, 35.

[26] The noun ἔθνη is normally translated "Gentiles" when a religious distinction between Israel and other people is implied by the context. But the term can be rendered "nations" and include Israel, especially when modified by "all" (as in 1:5; 16:27).

[27] Moo, *Romans*, 54. God's call is another way of talking about his choice of individuals to belong to Christ and experience the benefits of his saving work (1 Cor 1:26–31). The call comes through the preaching of the gospel by human agents in the power of the Spirit (1 Thess 1:4–5; 2 Thess 2:13–14). Contrast the special use of "called" in Rom 1:1 with reference to Paul's apostolic vocation.

he wants to visit them and impart "some spiritual gift" to strengthen them (v. 11). Put another way, he wants to have a fruitful ministry among them "just as . . . among the rest of the Gentiles" (v. 13). This letter is a first expression of that ministry (15:15–16) and a preparation for his projected visit (15:23–32). Even if their number included a number of Jewish believers (cf. 16:3–16), it would be reasonable for Paul to regard these Christians as falling within his sphere of responsibility as "an apostle to the Gentiles" (11:13).[28]

1:7. Three complementary expressions in the dative case constitute the formal epistolary address: "to all who are in Rome, loved by God, called as saints." "All" is in an emphatic position: their leaders are not singled out, and they are not described as a church. This may have been because a number of house groups in Rome did not meet as one assembly and the leaders were dispersed among them (cf. 16:3–16; §2.5).[29] God's love for them (5:5–8) and his calling of them to be "saints" (κλητοῖς ἁγίοις) set them apart from the other citizens of Rome. God's love is impartial and is experienced by all who believe the gospel about his Son.

They are "saints" because they are "called by Jesus Christ" (v. 6). Israel was called to be a "holy nation" (Exod 19:6 LXX, ἔθνος ἅγιον), meaning that those whom God rescued from Egypt were "set apart" to belong to God as his own special possession, to reflect his character and will to the nations. This holy status is now the privilege and responsibility of Jews and Gentiles who have responded to the gospel about God's Son and yielded their allegiance to him (Rom 10:9–13; 11:11–32). Paul regularly describes Christians as "saints" or "holy ones" (ἁγίοι), indicating that they are now the sanctified community, God's new covenant people, set apart to be faithful and obedient in every aspect of their lives (e.g., 8:27; 12:13; 15:25–26, 31; 16:2, 15). In common parlance the word "saint" is wrongly used to identify especially holy people, thus obscuring a

---

[28] Cf. Cranfield, *Romans*, 1:68. See more fully the assessment of Roman Christianity by Jewett, *Romans*, 59–74.

[29] Dunn (*Romans 1–8*, 19) follows those who suggest that there may have been factions or at least some tension between different groups of Christians in Rome. See my Introduction I.A. However, Moo (*Romans* 54) does not think much should be made of Paul's failure to address himself to the "church" in Rome since he does not consistently use the word in his letter openings (cf. Eph 1:1; Phil 1:1; Col 1:1). See also Schreiner, *Romans*, 37.

precious NT way of identifying *all* true believers. The designation "in Rome" is missing from v. 7 (and "to Rome" from v. 15) in a few ancient manuscripts, but the earliest and best texts include a specific address to Christians in Rome here.[30]

The concluding formula in v. 7b is exactly the same as in 1 Cor 1:3; 2 Cor 1:2; Gal 1:3; Eph. 1:2; Phil 1:2; Phlm 3 (abbreviated in Col 1:2; 1 Thess 1:1; 2 Thess 1:2). A wish-prayer (χάρις ὑμῖν, "grace to you"), instead of the ordinary Greek greeting (χαίρειν, "greetings"; cf. Acts 15:23; 23:26; Jas 1:1), refers to the grace of God that is mentioned numerous times in Romans. "Peace" (εἰρήνη, translating שָׁלוֹם) was the ordinary greeting of the Semitic world (e.g., Gen 43:23; Judg 19:20; 1 Sam 25:6), presumably here identifying the outcome of Christ's saving work as "peace with God" (Rom 5:1).[31]

> Paul seems to be using these terms here, as he does elsewhere in Romans (as well as in all of his other letters), to epitomize in compressed fashion something of the fullness of the Christian proclamation: that through the "grace" of God our Father, as expressed in the work of Christ (e.g., Rom 5:15–21), there has been brought about "peace" with God, as effected through the work of Christ (e.g., Rom 5:1–11).[32]

"God our Father and the Lord Jesus Christ" are together the source of these blessings, showing again Paul's high Christology. Believers already enjoy "grace and peace," but the apostle's wish-prayer effectively asks for his readers to keep experiencing the benefits (cf. 15:5; thirteen comments).

[30] Bruce M. Metzger (*A Textual Commentary on the Greek New Testament*, 2nd ed. [New York: American Bible Society, 1994], 446) considers that these omissions could be interpreted "either as the result of an accident in transcription, or, more probably, as a deliberate excision, made in order to show that the letter is of general, not local, application." The travel details in 15:23–32 confirm that the letter was originally directed to the Christians in Rome but shorter versions were later sent to other churches.

[31] Cranfield (*Romans*, 1.71–72) discusses more fully the background to Paul's usage here and its meaning.

[32] Richard N. Longenecker, *Introducing Romans: Critical Issues in Paul's Most Famous Letter* (Grand Rapids: Eerdmans, 2011), 381. Longenecker (204–25) discusses epistolary conventions in the ancient world and how they apply to this letter.

Bridge

Paul claims to be a personal envoy of Jesus Christ, with a divine commission to evangelize the nations and apply the gospel to every situation he encounters in the churches (cf. 16:25–27; Eph 3:1–12). The opening challenge of this letter is for the Romans to acknowledge his authority in writing to them as he does. Given the universal significance of Paul's divine calling (1:5–6), Christians in every age and place are faced with the same challenge. We either acknowledge or deny Paul's God-given authority by the way we respond to his teaching and apply it in our own context. Foundationally, Paul's gospel focuses on the fulfillment of God's promises in the person of his Son, the victorious Messiah, who calls people everywhere to acknowledge him with "the obedience of faith," and to experience the grace and peace he has to offer. To what extent does our presentation of the gospel convey these biblical perspectives? Do we proclaim a God-centered gospel, or are we mostly concerned about responding to human needs and aspirations? What place does the fulfillment of OT expectations have in our understanding of the gospel today? Have we so modified the message to suit our culture that we obscure or lose the foundational truths Paul addresses in this letter? Are we gripped by the privileges and responsibilities associated with being the new covenant people of God in a world where many are indifferent to the gospel and others determined to resist its message?

B. Thanksgiving, Prayer, and Thematic Introduction (1:8–17)

[8]First, I thank my God through Jesus Christ for all of you
because the news of your faith is being reported in all the world.
[9]God is my witness, whom I serve with my spirit in telling the
good news about his Son—that I constantly mention you, [10]al-
ways asking in my prayers that if it is somehow in God's will,
I may now at last succeed in coming to you. [11]For I want very
much to see you, so that I may impart to you some spiritual gift
to strengthen you, [12]that is, to be mutually encouraged by each
other's faith, both yours and mine.

[13]Now I don't want you to be unaware, brothers and sisters,
that I often planned to come to you (but was prevented until now)
in order that I might have a fruitful ministry among you, just as I

have had among the rest of the Gentiles. [14]I am obligated both to
Greeks and barbarians, both to the wise and the foolish. [15]So I am
eager to preach the gospel to you also who are in Rome.

[16]For I am not ashamed of the gospel, because it is the power
of God for salvation to everyone who believes, first to the Jew,
and also to the Greek. [17]For in it the righteousness of God is revealed from faith to faith, just as it is written: **The righteous will
live by faith.**

Context

Adapting the conventions of ancient Greek letter writing, Paul moves from introduction and greeting to assure his readers that he gives thanks for them and regularly prays to be able to visit them (vv. 8–10). He wants to strengthen them with "some spiritual gift" (v. 11), which effectively means preaching the good news to them (v. 15). When he reveals why he is not ashamed of the gospel (vv. 16–17), he indicates how that ministry might be expressed. Themes such as salvation, righteousness, faith, Jews and Gentiles, and new life in Christ are introduced here and expounded in the rest of the letter. Paul wants to benefit the Romans with such an understanding of the gospel and its implications before he visits them. As well as blessing them in this way, he hopes to gain their confidence and support for his future ministry (15:14–33).

Structure

Paul first describes how he gives thanks to God for his readers (v. 8) because news of their faith is being reported everywhere. His prayer report follows, beginning with an oath (v. 9), which is expanded in a statement about the service he renders to God "in telling the good news about his Son." Paul emphasizes how consistently he has been praying for them, before the content of his prayer is revealed (v. 10, "that if it is somehow in God's will, I may now at last succeed in coming to you").

An explanation for this prayer is introduced by the connective γάρ (v. 11, "*for* I want very much to see you"), and is filled out in the purpose clause that follows ("so that I may impart to you some spiritual gift to strengthen you"). A modification in v. 12 clarifies that he wishes this to be a mutually encouraging experience. The formal beginning to the letter is marked by a disclosure formula in v. 13 ("Now I don't want you to be unaware").[33] Possibly to counter the suggestion that he has neglected them, he stresses that his long-standing plan to visit Rome has often been frustrated. Another purpose clause expresses his intention more broadly: "in order that I might have a fruitful ministry among you, just as I have had among the rest of the Gentiles." Far from feeling any embarrassment about this, he regards it as part of his obligation to preach the gospel "both to Greeks and barbarians, both to the wise and the foolish" (vv. 14–15).

In the letter's theme statement (vv. 16–17), Paul declares that he is eager to preach the good news because he is not ashamed of it, and he is not ashamed "because it is the power of God for salvation to everyone who believes." The attached phrase "first to the Jew, and also to the Greek" qualifies what was said in v. 14 and gives priority to the Jew. A further clause argues that the gospel is the power of God for salvation because "in it the righteousness of God is revealed from faith to faith." Consistent with v. 2, this way of understanding the gospel is then related to a biblical text (Hab 2:4), which is introduced by the words "just as it is written."

Outline:

1. Paul's mission-focused thanksgiving and prayer (vv. 8–10)
2. Paul's ministry ambitions (vv. 11–15)
3. Paul's reasons for confidence in the gospel (vv. 16–17)

1:8. The first sentence of an ancient Greek letter after the introduction often informed recipients of the writer's thanksgiving and prayer for them. Paul adapts that convention by first telling the Romans that he thanks God because the news of their faith "is being reported in all the world" (v. 8). Then he assures them of his unceasing prayers to be able to visit them for mutual ministry (vv. 9–12). *Πρῶτον μέν* on its own means "from the very outset" or "above all" (cf. 3:2; 1 Cor 11:18), and may simply emphasize how important this thanksgiving is for the apostle. But it could be rendered "first"

[33] Peter T. O'Brien (*Introductory Thanksgivings in the Letters of Paul*, NovTSup 49 [Leiden: Brill, 1977], 197–202) argues that the formal thanksgiving period in Romans actually extends to 1:15. However, although Paul's personal travel plans continue to dominate vv. 13–15, these verses are more likely to be "the body opening" of the letter. Cf. Longenecker, *Introducing Romans*, 385–88.

to draw attention to the prayer report that follows as a second element in a sequence (without the expected grammatical link).[34] Paul's thanksgiving is directed to the one he calls "my God" (cf. 1 Cor 1:4; 2 Cor 12:21; Phil 1:3; 4:19; Phlm 4). Jesus Christ, who made this intimate relationship possible, now mediates his thanksgiving (cf. 5:11; 7:25; 1 Cor 15:57; Col 3:17).[35] Addition of the words "for all of you" (as in Phil 1:4; 1 Thess 1:2) continues the inclusive emphasis of v. 7, where the apostle addresses all the believers in Rome together, whatever their racial or religious background.

The ground and content of his thanksgiving is given in the causal clause introduced by ὅτι ("because [the news of] your faith is being reported in all the world").[36] CSB renders ἡ πίστις ὑμῶν "the news of your faith," because the verb καταγγέλλεται is used elsewhere with reference to the proclamation of "the good news" (1 Cor 2:1; 9:14; 11:26; Phil 1:17–18; Col 1:28). The fact that there are believers in the capital has been made known throughout the empire, wherever the gospel has been proclaimed (cf. 16:19, "[the report of] your obedience has reached everyone").

1:9–10. Paul often follows his thanksgivings with a prayer report, making known his concerns about his readers and effectively inviting them to pray for the same things (cf. Phil 1:9–11; Col 1:9–14). But rather than revealing what he has been praying for the Romans, he discloses what he has been praying about *himself*. His prayer report is introduced with an oath formula, which is closely linked to the preceding sentence (μάρτυς γάρ μού ἐστιν ὁ θεός, "for God is my witness"). As in other contexts (2 Cor 1:23; 11:31; Gal 1:20; Phil 1:8; 1 Thess 2:5, 10), Paul appeals to God to affirm something that only God can truly know, namely his inner motivation and

[34] This construction normally implies a sequence, with a linked clause beginning with something like ἔπειτα δέ (Heb 7:2, "then also") or ἔπειτα (Jas 3:17, "then"). Steven E. Runge (*Discourse Grammar of the Greek New Testament: A Practical Introduction for Teaching and Exegesis* [Peabody: Hendrickson, 2010], 74) contends that μέν is normally "anticipatory in nature, creating the expectation that another related point will follow."

[35] Cranfield (*Romans*, 1:74) observes that Christ is both mediator of God's approach to us and of our approach to God. Jewett (*Romans*, 119) views this thanksgiving as a further expression of Paul's apostolic allegiance (1:1).

[36] O'Brien (*Introductory Thanksgivings*, 7–8) shows that a causal use of ὅτι is the norm in introductory thanksgivings of this type.

the true character of his actions.[37] Some of the recipients may have had doubts about his message and ministry, and Paul was cautious about intruding into a situation where the gospel was already established, not wanting to build "on someone else's foundation" (15:20).

Although he speaks simply about serving God with his own spirit (ἐν τῷ πνεύματί μου, cf. 1 Cor 14:14; 16:18; 2 Cor 2:13), several factors suggest that we should understand the Spirit of God to be motivating and empowering Paul's spirit. A clear intersection between the human spirit and the divine Spirit is indicated in 8:16. Moreover, Paul describes his whole ministry in terms of the Spirit's activity in 15:18–19, and the same verb (λατρέυω, "serve") is used in combination with πνεύματι θεοῦ ("by the Spirit of God") in Phil 3:3 to describe new covenant worshippers.[38]

The next phrase (ἐν τῷ εὐαγγελίῳ τοῦ υἱοῦ αὐτοῦ) indicates that Paul's particular service to God is offered in the sphere of gospel ministry (cf. 15:16 comment). It is rightly translated "in telling the good news about his Son." This involved primary evangelism and church planting (cf. 15:19–20 comments). Other important facets of his work included writing letters to converts and praying for the progress of the gospel.[39]

God knows (lit.) "how constantly" (ὡς ἀδιαλείπτως) Paul has been (lit.) "making mention" (μνείαν ποιοῦμαι) of the Roman Christians. The following clause shows this is a way of speaking about intercessory prayer (πάντοτε ἐπὶ τῶν προσευχῶν μου δεόμενος, "always asking in my prayers"; cf. Eph 1:16; 1 Thess 1:2; Philm 4). Both adverbs ("always" and "constantly") point to "prayer offered at frequent and regular intervals."[40]

---

[37] Paul's formula here reflects an understanding that Jesus did not give a blank prohibition to oaths (cf. Matt 5:33–37).

[38] Paul's gospel ministry is a particular expression of the "understanding service" (τὴν λογικὴν λατρείαν) that all believers are to offer to God (12:1). Cf. David G. Peterson, *Engaging with God: A Biblical Theology of Worship* (Downers Grove: InterVarsity, 1992) 179–82.

[39] CSB ("in [telling] the good news about his Son") highlights the priority of preaching in Paul's gospel ministry. The noun εὐαγγέλιον here refers to the activity described by the verb εὐαγγελίζεσθαι (cf. 1:1 comment). Cranfield (*Romans*, 1.76–77) makes an artificial distinction between praying as the inward side of his service and preaching as the outward side.

[40] O'Brien, *Introductory Thanksgivings*, 214. However, Jewett (*Romans*, 121) disputes this.

The content of Paul's prayer is introduced by the awkward expression εἴ πως ἤδη ποτέ (lit., "if somehow now at last"). This betrays a degree of uncertainty on his part, though the following expression indicates genuine submission to God's will and complete dependence on God for the outcome. Paul is explicit about wanting to visit Rome, asking that (lit.), "I may have a good journey by the will of God to come to you" (εὐοδωθήσομαι ἐν τῷ θελήματι τοῦ θεοῦ ἐλθεῖν πρὸς ὑμᾶς). CSB translates the whole sentence, "If it is somehow in God's will, I may now at last succeed in coming to you."[41] By the will of God, he had been called to be an apostle and had been charged with bringing about "the obedience of faith for the sake of his name among all the Gentiles" (1:5). As he sought to fulfill that commission, he was open to the possibility that his prayer could be answered in a number of ways, and he confidently left the details to God (cf. 15:31–32). As it turned out, he arrived in the capital as a prisoner of the Roman government (Acts 28:14–31)!

1:11. At the end of the letter, Paul reveals a reason for wanting to visit the Roman believers related to his mission plan (15:22–32), but here his focus is more personal ("for I want very much to see you"). A purpose clause expresses the reason: he longs to share "some spiritual gift" with them (ἵνα τι μεταδῶ χάρισμα ὑμῖν πνευματικόν, "so that I may impart to you some spiritual gift"). The indefinite particle τι ("some") leaves open the possibility of sharing with them whatever is needed. The spiritual gift Paul has in mind is unlikely to be one of those mentioned in 12:6–8 or 1 Cor 12:8–10, since he affirms that they are already gifted and are "filled with all knowledge, and able to instruct one another" (15:14). It is best to link "some spiritual gift" with the sort of exposition of the gospel and its implications we find in Romans itself.[42] This letter shows what sort of contribution he would make if he were there in person: "This is what he now 'shares' since he cannot presently come to

---

[41] O'Brien (*Introductory Thanksgivings*, 217–21) notes the use of εὐοδόω in the LXX, either literally meaning "have a good journey," or figuratively meaning "succeed." Cf. 1 Cor 16:2; 3 John 2 (twice) and a parallel expression in 1 Thess 3:11.

[42] Dunn (*Romans 1–8*, 30) suggests that the reference is to "some act of ministry which is both of the Spirit and a means of grace." Moo (*Romans*, 60) similarly suggests "an insight or ability, given by the Spirit, that Paul hopes to 'share' with the Romans."

Rome."[43] A further purpose clause indicates that his ministry would be for their strengthening as disciples, with the passive verb implying that this would be God's doing (εἰς τὸ στηριχθῆναι ὑμᾶς, [lit.] "so that you may be strengthened"; cf. 16:25).

1:12. The expression τοῦτο δέ ἐστιν ("that is"), which only occurs here in the NT, amends slightly what has just been said by expressing a complementary truth. Rather than simply coming to *give* to the Romans, Paul also wants to *receive* from them, so that they might be "mutually encouraged" (συμπαρακληθῆναι ἐν ὑμῖν, [lit.] "to be encouraged together in your midst"). Here he applies his own teaching about giving and receiving in ministry (12:3–8; cf. 1 Cor 12:12–26). Mutual ministry takes place "by each other's faith, both yours and mine" (διὰ τῆς ἐν ἀλλήλοις πίστεως ὑμῶν τε καὶ ἐμοῦ). Faith in Christ (as in v. 8) is expressed in a variety of ministries. These bring encouragement and strength to others because God gives Christians different insights, experiences, and ways of articulating their faith (cf. 12:3–8). In 15:24 Paul hopes to receive their help in advancing his mission to Spain. In 15:29–32 he seeks their prayers concerning the immediate challenges facing him and looks forward to being refreshed in their company. Doubtless there were other ways he also expected to be encouraged by their faith in action.

1:13. In the pattern of ancient Greek letter writing, this would be the beginning of "the body opening," marked here by a pattern of speech Paul uses elsewhere when he wants to draw attention to the significance of what he is about to say (οὐ θέλω δὲ ὑμᾶς ἀγνοεῖν, "Now I don't want you to be unaware"; cf. 11:25; 1 Cor 10:1; 12:1; 2 Cor 1:8; 1 Thess 4:13).[44] The inclusive term "brothers" (ἀδελφοί) is used, as in 7:1, 4; 8:12; 10:1; 11:25; 12:1; 15:14, 30; and 16:17, to address the readers more directly and personally. It is rightly

---

[43] Fee, *God's Empowering Presence*, 488–89. Fee (486) notes, "A letter in antiquity was meant to serve as 'a second–best substitute for a personal visit.'" Longenecker (*Introducing Romans*, 158, 353–55) agrees that the "spiritual gift" Paul is uniquely able to give the Romans is his understanding of the gospel and its implications, as expressed in his letter (cf. 2:16; 16:25, "my gospel").

[44] The conjunction δέ ("now") signals a new development in the argument here (cf. Runge, *Discourse Grammar*, 32). Metzger (*Textual Commentary*, 447) notes two scribal modifications limited to Western witnesses, but the reading οὐ θέλω is widely attested and accords with Paul's usage elsewhere.

translated "brothers and sisters" since Paul is addressing "all" of the Roman believers together (v. 6; cf. 8:14–15 comment). Possibly to counter the suggestion that he has neglected them, he stresses that he often planned to come to them "but was prevented until now." Most obviously, his ministry "from Jerusalem all the way around to Illyricum" kept him from visiting Rome (15:18–22), but other undisclosed factors might also have been in Paul's mind. A purpose clause restates his intention to come "in order that I might have a fruitful ministry among you, just as I have had among the rest of the Gentiles." The expression τινὰ καρπόν (lit. "some fruit") should be read in the light of vv. 11–12, where he writes about wanting to give and receive in ministry for the sake of mutual encouragement. "Fruit" may include converts to the gospel, but Paul normally uses this metaphor to describe the character and behavior resulting from faith in Christ (6:1, 22: Gal 5:22; Eph 5:9; Phil 1:11; 4:17).[45] In practical terms this could include their support for the next stage of his apostolic mission (15:22–33).

1:14. Without a connective in Greek, Paul describes "the rest of the Gentiles" (v. 13) from two different perspectives ("both to Greeks and barbarians, both to the wise and the foolish").[46] "Greeks" will mean "all those Gentiles who are possessed of Graeco-Roman culture," and "barbarians" will mean "all non-Hellenized communities (Jews excepted), whether within the Roman Empire or outside it."[47] The second division ("both to the wise and the foolish") overlaps the first and is a different way of grouping the same totality: there were wise and foolish Greeks and wise and foolish barbarians![48] Paul believes himself to be obligated to them all (ὀφειλέτης,

---

[45] In Phil 1:22, "fruitful work" could include winning converts as well as strengthening believers. "This fruit" (CSB "the funds") in Rom 15:28 refers to the collection for the poor in Jerusalem from the Gentile churches, but the Roman Christians did not have an opportunity to contribute to this.

[46] Runge (*Discourse Grammar*, 20) observes that a sentence without a connective ("asyndeton") occurs "when the writer judges that the implicit relation between the two clauses is sufficiently clear."

[47] Cranfield, *Romans*, 1:84 and n. 2.

[48] Cranfield (ibid., 1.83–85) comes to this conclusion after evaluating five ways of viewing the pairs of contrasted terms. The word "barbarian" arose from an attempt to reproduce the sound of other languages on Greek ears. It came to stand for all those who were outside Greek culture. Romans could be regarded as "Greeks" if they adopted Greek language and culture. Cf. Moo, *Romans*, 61–62.

"debtor") because of his calling by God through the risen Christ "to bring about the obedience of faith for the sake of his name among all the Gentiles" (1:5). With this pair of opposites, Paul conveys "the sweeping inclusivity of the gospel of Christ crucified for all."[49]

1:15. The adverb at the beginning of this verse (οὕτως, "so") indicates that what follows is a direct consequence of what has been said in v. 14. With an unusual construction in Greek,[50] Paul tells his readers that he is "eager to preach the gospel to you also who are in Rome." As in 1:5–6, a broad statement about the apostle's commitment to all nations leads to a particular expression of concern for those who are in Rome.[51] He is not contradicting himself when he speaks about "preaching the gospel" (εὐαγγελίσασθαι) to them. According to Acts 28:15–31, he had an evangelistic engagement with unbelieving Jews in that city and then "welcomed all who visited him, proclaiming the kingdom of God and teaching about the Lord Jesus Christ with all boldness and without hindrance." However, "to preach the gospel" sums up Paul's lifelong obligation, and "its use can embrace the whole range of his ministry, including his explication of the gospel in this very letter."[52] The doxology in 16:25–26 claims God has the power to strengthen believers "according to my gospel and the proclamation about Jesus Christ, according to the revelation of the mystery kept silent for long ages but now revealed and made known through the prophetic Scriptures, according to the command of the eternal God." This gospel, expounded in the light of what is revealed in the prophetic Scriptures, will advance "the obedience of faith among all the Gentiles" (16:26; cf. 1:1–6). Paul's "gift" to the Romans (1:11) will be the sort of gospel proclamation and defense set forth in this letter. Believers need to have an ever-deepening understanding of the gospel and its significance to develop a biblical worldview and produce the "fruit" of obedient lives.

---

[49] Jewett, *Romans*, 131. He describes this verse as in several respects the "key to Romans" (130), since Roman culture was divided about ethnicity, class, and education.

[50] Cranfield (*Romans*, 1:85) argues that it is best to read τὸ κατ' ἐμὲ πρόθυμον ("my eager desire") as the subject of the sentence and (εὐαγγελίσασθαι, "to preach the gospel") as the predicate, understanding "is" as the link between them.

[51] See n. 30 above regarding the absence in some ancient manuscripts of the words "to Rome" in v. 7 and "in Rome" here.

[52] Dunn, *Romans 1–8*, 33–34. Cf. Schreiner, *Romans*, 53.

1:16. Paul's first definition of the gospel in vv. 2–4 described its "essence" (prophetic promises fulfilled in the Son). His second definition in vv. 16–17 builds upon the first by describing the gospel's "function." Here the gospel is expounded in terms of its saving power, the righteousness of God, and faith, which are distinctive themes in this letter (cf. 1 Cor 1:30; 2 Cor 5:21; Phil 3:8).[53] Another way of expressing the distinction would be to say that the summary in vv. 2–4 is Christological in focus, while the definition in vv. 16–17 is soteriological (see §2.1). Whether part of the body opening or the beginning of the body middle of the letter, these verses clearly form a bridge between Paul's disclosure of his mission plans in vv. 13–15 and the beginning of the letter proper.[54] Given the pattern of vv. 1–15, it is wise to note that he progressively discloses his agenda and continues to introduce a number of related ideas at once. The pastoral concerns in vv. 1–15 and the theological emphases in vv. 16–17 belong together in introducing this complex letter. Much development of these themes in concert must take place before the reader can properly discern Paul's purpose in writing. Nevertheless, at this point he begins to explain the gospel in a way that anticipates the argument in 3:21—5:11, which in turn lays the foundation for much of the teaching and exhortation that follows.

The conjunction γάρ ("for") links the opening words ("I am not ashamed of the gospel") with what Paul has just said about being eager to preach the gospel in Rome. He outlines why he is not ashamed of the gospel in a further explanatory sentence using γάρ ("*because* it is the power of God for salvation to everyone who believes, first to the Jew, and also to the Greek").[55] Some have taken

---

[53] Calhoun (*Paul's Definition*, 143) argues for the "essence"-"function" distinction by comparing what Greek philosophical and rhetorical texts say about definitions. Two terms occur earlier in the chapter ("power," "faith"), and two are introduced for the first time ("salvation," "the righteousness of God"). Cf. Moo, *Romans*, 64–65.

[54] Longenecker (*Introducing Romans*, 388–97) views the passage as the beginning of the "body middle" because Paul's "thesis statement" is repeated, expanded, supported and elucidated in 3:21–31. But Dunn (*Romans 1–8*, 37) thinks it is "the climax of the introduction" because of the gradual buildup of talk about the gospel (1, 9, 15, 16) and faith (vv. 5, 8–9, 12, 16–17). Moo (*Romans*, 64) argues that 1:16–17 is "technically part of the proem of the letter" but that these verses "serve as the transition into the body by stating Paul's theme."

[55] Runge (*Discourse Grammar*, 273–74) observes that δύναμις θεοῦ ("the power of God") is "in a marked position to emphasize the basis for not being ashamed of

the negative expression "I am not ashamed of the gospel" to be a form of speech called "litotes," making an understatement that actually has a positive meaning, such as "I am mighty proud of the gospel."[56] But it is better to understand the expression literally because Paul lived in a world where matters of honor and shame were taken seriously.[57] Elsewhere he identifies two particular reasons he might have been ashamed of the gospel: "For the Jews ask for signs and the Greeks seek wisdom" (1 Cor 1:22–23). But Paul responds by preaching Christ crucified, "a stumbling block to the Jews and foolishness to the Gentiles." Despite the cynicism and unbelief of people in both cultures, "the word of the cross" has proved to be "the power of God" to those who are being saved, "both Jews and Greeks" (1 Cor 1:17–24). In that context and here, Paul echoes biblical statements about the power of God's Word to deliver (e.g., Exod 9:16; Pss 77:14–15; 107:20; Isa 55:10–11) and to judge his people (e.g., Jer 16:21; 23:29–32). The message of the gospel is powerful to save because it conveys the benefits of the saving acts of God in Christ to all those who believe (1:4; 3:22; 4:11; 10:4, 11). It does this in the form of declarations and promises that, when believed, actually bring people into a relationship of dependence on God and his grace.[58]

"Salvation" for Paul fundamentally means deliverance from the final, eschatological expression of God's wrath (2:5; 5:9–10; 9:27; 13:11 cf. 1 Cor 3:15; 5:5; 1 Thess 1:10; 5:9). It also has a present, positive meaning, since believers have been saved *in hope* of "the redemption of our bodies" and anticipate sharing in the glory of God's new creation (8:23–24; cf. Eph 2:5, 8; 2 Tim 1:9; Titus 3:5). Indeed, salvation is secured in the present by believing the gospel and confessing Jesus as Lord (10:9–12; cf. 10:1; 11:14, 26). The singular expression "to everyone who believes, first to the Jew,

---

the gospel."

[56] Byrne, *Romans*, 30.

[57] Cf. G. M. Corrigan, "Paul's Shame for the Gospel," *BTB* 16 (1986): 23–27. Jewett (*Romans*, 136–37) notes that Greek orators used the "ashamed/not ashamed" formula in dealing with the social issues of honor and shame. Paul may also have known Jesus's warning in Mark 8:38//Luke 9:26 about not being ashamed of him and his word. Cf. 2 Tim 1:8, 11–12.

[58] Cf. 1 Cor 2:4–5; 1 Thess 1:4–5. Jewett (*Romans*, 138–39) draws attention to the significance of proclaiming such a gospel of power and salvation in a first-century Roman context.

and also to the Greek" signifies that there must be an individual faith response to the message of God's saving grace, whatever one's racial or religious background (cf. 3:27–4:25).[59] The present participle πιστεύοντι highlights believing as the essential response. The particle τε suggests the fundamental equality of Jew and Greek in the enjoyment of the benefits of the gospel, but πρῶτον emphasizes the priority of the Jew in God's plan of salvation (cf. 2:9–10). This is consistent with the covenant theology that is first expressed in Gen 12:1–3, where God's commitment to bless the offspring of Abraham makes it ultimately possible for "all the peoples on earth" to be blessed through them (cf. Rom 4:9–25). It is also the perspective of Isa 49:6, which seems to have influenced Paul's understanding of his calling from God (cf. Gal 1:15; Acts 13:46–47; 26:17–18). Romans 9–11 develops the theme of Jew and Gentile in the plan of God at some length but reveals a surprising twist in the way "all Israel" is to be saved (see especially 11:11–14, 25–26a; §2.5). God has acted to unite Jew and Gentile in praising him for his mercy (15:8–12).

1:17. Using the connective γάρ ("for") again, Paul provides the third explanatory clause in a sequence, articulating the meaning of the one before. The gospel is God's power for salvation to everyone who believes, "*for* in it the righteousness of God is revealed from faith to faith."[60] Since Paul has already used εὐαγγέλιον ("gospel") in v. 9 with reference to the activity described by the verb εὐαγγλίζεσθαι ("evangelize"), it is possible that he uses the noun in the same dynamic way here. If so, the present passive ἀποκαλύπτεται ("is revealed") signifies that the revelation of the righteousness of God takes place in the ongoing proclamation of the gospel, not simply in the message itself.[61] People from every nation are brought

[59] Mark A. Seifrid ("Unrighteous by Faith: Apostolic Proclamation in Romans 1:18–3:20," in *Justification and Variegated Nomism*, vol. 2: *The Paradoxes of Paul*, ed. Donald A. Carson, Peter T. O'Brien, and Mark A. Seifrid (Grand Rapids: Baker, 2004), 115) argues that Ἕλληνι ("to the Greek") here is a specific reference to the cultured Greco–Roman, not a simple equivalent for "Gentiles." However, contrast Schreiner, *Romans*, 62.

[60] Runge (*Discourse Grammar*, 274) argues that placing δικαιοσύνη θεοῦ ("the righteousness of God") in a marked position in the text "has the effect of attracting even more attention to it due to its importance in the context."

[61] Cf. Cranfield, *Romans*, 1:91–92. Wright ("Romans," 424) agrees that the revelation happens "every time the message about Jesus is announced, as God's

to faith in God's Son (1:3–4) when they hear about what God has accomplished in his death and resurrection (4:23–25).

But what does Paul mean by δικαιοσύνη θεοῦ ("the righteousness of God")? This term is found in 3:5, 21–22; 10:3 (twice in slightly different syntactical forms), with "his righteousness" (τῆς δικαιοσύνης αὐτοῦ) being mentioned in 3:25–26. Some have taken the righteousness of God to refer to an attribute of God, others to an activity of God, while still others have argued that it refers to a status given by God or the righteousness that "counts" in God's eyes. Biblical warrants have been found for each of these referents, but some combination of meanings in Paul's use of the terminology should be recognized.[62] As well as considering what the OT teaches about the righteousness of God, it is important to examine the use of this term in the wider context of Romans (see §2.4). A definition is required that adequately accounts for "the simultaneity of righteous wrath and the gift of righteousness of which Paul speaks (Rom 3:4–5; 3:21–26)."[63]

The Scriptures often speak of justification and righteousness in terms of the enactment of justice by God for the benefit of his people. Although the link is not so obvious in English, cognate words in Hebrew and Greek are used in ways that show how these themes are related. For example, in Ps 98:2 God's righteousness is associated with victory over his enemies when he judges the world righteously (v. 9; cf. Isa 46:13; 51:5; 63:1; 1 QS 11:12). In Isa 11:1–9 the work of the Messiah is to "judge the poor righteously and execute justice for the oppressed of the land." This manifestation of righteousness involves the punishment of the wicked and results in the transformation of the whole created order. Indeed, righteousness is regularly associated with God's rule and judgment beyond his relationship with Israel (e.g., Pss 9:5–8; 89:5–14; 97:1–12; 103:6). In some contexts God's righteousness is the basis or the motivation for

righteousness is unveiled before another audience." The passive suggests that the revelation of the righteousness of God in the proclamation of the gospel is God's doing.

[62] Cf. Moo, *Romans*, 70–75; Jewett, *Romans*, 142; Kruse, *Romans*, 70–71.

[63] Mark A. Seifrid, "Paul's Use of Righteousness Language against Its Hellenistic Background," in *Justification and Variegated Nomism*, vol. 2: *The Paradoxes of Paul*, 59. Cranfield (*Romans*, 1.96–99) argues that God's righteousness in Romans exclusively refers to the gift of righteousness from God, namely justification by faith.

his saving activity rather than a way of describing the activity itself (e.g., Pss 31:1; 35:24; 36:6, 10; 103:17; 143:1).

In v. 17 "the righteousness of God" is set between "the power of God for salvation" (v. 16) and "God's wrath" (v. 18), both of which expressions refer to a divine activity. According to 3:21–26, God's righteousness has been supremely revealed in the saving work of Christ and the justification of sinners this makes possible. According to 1:17, the revelation of God's righteousness continues in the proclamation of the message about this divine provision. God's righteousness involves granting mercy through judgment and putting things right for those who believe, as the argument in 1:18–3:26 indicates.[64] Righteousness is certainly an attribute of God, but the term is used to describe how God acts to establish justice for his people and put them right with himself.

The structure of Paul's sentence suggests that ἐκ πίστεως εἰς πίστιν should be connected with the verb ἀποκαλύπτεται, which immediately precedes it in the Greek text.[65] In relation to this verb, ἐκ πίστεως most likely denotes the means by which the revelation is received ("by faith") and εἰς πίστιν the purpose of the revelation ("for/with a view to faith"), namely, "the demand which it lays upon us."[66] Paul supports his claim by a citation from Hab 2:4b ("the righteous will live by faith"; cf. Gal 3:11; Heb 10:38). This establishes the continuity of God's way of salvation before and after Christ in the context of emphasizing the newness of the revelation of God's righteousness in the gospel. It is the first text Paul uses to show

---

[64] Schreiner (*Romans*, 66) contends that the righteousness of God in Romans is "both forensic and transformative": it is both gift and power, "a divine activity in which God vindicates his people" (68).

[65] Contrast Cranfield (*Romans*, 1:99–100), who links ἐκ πίστεως εἰς πίστιν to δικαιοσύνη θεοῦ and translates Hab 2:4, "He who is righteous by faith will live." He views εἰς πίστιν as an emphatic equivalent of ἐκ πίστεως and understands the whole expression to mean "a righteous status which is altogether by faith."

[66] Mark A. Seifrid, *Christ, Our Righteousness: Paul's Theology of Justification*, NSBT 9 (Downers Grove: InterVarsity, 2000), 38. Dunn (*Romans 1–8*, 44) suggests that ἐκ πίστεως refers to the faithfulness of God (cf. 3:3) and εἰς πίστιν to human faith, but no clues in the immediate context suggest this difference. Kruse (*Romans*, 72, 75–78) contends that the formula "from A to A" in Greek literature denotes progression in the same thing (e.g. "from strength to strength," "from glory to glory") and so means progression in human faith here, possibly from the faith response of Jews to the gospel to the faith response of Gentiles. Cf. Jewett, *Romans*, 143–44; Calhoun, *Paul's Definition*, 169–87.

how the gospel was "promised long ago through (God's) prophets in the Holy Scriptures" (1:2). The citation is preceded by the formula καθὼς γέγραπται ("just as it is written"), which establishes its biblical origin and consequent authority (cf. 1:17; 2:24; 3:4, 10; 4:17; 8:36; 9:13, 33; 10:15; 11:8, 26; 12:19; 15:3, 9, 21; see §2.2). Habakkuk proclaims that the righteous Israelite will be preserved alive through the terror of an enemy invasion because of his faith. In Paul's adaptation of this text, the personal pronoun is not translated so that the emphasis falls on faith generically as trust or reliance upon God.[67]

Contextually, ζήσεται ("will live") must refer to the salvation proclaimed in the gospel (1:16), which has present and future dimensions for the believer (cf. 5:17–21). "The righteous" will only enjoy the life promised in the gospel by responding to the message with faith. But the astute reader of Romans must ask who "the righteous" are in the light of later arguments about justification by faith (3:21–4:25). Paul may have intended his readers to draw out as much meaning as possible from Hab 2:4 and to understand that faith in the promises of God gives life (cf. Hab 2:2–3) *and* that those who have faith receive "the gift of righteousness" (Rom 5:17; cf. 9:30; 10:6) made possible by the work of Christ.[68] Paul's Christological explanation of the gospel in 1:3–4 undergirds the soteriological explanation in 1:16–17. His proclamation is about Messiah Jesus, the Son of God, in whose person and work the righteousness of God is fully and finally revealed.

---

[67] The MT of Hab 2:4 reads, "The righteous by *his* faith(fulness) shall live" (צַדִּיק בֶּאֱמוּנָתוֹ יִחְיֶה). The LXX reads, "The righteous by *my* faith(fulness) shall live" (ὁ δὲ δίκαιος ἐκ πίστεώς μου ζήσεται). Dunn (*Romans 1–8*, 44–46) suggests that Paul's failure to include either pronoun in his version of the text (cf. Gal 3:11) may have been prompted by a desire to avoid choosing between the alternatives and to embrace both forms or meanings. But K. W. McFadden ("Does ΠΙΣΤΙΣ Mean Faith[fulness] in Paul?" *TynBul* 66 [2015]: 251–70) questions the legitimacy of trying to read two meanings into the use of this noun in any context.

[68] A number of commentators take a "both/and" approach to this question, viewing the primary meaning as "the righteous will live by faith" and the secondary meaning that they are made righteous by faith. E.g., Davies, *Faith and Obedience*, 41–42; Dunn, *Romans 1–8*, 45–46; Schreiner, *Romans*, 74–75 (who shows how Paul uses Hab 2:4 in a way that is consistent with its original context).

Bridge

Paul establishes a relationship of confidence between himself and his Roman readers in anticipation of a visit to their city. He builds bridges of understanding and trust before launching into the sustained argument of his letter. His earnest concern for the welfare of his readers comes before any disclosure of his own needs. He wants them to benefit from his confirmation and defense of the gospel and to join with him in making it known (cf. 15:23–32). His thanksgiving and prayer report show the importance of being open and honest about ministry aspirations, especially when seeking to work with others to propagate the gospel. Disclosing how we pray for people reveals our best desires for them. Paul is both committed to the advancement of the gospel and to the spiritual maturation of the Roman Christians. But his approach is not one-sided: he wants to be encouraged by their faith and their ministry to him. In anticipation of the argument to come, he explains the gospel in terms of God's righteousness being revealed for the salvation of all who believe, "first to the Jew, and also to the Greek." There were reasons to be ashamed of the gospel in Paul's world, just as there are in ours. But understanding how the gospel is rooted in biblical theology and how it meets our need by being "the power of God for salvation" should deliver us from shame. Such confidence is critical for a fruitful gospel ministry.

II. God's Righteous Judgment against Sin Revealed (1:18–32)

18 For God's wrath is revealed from heaven against all godlessness and unrighteousness of people who by their unrighteousness suppress the truth, 19 since what can be known about God is evident among them, because God has shown it to them. 20 For his invisible attributes, that is, his eternal power and divine nature, have been clearly seen since the creation of the world, being understood through what he has made. As a result, people are without excuse. 21 For though they knew God, they did not glorify him as God or show gratitude. Instead, their thinking became worthless, and their senseless hearts were darkened. 22 Claiming to be wise, they became fools 23 and exchanged the glory of the immortal God for images resembling mortal man, birds, four-footed animals, and reptiles.

24 Therefore God delivered them over in the desires of their hearts to sexual impurity, so that their bodies were degraded among themselves. 25 They exchanged the truth of God for a lie, and worshiped and served what has been created instead of the Creator, who is praised forever. Amen.

26 For this reason God delivered them over to disgraceful passions. Their women exchanged natural sexual relations for unnatural ones. 27 The men in the same way also left natural relations with women and were inflamed in their lust for one another. Men committed shameless acts with men and received in their own persons the appropriate penalty of their error.

28 And because they did not think it worthwhile to acknowledge God, God delivered them over to a corrupt mind so that they do what is not right. 29 They are filled with all unrighteousness, evil, greed, and wickedness. They are full of envy, murder, quarrels, deceit, and malice. They are gossips, 30 slanderers, God-haters, arrogant, proud, boastful, inventors of evil, disobedient to parents, 31 senseless, untrustworthy, unloving, and unmerciful. 32 Although they know God's just sentence—that those who practice such things deserve to die—they not only do them, but even applaud others who practice them.

Context

When Paul proclaims that the gospel is the power of God for the salvation of everyone who believes (1:16–17), he presupposes a plight from which all must be rescued. In 1:18–3:20 this is explained in terms of God's righteous judgment against sin, both now and in the future. There are four stages in Paul's unfolding presentation (1:18–32; 2:1–16; 2:17–29; 3:1–20), each progressively building toward an exposition of the gospel in 3:21–31. This first stage of the argument shows how and why the eschatological wrath of God is already active among the nations. An immediate link to v. 17 is provided by repetition of the word "revealed" (v. 18), but the wrath of God is the subject now. God's wrath is experienced in the present as people are "delivered over" to the consequences of their sin (vv. 24, 26, 28). The ultimate revelation of the wrath of God is considered in the next passage (2:5, 6–11, 16). A contrast is made between "the righteous," who live by faith (v. 17) and those who "by their unrighteousness suppress the truth" (v. 18). The rest of the passage explains what this means and outlines the consequences. Paul prepares for the next stage of the argument by declaring that people not only do the things they know will merit God's judgment "but even applaud others who practice them" (v. 32).

Structure

Paul's opening thesis statement is that "God's wrath is revealed from heaven against all godlessness and unrighteousness of people who by their unrighteousness suppress the truth" (v. 18). This claim is supported by four arguments in the rest of the passage (vv. 19–21, 22–23, 24–27, 28–32).[1] Unrighteousness is developed in vv. 19–21 and godlessness in vv. 22–23. The truth Paul has in mind is "what can be known about God" (1:19). People are "without excuse" when they fail to respond appropriately to what God has revealed about himself (1:20). Rejection of the knowledge of God profoundly affects the way people think and act so that they give to idols the honor due to God.[2] In vv. 24–27 godlessness is described in terms of exchanging the truth about God for the lie of idolatry. Here we find the first of three statements about God's delivering people over in judgment against their sin (vv. 24, 26, 28). Idolatry is linked with sexual impurity and the degrading of their bodies among them-

[1] Following Jewett, *Romans*, 148.

[2] Seifrid ("Unrighteous by Faith," 108) identifies idolatry as "the primal sin," but the flow of the argument in vv. 18–23 suggests that the primal sin is suppressing what can be known about God and failing to glorify him or give him thanks.

selves. Particularly when people exchange natural sexual relations for unnatural, God's judgment is experienced as they receive "in their own persons the appropriate penalty of their error" (1:26–27). In vv. 28–32 Paul restates the fundamental problem exposed in the passage ("because they did not think it worthwhile to acknowledge God") and expresses God's judgment in a way that corresponds with this ("God delivered them over to a corrupt mind so that they do what is not right"). Various forms of unrighteous behavior are then described. This section concludes in v. 32 with an echo of Paul's claims in vv. 18–23, 28.

Outline:

1. Why God's wrath is being revealed (vv. 18–23)
    a. Unrighteous responses to what can be known about God (vv. 18–21)
    b. Godless behavior in the guise of religion (vv. 22–23)
2. How God's wrath is being revealed (vv. 24–32)
    a. Abandonment to the consequences of exchanging the truth of God for a lie (vv. 24–27)
    b. Abandonment to all forms of unrighteous behavior (vv. 28–32)

1:18. The conjunction *γάρ* ("for") suggests that the thesis presented here and argued in vv. 19–32 directly supports what is said about the gospel in vv. 16–17. An ongoing revelation (present passive *ἀποκαλύπτεται* ["is being revealed"], as in v. 17) of (lit.) "the wrath of God from heaven" (*ὀργὴ θεοῦ ἀπ̓ οὐρανοῦ*) manifests the righteousness of God in judgment against human sin.[3] Paul later refers to the imminent, final revelation of the wrath of God predicted in Scripture and other Jewish literature (2:5, 8; 3:5; 4:15; 5:9; 9:22; 12:19). But in this passage he points to observable, present expressions of God's wrath, not in fitful outbursts of anger but in delivering people up to the consequences of their sin. This is indicated by the threefold use of *παρέδωκεν αὐτοὺς ὁ θεός* ("God delivered

[3] Cranfield (*Romans*, 1:111) suggests that the expression "from heaven" emphasizes the utter seriousness of God's wrath: "It amounts in fact to an underlining of θεοῦ."

them over") in vv. 24, 26, 28.[4] Some commentators have argued that ἀποκαλύπτεται in v. 18 should be taken in parallel with its use in v. 17 to mean that the revelation of the wrath of God takes place through the preaching of the gospel. While Paul's gospel includes what may be called "a new understanding of wrath from the perspective of the gospel,"[5] the modifier ἐν αὐτῷ ("in it") or some equivalent is not found in this verse. Moreover, the apostle is directing the attention of his readers to a process that is going on in everyday human experience. People may not understand this as an expression of God's wrath until they hear the gospel or read the Scriptures, but the revelation takes place in human affairs whether they perceive it or not.

When Paul speaks about "all godlessness and unrighteousness of people who by their unrighteousness suppress the truth," he addresses human failure comprehensively. His use of πᾶσαν ("all") and ἀνθρώπων ("people") points in that direction. Although his critique of idolatry and the pretensions of human wisdom to some extent parallels descriptions of the Gentile world in Jewish writings (e.g., Wis 11–16), Paul knows well enough from the history of his own people that Jews could be idolaters and implies this in v. 23, where his language seems to reflect the condemnation of Israel's idolatry in Ps 106:20 (cf. Deut 4:15–19; Jer 2:11).[6] The terms ἀσέβειαν ("godlessness, impiety") and ἀδικίαν ("unrighteousness") are carefully chosen in anticipation of the argument to come. In Greco-Roman culture impiety was "the most heinous crime—the failure to respect deity, especially in the civic cult."[7] Unrighteousness included

[4] So Dunn (*Romans 1–8*, 54) concludes that "God's final judgment is simply the end of a process already in train (cf. particularly *1 En* 84:4; 91:7–9)," and Seifrid ("Unrighteous by Faith," 110) argues that "the final judgment does not inaugurate the contention between God and the fallen world. It rather culminates in it (3:1–5)."

[5] Jewett, *Romans*, 150. Cf. Wright, "Romans," 431–32. Cranfield (*Romans*, 1:110) views the death of Jesus as the historic manifestation of the wrath God, to which the gospel points. But this severs the link between 1:18 and what follows in 1:24–32.

[6] Cf. Cranfield, *Romans*, 1:105–6. Byrne (*Romans*, 63) says Paul aims to catch his Jewish dialogue partner in a rhetorical "trap" (2:1–3), "designed to drive home more effectively the thesis that there is no righteousness to be had on the basis of the law." But Moo (*Romans*, 96–97) and Seifrid ("Unrighteous by faith," 117–19) have a more nuanced approach.

[7] Jewett, *Romans*, 152. In Greek-speaking Judaism, ἀσέβεια refers to impious actions rather than attitudes or specifically proscribed crimes (cf. Werner Foerster,

wrongdoing, injustice, and law-breaking.[8] Various manifestations of unrighteousness are highlighted in vv. 24–32, but vv. 18–20 focuses on the injustice of suppressing what can be known about God. The second use of ἀδικία in v. 18 (τῶν τὴν ἀλήθειαν ἐν ἀδικίᾳ, "who by their unrighteousness suppress the truth") suggests that unrighteousness is fundamentally expressed in a refusal to acknowledge what God has revealed about himself.[9] The following verses define what Paul means by this (vv. 19–20). In v. 25 he calls it "the truth of God." Later contexts apply truth language to the specific revelation given to Israel (2:8, 20; 3:7; 15:8), but here the truth is what God manifests about himself in the created order. Paul's participial expression (κατεχόντων) could mean that people "possess" the truth but behave in a way that is inconsistent with that knowledge, which is the perspective that emerges in 2:1, 17–24. However, most commentators argue that the immediate context requires the meaning "hold down, suppress" the truth.[10]

1:19–20. The conjunction διότι ("since") indicates that what follows is an explanation of Paul's foundational claim in v. 18. "What can be known about God" (τὸ γνωστὸν τοῦ θεοῦ) identifies "the truth" that is suppressed. The claim that this is "evident among them" (φανερόν ἐστιν ἐν αὐτοῖς) continues the note of revelation, using different terminology.[11] What can be known about God apart

---

"ἀσεβής κτλ," *TDNT* 7:187–89).

[8] Cranfield (*Romans*, 1:112) contends that the terms ἀσέβειαν and ἀδικίαν in Paul's argument describe the same thing from a different perspective. But Paul differentiates these themes in the passage that follows, even as he weaves them together.

[9] The expression ἐν ἀδικίᾳ could be taken adverbially ("unrighteously"), rather than instrumentally ("by their unrighteousness"), to highlight this point. Godless and unrighteous acts flow from unrighteously suppressing the truth about God. Craig S. Keener (*The Mind of the Spirit: Paul's Approach to Transformed Thinking* [Grand Rapids: Baker Academic, 2016], 6–13) compares what ancient Greek and Jewish sources say about the knowledge of deity and the suppression of what can be known.

[10] Cf. BDAG, κατέχω. Bruce A. Baker ("Romans 1:18–21 and Presuppositional Apologetics," *BSac* 155 [1998]: 285) argues that both ways of reading this expression can be understood together. But the modifier ἐν ἀδικίᾳ suggests that the meaning here is specifically "suppress" or "hinder," as in 2 Thess 2:6–7; Phlm 13.

[11] Elsewhere in the NT γνωστόν refers to something that is known or being made known (Luke 2:44; 23:49; John 18:15–16; Acts 1:19; 2:14; 4:10, 16; 9:42; 13:38; 15:18; 19:17; 28:22, 28). Since Paul's point is that what is being manifested is not acknowledged (see comments on 1:21, 28), Moo (*Romans*, 103n55) justifies the translation "what can be known" in 1:19.

from special or supernatural revelation is manifest "in" or "among" human beings "because God has shown it to them" (ὁ θεὸς γὰρ αὐτοῖς ἐφανέρωσεν). The expression ἐν αὐτοῖς could refer to what is known inwardly and subjectively ("in them") or to what is known "publicly within each cultural group."[12] The latter is more likely to be Paul's meaning since he is arguing about a knowledge that is available to all, even if individuals choose not to acknowledge it (cf. Ps 19:1–2).

The conjunction γάρ ("for") introduces an explanation of what can be known about God and how God has manifested this knowledge. The *content* of the revelation is "his invisible attributes, that is, his eternal power and divine nature." God's invisible attributes (τὰ ἀόρατα αὐτοῦ) are mentioned generically, and then two are identified ("eternal power and divine nature").[13] Paradoxically, these invisible attributes have been "clearly seen" (καθορᾶται). This has happened "since the creation of the world, being understood through what he has made." CSB rightly takes ἀπὸ κτίσεως κόσμου in a *temporal* sense ("since the creation of the world") because the expression τοῖς ποιήμασιν (lit. "in what is made") indicates that the created order is *the place* where God manifests "his eternal power and divine nature." This includes human life, where his providential care is experienced every day (cf. Ps 104; Acts 14:15–17; 17:24–29).

Two verbs are used together to describe the apprehension of this revelation. The present indicative καθορᾶται ("clearly seen") describes ongoing, physical sight (LXX Exod 10:5; Num 24:2; Deut 26:15; Jdg 6:19; Job 10:4; 39:26), and the modifying present passive participle νοούμενα ("being understood") signifies the mental recognition of what is seen. The combination of these two verbs shows "unambiguously that an intellectual process is in view."[14] In short,

[12] Jewett, *Romans*, 153. Jewett claims that Jewish literature does not envisage a natural knowledge of God available for Gentiles. Compare Moo (*Romans*, 122–25) and my comments on the speeches to Gentiles in Acts 14:15–17; 17:22–31 (David G. Peterson, *The Acts of the Apostles*, PNTC [Grand Rapids: Eerdmans, 2009], 408–11, 493–503).

[13] Cf. Runge, *Discourse Grammar*, 328. The invisibility of God is stressed in passages such as Exod 33:19–20; John 1:18; 6:46; Col 1:15–16; 1 Tim 1:17; Heb 11:27. θειότης refers to "the quality or characteristics pertaining to deity, divinity, divine nature, divineness" (BDAG). Baker ("Romans 1:18–21," 289) identifies three attributes of God implied in this verse: he is personal, eternal, and powerful.

[14] Wilhelm Michaelis, "ὁράω κτλ," *TDNT* 5:380. Paul is not simply claiming a sensory perception of God's attributes in the created order. Baker ("Romans 1:18–21,"

then, throughout human history evidence for an all-powerful and eternal Creator has been perceived in humanity's experience of the natural order. But the unhappy result of God's self-manifestation in this way has not been a true knowledge of God, but a culpable ignorance.[15] The concluding clause (εἰς τὸ εἶναι αὐτους ἀναπολογήτους) could be read as statement of purpose (God has made this knowledge of himself available so that they are without excuse) or as a result clause, which is the way CSB renders it ("As a result, people are without excuse").[16] Such culpability makes the proclamation of the message of salvation through Christ an urgent necessity in every part of God's world.

1:21. A further phase of the argument begins with a second use of the conjunction διότι ("since"). Paul begins to outline the steps by which people have become idolaters, picking up the theme of knowing God from vv. 19–20, using the participle γνόντες in a concessive way ("though they knew God"). He also begins to define more specifically what is meant by "godlessness" (v. 18). Paul moves from the use of present-tense verbs (vv. 18–20), which provide general descriptive material, to a timeless use of aorist forms.[17] These provide an embedded narrative, giving a summary account of what has characterized human life from the beginning.[18] Although every race and culture have had some sense of God's eternal power and divine

---

292) concludes that the knowledge of God Paul has in mind "occurs through the conjunction of reflection and sensation."

[15] Kruse (*Romans*, 93–95) provides a helpful summary of contemporary views on Paul and natural theology. See also n. 12 above and nn. 66–67 below.

[16] Moo (*Romans*, 105n66) argues that Paul's general use of the articular infinitive with εἰς favors a purposive reading but acknowledges that result and purpose are closely linked when talking about God's revelatory activity.

[17] Constantine A. Campbell (*Verbal Aspect, the Indicative Mood, and Narrative: Soundings in the Greek of the New Testament* [New York: Peter Lang, 2007], 103–26) shows how the perfective aspect of aorist tense forms describes events from "an external viewpoint." The term "punctiliar" can only serve for perfectivity if "the *point* is understood to represent an *undefined whole*." The aorist characteristically carries the mainline in narratives.

[18] Some, such as Morna D. Hooker ("Adam in Romans 1," *NTS* 6 [1960]: 300–301) and Douglas J. W. Milne ("Genesis 3 in the Letter to the Romans," *RTR* 39 [1980]: 10–12), see a particular allusion to Adam's fall in Gen 3 here. However, Moo (*Romans*, 98, 109n85) and Joseph A. Fitzmyer (*Romans: A New Translation with Introduction and Commentary*, AB 33 [New York: Doubleday, 1993], 274) rightly critique this position. Cf. Keener, *The Mind of the Spirit*, 23–26.

nature, "they did not glorify him as God or show gratitude." Even the daily experience of God's providential care did not move people to praise him as the source of all the good things they enjoyed and to thank him for those benefits. Paul later declares that they did not think it worthwhile "to acknowledge God" (v. 28, τὸν θεὸν ἔχειν ἐν ἐπιγνώσει), meaning literally, "to have God in their knowledge." This suggests the possibility of being aware of God's existence and sovereign power but not taking that knowledge into account in everyday life.[19]

To "glorify him as God" (ὡς θεὸν ἐδόξασαν) means to give God the praise and honor that is due him. Since the cognate noun δόξα is widely used in Scripture to refer to the manifest character of God (e.g., "the glory of the immortal God," v. 23), to "glorify" God means to acknowledge and honor him as he has revealed himself.[20] Two particular examples of people glorifying God can be found later in this letter. First, we are told that Abraham continued to trust in God's promise despite his circumstances (4:19–20), glorifying God by his response (cf. 1 Cor 6:20). Second, Paul describes his missional task as bringing people everywhere to "glorify the God and Father of our Lord Jesus Christ with one mind and one voice" (15:6), facilitating the true worship of God through the ministry of the gospel (15:7–13, 16). Thanksgiving is a particular way of honoring or glorifying God as God—the logical outcome of recognizing our indebtedness to God's goodness and generosity. Although Jewish and Gentile writers identified the importance of giving thanks to God, "nowhere else in the ancient world was so universal a failure decried."[21] Paul uses other terms in vv. 23, 25 to show how the failure to worship God appropriately is foundational to the human plight (see §2.6).

---

[19] Cranfield (*Romans*, 1:128) argues that v. 28 points to "a knowledge which goes beyond that indicated by γνόντες τὸν θεόν in v. 21, and which in fact includes the δοξάζειν and εὐχαριστεῖν to which that verse refers." To acknowledge God is to respond to him appropriately. Cf. Dunn, *Romans 1–8*, 59.

[20] The LXX regularly uses δόξα to translate Heb. כָּבוֹד ("glory"), as in Ps 97:6 (LXX 96:6]); Exod 40:35; Isa 6:3; 40:5. Cf. Gerhard von Rad and Gerhard Kittel, "δοκέω, δόξα, δοξάζω κτλ.," *TDNT* 2:232–55; Dunn, *Romans 1–8*, 59.

[21] Jewett, *Romans*, 158. Jewett cites Greco-Roman sources pointing to the need to give thanks to God and claims that 2 Bar. 82:3–9 is the closest Jewish parallel to Paul's denunciation here. Cf. David W. Pao, *Thanksgiving: An Investigation of a Pauline Theme*, NSBT 13 (Downers Grove: InterVarsity, 2002).

The strong adversative ἀλλά ("but," "instead") introduces the next stage of the argument. Two passive verbs, ἐματαιώθησαν (v. 21b, [lit.] "made futile") and ἐσκοτίσθη ("were darkened") indicate "the state into which humans are placed when they fail to honor God as God."[22] Paul's combination of the first verb with ἐν τοῖς διαλογισμοῖς αὐτῶν (lit. "in their thoughts") echoes Ps 94:11 (LXX 93:11, "The Lord knows man's thoughts; they are meaningless"). A parallel expression (ἐσκοτίσθη ἡ ἀσύνετος αὐτῶν καρδία, "their senseless heart was darkened") echoes the Greek of Ps 76:5 (LXX 75:6, ἐταράχθησαν πάντες οἱ ἀσύνετοι τῇ καρδίᾳ, "all the senseless in heart were thrown into confusion"). No great distinction between mind and heart should be drawn here. Like the psalmist Paul uses the adjective ἀσύνετος ("senseless," "without understanding") to describe the heart that refuses to glorify God and give him thanks. In biblical usage "the heart" is a comprehensive term, embracing thoughts, emotions, and the will.[23] In human personalities the ability to think and to act appropriately is disabled or impaired when we fail to acknowledge the reality of God in our lives. "At the very center of every person, where the knowledge of God, if it is to have any positive effects, must be embraced, there has settled a darkness—a darkness that only the light of the gospel can penetrate."[24] When the mind is renewed through belief in the gospel, it becomes possible to discern and do "the good, pleasing, and perfect will of God" (12:2).

1:22–23. Wisdom was prized by Jews, Greeks, and Romans in the ancient world, though "it was widely assumed that one should never claim it for oneself."[25] Paul's dramatic assertion ("claiming to be wise, they became fools") lacks a connective in Greek and introduces his first attack on idolatry. The present participle φάσκοντες ("claiming") implies an ongoing or frequent claim to be wise. The aorist passive indicative ἐμωράνθησαν ("they became fools"), like

[22] Jewett (*Romans*, 158) only relates this comment to the first verb, but it is true of both. In the LXX the first verb is used to indicate the vanity of idolatry and the futility of ignorance. Cf. Otto Bauernfeind, "μάταιος," *TDNT* 4:521–22.

[23] James D. G. Dunn (*The Theology of Paul the Apostle* [Grand Rapids: Eerdmans; Edinburgh: T&T Clark, 1998], 73–75) argues that, "alongside *nous*, denoting 'the thinking I,' we may say that *kardia* denotes 'the experiencing, motivating I.'" What is going on in "the heart" is a crucial aspect of Paul's anthropology in Romans (1:21, 24; 2:5, 15, 29; 5:5; 6:17; 8:27; 9:2; 10:1, 6, 8–9, 10; 16:18).

[24] Moo, *Romans*, 107.

[25] Jewett, *Romans*, 159. Cf. Plato, *Apol.* 20c–23c.

the passives in the previous verse, could suggest a divine judgment ("they were made fools"). People who fail to acknowledge God, yet claim to be wise, become fools in the biblical sense of the word (e.g., Ps 14:1–4; Jer 4:22).[26] The ultimate act of foolishness is to exchange "the glory of the immortal God for images resembling mortal man, birds, four-footed animals, and reptiles." Paul apparently echoes the language of Ps 106:20 here (LXX 105:20, ἠλλάξαντο τὴν δόξαν αὐτῶν ἐν ὁμοιώματι μόσχου ἔσθοντος χόρτον, "they exchanged their glory for the image of a grass-eating ox").[27] This refers to Israel's quintessential act of rebellion, when they made the golden calf so soon after being rescued by God from Egypt (Exod 32:1–10). Paul also echoes Jer 2:11, where God's people at a later date are accused of having "changed his glory for something that does not profit" (ἠλλάξατο τὴν δόξαν αὐτοῦ ἐξ ἧς οὐκ ὠφεληθήσονται). So, by allusion to these biblical texts, the apostle includes Israel's sin in his condemnation of human idolatry.[28]

The seriousness of idolatry is emphasized in several ways here. First, it involves replacing God with something inferior as the object of devotion and the source of blessing. Particularly telling is the contrast between "the immortal God" (τοῦ ἀφθάρτου θεοῦ) and "mortal man" (φθαρτοῦ ἀνθρώπου). Even though humanity was created "in the image of God" (Gen 1:27, κατ' εἰκόνα θεοῦ), we now "fall short of the glory of God" (3:23) and perish. No person should take the place of God in our affections. Second, Paul's expression ἐν ὁμοιώματι εἰκόνος (lit. "in the likeness of the image") probably stresses the remoteness of an idol from what it represents: "an image twice removed, a distortion even of the proper shape of the creatures depicted in the idol."[29] Third, the fourfold description of "images resembling mortal man, birds, four-footed animals and reptiles" covers a range of beings mentioned in Gen 1:20–27 (without "the fish of the sea") and anticipates the accusation of worshipping and

[26] Cf. Chou-Wee Pan, "אֱוִיל," *NIDOTTE* 1:306–9.

[27] The LXX expression τὴν δόξαν αὐτῶν ("their glory") appears to refer to God as Israel's glory. Jewett (*Romans*, 159) observes that "Paul avoids the LXX's ambiguity in the use of δόξα ('glory') by a formulation closer to the MT that suggests the 'glory of God' as the target to be displaced by the idol."

[28] Byrne (*Romans*, 63) contends that these verses aim to catch Paul's Jewish dialogue partner in a rhetorical "trap" (2:1–3).

[29] Jewett, *Romans*, 161.

serving created things rather than the Creator (Rom 1:25). The same terms are used in Deut 4:15–18 (including "the fish of the waters"), where Israel is warned about acting corruptly and making idols of any sort. Dependence on idols or the created beings they represent denies the Creator the honor due him as the sole provider and sustainer of everything that exists. As well as in false religion, this can take place through devotion to money, possessions, art, entertainment, sensual pleasures, or human relationships.[30]

1:24. As in vv. 19, 21, the connective δίο ("since", "therefore") indicates a logical progression in the argument. Here we have the first of three statements about God's delivering people over (παρέδωκεν αὐτοὺς ὁ θεός) in judgment for their sin (vv. 24, 26, 28), amplifying what is meant by God's wrath being revealed from heaven (v. 18). Since God is clearly the subject of the verb παρέδωκεν, Paul is not simply speaking about "an inevitable process of cause and effect in a moral universe"[31] but about a process of retribution initiated by God himself. In everyday use, when followed by a dative form and an εἰς clause indicating purpose, this verb was "a technical expression for the police or courts in turning someone over to official custody for the purpose of punishment."[32] Paul does not simply mean that God withholds his help, which could have prevented judgment from falling. We are later told that "the creation was subjected to futility (ματαιότητι) not willingly, but because of him who subjected it" (8:20). As part of that response to human sin, God initiates and maintains a process of judgment in the world he created, expressing his wrath and showing the practical consequences of refusing to

[30] Moo (*Romans*, 113) observes that it is "putting some aspect of God's creation—whether it be an animal, a human, or a material object—in place of God that is the essence of idolatry." Cf. Raymond C. Ortlund Jr., *God's Unfaithful Wife: A Biblical Theology of Spiritual Adultery*, NSBT 2 (Downers Grove: InterVarsity, 2003).

[31] Charles H. Dodd, *The Epistle of Paul to the Romans* (London: Hodder & Stoughton, 1932; repr., London: Fontana, 1959), 50. Dodd (52) asserts that Paul's essential message in 1:24–32 is that "the retribution of sin is already at work, in the moral rottenness of pagan society." For Dodd, the act of God is "no more than an abstention from interference with their free choice and its consequences" (55).

[32] Jewett, *Romans*, 167. Cf. BDAG, παραδίδωμι, 1b. The verb is also simply used with an εἰς clause to express a handing over for punishment (e.g., Matt 10:21; 17:22; 24:9; Acts 8:3). In the LXX the verb is used when God "hands over" his people to judgment or delivers enemies into their hands (e.g., Gen 14:20; Lev 26:25; Num 21:34; Josh 7:7; Judg 2:14).

acknowledge him. "Like a judge who hands over a prisoner to the punishment his crime earned, God hands over the sinner to the terrible cycle of ever-increasing sin."[33] It may be that God permits people "to go their own way in order that they might at last learn from their consequent wretchedness to hate the futility of a life turned away from the truth of God."[34] But punishment rather than reformation is the purpose outlined here.

People are delivered over for judgment "in the desires of their hearts" (ἐν ταῖς ἐπιθυμίαις τῶν καρδιῶν αὐτῶν). This refers to the cravings already mentioned, as people assert themselves over against God and devote themselves to idols (vv. 18–23).[35] The prison into which they are delivered is literally "uncleanness" (εἰς ἀκαθαρσίαν), which in the present context will mean "a state of moral corruption" (BDAG). In view of the following clause, CSB narrows the meaning to "sexual impurity." The result is the abuse of their bodies: "so that their bodies were degraded among themselves" (τοῦ ἀτιμάζεσθαι τὰ σώματα αὐτῶν ἐν αὐτοῖς).[36] A distorted view of God brings a distorted view of human beings, made in the image of God (Gen 1:26–27), meaning that the proper use of our bodies in human relationships becomes obscured. Sexual immorality and idolatry are closely linked in paganism, but Paul is not simply exposing that link (as Wis 14:12–14 does). His fundamental thesis is that alienation from God brings practical, everyday expressions of God's wrath: sexual immorality and abusive human relationships of every kind are the result of that alienation. They are an ever-present expression of God's judgment against us as a race, showing how far we have fallen from God's purpose for us (cf. 3:23).

---

[33] Moo, *Romans*, 111.

[34] Cranfield, *Romans*, 1:121. Dunn (*Romans 1–8*, 63) suggests that Paul might have seen the divine handing over as "at least potentially redemptive, if it resulted in man's recoiling from the degenerate outworking of his own freedom (cf. 1 Cor 5:5), as no doubt had been the case with many of the Gentile God-worshippers who made up his audience."

[35] The noun ἐπιθυμία can refer to sinful lusts in general (6:12; 7:7–8; 13:14). The next expression (εἰς ἀκαθαρσίαν) narrows the focus to sexual immorality in the broadest sense. Cf. Rom 6:19; Gal 5:19; Eph 4:19; 1 Thess 4:17.

[36] The articular infinitive could also be read as an explanatory clause (Moo, *Romans*, 112n100). It is less likely to be a statement of purpose since εἰς ἀκαθαρσίαν expresses a state or condition and the following clause the resultant behavior. Cf. Cranfield, *Romans*, 1:122–23.

1:25. Most translations begin a new sentence here, but the indefinite relative pronoun οἵτινες introduces a subordinate clause, identifying those who are "delivered over" to judgment in the previous verse. Literally, they are "those who exchanged the truth of God for a lie, and worshipped and served what has been created instead of the Creator."[37] A rhetorical antithesis between "truth" and "lie" is matched by the antithesis between "Creator" and "creature" (κτίσις here could refer to the creation as a whole, but v. 23 points to particular creatures as the object of worship). Paul picks up terms from previous verses and modifies them to make his dramatic summary statement. "The truth" that is suppressed (v. 18) is "the truth of God," which has also been described as "what can be known about God" (v. 19) and "the glory of the immortal God" (v. 23). Those who "exchanged" (ἤλλαξαν) the glory of God for images (v. 23) have substituted (μετήλλαξαν) the truth about God "for the lie" (ἐν τῷ ψεύδει).[38] Use of the definite article and the singular noun ("the lie") points back to the suppression of the truth described in v. 18, leading to the worship of created things rather than the Creator (vv. 21–23). A lie was fundamental to "the primordial desire of humans to 'be like God' and to define evil and good for themselves (Gen 3:5)."[39] The worship of images and idols is a particular consequence of rejecting the truth about God as beneficent Creator.

The rare verb ἐσεβάσθησαν ("worshipped") only occurs here in the NT, conveying the sense of reverence or fear, though related terms are used elsewhere.[40] The second verb, ἐλάτρευσαν ("served"), refers to the cultic worship that was offered to idols in this context. In biblical teaching, the God of Israel demanded exclusive service from his people with no concession to idolatry (e.g., Exod 3:12;

[37] In this context the relative pronoun could have a qualitative or intensive sense ("these indeed"). Cf. Daniel B. Wallace, *Greek Grammar Beyond the Basics* (Grand Rapids: Zondervan, 1996), 343–44.

[38] Jewett (*Romans*, 169–17) suggests that the compound verb μετήλλαξαν may have the more intensive meaning "substituted." But Friedrich Büchsel ("ἀλλάσσω, κτλ.," *TDNT* 1:251–59) argues that the verbs are used in an equivalent way in vv. 23, 25.

[39] Jewett, *Romans*, 170. But see n. 18 above.

[40] The verb σέβομαι ("reverence, respect, worship") is used in Matt 15:9; Mark 7:7; Acts 13:43, 50; 16:14; 17:4, 17; 18:7, 13; 19:27. The noun σέβασμα ("object of worship") appears in Acts 17:23; 2 Thess 2:4, and the adjective σεβαστός ("revered") is in Acts 25:21, 25; 27:1. Cf. Werner Foerster, "σέβομαι, κτλ.," *TDNT* 7:168–91.

20:5). Moreover, cultic service to God was meant to encourage obedience to him in everyday life (e.g., Deut 6:13–19).[41] Using a typically Jewish formula, Paul declares that the Creator is to be "blessed" or "praised" forever (ὅς ἐστιν εὐλογητὸς εἰς τοὺς αἰῶνας), inviting his readers to share his response with an amen (cf. 9:5; 11:33–36; 16:27).[42] Paul's sudden injection of praise into the argument is an example of the gratitude he mentions in v. 21. Thanksgiving emerges again in 6:17–18; 7:25, showing how natural it was for the apostle to express himself in this way when talking about God.[43]

1:26–27. Once more God is described as having delivered people over to judgment (παρέδωκεν αὐτοὺς ὁ θεός, as in v. 24). Paul's threefold use of this expression does not point to a temporal sequence but refers to a single divine action. The causal expression διὰ τοῦτο ("for this reason") relates this specifically to the idolatry described in v. 25, while the prison into which they are delivered is now described as "disgraceful passions" (εἰς πάθη ἀτιμίας). "Passion" (πάθος) refers to "an involuntary state that simply comes over a person."[44] While this term could cover a range of impulses and desires, the noun ἀτιμίας (lit. "dishonor"), which is used adjectivally here (lit. "passions of dishonor"), points particularly to degrading sexual passions (cf. Col 3:5; 1 Thess 4:5).[45] Paul is not suggesting that this is somehow the journey of every individual but rather the broad history of humanity, which impacts individuals in different

---

[41] Cf. Peterson, *Engaging with God*, 64–66, and §2.6.

[42] To "bless" God means to acknowledge him as the source of different blessings (e.g., Gen 9:26; 14:20; 1 Sam 25:32; 2 Sam 18:28; 1 Kgs 1:48; 8:15). As in the LXX, εὐλογητός is used in the NT to introduce a Jewish form of praise called *berakah* (cf. Luke 1:68; 2 Cor 1:3; 11:31; Eph 1:3; 1 Pet 1:1; Hermann W. Beyer, "Εὐλογητός," *TDNT* 2:764). The expression εἰς τοὺς αἰῶνας (lit. "into the ages") portrays the future as an endless series of time periods (cf. Hermann Sasse, "αἰών, αἰώνιος," *TDNT* 1:199).

[43] A doxology is a formal expression of praise glorifying God for who he is or what he has done (11:36; 16:27; Eph 3:20–21; 1 Tim 1:17). Like a blessing (*berakah*), a doxology is an act of homage, confessing certain things about God.

[44] Jewett, *Romans*, 172. Greco-Roman philosophers spoke about being led away or ruled by passion. Hellenistic Judaism shared this view and urged the taming of the passions. Cf. Wilhelm Michaelis, "πάθος," *TDNT* 5:926–30; Keener, *The Mind of the Spirit*, 19–23.

[45] The genitive ἀτιμίας is "qualitative" (cf. Cranfield, *Romans*, 1.125; Wallace, *Greek Grammar*, 86–88). It can hardly be "partitive" (Jewett, *Romans*, 173).

ways. He is concerned with societal patterns, not with tracing in detail the genesis of every form of deviant behavior.[46]

The conjunction *γάρ* ("for") introduces two particular examples of "disgraceful passions" (linked by a *τε . . . τε* construction). Picking up the word "exchanged" (*μετήλλαξαν*) from v. 25, Paul says literally, "Their females exchanged natural sexual intercourse for what is unnatural." Repetition of this verb suggests that an exchange in human relationships is directly linked to exchanging the truth about God (cf. Wis 14:26; T. Naph. 3:3–4).[47] Same-sex behavior is portrayed as both evidence and consequence of humanity's rebellion against the Creator and his purpose for human life. Echoing Gen 1:27, "females" (*θήλειαι*) and "males" (*ἄρσενες*) are mentioned, rather than "women" and "men" (CSB; cf. Matt 19:4; Mark 10:6; Gal 3:28). This puts the focus on biological rather than sociocultural differences, which vary with time and place. The divine plan was for males and females to function together as "the image of God," propagating the race and exercising dominion in God's creation.

Paul literally speaks about females exchanging "the natural use for the unnatural" (*τὴν φυσικὴν χρῆσιν εἰς τὴν παρὰ φύσιν*), employing a well-established periphrasis for sexual intercourse (BDAG, *χρῆσις*, "use"). Following the pattern found in both Greco-Roman and Jewish literature, he describes this as either natural or unnatural. Plato (*Laws*, 636a–c), for example, described males uniting with males and females with females as "contrary to nature" (*παρὰ φύσιν*). The Stoics taught that "the proper use of objects is according to nature (*κατὰ φύσιν*) and that the failure to follow common sense and the inner law of one's being was against nature (*παρὰ φύσιν*). The expression for heterosexual intercourse was 'according to nature' (*ἡ κατὰ φύσιν ἐπιπλοκή*, Diodorus Siculus, *Hist.* 32.10.4.9), and a homoerotic relationship was *παρὰ φύσιν γάμος* ('marriage

[46] So Wright ("Romans," 435) observes that Paul's argument is that "the existence of homosexual practice in a culture is a sign that that culture as a whole has been worshiping idols and that its God-given male-and-female order is being fractured as a result." Wright suggests a number of ways in which contemporary Western culture has been engaged in idolatrous worship.

[47] Dunn (*Romans 1–8*, 64) asserts that "human respect (both self-respect and respect for others) is rooted in the recognition that only God has authority as Creator to order and dispose of that which is created."

against nature'; *Hist.* 32.10.9.3)."[48] In view of the way extrabiblical Jewish writers at the time considered same-sex intercourse, we may say that "minimally, Paul is referring to the anatomical and procreative complementarity of male and female."[49] For the apostle it was a simple matter of observation that homosexual intercourse was "contrary to nature" so that pagans who were ignorant of biblical teaching had no excuse for not knowing God's purpose for the sexual organs. However, given Paul's reflection on the biblical doctrine of creation, he must surely have meant κατὰ φύσιν to be understood theologically, as well as anatomically, to mean "in accordance with the intention of the Creator."[50]

For rhetorical reasons, the example of female same-sex relationships is mentioned first.[51] This is the only reference to lesbianism in the Bible, and there are infrequent, mostly negative references to it in Greco-Roman literature. Generally, however, a more positive evaluation of male homosexuality can be found in Greco-Roman sources. So Paul's introduction of the subject of male homoeroticism with the expression "in the same way also" (v. 27, ὁμοίως τε καί) is surprising. Linking it closely with his description of female behavior, he says (lit.), "The males left natural sexual intercourse with females." The participle ἀφέντες ("left") indicates a deliberate act of abandonment. However, since this is a corporate indictment of pagan society rather than a description of an individual's journey,

---

[48] Jewett, *Romans*, 175. Cf. Plutarch, *Amatorius*, 751c–e; 752b–c. On the Jewish side, see T. Naph. 3:4–5, Philo, *Abr.*, 135–37; *Spec.*, 3.39.2; *Mut.*, 111–12, and Josephus, *Ag. Ap.* 2.199; 2.275.

[49] Robert A. J. Gagnon, *The Bible and Homosexual Practice: Texts and Hermeneutics* (Nashville: Abingdon, 2001), 254. Paul was thinking of "nature" not as "the way things are usually done" (i.e., cultural convention) but rather as "the material shape of the created order" (126). See also n. 57 below.

[50] Cranfield (*Romans*, 1:125). Paul also uses the noun φύσις ("natural endowment, condition, or disposition," "nature") in 2:14, 27; 11:21, 24; 1 Cor 11:14; Gal 2:15; 4:8; Eph 2:3, though somewhat differently in each case.

[51] Cranfield (*Romans*, 1:125) argues that Paul deals with females first to give more emphasis to male homoeroticism and discuss it more fully. But mentioning lesbianism first and making it the basis for evaluating male homoeroticism would have been quite shocking for his first readers. His rhetorical purpose is to show how both behaviors involve the same error. Cf. Jewett, *Romans*, 173–77.

it cannot be argued that Paul is simply condemning heterosexual males who left their wives to engage in homoerotic behavior.[52]

The apostle speaks generally about males who abandon natural sexual intercourse with females and become "inflamed in their lust for one another" (ἐξεκαύθησαν ἐν τῇ ὀρέξει αὐτῶν εἰς ἀλλήλους).[53] This last expression picks up the preceding reference to "degrading passions" (v. 26), which in turn refers back to the cravings that result in the degrading of human bodies (v. 24). Although Paul does not address the issue of homosexual orientation or cover every aspect of homoerotic behavior here, he clearly highlights the lust that leads to homosexual intercourse, not simply the act itself.[54] In several respects he goes beyond the simple command of Lev 18:22 ("You are not to sleep with a man as with a woman; it is detestable"). But he echoes something of that text's abhorrence for sexual intercourse between males when he says (lit.), "Males committed with males the shameless act" (ἄρσενες ἐν ἄρσεσιν τὴν ἀσχημοσύνην κατεργαζόμενοι).[55]

The outcome of this choice is that they "received in their own persons the appropriate penalty of their error." Paul's language here recalls his previous argument. "The appropriate penalty" or "necessary recompense" (τὴν ἀντιμισθίαν ἥν ἔδει) alludes to God's punishment in handing people over to the consequences of their rebellion against him (vv. 24, 26, παρέδωκεν). "Their perversion" or "error"

[52] Schreiner (*Romans*, 95–97), Jewett (*Romans*, 176–81), and Kruse (*Romans*, 109–15) rightly take issue with those who argue that παρὰ φύσιν means "against a person's *own* nature" to establish that Paul is only condemning the perverse choice of "'naturally' heterosexual men and women." Paul's contemporaries did not understand "nature" in the individualized and psychological sense that is familiar to us.

[53] This is the only use of the noun ὄρεξις ("sexual desire, lust") in the NT. Jewett (*Romans*, 178–79) contends that, in the light of Greco-Roman usage, Paul's wording implies "an irrational bondage to an egoistic, empty, and unsatisfying expression of animalistic sexuality."

[54] "Neither distinguishing pederasty from relationships between adult, consenting males, nor distinguishing between active and passive partners as Roman culture was inclined to do, Paul simply follows the line of his Jewish cultural tradition by construing the entire realm of homosexual relations as evidence that divine wrath was active therein" (Jewett, *Romans*, 179).

[55] The term ἀσχημοσύνη commonly means "behavior that elicits disgrace" and so "the shameless deed" (BDAG). Although the singular form of the noun could refer to "the shameful member," Jewett's argument (*Romans*, 163, 179) for this application by Paul is unpersuasive.

(τῆς πλάνης) most obviously refers to "the cravings of their hearts," leading to sexual impurity and the degrading of their bodies among themselves (v. 24). In other words their sexual perversion itself is the punishment for abandoning the true God and his purpose for human life and relationships.[56]

Same-sex intercourse is one of the signs that our race has turned away from God.[57] Alienation from God affects the way we view one another and impacts our sexuality in a variety of ways. Different forms of sexual brokenness are hinted at in vv. 24, 26a, but Paul puts the focus on homoerotic behavior in vv. 26b–27 because it most obviously illustrates his point about using sexual organs in a way contrary to the Creator's purpose. Paul's description of same-sex behavior is not comprehensive since it serves a particular purpose in the flow of his argument. Contemporary Christians may feel the need to explore the reasons for people being drawn in this direction. Indeed, we are constantly pressured to share the growing acceptance of homosexuality in secular societies. But Paul wants us to understand theologically why homosexual desire and its bodily expression are a negative aspect of human experience and, if indulged, expose us to final judgment (2:1–11; cf. 1 Cor 6:9–10). Whatever the cause of homosexual desires, individuals must decide what to do about expressing those desires. The same thing could be said about all the other "passions" that Paul mentions in his letters. Moreover, his argument here is a preparation for his exposition of God's saving plan (3:21–6:14). With the gospel offer of freedom to change comes the challenge to become slaves of righteousness instead of being enslaved to sin (6:12–23; cf. 1 Cor 6:11, 18–20). So there is hope for those who struggle with same-sex attraction as much as there is hope for anyone caught in the pattern of sin Paul outlines in 1:18–32.

---

[56] So Cranfield (*Romans*, 1:126–27) argues that Paul is not referring to "a necessary or appropriate but unspecified punishment for their sexual perversion" beyond the perversion itself. Moo (*Romans*, 116) suggests that "eternal punishment" may be Paul's meaning, but there is nothing in the immediate context to support this.

[57] Gagnon (*The Bible and Homosexual Practice*, 264) argues that "along with idolatry, same-sex intercourse represents one of the clearest instances of conscious suppression of revelation in nature." Gagnon (270–303) deals with a number of challenges to the view he espouses.

1:28. For the third time Paul speaks about God's delivering people up to judgment, using again the formula found in vv. 24, 26 (παρέδωκεν αὐτοὺς ὁ θεὸς εἰς). This emphasizes that, "in striking free of God's immediate control, man has not escaped God's overall ordering of his creation."[58] Recalling the argument in vv. 18–23, he says the reason for this (καθώς, "since, because") is that "they did not think it worthwhile to acknowledge God" (οὐκ ἐδοκίμασαν τὸν θεὸν ἔχειν ἐν ἐπιγνώσει). The verb δοκιμάζω can mean "test" or "approve on the basis of testing" (BDAG, cf. 2:18; 12:2; 14:22). In this context it expresses the idea that they did not see fit to have God in their knowledge: "to know God in the sense of acknowledging him, reckoning with him, taking him into account in the practical affairs of one's life."[59] The prison into which they are delivered is "a corrupt mind so that they do what is not right" (ἀδόκιμον νοῦν ποιεῖν τὰ μὴ καθήκοντα). A play on words links the punishment with the crime: "Because they have rejected God as not worth reckoning with, God has delivered them into a condition in which their minds are fit only to be rejected as worthless, useless for their proper purpose, disreputable."[60] This parallels v. 21, where "their thinking became worthless, and their senseless hearts were darkened" because they failed to glorify God and give him thanks. But here the moral consequences of a debilitated, godless way of thinking are set forth in an extensive catalogue of vices, beginning with the clause "to do what is not right" (ποιεῖν τὰ μὴ καθήκοντα).[61]

---

[58] Dunn, *Romans 1–8*, 75. Dunn goes on to point out that "it is God who has handed man over to his desires and the endless pursuit of their satisfaction: man's freedom to go his own way still leaves him within the limits set by God."

[59] Cranfield, *Romans*, 1:128. Dunn (*Romans 1–8*, 75) observes that this refusal to acknowledge God is presented as "a deliberate act of human pride and self-sufficiency." See also n. 19 above.

[60] Cranfield, *Romans*, 1:128. The adjective ἀδόκιμος means "not standing the test," thus "unqualified, worthless, base" (BDAG; cf. 1 Cor 9:27; 2 Cor 13:5, 6, 7; 2 Tim 3:8; Titus 1:16; Heb 6:8). Cf. Walter Grundmann, "δόκιμος, κτλ," *TDNT* 2:255–60. "Paul stresses that people who have turned from God are fundamentally unable to think and decide correctly about God and his will" (Moo, *Romans*, 118).

[61] The infinitive ποιεῖν functions like ἀτιμάζεσθαι ("dishonor") in 1:24, expressing the practical result of a certain condition of mind or heart. The verb from which the participle καθήκοντα comes means "be appropriate, proper" (BDAG, καθήκω). Greek writers used it with reference to duty or moral responsibility.

1:29–31. Paul's list of things that are morally wrong follows to a certain extent the pattern of vice catalogs in Greco-Roman literature.[62] He employs similar lists elsewhere for different purposes (1 Cor 5:10–11; 6:9–10; 2 Cor 12:20; Gal 5:19–21; Eph 4:31; 5:3–5; Col 3:5, 8; 1 Tim 1:9–10; 6:4–5; 2 Tim 3:2–4; Titus 3:3). Here we have a depiction of the moral chaos that pervades human life as a result of refusing to acknowledge God. The first four terms are general in scope and are introduced by the perfect passive participle πεπληρωμένος ("filled"), suggesting that people are totally controlled by these pursuits ("with all unrighteousness, evil, greed, and wickedness"). Breaking with the traditional pattern of fours that characterize some Greco-Roman catalogs, Paul introduces five more terms with the adjective μεστούς ("full"), expressing more precisely the diversity of behavior he has in mind ("of envy, murder, quarrels, deceit, and malice").[63]

A sudden change of syntax introduces eight character types. The first two terms ("gossips, slanderers") describe those who seek to destroy another's reputation by misrepresentation. Four terms then identify different expressions of arrogance ("God-haters, arrogant, proud, boastful"). The final two terms ("inventors of evil, disobedient to parents") describe those who are always discovering new ways to be evil and those who persistently deny the authority of their parents. This switch from vices to persons appears to be without parallel in contemporary lists of this kind and has the effect of highlighting established lifestyles.

The final set of four terms in v. 31 all begin with the same letter in Greek, identifying the qualities people lack (ἀσυνέτους ["undiscerning"; CSB: "senseless"], ἀσυνθέτους ["untrustworthy"], ἀστόργους ["unloving"], ἀνελεήμονας ["unmerciful"]).[64] In this overall list

[62] Jewett, *Romans*, 165, 183–90. Jewett notes that the rhetorical effect of asyndeton (lack of connectives in the Greek) is to make the items in the list appear to be "more numerous than they really are" (citing Quintilian, *Inst.* 9.3.50).

[63] Cranfield (*Romans*, 1:130) says that in other contexts "all the evils denoted by the four genitives which follow φθόνου ['envy'] are very often to be explained as fruits of envy."

[64] The four terms after the participle πεπληρωμένος are all in the dative case, but the five terms after μεστούς are all in the genitive case. Twelve character descriptions in vv. 29–31 are in the accusative case, agreeing with ἀυτούς in v. 28. Four of these terms are nouns (ψιθυριστάς ["gossips"], ὑβριστάς ["arrogant"], ἐφευρετάς ["inventers

> we have a social pathology that is oriented not to the character flaws of individuals or groups but to the collective experience of the human race since the corruption of creation, viewed in the radical light shed by the gospel. This catalogue undercuts in the most sweeping manner any potential claims of individual, group, or national exceptionalism.[65]

Paul's description of human behavior in this passage has a surprising number of positive and negative echoes in later chapters. Using related terms, he either urges his readers to avoid certain vices or encourages them to adopt alternative attitudes arising from their new life in Christ. So generosity is urged instead of greed and good instead of evil (12:8, 9, 21). Love without hypocrisy is expounded as the positive alternative in every situation (12:9–21; cf. 13:9). Walking with decency is the antidote to all forms of sexual impurity, quarreling, and jealousy (13:13). Blessing rather than cursing and humility rather than pride or boasting are commanded (12:3–4, 9, 14, 16). The alternative to being undiscerning, untrustworthy, unloving, and unmerciful is the ability to test and approve God's will (12:2), being faithful in prayer (12:12), being devoted to one another (12:10), and showing mercy with cheerfulness. In other words, Paul shows how the gospel makes it possible for people to exhibit a totally different pattern of life (see §2.6).

1:32. The final description of those whom God has delivered over to "a corrupt mind so that they do what is not right" (v. 28) is introduced with the relative pronoun οἵτινες ("those who," as in v. 25; CSB: "they"). A concessive clause with the aorist participle ἐπιγνόντες introduces a summary description of human behavior ("although they know"), returning to a major theme of the passage (cf. γνόντες, v. 21). People have a knowledge of God that they will not allow to influence their thinking and behavior (vv. 18–21, 28). This includes knowledge of "God's just sentence" (τὸ δικαίωμα τοῦ θεοῦ) "that those who practice such things deserve to die." In 2:26; 8:4 δικαίωμα is used to express the just requirement of the law given to Israel. However, as in 1:18, the reference here is more generally to

{of evil}"], ἀνελεήμων ["unmerciful"]) and the rest are adjectives or participles used substantivally.

[65] Jewett, *Romans*, 184. Jewett examines in detail the way Greco-Roman writers viewed the various vices in this list.

what God manifests about himself apart from his special revelation to Israel.[66] In various ways people of different cultures have demonstrated an awareness of God's righteous character and expectations for human life and relationships. This includes a knowledge of "his uncompromising hostility to evil, and therefore of the ultimate penalty of their evil-doing."[67] Some perception that death is the penalty for sin is indicated. Moreover, the implication here is that "some knowledge of God remains even after a person has fallen into the degenerate state that Paul depicts in these verses."[68] People are willing to risk God's condemnation in order to pursue their own desires and ambitions. Humans are culpable in this connection because they not only do the things they know to be worthy of God's judgment but "even applaud others who practice them." In this way the apostle "completes the case for individual and corporate accountability."[69]

Bridge

The problem of evil demands answers and is a key obstacle to belief in a good God for many people. But if we truly face the problem of evil as this passage exposes it, we will see the need for the solution that a good God has provided (1:16–17; 3:21–26). The issue is humanity's unwillingness to acknowledge their Creator and to live in a way that honors his character and intentions. People prefer to be wise in their own eyes and to pursue godless and unrighteous patterns of thinking and behavior. Idolatry and sexual immorality

[66] A revelation of God's "eternal power and divine nature" exists in the natural world and has been perceived and understood to some extent (vv. 18–20), but "the purpose and effect of that revelation are wholly negative" (Moo, *Romans*, 124).

[67] Cranfield, *Romans*, 1:134. Cranfield rightly points out that the reference here is to death as the ultimate penalty for sin in God's creation rather than death as a penalty for particular wrongdoings according to an actual code of law.

[68] Moo, *Romans*, 124. Moo notes that the present tenses in v. 32, "long with the fact that Paul is trying to establish the seriousness of the sinning he has depicted, make it probable that 'knowing the righteous ordinance of God' is contemporaneous with the panoply of sinning outlined in vv. 29–31."

[69] Jewett, *Romans*, 190. Cranfield (*Romans*, 1:133–35) discusses the textual variants that arose as an attempt to deal with the implication that approval of evil deeds is even worse than doing such things. He wisely discerns that "those who condone and applaud the vicious actions of others are actually making a deliberate contribution to the setting up of a public opinion favourable to vice, and so to the corruption of an indefinite number of other people" (135).

are two particular consequences of rejecting what can be known about God from the created order. But Paul's concluding list identifies many ways human life is affected by this refusal to acknowledge God. A Christian assessment of the moral and social evils that characterize human life must include this theological perspective. The justice of God's wrath needs to be faced, as he abandons humanity to the consequences of sin. Our present experience of God's judgment anticipates, but does not replace, the ultimate "day of wrath" (2:5). It functions as a warning of final judgment and as a stimulus to seek reconciliation with God. Convincing people of the rightness of God's present and future judgment against sin is an important preliminary to proclaiming and explaining the saving righteousness of God. The more we understand the enormity of our disregard for God and his intentions for our lives, the more we will see our need for his saving grace and the transforming power of the gospel.

III. Judgment and Identity: Revealing the True Children of God (2:1–3:20)

In this first defensive section of the letter (see Introduction II.C), Paul begins to focus his attention on Jewish beliefs and practices, though his rhetorical strategy dictates that Jews are not named until 2:17.[1] He moves from exposing present manifestations of the wrath of God (1:18–32) to considering the way God will act "in the day of wrath," when his righteous judgment is fully revealed (2:5, 6–16). As Paul deals with the failure of his fellow Jews to live up to their calling, he identifies those who will receive the gift of eternal life and those who will experience God's condemnation. A concentric structure can be identified in the section as a whole:[2]

- A Jews are judged if they do the same things as Gentiles (2:1–5)
  - B God's impartiality in judgment (2:6–11)
    - C External and internal law (2:12–16)
      - D God is blasphemed among Gentiles by Jewish sin (2:17–24)
    - C´ External and internal circumcision (2:25–29)
  - B´ God's righteousness in judgment (3:1–8)
- A´ The law condemns Israel for doing the same things as Gentiles (3:9–20)

For the purpose of exposition, however, three major subdivisions are suggested, drawing together elements of this structure: God's Impartiality in Judgment (2:1–16), Misplaced Confidence (2:17–29), and God's Righteousness in Judgment (3:1–20).

A. God's Impartiality in Judgment (2:1–16)

[1]Therefore, every one of you who judges is without excuse. For when you judge another, you condemn yourself, since you, the judge, do the same things. [2]We know that God's judgment on those who do such things is based on the truth. [3]Do you re-

[1] Cranfield (*Romans*, 1:138–39) offers seven reasons for seeing a Jewish audience from the beginning of this section. See also Seifrid, "Unrighteous by Faith," 120–21; Simon J. Gathercole, *Where Is Boasting? Early Jewish Soteriology and Paul's Response in Romans 1–5* (Grand Rapids: Eerdmans, 2001), 197–200.

[2] I am indebted to my colleague Richard Gibson for this observation.

ally think—anyone of you who judges those who do such things
yet do the same—that you will escape God's judgment? [4]Or do
you despise the riches of his kindness, restraint, and patience,
not recognizing that God's kindness is intended to lead you to
repentance? [5]Because of your hardened and unrepentant heart
you are storing up wrath for yourself in the day of wrath, when
God's righteous judgment is revealed. [6]**He will repay each one
according to his works**: [7]eternal life to those who by persistence
in doing good seek glory, honor, and immortality; [8]but wrath and
anger to those who are self-seeking and disobey the truth while
obeying unrighteousness. [9]There will be affliction and distress for
every human being who does evil, first to the Jew, and also to the
Greek; [10]but glory, honor, and peace for everyone who does what
is good, first to the Jew, and also to the Greek. [11]For there is no
favoritism with God.

[12]All who sin without the law will also perish without the
law, and all who sin under the law will be judged by the law.
[13]For the hearers of the law are not righteous before God, but the
doers of the law will be justified. [14]So, when Gentiles, who do
not by nature have the law, do what the law demands, they are a
law to themselves even though they do not have the law. [15]They
show that the work of the law is written on their hearts. Their
consciences confirm this. Their competing thoughts either accuse
or even excuse them [16]on the day when God judges what people
have kept secret, according to my gospel through Christ Jesus.

Context

Many terms and themes from the previous passage reappear here, showing the continuity of Paul's argument. The people addressed in vv. 1–3 condemn others who practice the things just described while doing the same things themselves. Paul warns about the need to repent and avoid "storing up wrath for yourself in the day of wrath" (vv. 4–5). This leads to an explanation of how God will "repay each one according to his works" and an identification of those who will receive the gift of eternal life (vv. 6–11). The process of final judgment is then specifically related to doing what God's law requires (vv. 12–16). This prepares for the challenge in vv. 17–24 about boasting in God and his law but dishonoring him by breaking it.

Structure

Three subsections in this passage can be discerned by observing thematic and stylistic variations. In vv. 1–5 Paul uses the second-person singular in a *diatribe style* to address someone who passes judgment on others who practice the things listed in 1:29–31 yet acts in the same way.[3] God will judge such people on the coming "day of wrath."

Then, using the more objective third-person form, vv. 6–11 provide a *description* of the way God acts impartially in judging Jew and Greek alike. The principle of retributive justice is stated first ("he will repay each one according to his works"). This is followed by two contrasting descriptions of human behavior: "those who by persistence in doing good seek glory, honor, and immortality" and "those who are self-seeking and disobey the truth while obeying unrighteousness." The outcome for the latter is "wrath and anger," further defined in v. 9 as "affliction and distress for every human being who does evil, first to the Jew, and also to the Greek." The outcome for the former is "eternal life" (v. 7), further defined in v. 10 as "glory, honor, and peace for everyone who does what is good, first to the Jew, and also to the Greek." The segment concludes with an assertion about God's impartiality (v. 11), supporting the claim in v. 6 about God's pattern of justice.[4]

The twofold reference to Jew and Greek in vv. 9–10 leads Paul to a *definitive statement* about the judgment of those who sin "without the law" and those who sin "under the law" in v. 12.[5] There are eleven references to law in vv. 12–16 (nine in the Greek text), indicating that this is a critical issue for the apostle. But, in preparation for the denunciation of the disobedient Jew in 2:17–24, he makes clear that "the hearers of the law are not righteous before God, but the doers of the law will be justified" (v. 13). Then, as a challenge to his fellow Jews, he points to Gentiles "who do not by nature have

[3] A diatribe is a way of engaging in debate with imaginary opponents, "putting them on the spot, asking them rhetorical questions, answering their supposed objections" (Wright, "Romans," 437). Cf. Stanley K. Stowers, *The Diatribe and Paul's Letter to the Romans*, SBLDS 57 (Chico: Scholars Press, 1981), 93–96, 110–12.

[4] A chiastic structure is apparent in vv. 6–11 (an outline is given below in the comment on v. 6), which is the centerpiece of the argument in vv. 1–16.

[5] Once again a new stage in the argument is linked to the previous paragraph by γάρ ("for"), which is not translated by CSB.

the law" but who "do what the law demands" (v. 14). This is immediately followed by the declaration that "they show that the work of the law is written on their hearts" and that "their consciences confirm this" (v. 15).[6] The judgment of God, which according to Paul's gospel will take place "through Christ Jesus," will expose the secrets of the human heart and reveal those whose hearts are set on doing what God requires (v. 16).

Outline:

1. God's judgment is based on truth (vv. 1–5).
2. God's judgment is based on works (vv. 6–11).
3. God's judgment reveals those whose hearts are set on pleasing him (vv. 12–16).

2:1. The conjunction Δίο ("therefore") should be understood "in the full logical sense, drawing the inference from the preceding paragraph."[7] A direct consequence of the argument in 1:28–32 is that those who know "God's just sentence" cannot be excused when they judge others but act "in a similarly arrogant manner, suppressing the truth."[8] Like those described in 1:20, they are "without excuse" (ἀναπολόγητος). Paul addresses a broad category of individuals here (πᾶς ὁ κρίνων, "everyone who judges"), though he uses the second-person singular (εἶ, "you are"; κρίνεις, "you judge"; πράσσεις, "you do") and the vocative expression ὦ ἄνθρωπε ("O man") in a diatribe style, addressing a hypothetical dialogue partner. Present-tense verbs suggest that such judging is habitual. Paul's manner of argument could convey the substance of "many actual debates and conversations with those to whom he was preaching the gospel,"[9] but his rhetoric also draws the readers into the warning (CSB: "Every one of you who judges is without excuse"). The reason for this is given in two linked explanatory clauses: "For (γάρ) when you judge another, you condemn yourself, since (γάρ) you, the judge,

[6] No conjunction links this verse to the previous one. Runge (*Discourse Grammar*, 20) observes that this pattern of speech (asyndeton) is used "when the writer judges that the implicit relation between to the clauses is sufficiently clear."

[7] Jewett, *Romans*, 196. Cf. Cranfield, *Romans*, 1:141.

[8] Jewett, *Romans*, 196.

[9] Moo, *Romans*, 126. Runge (*Discourse Grammar*, 329) observes how the overspecification in this verse lets the reader know how the writer conceived of such people. Cf. Stowers, *Diatribe*, 110–12; Wright, "Romans," 437–38.

do the same things." Condemnation is not due to the act of judging itself but because people practice what they condemn.[10]

Some have argued that Paul attacks moralists in general in these verses since he only specifically addresses Jews from v. 17. However, although the issue in vv. 6–11 is God's impartial judgment of Jews and Greeks alike, God's judgment will come "first to the Jew" (v. 9). Then vv. 12–13 focus on the need for those who have the law of God to obey it. Most likely Jewish opponents of Paul's gospel are the target of his argument from the beginning of the chapter, though he does not name them until 2:17.[11] Nevertheless, the idea that "when you judge another, you condemn yourself" recalls Jesus's general warning to his disciples that "you will be judged by the same standard with which you judge others, and you will be measured by the same measure you use" (Matt 7:1–2). So Paul's immediate concern to challenge the hypocrisy of judging another while doing the same things has wider implications. In fact, it prepares for his later critique of the judgmental spirit among the Roman Christians (14:1–23).

2:2. A sudden switch to the first person plural (οἴδαμεν, "we know") introduces a belief shared by Paul and those he is addressing (cf. 3:19; 7:14; 8:22, 28; 2 Cor 5:1; 1 Tim 1:8).[12] The belief is "that God's judgment on those who do such things is based on the truth (κατὰ ἀλήθειαν, "according to truth")." In other words, God's judgment is "in accordance with the facts (i.e., is just)."[13] Those who knew the teaching of Moses and the prophets would not have been surprised by such a claim (cf. Deut 7:9–10; 32:4; Ps 96:13; Isa 2:12–22; 10:22–23).

---

[10] Cf. Schreiner, *Romans*, 107.

[11] Dunn (*Romans 1–8*, 76–78) observes, "The increasing specificity of the Jewish identity of the viewpoint rebutted" in vv. 1–29. Cranfield (*Romans*, 1:138–39) contends that Paul has the Jews in mind from v. 1.

[12] The conjunction δέ, which is not translated by CSB, signals a new development in the argument and should be rendered "now" here (cf. 3:19). The variant γάρ ("for") is not as well attested and was probably a scribal insertion motivated by the observation that Paul normally uses γάρ in combination with the verb οἶδα.

[13] Cranfield, *Romans*, 1:143. The word κρίμα ("judgment") normally refers to a judge's unfavorable decision or "sentence of condemnation." Cf. Friedrich Büchsel and Volkmar Herntrich, "κρίνω κτλ.," *TDNT* 3:942; Mathias Rissi, "κρίμα," *EDNT* 2:317–18.

2:3. Returning to the second-person singular, Paul confronts his imaginary opponent more directly, as in v. 1. A category of persons is indicated by the substantive ὁ κρίνων ("the one who judges"), but the second-person singular verb λογίζῃ ("do you really think"), the vocative expression ὦ ἄνθρωπε ("O man"), and the personal pronoun σύ ("you") individualize the address. Two rhetorical questions are posed. The first one is, "Do you really think—anyone of you who judges those who do such things yet do the same—that you will escape God's judgment?" This is the first of nineteen uses of the verb λογίζομαι in Romans, which has a broad semantic range.[14] CSB has rendered it "really think" to emphasize the absurdity of the proposition. In essence, the question is, Do you consider yourself to be a special case when it comes to God's judgment?

2:4. Paul's second rhetorical question (introduced by ἤ, "or") expresses the same challenge in a different way: "Do you despise the riches of his kindness, restraint, and patience, not recognizing that God's kindness is intended to lead you to repentance?"[15] Paul often mentions the richness or generosity of God toward his people (e.g., Rom 9:23; 2 Cor 8:9; 9:14–15; Eph 1:7, 18; 2:7 3:16; Col 1:27; 2:2). God's kindness is the leading idea in this verse, the same word being picked up again in the second clause (τῆς χρηστότητος . . . τὸ χρηστὸν τοῦ θεοῦ). There are significant references to God's kindness in the Psalms, regularly translating the Hebrew טוֹב ("good," e.g., Pss 25:7–8 [LXX 24:7–8]; 34:8 [LXX 33:9]; 100:5 [LXX 99:5). This aspect of God's character is also highlighted in key NT contexts (Luke 6:35; Rom 11:22; Eph 2:7; Titus 3:4; 1 Pet 2:3). A particular dimension of God's kindness is his "restraint" (ἀνοχή).[16] The only other NT use of this noun is in 3:26, where Paul refers to God's passing over sins previously committed, restraining his

[14] Cf. BDAG; Hans-Werner Bartsch, "λογίζομαι," *EDNT* 2:354–55. The verb is found in Rom 2:3, 26; 3:28; 4:3, 4, 5, 6, 8, 9, 10, 11, 22, 23, 24; 6:11; 8:18, 36; 9:8; 14:14, and elsewhere in Paul's writings.

[15] The participle ἀγνοῶν is used here to explain the means by which God's kindness is despised ("by being ignorant"). Cf. Wallace, *Greek Grammar*, 628–30. The verb ἄγει is used in a conative sense, pointing to an intended outcome ("intended to lead"). Cf. Wallace, *Greek Grammar*, 534–35.

[16] Cf. Heinrich Schlier, "ἀνέχω, ἀνεκτός, ἀνοχή," *TDNT* 1:359–60. This noun is only used once in the LXX (1 Macc 12:25), though the cognate verb is found in Isa 42:14; 63:15; 64:11 (ET 64:12). The verb has different applications in the NT (e.g., 2 Cor 11:4; 2 Thess 1:4; 2 Tim 4:3; Heb 13:22).

wrath. God's "patience" (μακροθυμία; cf. 9:22; 1 Tim 1:16; 2 Pet 3:9 [μακροθυμεῖ]) is another way of expressing his restraint in judging. The foundational revelation of God's patience was given to Moses in terms of his being "slow to anger" (Exod 34:6, translating אֶרֶךְ אַפַּיִם, [lit] "delaying your wrath").[17] The same formula is repeated in later biblical contexts (e.g., Num 14:18 [μακρόθυμος καὶ πολυέλεος, "slow to anger and rich in faithful love"]; Neh 9:17), and is specifically used as a motivation for Israel's repentance in Joel 2:13.

The danger is that those who view themselves as the beneficiaries of God's kindness, restraint, and patience can "despise" or show contempt for these attributes by refusing to recognize (ἀγνοῶν implies a wilful ignorance) that "God's kindness is intended to lead you to repentance." Repentance is mostly mentioned in the NT in connection with the initial turning of people to Christ in response to the preaching of the gospel (e.g., Mark 1:15; Luke 5:32; Acts 2:38; 3:19; 17:30–31; 20:21). This echoes the appeal of the prophets to the people of Israel to turn from their sin and return to their covenant Lord (e.g., Jer 3:12–18; Hos 6:1–3; Joel 2:12–14; cf. Wis 11:23). Those addressed by Paul need to forsake their judgmental attitude and acknowledge their need for the salvation offered to them in the gospel (cf. 1:16–17).

2:5. Paul's prophetic-type challenge continues with the claim that (lit.) "because of your hardness and unrepentant heart you are storing up wrath for yourself in the day of wrath, when God's righteous judgment is revealed."[18] The noun "hardness" (σκληρότης) echoes the description of Israel in Deut 9:27, and "unrepentant heart" (ἀμετανόητον καρδίαν) recalls Moses's subsequent challenge to "circumcise your hearts and don't be stiff-necked any longer" (Deut 10:16).[19] Mostly, the verb θησαυρίζω is used with reference

---

[17] Johannes Horst ("μακροθυμία κτλ.," *TDNT* 4:377) rightly observes that in Exod 34:6–7 God's patience does not mean the complete end of wrath. There is no overlooking or renouncing of the grounds for wrath, but alongside wrath "there is a divine restraint which postpones its operation."

[18] The preposition κατά is used in a causal sense here ("because"; cf. BDAG, κατά 5δ). CSB reads σκληρότητα σου ("your hardness") adjectivally in relation to καρδίαν ("heart").

[19] Although σκληρότης ("hardness") only occurs here in the NT, cognate terms are used in Matt 19:8; Mark 10:5; Acts 7:51; 19:9; Rom 9:19; Heb 3:8, 13, 15; 4:7. Schreiner (*Romans*, 1–8) suggests that Rom 2:5 anticipates 2:29, "where a circumcised heart becomes a reality only by the work of the Holy Spirit."

to storing up something good (e.g., Prov 2:7; Matt 6:19–20), but ironically here it refers to an accumulation of wrath that is soon to be experienced (cf. Jas 5:3; 2 Pet 3:7).[20] Most obviously, Paul is refuting Jewish claims of covenant privilege, by which "they believed themselves protected from God's wrath even if they transgressed."[21] "The day of wrath" is a quasi-technical term for "the day of the Lord" or the final judgment of God (e.g., Ps 110:5; Isa 2:12–22; Amos 5:18–20; Zeph 1:14–15; Rev 6:17). Paul goes on to speak about it as "the day when God judges what people have kept secret" (2:16). Elsewhere he describes it as "the day of our Lord Jesus Christ" (1 Cor 1:8), "the day" (1 Cor 3:13), "the day of the Lord" (1 Cor 5:5; 1 Thess 5:2; 2 Thess 2:2), "the day of our Lord Jesus" (2 Cor 1:14); "the day of Christ Jesus" (Phil 1:6, 10; 2:16); and "that day" (2 Thess 1:10; 2 Tim 1:12, 18). "The day of wrath" will be the occasion for the judgment of God that is "based on truth" (v. 2), which is here described as his "righteous judgment" (δικαιοκρισίας; cf. 2 Thess 1:5). The following verses spell out what that righteous judgment involves.

2:6. Paul's style of argument changes as he continues the long sentence in Greek that began in v. 5. A relative pronoun (ὅς, "who"; CSB: "he") indicates that God is the primary subject, and a third-person verb introduces a formal declaration of how God's righteous judgment takes place. An apparent conflation of Prov 24:12 and Ps 62:12 (LXX 61:13) affirms the common Jewish belief that God "will repay each one according to his works."[22] The verb ἀποδίδωμι is used here in the sense of "recompense, whether in a good or bad sense, *render, reward, recompense*" (BDAG). The principle of judgment according to works is reaffirmed in several NT contexts (e.g., Matt 16:27; 2 Cor 11:15; 2 Tim 4:14). A chiastic structure emerges in vv. 6–11 as Paul explains the implications of this judgment. There

[20] Jewish literature has an emphasis on storing up good works so as to enjoy future bliss (e.g., Pss. Sol. 9:5, "The one who does what is right saves up life for himself with the Lord"; cf. Tob 4:9–10; 2 Esd 6:5; 7:77; 8:33, 36; 2 Bar. 14:12).

[21] Schreiner, *Romans*, 109. So also, Dunn, *Romans 1–8*, 81–83; Moo, *Romans*, 131. Cf. Wis 3:9–10; 11:9–10; 12:22; 15–12; Pss. Sol. 1:4–8; 2:3–18; 4:1–8; 8:1–15; 9:1–3; 15:8; 17:5–20.

[22] Cf. Job 34:11; Eccl 12:14; Jer 17:10; Hos 12:2. Paul teaches that the final judgment of God will be on the basis of works in 2 Cor 5:10 and lists the sort of behavior that will exclude people from the kingdom of God in passages such as 1 Cor 6:9–10; Gal 5:19–21.

is a positive outcome for those who "seek glory, honor, and immortality" (v. 7), namely "eternal life."[23] In v. 10 they receive what they seek, namely "glory, honor, and (eschatological) peace." There is a negative outcome for those who are "self-seeking and disobey the truth" (v. 8), namely "wrath and anger," which involves "affliction and distress" (v. 9). The concluding verse explains that this will happen because "there is no favoritism with God" (v. 11). In this recursive structure, the turning point is vv. 8–9, where there is a piling up of words to describe the outcome for those who will be judged unfavorably:

6 (God) will repay each one according to his works
  7 eternal life to those who by persistence in doing good seek glory, honor, and immortality
    8 but wrath and anger to those who are self-seeking and disobey the truth while obeying unrighteousness
    9 affliction and distress for every human being who does evil, first to the Jew, and also to the Greek
  10 but glory, honor, and peace for everyone who does what is good, first to the Jew, and also to the Greek
11 for there is no favoritism with God.

2:7. Although vv. 1–5 primarily address complacent and hypocritical Jews, Paul's argument in vv. 6–11 is more obviously universal. The expression "to each" (v. 6, ἑκάστῳ) is amplified by a description of two different lifestyles, introduced in vv. 7 and 8 by contrasting plural expressions (τοῖς μέν . . . τοῖς δέ). The first group is defined as "those who by persistence in doing good seek glory, honor, and immortality." Elsewhere in the Pauline corpus the fruit of a genuine relationship with God is "every good work" or "good works" (e.g., 2 Cor 9:8; Eph 2:10; Col 1:10; 2 Thess 2:17; 1 Tim 2:10; 5:10; 2 Tim 2:21; Titus 1:16; 3:1). Such a meaning is likely here also. A God-focused pattern of life is indicated by the

[23] The expression "eternal life" (ζωὴ αἰώνιος) first appears in Dan 12:2 and then in later Jewish writings (cf. Rudolph Bultmann, "ζάω κτλ.," *TDNT* 2:855–61). The full expression is used four times in Romans with reference to "the life of the Age to Come" (2:7; 5:21; 6:22, 23). ζωή appears to have the same reference in 5:17, 18; 6:4; 7:10; 8:2, 6, 10; 11:15, though sometimes it identifies the newness of life that the Spirit brings in anticipation of the resurrection of the dead.

description of these people as "those who. . . seek glory, honor, and immortality." The participle ζητοῦσιν (present tense) indicates a continuous or regular pattern of behavior. They seek "the eschatological gifts of God already firmly associated in Jewish thought with the resurrection of the blessed."[24] In effect, they seek "eternal life," and this is what God gives them (ζωὴν αἰώνιον ["eternal life"] being the direct object of ἀποδώσει [v. 6, "he will render"]). But the measure by which they are judged is, literally, "by perseverance in a good work" (καθ ὑπομονὴν ἔργου ἀγαθοῦ).[25] Although some have taken the singular "good work" to refer to faith, the flow of Paul's argument suggests he means the ongoing evidence of faith in the practical goodness of their lives (CSB, "in doing good").[26] More will be said about the identity of those in view here in my comment on v. 10.

2:8. A negative triad of characteristics contrasts a second group of people with those just mentioned. These are "self-seeking and disobey the truth, while obeying unrighteousness." The first expression (ἐξ ἐριθείας) literally means "factious." Elsewhere it refers to rivalry and partisanship in human relationships (e.g., Phil 1:17), but in the sequence of thought here, it means they constitute "a faction in opposition to God."[27] A God-rejecting dimension to their behavior is suggested by the expression καὶ ἀπειθοῦσι τῇ ἀληθείᾳ ("and disobey the truth"). This recalls the earlier charge against those who "by their unrighteousness suppress the truth" (1:18), meaning "the truth of God" (1:25). Paul's third description of their behavior in v. 8 (πειθομένοις δὲ τῇ ἀδικίᾳ, "obeying unrighteousness") also points

---

[24] Cranfield, *Romans*, 1:147. Note that the terms in v. 10 describing God's gift to them are virtually the same (δόξα ["glory"], τιμή ["honor"], εἰρήνη ["peace"]). Compare 1 Pet 1:7. Jewett (*Romans*, 205) obscures this eschatological reference by suggesting that Paul used honorific terms from Greco-Roman culture to appeal to his audience.

[25] The preposition κατά is used here, as in v. 6 and the texts to which that verse alludes, to indicate "the norm according to which a judgment is rendered, or rewards or punishments are given" (BDAG). The singular ἔργου ("work") is used in a collective way, as in 2:15, to express the idea of a lifework.

[26] Cf. Cranfield, *Romans*, 1:147, 152; Moo, *Romans*, 137. The word "good" (ἀγαθός) occurs twenty-one times in Romans, indicating its importance for Paul.

[27] Cranfield, *Romans*, 1:148. Jewett (*Romans*, 206) thinks factional behavior toward others is meant because Paul is implicitly challenging the Roman believers, whom he finally charges with partisanship in Rom 14. But the Godward nature of their factionalism is much more obvious from v. 8 than Jewett allows.

back to the general charge against humanity in 1:18. Jews, who have the truth of God expressed more fully to them in the law, disobey the truth by rebelling against God's revealed will for them as his people (vv. 17–24). At the end of the verse in Greek, two words appear in the nominative case without a finite verb: ὀργὴ καὶ θυμός ("wrath and anger").[28] This is like an exclamation, indicating the ultimate outcome for those who are set on such a pattern of living. CSB has moved the words to the beginning of the verse and made them the notional object of the verb ἀποδώσει (v. 6, "render").

2:9. The turning point in the chiastic structure of vv. 6–11 is indicated by the use of the words θλῖψις καὶ στενοχωρία ("affliction and distress"). These match the two words at the end of v. 8 (ὀργὴ καὶ θυμός) and express the outcome or effect of God's "wrath and anger." Both terms are used again in 8:35, associated with experiences of "persecution," "famine," "nakedness," "danger," and "sword" in this life. Paul also uses these words in connection with the hardships and pressures of his own ministry (2 Cor 6:4). However, in the flow of his argument in vv. 8–9, they refer to affliction and distress experienced beyond this life as a consequence of God's final judgment of humanity.[29] The universality of that punishment is indicated by the expression "for every human being who does evil."[30] Repetition of the phrase "first to the Jew, and also to the Greek" from 1:16 is ironic here. It reinforces the note of universality in the previous expression by insisting that if salvation is for the Jew first (as restated in v. 10), judgment must also begin with the people of God (cf. Amos 3:1–2; Luke 19:41–44; 1 Pet 4:17–18).[31]

---

[28] These two terms often occur together in the LXX (e.g., Deut 9:19; Ps 2:5; Hos 13:11). Cf. Rudolf Pesch, "ὀργή," *EDNT* 2:530; Friedrich Büchsel, "θυμός κτλ.," *TDNT* 3:168. θυμός can be translated "fury" or "indignation" and may suggest moral outrage here.

[29] Jewett (*Romans*, 207–8) lists ways these terms were employed in the LXX in connection with the struggles and pressures of life, noting that sometimes they have the specific connotation of divine judgment (e.g., Ps 78:49 [LXX 77:49]; Isa 8:22).

[30] The Semitic formula πᾶς ψυχὴ ἀνθρώπου (lit. "every human person") can be found in LXX Num 19:11; Isa 13:7. Ψυχή translates the Hebrew word for "person" (נֶפֶשׁ) and does not refer merely to the inner life or "soul" of a person.

[31] As noted in connection with 1:14, "Greeks" can have a narrow meaning when contrasted with "barbarians." However, in 1:16 the term "Greek" is linked with "Jew"

2:10. In the parallelism of the structure in vv. 6–11, Paul restates the positive outcome for "those who by persistence in doing good seek glory, honor, and immortality" (v. 7). In almost the same terms, he indicates that what they seek is given to them by God, namely "glory, honor, and peace" (these nouns are in the nominative case in Greek, and we should understand the verb "to be": "there shall be"). The word "peace" (εἰρήνη) in this context will be a synonym for eschatological salvation.[32] The availability of that salvation for "everyone who does what is good" (παντὶ τῷ ἐργαζομένῳ τὸ ἀγαθόν) is stressed by repetition of the word "all" from v. 9 (in the dative form here) and by a positive restatement of the priority of Israel in God's plan of salvation for humanity (as in 1:16).

In the positive statements of vv. 7, 10 about those who receive eternal life and its blessings, Paul is not contradicting his later teaching about justification by faith (see especially 3:21–4:25). Nor is he speaking hypothetically since the argument that follows in vv. 12–16 draws attention to those who genuinely show by their behavior that "the work of the law is written on their hearts." The main purpose of vv. 6–11 is to establish the righteousness and impartiality of God's judgment "according to works." Paul specifically challenges Jews who are complacent about their knowledge of God and do not take seriously the need for repentance and an obedient lifestyle. But in making this point he also outlines how people generally are saved from the wrath of God. Since his argument is progressive and cumulative, he does not yet explain how God has made that possible. In simple terms he reveals that certain people receive the gift of eternal life because their lifestyle demonstrates that they are truly seeking after God. Some have argued that this refers to the possibility of salvation for Gentiles apart from faith in Christ.[33] But the terms "glory,

---

in a way that suggests the meaning "Gentile." Note that in 1 Cor 1:22–24 "Greeks" and "Gentiles" are interchangeable.

[32] Cf. Werner Foerster, "εἰρήνη κτλ.," *TDNT* 2:406–17. Jewett (*Romans*, 209) plays down the eschatological nature of "peace" here because he is so committed to the idea that Paul is addressing the need for peace in the Roman Christian community, in anticipation of 14:17, 19.

[33] Moo (*Romans*, 140–42) summarizes and critiques a number of these views and concludes that "Paul sets forth the biblical conditions for attaining eternal life apart from Christ." But Moo concludes that the promise can never be realized because all are under the power of sin (3:9). My understanding of Paul's argument here is different.

honor, and immortality" specifically recall the promises of God to his people in Scripture. Those who desire an eternal relationship with God could include Jews and Gentiles who responded appropriately to God's promises before the coming of Christ. But Paul most likely means that those who now believe the gospel and express their commitment to Christ in obedience to his will receive this gift and escape the wrath of God (cf. vv. 13–15 comments).

2:11. This verse corresponds to v. 6 in the chiastic structure of the segment. The connective γάρ ("for") introduces a theological justification for the preceding argument: God's judgment "according to works" is without partiality or favoritism. Although the theme of God's impartiality is widely expressed in biblical and postbiblical writings, the noun προσωπολημψία mostly only occurs in Christian writings (cf. Eph 6:9; Col 3:25; Jas 2:1).[34] It is based on an LXX rendering of the Hebrew expression for "lifting up the face" (sometimes represented by πρόσωπον λαμβάνειν). In some contexts this means "be gracious to," "show consideration for" (e.g., Deut 28:50; 2 Kgs 3:14; Job 42:8–9; Lam 4:16), but in other contexts it means "be unduly influenced by," "show partiality towards" (e.g., Lev 19:15; Deut 10:17; Ps 82:2; Prov 18:5).[35] God's impartiality in judgment is axiomatic in Jewish literature, but nowhere is this divine attribute developed as it is here, "in a universalistic manner that undermines the distinction between Jews and Gentiles."[36]

2:12. A link to the preceding section is indicated by the connective γάρ ("for"), which is not translated by CSB. Paul continues to explain how the judgment of God will fall on Jews and Gentiles alike, but in a different way. With two parallel clauses introduced by the relative adjective ὅσοι ("as many as, whoever"), he claims that (lit.) "as many as sin without the law will also perish without the

[34] Cf. T. Job 43.13. In Gal 2:6 Paul uses a verbal expression that more literally reflects the way the LXX translates the Hebrew idiom (πρόσωπον [ὁ] θεὸς ἀνθρώπου οὐ λαμβάνει, [lit.] "God does not receive the face of man"). Acts 10:34 uses the related noun προσωπολήμπτης.

[35] Cf. Eduard Lohse, "πρόσωπον κτλ.," *TDNT* 6:779–80. In the foundational expression of God's impartiality in Deut 10:17, another verb is used in the Greek translation (οὐ θαυμάζει πρόσωπον).

[36] Jewett, *Romans*, 209, following Jouette M. Bassler, *Divine Impartiality: Paul and a Theological Axiom*, SBLDS 59 (Chico: Scholars Press, 1982), 43–44.

law, and as many as sin under the law will be judged by the law."[37] Although this is the first explicit mention of sin in the letter, the nature of sin in its various manifestations has already been exposed (1:18–2:5). Evidence from Greco-Roman and Jewish sources indicates the verb ἁμαρτάνω ("sin") had the same meaning across these cultures, namely, "failure to meet a standard," to "miss the mark," or to "transgress."[38] Sinning "without the law" (ἀνόμως) describes the sort of behavior outlined in 1:18–32 (cf. 2 Macc 8:17). Perishing "without the law" means experiencing the wrath and indignation of God without knowing the judgments of the law or its merciful provisions for repentant sinners. Paul formulates the principle differently for Jews, who sin "under the law," or in the context of knowing the law (ἐν νόμῳ). They will be judged "by the law" (διὰ νόμου), meaning that God will judge them by the standard and teaching he gave to them.[39] Verses 12–16 have eleven references to law, as Paul explicitly mentions this important topic for the first time (an indirect reference may be recognized in vv. 1, 3) (see §1.4).[40]

2:13. The conjunction γάρ ("for") signals a further explanation of how God will use the law in judging his people. Paul's point-counterpoint argument insists that it is not those who are merely "hearers of the law" who are "righteous before God" (δίκαιοι παρὰ [τῷ] θεῷ).[41] Rather, "the doers of the law will be declared righteous" (δικαιωθήσονται). A true hearing of the law involves heeding and obeying it, as many biblical texts indicate (e.g., Deut 6:4–9, 24–25; Jer 11:3–4; 12:17; Jas 1:22–25; cf. Matt 7:24–27). "Like his

---

[37] Runge (*Discourse Grammar*, 215) observes that the two topical frames of v. 12 (ὅσοι ἀνόμως ἥμαρτον and ὅσοι ἐν νόμῳ ἥμαρτον) provide "a significant aid in tracking who is doing what to whom." Having similar yet completely opposite frames of reference creates a sharp contrast (Runge, 199).

[38] Cf. Jewett, *Romans*, 210, citing Peter Fiedler, "ἁμαρτία κτλ.," *EDNT* 1:66.

[39] Such teaching is expressed in the law itself (e.g., Deut 27:9–26; 28:15–68), in various prophetic oracles (e.g., Jer 7:1–34; 11:1–13), and in later Jewish literature (e.g., 2 Bar. 48:46–47).

[40] Cranfield (*Romans*, 1:154n2) rightly observes that, even though Paul uses νόμος without an article, the context makes clear that he is talking about the law of God, not law in general.

[41] Jewett (*Romans*, 211) takes "hearers of the law" literally to refer to "Jewish worshipers who participate in public readings (of the law) on the Sabbath." He (193) notes that the absence of the definite article τῷ in some manuscripts is puzzling (B D* 056 1874*) but that there is stronger textual evidence for its inclusion.

fellow Jews and the whole prophetic tradition, Paul is ready to insist that a doing of the law is necessary for final acquittal before God."[42] However, v. 13 needs to be read in the light of Paul's teaching about justification by faith later in the letter. This is the first of fifteen uses of the verb δικαιόω, which means "acquit" or "pronounce and treat as righteous" (BDAG; cf. §2.4).[43] The ground of justification is the redemptive work of Christ (3:22–26; 4:25; 5:9, 18–19), and faith is the means by which the benefits of that redemption are appropriated (3:28, 30; 5:1). The future passive form here refers to the ultimate eschatological verdict of God (note the parallel with κριθήσονται ["they shall be judged"] in v. 12). In that judgment "works" will be evaluated as an indicator of genuine faith, not as something added to faith to make it more acceptable (vv. 6–11). On that occasion the believer's present justification by faith will become publicly manifest.[44] As argued above, neither here nor in vv. 7, 10 does Paul argue for justification by obedience apart from faith in Christ.[45] "Works righteousness" is excluded in passages such as 3:19–20, 27–31; 9:30–33, but Paul has in mind a different way of "doing the law" in v. 13, "a doing . . . commensurate with 'the obedience of faith.'"[46]

2:14. Once more, γάρ ("for"; CSB: "so") indicates a development of the foregoing argument. Paul continues to challenge Jewish unbelief and hypocrisy by drawing attention to the fact that "when Gentiles, who do not by nature have the law, do what the law

[42] Dunn, *Romans 1–8*, 98.

[43] The verb δικαιόω is forensic and positive in meaning: "to 'justify' someone is to vindicate them, not to punish them." Cf. Mark A. Seifrid, *Justification by Faith: The Origin and Development of a Central Pauline Theme*, NovTSup 68 (Leiden: Brill, 1992).

[44] N. T. Wright (*Justification: God's Plan and Vision* [London: SPCK, 2009], 167–68) appears to give the future verdict of justification rather than present justification, the primacy in Paul's thought. Contrast Guy P. Waters, *Justification and the New Perspectives on Paul: A Review and Response* (Phillipsburg: P&R, 2004), 131.

[45] Moo (*Romans*, 148) argues, "This verse confirms and explains the reason for the Jews' condemnation in v. 12b; and this suggests that its purpose is not to show how people can be justified but to set forth the standard that must be met if a person is to be justified." But Schreiner (*Romans*, 115) contends, "Paul's insistence elsewhere that works are necessary to enter the kingdom suggests that the similar theme here cannot be dismissed as hypothetical."

[46] Don B. Garlington, *Faith, Obedience and Perseverance: Aspects of Paul's Letter to the Romans*, WUNT 79 (Tübingen: Mohr-Siebeck, 1994), 59. Cf. Seifrid, "Unrighteous by Faith," 124–26.

demands, they are a law to themselves even though they do not have the law." CSB has rightly taken the noun φύσει (lit. "by nature") to modify the participle immediately preceding it (ἔχοντα, "having") rather than the indicative verb that follows in the expression "do what the law demands" (τὰ τοῦ νόμου ποιῶσιν). Many take these verses to mean that certain Gentiles (ἔθνη without an article), apart from special revelation, "do by nature (or 'instinctively') what the law demands." In effect, "they have the moral norms of the Mosaic law, evidenced by occasionally keeping the commandments of that law."[47] Paul is said to have borrowed the popular Greek conception of a natural law written on the heart (v. 15) and coupled this with another stereotypical Greek expression: "They are a law to themselves" (ἑαυτοῖς εἰσιν νόμος).[48] The conclusion is that Gentiles will be judged on the basis of natural law whereas Jews will be judged on the basis of the law given to Moses.

However, there are several reasons for believing that Paul specifically draws attention to *Gentile Christians* here, identifying them as those who enjoy the transformation promised under the new covenant, having the knowledge of God's will inscribed in their hearts and embodying the teaching of the law in their persons.[49] First, φύσις in Paul's writings normally qualifies *identity* rather than *behavior* (e.g., 2:27; 11:21; Gal 2:15; 4:8; Eph 2:3). Second, φύσει is more likely to modify the verb that immediately precedes it rather than the verb that follows. So it is more likely that the meaning is "they do not have the law *by virtue of their birth*."[50] This removes the

---

[47] Schreiner, *Romans*, 122. Schreiner (120–24) opposes the view that Paul speaks of Christian Gentiles here. He takes v. 16 to imply that "the doing of the law described in verse 14 should not be understood as a consistent and regular observance of the law." Dunn (*Romans 1–8*, 98–99) argues that this knowledge of rightness and wrongness by "the godly pagan" has already been hinted at in 1:26–28, 32.

[48] Moo (*Romans*, 150) says Paul presses into service "a widespread Greek tradition to the effect that all human beings possess an 'unwritten' or 'natural' law—an innate moral sense of 'right and wrong.'"

[49] Cf. Simon J. Gathercole, "A Law unto Themselves: The Gentiles in Romans 2:14–15 Revisited," *JSNT* 85 (2002): 27–49. Others who argue that the passage is about Gentile Christians include Cranfield, *Romans*, 1:155–59; N. T. Wright, "The Law in Romans 2," in *Paul and the Mosaic Law*, ed. James D. G. Dunn (Grand Rapids: Eerdmans, 2000), 131–50; Jewett, *Romans*, 213–17; Kruse, *Romans*, 130–40.

[50] Gathercole ("A Law unto Themselves," 35–37) cites examples where φύσει occurs at the end of a phrase (e.g., Wis 13:1; Josephus, *Ant.* 8.152; Ign., *Eph.* 1:1), and argues that "it is a common rule in the grammar books that adverbs *follow* their

need to speculate about unbelieving Gentiles having a natural law written on the heart. Jews have the law as their natural inheritance; Gentiles do not (cf. 2:17–23). Third, the expression "the work of the law written on their hearts" (v. 15) most obviously alludes to Jer 31:33 (LXX 38:33; cf. Ezek. 36:26, "a new heart"). Elsewhere Paul uses the plural expression "works of the law" negatively (3:20, 28; Gal 2:16; 3:2, 5, 10), but the singular expression "the work of the law" (τὸ ἔργον τοῦ νόμου) signifies "the essential unity of the law's requirements,"[51] which God writes on the hearts of his new covenant people. Those who take the natural law approach to Rom 2:14–16 either deny that this is an allusion to Jeremiah's prophecy, or take Paul's expression to be "a more open-ended formula, which has at least the potential of wider application."[52] Given the eschatological significance of the promise in Jer 31:33, it is hard to believe Paul used the expression "the work of the law written on their hearts" simply to refer to a fact of everyday life among the Gentiles. Even more odd is the suggestion that he borrowed a stereotypical Greek expression that was similar to Jeremiah's promise, but conveyed a different meaning, and used it at the beginning of a letter that regularly alludes to the fulfillment of Jeremiah's promise in other ways (cf. 2:26–29; 5:5; 6:17; 7:4–6; 8:4; 10:9–13; 11:26; 12:2)![53] Fourth, the expression "they are a law to themselves even though they do not have the law" should be understood in relation to the claim about "the work of the law written on their hearts." Possession of the law

verbs." He also observes that "if the first half of 14a did not include the φύσει, the clause would be merely repeated exactly in the first half of 14b."

[51] Cranfield, *Romans*, 1:158. Cf. Rom 8:4, "the righteous requirement of the law" (τὸ δικαίωμα τοῦ νόμου). Gathercole ("A Law unto Themselves," 41–43) deals with objections to the view that 2:15 proclaims the fulfillment of Jer 31:33 (LXX 38:33).

[52] Dunn, *Romans 1–8*, 100. Dunn is prepared to admit that Jer 31:33 is probably evoked in Rom 2:15 but says it is deliberately modified to have a wider application. Gathercole ("A Law unto Themselves," 41) observes four specific verbal links between the LXX version of this text (Jer 38:33) and Rom 2:15.

[53] Cf. David G. Peterson, *Transformed by God: New Covenant Life and Ministry* (Downers Grove: InterVarsity, 2012), 136–55. In 2 Cor 3:2–3, 6, Paul modifies Jeremiah's promise about God's writing his law upon the heart and combines this with Ezekiel's promise of the renewing work of the Spirit.

by birthright is contrasted with knowing it and "actually having in their hearts the earnest desire to obey it."[54]

2:15–16. As Paul sets out to undermine Jewish self-confidence based on the possession of the Mosaic law and circumcision (vv. 17–29), he draws attention to the fact that certain Gentiles are enjoying the blessings of the new covenant promised to Israel (vv. 14–16, cf. Jer 31:33–34; Ezek 36:26–27).[55] Consistent with his missionary strategy in 11:14—to provoke unbelieving Jews to jealousy and thus "save some of them"—he wants *Jews* to see their need for Christ. Using the relative adjective οἵτινες ("those who"; CSB: "they"), he declares that those described in the previous verse "show that the work of the law is written on their hearts." They have been transformed by a remarkable work of God. The verb "show" (ἐνδείκνυνται) most likely indicates that there are present, outward proofs of this heart transformation, but it could also refer to the future judgment of God because of the linked clauses that follow (CSB has made separate sentences out of the two subordinate clauses in v. 15).[56]

First, a genitive absolute expression with a participle in the present tense (συμμαρτυρούσης αὐτῶν τῆς συνειδήσεως) points to their conscience as a present, accompanying witness to "the law written on their hearts."[57] The closest parallel is 9:1, where Paul claims the Holy Spirit confirms the witness of his conscience that he is speaking the truth in Christ and not lying. In both passages conscience is not an independent way of knowing God's will but

---

[54] Cranfield, *Romans*, 1:158. The expression ἑαυτοῖς εἰσιν νόμος is used by Greek writers "with reference to the man of superior virtue who does not need the guidance or sanctions of external law." But this is hardly Paul's meaning here.

[55] Wright ("The Law in Romans 2," 134–35) points to the close parallels between vv. 14–15 and 25–29. Note also what is said about Christian believers in Rom 7:6; 8:2; 2 Cor 3:6; Phil 3:3.

[56] Moo (*Romans*, 151) allows for a transition from present to future in Paul's argument by contending that, "although the implicit testimony of the works of Gentiles reaches its climax in the judgment, Paul's focus in this verse is still on the implications of these works in this life." Cranfield (*Romans*, 1:161–62) gives "show" a present reference but restricts the testimony of conscience and competing thoughts to the final judgment.

[57] A genitive absolute construction functions in an adverbial (circumstantial) way in relation to a principal clause (Wallace, *Greek Grammar*, 654–55). There are three uses of the compound verb συμμαρτυρέω in Romans (2:25; 8:16; 9:1), and in each case the prefix συν- ("with") is to be given its full force so that the meaning is "to provide supporting evidence by testifying, *confirm, support by testimony*" (BDAG).

simply a "knowledge shared with oneself whether of one's having done wrong or of one's innocence."[58] So the conscience of these Gentiles evaluates whether their behavior is consistent with "the law written on their hearts." Two further genitive absolute clauses then refer to the activity of "their competing thoughts." The expression μεταξὺ ἀλλήλων τῶν λογισμῶν literally means "their thoughts among themselves" and, in the flow of the argument, most likely refers to personal reflection rather than thoughts shared with other people.[59] Accusation is given greater emphasis than defense in the expression κατηγορούντων ἢ καὶ ἀπολογουμένων (lit., "accusing or even excusing"), but this is not a reason for denying that Christians could be on view in this passage. According to 1 John 3:20, Christians may have accusing "hearts" and still be vindicated by God. Gentiles are condemned in Rom 1:20–21 because of their wrong thinking, but in 2:15–16 "accusing or even excusing thoughts" are evidence of honest self-assessment before God.[60] Although these competing thoughts might be a further description of the role of conscience, "it is not the moral quality of the thoughts, but their forensic function on the day of judgment which is in view here."[61]

In effect Paul mentions three witnesses to the transforming work of God: a lifestyle showing that "the work of the law is written on their hearts," consciences testifying in support of this, and "accusing or even excusing thoughts among them." These witnesses have a present role (indicated by present tense verbs and genitive absolute constructions in v. 15), but the opening words of v. 16 (ἐν ἡμέρᾳ ὅτε,

[58] Cranfield, *Romans*, 1.160. Christian Maurer ("σύνοιδα, συνείδησις," *TDNT* 7:917) argues that the role of conscience for Paul is no longer simply that of the accusing and convicting inner voice, as in Hellenistic-Jewish writings, but "the central self-consciousness of knowing and acting man." However, Jewett (*Romans*, 215) contends that conscience here simply means "an autonomous witness as to whether a particular action is consistent with the internalized standard." See further on 13:5.

[59] Jewett (*Romans*, 216–17) takes the public alternative and endorses the rendering of Charles K. Barrett (*A Commentary on the Epistle to the Romans*, BNTC [London: Black, 1971], 53): "their inward thoughts in mutual debate."

[60] Schreiner (*Romans*, 124) argues that saving obedience is not envisioned in vv. 14–15 because "accusing" thoughts predominate. But this suggests a perfectionist view of saving obedience. Kruse (*Romans*, 134) rightly observes that 2 Cor 5:10 is "sufficient to cause even believers to approach the Day of Judgment with some apprehension."

[61] Gathercole, "A Law unto Themselves," 46.

"on the day when") clearly indicate that they have a climactic role to play "on the day when God judges what people have kept secret."[62] This whole sequence indicates that inner transformation is the true focus of God's judgment, with lifestyle and behavior indicating what is happening in human hearts (cf. 1 Cor 4:4–5). "The inner witness of the conscience and conflicting thoughts (v. 15) are known to God and destined to be revealed on the day of judgment."[63] Such teaching would not have come as a shock to those familiar with biblical teaching about the way God knows the secrets of human hearts (e.g., 1 Sam 16:7; 1 Chr 28:9; Ps 139:1–2; Jer 17:10). But Paul makes the disturbing claim in his gospel that this judgment will take place for Jews and Gentiles alike, and it will be "through Christ Jesus" (cf. 10:9–12; Acts 17:31; 2 Tim 4:1).

Bridge

Although Paul is specifically developing an argument against Jews who are complacent about their sin, hypocritical in judging others, and falsely reliant on their covenant status to protect them from God's wrath, this passage clearly has a wider application. Those who know that God judges righteously and impartially must understand that they will be judged in the same way as everyone else. When they condemn others for doing the things they themselves do, they condemn themselves in advance of God's universal judgment. What really counts with God is a life moved by repentance in response to "the riches of God's kindness, restraint, and patience." In positive terms this means persevering in doing God's will, motivated by a sense of his goodness and the desire for an eternal relationship with God in Christ. The alternative is a life of self-seeking and disobedience to the truth. So the impetus for godly living is the reality of God's coming judgment according to works and God's promise of "glory, honor, and peace" to "everyone who does what is good." Those who live in this way show that God's law is written in their hearts and that they are truly the beneficiaries of the new covenant (Jer 31:31–34). They present a vital challenge to

[62] The verb κρινει is without accent in some significant manuscripts but is accented as a present tense (κρίνει) or as a future tense (κρινεῖ) in others. However, this variation has no significance for exegesis since the present tense can have a future meaning. Cf. Schreiner, *Romans*, 125–26.

[63] Moo, *Romans*, 154.

those who are hearers but not actually doers of God's law (cf. Jas 2:14–26).

B. Misplaced Confidence (2:17–29)

17 Now if you call yourself a Jew, and rely on the law, and
boast in God, 18 and know his will, and approve the things that are
superior, being instructed from the law, 19 and if you are convinced
that you are a guide for the blind, a light to those in darkness, 20 an
instructor of the ignorant, a teacher of the immature, having the
embodiment of knowledge and truth in the law—21 you then, who
teach another, don't you teach yourself? You who preach, "You
must not steal"—do you steal? 22 You who say, "You must not commit adultery"—do you commit adultery? You who detest idols, do
you rob their temples? 23 You who boast in the law, do you dishonor
God by breaking the law? 24 For, as it is written: **The name of God
is blasphemed among the Gentiles because of you.**

25 Circumcision benefits you if you observe the law, but if
you are a lawbreaker, your circumcision has become uncircumcision. 26 So if an uncircumcised man keeps the law's requirements,
will not his uncircumcision be counted as circumcision? 27 A man
who is physically uncircumcised, but who keeps the law, will
judge you who are a lawbreaker in spite of having the letter of
the law and circumcision. 28 For a person is not a Jew who is one
outwardly, and true circumcision is not something visible in the
flesh. 29 On the contrary, a person is a Jew who is one inwardly,
and circumcision is of the heart—by the Spirit, not the letter. That
person's praise is not from people but from God.

Context

This section continues the diatribe with an imaginary opponent that began in vv. 1–5, though the person addressed is now explicitly a Jew who approves what the law teaches, commends it to others, but fails to obey it. Following on from his reference to *Gentiles* who show that "the work of the law is written on their hearts" (vv. 14–15), Paul asserts that a true *Jew* will have a circumcised heart (vv. 25–29). An inclusion is formed between the use of the word "Jew" at the beginning and the end of this passage. There is an echo of vv. 14–15 in vv. 26–27 with the claim that Gentiles who are physically uncircumcised, yet fulfill the law's demands, expose the failure of those who are lawbreakers "in spite of having the letter of the law and circumcision." Echoes of 1:18–32 can also be discerned. In contrast with those who "did not think it worthwhile to have God in their knowledge" (1:28), Jews who know God's will "approve the things that are superior" (2:18). But Paul challenges whether in fact they dishonor God by their conduct among the nations. This condemnation of Jewish hypocrisy and failure to live before the world as the covenant people of God prepares for the next stage of Paul's argument (3:1–8). There he returns to the twin themes of humanity's culpability before God and God's righteousness in condemning both Jews and Gentiles.

Structure

The first part of the argument (vv. 17–24) explains why Jews cannot be exempt from God's judgment. The person addressed here is confident about possessing God's law and having a vocation to commend it to the nations (vv. 17–20).[64] But four rhetorical questions challenge whether he is guilty of the sins he condemns in others (vv. 21–22). A summary statement clarifies that Paul has been speaking about Jews who boast in the law but dishonor God by breaking it (v. 23).[65] Citing Isa 52:5, Paul concludes that they have failed to live up to their calling, since "the name of God is blasphemed among the Gentiles because of you" (v. 24).

The second part (vv. 25–29) deals with outward and inward circumcision and the fulfillment of God's law. Two contrasting hypothetical situations are outlined (v. 25, "for circumcision benefits you if you observe the law, but if you are a lawbreaker, your circumcision has become uncircumcision"). A third conditional clause appears in the form of a question (v. 26, "if an uncircumcised man keeps the law's requirements, will not his uncircumcision be counted as circumcision?") This person is then described in slightly different

[64] The participial clause κατηχούμενος ἐκ τοῦ νόμου ("being instructed from the law") functions in a causal way with reference to the whole of vv. 17–18. A matching participial clause ἔχοντα τὴν μόρφωσιν τῆς γνώσεως καὶ τῆς ἀληθείας ἐν τῷ νόμῳ ("having in the law the full expression of knowledge and truth") concludes the description of the Jew in vv. 19–20. Cf. Dunn, *Romans 1–8*, 109.

[65] CSB reads v. 23 as a further question (so also NRSV, NIV), but the change of syntax in this verse suggests it should be read as a statement (so ESV), with v. 24 being a confirmation of its truth (γάρ). Cf. Cranfield, *Romans*, 1:170; Schreiner, *Romans*, 132.

terms as "a man who is physically uncircumcised, but who keeps the law." Such a person will judge the Jew who is "a lawbreaker in spite of having the letter of the law and circumcision" (v. 27). In the conclusion to this section (vv. 28–29), Paul contrasts one who is a Jew "outwardly" and physically circumcised with one who is a Jew "inwardly," whose circumcision is "of the heart—by the Spirit, not the letter," whose praise is "not from people but from God."

Outline:

1. The deceit of hypocrisy (vv. 17–24)
2. Seeking God's praise (vv. 25–29)

2:17. Paul resumes the diatribe style employed in vv. 1–5, addressing an imaginary opponent with second-person singular verbs and the emphatic pronoun *σύ* ("you"). But the connective δέ ("but, now") sets this section in an adversative relation to vv. 1–16.[66] Paul sets out to challenge the complacency of mainstream Judaism and highlight its failure to live up to God's calling. He lets his Christian audience overhear this challenge, "in order to lay the groundwork to persuade them to accept his own view of Jewish identity and Jewish vocation, and thus to accept his apostolic ministry, along with its implications for Jew-Gentile relationships in the Roman community itself."[67]

A modified conditional clause, beginning with εἰ ("if"), is followed by five indicative verbs and two participles in an extended protasis but with no formal apodosis.[68] The person addressed is someone who "calls himself" (*ἐπονομάζῃ* [present middle]) a Jew. For centuries the term Ἰουδαῖος had been used by foreigners to identify a person belonging to Judea. But from the Maccabean period onward, it was adopted by Jews themselves as a replacement for

[66] In place of εἰ δέ ("now if"), which the best ancient manuscripts strongly support, later texts read ἴδε ("behold," as in KJV). Metzger (*Textual Commentary*, 448) suggests why this alternative may have arisen.

[67] Windsor, *Vocation*, 151. Windsor (142–52) identifies the similarities and differences between vv. 1–16 and vv. 17–29 in Paul's argument.

[68] A first-class conditional sentence normally expresses a logical sequence: if certain things are true (expressed in the protasis), then other things follow (expressed in the apodosis). But Paul adapts the format and replaces the apodosis with a series of questions. Schreiner (*Romans*, 128) calls it "a conceptual apodosis." Cf. Wallace, *Greek Grammar*, 450–51, 690–94.

the older designations "Israelite" or "Hebrew."[69] Paul addresses his fellow Jews collectively in this way, implying that "the presence of misbehavior within ethnic Israel renders void the national, ethnic boast; it prevents Israel from fulfilling its calling to be the light of the world."[70] Several expressions are used in vv. 17–20 to identify what it meant to be a Jew in Paul's world. The first is "you rely on the law" (ἐπαναπαύῃ νόμῳ), the preceding context suggesting that confidence before God on the day of judgment is meant. Compare Mic 3:11 LXX where corrupt leaders "lean on the Lord" (ἐπὶ τὸν κύριον ἐπανεπαύοντο) and consider that no calamity will come upon them. The second identifying expression is "you boast in God" (καυχᾶσαι ἐν θεῷ). Such boasting is commendable if it means allowing the knowledge of God and his will to determine the character of your life (Deut 10:21; Jer 9:23–24; 1 Cor 1:28–31; 2 Cor 10:12–18; Phil 3:3; cf. Pss. Sol. 17:1). But the terminology could be used to describe a self-confident and arrogant approach to God.[71] Paul's dialogue partner is unrepentant and heading for condemnation. He is about to be exposed for having a misplaced confidence in God, the law, and his own covenant status (vv. 21–24; cf. 3:27–28; 4:2).

2:18. The positive potential of relying on God's law and boasting in God is now described: "[You] know his will and approve the things that are superior." Knowing the will of God makes possible appropriate decisions in life. The verb δοκιμάζειν can mean "to make a critical examination of something to determine genuineness, *put to the test, examine*" (BDAG). Contextually, however, the meaning is more likely to be "draw a conclusion about worth on the basis of

---

[69] Cf. Walter Gutbrod, "Ἰσραήλ, κτλ.," *TDNT* 3:369–75. "Jew" denoted the special status enjoyed by Israelites in comparison with other nations. Cf. 1:16; 2:9, 11.

[70] Wright, "Romans," 445. Gathercole (*Boasting*, 37–194) examines the theme of obedience and final vindication in Jewish literature from the Second Temple period, concluding that obedience as well as election was the basis of the Jews' confidence before God. Cf. 2 Bar. 48:22–24. Dunn (*Romans 1–8*, 110–11) sees the boasting in 2:17 as purely "nationalistic" and does not allow that it includes confidence in the face of judgment. Cf. Seifrid, "Unrighteous by Faith," 127–35.

[71] The verb καυχᾶσθαι ("boast") is used again in 2:23; 5:2, 3, 11, the cognate noun καύχησις in 3:27; 15:17, καύχημα in 4:2 and κατακαυχᾶσθαι in 11:18. These words are used in the LXX in two senses: boastful self-confidence and self-glorification in relation to God and other people, but also the kind of boasting in God that looks away from self and glories in the character and deeds of God. Cf. Josef Zmijewski, "καυχάομαι, κτλ.," *EDNT* 2:276–79.

testing, *prove, approve*," where the focus is on the result of a procedure or examination (BDAG). In 1:28 (DLNT) the apostle condemns those who literally "did not approve [οὐκ ἐδοκίμασαν] to have God in their knowledge," but here he expects better things of the Jew who has the law of God. The expression τὰ διαφέροντα could simply mean "the things that differ," but more likely, "the things that really matter (or are essential)" (CSB: "the things that are superior").[72] The participial clause κατηχούμενος ἐκ τοῦ νόμου ("being instructed from the law") relates to both preceding verbs in a causal way and establishes the means by which God's will is known and the things that are superior can be approved.[73]

2:19–20. With an introductory perfect participle (πέποιθάς, "you are convinced"), Paul begins to describe the Jew's confidence in relation to those outside the law. Israel's divine vocation was to be a blessing to the nations (Gen 12:3; 18:18; 22:18; 26:4–5; Exod 19:5–6). The nature and significance of that calling is explored in many biblical passages and in a variety of extrabiblical writings. The first two terms allude to Isa 42:6–7, where Israel as the Lord's servant is meant to be "a guide for the blind, a light to those in darkness" (cf. Wis 18:4; 1 En. 105:1; Sib. Or. 3:194–95; T. Levi 14:4; 18:9; 1QSb 4:27–28). The next two expressions identify the Jew as "an instructor of the ignorant, a teacher of the immature" (παιδευτὴν ἀφρόνων, διδάσκαλον νηπίων). Such terms were frequently used in Greek and Hellenistic Jewish culture to describe tutors and educators. We know Jewish teachers gave formal instruction to Gentile proselytes, but the meaning here is probably broader.[74] Jews in the Dispersion had everyday opportunities to tell Gentiles about the values given to them in their law and to model those values.

---

[72] Cf. Moo, *Romans*, 157–58. Cf. Phil 1:10. Cranfield (*Romans*, 1:166) suggests that Paul's claim can be compared with Matt 23:23, where the Jew, with a knowledge of passages such as Deut 6:4–6; Lev 19:18, should be able to discern and approve "the more important matters of the law."

[73] The verb κατηχεῖν can have the more general sense "to share a communication one receives, report, inform" (Acts 21:21, 24), or the more specific sense "to teach, instruct" (Acts 18:25; 1 Cor 14:19; Gal 6:6), which is applicable here (BDAG). Instructed by the law, Jews should have been in a position to teach others.

[74] Responding to Stanley K. Stowers (*A Rereading of Romans: Justice, Jews and Gentiles* [New Haven: Yale University, 1994], 144–58), Windsor (*Vocation*, 162) argues that Paul's interlocutor is "both a talented Law-teacher and, at the very same time, a representative and exemplar of Jewish identity itself."

The basis for teaching others about the character and will of God is given in the participial clause that follows: "having the embodiment of knowledge and truth in the law." The noun μόρφωσις means "the state of being formally structured, embodiment" (BDAG), and so Paul's full expression signifies that the law provides "knowledge and truth in a form which can be grasped, expressed clearly and understandably."[75] Knowledge and truth are important biblical notions, though they clearly also figure in the aspirations and claims of many human philosophies and religions. God's special revelation to Israel put his people in a unique position to know him, understand his will for humanity, and have their behavior formed by it (cf. 3:1–2; 9:4).

2:21–22. Four consequential questions are linked to the preceding verses by οὖν ("then"). Paul's affirmations about the law and Israel's role in God's plan for the world (vv. 17–20) are the basis for a series of challenges to Jews about their faithfulness to God's revelation in everyday lifestyle and behavior. The first question functions as the fundamental charge. This is amplified in three specific challenges that follow.[76] It provides an immediate link with the previous verse and establishes the pattern for what follows: "You then, who teach another, don't you teach yourself?" The hypocrisy of teaching something and not adhering to it yourself was widely recognized in the ancient world.[77] Paul suggests that some of his fellow Jews, who preached against stealing, stole themselves. Others spoke against adultery but were guilty of adultery themselves. The fourth accusation suggests that even those who "detest idols" (ὁ βδελυσσόμενος τὰ εἴδωλα) had in some way compromised with idolatry.[78] The verb ἱεροσυλεῖς literally means "rob a temple" (cf. 2 Macc

[75] Cranfield, *Romans*, 1:167. Cranfield observes that Paul nowhere contradicts this statement about the law even though he indicates that many Jews have misunderstood the law and its purpose. Jewett (*Romans*, 226–27) wrongly implies that the expression suggests a claim by Jews to embody the truth of God's law in themselves.

[76] Moo, *Romans*, 163. A series of statements could be read here, rather than questions. However, rhetorical questions raise possibilities rather than claiming that every Jew is guilty of every sin described, which fits better with the tenor of Paul's argument in this section. The syntax in vv. 24–25 points to a statement, rather than another question, followed by a supportive argument from Scripture.

[77] Jewett, *Romans*, 227–28. Cf. Ps 50:16–21; 'Abot R. Nat. 29[8a]; Matt 23:3.

[78] The verb βδελύσσομαι means "to detest something because it is utterly offensive or loathsome" (BDAG). Werner Foerster ("βδελύσσομαι, κτλ.," *TDNT* 1:598–600)

9:2; Josephus, *Ant.* 17.163). Some Jews may have been guilty of plundering items from temples devoted to false gods, justifying this on the ground that the gods have no real existence.[79] If this was so, they were ignoring Deut 7:25–26, which explicitly prohibits taking silver and gold from an idol and being ensnared by it. Against the view that Paul's accusation relates to the misappropriation of funds intended for the Jerusalem temple or to sacrilege in a more general sense, it should be noted that such behavior would not involve "a contradiction to the Jews' abhorrence of idols."[80]

Paul may have chosen the particular sins listed here because he wanted to highlight the way specific commands in the Decalogue were being broken (stealing, adultery, idolatry). Perhaps also his desire was "to show the equivalence between the sins of Jews and of Gentiles (cf. 2:3)."[81] He does not argue that *all* Jews were guilty of the same transgressions but that in different ways they failed to keep the law they possessed and to fulfill their calling to commend it to the nations.

2:23. Paul turns from rhetorical questioning to a concluding statement, supporting this with a citation from Scripture. The syntax here is different from the repeated pattern of questioning in vv. 21–22. The first clause uses an indicative form rather than a participle (ὃς ἐν νόμῳ καυχᾶσαι, "you who boast in the law") and echoes the language of v. 17. This suggests that a conclusion to the section is being drawn: "Just as there is a right, but also a wrong, boasting or exulting in God, so too with the law."[82] What makes boasting in the law empty and inappropriate is breaking the law (διὰ τῆς παραβάσεως τοῦ νόμου, "by breaking the law"), which summarizes

points out that in the LXX this term is used of things that are particularly abominable to God. The cognate noun (βδέλυγμα, "abomination") is frequently used with specific reference to idolatry (e.g., Deut 7:25–26; Isa 2:8, 20; Dan 11:31; 1 Macc 1:54; Wis 14:11).

[79] Cf. Dunn, *Romans 1–8*, 114–15; Schreiner, *Romans*, 132–33 (citing 2 Macc 4:39, 42; 9:2; 13:6; Sib. Or. 2:14; 13:12; Josephus, *Ant.* 16.2.4 §45; 16.6.2 §164; *War* 5.13.6 §562).

[80] Moo, *Roman*, 164. Moo discusses three ways in which ἱεροσυλεῖς could be understood and concludes that the natural, literal sense is the best option.

[81] Ibid., 165.

[82] Cranfield, *Romans*, 1:170. In v. 17 the boast is in God, though this is closely linked with relying on the law and being instructed from the law (v. 18). The common language indicates an inclusion or return to the ideas with which the paragraph began.

the accusations in vv. 21–22.[83] Jews who transgress God's law and still express confidence in their covenant status actually "dishonor God" (τὸν θεὸν ἀτιμάζεις). This is another way of saying they fail to glorify God (cf. 1:21).

2:24. Linked to this conclusion by *γάρ* ("for"), the citation from Isa 52:5 makes clear that this dishonoring of God by his chosen people has caused the blaspheming of his name among the Gentiles (ἐν τοῖς ἔθνεσιν).[84] Such blasphemy shows the failure of Israel to be "a guide for the blind, a light to those in darkness" (v. 19). As in 1:17, *καθὼς γέγραπται* ("as it is written") draws attention to the biblical source and authority of the citation. Paul's wording differs slightly from the LXX: he omits "continually" (*διὰ παντός*) and substitutes "the name of God" (τὸ ὄνομα τοῦ θεοῦ) for "my name" (τὸ ὄνομά μου).[85] At the time of the Babylonian exile, Gentiles denigrated the God of Israel because his people had become subject to foreigners, making their God seem weak and ineffective. But the prophet insisted that God was actively judging his people for their unfaithfulness and continuing transgression of his law (Isa 40:2; 42:24–25; 43:22–28; 50:1; cf. Ezek 36:17–23). So Paul's use of this text is in keeping with its contextual meaning. Israel is under judgment for continuing to forsake her God-given vocation to be a light to the nations.

> It is not just particular acts of transgression, but the whole attitude to the law expressed in the previous verses, which amounts to a perversion of God's purpose for Israel and the nations, and which results in the nations continuing to regard

---

[83] Παράβασις ("transgression") is used again in 4:15; 5:14; and the cognate *παραβάτης* ("transgressor") is found in 2:25, 27. This terminology means "deviating from an established boundary or norm" (BDAG), and in biblical usage a deliberate breaking of a known commandment of God. Cf. Johannes Schneider, "*παραβαίνω, κτλ.*," *TDNT* 5:738.

[84] The verb βλασφημέω ("blaspheme") means "speak in a disrespectful way that demeans, denigrates, maligns" (BDAG). Both the verb and the cognate noun are used in Greco-Roman and Jewish literature with particular reference to "disrespect shown or harm done to a deity's reputation." Cf. Hermann W. Beyer, "βλασφημέω, κτλ.," *TDNT* 1:621–25.

[85] The Hebrew text of Isa 52:5 is shorter וְתָמִיד כָּל־הַיּוֹם שְׁמִי מִנֹּאָץ, "and my name is continually blasphemed all day long"). Clearly the LXX version suited Paul's purpose more precisely.

God simply as the national God of a small nation and thus to dishonor him who is the only God, God of all (3:29).[86]

2:25. The second main section of the argument begins with the keyword περιτομή ("circumcision"), which occurs six times in this short passage (the contrasting term ἀκροβυστία ["uncircumcision"] occurs four times). A clear link with the preceding argument is provided by the connective γάρ ("for"), suggesting that circumcision might be a particular reason for Jews to boast in the law and have confidence about their relationship with God. In Gen 17:1–14 circumcision is the God-given sign of the eternal covenant God established with Abraham and his descendants (cf. Rom 2:11). When Antiochus Epiphanes banned circumcision in the second century BC (cf. 1 Macc 1:48, 60–61; 2 Macc 6:10), it led to a strong counterreaction, affirming the importance of the rite for Jews and the need to circumcise foreigners who wanted to be counted as beneficiaries of God's covenant.[87] But a significant qualification is made in Paul's opening statement about circumcision when he uses the contrasting terms μέν and δέ. This construction allows him to affirm that "circumcision benefits you if you observe the law," meaning if you faithfully keep the law.[88]

In view of what he previously argued about facing the ultimate judgment of God (vv. 1–16), the "benefit" (ὠφελεῖ) he has in mind is salvation from the wrath of God. Syntactically, however, the emphasis falls on the contrary proposition: "*But* if you are a lawbreaker, your circumcision has become uncircumcision." The expression "a lawbreaker" (παραβάτης νόμου) picks up the language of v. 23 and identifies someone who is a habitual or fundamental transgressor of God's law (cf. Gal 2:18). Paul's judgment is that such a person has effectively become uncircumcised, meaning that his membership of the covenant people is called into question and he has no

---

[86] Dunn, *Romans 1–8*, 116. Contrast Christopher D. Stanley, *Arguing with Scripture: The Rhetoric of Quotations in the Letters of Paul* (New York: T&T Clark, 2004), 145–50.

[87] Cf. Esth 8:17 LXX; Jdt 14:10; Josephus, *Ant.* 1.10.5 §192; 13.9.1 §257–58; 13.11.3 §318–19; *War* 2.17.10 §454; *Life* 23 §113; Philo, *Migr.* 16 §89–93.

[88] Cranfield (*Romans*, 1:171n3, 173) rightly argues that this and parallel expressions do not mean perfectly obeying the law. Parallels in the immediate context are "doers of the law" (v. 13, οἱ ποιηταὶ νόμου), "keeps the law's requirements" (v. 26, τὰ δικαιώματα τοῦ νόμου φυλάσσῃ), and "fulfills the law" (v. 27, τὸν νόμον τελοῦσα).

basis for confidence before God as judge.[89] Paul's opponents would have challenged the starkness of his claim. Contemporary Jewish teachers held that "only a radical decision to renounce the covenant invalidated one's circumcision."[90] In positive terms the apostle contends that the advantage of circumcision accrues only if you observe the law's other demands (cf. Gal 5:3). Of course, males are the focus of attention here because of the nature of circumcision itself. But the challenge about genuine covenant membership could equally apply to females who were only superficially devoted to God and his law.

2:26. A further stage in Paul's argument is introduced with the connective οὖν ("therefore"). The noun previously used to describe the state of being uncircumcised is now employed with reference to "the uncircumcised" (ἡ ἀκροβυστία), which CSB renders "an uncircumcised man."[91] When Paul writes about the possibility of a Gentile keeping "the law's requirements" (τὰ δικαιώματα τοῦ νόμου φυλάσσῃ, cf. Exod 15:26; Deut 4:40; Ezek 11:20 etc.), he most likely restates in different terms the theme announced in v. 14 (ἔθνη . . . τὰ τοῦ νόμου ποιῶσιν, "Gentiles . . . do what the law demands"). Once again, he has in mind that Gentile Christians show by their *behavior* that "the work of the law is written on their hearts" (v. 15).[92] But here the outcome is expressed in an extraordinary question expecting a positive answer: "Will not his uncircumcision be counted as circumcision?" Paul uses the verb λογισθήσεται in this context to

---

[89] Cranfield (*Romans*, 1:172) suggests that the Jew's circumcision has not been annulled in God's sight but "he has become uncircumcised in heart (i.e., one whose heart is far from God and whose life is a contradiction of his membership of the Covenant people)." It might be better to say that such a person has never been circumcised inwardly and is no better than a Gentile in God's sight (cf. Eph 2:11–12).

[90] Moo, *Romans*, 169, citing Ed P. Sanders, *Paul and Palestinian Judaism: A Comparison of Patterns of Religion* (Philadelphia: Fortress, 1977), 157–82. See, however, Daniel Boyarin, *A Radical Jew: Paul and the Politics of Identity* (Berkley: University of California, 1994), 92–93.

[91] The term ἡ ἀκροβυστία literally means "the foreskin," but it is also used for the state of being uncircumcised and for the community of the uncircumcised or for individual Gentiles. Dunn (*Romans 1–8*, 119–20) provides Jewish and Greco-Roman evidence for the circumcision/uncircumcision distinction being used in Paul's time as equivalent to the Jew/Gentile distinction. Cf. Rom 3:30; Gal 2:7; Col 3:11.

[92] Windsor (*Vocation*, 145–46, 176–79) disputes the identification of v. 26 with the situation described in vv. 14–15. He contends that v. 26 simply reflects debates among Jews about whether Gentile proselytes needed to be circumcised. But Paul's escalating argument demands a more radical implication.

mean that God will "reckon," "count," or "credit" the uncircumcised man who keeps the law's requirements to be a member of his covenant people.[93] Rabbinic Judaism would have rejected this proposal, especially in view of the requirement about circumcising foreigners in Gen 17:12–14. But Paul explains his argument more fully in the rest of Romans. In 3:21–4:25 he indicates that Gentiles can be justified by faith together with Jews who trust in Jesus and thus be reckoned as Abraham's true descendants. The outcome of such a relationship with God is then revealed to be a life of faithful obedience to the will of God, directed and empowered by his Spirit (6:12–14; 7:4–6; 8:1–5; 12:1–2). In 11:25–32 he argues that even Jews who remain hardened against the gospel may yet come to experience God's mercy in Jesus the Messiah.

2:27. The Gentile Paul has in mind is now described as "a man who is physically uncircumcised, but who keeps the law" (ἡ ἐκ φύσεως ἀκροβυστία τὸν νόμον τελοῦσα).[94] The expression ἐκ φύσεως draws attention to the fact that the Gentile is "naturally" or "by virtue of [his] birth" uncircumcised (cf. φύσει, "by nature" in 2:14). Although it has been argued that "Gentiles keep the moral norms of the law, while the laws that culturally distinguished Jews from Gentiles, such as circumcision, are no longer in force (cf. 1 Cor 7:17),"[95] Paul nowhere suggests the need for a partial or nuanced attachment of Gentiles to the law. His previous claim that Gentile Christians "show that the work of the law is written on their hearts" (v. 15) points to the fact that what the law essentially required is produced by the Spirit in their lives (cf. 8:4; §1.4). When he claims that such a person will "judge" the Jew, he is not encouraging Gentiles to adopt a judgmental attitude toward unbelieving Jews (cf. 2:1–3; 11:17–24). As in Matt 12:41–42; Luke 11:31–32, the believing Gentile will function like "a witness for the prosecution in the sense

[93] Schreiner (*Romans*, 141) takes the future passive λογισθήσεται to refer to eschatological judgment, God being the implied agent (cf. Moo, *Romans*, 169n17; Byrne, *Romans*, 102). This fits the judgment context in Rom 2. Contrast Jewett, *Romans*, 233.

[94] The verb τελεῖν (BDAG, "to carry out an obligation or demand, carry out, accomplish, perform, fulfill, keep") is also used in connection with the law in Jas 2:8. As argued in n. 88 above, it parallels the other expressions Paul uses in vv. 13, 26 to describe faithful obedience rather than perfect obedience to the law. The participle is used conditionally here (Wallace, *Greek Grammar*, 632–33).

[95] Schreiner, *Romans*, 139.

that his obedience will be evidence of what the Jew ought to have been and could have been."[96]

The Jew who is identified as "a lawbreaker" (παραβάτην νόμου, cf. v. 25) is further described with a complex adjectival clause (τὸν διὰ γράμματος καὶ περιτομῆς, [lit.] "who through the letter and circumcision"). The preposition διά with the genitive may refer to attendant circumstances ("in spite of having the letter of the law and circumcision").[97] "The letter" may simply emphasize the written character of the law. Although the Jew has "the written code and circumcision" (NIV), he still fails to do what the law requires. But it is also possible to read the Greek construction instrumentally ("who through the letter of the law and circumcision is a transgressor"), suggesting that the Jew is at fault for taking the law literally and relying too much on the outward sign of circumcision.[98] The letter-Spirit contrast in vv. 28–29 is a salvation-historical one (cf. 7:6), and Paul prepares for that by identifying the law as "letter" in v. 27. The implied contrast in vv. 28–29 is between the externality of the law given to Israel on tablets of stone with the inward working of the Holy Spirit under the new covenant (cf. 2 Cor 3:3–11).

2:28–29. Paul turns from his second-person style of address to summarize in principle what it means to be a true Jew. The Greek in these verses is elliptical, requiring the translator to add words to bring out the meaning. So CSB draws a contrast between "a person who is a Jew outwardly" (ὁ ἐν τῷ φανερῷ Ἰουδαῖος) and "a person who is a Jew inwardly" (ὁ ἐν τῷ κρυπτῷ Ἰουδαῖος).[99] The difference

[96] Cranfield, *Romans*, 1:174. Cf. Jewett, *Romans*, 234. Dunn (*Romans 1–8*, 127) points out that the tables are neatly turned on the Jew who sits in judgment on others, and "the counsel for the prosecution (2:1–3) finds himself in the dock!"

[97] Cf. Cranfield, *Romans*, 1:174; Moo, *Romans*, 172–73; Schreiner, *Romans*, 139; Jewett, *Romans*, 234. Most English versions understand the expression in this way.

[98] Brian S. Rosner (*Paul and the Law: Keeping the Commandments of God*, NSBT 31 [Downers Grove: InterVarsity, 2013], 98–100) concludes that "the law, if not to blame, is at least complicit in the condemnation of the Jews." Dunn (*Romans 1–8*, 123) makes the point that "circumcision as valued typically within Judaism focused too much on the outward rite."

[99] The expression ὁ ἐν τῷ κρυπτῷ Ἰουδαῖος recalls the warning about God's judging "what people have kept secret" (v. 16, τὰ κρυπτὰ τῶν ἀνθρώπων). Windsor (*Vocation*, 183–89) contends that Paul redefines Jewish identity in these verses. The distinct privilege and vocation of Jews is realized "*apart from* the mainstream Jewish community, within the Christ-believing community" (emphasis in original).

is explained in terms of "[true] circumcision" being "not something visible in the flesh" (ἡ ἐν τῷ φανερῷ ἐν σαρκὶ περιτομή, [lit.] "outward circumcision in the flesh") but "of the heart—by the Spirit, not the letter" (περιτομὴ καρδίας ἐν πνεύματι οὐ γράμματι). Here Paul echoes the language of v. 27 but adds the perspective that circumcision of the heart is accomplished by the Spirit of God.[100] This recalls God's demand in Deut 10:16 ("circumcise your hearts"; cf. Lev 26:41) and his promise in Deut 30:6 ("The LORD your God will circumcise your heart and the hearts of your descendants"). Israel's failure to respond to this demand is picked up by Jeremiah (4:4; 9:26), who announces God's intention to transform the hearts of his people by the provision of a new covenant (Jer 31:33; cf. 24:7; 32:40). Ezekiel 36:26–27 makes a similar promise but clarifies that this profound change will be brought about by God's placing his Spirit within his people, causing them to follow his statutes and carefully observe his ordinances. In effect, Paul links these promises together and expects to see their fulfillment in the lives of Jews like himself, who have put their trust in Jesus and his saving work (cf. Phil 3:3). But Gentile believers can also experience the transforming work of the Holy Spirit as beneficiaries of the new covenant (vv. 14–15, 26–27; cf. 2 Cor 3:1–18; Col 2:11).[101]

A concluding clause describes the Jew who is "one inwardly" as a Jew whose "praise is not from people but from God." The Hebrew word for "Jew" (*yehudi*) is derived from "Judah" (*yehudah*), which sounds like the Hiphil form of the Hebrew verb "praise" (*yadah*). When Judah was named, his mother declared, "This time I will praise the LORD" (Gen 29:35). When his father was at the end of his life, he predicted, "Judah, your brothers will praise you" (Gen 49:8). This play on words is not obvious in Greek or English, but Paul

[100] It is unlikely that πνεῦμα means the human spirit here since the inwardness of this circumcision is expressed by καρδίας. In contrast with γράμμα, πνεῦμα most obviously refers to the Holy Spirit in 7:6; 2 Cor 3:6, and there is a link between true circumcision and the Holy Spirit in Phil 3:3. Cf. Moo, *Romans*, 174–75.

[101] See Peterson, *Transformed by God*, 17–43, for a review of OT teaching on this subject. Paul's combination of Jer 31:33 and Ezek 36:26–27 in 2 Cor 3:1–18 is critical for understanding new covenant allusions elsewhere in his writings (cf. *Transformed by God*, 105–55). Although Second Temple Judaism emphasized the need for a transformed heart, both spiritual and physical circumcision were considered necessary (e.g., Jub. 1:23; Odes Sol. 11.1–3; 1QS 5:5; 1QH 2:18; Philo, *Spec.* 1.1 §6; 1.61 §304–5; *Migr.* 16 §89–93).

presumes Jews will know the Hebrew significance of the name. It is natural to live for the praise of others and put great value on physical, visual, and ritual matters. Any form of religion can be captivating in that way. But the Jew whom God praises has something that can never be measured in such terms: "It is something hidden, of the heart, by the Spirit."[102] The true Jew lives to please God because he has been circumcised inwardly by the transforming work of the Holy Spirit. Jews who acknowledge Jesus as Messiah and enjoy the benefits of the new covenant cannot expect praise from fellow Jews who are resistant to the gospel, but they can certainly expect praise from God.[103] In the context of approaching judgment, "praise" from God will involve an eschatological reward (cf. 1 Cor 4:5; 1 Pet 1:7), equivalent to eternal life in 2:7, 10.

Bridge

As Paul exposes the false confidence that kept many of his fellow Jews from recognizing their need for salvation, he draws attention to their hypocrisy and failure to be true to God's calling. Although they were convinced about having "the embodiment of knowledge and truth in the law," they dishonored God by breaking his law. When they attempted to instruct Gentiles from the law, God was maligned. Positively, Paul suggests the possibility of fulfilling their identity and vocation by means of the new covenant gift of the Holy Spirit resulting from commitment to Jesus (cf. 2:29; 5:5; 8:14). Christians need to consider how these warnings and encouragements might be applicable to them. If we genuinely trust in Christ and are convinced about the truth of the gospel, we can rejoice to know God's will and share that knowledge with unbelievers. But if we fail to practice what we preach, the name of God will be blasphemed or derided by those we seek to influence. The hypocrisy of churchgoers in everyday life is often a significant obstacle in the way of others coming to faith. But Spirit-directed obedience honors God and demonstrates the transforming effect of being in Christ. Certainty about our relationship with God should not come from ceremonies,

[102] Dunn, *Romans 1–8*, 124. Jesus also challenged his contemporaries about accepting glory or praise from one another rather than seeking the glory that comes from God (John 5:41–44; cf. Matt 23:5–7; Mark 12:38–39). Cf. John 12:42–43.

[103] Cf. Kruse, *Romans* 157.

religious activities, or the praise of others. The sign of God's work in our heart is that we live for his praise and glory (cf. 15:8–12).

C. God's Righteousness in Judgment (3:1–20)

1 So what advantage does the Jew have? Or what is the benefit of circumcision? 2 Considerable in every way. First, they were
entrusted with the very words of God. 3 What then? If some were
unfaithful, will their unfaithfulness nullify God's faithfulness?
4 Absolutely not! Let God be true, even though everyone is a liar,
as it is written:

> **That you may be justified in your words**
> **and triumph when you judge.**

5 But if our unrighteousness highlights God's righteousness,
what are we to say? I am using a human argument: Is God unrighteous to inflict wrath? 6 Absolutely not! Otherwise, how will God
judge the world? 7 But if by my lie God's truth abounds to his glory, why am I also still being judged as a sinner? 8 And why not say,
just as some people slanderously claim we say, "Let us do what
is evil so that good may come"? Their condemnation is deserved!

9 What then? Are we any better off? Not at all! For we have
already charged that both Jews and Gentiles are all under sin, 10 as
it is written:

> **There is no one righteous, not even one.**
> 11 **There is no one who understands;**
> **there is no one who seeks God.**
> 12 **All have turned away;**
> **all alike have become worthless.**
> **There is no one who does what is good,**
> **not even one.**
> 13 **Their throat is an open grave;**
> **they deceive with their tongues.**
> **Vipers' venom is under their lips.**
> 14 **Their mouth is full of cursing and bitterness.**
> 15 **Their feet are swift to shed blood;**
> 16 **ruin and wretchedness are in their paths,**
> 17 **and the path of peace they have not known.**
> 18 **There is no fear of God before their eyes.**

19 Now we know that whatever the law says, it speaks to those
who are subject to the law, so that every mouth may be shut and

the whole world may become subject to God's judgment. [20]For no one will be justified in his sight by the works of the law, because the knowledge of sin comes through the law.

Context

This passage provides the final two segments of a concentric structure that began in 2:1 (see above commentary under III). Paul's insistence on God's righteousness in judgment (3:1–8) corresponds with his previous teaching about God's impartiality in judgment (2:6–11). The use of biblical citations to establish that "both Jews and Gentiles are all under sin" (3:9–20) supports his previous contention that Jews will be condemned if they do the same things as Gentiles (2:1–5). This whole section (2:1–3:20) continues the exposition of God's judgment against sin that began in 1:18–32, highlighting the profound consequences of rebellion against God in its Gentile and Jewish forms. But the wider unit (1:18–3:20) is bracketed by Paul's announcement that God's saving righteousness is revealed in the gospel (1:16–17), and the development of that theme in 3:21–26. So Paul's ultimate aim in 1:16–3:26 is to show how extensive and profound is the deliverance achieved by Christ. A specific link with the preceding section is provided by the questions in 3:1. A transition to the next section is indicated by the declaration in 3:20 that no person will be justified in God's sight by "works of the law."[104]

Structure

Paul uses a series of questions and answers to continue the debate with an imaginary Jewish opponent in 3:1–8. "Each set of questions is succinctly and vehemently answered before the next set begins."[105] Two introductory questions (v. 1) express objections that might be made to his argument in the preceding chapter: "What

[104] Dunn (*Romans 1–8*, 129–30) also notes how 3:1–8 provides a transitional bridge to later chapters, concluding that it is "like a railway junction through which many of the key ideas and themes of the epistle pass." Most obviously, 3:1–4 anticipates Romans 9–11 and 3:5–8 anticipates Romans 6–7.

[105] Jewett, *Romans*, 240. Jewett (239) observes four pairs of questions in 3:1–8 and argues that "the doubling of the questions gives the impression of satisfying completeness and matches the stylistic inclination of Greco-Romans rhetoric." Cf. Stanley K. Stowers, "Paul's Dialogue with a Fellow Jew in Romans 3:1–9," *CBQ* 46 (1984): 707–22.

advantage does the Jew have?" and "What is the benefit of circumcision?" Paul's emphatic answer ("considerable in every way") leads him to affirm only the truth that "they were entrusted with the very words of God" (v. 2). The next two questions take up the issue of Jewish unfaithfulness and God's faithfulness (v. 3). Paul asserts that God must be true, even though every human being is a liar, supporting this with a quote from Ps 51:4b. This gives rise to another pair of questions concerning God's righteousness in inflicting wrath (v. 5), followed by a question affirming God's right to judge the world (v. 6). A further question in v. 7 expresses in a different form the false proposal put forward in v. 5, asking, "If by my lie God's truth abounds to his glory, why am I also still being judged as a sinner?" This question is answered with a further question in v. 8, expressing a dangerous misrepresentation of Paul's teaching ("Let us do what is evil so that good may come"), which is summarily dismissed.

The second part of this passage begins with another pair of questions, restating the issue raised in v. 1 ("What then? Are we any better off?") or, if the verb is passive, raising a new possibility in the light of vv. 1–8 ("Are we [Jews] excelled [by Gentiles]?"). Paul's answer summarizes the argument in 1:18–2:29 by saying, "For we have already charged that both Jews and Gentiles are all under sin." This claim is then supported from biblical texts (vv. 10–18) woven together to emphasize the universality of sin and its impact on every aspect of human life. An abrupt change of style in v. 19 introduces Paul's conclusion. This carefully worded statement is linked to vv. 9–18 by the repetition of certain key words, but it also prepares for the argument to come in vv. 21–31 with four uses of νόμος ("law"), the expression ἔργων νόμου ("works of the law"), and the verb δικαιωθήσεται ("justified").

Outline:

1. God's righteous judgment is an expression of his faithfulness (vv. 1–8)
2. God's law makes everyone accountable to him (vv. 9–20)

3:1–2. The inferential conjunction οὖν ("therefore, so") introduces two questions that logically follow from the argument so far. If being a circumcised Jew provides no exemption from the judgment of God, "what advantage does the Jew have? Or what is the benefit of circumcision?"[106] God chose Abraham and his offspring to be his special possession among the nations and gave them circumcision as the sign of that covenanted relationship (Gen 17:1–14). But Paul has already made the point that circumcision is only a benefit "if you observe the law" (2:25). So now he considers the "advantage" (τὸ περισσόν) of the Jew over the Gentile but not the specific "benefit" (ἡ ὠφέλια) of circumcision (until 4:9–12). His brief but emphatic πολὺ κατὰ πάντα τρόπον ([lit.] "much in every way") introduces what looks like the first in a list of privileges (πρῶτον μέν, "first"), but only one is mentioned: "They were entrusted with the very words of God" (ἐπιστεύθησαν τὰ λόγια τοῦ θεοῦ).[107] Other advantages are listed in 9:4–5, all of which flow from receiving "the very words of God." The passive verb ἐπιστεύθησαν ("they were entrusted") implies a God-given responsibility to preserve and live in obedience to God's "oracles."[108] In ancient Greek literature, the singular noun λόγιον mostly referred to "short divine sayings" (BDAG). In Jewish and Christian circles the plural was used with reference to God's spoken and written words (e.g. Acts 7:38; Heb 5:12; 1 Pet 4:11). Here, τὰ λόγια τοῦ θεοῦ (lit., "the oracles of God") could simply refer to the promises of God,[109] but 2:17–29 points to Israel's unfaithfulness to God's *laws* as well as his promises. Furthermore, citations from the entire canon of OT Scripture are used in 3:19–21 to convict both Jews and Gentiles of their sin, suggesting that "the very words of God" means everything God revealed to his people (1:2, "the Holy Scriptures").

[106] The first of these rhetorical questions is answered in 3:1–20, and the second, in 3:27–4:12. They telegraph Paul's desire to attract attention to two new phases of his argument (cf. Runge, *Discourse Grammar*, 65).

[107] Jewett (*Romans*, 243–44) argues that Paul did not intend further enumeration and renders πρῶτον "primarily." But his translation is awkward and cumbersome. See my comment on πρῶτον μέν ("first") in 1:8.

[108] A passive form of the verb πιστεύειν with an accusative noun can also be found in 1 Cor 9:17; Gal 2:7; 1 Thess 2:4; 1 Tim 1:11, where the gospel or stewardship of the gospel is entrusted by God to Paul.

[109] Jewett (*Romans*, 243) follows Sam K. Williams ("The 'Righteousness of God' in Romans," *JBL* 99 [1980]: 267–68) in arguing that the "oracles of God" in Rom 3:2 refers to the divine promises regarding the salvation of Israel and the nations, but the flow of Paul's argument suggests a broader meaning.

3:3–4. An introductory question from an imaginary opponent (*τί γάρ*, "What then?") signals a new stage in the argument.[110] The related question is in the form of a conditional sentence. It picks up *ἐπιστεύθησαν* from v. 2 ("they were entrusted") and restates Paul's charge in 2:17–24 about the unfaithfulness of his fellow Jews to God's law (*εἰ ἠπίστησάν τινες*; "if some were unfaithful"). This forms the basis for a question expecting a negative answer, considering the impact of such behavior on the faithfulness of God (*μὴ ἡ ἀπιστία αὐτῶν τὴν πίστιν τοῦ θεοῦ καταργήσει*; [in effect]: "Their unfaithfulness will not cancel God's faithfulness, will it?"). The noun *πίστις* ranges in meaning from "faith" (as in 1:17) to "faithfulness." Although the verb *ἀπιστέω* strictly means "disbelieve, refuse to believe" and the noun *ἀπιστία* means "unbelief," these words can also be translated "be unfaithful" and "unfaithfulness" (BDAG). This is the best rendering when human behavior is contrasted with the faithfulness of God (cf. 2 Tim 2:13 [*πιστός*]). God's faithfulness is extensively proclaimed throughout Scripture. It is experienced in the created order and in his special commitment to the welfare of his chosen people (e.g., Ps 33:4; Lam 3:23; Hos 2:20; 1 Cor 1:9; 10:13; 2 Cor 1:18).[111]

Beginning with the emphatic *μὴ γένοιτο* ("absolutely not!"), Paul denies the possibility that God's faithfulness may somehow be invalidated or nullified (*καταργήσει*) by human sin.[112] In chapters 9–11 he argues that God's saving plan has not even been frustrated by the failure of Jews to respond to the gospel about their Messiah (11:17, using *τινες* ["some"] as here). Paul asserts God's faithfulness as strongly as any covenant-conscious Jew, but in what follows he

[110] Jewett (*Romans*, 244) argues that *τί γάρ* should not be read as a separate question or as the introduction to a single question in v. 3. Rather, it introduces the first question ("What then if some were unfaithful?"), which is directly related to Paul's answer in v. 2 about "the oracles of God being given in faith to the Jews."

[111] The Hebrew word for faithfulness (אֱמוּנָה) denotes firmness and reliability. This is translated by *πίστις* and *ἀλήθεια* in the LXX. Cf. Kevin W. McFadden, "Does ΠΙΣΤΙΣ Mean Faith(fulness) in Paul?" *TynBul* 66 (2015): 251–70.

[112] The verb *κατεργεῖν* here probably means "to cause something to lose its power or effectiveness, invalidate, make powerless" (as in 3:31; 4:14), though it can have the stronger sense of causing something "to come to an end or to be no longer in existence, abolish, wipe out, set aside" (BDAG; CSB ["nullify"]; cf. 6:6; 1 Cor 13:11; 15:24, 26; Heb 2:14). The strong negation *μὴ γένοιτο* is used frequently in Romans after rhetorical questions (3:6, 31; 6:2, 15; 7:7, 13; 9:14; 11:1, 11).

highlights "God's faithfulness as righteous Creator and Judge, and not just as God of Israel."[113] The imperative expression γινέσθω δὲ ὁ θεὸς ἀληθής ("let God be true") could simply be "a vigorous way of stating the true situation after the emphatic rejection of an altogether false suggestion."[114] But the truthfulness of God is another way of speaking about his faithfulness (cf. ἀλήθεια in Pss 89:1–2 [LXX 88:2–3]; 98:3 [LXX 97:3]). In 2:2 God's judgment was said to be κατὰ ἀλήθειαν ([lit.] "according to truth"), and here Paul asserts that God must be "true" even though every person proves to be a liar (πᾶς δὲ ἄνθρωπος ψεύστης). These last words recall an observation in Ps 116:11 (LXX 115:2) about the extent of human dishonesty, and they echo Paul's earlier discussion about those who suppress or disobey the truth (1:18, 25; 2:8, 20). This accusation clearly applies to Gentiles as well as to Jews. God's faithfulness is a fundamental aspect of his character that cannot be set aside or modified under any circumstance!

So important is this assertion that the apostle backs it up with a citation of Ps 51:4b (MT 51:6; LXX 50:6b): "that you may be justified in your words and triumph when you judge." This is introduced by the now familiar καθὼς γέγραπται ("as it is written", cf. 1:17; 2:24), confirming the scriptural origin and authority of the words.[115] The expression ὅπως ἂν with the subjunctive normally indicates purpose ("in order that you might be justified"). Although there is debate about the best way to interpret the text in its original context, in the sequence of Paul's argument its function is to relate God's faithfulness to his righteousness in judgment.[116] "The oracles of God" contain many warnings of judgment as well as promises of blessing: "God is equally faithful when he judges his people's

---

[113] Dunn, *Romans 1–8*, 129.

[114] Cranfield, *Romans*, 1:181. The verb does not convey any sense of "becoming" here. Cranfield suggests that it effectively means "we confess rather that God is true."

[115] The variant καθάπερ ("even as") is found in some Greek manuscripts (cf. 4:6; 9:13; 10:15; 11:8; 12:4, where there is a similar divergence in the textual tradition). Jewett (*Romans*, 238) argues that the comparative function of καθώς "seems slightly awkward in the context of the citation it introduces and thus should be preferred as the more difficult reading."

[116] Moo (*Romans*, 187n50) discusses a variety of possible meanings. Marvin E. Tate (*Psalms 51–100*, WBC 20 [Dallas: Word, 1990], 17–18) argues that it is best to read a result clause in both the Hebrew and the Greek version of the psalm. Cf. Schreiner, *Romans*, 151–52, 159–60.

sin and when he fulfills his promises."[117] Three significant verbs are used in the psalm text. The first is δικαιωθῇς ("be justified"), which is the second occurrence of a key term in the argument of Romans (cf. 2:13 comment; 3:20, 24 comment, 26, 28, 30; 4:2, 5; 5:1, 9; 6:7; 8:30, 33), not always with the same meaning. Here God is justified or "proved to be right" (BDAG) in his "words" (ἐν τοῖς λόγοις σου), which contextually means when he pronounces judgment. The second and third verbs confirm that he will "triumph" when he "judges" (νικήσεις ἐν τῷ κρίνεσθαί σε). CSB has rightly taken κρίνεσθαι as a middle ("when you judge") rather than as a passive ("when you are judged").[118] In the context of Paul's argument with a Jewish objector, he alludes to this confession by David, who made no attempt to argue a special relationship, prerogative, or merit as a way of averting God's wrath. David "accepted God's condemnation as wholly justified."[119]

3:5–6. The next question picks up the language of justification from the psalm citation (δικαιωθῇς). Seeing that a false inference could be drawn from what he has just said, the apostle introduces another conditional sentence, assuming for the sake of the argument that our unrighteousness (ἀδικία) highlights or establishes God's righteousness.[120] Once again this could be reflecting the sort of challenges presented to him by opponents. The term θεοῦ δικαιοσύνη ("the righteousness of God") was discussed in connection with 1:17, where it was argued that we need a definition that adequately accounts for Paul's emphasis on God's righteousness in

---

[117] Moo, *Romans*, 188. Cf. Neh 9:32–33; Lam 1:18. Moo points out that this becomes a key motif in Pss. Sol. 2:18; 3:5; 4:8; 8:7, where δικαιόω ("be just," "justify") is used, as in Ps 51:4b (LXX 50:6b), to state the "justness" of God in his judgment of his people.

[118] Cf. Cranfield, *Romans*, 1:182n4. Paul's citation of LXX Ps 50:6b is exact, except that he has the future indicative νικήσεις instead of the subjunctive νικήσῃς. Some manuscripts of Romans have the subjunctive, but the indicative is the harder reading and more likely to be what Paul actually wrote. Moo (*Romans*, 186n49) compares the LXX with the Hebrew text, where תִּזְכֶּה means "in the clear."

[119] Dunn, *Romans 1–8*, 140.

[120] The verb συνίστησιν here means "provide evidence of a personal characteristic or claim through action, demonstrate, show, bring out" (BDAG, cf. 5:8; 2 Cor 6:4; 7:11; Gal 2:18). This is the protasis of a first-class condition in form, even though the assumption it contains is false (cf. Wallace, *Greek Grammar*, 762–63).

both judgment and salvation.[121] In the present context, God's righteous judgment is the primary focus, though the parallel with God's faithfulness (v. 3) might also suggest that the saving dimension of his righteousness is in view. God's righteousness cannot simply be equated with his faithfulness, though a certain overlap of meaning is suggested by the use of the terms together in some contexts (e.g., Pss 33:4–5; 36:5–7; 98:2–3; Isa 51:1–6).[122] Here the expression points to the fact that God rules his creation with justice and intends to subdue all forms of opposition to his rule (cf. Pss 96:10–13; 97:2, 6–9; 98:7–9). In 3:21–26 the saving aspect of God's righteousness comes more to the fore.

The second part of Paul's conditional sentence begins with an attention-grabbing question ("What are we to say?" cf. vv. 3, 9). This introduces the real question he wishes to pose, expecting a negative answer (μὴ ἄδικος ὁ θεὸς ὁ ἐπιφέρων τὴν ὀργήν; "Is God unrighteous to inflict wrath?"). This is immediately qualified by the claim that he is using "a human argument" (κατὰ ἄνθρωπον λέγω, [lit.] "I speak in a human way").[123] Denying the proposal emphatically (μὴ γένοιτο [see on v. 4]), Paul asks a further question (v. 6, ἐπεὶ πῶς κρινεῖ ὁ θεὸς τὸν κόσμον; "Otherwise, how will God judge the world?"). It is a biblical axiom that God must judge the world and that he will do this with perfect justice (e.g., Gen 18:25; Deut 32:4; Job 8:3; Pss 96:10–13; 97:2, 6–9; 98:7–9). To deny the righteousness of God in inflicting wrath is to deny God the role of judge in his creation.

3:7. The first of two other linked questions expresses in different terms the false proposal put forward in v. 5: "But if by my lie God's truth abounds to his glory, why am I also still being judged as a sinner?"[124] The expression "God's truth" (ἡ ἀλήθεια τοῦ θεοῦ)

---

[121] Cf. Seifrid, "Paul's Use of Righteousness Language," 39–74. John Piper (*The Justification of God: An Exegetical and Theological Study of Romans 9:1–23*, 2nd ed. [Grand Rapids: Baker, 1993], 133) similarly argues that in 3:2–4 "God's righteousness embraces both his gracious faithfulness to his promises and his punitive judgment on sin."

[122] Righteousness language applied to God in Scripture may allude to his character or to the defining actions by which his righteousness is experienced (cf. David J. Reimer, "צדק," *NIDOTTE* 3:752). Cf. §2.4.

[123] Cranfield (*Romans*, 1:184) takes this to mean "a thought which is all too human in its weakness and folly."

[124] The connective δέ ("and, but") is more likely to be original in v. 7 even though the alternative γάρ ("for") is widely attested and would be the harder reading. The

refers to "God's faithfulness" (v. 3, τὴν πίστιν τοῦ θεοῦ), which is equated with his being "true" (v. 4, ἀληθής). It is a further reference to his character, as revealed in Scripture, which involves a commitment to fulfil his own promises and warnings. "By my lie" (ἐν τῷ ἐμῷ ψεύσματι) picks up Paul's claim about everyone being "a liar" (v. 4, ψεύστης) and the preceding discussion about different ways human beings suppress or disobey the truth (1:18, 25; 2:8, 20). Paul adopts the position of a Jewish opponent when he introduces the first-person singular (κἀγὼ ὡς ἁμαρτωλὸς κρίνομαι: "Why am I also still being judged as a sinner?"). But his opponent's question plays down the seriousness of the situation by asking how a Jew could be blamed when his faithlessness "abounds" (ἐπερίσσευσεν) to God's glory. The assumption is that his sin "serves to display God's glory when he forgives his people,"[125] but the rhetorical effect is to show the absurdity of the conclusion. In fact, God is glorified when his faithfulness in judging his people is manifested. Paul's dialogue partner reflects the sort of misrepresentation of the gospel reflected in the next verse.

3:8. The apostle's introductory words indicate how he personally felt about the charge of antinomianism being leveled at him ("And why not say, just as some people slanderously claim we say").[126] His use of βλασφημούμεθα ([lit.] "we are slandered") is particularly striking, suggesting that he was both sensitive about this false claim and personally demeaned by it.[127] The first-person plural possibly includes his mission partners, and even the Roman Christians, as recipients of this slander. In essence his opponents were saying that he or they proclaimed, "Let us do what is evil that good may come" (ποιήσωμεν τὰ κακά, ἵνα ἔλθῃ τὰ ἀγαθά). When

---

latter obscures the parallel between v. 5 and v. 7 and suggests the introduction of a new argument. Cf. Metzger, *Textual Commentary*, 448.

[125] Stowers, "Paul's Dialogue," 718. Jewett (*Romans*, 249) takes the first-person references to be literal rather than fictive or hypothetical and translates the emphatic τί ἔτι κἀγὼ ὡς ἁμαρτωλὸς κρίνομαι: "Why then should *I* be judged as a sinner?" Cf. Cranfield, *Romans*, 1.185.

[126] Cranfield (*Romans*, 1:186) observes that "the construction of the verse is unusually clumsy and tangled" and discusses different ways it could be punctuated.

[127] With reference to human beings, as in this verse, βλασφημέω means, "to speak in a disrespectful way that demeans, denigrates, maligns" (BDAG). Used in relation to pagan deities or the God of the Bible, it means, "slander, revile, defame, speak irreverently/impiously/disrespectfully of or about" (as in 2:24).

they heard the teaching about salvation by grace alone, they misunderstood this to be promoting lawlessness.[128] In Paul's gospel "the good" (τὰ ἀγαθά) would include justification by faith and vindication at the ultimate judgment of God. So his opponents concluded that sin could be encouraged because it allowed God to show mercy! This was a dangerous misrepresentation of Paul's teaching, and he simply concludes, "Their condemnation is deserved" (ὧν τὸ κρίμα ἔνδικόν ἐστιν). "All the moral force of the Judeo-Christian tradition of a righteous God who maintains the right in God's judgment lies behind this short final sentence."[129] When God justifies someone by faith (3:28), he intends to promote righteous behavior, not lawlessness (cf. 6:1–4, 15–19).

3:9. Paul's engagement with a Jewish objector continues with an introductory question, (Τί οὖν: "What then?"), clearly linking the next question to the preceding argument. But there is debate about the precise meaning of the verb προεχόμεθα here.[130] Most translators and commentators understand it as a middle form with an active meaning (CSB: "Are we any better off?"). It is possible, however, to read this as a passive meaning, "Are we excelled?" (ESV margin: "Are we at any disadvantage?").[131] As a sequel to the demolition of the objector's position in vv. 1–8, the question could be asking whether Jews are actually worse off than Gentiles! A decision

---

[128] Schreiner (*Romans*, 153–54) argues that Paul's opponents here were probably Jewish, who "accused Paul of teaching an antinomian gospel because of his emphasis on divine sovereignty and the inability of human beings to keep God's law." These adversaries "drew out what they believed were the logical implications of the Pauline gospel in order to reject its validity."

[129] Jewett, *Romans*, 251–52. The noun κρίμα may refer to the legal decision rendered by a judge (BDAG), who is most obviously God in this context (cf. 5:16). Dunn (*Romans 1–8*, 143) concludes, "Anyone who could think Paul was so perverse in his reasoning is hardly worth arguing with!"

[130] Among a series of textual variations, the best attested option is προεχόμεθα οὐ πάντως, which is also the most difficult reading. Cf. Cranfield, *Romans*, 1:187–89; Jewett, *Romans*, 253.

[131] The case for the former is argued by Cranfield (*Romans*, 1.188–90); Schreiner, *Romans*, 162–63, and Kruse, *Romans*, 163–64. The case for the latter is argued by Jewett (*Romans*, 256–57), who cites BDAG and agrees with Fitzmyer (*Romans*, 331) that this best suits this "climactic question in Paul's dialogue with the Jewish interlocutor." Dunn (*Romans 1–8*, 146–48) understands it as a genuine middle and renders the whole expression, "What then do we put forward on our own behalf?" But this involves a tortuous exegesis of the verse.

between these alternatives is difficult, though both lead to the same conclusion (οὐ πάντως, "not at all!").[132]

Paul claims that in his argument so far he has "already charged that both Jews and Greeks are all under sin." In other words, neither Jews nor Greeks have any advantage because of the controlling power of sin in their lives. As in 1:16, the formula Ἰουδαίους τε καὶ Ἕλληνας ("both Jews and Greeks") highlights the major cultural and religious backgrounds from which the Roman Christians would have come. But CSB renders the expression "both Jews and Gentiles," understanding that Paul intended to expose the sinfulness of the nations more generally ("Greeks" being a metonym for "Gentiles"). The verb προῃτιασάμεθα does not appear in extant literature until later than Paul's era, but by etymology it means "ask beforehand," and so "reach a charge of guilt prior to an implied time" (BDAG).[133] In God's indictment of the nations, Paul has already set forth the charges in his argument thus far.

The noun "sin" (ἁμαρτία) is used for the first time here in Romans, though the verb "sinned" was introduced in 2:12 and the noun "sinner" in 3:5. In fact, the character of sin in its various manifestations has been explored from 1:18, where Paul employs the related terms "unrighteousness" (ἀδικία, cf. 1:29; 2:8; 3:5) and "godlessness" (ἀσέβεια). The notion of being "under sin" (ὑφ' ἁμαρτίαν) surfaces again in 7:14 (cf. Gal 3:22). With the early chapters of Genesis particularly in view, sin is portrayed as a power controlling human life and directing people away from honoring and serving God (cf. 5:12–21; 6:12–23; Sir 21:2; 27:10; 1 QH 1:27; 4:29–30). The sweeping declaration that "all" (πάντας) are under the power of sin "means that they participate in various cultures of lies from

---

[132] Strictly speaking, οὐ πάντως means "not altogether" (1 Cor 5:10) and πάντως οὐ means "altogether not" (1 Cor 16:12), but Jewett (*Romans*, 257) gives evidence for the former being used in diatribes to mean "not at all." Cf. Moo, *Romans*, 200n16; Schreiner, *Romans*, 163–64.

[133] The first person plural is most obviously an epistolary plural, referring to Paul alone (cf. Wallace, *Greek Grammar*, 394–96). Stowers's view (*Rereading Romans*, 180) that "the plural is a dialogical 'we,' that is, 'I Paul, and you, the interlocutor, in our discussion have already concluded'" seems unlikely because the dialogue with the Jew has really only taken place in 2:1–3:8, with the case against Gentiles being made by Paul in another way in 1:18–32. So Jewett (*Romans*, 257–58) really has no basis for concluding that Paul's conversation partner has dramatically changed his opinion.

which they do not seem to be able to escape without outside exposure and intervention."[134]

3:10–12. The claim that "both Jews and Gentiles are all under sin" is supported by a catena (linked collection) of biblical texts in vv. 10–18, beginning with the words καθὼς γέγραπται ("as it is written," cf. 2:24; 3:4).[135] The topic sentence is adapted from Eccl 7:20 ("There is certainly no righteous man on the earth who does good and never sins"), abbreviated to read οὐκ ἔστιν δίκαιος οὐδὲ εἷς ("There is no one righteous, not even one"). Here we have the first of six uses of the expression οὐκ ἔστιν ("there is not," vv. 10, 11, 12, 18), which reinforces the claim of v. 9 (πάντας, "all") and ties these texts together. Paul focuses on identifying the universal characteristics of "the wicked" and says nothing about "the righteous" who are mentioned in some of the psalms from which he quotes.[136] This selective approach enables him to say that, if human behavior is the measure of righteousness, all are condemned. When he later speaks about those who are righteous by faith, he makes clear that both Abraham and David needed to believe in the one who "declares the ungodly to be righteous" and forgives sin (4:5–10).

Linking Eccl 7:20 to a slightly emended version of LXX Ps 13:2–3 (ET 14:1–3; cf. 53:2–3 [LXX 52:3–4]), Paul effectively defines unrighteousness in terms of not understanding or seeking after God. The psalm is about the fool who says in his heart "God does not exist." It portrays the kind of foolishness outlined in 1:18–32, where the practical consequences of turning away from the true and living God are outlined. Following his disclosure of Jewish hypocrisy, unfaithfulness, and unrighteousness (2:1–3:8), the apostle uses this text with reference to *all* who fail to understand and truly seek after God (cf. 2 Chr 12:14; 15:13; 16:12). Paul simplifies

---

[134] Jewett, *Romans*, 259. Paul's view of sin involves more than transgression of God's law: Paul has chosen to conceptualize sin as "an enslaving master" (Moo, *Romans*, 201n20). Cf. Walter Grundmann, "ἁμαρτάνω κτλ.," *TDNT* 1:309.

[135] Cranfield (*Romans*, 1.192) observes that this collection of texts may already have been in use in Christian circles and that Paul adapted it for his purpose. However, Jewett (*Romans*, 254n3) presents reasons for believing it originated in Jewish circles. I discuss Paul's use of Scripture in §2.2.

[136] Cf. Davies, *Faith and Obedience*, 80–104. Schreiner (*Romans*, 167–68) contends that Paul deliberately uses passages about the wicked to show that the sin of Jews places them in the same situation as Gentiles: guilty before God. Cf. Moo, *Romans*, 202–3.

and abbreviates the second verse of the psalm and then cites the third verse almost exactly: "There is no one who understands, there is no one who seeks God. All have turned away; all alike have become worthless. There is no one who does what is good, not even one."[137]

3:13–14. The first two lines of the next citation correspond with LXX Ps 5:10 (ET 5:9) and focus on the deadly effects of speech ("Their throat is an open grave; they deceive with their tongues"). Just as an open grave can allow pollution to spread or cause injury to people who stumble into it, so dishonest speech can damage those who encounter it. Paul reported his own experience of such slander in 3:8, most likely from Jewish opponents. A line from LXX Ps 139:4 (ET 140:3) is added to reinforce the poisonous consequences of different patterns of speech ("Vipers' venom is under their lips"). A fitting conclusion to this focus on sinful speech is provided by an adaptation of LXX Ps 9:28 (ET 10:7, οὗ ἀρᾶς τὸ στόμα αὐτοῦ γέμει, "His mouth is full of cursing"), expressed as ὧν τὸ στόμα ἀρᾶς καὶ πικρίας γέμει ("Their mouth is full of cursing and bitterness"). A shift from the singular to the plural brings the citation in line with the "all" in v. 12 and the plurals of v. 13. Destructive speech is a universal human problem (cf. Jas 3:1–12).

3:15–18. An abridgement of LXX Isa 59:7–8a follows, identifying the violence that was sadly evident in Israel's life and brought the judgment of the Babylonian exile upon them: "Their feet are swift to shed blood; ruin and wretchedness are in their paths, and the path of peace they have not known." Finally, a slight modification of LXX Ps 35:2b (ET 36:1b) restates the idea of not seeking God ("There is no fear of God before their eyes").[138] This forms an inclusio with v. 11. The psalm begins with the words "an oracle within my heart concerning the transgression of the wicked" and goes on to describe the self-deceit and maliciousness of those have stopped acting wisely and doing good. From Israel's own Scriptures Paul

[137] The second instance of οὐκ ἔστιν ("there is not") in 3:12 is missing in a few manuscripts (B 1739 syr^{p} Origen). Normally the shorter reading would be preferred, the longer reading being understood as an assimilation to Ps 13:3 LXX. However, in this case Metzger (*Textual Commentary*, 448–49) argues that the longer reading is to be preferred, supported as it is by the mass of witnesses.

[138] As with the adaptation of LXX Ps 9:28 (10:7) in v. 14, a shift from the singular to the plural brings the citation in line with the "all" in v. 12 and the plurals of v. 13.

points to the same sinfulness among his own people as was evident among the Gentiles.[139]

3:19. CSB rightly translates the conjunction δέ "now" to signal a new development in the argument.[140] The apostle appeals to a knowledge shared with his readers ("Now we know that," as in 2:2), namely, God's purpose in giving "the law" to Israel. Following the citations from Ecclesiastes, Psalms, and Isaiah, it is possible that ὁ νόμος refers to the whole body of Scripture here, previously identified as "the very words of God" (3:2).[141] God's chosen people are described as "those who are subject to the law" (τοῖς ἐν τῷ νόμῳ), which in the broadest sense may mean those who live "within the sphere of the revelation of God given in the Scripture/law."[142] However, as the argument in vv. 19–20 develops, it becomes clear that Paul focuses more narrowly on "the law" as a collection of commandments and judgments. As a revelation of the character and will of God, the law showed the standard by which his people would be judged (2:12), and "the whole world" would become accountable to God. This should have happened as Israel taught and lived in obedience to the law of God (cf. 2:17–24). A specific link to vv. 10–18 is provided by the repetition of certain key words (στόμα ["mouth"], as in v. 14, and three variations of πᾶς ["all, every"], as in vv. 9, 12). The purpose clause incorporating these key words has two parts.

First, it is said that God's law was given "so that *every* mouth may be shut" (ἵνα πᾶν στόμα φραγῇ). The image here is of people being prevented from speaking with no more challenges or objections being voiced (cf. Job 5:16; Pss 63:11; 107:42). Convicted of their sin, God's people were meant to see their need for his mercy, which would ultimately be expressed in the work of Christ. Second, it is said that "the whole world may become subject to God's

[139] Dunn's claim that Paul turns the tables on "Jewish overconfidence in their nation's favored status before God" (*Romans 1–8*, 151) leaves the issue at a corporate, covenantal level. This ignores the rhetoric in 2:17–29, which is clearly addressed to Jews individually, and focuses on the sort of moral failure described in 3:10–18.

[140] Cf. Runge, *Discourse Grammar*, 28–36.

[141] Compare the use of νόμος with reference to Scripture other than the Pentateuch in John 10:34; 15:25; 1 Cor 14:21. This reflects wider Jewish usage of the term (cf. Str-B 3:159, 463).

[142] Moo, *Romans*, 205. Moo concludes that the passages quoted in vv. 10–18, "while not all originally directed to Israel as a whole, are, indeed, 'speaking to' the Jews generally. They cannot be excluded from the scope of sin."

judgment" (ὑπόδικος γένηται πᾶς ὁ κόσμος τῷ θεῷ). The law was given to silence human presumption in its Jewish and Gentile forms and to convince people everywhere of their culpability before God (ὑπόδικος, "liable to punishment" [BDAG]).[143] Jews cannot claim a special exemption at the judgment seat of God since the oracles entrusted to them (3:2) expose their own transgressions. Their testimony to the nations lacked this essential message because they had not first grasped it for themselves.

3:20. A further explanation of the preceding verse is provided by a sentence beginning with the conjunction διότι ("for, because"). Paul adapts Ps 143:2 (LXX 142:2) to read οὐ δικαιωθήσεται πᾶσα σὰρξ ἐνώπιον αὐτοῦ ("no one will be justified in his sight"),[144] recalling the claim that began his catena of citations in 3:10 ("There is no one righteous, not even one"). Aware of his own unrighteousness, the psalmist asks the Lord not to enter into judgment with him, confessing that, like the rest of humanity, he cannot hope to be acquitted or vindicated. Most importantly, Paul's allusion to Ps 143:2 adds that justification by God (cf. 2:13; 3:24, 26, 28, 30; 4:2, 5; 5:1, 9; 6:7; 8:30, 33) will not take place "by the works of the law" (ἐξ ἔργων νόμου, cf. 3:27, 28; Gal 2:16 [3 times]; 3:2, 5, 10). As in 2:13, the future tense of the verb δικαιωθήσεται ("will be justified") could refer to the ultimate verdict of God, or the meaning could be logical and refer to a present possibility, as Paul's concluding clause suggests.

The expression ἐξ ἔργων νόμου narrows the focus of νόμος to the demands of God in the law and is obviously designed to challenge any sense of special exemption for Jews. This term is introduced without explanation, and so the apostle must have expected that its meaning was well-known or largely made clear by the context.[145] It

---

[143] Christian Maurer ("ὑπόδικος," *TDNT* 8:558) says this word conveys "the state of an accused person who cannot reply at the trial initiated against him because he has exhausted all possibilities of refuting the charge against him and averting the condemnation and its consequences which ineluctably follow."

[144] Paul's version changes the word order, makes the pronoun third person instead of second person, and substitutes the expression πᾶσα σάρξ ("all flesh"; cf. Gal 2:16) for πᾶς ζῶν ("everyone alive"), thus highlighting human weakness and corruptibility (cf. Gen 6:12, 17; 7:21; 9:11). Cf. Richard B. Hays, *Echoes of Scripture in the Letters of Paul* (New Haven: Yale University, 1989), 51–53.

[145] Seifrid ("Unrighteous by faith," 141) makes this point and argues that "works of the law" must mean deeds of obedience to the law's demands, "which were thought

is sometimes rendered "nomistic service," meaning "a mode of existence marked out in its distinctiveness as determined by the law."[146] In particular it is argued that this involved observing "boundary markers" such as Sabbath keeping, circumcision, and food laws, which distinguished Jews from Gentiles. But the apostle has not simply been concerned to expose Jewish false confidence in the observance of covenantal boundary markers. He has highlighted the hypocrisy of Jews who condemn the behavior of Gentiles while doing exactly what they do and who fail in their everyday lives to be genuinely different: "a guide for the blind, a light to those in darkness" (2:19). The term "works" appears to be a substitute for "works of the law" more generally in 4:2, 6; 9:11, 32; 11:6, where the contrast is fundamentally with faith and grace (cf. Eph 2:8–10).[147]

The reason (γάρ, "because") justification cannot be on the basis of "works of the law" is that "the knowledge of sin comes through the law" (διὰ γὰρ νόμου ἐπίγνωσις ἁμαρτίας, cf. 4:15; 5:13; 7:13). Sin, not human righteousness, is revealed through the law (see §1.4). "The law was *not* intended to provoke a sense of merit and security, but to make those to whom it was addressed conscious of the fact that even as members of the people of God their continuing need of grace was no different from that of the gentile sinner."[148] Put another way, Paul is opposing

---

to secure or confirm divine favor." However, without belief in the oracles of God that speak of human failure, "works of the law" cannot bring justification but only "the experiential knowledge of sin as a comprehensive and therefore enslaving reality."

[146] Dunn, *Romans 1–8*, 154; cf. lxiii–lxxii. Dunn (155) argues that Paul's target is "the devout Jew in his presumption that as a member of the covenant people he could expect God's righteousness to be put forth in his favor because he was 'within the law.'" Dunn (158–59) contends that "works of the law" operate at the level of "the letter" (2:27, 29), "an outward mark indicative of ethnic solidarity (2:28), something more limited than 'the patient perseverance in good work' (2:7)." Cf. Wright, "Romans," 459–61. Gathercole (*Boasting*, 218–22, 248–49) critiques this argument, as do Moo, *Romans*, 206–17; Byrne, *Romans*, 120–21; and Schreiner, *Romans*, 169–73.

[147] Cf. I. Howard Marshall, "Salvation, Grace and Works in the Later Writings in the Pauline Corpus," *NTS* 42 (1996): 339–58. Moo (*Romans*, 209) argues that "works of the law" are simply "good works" defined in Jewish terms ("things done in obedience to the law").

[148] Dunn, *Romans 1–8*, 156; cf. 160; Schreiner, *Romans*, 172.

a Jewish confidence at the final judgment that is based on election in conjunction with obedient fulfilment of the Torah. Paul is trying to persuade his interlocutor that his sin runs much deeper than he thought, and so the interlocutor's obedience to Torah is by no means comprehensive enough for his justification. Rather, because of his lack of repentance (and thus, lack of qualification for atonement), he is storing up wrath (2:5).[149]

Bridge

Paul demonstrates how the failure of Jews to be true to their calling highlights the faithfulness and righteousness of God in dealing with his people. In so doing he exposes the sort of objections to the gospel he had to deal with in the course of his ministry. Paul's argument challenges those who want to avoid any sense of accountability to God or who use clever arguments to justify their hypocrisy and unbelief. Biblical revelation was given to expose sin, not to provide a means of self-justification. By bringing condemnation to Israel first and then to the nations, the law testified to the need of all for the manifestation of the righteousness of God in the saving work of the Messiah (3:21–31). In today's world people continue to ignore God and the challenge of the gospel. Some see no need to rely on God's merciful provision in Jesus Christ because of their own beliefs and achievements. Such false confidence may be based on religious activity that is divorced from a genuine relationship with God. Others distort the gospel and claim immunity from judgment because of a simplistic view of the love of God. Many use deceptive moral and intellectual arguments to challenge the truthfulness of the Christian position, to malign believers, and to justify their own unbelief and rebellion against God. Paul's use of Scripture in this passage invites us to examine the depths of sin in our own lives, to challenge the superficial and self-serving views of unbelievers, and to demonstrate the universal need for the gospel of grace.

[149] Gathercole, *Boasting*, 214–15. Gathercole (223) argues, "The statement in 3:20 makes perfect sense as a denial that 'flesh' can be justified through an obedience to the terms of the Torah" (cf. Rom 7; 8:3, 7).

IV. God's Saving Righteousness Revealed: The Redemptive Sacrifice That Makes Justification Possible (3:21–26)

After a long defensive argument with an imaginary Jewish opponent (2:1–3:20), Paul provides a short but memorable exposition of the gospel he proclaims, developing some of the themes announced in 1:16–17 (see §2.1). He has brought his readers to face the reality of sin in its various manifestations and the prospect of divine judgment for Jews and Gentiles alike, notwithstanding any human achievement. Now he celebrates the revelation of the righteousness of God in Jesus Christ, making possible the salvation of all who believe. Paul adopts an elevated style for "the exposition of a vivid and elevated subject matter."[1] The passage reads like a solemn proclamation and forms the theological heart of Paul's message in the body of this letter. Some have argued that a pre-Pauline formula such as a hymn is adapted by the apostle to suit his purpose here, but "it is very much more probable that these verses are Paul's own independent and careful composition reflecting his own preaching and thinking."[2] In later expository sections (5:1–11; 6:1–23; 8:1–39), the apostle continues to establish the coherence and efficacy of his gospel before resuming a more defensive approach in each of the passages that follow (cf. Introduction II.C). So in the present context his celebration of the saving righteousness of God (3:21–26) introduces a segment in which God's people are defined by faith in Christ, not racial descent or obedience to the Mosaic law (3:27–4:25).

> 21 But now, apart from the law, the righteousness of God has
> been revealed, attested by the Law and the Prophets. 22 The righ-
> teousness of God is through faith in Jesus Christ to all who be-
> lieve, since there is no distinction. 23 For all have sinned and fall
> short of the glory of God. 24 They are justified freely by his grace
> through the redemption that is in Christ Jesus. 25 God presented
> him as an atoning sacrifice in his blood, received through faith,
> to demonstrate his righteousness, because in his restraint God
> passed over the sins previously committed. 26 God presented him

[1] Jewett, *Romans*, 269.

[2] Cranfield, *Romans*, 1:200n1. Jewett (*Romans*, 270–71) outlines how Paul may have adopted pre-Pauline material in writing this letter. But see Schreiner, *Romans*, 187–89. Moo (*Romans*, 220–21) argues that Paul wrote these verses "in dependence on a certain Jewish-Christian interpretation of Jesus' death."

to demonstrate his righteousness at the present time, so that he would be righteous and declare righteous the one who has faith in Jesus.

Context

A contrast with the preceding argument is suggested by the introductory words "but now" (v. 21) and the expression "apart from the law" (cf. vv. 19–20). Other verbal links include the phrase "the righteousness of God" (vv. 21, 22, 25, 26; cf. v. 5), the claim that "all have sinned and fall short of the glory of God" (v. 23; cf. vv. 9, 19–20), and the mention of justification (vv. 24; 26; cf. v. 20). As previously noted, vv. 21–26 expound and develop key themes announced in 1:16–17. This passage also raises topics that need to be explored and defended in the following section (3:27–4:25). In particular Paul goes on to discuss the nature and significance of saving faith and the implications for Jews and Gentiles of justification by God's grace (see §2.4).

Structure

This paragraph opens and closes with two references to the righteousness of God (vv. 21–22, 25–26). The first claims a new revelation of God's righteousness in the gospel era (νυνὶ δέ, "but now"). This revelation is "apart from the law," though "attested by the Law and the Prophets." The second reference shows how the revelation of the righteousness of God benefits humanity: it is "through faith in Jesus Christ to all who believe." A new stage in the argument begins with the words "since there is no distinction" (v. 22d), which is explained by the sentence "for all have sinned and fall short of the glory of God" (v. 23).[3] This recalls the argument in 1:18–3:20, which revealed the universal human need for salvation from the wrath of God. A participial clause in v. 24 indicates that salvation is experienced when sinners are "justified freely by his grace through

[3] Douglas A. Campbell (*The Rhetoric of Righteousness in Romans 3.21–26*, JSNTSup 65 [Sheffield: Sheffield Academic, 1992], 81) argues that Paul uses "extended periodic syntax" that fuses the entire paragraph into one sentence (cf. Jewett, *Romans*, 268). But UBS GNT (5th rev. ed.) begins a new sentence with οὐ γάρ ἐστιν διαστολή ("since there is no distinction"). CSB begins a new sentence in almost every verse. Since early manuscripts often lack punctuation, editors must decide on the arrangement that best brings out the sense.

the redemption that is in Christ Jesus." A relative clause in v. 25a–c outlines how God accomplished this redemption (lit., "whom God presented as an atoning sacrifice in his blood, received through faith"). Two assertions about God demonstrating his righteousness in this way conclude the paragraph (vv. 25d–26 in the Greek text). First, it was "because in his restraint God passed over the sins previously committed." Second, this eschatological demonstration of the righteousness of God (ἐν τῷ νῦν καιρῷ, "at the present time") took place so that God might "be righteous and declare righteous the one who has faith in Jesus."

Outline:

1. How the righteousness of God is revealed in the present time (vv. 21–22c)
2. How justification is now possible for all who believe (vv. 22d–25c)
3. Why God demonstrated his righteousness in this way (vv. 25d–26)

3:21. A direct link with the preceding passage is provided by the introductory words "but now" (νυνὶ δέ) and the contrasting expression "apart from the law" (χωρὶς νόμου). A temporal meaning for νυνί is confirmed by the parallel in v. 26 (ἐν τῷ νῦν καιρῷ, "at the present time"; cf. 2 Cor 6:2). Paul celebrates the eschatological revelation of the righteousness of God, which has taken place in Christ "apart from the law" (χωρὶς νόμου).[4] This adverbial phrase modifies πεφανέρωται ("has been revealed") rather than δικαιοσύνην θεοῦ (KJV: "the righteousness of God without the law"). The old era, when the righteousness of God was revealed to Israel through the law, is contrasted with the revelation of the righteousness of God in the gospel era.[5]

---

[4] Byrne (*Romans*, 122) describes it as the "'eleventh hour' on the apocalyptic time-scale when all is rushing to destruction and ruin." Jewett (*Romans*, 272) misses this salvation-historical reference when he argues that νυνὶ δέ indicates "a logical contrast with the preceding argument" rather than a contrast of eras (compare 16:26; 2 Cor 6:2; Col 1:26). See §1.6 on Paul's eschatology.

[5] Runge (*Discourse Grammar*, 222–23) observes that two adverbial "frames" (νυνὶ δέ and χωρὶς νόμου) attract attention to the discontinuity of time and situation in which this revelation of the righteousness of God takes place.

Some have related χωρὶς νόμου to ἐξ ἔργων νόμου ("by the works of the law") and διὰ νόμου ("through the law") in 3:20, equating it with χωρὶς ἔργων νόμου (3:28, "apart from works of the law") and χωρὶς ἔργων (4:6, "apart from works").[6] However, to say that righteousness is "*now* obtained without any contribution from the 'works of the law' would be to imply that it was *once* obtained with (at least some) contribution from 'the works of the law'—and that is precisely what Paul has ruled out in the previous verses."[7] Others have taken χωρὶς νόμου to mean "outside the national and religious parameters set by the law, without reference to the normal Jewish hallmarks,"[8] understanding Paul's focus to be specifically on the justification of Gentiles who are beyond the sphere of the law. But the preceding context has shown a concern for Jews as well as Gentiles, and Paul's aim is to demonstrate how the righteousness of God comes to *all* who believe in the Messiah Jesus (v. 22). This obviously puts Jews and Gentiles on the same footing, though this is not articulated until 3:29–31. As the argument about the law in 5:20–21; 6:14; 7:1–6 suggests, the shift in salvation history to which Paul alludes in 3:21–22 is more radical than a setting aside of the "identity markers" separating Jews and Gentiles.

The perfect passive πεφανέρωται ("has been revealed") recalls the use of the present passive ἀποκαλύπτεται ("is revealed") in 1:17.[9] The latter indicates that the righteousness of God is revealed in the ongoing proclamation of the gospel, which brings people to faith in Christ. The perfect tense in 3:21 is normally taken to refer to the historic manifestation of the righteousness of God in the redemptive work of Christ. However, the perfect could also be rendered "is revealed," with the context suggesting that the revelation of the righteousness of God takes place as people hear the gospel about God's

---

[6] E.g., Cranfield, *Romans*, 1:201; Jewett, *Romans*, 272.

[7] Donald A. Carson, "Atonement in Romans 3:21–26," in *The Glory of the Atonement: Biblical, Theological and Practical Perspectives*, ed. Charles E. Hill and Frank A. James (Downers Grove: InterVarsity, 2004): 122–23.

[8] Dunn, *Romans 1–8*, 165. Dunn contrasts ἐξ ἔργων νόμου with ἐν τῷ νόμῳ (3:19, [lit.] "those within the law"), despite the fact that the syntax does not suggest a connection between these expressions in the flow of the argument.

[9] These verbs are effectively synonymous, but φανεροῦν is used more frequently in the NT than ἀποκαλύπτειν. Φανεροῦν means "to cause to become visible, reveal, expose publicly" (BDAG). It is used in 1:19; 3:21; 16:26 (cf. φανερός in 1:19; 2:28).

saving action in the death and resurrection of Jesus and are justified by faith (vv. 22–24).[10]

In short, God has manifested his righteousness "apart from the law as an entire system that played its crucial role in redemptive history," that is, apart from "the law-covenant."[11] But the righteousness that is now revealed is "attested by the Law and the Prophets" (μαρτυρουμένη ὑπὸ τοῦ νόμου καὶ τῶν προφητῶν). This designation for what we call the OT is employed elsewhere in the NT (Matt 5:17; 7:12; 22:40; Luke 16:16; John 1:45; Acts 13:15; 24:14; 28:23) and in some Jewish writings (e.g., Sirach Prologue; 2 Macc 15:9; 4 Macc 18:10) but nowhere else by Paul. The apostle stresses the continuity of divine revelation even as he proclaims the newness of the gospel message. In particular, he knows from Scripture and his own encounter with the risen Lord about the righteousness of God being manifested in a new and decisive way through the messianic deliverance (see §2.4).

As noted in connection with 1:17, "the righteousness of God" (δικαιοσύνη θεοῦ) has been interpreted as an attribute of God, an activity of God, a status given by God, the righteousness that "counts" in God's eyes, or some combination of these ideas. It is clear from 3:5 that Paul regards God's righteousness as an attribute that is expressed in the way God rules his creation with justice and subdues all forms of opposition to his rule (cf. Pss 96:10–13; 97:2, 6–9; 98:7–9). Indeed, it could be said that 1:18–3:20 as a whole explores the way God's righteousness is expressed in judgment, now and in the future. But τῆς δικαιοσύνης αὐτοῦ ("his righteousness") in 3:25–26 has a more salvific sense, describing his justice in presenting Jesus as "an atoning sacrifice" for sins and justifying those who have faith in him. These verses at the end of the section suggest that δικαιοσύνη θεοῦ in vv. 21–22 should be read similarly, taking θεοῦ as a subjective genitive and viewing his justifying or

[10] Campbell (*Verbal Aspect*, 185) points out, "The striking overlap of the perfect indicative with the present in discourse contexts strongly suggests that it shares the same aspect as the latter tense form." The most likely aspectual value of the perfect is "imperfectivity": "its spatial value is one of proximity rather than remoteness" (196), but "the perfect semantically encodes a higher level of proximity" (197). Schreiner (*Romans*, 182, 184) discusses the use of the perfect tense here in relation to the expression διὰ πίστεως Ἰησοῦ Χριστοῦ in 3:22.

[11] Carson, "Atonement," 123. Cf. Moo, *Romans*, 222–23.

vindicating activity as an expression of his own intrinsic righteousness (vv. 25–26).[12]

As Rom 4 will confirm, believers enjoy a righteous status as the outcome of God's justifying activity, but this does not mean the expression in 3:21 should be rendered "a righteousness from God." Some would equate "the righteousness of God" with "the faithfulness of God to the promises long ago announced to Israel."[13] This understanding has been linked to the fulfillment of the promise to Abraham, which dominates the argument in Rom 4. God's righteousness is thus defined as his "covenant faithfulness." However, 1:18–3:20, with its emphasis on the culpability of all humanity before God as judge, provides the ground for understanding Paul's meaning in 3:21–26. The coming together of Jew and Gentile through faith in Christ to fulfill God's covenant plan emerges as a consequence that is explored in 3:27–4:25. The apostle's first concern is to show how God in his righteousness can be both judge of the nations and the savior of those who turn to him in faith (cf. Ps 98; Isa 47:22–25).[14]

3:22. The connective δέ with the repeated δικαιοσύνη θεοῦ suggests that Paul is about to give a closer definition of the righteousness of God than is now manifested.[15] It is experienced or encountered "through faith *in* Jesus Christ" (διὰ πίστεως Ἰησοῦ Χριστοῦ), understanding an objective genitive in the expression Ἰησοῦ Χριστοῦ.[16]

[12] Moo, *Romans*, 74. Moo (219) observes that "the righteousness of God" in vv. 21–22 strictly refers to the justifying act of God, whereas in vv. 25–26 "his righteousness" refers to "the 'integrity' of God, his always acting in complete accordance with his own character." But the jump from the one to the other is not as great as might first appear, since "righteousness" language applied to God may allude to his character, as experienced in revelatory actions. Cf. David J. Reimer, "צדק," *NIDOTTE* 3:752.

[13] Wright, "Romans," 464. See more fully, ibid., 397–406; and Dunn, *Romans 1–8*, 40–44.

[14] While Jewett (*Romans*, 272–73) is correct to observe that there are social and cosmic dimensions to the justifying activity of God, Paul's focus in 3:21–26 is on the implications for believers individually in relation to God as judge.

[15] Compare the use of this connective in 9:30; Phil 2:8. CSB begins a new sentence in 3:22.

[16] Paul prefers ἐκ ("from," "on the basis of") with πίστις (as in 1:17; 3:26, 30; 4:16; 9:30; and many other verses), but διὰ τῆς πίστεως ("through faith") is clearly a parallel expression in 3:30. Διά is also used with πίστις in 3:25 (cf. 2 Cor 5:7; Gal 2:16; 3:14, 26; Eph 2:8; 3:12, 17; Phil 3:9; Col 2:12; 1 Thess 3:7; 2 Tim 3:15).

Moreover, it is "to" or "for *all* who believe" (εἰς πάντας τοὺς πιστεύοντας), recalling 1:16 and anticipating the emphasis in 3:23–24 on the need for all to believe in the justifying grace of God.[17] In 9:30 the righteousness that can be "obtained" (κατέλαβεν) under the new covenant is expressed as "the righteousness that comes from faith" (δικαιοσύνην δὲ τὴν ἐκ πίστεως). In Phil 3:9 Paul speaks about not having a righteousness of his own from the law but "one that is through faith in Christ—the righteousness from God based on faith" (τὴν διὰ πίστεως Χριστοῦ, τὴν ἐκ θεοῦ δικαιοσύνην ἐπὶ τῇ πίστει). These verses identify a righteousness that is attributed to believers in Christ through justification by faith. Paul comes close to expressing himself in that way here, though the full sequence of his thinking is not revealed until the next chapter. God has acted in his righteousness to make it possible for all to be justified by faith on the basis of the redemptive work of Jesus (vv. 24–26). In this way righteousness is attributed to those who believe (4:22–25).

However, some commentators have understood the genitives in the expression διὰ πίστεως Ἰησοῦ Χριστοῦ as subjective, giving the meaning "through the faith of Jesus Christ" or, taking πίστις to mean "faithfulness," "through the faithfulness of Jesus Christ."[18] It is pointed out that πίστις followed by a genitive in 3:3 refers to "the faithfulness of God," and in 4:12, 16 it refers to "the faith of Abraham." If δικαιοσύνη θεοῦ refers to the eschatological manifestation of God's righteousness, διὰ πίστεως Ἰησοῦ Χριστοῦ could indicate that this happened through the faith or faithfulness of Jesus, leaving εἰς πάντας τοὺς πιστεύοντας to point to the faith of those who

[17] The name "Jesus" is overwhelmingly attested in the manuscript evidence but is strangely missing from manuscript B and Marcion. In place of εἰς πάντας ("for all"), which is widely attested, a few witnesses have ἐπὶ πάντας ("upon all"). Following א[c] D G K 33 and others, TR combines the two readings, but this produces "an essentially redundant and tautological expression" (Metzger, *Textual Commentary*, 449). The KJV adopts this composite reading.

[18] E.g., Donald W. B. Robinson, "'Faith of Jesus Christ'—a New Testament Debate," *RTR* 29 (1970): 71–81; Luke T. Johnson, "Rom 3:21–26 and the Faith of Jesus," *CBQ* 44 (1982): 77–90; Sam K. Williams, "The 'Righteousness of God' in Romans," *JBL* 99 (1980): 272–78; Williams, "Again Pistis Christou," *CBQ* 49 (1987): 431–47; Richard B. Hays, *The Faith of Jesus Christ: An Investigation of the Narrative Structure of Galatians 3:1–4:11*, 2nd ed., SBLDS 56 (Grand Rapids: Eerdmans, 2001).

benefit from his sacrificial death.[19] This understanding of the text could anticipate Paul's argument in 5:18–19 that "through one righteous act there is justification leading to life for everyone," referring to the obedience of Christ by which "the many will be made righteous" (compare also Phil 2:6–8; Heb 5:7–9; 9:14; 10:10).

But there are difficulties with this approach. Given the widespread use of πίστις with reference to the faith of believers in general, both before (1:5, 8, 12, 17) and after this passage (3:27–4:25), there would need to be clearer indications in the context that Paul was employing the term differently in 3:22.[20] In fact, nowhere in his writings does he unambiguously use the terminology of faith or faithfulness with reference to the obedience of Jesus.[21] In Gal 2:16 διὰ πίστεως Ἰησοῦ Χριστοῦ is most naturally translated "by faith in Jesus Christ," and this is followed by καὶ ἡμεῖς εἰς Χριστὸν Ἰησοῦν ἐπιστεύσαμεν ("and *we* have believed in Christ Jesus"). Similarly in Rom 3:22, if διὰ πίστεως Ἰησοῦ Χριστοῦ is rendered "by faith in Jesus Christ," the next clause (εἰς πάντας τοὺς πιστεύοντας, "to all who believe") is not redundant because it highlights the universal implications of the first.[22] Paul continues to emphasize the need for *all* to have faith in Christ with the expression οὐ γάρ ἐστιν διαστολή ("since there is no distinction"). This qualifies the previous clause and provides a link to the next verse. It has the effect of applying both the preceding and the immediately following "all" to both Jew

[19] So Wright ("Romans," 467) says, "On the cross Jesus accomplished what God had always intended the covenant to achieve. Where Israel as a whole had been faithless, he was faithful: 3:22 answers to 3:2–3." However, this leads Wright (468) to define Christian faith in terms of faithfulness, which suggests a different view of what it means to be justified by faith. See further my comments on διὰ [τῆς] πίστεως in v. 25 and ἐκ πίστεως Ἰησοῦ in v. 26.

[20] Furthermore, Schreiner (*Romans*, 182–83) demonstrates how the use of objective genitives in the expression διὰ πίστεως Ἰησοῦ Χριστοῦ is not as grammatically unlikely as some suggest (so also Fitzmyer, *Romans*, 345–46). Contrast Wallace, *Greek Grammar*, 114–18

[21] This is one of four decisive reasons given by Schreiner (*Romans*, 185–86) for reading "through faith in Jesus Christ" in Rom 3:22. See also James D. G. Dunn, "Once More, Πίστις Χριστοῦ," in *Society of Biblical Literature 1991 Seminar Papers*, ed. E. H. Lovering Jr. (Atlanta: Scholars Press, 1991): 730–44.

[22] Jewett (*Romans*, 278) argues, "The reiteration of the inclusive social scope of 'all who have faith' in 3:22 suggests that Paul is focusing on the faith of believers rather than the faithfulness of Christ."

and Gentile (cf. 10:12).[23] In this way Paul prepares for the argument that the promise to Abraham about the whole world's being blessed through his offspring is fulfilled in Christ (4:9–25).

3:23. This verse, together with the linking clause "since there is no distinction" (v. 22), begins a new phase of the argument. On the one hand, it recalls and summarizes what is said in 1:18–3:20 about the universal human need for salvation from the wrath of God. On the other hand, it paves the way for Paul to say that justification is universally available for those who trust in the redemptive work of the Messiah Jesus (v. 24). The paradox that God justifies sinners is restated in 4:5, where Paul claims that God justifies "the ungodly" (τὸν ἀσεβῆ).[24] The aorist verb ἥμαρτον may have a summary meaning ("have sinned") or be used in a gnomic way ("all sin"). The present tense of ὑστεροῦνται ("fall short") is more obviously gnomic, expressing what all who sin characteristically lack. "The glory of God" (τῆς δόξης τοῦ θεοῦ) reflects the Jewish tradition that when Adam sinned he lost the glory that was his when he was created in the image and likeness of God (Gen 1:26–27; Ps 8:5).[25] All men and women have been caught up in Adam's sin and its consequences (5:12–19), but Paul later affirms that believers will encounter the glory of God at the consummation of the age through physical resurrection and transformation into the image of God's Son (5:2; 8:18–21, 29–30). Elsewhere he suggests that something of the glory of God is experienced in advance by meeting Christ through the gospel and receiving the promised Holy Spirit (e.g., 2 Cor 3:18; 4:4–6).[26]

3:24. The present passive participle δικαιούμενοι ("being justified, set right") agrees with πάντες ("all") at the beginning of v. 23. CSB begins a new sentence here. All who have sinned and fall short

---

[23] Campbell (*Rhetoric of Righteousness*, 86–92, 182–83) contends that vv. 22d–24a form a parenthesis, elaborating the theme of "all who have faith."

[24] So Carson ("Atonement," 120) concludes that the problem is "not first and foremost the failure of Israel (national or otherwise), or inappropriate use of the law, or the urgency of linking Jews and Gentiles (all genuine themes in these chapters), but the wrath of God directed against every human being, Jew and Gentile alike—a wrath elicited by universal human wickedness." Contrast Wright, "Romans," 464–68.

[25] Cf. §1.1; Apoc. Mos. 20:2–3; 21.6; 3 Bar. 4.16; Gen. Rab. 12:6; 1QS 4:22–23; CD 3:19–20; 4QpPs[a] 3:1–2.

[26] Gerhard Kittel ("δοκέω, δόξα κτλ.," *TDNT* 2:250) concludes, "Participation in δόξα, whether here in hope or one day in consummation, is participation in Christ." Cf. Peterson, *Transformed by God*, 113–22.

of the glory of God are "justified freely by his grace through the redemption that is in Christ Jesus."[27] This verb is a cognate of the noun δικαιοσύνη ("righteousness") in vv. 21–22. Paul does not envisage automatic justification for all since he has clearly emphasized the need for faith. But the flow of the argument indicates that all who have sinned and have faith in the Messiah and his atoning death may receive this gift. Three important terms are used in vv. 24–25 to explain how God's righteousness is manifested "at the present time." These are not simply alternative ways of portraying the work of Christ but interdependent ideas that linked together syntactically and theologically: *justification* is made possible by a divine act of *redemption*, which involves *an atoning sacrifice*.

With its lawcourt associations the language of justification recalls the argument about God's wrath against sinners in 1:18–2:16. The verb δικαιόω is forensic and positive in meaning: "to 'justify' someone is to vindicate them, not to punish them."[28] Justification was first mentioned in connection with the day when God judges Jew and Gentile alike (2:13). In that judgment "works" will be evaluated as an indicator of genuine faith, not as something added to faith to make it more acceptable (2:6–11). But in 3:24 Paul indicates that the righteous judge has "acted ahead of time in history and in his grace has pronounced a pardon on those who have faith in Christ, so that their guilt can no longer be cited against them."[29] The ground of acquittal is not "works of the law" (3:20) but the "the redemption that is in Christ Jesus." To emphasize the gift character of God's justifying action, Paul adds "freely by his grace" (δωρεὰν τῇ αὐτοῦ χάριτι), using the accusative noun δωρεάν ("gift") adverbially (cf. δωρεά in 5:15, 17; 2 Cor 9:15; Eph 3:7; 4:7). Grace is mentioned twenty-five times in Romans, mostly with reference to the unmerited favor of God revealed in the person and work of Christ.[30] Reciprocity

---

[27] Cranfield (*Romans*, 1.205) discusses how this clause could relate to the preceding verse and concludes that it fills out the explanation of v. 22b ("there is no distinction") while conveying the other side of the picture presented in v. 23.

[28] Seifrid, "Paul's Use of Righteousness Language," 52. Cf. §2.4.

[29] Anthony T. Lincoln, "From Wrath to Justification: Tradition, Gospel, and Audience in the Theology of Romans 1:18–4:25," in *Pauline Theology, Volume III: Romans*, ed. David M. Hay and E. Elizabeth Johnson (Minneapolis: Fortress, 1995), 148.

[30] Hans Conzelmann and Walther Zimmerli ("χαίρω, χαρά κτλ.," *TDNT* 9:372–99) point out that the fundamental meaning of χάρις in Greek literature is "what delights,"

was a central feature of benefaction in the Greco-Roman world, but Paul stresses the *unilateral* nature of God's grace, expressed in the gift of his Son and everything flowing from his saving work.[31] As 4:6–8 makes clear, justification by faith involves being graciously set in a right relationship with God by his judicial verdict of pardon. There are covenantal implications that Paul goes on to outline, but justification is not primarily explained in covenantal terms.[32]

Justification by faith is made possible "through the redemption that is in Christ Jesus" (διὰ τῆς ἀπολυτρώσεως τῆς ἐν Χριστῷ Ἰησοῦ). Redemption terminology is linked to freedom from slavery in both Greco-Roman and Jewish sources. From a biblical point of view, Israel was redeemed from bondage in Egypt (e.g., Deut 7:8; 9:26; 15:15), and this became the pattern for prophecies about release from captivity in Babylon (e.g., Isa 43:1, 14; 44:22–24; 51:11; 52:3). Having previously charged that all are under the power of sin (3:9), Paul now claims that redemption from this universal captivity has taken place "in the Messiah Jesus."[33] Some have argued that the noun ἀπολύτρωσις simply means "deliverance" or "emancipation," without any reference to a ransom (λύτρον),[34] but several factors suggest otherwise. First, there is the use of λύτρον and its cognates

and that it can therefore denote an act of kindness that brings pleasure. In the LXX it translates חֵן, which is used in a variety of ways to mean "favor." They argue that the linguistic starting point for Paul's use of χάρις is "the sense of 'making glad by gifts,' of showing free, unmerited grace."

[31] Dunn (*Theology of Paul*, 320–23) argues that Paul's understanding of grace incorporates notions expressed by related terms in OT confessions about God, such as Exod 34:6 ("a compassionate and gracious God, slow to anger and abounding in faithful love and truth"). For Greco-Roman usage, see James R. Harrison, *Paul's Language of Grace in Its Graeco-Roman Context*, WUNT 172 (Tübingen: Mohr Siebeck, 2003).

[32] Cf. John Piper, *The Future of Justification: A Response to N. T. Wright* (Wheaton: Crossway, 2007), 39–55.

[33] In the expression ἐν Χριστῷ Ἰησοῦ the title precedes the personal name. As in 1:1–4, the reference is to the Messiah, though more specifically to his redeeming work here. However, this first use of the formula ἐν Χριστῷ may also imply that the benefits of redemption are experienced by those who have been incorporated into Christ by faith. Cf. Constantine R. Campbell, *Paul and Union with Christ: An Exegetical and Theological Study* (Grand Rapids: Zondervan, 2012), 114–15, 198–99.

[34] Cf. Otto Procksch and Friedrich Büchsel, "λύω, ἀναλύω κτλ.," *TDNT* 4:354–55; Dodd, *Romans*, 77–78. The noun ἀπολύτρωσις, which occurs in Rom 3:24; 8:23 (cf. Luke 21:28; 1 Cor 1:30; Eph 1:7, 14; 4:30; Col 1:14; Heb 9:15; 11:35), derives from ἀπολυτρόω. This verb, which means "set free for a ransom (λύτρον)," does not occur

in Greek literature with implications of payment and the fact that freedom from slavery by payment of a price would have been a familiar idea to Paul's readers. Second, the freedom of justification for believers is directly linked to the redemption God provides, suggesting that the latter includes the idea of a price being paid or a cost on God's part.[35] Third, the following verse speaks of Christ's sacrificial death, using the expression "in his blood." The sequence suggests that Jesus frees people from sin's penalty, which is death (5:12; 6:23), by offering himself in a substitutionary way (5:17–21). Fourth, although a different verb is used, there are references to Christians having been bought with a price in 1 Cor 6:20; 7:23 (cf. Gal 3:13; 4:5). By this redemptive act God has made it possible for believers to be freed from the penalty he himself imposed for sin and to be justified by faith (cf. Ps 130:7–8). "The 'cost' of redemption is thus the death of Christ, seen as the gift of divine grace, and the 'price' of it is the sacrificial offering made to God."[36]

3:25. Paul's third explanation of how the righteousness of God is revealed in the gospel era employs the language of Israel's sacrificial system. Redemption is accomplished in Christ Jesus, "whom God presented as an atoning sacrifice" (ὃν προέθετο ὁ θεὸς ἱλαστήριον). God's initiative is emphasized with the words προέθετο ὁ θεός. This verb is used in the LXX for the priestly task of setting forth bread before the Lord (Exod 29:23; 40:23; Lev 24:8; 2 Macc 1:8, 15), but here God himself "set forth publicly" (BDAG) the crucified Christ as a way of dealing with the problem of human sin.[37] The term ἱλαστήριον is used twenty-one times in the LXX as a noun referring to the golden cover over the ark in the inner sanctuary of

---

in the NT, though the noun λύτρον is used in Mark 10:45/Matt 20:28. Related terms can be found in Luke 1:68; 2:38; 24:21; Acts 7:35; Titus 2:14; Heb 9:12; 1 Pet 1:18.

[35] Schreiner, *Romans*, 190. Although Leon L. Morris (*The Apostolic Preaching of the Cross* [Grand Rapids: Eerdmans, 1965], 16–55) argues that the notion of price is almost always present in this use of this terminology, Schreiner has a more nuanced approach to the evidence.

[36] I. Howard Marshall, "The Development of the Concept of Redemption in the New Testament," in *Reconciliation and Hope: New Testament Essays on Atonement and Eschatology Presented to L. L. Morris on His 60th Birthday*, ed. Robert J. Banks (Exeter: Paternoster, 1974), 163. Cf. Kruse, *Romans*, 183–85.

[37] Cranfield's view (*Romans*, 1:208–9) that the verb means "purpose, intend" here (as in 1:13) is less likely in this context, where the focus is on the manifestation or demonstration of God's righteousness (3:21, 25–26).

the tabernacle/temple (e.g., Exod 25:17–22).[38] Sacrificial blood was sprinkled here by the high priest on the annual Day of Atonement (Lev 16:2, 13, 14, 15) as part of the ritual to make atonement for "the whole assembly of Israel" (16:17). Paul apparently uses this term to portray Jesus as the new covenant antitype to the old covenant "place of atonement" and "derivatively, to the ritual of atonement itself."[39] For reasons that will be argued below, "propitiation" is a valid rendering of the term in this context.

The atoning significance of Jesus's death is further specified by the phrase "in his blood" (ἐν τῷ αὐτοῦ αἵματι), which most likely modifies ἱλαστήριον ("a propitiation in/by his blood"). When the lifeblood of animals was shed in sacrificial rituals under the old covenant, it was said to "make atonement" for the lives of God's people (Lev 17:11, ἐξιλάσκεσθαι). Christ is now the decisive sin offering for all who believe (cf. 8:3 comment). Although Paul's word order suggests the possibility of translating διὰ [τῆς] πίστεως ἐν τῷ αὐτοῦ αἵματι as "through faith in his blood," he nowhere else makes Christ's blood an object of faith.[40] The sense is that God has publicly set forth the crucified Messiah as the new means of propitiation, accessible to all by faith, in his atoning death. It has been argued that διὰ [τῆς] πίστεως refers once more to the faithfulness of Jesus,[41] but this could only be so if it could be firmly established that διὰ πίστεως Ἰησοῦ Χριστοῦ in v. 22 had this meaning. Paul is talking about *our* faith in the crucified Christ, so that διὰ [τῆς] πίστεως in v. 25 is rightly paraphrased by CSB "received through faith."

Given the use of ἱλαστήριον in Greek literature more widely, some have contended that the apostle employs this term to make "a

---

[38] The rendering "mercy seat" comes from Tyndale's translation. The "cover" (כַּפֹּרֶת) over the ark came to represent the atoning action that took place there (Lev 16:17, לְכַפֵּר [ἐξιλάσασθαι], "to make atonement"), by which God's mercy was sought.

[39] Moo, *Romans*, 232. Moo cites numerous supporters of this interpretation and observes that it is attractive because it gives ἱλαστήριον a meaning that is derived from its "customary" biblical usage (cf. Heb 9:5). It "creates an analogy between a central OT ritual and Christ's death that is both theologically sound and hermeneutically striking."

[40] The reading διὰ τῆς πίστεως is attested by $\mathfrak{P}^{40}$ (apparently) B Ψ, the correctors of C and D, and other witnesses. It is certainly used in vv. 30–31. Διὰ πίστεως is attested by א, the original texts of C and D, and other witnesses. As the shorter option, it is more likely to have been the original in v. 25.

[41] Cf. Wright, "Romans," 476–77.

general reference to the removal of the wrath of God, rather than a specific reference either to the mercy-seat, or to the Day of Atonement ceremonies."[42] However, if the expression "attested by the Law and the Prophets" (v. 21) is taken as a guide to the way Paul argues throughout this passage, and the close link between ἱλαστήριον and ἐν τῷ αὐτοῦ αἵματι is observed, then a specific allusion to the "mercy seat" in the holy of holies and the Day of Atonement ritual is more likely.[43] But some would question the appropriateness of translating ἱλαστήριον as "a propitiation" because they deny that the sacrifice of Christ is in any sense a means of appeasing God's wrath. Words from the ἱλασκ- root regularly express the notion of propitiating the gods in ancient Greek sources, but in biblical usage they are said to refer to the expiation of sin, which means, "to perform an act whereby guilt or defilement is removed."[44]

Pagan ideas of wrath and propitiation are absent from the biblical text, but we must still ask why the LXX translators chose to use this terminology when rendering the Hebrew verb כפר and its cognates.[45] The wider context for understanding blood rituals in the OT is the need to avert the wrath of God. In passages such as Leviticus 26 and Deuteronomy 27–28, Israel is warned about unfaithfulness to God and the possibility of experiencing the covenant curses, ultimately being excluded from the land and God's presence.[46] The sacrificial system provided a means of maintaining Israel's relationship

[42] Morris, *Apostolic Preaching*, 198. A history of the interpretation of this term is provided by Arland J. Hultgren, *Paul's Gospel and Mission* (Philadelphia: Fortress, 1985). Kruse (*Romans*, 188–91) also surveys the issues briefly.

[43] Jewett (*Romans*, 287) says the reference here is to "the provision of a new institutional vehicle for atonement." Cf. Schreiner, *Romans*, 192–93; Wright, "Romans," 474–77; Daniel P. Bailey, "Jesus as the Mercy Seat: The Semantics and Theology of Paul's use of *Hilasterion* in Romans 3:25," *TynBul* 51 (2000): 155–58.

[44] Dodd, *Romans*, 78. Dodd's argument is more fully expressed in *The Bible and the Greeks* (London: Hodder & Stoughton, 1935), 82–85. See also Friedrich Büchsel and Johannes Hermann, "ἵλεως, ἱλάσκομαι, ἱλασμός, ἱλαστήριον," *TDNT* 3: 300–323.

[45] Richard E. Averbeck ("כפר," *NIDOTTE* 2:689–710) argues that the base meaning of the verb is "wipe away." The derived meaning is "ransom" when it refers to the overall effect of the action. Averbeck concludes, "If the issues that would cause God's wrath to be turned against us are wiped away, expiation, then there is no reason for God to be angry anymore—he is propitiated." Cf. P. Garnet, "Atonement Constructions in the Old Testament and the Qumran Scrolls," *EvQ* 46 (1974): 13–63.

[46] Morris (*Apostolic Preaching*, 149–54) outlines more fully the way God's wrath is expressed and must be averted in OT thought. He (155–74) goes on to argue that

with the Holy One and enjoying the blessings of the covenant. But when God's judgment was experienced in the Babylonian exile, the system could no longer operate, and another form of sacrifice for sin was promised in the affliction of the Suffering Servant (Isa 53:4–12). In a later era the Maccabean literature expressed the need for God's wrath to be appeased by the blood of the martyrs, atoning for the sins of Israel (e.g., 2 Macc 7:18, 37–38; 4 Macc 6:27–29; 17:21–22 [where ἱλαστήριον is actually used]). Against this background the logic of Paul's argument is that the wrath of God (1:18–3:20) is averted by Jesus's death as a substitute for believers, bearing the penalty for their sin (cf. 8:3 comment). However, in presenting God as both subject and object of the atoning work of Christ, the apostle's view of propitiation differs from pagan notions.[47] The cross proceeds from God's grace, and it does not make God gracious. God in his mercy provides the way by which his own wrath is expressed and satisfied. As with the provisions for atonement in the Mosaic law, God is both originator and recipient of this sacrifice.

Paul's vivid explanation of how the righteousness of God is revealed in the gospel era (vv. 21–25c) leads him to state why God has acted in this way (vv. 25d–26). God's purpose in providing a propitiation accessible to all by faith in the sacrifice of the Messiah was (lit.) "for a demonstration of his righteousness" (v. 25d, εἰς ἔνδειξιν τῆς δικαιοσύνης αὐτοῦ).[48] This continues the theme of God's triumph over human opposition announced in 3:4 (citing Ps 51:4) but focusing now on God's righteousness in salvation as well as in judgment. Although God's righteousness cannot simply be defined as the desire to maintain his glory, "the desire for his glory undergirds his desire to demonstrate his righteousness."[49] An apologetic

---

the sense of propitiation is regularly established by the context when the Hebrew and Greek terms are used.

[47] Dunn (*Romans 1–8*, 171) argues that the passage portrays God as "offerer of the sacrifice rather than its object." But if God's wrath is to be averted in any *personal sense*, God himself must be the object of any action he prescribes (e.g., Num 25:1–13).

[48] John Piper ("The Demonstration of the Righteousness of God in Rom 3:25, 26," in *The Pauline Writings*, ed. Stanley E. Porter and Craig A. Evans, Biblical Seminar 34 [Sheffield: Sheffield Academic, 1995]: 183–91) shows that attempts to distinguish sharply between "proof" and "demonstration" as renderings of ἔνδειξις cannot be supported by the linguistic evidence.

[49] Schreiner, *Romans*, 198–99, responding to Piper, *Justification of God*, 135–50.

agenda is indicated by the next two linked phrases: (lit.) "because of the passing over of sins previously committed" (v. 25e, διὰ τὴν πάρεσιν τῶν προγεγονότων ἁμαρτημάτων) and "in the restraint of God" (v. 26a [Greek text], ἐν τῇ ἀνοχῇ τοῦ θεοῦ). God's "passing over" of sins implies "deliberate disregard," or "letting them go unpunished" (BDAG, πάρεσις), but not pardoning them.[50] "God's past restraint in punishing sins with the full measure of punishment they deserved calls into question his fair and impartial 'justice,' or holiness, creating the need for his justice to be 'satisfied,' a satisfaction rendered by the propitiatory sacrifice of Christ."[51] Mention of God's "forbearance" or "restraint" (ἀνοχή) supports this view. This term in 2:4 was linked with God's kindness and patience, providing an opportunity for repentance. "Sins previously committed" most likely includes every transgression before the sacrifice of Christ (cf. Heb 9:15), since "up to that time sins were neither punished as they deserved nor atoned for as they were going to be."[52]

3:26. God's purpose in presenting Christ as "a propitiation" is expressed again with a prepositional phrase like the one in v. 25: (lit.) "for a demonstration of his righteousness" (πρὸς τὴν ἔνδειξιν τῆς δικαιοσύνης αὐτοῦ).[53] This time the emphasis falls on the timing of the demonstration (ἐν τῷ νῦν καιρῷ, "at the present time"; cf. v. 21, νυνὶ δέ). Paul's eschatological allusion suggests "both that the past problem has reached a present conclusion and that the future verdict has been brought forward into the present time."[54] Instead of a causal clause (as in v. 25), Paul uses a further purpose clause to

---

[50] Cf. Jewett, *Romans*, 290–91. Schreiner (*Romans*, 196–98) and Carson ("Atonement," 136–38) discuss alternative views about Paul's language in this verse.

[51] Moo, *Romans*, 238. Moo (242) comments further on the appropriateness of viewing the atoning work of Christ in terms of the "satisfaction" of God's justice.

[52] Cranfield, *Romans*, 1:212n1. Jewett (*Romans*, 290) limits the reference to "sins not covered by temple rites, which would have included all transgressions outside Israel's ethnic boundaries." However, Cranfield's more comprehensive approach allows for the possibility that Paul saw the cultic provisions of the OT law as only an anticipation of the reality to come in the Messiah's sacrifice for sin (cf. Heb 10:1–10, 14–18). Cf. Dunn, *Romans 1–8*, 173–74.

[53] CSB begins a new sentence in v. 26 and includes the words "God presented him" to show the link back to those words in v. 25a.

[54] Wright, "Romans," 473. In 8:18; 11:5 Paul refers to "the present time" as a time of suffering and of Israel's hardening. But the use of νυνὶ δέ in v. 21, in contrast with the era of the law, suggests that a positive reference to the present as the time of fulfillment is intended in vv. 21, 26. Cf. Cranfield, *Romans*, 1.212n2.

explain what he means: "so that he would be righteous and declare righteous the one who has faith in Jesus" (εἰς τὸ εἶναι αὐτὸν δίκαιον καὶ δικαιοῦντα τὸν ἐκ πίστεως Ἰησοῦ). God's righteousness is demonstrated when he maintains his justice *even* in justifying sinners (understanding καί as concessive, rather than as the coordinating "and").[55] Both aspects of the righteousness of God revealed in the law and the prophets come together in this claim: the perfect justice by which God judges humanity and the deliverance he graciously provides, even from his own judgments. The basis of such justification was explained in vv. 24–25c, and the required response is once again "faith in Jesus." Although some would render the expression τὸν ἐκ πίστεως Ἰησοῦ "the one who rests on the faithfulness of Jesus," or "the one who shares the faith that Jesus had," the reasons for not reading a subjective genitive in vv. 22, 25 apply here also.[56]

Bridge

As anticipated in 1:16–17, the focus of Paul's gospel exposition is the public exhibition of God's righteousness "at the present time." Here is why the gospel is "the power of God for salvation to everyone who believes, first to the Jew, and also to the Greek." The background to this is Paul's teaching about God's rightly judging humanity in this life and the next (1:18–3:20). God's wrath is expressed because "all have sinned and fall short of the glory of God." But the good news is that God has acted to justify all who have faith in Jesus through the redemption he has provided in the propitiatory sacrifice of the Messiah. God's saving justice enables him to remain just when he justifies or puts sinners right with himself. Each of the critical terms in this complex declaration needs to be understood in the light of biblical precedents. Justification brings assurance, redemption brings deliverance, and propitiation brings forgiveness. These are not independent notions but interrelated

---

[55] Jewett (*Romans*, 292–93) discusses five possible ways in which the conjunction καί has been interpreted here.

[56] Cf. Wright, "Romans," 473–74. Compare the use of οἱ ἐκ πίστεως ("those who have faith") in Gal 3:7, 9. Paul's focus on faith in Jesus, using two different expressions in vv. 22, 26, is related to the fact that the paragraph focuses on what Jesus accomplished to make justification possible. Cf. John W. Pryor, "Paul's Use of Ἰησοῦς—a Clue for the Translation of Romans 3:26?" *Colloquium* 16, no. 1 (1983): 40–41.

divine provisions in the death of Jesus. Paul emphasizes the beginning of a new era in human history in which familiar teaching takes on a radical new meaning "in Christ" and is applicable to people everywhere. So the missional implications of this passage need to be exposed. Whenever and wherever the saving justice of God is proclaimed and believed, there is hope of deliverance from the penalty and power of sin. The righteousness of God manifested in the saving work of Christ and experienced through justification by faith has life-changing implications for people in every culture, in every age.

V. God's Saving Righteousness Revealed: Faith, Not Law, the Defining Characteristic of God's People (3:27–4:25)

A second defensive section in Paul's letter begins with a series of questions and answers (3:27–31), resuming the diatribe style of 3:1–9. As part of his strategy to address Jewish objections and misunderstandings, this exchange develops from his exposition of the gospel in 3:21–26.[1] Paul reasserts that justification is by faith and reinforces this claim by addition of the words "apart from the works of the law." He then clarifies that justification by faith is for Jews and Gentiles alike and contends that, far from cancelling the law, his gospel upholds the law. Paul's diatribe continues in 4:1–12 with a series of questions and answers focusing on Abraham's righteousness and the identity of his true descendants. In this way he engages with some of the issues raised about Abraham in postbiblical Jewish tradition and shows how "God always intended and promised that the covenant family of Abraham would include Gentiles as well as Jews."[2] Further reflection on the story of Abraham enables Paul to consider the issues of faith apart from the law (4:13–16) and faith apart from sight (4:17–21) before linking Abraham's faith explicitly with Christian faith (4:22–25).

> [27]Where, then, is boasting? It is excluded. By what kind of
> law? By one of works? No, on the contrary, by a law of faith.
> [28]For we conclude that a person is justified by faith apart from the
> works of the law. [29]Or is God the God of Jews only? Is he not the
> God of Gentiles too? Yes, of Gentiles too, [30]since there is one God
> who will justify the circumcised by faith and the uncircumcised
> through faith. [31]Do we then nullify the law through faith? Absolutely not! On the contrary, we uphold the law.
>
> [1]What then will we say that Abraham, our forefather according to the flesh, has found? [2]If Abraham was justified by works,
> he has something to boast about—but not before God. [3]For what
> does the Scripture say? **Abraham believed God, and it was credited to him for righteousness.** [4]Now to the one who works,
> pay is not credited as a gift, but as something owed. [5]But to the

[1] See Stowers, *Diatribe*, 164–67; and my Introduction II.C. Verbal links with the previous defensive section include "boast" (2:17, 23), "law" (2:11–15, 17–18, 20, 23, 25–27; 3:19–20), "works" (3:20), "justification" (2:13; 3:20), "Jews" and "Gentiles" (2:17–29; 3:1–9), "circumcised" and "uncircumcised" (2:25–29).

[2] Wright, "Romans," 488.

one who does not work, but believes on him who declares the
ungodly to be righteous, his faith is credited for righteousness.

[6]Just as David also speaks of the blessing of the person to
whom God credits righteousness apart from works:

7 **Blessed are those whose lawless acts are forgiven**
and whose sins are covered.
8 **Blessed is the person**
the Lord will never charge with sin.

[9]Is this blessing only for the circumcised, then? Or is it also
for the uncircumcised? For we say, **Faith was credited to Abraham for righteousness.** [10]In what way then was it credited—
while he was circumcised, or uncircumcised? It was not while
he was circumcised, but uncircumcised. [11]And he received the
sign of circumcision as a seal of the righteousness that he had by
faith while still uncircumcised. This was to make him the father
of all who believe but are not circumcised, so that righteousness
may be credited to them also. [12]And he became the father of the
circumcised, who are not only circumcised but who also follow
in the footsteps of the faith our father Abraham had while he was
still uncircumcised.

[13]For the promise to Abraham or to his descendants that he
would inherit the world was not through the law, but through the
righteousness that comes by faith. [14]If those who are of the law
are heirs, faith is made empty and the promise nullified, [15]because
the law produces wrath. And where there is no law, there is no
transgression.

[16]This is why the promise is by faith, so that it may be according to grace, to guarantee it to all the descendants—not only
to those who are of the law but also to those who are of Abraham's
faith. He is the father of us all. [17]As it is written: **I have made you
the father of many nations.** He is our father in God's sight, in
whom Abraham believed—the God who gives life to the dead and
calls things into existence that do not exist. [18]He believed, hoping
against hope, so that he became **the father of many nations** according to what had been spoken: **So will your descendants be.**
[19]He did not weaken in faith when he considered his own body to
be already dead (since he was about a hundred years old) and also
the deadness of Sarah's womb. [20]He did not waver in unbelief at
God's promise but was strengthened in his faith and gave glory to
God, [21]because he was fully convinced that what God had promised, he was also able to do. [22]Therefore, **it was credited to him
for righteousness.** [23]Now **it was credited to him** was not written

for Abraham alone, [24]but also for us. It will be credited to us who believe in him who raised Jesus our Lord from the dead. [25]He was delivered up for our trespasses and raised for our justification.

Context

An immediate link with the preceding passage is provided by the inferential conjunction οὖν ("then"), along with references in 3:27–28 to "faith" (cf. 3:22, 25, 26) and being "justified by faith" (cf. 3:24, 26). The claim that there is "no distinction" (3:22–24) is reinforced when Paul stresses that justification by faith is for "Jews" and "Gentiles," "circumcised" and "uncircumcised" (3:29–30). Paul's reference to the testimony of the law and the prophets (3:21) also finds an echo in his claim to "uphold the law" (3:31). These themes surface again in the next chapter, where they are developed more fully: justification by faith apart from works (4:1–8); no distinction between circumcised and uncircumcised in the enjoyment of this blessing (4:9–12); the law is upheld by showing how the covenant promise to Abraham is fulfilled in Christ (4:13–25). So 3:27–31 is a bridge passage, preparing for the exposition of these important themes in 4:1–25. This whole unit concludes with the assertion that Jesus was "raised for our justification" (4:25), which prepares for the opening words of the next section, "Therefore, since we have been declared righteous by faith" (5:1).

Structure

The bridge passage in 3:27–31 includes six rhetorical questions. The first allows Paul to exclude the possibility of a particular form of boasting. Two further questions clarify that this exclusion is "by a law of faith," which is explained (γάρ, "for") in terms of a person's being "justified by faith apart from the works of the law."[3] The fourth and fifth questions lead to the affirmation that God is for Jews and Gentiles alike, "since there is one God who will justify the circumcised by faith and the uncircumcised through faith." Paul's final question ("Do we then nullify the law through faith?")

[3] The external evidence supporting γάρ in 3:28 (א A D* Ψ etc.) is slightly superior to that supporting οὖν (B C D^c K P etc.). "The context, moreover, favors γάρ, for ver. 28 gives a reason for the argument in ver. 27, not a conclusion from it" (Metzger, *Textual Commentary*, 450).

is answered emphatically ("Absolutely not! On the contrary, we uphold the law.") The next chapter illustrates what he means by this.

A further series of questions in 4:1, 3, 9, 10 continues the dialogical exchange. The first introduces the possibility that Abraham was "justified by works" and "has something to boast about." Yet the emphatic response "but not before God" clearly rejects this. A second question asks what Scripture says about this and introduces a quote from Gen 15:6. This text is critical to the argument that follows. Developing his previous claim that justification is "by faith apart from the works of the law," Paul contrasts "one who works" with "one . . . who believes." A citation from Ps 32:1–2 is added to fill out the picture. The next section considers faith in relation to circumcision (vv. 9–12), asking whether the blessing of righteousness by faith is only for the circumcised. Paul restates Gen 15:6 in his own words and argues that Abraham "received the sign of circumcision as a seal of the righteousness that he had by faith while still uncircumcised." This happened so that he might be the father of uncircumcised and circumcised believers alike. Paul continues to reflect on faith in relation to the story of Abraham, considering faith apart from the law (vv. 13–16), then faith apart from sight (vv. 17–21), before demonstrating how Abraham's faith anticipated Christian faith (vv. 22–25). Righteousness will be credited to those who share the resurrection faith of Abraham and "believe in him who raised Jesus our Lord from the dead." A concluding statement ("he was delivered up for our trespasses and raised for our justification") enables Paul to outline more fully the particular shape of Christian faith.

Outline:

1. Justification by faith for Jews and Gentiles alike (3:27–31)
2. Abraham the father of all who are justified by faith (4:1–12)
3. The promises to Abraham fulfilled in Christ (4:13–25)

3:27–28. Paul resumes the diatribe mode of discourse used in 2:1–3:9, once more allowing readers to overhear an argument with a Jewish dialogue partner. His first question ("Where, then, is boasting?" Ποῦ οὖν ἡ καύχησις) is decisively answered by the statement that "it is excluded" (ἐξεκλείσθη; cf. Gal 4:17). The inferential conjunction οὖν ("then") links this question closely to the preceding argument about the manifestation of the righteousness of God in the gospel era. This has made justification possible for all who have faith in the crucified Messiah. So the passive verb ἐξεκλείσθη implies that boasting is excluded by God's action in justifying sinners on the basis of Christ's redemptive sacrifice.[4] But two further questions are posed for clarification: "By what kind of law? By one of works?" (διὰ ποίου νόμου; τῶν ἔργων;).[5] The emphatic answer is "No, on the contrary, by a law of faith" (οὐχί, ἀλλὰ διὰ νόμου πίστεως).

Paul's play on the word νόμος could be understood metaphorically to mean "principle" or "rule." It is more likely, however, that νόμος is used consistently throughout this passage to refer to the Mosaic law (see §1.4).[6] So "the law of works" (νόμου τῶν ἔργων) will be the inverse of ἔργων νόμου (vv. 20, 28, "works of the law"), and the sense will be "the law understood as teaching righteousness by works." On this reading, "the law of faith" (νόμου πίστεως) will be "the law understood as teaching righteousness by faith."[7] Paul's conclusion in v. 31 supports this view. His teaching about justification by faith upholds the law and is consistent with a true understanding of the law and its purpose (cf. 10:5–10 comment). Viewing the law as a means of obtaining righteousness by obedience to God's commands leads to the sort of boasting that Paul says is excluded by the gospel.

Given Paul's earlier use of the verb καυχᾶσαι ("boast") in connection with Israel's knowledge of God and possession of the law (2:17, 23), the related noun καύχησις has a special application to Jewish boasting or false confidence in 3:27 (cf. 4:2, καύχημα ["boast"]). The apostle does not oppose boasting of every sort here,

[4] Cf. Dunn, *Romans 1–8*, 185. Cranfield (*Romans*, 1:219) considers that boasting is excluded "in the sense that (God) has shown it to be futile and absurd through the OT scriptures." It is certainly excluded in the case of Abraham (4:1–5).

[5] Cf. Runge, *Discourse Grammar*, 66.

[6] So Cranfield, *Romans*, 1:219–20. Moo (*Romans*, 251–53) argues for the metaphorical view, as does Rosner, *Paul and the Law*, 119–20. Schreiner (*Romans*, 201–2) explains why he has shifted from the metaphorical to the literal view. Cf. 9:31–32; 10:1–4 comments.

[7] Dunn (*Romans 1–8*, 186–87) argues that the law understood in terms of works gives prominence to certain features such as circumcision that exclude Gentiles, but the law understood in terms of faith does not. This, however, ignores the moral dimension to "works" in Paul's argument.

though the gospel certainly challenges all forms of self-confidence before God.[8] He later employs the terminology in a positive way, implying a transformation of human values and attitudes when the gospel is believed (5:1–2, 11; 15:17; cf. 1 Cor 1:29–31).[9]

Proponents of the so-called New Perspective on Paul contend that 3:20, 27–29 merely describe Paul's opposition "to Jewish confidence in national privilege and to exclusivism, not a legalistic works-righteousness that earns salvation."[10] However, several arguments challenge the adequacy of this conclusion. First, as already noted in connection with 3:1–20, Paul argues that Jews cannot claim a special exemption at the judgment seat of God on the basis of their election and obedience to the law since the oracles entrusted to them (3:2) expose their moral transgressions and accountability to God's judgment. Indeed, "no one will be justified in his sight by the works of the law, because the knowledge of sin comes through the law" (3:20). Second, Paul's contrast between the law of works and the law of faith in 3:27 appears to be amplified and explained in 9:31–32. Unbelieving Israel, "pursuing the law of righteousness, has not achieved the righteousness of the law" because "they did not pursue it by faith, but as if it were by works."[11] Third, as a development from 3:20, two ways of seeking justification are contrasted in 3:28: "For we conclude that a person is justified by faith apart from the works of the law." These two ways are explained in 4:1–5 with reference to Abraham's faith and the works for which he was praised

---

[8] Jewett (*Romans*, 295–96) argues that Rome was "the boasting champion of the ancient world" and contends that Paul takes Jewish boasting as illustrating "a universal phenomenon in Paul's social environment." However, the issue here is not "competitive boasting" but boasting before God (cf. 4:2).

[9] Cf. Gathercole, *Boasting*, 252–62. Paul uses καύχησις in a negative sense in 3:27; 15:17 but positively in 1 Cor 15:31; 2 Cor 1:12; 7:4, 14; 8:24; 11:10, 17; 1 Thess 2:19. Jewett (*Romans*, 295n10) points to negative applications in the LXX (e.g., Sir 31:10; Prov 16:31) and other Greek texts.

[10] Gathercole, *Boasting*, 222. Gathercole summarizes the views of Sanders, Dunn, and Wright here. Arguing against their conclusions, Gathercole exposes teaching about obedience and final vindication in Jewish literature from the Second Temple period.

[11] See how Gathercole (*Boasting*, 226–30) critiques interpretations of 9:30–33; 10:3 by representatives of the New Perspective.

in Jewish tradition. Paul's "we conclude" (λογιζόμεθα) refers to "a faith-judgment, a conviction reached in the light of the gospel."[12]

Although it would be wrong to caricature first-century Judaism as being consumed with works-righteousness and petty legalism, "it is probably the case that Paul detected a reliance on one's own works in those Jews who had heard and rejected the gospel, for they trusted in their own adherence to the law rather than in Christ for salvation."[13] If righteousness before God depends on faith, it cannot be achieved by pursuing "the works of the law" in any form. Paul does not yet focus on the inclusion of the Gentiles, though this verse lays the foundation for what he says in vv. 29–30. The term ἄνθρωπον ("a person") in v. 28 embraces all humanity.

3:29–30. Paul's fourth and fifth questions focus on the possibility of justification by faith for Jews and Gentiles alike. His rapid-fire style suggests "a line of argument finely tuned as a result of many exposures in debate."[14] The expression ἢ Ἰουδαίων ὁ θεὸς μόνον; ("Or is God the God of Jews only?") makes a conclusion about "what would necessarily follow, if what is stated in v. 28 were not true."[15] The related question clearly expects a positive answer ("Is he not the God of Gentiles too?" [οὐχὶ καὶ ἐθνῶν;]), which is immediately given ("Yes, of Gentiles too" [ναὶ καὶ ἐθνῶν]). This response is supported by the claim, "Since there is one God" (εἴπερ εἷς ὁ θεός). Paul alludes to the *Shema*, which was the basic creed of Judaism ("Listen, Israel: The LORD our God, the LORD is One," Deut 6:4), to challenge Jewish exclusivity and false confidence. The oneness of God means that he is the God of every race and nation and is concerned for the welfare of all. This is expressed in the relative clause that follows: "Who will justify the circumcised by faith and the uncircumcised

---

[12] Cranfield, *Romans*, 1:220. According to BDAG, the verb can mean "reckon" in the sense of "calculate, credit" (as in 4:4, 5, 6, 8), "consider" as a result of evaluating or calculating (as in 6:11; 8:36; 9:8), or "think, believe" (as in 2:3; 8:18). Cf. Hans W. Heidland, "λογίζομαι, λογισμός," *TDNT* 4:284–92.

[13] Schreiner, *Romans*, 205.

[14] Dunn, *Romans 1–8*, 188. Dunn highlights the tension in Jewish literature over the question of God's relationship to Gentiles.

[15] Cranfield, *Romans*, 1:221. Cranfield says no Jew of Paul's day would have questioned that God is the Creator, Ruler, and Judge of all, but the context here also implies that he is concerned for the salvation of all, as the promise to Abraham indicates (Gen 12:3; 17:4–6 cf. Rom 4:9–18).

through faith."[16] The religious and cultural division between Jews and Gentiles in Paul's world is highlighted by designating them "the circumcision" (περιτομήν) and "the uncircumcision" (ἀκροβυστίαν). But their common need for justification by faith is emphasized by the parallel expressions "by faith" (ἐκ πίστεως) and "through faith" (διὰ τῆς πίστεως).[17]

3:31. The final question in this section is "Do we then nullify the law through faith?" (νόμον οὖν καταργοῦμεν διὰ τῆς πίστεως;). This requires a strongly negative response ("Absolutely not!" μὴ γένοιτο) because it draws a wrong conclusion to what has just been argued. The premise that God is one and that he justifies Jews and Gentiles on the same basis is entirely consistent with the teaching of the law. The verb καταργέω can mean "invalidate, make powerless" (BDAG), as in 3:3; 4:14, but most likely means "abolish, wipe out, set aside" here (cf. 6:6). When Paul says, "On the contrary, we uphold the law" (ἀλλὰ νόμον ἱστάνομεν), he uses a verb that reflects biblical and later Jewish discussions of the law.[18] In this way he claims to be treating God's law appropriately. But what does he mean by "law" in this context? In 3:19–20 he talks about the law revealing and condemning sin, and there is an echo of that in 4:14–15. In 3:21 he claims that "the righteousness of God" is revealed in the gospel era "apart from the law" (meaning the law as "law-covenant"), though it is "attested by the Law and the Prophets." This is illustrated in 4:1–8 when he provides from Gen 15:6 and Ps 32:1–2 an explanation of the righteousness that is by faith. In 4:9–25 he shows how the covenant promises to Abraham are fulfilled in Christ, enabling Jews and Gentiles to trust in the Messiah and benefit from his saving work. Fundamentally, then, Paul means that the law is upheld in its prophetic role as a preparation for the gospel era,

---

[16] Jewett (*Romans*, 300) observes that εἴπερ ("if, as is indeed true," "seeing that") introduces the protasis, "presented as a fact in v. 30, which supplies the premise of the apodosis in v. 29." Jewett explains how Paul's openness to Gentiles differed from the developing views of rabbinic Judaism. Cf. Dunn, *Romans 1–8*, 189.

[17] Moo (*Romans*, 252) rightly argues that no distinction in meaning can be made between ἐκ πίστεως (cf. 1:17; 3:26; 4:16; 5:1) and διὰ τῆς πίστεως (cf. 3:22, 25). The future indicative δικαιώσει could be "simply logical" (Cranfield, *Romans*, 1.222) or a reference to final justification (Dunn, *Romans 1–8*, 188; Schreiner, *Romans*, 206).

[18] Cf. Dunn, *Romans 1–8*, 190; Jewett, *Romans*, 302–3; M. Wolter, "ἵστημι, ἱστάνω," *EDNT* 2:207. But Richard W. Thompson "The Alleged Rabbinic Background of Rom 3:31," *ETL* 63 [1987]: 136–48) disputes this.

"in which both Jews and Gentiles will be justified by grace through faith"[19] (see §§1.4; 2.2).

4:1. Paul's dialogical exchange continues with a further series of rhetorical questions (vv. 1, 3, 9, 10). As in 3:27, 31, the inferential conjunction οὖν ("then") signifies a new stage in the argument, making a logical connection with what has gone before. But the immediate link is not with "the law" (3:31) but with "boasting" (3:27). The first question is an odd construction because τί οὖν ἐροῦμεν ("What then will we say?") is normally followed by a statement and answer or a second question (cf. 6:1; 7:7; 8:31; 9:14, 30). This observation has led some to propose alternative translations (e.g., "What then will we say? Have we found Abraham to be our forefather according to the flesh?"). But this is not the most natural way to read the Greek, and it has suggested different lines of interpretation.[20] The traditional rendering makes good sense in the flow of the argument. Abraham is introduced as "our forefather according to the flesh" (τὸν προπάτορα ἡμῶν κατὰ σάρκα), suggesting that this is a question for Jews, who are related to Abraham by birth.[21] Later in the chapter he describes Abraham as the spiritual "father" of both Gentiles and Jews who believe (vv. 11–12, 16–17). The infinitive εὑρηκέναι ("to have found") is probably chosen to recall LXX expressions such as "find grace [mercy]" (εὑρίσκειν χάριν [ἔλεος]).[22] In effect, Paul's

[19] Rosner, *Paul and the Law*, 154. Cf. Byrne, *Romans*, 138, 140–41. Jewett's interpretation of νόμος as "law in general" (*Romans*, 303) is forced and inappropriate in this context. Schreiner's view (*Romans*, 207–8) that Paul refers specifically to the "moral norms of the law" is also not supported by the context (cf. Moo, *Romans*, 254–55).

[20] Cf. Richard B. Hays, "Have We Found Abraham to Be Our Forefather according to the Flesh? A Reconsideration of Rom 4:1," *NovT* 27 (1985): 76–98; Wright, "Romans," 489–90. Both have different ways of arguing that the primary issue in Rom 4 is the definition of Abraham's family rather than soteriology. Note the critique by Schreiner, *Romans*, 213, and Gathercole, *Boasting*, 234–35. Jewett (*Romans*, 307–8) also argues against Hays but relates κατὰ σάρκα unnaturally to the verb ("What shall we say our forefather Abraham found according to the flesh?")

[21] Προπάτορα ("forefather"), which only occurs here in the NT, is found in the earliest manuscripts but is replaced by πατέρα ("father") in later ones. Some correctors of early manuscripts also insert πατέρα, presumably because it was the customary designation for Abraham. But the harder reading is surely original.

[22] Cf. Sigfred Pedersen, "εὑρίσκω," *EDNT* 2:83–84 (e.g., Gen 6:8; 18:3; 19:19; 30:27). The position of εὑρηκέναι differs in some manuscripts, being found before Ἀβραάμ in ℵ A C D G Ψ etc., and after ἡμῶν in K P 33 88 etc. This variation could indicate that texts omitting the word (B 1739 Origen) were original, but Metzger

question is about how Abraham found favor with God (Gen 18:3; cf. 6:8; 30:27; 32:5 [LXX 32:6]; 33:8, 10).

A critical issue for understanding the argument that follows is an awareness of how some Jewish literature presents Abraham as the type or model for the devout Jew. In one strand he is described as "the great father of a multitude of nations, and no one has been found like him in glory. He kept the law of the Most High, and entered into a covenant with him; he certified the covenant in his flesh, and when he was tested he proved faithful" (Sir 44:19–20 [NRSV]; cf. 1 Macc 2:52). In another strand Abraham's faithfulness in testing leads to his being "accounted" as a friend of God: "Abraham did not walk in (evil), and he was accounted a friend of God because he kept the commandments of God and did not choose his own will" (CD 3:2–4; cf. Jub. 19:8–9; 23:9–10). Crucial to the Jewish presentation of Abraham is the view that "he was righteous on the basis of his obedience at the time of his justification, and thus the divine declaration (in Gen 15:6) is a *descriptive* judgment."[23] In these Jewish texts faithful obedience is counted for righteousness by God: "Abraham in the Jewish expository tradition was not marked out merely by his circumcision (though it was very significant); he was thought of as faithful and a friend of God because of his *comprehensive obedience*."[24]

4:2. A conditional clause, linked by the conjunction γάρ ("for"), explains the issue underlying the question just posed: "If Abraham was justified by works, he has something to boast about." The noun καύχημα ("boast"; cf. Sir 44:7) forms an obvious link with Paul's previous question about "boasting" (καύχησις) and his response in 3:27–28.[25] There he argues that boasting is excluded by the divine act of justification by faith "apart from the works of the law" (χωρὶς

(*Textual Commentary*, 450) argues that there was no reason for copyists to add this word if it was not part of the original. Manuscript variations may be attempts to improve the sense of the sentence. Cf. Cranfield, *Romans*, 1:226–27.

[23] Gathercole, *Boasting*, 237 (author's emphasis). Gathercole (37–194) provides a thorough analysis of the role of obedience in final vindication in a vast array of Jewish texts.

[24] Ibid., 238 (emphasis added).

[25] According to BDAG, καύχημα and καύχησις overlap in meaning. However, the latter is used in 3:27 with the sense of "taking pride in something, boasting" and the former is used in 4:2 with the sense of "that which constitutes a source of pride, boast."

ἔργων νόμου). Paul's expression in 4:2 also recalls 3:20, where he denies the possibility of being justified "by the works of the law" (*ἐξ ἔργων νόμου*). His emphatic response, "But not before God" (*ἀλλ' οὐ πρὸς θεόν*), prepares for the argument from Gen 15:6 that follows. The expression *πρὸς θεόν* is probably equivalent to *ἐνώπιον αὐτοῦ* (3:20, "before him"). It need not imply that Abraham had a boast before human beings but simply states his position "in reference to God."[26]

4:3. Paul's second rhetorical question ("For what does the Scripture say?") introduces a critical text into this debate. Scripture is treated as the ultimate authority. According to one line of Jewish thinking, Abraham was "found *faithful* (*πιστός*) when tested, and it was reckoned to him as righteousness" (1 Macc 2:52; cf. Mekilta 35[b]; 40[b]).[27] But Gen 15:6 states that "Abraham *believed* God and it was credited to him for righteousness" (*ἐπίστευσεν δὲ Ἀβραάμ* [LXX *Ἀβράμ*] *τῷ θεῷ καὶ ἐλογίσθη αὐτῷ εἰς δικαιοσύνην*).[28] This does not imply that Abraham's faith was a meritorious act that God recognized and rewarded. Paul clearly distinguishes between "working" and "believing" (vv. 4–5). The challenge facing Abraham was to rely on God's promise to supply numerous descendants even though he was childless and anticipated that his slave would be his heir (Gen 15:2–5). Later passages in Genesis illustrate the testing of Abraham's faith, but the verb *ἐλογίσθη* ("it was credited") in 15:6 must signify "a counting which is not a rewarding of merit but a free and unmerited decision of divine grace."[29] The "crediting" on view here is a "reckoning" of something that is not inherent to that person, in this case righteousness before God.

---

[26] Jewett, *Romans*, 304, 310. Cf. Cranfield, *Romans*, 1:228; and Gathercole, *Boasting*, 241–42.

[27] Cf. Cranfield, *Romans*, 1:229. Gathercole (*Boasting*, 243) observes, "In the Jewish literature, God responds to Abraham with the fully *appropriate* verdict of the justification of that faithful Abraham." But Paul infers in v. 5 that Abraham was "ungodly" when righteousness was "credited to him."

[28] The first verb in the Hebrew text (וְהֶאֱמִן, "he believed") "probably indicates repeated or continued action" (Gorndon J. Wenham, *Genesis 1–15*, WBC 1 [Waco: Word, 1987], 329). The second verb is active (וַיַּחְשְׁבֶהָ, "and he credited it"), rather than passive (LXX *ἐλογίσθη*, "it was credited"; see n. 12 above for different uses of this verb).

[29] Cranfield, *Romans*, 1.231. Cf. Moo, *Romans*, 265.

Paul understands Gen 15:6 to express what he means by justification by faith. In vv. 4–8 he explains what the text means by "it was credited" and, in vv. 9–21, how Abraham "believed." God's pronouncement initiated a new stage in the patriarch's relationship with God. The sequel was a restatement of God's promise to give the land to Abraham's offspring. A sacrificial ritual confirmed that this would eventually happen because of God's covenant commitment to him (Gen 15:7–20). Paul goes on to indicate that there was a forensic dimension to this reckoning when he speaks about God justifying "the ungodly" (v. 5), and he relates the reckoning of righteousness to the nonreckoning of sin (v. 8; cf. Ps 32:2). The apostle has in mind "a creative act, whereby the believer is given a new 'status.'"[30]

4:4–5. As in 3:19, the conjunction δέ ("now") signals a new development in the argument.[31] The significance of Gen 15:6 is developed in two parallel claims. On the one hand, Paul considers the situation of "the one who works" (τῷ δὲ ἐργαζομένῳ). To such a person, "pay is not credited as a gift, but as something owed" (ὁ μισθὸς οὐ λογίζεται κατὰ χάριν ἀλλὰ κατὰ ὀφείλημα, [lit.] "the reward is not reckoned according to grace but according to debt").[32] On the other hand, Paul compares the situation of "the one who does not work, but believes on him who declares the ungodly to be righteous" (τῷ δὲ μὴ ἐργαζομένῳ πιστεύοντι δὲ ἐπὶ τὸν δικαιοῦντα τὸν ἀσεβῆ). To such a person, "his faith is credited for righteousness" (λογίζεται ἡ πίστις αὐτοῦ εἰς δικαιοσύνην). Several OT texts insist that God does not justify the guilty and warn human judges about doing this (e.g., Exod 23:7; Prov 17:15; Isa 5:23). But Paul's startling claim that God justifies the ungodly arises from what he proclaimed in 3:23–26. Only because of the redemptive and propitiatory death of Jesus can God be righteous and declare sinners righteous. Abraham's dependent faith prefigured this gospel-informed trust in God (cf. 4:23–25).

---

[30] Moo, *Romans*, 264. Donald A. Carson ("The Vindication of Imputation: On Fields of Discourse and Semantic Fields," in *Justification: What's at Stake in the Current Debates*, ed. Mark Husbands and Daniel J. Treier [Downers Grove: InterVarsity, 2004]: 56–68) considers the extent to which this may be described as an imputation of righteousness.

[31] Cf. Runge, *Discourse Grammar*, 28–36.

[32] For Paul's use of χάρις with reference to divine grace, see 1:5, 7; 3:24 (comment); 4:16; 5:2, 15, 17, 20, 21; 6:1, 14, 15; 11:5, 6; 12:3, 6; 15:5; 16:20, 24.

Paul's stark contrast between a "worker" and a "believer" has been described as not truly mirroring Jewish theology, which often indicates that good works flow from God's grace.[33] But metaphors of repayment or commutative justice can also be found in the literature, and "the soteriology of Second Temple Judaism more than justifies a 'mirror reading' in this case."[34] Paul speaks here about works that are not rooted in faith, continuing his engagement with the sort of Judaism reflected in 2:1–3:20. There he portrays "one who works" as fundamentally unbelieving and unrepentant (2:2–5), with a false confidence in his status before God and his obedience to Torah. As the context of Gen 15:6 makes clear, however, Abraham is a genuine believer who trusts the promises of God and acts accordingly. Moreover, Paul implies that Abraham was "ungodly" (ἀσεβῆ) when he was justified and unable to make a claim on God because of his obedience and faithfulness. Biblical and later Jewish tradition portrayed Abraham as having come from a pagan background (e.g., Gen 11:31–12:3; Josh 24:2–3; Jub. 12:1–8, 12–14, 16–20; Apoc. Abr. 1–8; Josephus, *Ant.* 1.155). In response to God's initiative, Abraham became a believer in the one true God, but the term "ungodly" cannot simply be a reference to his origins. Paul applies the term generally in 5:6 (ἀσεβῶν) to all for whom Christ died, and it is likely that he simply regards Abraham as a sinner needing God's forgiveness and justifying grace.[35]

4:6–8. Against those who argue that the issue addressed by Paul in this chapter is Jewish ethnocentricity and unwarranted confidence in external signs of covenant membership, these verses point

[33] So Dunn (*Romans 1–8*, 204) says, "The language used here (working, reckoning reward) should not be taken as a description of the Judaism of Paul's day." Wright ("Romans," 479) contends that first-century Jews "were not bent on earning their justification, or their salvation, from scratch by performing the 'works of the law.'" He describes the metaphor in 4:5 as a "unique and brief sidelight" (491). But how adequately does this view of Judaism square with the challenges Paul presents?

[34] Gathercole, *Boasting*, 244. He cites Pss. Sol. 2:34; 9:1–5; T. Job 4:6–7; Sib. Or. 2:304; Josephus, *Ant* 3.10; 2 En. 2:2; 45:1–2. "Mirror reading" involves understanding a text as a reflection of beliefs or practices in the situation addressed.

[35] The related term ἀσέβειαν ("godlessness") is used in 1:18 with reference to the sort of idolatrous lifestyle that Paul goes on to describe. But the narrative in Gen 12:4–14:24 indicates that Abraham had already left his pagan background behind. Contrast Byrne, *Romans*, 146.

to a more fundamental problem.[36] The comparative conjunction καθάπερ ("just as") introduces what "David also says" (καὶ Δαυὶδ λέγει) about justification (καθώς similarly introduces a biblical citation in 3:4; 9:13; 10:15; 11:8). David is portrayed as an ungodly and sinful Israelite who speaks of "the blessing of the person to whom God credits righteousness apart from works."[37] Examples of David's godlessness can be gleaned from the narratives about his life (most obviously 2 Sam 11). But Ps 32:1–2 (LXX 31:1–2), which is attributed to David, presents his own testimony about this matter. Paul's introduction includes the word "blessing" (μακαρισμόν) because the related term "blessed" occurs twice in the citation (μακάριοι, μακάριος). He also picks up terms from the preceding argument (ὁ θεὸς λογίζεται δικαιοσύνην χωρὶς ἔργων, "God credits righteousness apart from works") and makes a verbal connection with Gen 15:6.[38] A literal translation of Ps 32:1–2 shows the links more clearly: "Blessed are those whose lawless acts are forgiven and whose sins are covered; blessed is the person whose sin the LORD will never credit." With this text the apostle links the reckoning of righteousness apart from works with the forgiveness of lawless acts (ἀφέθησαν αἱ ἀνομίαι) and the nonreckoning of sin (οὐ μὴ λογίσηται κύριος ἁμαρτίαν).

Although the verb "forgive" occurs nowhere else in the Pauline writings, he uses the noun "forgiveness" (ἄφεσις) in two significant contexts (Eph 1:7; Col 1:14). "Lawless acts" (αἱ ἀνομίαι) are deliberate and open expressions of rebellion against God and his commands (cf. 6:19; 2 Cor 6:14; 2 Thess 2:3, 7; Titus 2:14), while "sins" (αἱ ἁμαρτίαι) are more generally offenses against God.[39] The

[36] Schreiner (*Romans*, 217–21) points to several inadequacies in the approach to this passage by exponents of the New Perspective. Cf. Gathercole, *Boasting*, 246–48.

[37] Paul's introduction challenges the view of David presented in CD 5:5, which talks about his works (apart from the murder of Uriah) going up before God, and 4QMMT, which speaks of David as "a man of righteous deeds," whose salvation from afflictions and forgiveness resulted from his obedience.

[38] Paul follows the Rabbinic pattern of biblical interpretation called *gezerah shawah* (analogy), joining two passages on the basis of a particular word or phrase, in this case ἐλογίσθη (Gen 15:6) and λογίσηται (LXX Ps 31:2). Cf. Richard N. Longenecker, *Biblical Exegesis in the Apostolic Period* (Grand Rapids: Eerdmans, 1975), 34, 117. Paul uses the second passage to explain the significance of the first.

[39] Paul mostly uses the singular form of this word with reference to "a state which embraces all humanity" (Walter Grundmann, "ἁμαρτάνω, ἁμάρτημα, ἁμαρτία,"

covering of sin by God (ἐπεκαλύφθησαν αἱ ἁμαρτίαι) is another way of speaking about his forgiveness and refusal to take into account what causes someone to be guilty (cf. Ps 85:2; LXX 84:3).[40] An emphatic negative (οὐ μὴ λογίσηται) highlights God's intention *never* to reckon sin and its punishment against the person whose sin has been forgiven. So David is

> the paradigmatic sinner whose sins need, in the threefold assertion of 4:7–8, forgiveness, covering, and "nonreckoning." God's declarative act of the justification of the sinner (4:5) requires his act of the "nonreckoning" of sin (4:8). However, this is simultaneous with God's *positive* reckoning of righteousness on the other side of the ledger.[41]

The implication of Paul's argument is that God's reckoning of righteousness to Abraham involved also the nonreckoning of his sin. Moreover, by citing a text from Genesis and another from Psalms, "Paul makes good his earlier claim that 'the Law and the Prophets bear witness' to the righteousness of God that stands revealed 'apart from the law' (3:21b)."[42]

4:9–10. Paul moves to a new stage in his argument, once again using the inferential conjunction οὖν ("then," as in 3:27, 31; 4:1, 10). But his third question actually returns to the claim in 3:29–30 that justification by faith is possible for Jews and Gentiles equally. Paul asks, "Is this blessing only for the circumcised, then? Or is it also for the uncircumcised?" At first glance the blessing promised in Ps 32:1–2 was relevant to Jews alone (τὴν περιτομήν, "the circumcision") and not to Gentiles (τὴν ἀκροβυστίαν, "the uncircumcision").

TDNT 1:309).

[40] Although the rabbis related this psalm to the cleansing made possible by the Day of Atonement ritual (e.g., Pesiq. Rab. 45 [185^b]), there is no indication in Ps 32 that this is specifically in view. Rather, the psalm speaks of David's personal struggle to acknowledge his sin to God and experience his forgiveness. Cf. Cranfield, *Romans*, 1.234nn1,4.

[41] Gathercole, *Boasting*, 248 (emphasis in original). Carson ("The Vindication of Imputation," 61–68) argues that it is not faith in some purely psychological sense that is credited as righteousness but "faith with a certain object." Justification is parallel to the imputation of righteousness in vv. 5–6, and what is imputed is "an alien righteousness" because God is said to justify "the ungodly."

[42] Byrne, *Romans*, 147.

After all, David himself was a circumcised man! But the apostle challenges that exclusive view by first restating Gen 15:6 in his own words ("For we say, 'Faith was credited to Abraham for righteousness'"). Then, he poses a fourth question about the context of that divine pronouncement ("In what way then was it credited—while he was circumcised, or uncircumcised?" *πῶς οὖν ἐλογίσθη; ἐν περιτομῇ ὄντι ἢ ἐν ἀκροβυστίᾳ;*). This allows him to make a simple observation from Scripture ("Not while he was circumcised, but uncircumcised," *οὐκ ἐν περιτομῇ ἀλλ᾽ ἐν ἀκροβυστίᾳ*).

4:11–12. Paul adds a supporting observation to his previous one, using the coordinating conjunction *καί* ("and"). When God commanded Abraham and his offspring to be circumcised, he described the action as "a sign of the covenant between me and you" (LXX Gen 17:11, *ἐν σημείῳ διαθήκης ἀνὰ μέσον ἐμοῦ καὶ ὑμῶν*). Paul adapts this wording and speaks of "the sign of circumcision" (*σημεῖον περιτομῆς*), which was "a seal of the righteousness that he had by faith while still uncircumcised" (*σφραγῖδα τῆς δικαιοσύνης τῆς πίστεως τῆς ἐν τῇ ἀκροβυστίᾳ*).[43] That reckoning of righteousness to Abraham took place on an earlier occasion (Gen 15:6). So Paul views circumcision as "the outward and visible authentication, ratification and guarantee of the righteousness by faith which was already his while he was still uncircumcised."[44] Circumcision did not confer righteousness on him since righteousness was the gracious gift of God in a previous encounter.

A purpose clause shows God's intention for Abraham with respect to the uncircumcised: (lit.) "so that he might be the father of all who believe in a state of uncircumcision" (*εἰς τὸ εἶναι αὐτὸν πατέρα πάντων τῶν πιστευόντων δι᾽ ἀκροβυστίας*). A subsidiary clause shows that, in justifying Abraham when he was uncircumcised, God intended that believing Gentiles might similarly have righteousness credited to them (*εἰς τὸ λογισθῆναι [καὶ] αὐτοῖς [τὴν] δικαιοσύνην*, "so

---

[43] "The sign which is circumcision" (*σημεῖον περιτομῆς* [genitive of apposition]), was received as *σφραγῖδα*, meaning "attestation, confirmation, certification" (BDAG), of the righteousness he had by faith. Cf. Tim Schramm, "*σφραγίς*," *EDNT* 3:317. "Righteousness" is not simply a substitute for "covenant membership," as Wright ("Romans," 495) argues.

[44] Cranfield, *Romans*, 1:236. Circumcision pointed beyond itself to "a righteousness that is far more universally available" through faith (Byrne, *Romans*, 147).

that righteousness may be credited to them [also]").[45] Paul reverses the order expressed in 1:16 ("first to the Jew and also to the Greek") in his desire to highlight God's commitment to justifying Gentiles by faith. The main purpose clause is resumed in v. 12, when the word "father" (*πατέρα*) is repeated. Now it is asserted that God made Abraham "the father of the circumcised" (*καὶ πατέρα περιτομῆς*). But there is an important qualification to this claim: "who are not only circumcised, but who also follow in the footsteps of the faith our father Abraham had while he was still uncircumcised" (*τοῖς οὐκ ἐκ περιτομῆς μόνον ἀλλὰ καὶ τοῖς στοιχοῦσιν τοῖς ἴχνεσιν τῆς ἐν ἀκροβυστίᾳ πίστεως τοῦ πατρὸς ἡμῶν Ἀβραάμ*). Paul is not thinking about two different Jewish groups here, but one. Abraham is only "the father of the circumcised" in a limited sense. He is the father of those who do not rely on circumcision alone but who exhibit the same faith as Abraham did. Summarizing vv. 11–12, then, Abraham is "the point of union between all who believe, whether circumcised or uncircumcised."[46] This spiritual fatherhood should be contrasted with the fatherhood "according to the flesh" mentioned in v. 1.

4:13. Paul continues his reflection on Abraham and his faith, using *οὐ γάρ* ("for not") to introduce an important thesis statement (cf. 1:16). A note of eschatological fulfillment is struck when he explains that the promise to Abraham or to his offspring was that "he would inherit the world" (*τὸ κληρονόμον αὐτὸν εἶναι κόσμου*). Such an amazing outcome would not be "through the law" (*διὰ νόμου*) but "through the righteousness that comes by faith" (*διὰ δικαιοσύνης πίστεως*). Paul could simply be reflecting on the biblical sequence of events here: the law was given through Moses long after God's promises were made to Abraham (cf. Gal 3:17–18). But the preposition *δία* ("through") is most likely used in an instrumental sense,

---

[45] This second clause could be consecutive, expressing result (Cranfield, *Romans*, 1:237), but the same syntactical form in a sequence like this (*εἰς τό* with an infinitive) is more likely to express purpose on both occasions. Although the word *καί*, meaning "also" here, is found in a range of manuscripts, the shorter reading is well attested and is more likely to be original. Copyists could have added this word to sharpen the argument. It is hard to decide from the manuscript evidence whether the definite article *τήν* should be read before *δικαιοσύνην*.

[46] Cranfield, *Romans*, 1:237. Considering the double use of *τοῖς* in v. 12, Moo (*Romans*, 270–71) argues that Paul refers to Jewish Christians here. But Dunn (*Romans 1–8*, 211) rightly claims that the complex syntax simply refers to "the circumcised who believe." See n. 57 below and Schreiner, *Romans*, 226.

conveying the idea that "the promise was not given on the condition of its being merited by fulfillment of the law but simply on the basis of the righteousness of faith."[47]

Paul's expansion of "the land" to "the world" is in line with Jewish thinking (e.g., Sir 44:21; Jub. 19:21; Philo, *Mos.* 1.155; cf. 1 En. 5:7b), which came to identify this with "the world to come" (e.g., Pss. Sol. 12:6; Josephus, *Ant.* 32.3; Sib. Or. 3:768–69; 4 Ezra 6:59; 7:9; 2 Bar. 14:13; 44:13; 51:3).[48] This inheritance would be the eventual outcome of the promises made to Abraham: that he would have an immense number of descendants, encompassing "many nations" (Gen 12:2; 13:16; 15:5; 17:4–6, 16–20; 22:17); that he would possess the land of Canaan (Gen 13:15–17; 15:12–21; 17:8); and that he would be the medium of blessing to "all the peoples on earth" (Gen 12:3; 18:18; 22:18).[49]

For the first time in this letter, Paul uses the word "promise" (ἐπαγγελία) in relation to these covenant commitments (cf. 4:14, 16, 20; 9:4, 8, 9; 15:8; §1.2). This terminology came into favor in Hellenistic Jewish writings (e.g., 3 Macc 2:10–11; Pss. Sol. 12:6; T. Jos. 20:1), even though it had no preliminary history in the OT.[50] Paul makes clear in vv. 14–16 his reasons for preferring this way of speaking about God's covenant with Abraham. Abraham's God-given faith was to be the means by which the divine plan was advanced in his own lifetime, and this depended on God's gracious promises. The ultimate fulfillment of God's promises occurred through Christ, who made it possible for believing Jews and Gentiles to share his resurrection glory and reign with him in the world to come (e.g., 4:23–25; 5:2, 17; 8:11, 17, 19–23; cf. 1 Cor 3:21b–23).[51]

---

[47] Cranfield, *Romans*, 1:239. Cranfield notes rabbinic sources where it was claimed that Abraham knew the law of Moses and performed it in its completeness.

[48] Byrne (*Romans*, 157) points out that in Jub. 22:14; 32:19 Israel's lordship of the world brings about the fulfillment of Gen 1:26–28 via the Abrahamic promise.

[49] Moo (*Romans*, 274) notes the special significance of Gen 22:17 ("your offspring will possess [κληρονομήσει] the city gates of their enemies") and the beatitude of Jesus in Matt 5:5 ("Blessed are the humble, because they will inherit the earth" [γή]).

[50] Cf. Julius Schniewind and Gerhard Friedrich, "ἐπαγγέλλω κτλ.," *TDNT* 2:579. The word διαθήκη ("covenant") is only used in 9:4; 11:27 (cf. 1 Cor 11:25; 2 Cor 3:6, 14; Gal 3:15, 17; 4:24).

[51] However, τῷ σπέρματι αὐτοῦ should be understood collectively in this context ("to his descendants," as in vv. 16, 18; 9:7–8), rather than being a particular reference to Christ, as in Gal 3:16.

4:14–15. Paul's thesis in the previous verse is supported negatively in two ways. First, the reason (γάρ, "for") the inheritance promised to Abraham is not "through the law" is that "if those who are of the law are heirs, faith is made empty and the promise is nullified." The beginning of this conditional clause (εἰ οἱ ἐκ νόμου κληρονόμοι) raises the possibility that adherence to the law is necessary for someone to "inherit the world."[52] But Paul's conclusion counters this by pointing to the unacceptable consequences. Faith is "reduced to nothing" (κεκένωται ἡ πίστις) or "caused to be without result or effect" (BDAG; cf. 1 Cor 15:14, κενὴ καὶ ἡ πίστις ὑμῶν), and the promise is "made powerless" or "set aside" (κατήργηται, cf. 3:31 comment). In view of what follows, the apostle is not simply claiming that the words "faith" and "promise" would lose their meaning. Rather, the exercise of faith would fail to attain its end, and the promise would never be fulfilled.[53]

The second reason (γάρ) the inheritance promised to Abraham is not through the law is that "the law produces wrath" (ὁ νόμος ὀργὴν κατεργάζεται). This suggests that any attempt to establish a claim on God by obedience to the law is futile because the law exposes sin and brings God's wrath (cf. 3:20; 5:20; 7:7–13). Paul clarifies this point by claiming that "where there is no law, there is no transgression" (οὗ δὲ οὐκ ἔστιν νόμος οὐδὲ παράβασις). Of course, sin exists where there is no law, but the character of sin as transgression is revealed by the law (cf. 2:23 [παραβάσεως]; 5:12–14). Consequently, "the law renders people even more accountable to God than they were without the law"[54] (see §1.4).

4:16. The thesis in v. 13 is developed positively in vv. 16–22 as Paul argues that faith is the key to the fulfillment of God's promise about inheriting "the world." The reason the promise is "by faith"

---

[52] Dunn (*Romans 1–8*, 213) and Jewett (*Romans*, 326) argue that the expression οἱ ἐκ νόμου ("those of the law") reflects the technical Jewish expression for "the sons of the law." Moo (*Romans*, 275) takes the expression to mean "those who are basing their hope for the inheritance on the law."

[53] So Moo, *Romans*, 275; Cranfield, *Romans*, 1:240. Dunn (*Romans 1–8*, 214) and Jewett (*Romans*, 326) take the definite article before πίστις to refer back to Abraham's faith in Gen 15:6, but the reference could also be to faith generically.

[54] Moo, *Romans*, 277. Moo considers a variety of interpretations of v. 15. Jewett (*Romans*, 327) suggests that "the law produces wrath" is Paul's "combat slogan" against the premise of his opponents that the law produces life and is the means to inherit what was promised to Abraham. See also Schreiner, *Romans*, 230.

(Διὰ τοῦτο ἐκ πίστεως, cf. 1:17) is first explained with a purpose clause: "so that it may be according to grace" (ἵνα κατὰ χάριν), that is, according to God's free and unmerited favor. "God has made his plan of salvation to depend, on man's side, not on fulfillment of the law but solely on faith, in order that, on his side, it might be a matter of grace."[55] A further clause, which could express result but more likely purpose, explains this in terms of the promise being guaranteed to every descendant of Abraham (εἰς τὸ εἶναι βεβαίαν τὴν ἐπαγγελίαν παντὶ τῷ σπέρματι, [lit.] "so that the promise might be unwavering for every descendant"). Given what Paul has already said about the law in v. 15, God's plan could not be (lit.) "something that can be relied on" (βεβαίαν, BDAG) unless it were a matter of grace.[56] Since the promise calls for faith in God's grace for its fulfillment, the blessing is available to every believing descendant.

The expression "not only to those who are of the law but also to those who are of Abraham's faith" (οὐ τῷ ἐκ τοῦ νόμου μόνον ἀλλὰ καὶ τῷ ἐκ πίστεως Ἀβραάμ) parallels the claim at the end of v. 12 about Abraham being "the father of the circumcised, who are not only circumcised but who also follow in the footsteps of the faith our father Abraham had while he was still uncircumcised." In both contexts the reference is to Jews who share the faith of Abraham.[57] An allusion to Gen 17:5 confirms that Abraham is "father of us all" (ὅς ἐστιν πατὴρ πάντων ἡμῶν), embracing also believing Gentiles (as in v. 11). So Paul's concentration on the law and faith in relation to Abraham's Jewish offspring (vv. 13–16) concludes with a reminder that God is the father of *all* who share Abraham's faith (cf. vv. 11–12).

---

[55] Cranfield, *Romans*, 1:242. He contends that διὰ τοῦτο ("for this reason") refers forward to the purpose clause beginning with ἵνα rather than backward to the argument of the preceding verses (cf. 2 Cor 13:10; Phlm 15; 1 Tim 1:16).

[56] In a technical sense, βεβαίος was used to denote legally guaranteed security (Dunn, *Romans 1–8*, 216). See n. 32 above for references to divine grace in Romans, and Klaus Berger, "χάρις," *EDNT* 3:458–59.

[57] Cranfield's proposal (*Romans*, 1.242–43) that τῷ ἐκ τοῦ νόμου refers to Jewish Christians and τῷ ἐκ πίστεως Ἀβραάμ refers to Gentile Christians is forced and out of place here. Byrne (*Romans*, 150, 159) sees a reference to Christians in both vv. 11–12 and v. 16. But Paul cannot be excluding Jews and Gentiles who shared the faith of Abraham before the time of Christ from experiencing justification. His application to Christian believers comes in vv. 23–25. So, rightly, Dunn, *Romans 1–8*, 216.

4:17. Genesis 17:5 is now quoted from the LXX (πατέρα πολλῶν ἐθνῶν τέθεικά σε, "I have made you the father of many nations"), introduced by the familiar formula καθὼς γέγραπται ὅτι ("as it is written"). God spoke these words after he reconfirmed the promise to multiply Abraham's offspring. At the same time, he declared that Abram's name would be changed to Abraham ("father of a multitude"). Then came a restatement of the promise about inheriting the land and the command to circumcise. The next words in Paul's argument (κατέναντι οὗ ἐπίστευσεν θεοῦ, [lit.] "before the God in whom he believed") could relate to the clause at the end of v. 16 (ὅς ἐστιν πατὴρ πάντων ἡμῶν), which is why CSB translates, "He is our father in God's sight, in whom Abraham believed." However, if all the Greek words after the citation are taken together as a reminder of the nature of the God in whose presence the promise was given and accepted, they explain the certainty expressed by τέθεικά σε ("I have made you").[58] Paul's syntax is difficult because he is defining the context in which Abraham received this promise ("in the presence of the God in whom he believed") *and* highlighting two attributes of God that made belief in the promise possible ("who gives life to the dead and calls things into existence that do not exist"). It would be better to represent this literally as an incomplete sentence, linked with an em dash to the citation from Gen 17:5 (so ESV).

The first divine attribute (τοῦ ζῳοποιοῦντος τοὺς νεκρούς, "who gives life to the dead") corresponds to the second of the Eighteen Benedictions, which could have been known to the apostle (Str-B, 3.212; see also Wis 16:13; Tob 13:2; Jos. Asen. 20:7). This prepares for the claim in vv. 18–19 that Abraham believed he could have many descendants, although he and Sarah were as good as "dead" (νενεκρωμένον, νέκρωσιν). The second attribute (καὶ καλοῦντος τὰ μὴ ὄντα ὡς ὄντα, "and calls things into existence that do not exist") probably reflects the common Jewish belief that by his word of command God created everything that exists out of nothing (e.g., Ps 33:6, 9; Isa 48:13; Wis 11:25; 2 Macc 7:28; Jos. Asen. 8:9; Philo, *Spec.*

[58] So Moo (*Romans*, 280) concludes after reviewing other possibilities. Moo observes that Paul's relative clause acts as a pivot in his argument, looking backward to the giving of this promise and forward to what is said about Abraham's faith in subsequent verse.

4.187; 2 Bar. 21:4; 48:8).[59] Paul's twofold confession about the character of God implies that this is what Abraham believed when he received the promise about becoming "father of many nations."

4:18–19. With such a conviction about God's ability to fulfill his promises, Abraham (lit.) "believed against hope on the basis of hope" (παρ' ἐλπίδα ἐπ' ἐλπίδι ἐπίστευσεν). This paradoxical expression suggests that Abraham's God-given hope "flew in the face of that hope which is founded on the evidence of reason and common sense—'hope' as we often use the word ('I hope to win the lottery')."[60] As a result, "he became the father of many nations" (εἰς τὸ γενέσθαι αὐτὸν πατέρα πολλῶν ἐθνῶν), according to what had been previously said to him in Gen 15:5 ("so will your descendants be"). The effect of this citation is to connect the words from Gen 17:5 with that earlier promise, which gave Abraham the hope he needed. When Paul concludes that Abraham "did not weaken in faith" (μὴ ἀσθενήσας τῇ πίστει), the reference is to faith in a generic sense rather than to "the faith" as a set of beliefs.[61] The indicative verb κατενόησεν, rather than the aorist participle, expresses the subordinate idea in this sequence ("when he considered").

There is some textual evidence for reading the negative οὐ κατενόησεν ("he did not consider"), meaning that Abraham did not weaken in faith *and* did not concentrate on the age of his own body or that of his wife. But the textual evidence for the positive reading is stronger.[62] According to Gen 17:17, "Abraham fell to the ground,

---

[59] Moo (*Romans*, 282) claims that Paul simply describes God as "speaking of" or "summoning" that which does not yet exist as if it does. Schreiner (*Romans*, 237) argues similarly, noting the difficulty of reading ὡς as expressing result. Cranfield (*Romans*, 1:244–45) discusses different ways the Greek syntax could be understood and affirms the possibility that it refers to God's creative power. Cf. Dunn, *Romans 1–8*, 218; Jewett, *Romans*, 334.

[60] Moo, *Romans*, 282. Abraham's faith was "exercised in the confident hope which the promise of God engendered" (John Murray, *The Epistle to the Romans: The English Text with Introduction, Exposition, and Notes*, NICNT repr. [Grand Rapids: Eerdmans, 1997], 148).

[61] Cf. Moo, *Romans*, 283. The dative of respect τῇ πίστει relates back to the faith of Abraham just mentioned (ἐπίστευσεν). Compare the dative of cause τῇ ἀπιστίᾳ ("because of unbelief"), followed by another dative of respect τῇ πίστει in v. 20.

[62] The negative οὐ is found in D and later manuscripts (F G Ψ 33 104 etc.) but not in earlier manuscripts (א A B C etc.). Metzger (*Textual Commentary*, 451) observes that "Paul does not wish to imply that faith means closing one's eyes to reality, but that Abraham was so strong in faith as to be undaunted by every consideration."

laughed and thought in his heart, 'Can a child be born to a hundred-year-old man? Can Sarah, a ninety-year-old woman, give birth?'" Paul's more sober account stresses that "he considered his own body to be already dead" (κατενόησεν τὸ ἑαυτοῦ σῶμα [ἤδη] νενεκρωμένον), "since he was about a hundred years old." He also considered "the deadness of Sarah's womb" (τὴν νέκρωσιν τῆς μήτρας Σάρρας).[63] The language of death is used twice here to highlight the need for the sort of resurrection faith mentioned previously (v. 17). Abraham could "laugh at human weakness but refused to give up hope in the superior power of God."[64]

4:20–21. In Paul's Greek text the expression εἰς δὲ τὴν ἐπαγγελίαν τοῦ θεοῦ ([lit.] "with reference to the promise of God") is in an emphatic position before the words οὐ διεκρίθη τῇ ἀπιστίᾳ ("he did not waver in unbelief"). This highlights that Abraham's faith was "wholly based on, and controlled by, the divine promise."[65] There are incidents in the Genesis record where Abraham seems to deviate from the pathway of faith (e.g., 16:1–16; 20:1–18), but he "avoided a deep-seated and permanent attitude of distrust and inconsistency in relationship to God and his promises."[66] The passive verb ἐνεδυναμώθη ("he was strengthened") suggests the agency of God with reference to Abraham's faith, making τῇ πίστει a dative of respect ("in faith") rather than an instrumental dative ("by faith"). Instead of having "something to boast about" (v. 2, καύχημα), Abraham "gave glory to God" (δοὺς δόξαν τῷ θεῷ). He did "what humans had refused to do in the lapse into idolatry presented in 1:21–23 as the paradigm of human alienation from God."[67] Abraham glorified God as Creator by believing in his promises and by being

---

[63] The word ἤδη ("already") is found in a range of important manuscripts (א A C D Ψ etc.) but is missing from others (B F G etc.). Since it gives the impression of "a certain heightening of the account" (Metzger, *Textual Commentary*, 451), it could be regarded as a later addition. Moreover, unless by accident, why would it have been omitted had it stood in the text originally?

[64] Jewett, *Romans*, 337.

[65] Cranfield, *Romans*, 1:248. Abraham did not believe in the impossible simply because it was impossible! The verb διακρίνομαι in the sense of "be divided within oneself, waver, doubt" is also used in 14:23 (cf. Matt 21:21; Mark 11:23; Acts 10:20; Jas 1:6; 2:4; Jude 22).

[66] Moo, *Romans*, 285.

[67] Byrne, *Romans*, 154–55. Cf. 15:6–12. Note the detailed comparison of 4:17–21 with the language of 1:20–21, 24–25, 26–27 by Wright, "Romans," 500.

"fully convinced that what God had promised, he was also able to do" (πληροφορηθεὶς ὅτι ὃ ἐπήγγελται δυνατός ἐστιν καὶ ποιῆσαι). In other words, his faith was in "the God who had promised, not merely in what had been promised."[68]

4:22–24. Paul's biblical argument comes to its climax (δίο, "therefore") with a restatement of the key words from Gen 15:6 ("it was credited to him for righteousness").[69] An application of this text to the gospel era follows. God's promise to Abraham was not written for him alone but "also for us" (ἀλλὰ καὶ δι' ἡμᾶς). Abraham heard these words directly, but they were recorded for the benefit of the eschatological people of God (cf. 15:4; 1 Cor 9:8–10; 10:1–11; Gal 4:21–31). Paul includes his readers in this blessing, addressing them directly for the first time since 1:1–15.[70] Righteousness will be credited to all who share the resurrection faith of Abraham and "believe in him who raised Jesus our Lord from the dead."

Some have taken the words μέλλει λογίζεσθαι ("it will be credited"), together with the future tense in 3:30 (δικαιώσει, "will justify"), as a reference to final vindication on the day of judgment (cf. 2:13 comment). But Paul's immediate insistence on justification as a present reality for his readers in 5:1, 9 suggests otherwise. Moreover, Abraham has been consistently presented in Rom 4 as a beneficiary of justification in the course of his earthly life. If the aorist indicative ἐγράφη establishes that what was written about Abraham was in the past, the future construction μέλλει λογίζεσθαι relates to those who come after the Genesis account was written.[71]

A close link with Abraham's situation is emphasized when justification is promised to those "who believe in him who raised Jesus our Lord from the dead." In relation to physical descendants

[68] Cranfield, *Romans*, 1:249.

[69] Against Byrne (*Romans*, 155), it is not correct to say this sequence shows that the persevering character of Abraham's faith played some part in the "reckoning" to him of righteousness. Paul's recall of Gen 15:6 takes us back to the preceding argument about Abraham's simple assertion of belief in God's promise as the basis of his justification.

[70] As he shifts from debating Jewish issues to addressing the Christians in Rome, Paul prepares for a further exposition of the gospel and its implications in 5:1–11.

[71] Cf. Schreiner, *Romans*, 242; Jewett, *Romans*, 341. Jewett takes issue with the eschatological reading of μέλλει λογίζεσθαι but also disputes the view of BDAG and Cranfield (*Romans*, 1:250) that it refers to "an action that necessarily follows a divine decree."

and the fulfillment of God's promises, Abraham believed in God "who gives life to the dead and calls things into existence that do not exist" (v. 17). Belief in the resurrection of Jesus is similarly critical for Christian faith. NT writers consistently refer to his resurrection as God's act (e.g., Acts 2:31–36; 3:15; 4:10; 13:30; Rom 8:11; 10:9; 1 Cor 6:14; 15:15; 2 Cor 4:14; 1 Pet 1:21), often using the verb ἐγείρω ("raise") and the phrase ἐκ νεκρῶν ("from the dead"). They view it as God's vindication of his Son as Lord and Christ, the means by which he was exalted to the right hand of God, poured out the promised Holy Spirit, and made it possible for the forgiveness of sins to be proclaimed in his name to all nations. Consequently, for those who believe that Jesus was raised from the dead, there is the possibility of experiencing new life in the present and resurrection from physical death to share eternal life with him. Paul explores these issues in Rom 5–8 (see §1.6; 2.1).

4:25. A confessional statement ("he was delivered up for our trespasses and raised for our justification," ὃς παρεδόθη διὰ τὰ παραπτώματα ἡμῶν καὶ ἠγέρθη διὰ τὴν δικαίωσιν ἡμῶν) enables Paul to return to his main theme and provides a bridge to the next passage (5:1–11). There are formal aspects of this statement that might suggest pre-Pauline usage as a primitive Christian creed, but its ultimate source is the language of Isa 52:13–53:12.[72] The LXX version of this prophecy proclaims that the Lord "delivered up" his servant "for our sins" (53:6, κύριος παρέδωκεν αὐτὸν ταῖς ἁμαρτίαις ἡμῶν). This is repeated in a slightly different form in 53:12, where it is said that "his soul was delivered up to death" (παρεδόθη εἰς θάνατον ἡ ψυχὴ αὐτοῦ) and "he was delivered up for the sake of their sins" (διὰ τὰς ἁμαρτίας αὐτῶν παρεδόθη). The Hebrew text also implies that the servant enjoys new life after his death as a sin offering, making it possible for him to "justify" many (53:11, יַצְדִּיק).[73] This may explain the reason for justification and Jesus's resurrection being

[72] Cf. Moo, *Romans*, 288–89. Isaiah's Servant theology plays an important role in Paul's Christology and understanding of his own apostolic ministry (8:32; 10:16; 15:8, 21).

[73] The LXX has δικαιῶσαι in Isa 53:11, though the rest of the verse differs widely from the Hebrew. Note that παραπτώματα ("transgressions") is used by Paul rather than ἁμαρτίαις ("sins"). In view of the extensive use of the former in 5:15, 16, 17, 18, 20, this suggests Pauline authorship of the confession in 4:25.

linked in the concluding words of v. 25 (ἠγέρθη διὰ τὴν δικαίωσιν ἡμῶν, "raised for our justification").

It is clear from 5:9 that we are justified by Christ's "blood," which is the meaning of Paul's argument in 3:24–25. But we are also saved by Christ's "life" (5:10; cf. 10:9; Eph 2:5–6). Those who receive the gift of righteousness made possible by his death will "reign in life through the one man, Jesus Christ" (5:17). If Christ's sacrifice had not been followed by his resurrection, "it would not have been God's mighty deed for our justification."[74] The resurrection of Jesus represented "*his* vindication, the public declaration of his righteousness by God, in other words, his *justification*."[75] By faith Christians are united with Christ and are associated with that verdict, experiencing through him "justification leading to life" (5:18).

Bridge

Although the boasting that Paul attacks in 3:27–30; 4:1–3 is specifically Jewish in character, the preceding context has exposed that all are "under sin" (3:9; cf. 3:23). So any form of human boasting or exclusivism before God based on moral or religious achievement, social status, or ethnic background must be challenged. The claim that God "justifies the ungodly" (ESV) calls for an acknowledgment that one's lawless acts need to be forgiven and one's sins covered (4:5–8). Abraham's faith was not something to boast about. It involved total reliance on God for acceptance and the fulfillment of his promises (4:9–21). Abraham is both a model of saving faith and the one whose God-given faith uniquely advanced the plan of God. Biblical heroes such as Abraham and David depended on the grace of God for forgiveness and justification but did not know the basis on which this could be given. The gospel reveals that this blessing is possible because Jesus was "delivered up for our trespasses

---

[74] Cranfield, *Romans*, 1:252. Cranfield points out that the formation of the two clauses in 4:25 was controlled by theological rather than solely rhetorical considerations. The first use of the preposition δία is causal (διὰ τὰ παραπτώματα ἡμῶν, "because of our sins"), and the second is final (διὰ τὴν δικαίωσιν ἡμῶν, "for our justification"). Cf. Dunn, *Romans 1–8*, 225; Moo, *Romans*, 289–90.

[75] Peter M. Head, "Jesus' Resurrection in Pauline Thought: A Study of Romans," in *Proclaiming the Resurrection*, ed. Peter M. Head (Carlisle: Paternoster, 1998): 69. Cf. Rom 1:3–4; 1 Tim 3:16.

and raised for our justification" (4:25, echoing Isa 53:6, 11, 12). So Christian faith is more specifically a Christ-focused confidence in God, relying solely on the atoning work of Jesus and his victorious resurrection. On this basis all who seek after God, whether religious or not, morally bankrupt, or righteous in the sight of others, may be justified by faith. A new life in Christ is made possible by the justifying action of God, uniting believers in a common dependence on his grace. Such trust is the means by which the blessings promised in the gospel are received and enjoyed.

VI. The Fruit of Justification: Present and Future (5:1–11)

With its celebratory tone and confessional style, this passage differs in genre from the more defensive sections that precede and follow it and is more like 3:21–26. Thematically there are obvious links with what has gone before. Justification is highlighted (vv. 1, 9; cf. 3:24–26; 4:3–12, 22–25) as Paul explores its present implications and the hope it provides for believers. A new dimension is added to the argument when the theme of peace or reconciliation with God is developed (vv. 1, 10, 11). A further link with what has gone before can be seen in the threefold use of boasting terminology (vv. 2, 3, 11 [CSB: "rejoice"], cf. 2:17, 23; 3:37; 4:2). At the same time themes such as suffering, endurance, glory, the love of God, and the Holy Spirit are introduced into the argument. When these terms reappear in 8:18–39, it is clear that a large inclusion has been formed between these passages. A new major division in Paul's argument begins in 5:1–11, which is the first part of a "ring composition" or chiasm.[1] In the structure of the letter as a whole, 5:1–8:39 has a central role, with its focus on living in the light of what God has already accomplished for us in Christ while we await the consummation of his purpose for us (cf. Introduction II.C).[2] In short, 5:1–11 has a transitional function, continuing Paul's exposition of the gospel from 3:21–26 and exploring more of its implications.

> [1]Therefore, since we have been declared righteous by faith,
> we have peace with God through our Lord Jesus Christ. [2]We have
> also obtained access through him by faith into this grace in which
> we stand, and we rejoice in the hope of the glory of God. [3]And not
> only that, but we also rejoice in our afflictions, because we know
> that affliction produces endurance, [4]endurance produces proven
> character, and proven character produces hope. [5]This hope will

[1] Moo, *Romans*: 293–94. Cf. Wright, "Romans," 508–14.

[2] For different views on the theological significance of Rom 5–8 and its relation to what has gone before, see Frank Thielman, "The Story of Israel and the Theology of Romans 5–8," and Charles B. Cousar, "Continuity and Discontinuity: Reflections of Romans 5–8: In Conversation with Frank Thielman," in *Pauline Theology, Volume III: Romans*, ed. David M. Hay and E. Elizabeth Johnson (Minneapolis: Fortress, 1995), 169–210; Richard N. Longenecker, "The Focus of Romans: The Central Role of 5:1–8:39 in the Argument of the Letter," in *Romans and the People of God: Essays in Honor of Gordon D. Fee on the Occasion of His 65th Birthday*, ed. Sven K. Soderlund and N. T. Wright (Grand Rapids/Cambridge: Eerdmans, 1999), 49–69.

not disappoint us, because God's love has been poured out in our hearts through the Holy Spirit who was given to us.

[6]For while we were still helpless, at the right time, Christ
died for the ungodly. [7]For rarely will someone die for a just person—though for a good person perhaps someone might even dare
to die. [8]But God proves his own love for us in that while we were
still sinners, Christ died for us. [9]How much more then, since we
have now been declared righteous by his blood, will we be saved
through him from wrath. [10]For if, while we were enemies, we
were reconciled to God through the death of his Son, then how
much more, having been reconciled, will we be saved by his life.
[11]And not only that, but we also rejoice in God through our Lord
Jesus Christ, through whom we have now received this reconciliation.

Context

A link to the preceding argument is made with the opening words ("Therefore, since we have been declared righteous by faith"). The most immediate reference to justification is in 4:25, though Paul's conclusion there recalls his more extensive celebration of God's justifying activity in 3:21–26. Faith as the means of responding to God's promise and experiencing justification was the focus of 3:27–4:25. So 5:1–11 picks up these and other strands from Paul's developing exposition of the gospel and adds new elements. He does this to focus on the hope provided by the gospel and the assurance it offers even in the face of suffering. The implications for individual Christian living are further explored in 6:1–23, but before Paul moves in that direction, he provides another defensive section (5:12–21).[3]

Structure

The first half of this passage highlights the present consequences of justification by faith: peace with God, boasting in the hope of the glory of God, boasting in afflictions, knowing that afflictions further God's purpose for us, and being assured by the Spirit of God's love (vv. 1–5). The second half grounds these realities in Christ's death

[3] Dunn (*Romans 1–8*, 243) observes that the focus in 5:1–11 and in 6–8 is primarily on the individual believer, whereas the focus in 5:12–21 and from 8:14 onwards is more and more on God's purpose for humanity at large.

for us and gives further assurance about the future consequences of his saving work (vv. 6–11). Justification "by (Christ's) blood" and reconciliation to God "through the death of his Son" are two different but related ways of providing this assurance. The passage finishes in a way that parallels the opening verses, with a claim that boasting in God is possible "through our Lord Jesus Christ, through whom we have now received this reconciliation." A concentric structure can thus be discerned, with the death of Jesus at the center:

A Peace with God through our Lord Jesus Christ (vv. 1–2a)
  B Hope of sharing the glory of God (vv. 2b–4)
    C God's love poured out in our hearts (v. 5)
      D Christ died for the ungodly (vv. 6–7)
    C´ God's love demonstrated in Christ's death (v. 8)
  B´ Hope of salvation from the wrath of God (vv. 9–10)
A´ Reconciliation with God through our Lord Jesus Christ (v. 11)

The following outline draws together elements of this structure topically:

1. Peace with God (vv. 1–2a)
2. Hope in sufferings (vv. 2b–5)
3. The ground of hope (vv. 6–11)

5:1. This section is linked to the preceding one by the connective οὖν ("therefore"). It is also linked by the aorist passive participle δικαιωθέντες used in a causative way (lit., "since we are justified")[4] and by ἐκ πίστεως, reaffirming that we are declared righteous on the basis of faith alone (3:26, 30; 4:16). Most immediately, this recalls the claim in 4:3–12 that righteousness was credited to Abraham when he believed God and trusted in his promises. But Paul contends that Gen 15:6 "was not written for Abraham alone, but also for *us*" (4:23–24), including himself with all Christian believers.[5] Justification by faith is possible because Jesus was "delivered up for our trespasses and raised for our justification" (4:25, δικαίωσιν),

[4] The aorist participle does not necessarily indicate past tense but merely the fact of justification viewed comprehensively. CSB translates "declare(d) righteous" here and in 3:26; 5:9.

[5] This use of the first-person plural to refer to Christians continues into 5:1–11. In previous contexts the first-person plural seems mostly to be used with reference to fellow Jews with whom he is in debate (e.g., 2:2; 3:5, 8–9; 4:1).

restating 3:21–26 in different terms (see §2.4). The new idea in 5:1 is that "we have peace with God through our Lord Jesus Christ."[6]

Peace "in relation to God" (πρὸς τὸν θεόν) is more than an inner sense of well-being or contentment, though this may arise from the certainty of being reconciled to God.[7] Paul previously linked glory, honor, immortality, and peace with eternal life (2:7, 10), contrasting these eschatological gifts with wrath and indignation, affliction and distress (2:8, 9). The prophetic hope of peace in the messianic age envisaged rescue from enemies and restored relationships in a new creation, resulting from God's renewal of his covenant with Israel (e.g., Isa 9:6–7; 32:17–18; 54:10–17; Ezek 34:25–31; 37:26; Mic 5:4–5; Hag 2:9). Paul's claim that we now have peace with God "through our Lord Jesus Christ" indicates that these promises are in the process of fulfillment. Israel's Messiah has now achieved the redemption that can bring peace to all nations (cf. Luke 2:14; Acts 10:36), though the complete outworking of that peace awaits us in the resurrection to eternal life (Rom 8:18–23). The accomplishment of peace through God's reconciling work in Christ is the parallel notion in v. 10, where the end of hostility between God and his enemies is proclaimed. Deliverance from the wrath of God has already been achieved by the shedding of the Messiah's blood (v. 9), and reconciliation may be received and experienced by faith (v. 11 comment).

The refrain "through our Lord Jesus Christ" reappears in different forms at significant points in the rest of the letter (5:11; 6:23; 7:25; 8:39; 13:14; 15:6). It recalls and combines declarations about "the redemption that is in *Christ* Jesus" (3:24) and the fact that God "raised Jesus our *Lord* from the dead" (4:24) (see §2.3).

Justification and reconciliation are two different but related ways of describing the outcome of Christ's death and resurrection

---

[6] Runge (*Discourse Grammar*, 43) observes that Paul transitions "from the means of justification to a discussion of the results that it brings about."

[7] There is impressive textual evidence for the subjunctive ἔχωμεν (א* A B* C D K L 33 81 etc.), which could mean, "Let us have [peace with God]." But such an exhortation would be inconsistent with the argument in vv. 6–11, where justification and reconciliation are accomplished and received. The subjunctive could mean, "Let us enjoy [peace with God]," but Paul does not otherwise begin exhorting on the basis of justification until 6:11. It seems more likely that the subjunctive is an early copyist's error and that the indicative ἔχομεν (א[a] B[3] G P Ψ etc.) is the original. Cf. Metzger, *Textual Commentary*, 452; Schreiner, *Romans*, 258.

for us. Reconciliation does not follow justification as a separate event. In 5:9–11 God's justifying activity is shown to involve the sort of self-engagement with sinners expressed by the idea of reconciliation.[8]

> [God] does not confer the status of righteousness upon us without at the same time giving himself to us in friendship and establishing peace between himself and us—a work which, on account of the awful reality of both his wrath against sin and of the fierce hostility of our egotism against the God who claims our allegiance, is only accomplished at unspeakable cost to him.[9]

5:2. A relative clause, introduced by δι' οὗ καί ([lit.] "through whom also"), makes a further statement about what God has achieved "through our Lord Jesus Christ." Two verbs are used in the perfect tense to say more about the present state in which believers find themselves as a result of justification: (lit.) "we have access by faith to this grace in which we stand" (τὴν προσαγωγὴν ἐσχήκαμεν [τῇ πίστει] εἰς τὴν χάριν ταύτην ἐν ᾗ ἑστήκαμεν).[10] Prominence is given to "access" and "standing" by this use of the perfect tense. The noun προσαγωγή (BDAG "way of approach, access") can have a cultic meaning and could imply access to God's heavenly sanctuary (cf. Eph 2:18–22; Heb 4:16; 10:19–22) or access to God's royal presence.[11] But the object is specifically "this grace in which

---

[8] Similarly, in 2 Cor 5:18–21 reconciliation is linked with "not counting their trespasses against them," which is an expression of justification reminiscent of Rom 4:7–8.

[9] Cranfield, *Romans*, 1:258. Dunn (*Romans 1–8*, 259–60) rightly opposes the view of Ralph P. Martin (*Reconciliation: A Study of Paul's Theology*, rev. ed. [Grand Rapids: Zondervan, 1989], 153) that Paul preferred the notion of reconciliation to that of justification because the former has more universal appeal in preaching to Gentiles. Martin's view is restated in "Reconciliation: Romans 5:1–11," in Soderlund and Wright, eds., *Romans and the People of God*, 36–48.

[10] The textual evidence is fairly evenly balanced between the inclusion of τῇ πίστει (ℵ A [with ἐν] C K P etc.) and its omission (B D G etc.). Paul has already declared that justification is "by faith" (v. 1, ἐκ πίστεως), and so copyists may have dropped τῇ πίστει ("by faith") as redundant and superfluous. Cf. Metzger, *Textual Commentary*, 452–53. The perfect indicative ἑστήκαμεν should simply be rendered "we have."

[11] Dunn (*Romans 1–8*, 248–49) suggests that the language of access and grace is more likely court imagery. God's kingly favor enables us to stand in his presence as

we stand." Paul simply means that, trusting in the promise of justification "freely by his grace" (3:24), believers are enabled by the work of Christ to have continuing access to the grace of God. Grace emerges as a significant theme in this chapter, specifically linked to "the free gift of righteousness" in Christ (vv. 15, 17, 20–21 ESV).

A significant implication of this continuing access to the grace of God is that (lit.) "we boast in the hope of the glory of God." CSB, like most English versions, renders καυχώμεθα as "we rejoice."[12] But the normal meaning of this terminology is "boast" (cf. 2:17, 23; 3:37; 4:2), and it is better to translate the verb that way here and in vv. 3, 11. A deliberate contrast with the preceding usage is intended, showing that there is an appropriate form of boasting or glorying, expressing confidence in God and what he has promised us (e.g., Deut 33:29; Ps 4:11; Rom 15:27; 1 Cor 1:29–31).[13] Such confidence could be expressed individually or corporately, in prayer, praise, or testimony, to honor God and encourage others. Genuine boasting is only possible for those who rely on God's grace and do not claim any special rights or privileges. Jesus's death and resurrection give believers the only real ground for confidence about their relationship with God and their future (cf. v. 11 comment). The glory of God, which is central to that hope, is now obscured and unattainable in ordinary human life because of idolatry and sin (1:23; 3:23). But God promises that those who seek it will experience the ultimate revelation of his glory (2:7, 10). This will happen when believers are set free from "the bondage to decay" in "the redemption of our bodies" (8:18–23) and are "glorified" (8:30). Experiencing the glory of God involves being transformed by it, a process that has begun in part for those who have seen God's glory "in the face of Jesus Christ" (2 Cor 4:6; 3:18; cf. Rom 8:18, 28–30 comments).

---

those who have been reconciled to him. Moo (*Romans*, 301) insists that the notion of grace here "goes beyond justification to all that is conveyed to us by God in Christ."

[12] The verb καυχάομαι and related terms are occasionally employed in the LXX with the context giving the sense of rejoicing or praise (e.g., Ps 31:11 [καυχᾶσθε, ET 32:11]; 1 Chr 16:27; 29:11; Ps 88:18; Jer 17:14 [καύχημα]). "Exult" or "glory" could be alternative renderings, though "glory in the hope of glory" would be awkward.

[13] Cf. Rudolph Bultmann, "καυχάομαι, καύχημα κτλ," *TDNT* 3:645–54; Jewett, *Romans*, 351. The verb καυχώμεθα could be read as a subjunctive ("let us boast") or as an indicative ("we boast"). The latter alternative is logical after the indicative ἔχομεν ("we have") in v. 1 (cf. n. 7 above).

5:3–4. With the emphatic words *οὐ μόνον δέ, ἀλλὰ καί* ("and not only that, but also," cf. v. 11; 8:23; 9:10), Paul's adds the surprising claim that (lit.), "we boast in our afflictions." In 2:9 "affliction" (θλῖψις) refers to the distress experienced beyond this life as a consequence of God's final judgment, but here the reference is to present suffering or oppression. This can come from persecution or difficulties in ministry (e.g., 8:35; 12:12; 2 Cor 1:4, 8; 2:4) but also from everyday relationships or sickness (e.g., 1 Cor 7:28; 2 Cor 12:9). The preposition ἐν ("in") could imply that believers boast "in the midst of afflictions," but, considering the parallels (v. 2 [ἐπ' ἐλπίδι], v. 11 [ἐν τῷ θεῷ]), the meaning is more obviously "with respect to afflictions." People normally boast about their status or achievements but not about their frustrations and weaknesses![14]

The reason for this confident attitude is given in the sequence of clauses beginning with εἰδότες ὅτι ("because we know that"), where the focus is on experiential knowledge. First, we know that "affliction produces endurance" (ἡ θλῖψις ὑπομονὴν κατεργάζεται). Paul has already indicated that endurance is a necessary quality of those who hope to enjoy eternal life (2:7; cf. 8:25; 15:4, 5–6). God uses affliction as a discipline by which he teaches us to wait patiently for final salvation (1 Cor 11:32; Heb 12:3–13). Second, we know that "endurance produces proven character" (ἡ δὲ ὑπομονὴ δοκιμήν). The process of testing reveals the genuineness of a person's trust in God and his promises. Paul uses the rare noun δοκιμή to describe the authentication or proving that God requires and makes possible (2 Cor 2:9; 8:2; 9:13; 13:3; Phil 2:22).[15] As when precious metals are passed through fire to remove baser metals, so a greater Christlikeness may emerge from the refinement of suffering (12:14–21; Jas 1:2–4). The proving of believers in spiritual and moral terms prepares us for final assessment by God. Third, at the end of this

[14] Jewett (*Romans*, 352–54) shows how such boasting would have been a countercultural challenge for Paul's Roman readers. Cranfield (*Romans*, 1:261) observes that people are more naturally moved by afflictions to "murmur against God, and even to curse him."

[15] Walter Grundmann ("δόκιμος ἀδόκιμος κτλ," *TDNT* 2:255–60) points to OT influences on the way this notion develops in the NT. The noun δοκιμή can refer to a testing process (2 Cor 8:2) or to the result of testing, namely, proven character (cf. 2 Cor 2:9; 9:13; Phil 2:22). Compare the use of δόκιμος ("approved" in Rom 14:18; 16:10), δοκιμάζω ("approve" in Rom 1:28; 2:18; 12:2; 14:22), and δοκίμιον ("testing" in Jas 1:3; 1 Pet 1:7).

sequence, we know that "proven character produces hope" (ἡ δὲ δοκιμὴ ἐλπίδα). Confidence in the promises of God can be strengthened by the process of suffering patiently and being changed by it. The objective basis of Christian hope is the death and resurrection of Jesus, but experiencing God's grace in times of testing makes it possible to "overflow with hope" (15:13).

5:5. Such hope "will not disappoint" (ἡ δὲ ἐλπὶς οὐ καταισχύνει) or "put those who cherish it to shame by proving illusory."[16] This is so "because God's love has been poured out in our hearts." "If the normal goal of boasting is to achieve honor and avert shame, here it is claimed that the avoidance of shame is accomplished in a revolutionary manner."[17] As in v. 2, the perfect tense can function like a present, expressing a continuing reality (ἐκκέχυται, "is [being] poured out").[18] God provides ongoing assurance of his love to sustain hope in the midst of trials (cf. 2 Cor 5:14–15). Although the verb "poured out" is elsewhere used with reference to the gift of God's Spirit (Acts 2:17, 18 [citing Joel 2:28–29]; 2:33; 10:45; Titus 3:6), the subject here is explicitly "God's love," and the Spirit is the agent (διὰ πνεύματος ἁγίου, "through the Holy Spirit"). Contextually, God's love for us (subjective genitive) is the primary focus, not our love for God (objective genitive).

The supreme demonstration of God's love was the provision of his Son as a sacrifice for our sins (5:8; 8:37; cf. John 3:16; 1 John 4:7–12). What is proclaimed in the gospel is "actually brought home to our hearts (so that we have recognised it and rejoice in it) by the Holy Spirit who was given to us."[19] God as Trinity is involved in this revelation of his love for sinners (see §2.3). The aorist passive

---

[16] Cranfield, *Romans*, 1:261–62. Cranfield reads the verb καταισχύνει as present tense, but it could be read as future, denoting the confidence believers can have at the judgment of God (Schreiner, *Romans*, 256–57). Cf. Pss 22:5 (LXX 21:6); 25:3 (LXX 24:3); Isa 28:16 (cited in Rom 9:33; 10:11); Joel 2:26–27.

[17] Jewett, *Romans*, 355. "Divine love addresses shame at its deepest level and reveals the motivation behind 'peace' and 'reconciliation'" (Jewett, 356).

[18] Cf. Campbell, *Verbal Aspect, the Indicative Mood,* 184–85. Against Jewett (*Romans*, 356), the perfect tense need not refer to any initiating event such as baptism or conversion here.

[19] Cranfield, *Romans*, 1:263. Dunn (*Romans 1–8*, 253) says that this use of "Spirit vocabulary" when talking of God's love suggests that Paul was not greatly concerned to make a distinction between the gift of the Spirit and the outpouring of love. Cf. 2 Cor 1:22; Gal 4:6; 2 Thess 2:16–17; 3:5.

participle δοθέντος ("given") is used adjectivally, highlighting the *fact* that the Spirit was given by God. As in 1:21, 24; and 2:5, "heart" is used to refer to the control center of human personalities. Paul alludes to the fulfilment of biblical promises about the eschatological renewal of the hearts of God's people to love and fear him (e.g., Jer 31:33–34; 32:39–40; Ezek 36:26–27). So it is ultimately true that "God's gift of love kindles believers to love him in return."[20] What was implicit in Rom 2:14–15, 26–28 is made explicit here (cf. 6:17 comment): the new covenant has been inaugurated, making it possible for hearts to be renewed in love by the Holy Spirit because of the work of Christ (cf. 2 Cor 3:3–11).

5:6. A link with the preceding verse is indicated by the inferential γάρ ("for"). Paul returns to the subject of Jesus's death, which secures for believers every benefit previously mentioned. The Holy Spirit persuades us of the love of God by convincing us about the significance of what is stated here. In a carefully crafted Greek sentence, the subject "Christ" is emphatically at the beginning, and the verb "died" is at the end. In between is the important qualification "while we were still helpless" (ἔτι . . . ὄντων ἡμῶν ἀσθενῶν ἔτι), meaning while we were unable to rescue ourselves.[21] The principal clause expresses the fact that Christ's death took place "at the right moment" (κατὰ καιρόν).[22] Those for whom Christ died are further described as "the ungodly" (ὑπὲρ ἀσεβῶν, cf. 4:5). Human beings are not merely weak and helpless but also ungodly in the way they suppress the truth and pursue all forms of idolatry and unrighteousness, warranting God's wrath and his just sentence of death (1:18–32). "What Paul is here concerned to bring out is the fact that the

[20] Schreiner, *Romans*, 257. Wallace (*Greek Grammar*, 121) argues that the genitive may be read as both subjective and objective in this context.

[21] The genitive absolute with a present participle indicates the temporal context in which Christ died but also, by implication, a reason for his death. The textual evidence for ἔτι γὰρ . . . ἔτι is strong (א A C D* etc.). The variants are likely to have been attempts by scribes to avoid the awkward repetition of ἔτι. Cf. Metzger, *Textual Commentary*, 453. The first ἔτι is used for the sake of special emphasis and need not be translated, while the second one more obviously functions to modify the participle ὄντων.

[22] Cf. Gal 4:4. The word καιρός may refer to a time of special crisis or significance (BDAG). Dunn (*Romans 1–8*, 255) thinks the reference is to the time "to which God's purpose has been moving and in which he acted decisively." Cf. Schreiner, *Romans*, 260.

divine love is love for the undeserving, love that is not the result of any worth in its objects but is self-caused and in its freedom itself confers worth upon them."[23]

The preposition ὑπέρ with the genitive can express representation or advantage ("on behalf of, for the sake of"), reference ("concerning, with reference to"), or substitution ("in place of, instead of"). It is used in a substitutionary sense in texts that have no soteriological significance (e.g., Rom 9:3; Phlm 13) and in texts that are clearly soteriological (e.g., John 11:50; 2 Cor 5:14; Gal 3:13; 1 Tim 2:6). A substitutionary meaning should be understood in 5:6–8; 8:32; 14:15, where the death of Jesus is in view.[24] Paul's teaching about death as the penalty for sin (5:12–21) is foundational for understanding this text.

5:7–8. Highlighting the extraordinary nature of Christ's sacrifice for us, Paul first compares two different human situations. Again using the inferential γάρ ("for"), he asserts that "rarely will someone die for a just person." A second γάρ introduces what appears to be a qualification of what has just been said, (lit.) "Though for a good person perhaps someone might even dare to die."[25] This sentence is worded in such a way as to suggest a development in Paul's argument. The good person appears to be more attractive than the just person, and a note of greater possibility is introduced by the use of τάχα ("perhaps") with the adverbial καί ("even") and the verb τολμᾷ ("dare"). If someone was good to you, you might just be willing to die for him![26] But the contrast (δέ) with God's love is stark. God "demonstrates" or "shows" (συνίστησιν, cf. 3:5; Gal 2:18) "his own love for us" (τὴν ἑαυτοῦ ἀγάπην εἰς ἡμᾶς) in that (ὅτι) "while we

[23] Cranfield, *Romans*, 1.264.

[24] Wallace (*Greek Grammar*, 383–89) discusses the substitutionary use of ὑπέρ in several LXX texts and Greek papyri as well as in the NT (cf. 1 Cor 15:3; 2 Cor 5:14; 1 Thess 5:9–10). Christ took the punishment we deserved (Moo, *Romans*, 307n65; Schreiner, *Romans*, 260). Cf. Simon J. Gathercole, *Defending Substitution: An Essay on Atonement in Paul* (Grand Rapids: Baker, 2015).

[25] A concessive use of the second γάρ is unusual, but it is suggested by the adverbial καί ("even").

[26] Schreiner (*Romans*, 261–62) concludes that "the good person" could be someone's benefactor. The contrast with the masculine adjective δικαίου means that τοῦ ἀγαθοῦ most likely refers to a person rather than to "a good cause" (cf. 2:7, 10). Cf. Andrew D. Clarke, "The Good and the Just in Romans 5:7," *TynBul* 41 (1990): 128–32.

were still sinners, Christ died for us" (ἔτι ἁμαρτωλῶν ὄντων ἡμῶν Χριστὸς ὑπὲρ ἡμῶν ἀπέθανεν). As in v. 6, the adverb ἔτι ("still") and a genitive absolute construction with the participle in the present tense point to the ongoing condition of those for whom Christ died. No escalation is suggested by the sequence "ungodly" (v. 6), "sinners" (v. 8), and "enemies" (v. 10), but the rhetorical effect of this variation is to emphasize the unmerited character of God's love. A threefold repetition of the preposition "us" (v. 8, ἡμᾶς, ἡμῶν [twice]) includes Paul and his readers among the beneficiaries. The reflexive pronoun ἑαυτοῦ indicates that God's "own" love for believers is shown in the Messiah's death. The personal nature of God's love is amplified by reference to "the death of his Son" in v. 10 (cf. 8:32). This is the message that is brought home to our hearts by the Holy Spirit (v. 5; cf. Gal 2:20b ["the Son of God, who loved me and gave himself for me"]).

5:9. Paul returns to the theme of hope not disappointing us. The inferential conjunction οὖν ("then") signals a logical development of what has gone before. Using the comparative expression πολλῷ μᾶλλον ("how much more"), Paul argues that we who are (lit.) "now justified by his blood" (δικαιωθέντες νῦν ἐν τῷ αἵματι αὐτοῦ) will undoubtedly be "saved through him from wrath" (σωθησόμεθα δι' αὐτοῦ ἀπὸ τῆς ὀργῆς).[27] Use of the word "blood" picks up the sacrificial connotation of 3:25 and the link to justification by faith in that context. The divine act of justifying sinners took place by means of the atoning death of Christ (ἐν τῷ αἵματι αὐτοῦ), the benefits of which are now (νῦν) applied to those who put their trust in him.[28] Salvation from future wrath (2:5, 8) is the assured outcome. The verb σώζω ("save") is used again in 5:10; 8:24; 9:27; 10:9, 13; 11:14, 26, and the noun σωτηρία ("salvation") in 1:16; 10:1, 10; 11:11; 13:11.

---

[27] Paul uses this sort of argument in several contexts (5:9–10, 15, 17; 2 Cor 3:9, 11; Phil 1:23; 2:12), possibly influenced by his rabbinic training, where the *qal wāhōmer* ("light and heavy") exegetical rule was followed (Str-B 3.223–26; cf. Jewett, *Romans*, 362). Moo (*Romans*, 310) and Schreiner (*Romans*, 262) describe this as a greater-to-the-lesser argument on the ground that the death of Jesus guarantees ultimate salvation be obtained. But Paul's rhetorical style need not imply that one act of God is greater in significance than another.

[28] Dunn (*Romans 1–8*, 257) says the language of blood sacrifice "presupposes the rationale of the covenant relationship between God and his people." Christ's death establishes the new covenant (cf. 1 Cor 11:25) and renders further sacrifice unnecessary.

Essentially salvation means deliverance from wrath "in the day of wrath, when God's righteous judgment is revealed" (2:5; cf. 1 Thess 1:10; 5:9). Jesus is the mediator who turns aside the ultimate expression of God's wrath (cf. Ps 106:23 [Moses]; Wis 18:20–25 [Aaron]; Sir 45:23 [Phinehas]). However, salvation also has a positive dimension for Paul, putting believers in a position where they can share eternal life with Christ (5:10; 8:24; 13:11). Salvation is secured in the present by believing the gospel and confessing Jesus as Lord (10:9–12). So when Paul prays for people to be saved (10:1), he preaches the gospel so they might have the opportunity to respond with faith (11:14, 26; see §2.1).

5:10. An explanatory γάρ ("for") introduces an expansion of the preceding argument in the form of a conditional clause. The first part of the construction (the protasis) makes an important assumption: "If, while we were enemies, we were reconciled to God though the death of his Son" (εἰ . . . ἐχθροὶ ὄντες κατηλλάγημεν τῷ θεῷ διὰ τοῦ θανάτου τοῦ υἱοῦ αὐτοῦ). As in vv. 6, 8, a present participle (ὄντες) stresses that God took the initiative while "we" remained in steadfast opposition to him. "Enemies" (ἐχθροὶ) is an appropriate description here because reconciliation involves "the exchange of hostility for a friendly relationship" (BDAG). Paul uses a verb with particular significance in the world of diplomacy to describe God's sovereign action in this situation (κατηλλάγημεν [passive] τῷ θεῷ, "we were reconciled to God").[29] Reconciliation played no real part in the language of Greek religion "since the relation between deity and man was not conceived of in ancient paganism as the deeply personal thing that it is in the Bible."[30] But Paul's use of the terminology in 2 Cor 5:18–21 suggests it became significant for him as a result of his conversion. Convinced that he had been acting as

[29] The verb καταλλάσσω is only found elsewhere in the NT in 1 Cor 7:11; 2 Cor 5:18, 19, 20, and the related noun καταλλαγή ("reconciliation") in 5:11; 11:15; 2 Cor 5:18, 19. The compound ἀποκαταλλάσσω is used in Col 1:20, 22; Eph 2:16. The root verb ἀλλάσσω ("change, exchange") is also rare (Acts 6:14; 1 Cor 15:51, 52; Gal 4:20; Heb 1:12) but is used by Paul in 1:23, and the compound μεταλλάσσω is in 1:25, 26.

[30] Cranfield, *Romans*, 1:267. Dunn (*Romans 1–8*, 259) gives examples of the occasional use of this terminology in Greek-speaking Judaism (e.g., 2 Macc 5:11–20; 7:32–3; 8:29; 4 Macc 7:28–9; 17:22). Cf. I. Howard Marshall, "The Meaning of 'Reconciliation,'" in *Jesus the Saviour: Studies in New Testament Theology* (London: SPCK, 1990), 258–74.

an enemy of God, he came to experience God's reconciling love in Christ and was called to proclaim the message of reconciliation to others.[31]

Hostility toward God is certainly implied by the designation "enemies" (cf. 8:7 [ἔχθρα εἰς θεόν, "hostile to God"]), but the previous verse indicates that God's hostility against sinners was dealt with by means of the atoning death of Jesus. As the offended party, God took the initiative in reconciliation. This action "through the death of his Son" (v. 10) opened the way for *our* hostility to cease. So when the message of reconciliation is proclaimed, God calls upon us to "be reconciled" to him (2 Cor 5:20) and to receive what is offered in the gospel.

The second part of Paul's conditional clause (the apodosis) asserts what follows from the first part: "how much more, having been reconciled, will we be saved by his life" (πολλῷ μᾶλλον καταλλαγέντες σωθησόμεθα ἐν τῇ ζωῇ αὐτοῦ). As in v. 9, the comparative expression πολλῷ μᾶλλον ("how much more") introduces the claim that what is presently true ("having been reconciled") gives assurance about a future event ("will we be saved by his life"). Paul has already claimed that Jesus's resurrection was an essential part of God's justifying activity (4:24–25). Moreover, because Jesus has been raised, "he also is at the right hand of God and intercedes for us" (8:34). The expression "by his life" points to Christ's risen life and his power to save those who identify with him.[32] Salvation in the ultimate sense is rescue from the penalty for sin (v. 9, "from wrath") in order to live with Christ in God's eternal kingdom.[33]

---

[31] Seyoon Kim (*The Origin of Paul's Gospel*, WUNT 2.4 [Grand Rapids: Eerdmans, 1982], 13–20, 312–15) argues that this link to Paul's conversion explains why reconciliation remains limited to the Pauline tradition in the NT. Friedrich Büchsel ("ἀλλάσσω, κτλ," *TDNT* 1:256–58) observes that reconciliation was achieved in the death of Jesus, but the process of offering this to "the world" continues through the preaching of the gospel (2 Cor 5:18–20).

[32] Cf. Moo (*Romans*, 321); Schreiner (*Romans*, 264). Dunn (*Romans 1–8*, 261) points out that, "the hope of resurrection was familiar to contemporary Judaism, but not of resurrection as mediated through a particular salvific figure."

[33] When Paul reflects further on the resurrection of Jesus in 6:4–14; 7:4–6; 8:11, his focus is on the present possibility of living a life of obedience to God in anticipation of being resurrected to eternal life with Christ.

5:11. Concluding his focus on God's reconciling work and its consequences, Paul refers again to boasting.[34] The introductory words *οὐ μόνον δέ, ἀλλὰ καί* ("and not only [that], but also") recall v. 3. Here they link the Christian's boasting with the assurance of being saved by the resurrection life of Christ. But Paul's point is that boasting should not simply be "in the hope of the glory of God," which is based on the resurrection of Jesus, or in the afflictions that are part of the process by which our grasp of that hope is strengthened. We also boast "in God through our Lord Jesus Christ." Believers are confident about knowing God and his reconciling love in Christ (cf. Phil 3:3, "boast[ing] in Christ Jesus").[35] Paul stresses the role of Christ in securing this relationship when he says, "Through whom we have now received this reconciliation" (δι' οὗ νῦν τὴν καταλλαγὴν ἐλάβομεν).[36] When the boasting of the Jew "in God" (2:17) and "in the law" (2:23) was exposed as false, it was because of an unrepentant heart (2:1–5) and a lifestyle demonstrating that the person concerned was not a Jew inwardly (2:17–29). "Furthermore, since Israel is under sin just as the gentiles are, the Jewish boast over against the gentile must also fall to the ground."[37] But when the subject of boasting is raised again in 5:2–3, 11, the difference is that it is grounded solely on God's action in Christ and the relationship with sinners he graciously makes possible.

Bridge

For many reasons professing Christians may lack assurance about their relationship with God in the present and have doubts about enjoying an eternal future in his presence. Some may never have understood justification by faith, with the result that guilt about sin makes them feel unworthy and causes them to question God's

---

[34] The present participle καυχώμενοι ("boasting") has the force of an indicative in this context, indicating that "boasting is a continuous feature for the believer, even in the period between reconciliation and salvation, characterized by suffering" (Dunn, *Romans 1–8*, 261).

[35] Gathercole (*Boasting*, 259) notes that "God is now the ground for the boast because he has accomplished the reconciliation that has been won though the cross." Cf. 1 Cor 1:31.

[36] CSB has taken the definite article τήν to be "anaphoric" ("this reconciliation"), pointing back to the reconciliation mentioned in the previous verse. Cf. Wallace, *Greek Grammar*, 217–20.

[37] Gathercole, *Boasting*, 261.

acceptance of them. Those who have not grasped and appreciated the grace of God in the gospel may feel the need to prove themselves and earn God's favor. Others may think of the Christian hope as merely an aspiration rather than a certainty offered to them in the death and resurrection of Jesus. Some may doubt the love of God because of affliction, whereas Paul talks about the positive benefits of suffering, such that one may even glory in it. Some may know about justification but have not thought about their relationship with God in the more personal sense of reconciliation. Others may need to be assured about the link between the present state of being justified and reconciled to God and being saved from wrath to enjoy eternal life with him. This passage invites us to be certain about all these matters and to express our confidence in God and the hope he gives us through our Lord Jesus Christ, even as we face affliction. Experiential knowledge of God's love in the struggles of Christian living arises from knowing that we are among those for whom Christ died. As we contemplate the love of God revealed in Christ's death for us, the Holy Spirit makes this palpable and moves us to love God in return.

VII. Adam's Transgression and Christ's Gift: Grace, Not Law, the Source of Life (5:12–21)

Two things indicate that this is a new, defensive section of the letter. First, there is a change of style from the flowing, expansive sentences in vv. 1–11 to more cryptic and elliptical ones.[1] Second, God's law comes into focus again as the apostle resumes his treatment of Jewish objections to the gospel. Adam is exposed as the first lawbreaker who ushered in the universal reign of sin and death. The law given to Moses was not God's definitive response to this problem (vv. 13–14, 20–21). In salvation-historical terms this passage is about what happens when "the reign of Christ confronts the reign of sin and death initiated by Adam."[2] Only by relying on the Messiah's sacrificial death, rather than the law, can anyone receive justification and "reign in life through the one man, Jesus Christ." Adam and Christ are epochal figures: Adam's sin determines the character of the present age, and Christ's saving action determines the character of the coming age (cf. 1 Cor 15:22; see §§1.1, 1.6).

> 12 Therefore, just as sin entered the world through one man,
> and death through sin, in this way death spread to all people, be-
> cause all sinned. 13 In fact, sin was in the world before the law,
> but sin is not charged to a person's account when there is no law.
> 14 Nevertheless, death reigned from Adam to Moses, even over
> those who did not sin in the likeness of Adam's transgression. He
> is a type of the Coming One.
>
> 15 But the gift is not like the trespass. For if by the one man's
> trespass the many died, how much more have the grace of God
> and the gift which comes through the grace of the one man Jesus
> Christ overflowed to the many. 16 And the gift is not like the one
> man's sin, because from one sin came the judgment, resulting in
> condemnation, but from many trespasses came the gift, resulting
> in justification. 17 Since by the one man's trespass, death reigned
> through that one man, how much more will those who receive

---

[1] There is also a shift from first-person plural verbs in vv. 1–11, where Christians are addressed, to third-person plural verbs in vv. 12–21, where the universal consequences of Adam's sin and the universal implications of the work of Christ are identified.

[2] Ernst Käsemann, *Commentary on Romans*, trans. Geoffrey Bromiley (Grand Rapids: Eerdmans, 1980), 142. Cf. Thomas H. Tobin, "The Jewish Context of Rom 5:12–14," *Studia Philonica Annual* 13 (2001): 159–75.

the overflow of grace and the gift of righteousness reign in life through the one man, Jesus Christ.

[18]So then, as through one trespass there is condemnation for everyone, so also through one righteous act there is justification leading to life for everyone. [19]For just as through one man's disobedience the many were made sinners, so also through the one man's obedience the many will be made righteous. [20]The law came along to multiply the trespass. But where sin multiplied, grace multiplied even more [21]so that, just as sin reigned in death, so also grace will reign through righteousness, resulting in eternal life through Jesus Christ our Lord.

Context

The themes of grace, righteousness, and life are developed from vv. 1–11, as the extraordinary outcome of Jesus's obedience is compared with the effect of Adam's disobedience. Redemption is portrayed in terms of moving "from the sphere of Adam to the sphere of Christ."[3] Paul's conclusion (v. 21) serves as a transition to the next chapter, where dying and rising with Christ is identified as the means of transfer from the reign of sin and death to the reign of righteousness and life.

Structure

The opening statement ("just as sin entered the world through one man, and death through sin") is not completed until v. 18, where the claim is repeated in different words and the critical comparison is made ("so also through one righteous act there is justification leading to life for everyone"). Meanwhile, Paul introduces several explanatory asides. The first is that "death spread to all people, because all sinned" (v. 12c). This is linked to the role of law by the claim that "sin was in the world before the law, but sin is not charged to a person's account when there is no law" (v. 13). Paul adds a significant qualification to this claim when he says, "Nevertheless, death reigned from Adam to Moses, even over those who did not sin in the likeness of Adam's transgression." Three uses of the aorist verb ἐβασίλευσεν ("reigned") in connection with sin and death

[3] Morna D. Hooker, *From Adam to Christ: Essays on Paul* (Cambridge: Cambridge University, 1990; repr., Eugene: Wipf and Stock, 2008), 41. Cf. Dunn, *Romans 1–8*, 289–90.

(vv. 14, 17, 21) are significant in the structure of this passage. They are matched by two uses of the future tense with reference to believers reigning "in life through the one man, Jesus Christ" (v. 17), and grace reigning "through righteousness, resulting in eternal life through Jesus Christ our Lord" (v. 21).

The description of Adam as "a type of the Coming One" (v. 14c) introduces a series of *contrasts* between Adam and Christ (vv. 15–17) before a simple comparison is made in v. 18. The comparison is repeated in v. 19, with Adam's trespass described as an act of disobedience and Christ's righteous act as an expression of obedience. The universal effect of the former is that "the many were made sinners," and the universal potential of the latter is that "the many will be made righteous." The conclusion to the whole argument comes in vv. 20–21. Law is said to have entered into the situation "to multiply the trespass. But where sin multiplied, grace multiplied even more." This startling claim is amplified in the final clause, linking together several key terms from the preceding verses: "So that, just as sin reigned in death, so also grace will reign through righteousness, resulting in eternal life through Jesus Christ our Lord."

Outline:

1. The reign of sin and death (vv. 12–14)
2. The gift of Christ (vv. 15–17)
3. The reign of grace (vv. 18–21)

5:12. The expression διὰ τοῦτο ("therefore") introduces both a conclusion to what has gone before and a new stage in the argument. Paul's focus on sin and death continues the teaching in 1:18–3:20, and his focus on justification and life connects with the progressive development of those themes in 3:21–5:11. This passage recalls some of that extended discussion and presents it in a new light. A comparative construction beginning with ὥσπερ ("just as") would normally be followed by οὕτως καί ("so also"), as in vv. 19, 21. But in v. 12 καὶ οὕτως ("and so"), meaning "as a result" or "in this way," draws an implication rather than a comparison.[4] In fact, Paul's intended comparison between Adam and Christ is not expressed until v. 18, where the claim is repeated in different words ("as through one trespass there is condemnation for everyone"). Then the conclusion is made

[4] Jewett, *Romans*, 373; cf. Cranfield, *Romans*, 1:272n5; Dunn, *Romans 1–8*, 272.

("so also through one righteous act there is justification leading to life for everyone"). This interruption to Paul's argument is due to "the wealth of ideas and associations which crowd in upon him, and here especially to the balancing of given motifs with his own purpose."[5] Given the fact that several contrasts are made between Adam and Christ in vv. 15–17, it seems that the apostle was particularly concerned to show the *dissimilarity* between them before drawing the comparison in v. 18.

The claim that "sin entered the world through one man" (δι' ἑνὸς ἀνθρώπου ἡ ἁμαρτία εἰς τὸν κόσμον εἰσῆλθεν) refers to Adam's disobedience in Gen 3. Although that passage highlights the role of Eve in the process (cf. 2 Cor 11:3; 1 Tim 2:14), Paul treats Adam as ultimately responsible. Sin is viewed as a power released into human life by his primal act of rebellion against God. Adam's sin is "the bridgehead that paves the way for 'sinning' as a condition of humanity."[6] Death as a related power followed the entry of sin (καὶ διὰ τῆς ἁμαρτίας ὁ θάνατος, "and death through sin") since death was the prescribed punishment for transgressing the command of God (Gen 2:17; 3:3). Paul's reflection on this biblical narrative is less complicated than the views expressed in various ancient Jewish writings.[7] From his perspective the simple consequence (καὶ οὕτως, "and so, in this way") was that (lit.) "death spread to all people, because all sinned" (εἰς πάντας ἀνθρώπους ὁ θάνατος διῆλθεν, ἐφ' ᾧ πάντες ἥμαρτον). Without denying the responsibility of each person individually, he presents sin and death as "cosmic forces under which all humans are in bondage."[8] Adam's sin decisively determined the

[5] Käsemann, *Romans*, 146. Moo (*Romans*, 321) takes καὶ οὕτως to mean "in this way" and sees a chiasm in this verse.

[6] Moo, *Romans*, 319. Moo notes that "sin" in the singular is a characteristic of 5:12–8:13, where it is personified as a power that holds sway in the world.

[7] Kruse (*Romans*, 255–57) records some of the key Jewish texts in chronological order. The classic statement is in 4 Ezra 3:7–8 (cf. 2 Bar. 17:2–3; 23:4; 48:42–43; 54:15–19; Josephus, *Ant.* 13.8). Some texts blame the devil (Wis 2:24), and others blame Eve (Sir 25:24; Apoc. Mos. 14). Some speak of the "evil heart" of Adam, which was passed on to all who were born of him (e.g., 4 Ezra 3:21–22; 4:30–32). Cf. Tobin, "The Jewish Context," 160–69.

[8] Jewett, *Romans*, 374. Byrne (*Romans*, 176) comments, "By giving entrance to the tyranny of sin, Adam genuinely facilitated its subsequent dominance in human affairs."

behavior of his descendants. But the meaning of the expression ἐφ' ᾧ πάντες ἥμαρτον continues to be much debated.

Some have taken the relative pronoun ᾧ as masculine and related it to ὁ θάνατος ("death"), understanding death as the realm "in which all sinned." Alternatively, the expression has been taken to mean "with the result that all sinned," or "upon the basis of which all sinned." We enter the world alienated from God and spiritually dead "by virtue of Adam's sin," and as a result all sin. [9] However, "the way in which πάντες picks up εἰς πάντας ἀνθρώπους in the previous clause strongly suggests that the last clause of the verse was intended to explain why death came to all men."[10] Sin is not being presented as the result of death but death as the result of sin. Others link the pronoun to ἑνὸς ἀνθρώπου ("one man"), giving the sense "in whom all sinned." All sinned when Adam sinned and share his punishment, which is the emphasis in vv. 15–17. But the antecedent ἑνὸς ἀνθρώπου is too far away in the sentence for this to be the natural meaning, and ἐν ("in") would be the more appropriate preposition to express this. It is more likely that ᾧ is neuter and that ἐφ' ᾧ is a conjunctional expression meaning "because" (cf. 2 Cor 5:4; Phil 3:12). The construction ἐφ' ᾧ πάντες ἥμαρτον does not relate to any antecedent but explains how death passed to all: "Death is universal for the precise reason that sin is universal."[11] Paul later asserts that through Adam's disobedience "the many were made sinners" (v. 19 comment). This has been taken to mean that "the nature passed on by him to his descendants was a nature weakened and corrupted,"[12] though the passage is not explicit about this. The so-called

---

[9] Schreiner, *Romans*, 276. Cf. Joseph A. Fitzmyer, "The Consecutive Meaning of ἐφ' ᾧ in Romans 5.12," *NTS* 39 (1993): 321–39. Schreiner's argument is persuasive, but I am not convinced it is adequate for the context.

[10] Cranfield, *Romans*, 1:275. He discusses and evaluates six possible understandings of ἐφ' ᾧ, arguing for a conjunctional reading ("because").

[11] S. Lewis Johnson, "Romans 5:12—an Exercise in Exegesis and Theology," in *New Dimensions in New Testament Study*, ed. Richard N. Longenecker and Merrill C. Tenney (Grand Rapids: Zondervan, 1974): 305. Cf. Wallace, *Greek Grammar*, 342–43; Byrne, *Romans*, 183.

[12] Cranfield, *Romans*, 1:279. Byrne (*Romans*, 177) observes that the two "causes" of death (Adam's sin and subsequent human sinning) are "not separate but intimately connected." Moo (*Romans*, 328n61) concludes that "Paul affirms the reality of a solidarity of all humanity with Adam in his sin without being able to explain the exact nature of that union."

Augustinian view has been rehabilitated by taking ἐφ' ᾧ to mean "on the basis of which" and arguing that "since all were in Adam, the head, sin could be reckoned to them according to the terms of the Adamic covenant, as offshoots of his sin."[13] Adam's role was "to make possible the imputation, the judicial treatment, of human sins."[14] While this is a possible reading, it seems more likely that Paul's expression means "because all sinned" and that he is linking Adam's primal sin with a previous claim about the universal phenomenon of sin (cf. 3:23). Human beings became sinners not merely by imitating Adam's transgression, but "they were constituted sinners by him and his act of disobedience."[15]

Some would argue that the theological point here does not depend on Adam's being a historical individual or his disobedience being a historical event. But if Genesis 2–3 only represents "mythic history," we are left with the conclusion that sin and death are simply a natural part of our existence.[16] Culpability for sin is reduced to the level of personal failure, and the notion of death as the punishment for sin is removed. Paul is not simply talking about the entrance of spiritual death into the world but death in both its physical and spiritual dimensions.[17]

5:13–14. When Paul asserts that "sin was in the world before the law" (ἄχρι νόμου ἁμαρτία ἦν ἐν κόσμῳ), his argument is clearly linked to the preceding verse by the connective γάρ (CSB: "in fact"). His return to the theme of law at this point continues his pattern of confronting specifically Jewish issues when they are relevant to his

---

[13] Henri Blocher, *Original Sin: Illuminating the Riddle*, NSBT 5 (Downers Grove: InterVarsity, 1997), 78.

[14] Ibid., 77.

[15] Fitzmyer, *Romans*, 421 (commenting on 5:19). Cf. Cranfield, *Romans*, 1:277–79.

[16] Dunn (*Romans 1–8*, 289–90) is representative of those who take Gen 2–3 to be mythic history, believing the argument in Romans works because the original readers accepted this sad tale of human failure.

[17] Cf. Moo, *Romans*, 320; Blocher, *Original Sin*, 37–62; Kruse, *Romans*, 242–44. William VanDoodewaard (*The Quest for the Historical Adam: Genesis, Hermeneutics, and Human Origins* [Grand Rapids: RHB, 2015]) outlines the theological consequences of arguing for a mythical Adam, or a historical Adam of evolutionary origins. See also Hans Madueme and Michael Reeves, eds., *Adam, the Fall, and Original Sin: Theological, Biblical, and Scientific Perspectives* (Grand Rapids: Baker Academic, 2014).

argument.[18] Here he lays the ground for a more negative statement about the law in v. 20. Previously he claimed that "the knowledge of sin comes through the law" (3:20b) and "where there is no law, there is no transgression" (4:15). Without the law, people knew something about the nature and consequences of sin (cf. 1:18–32), but sin's character as transgression was shown when God's will for humanity was revealed to Israel and rejected. Paul clarifies the situation by saying, "But sin is not charged to a person's account when there is no law" (ἁμαρτία δὲ οὐκ ἐλλογεῖται μὴ ὄντος νόμου). The commercial term ἐλλογεῖται means, "to charge with a financial obligation" (BDAG, cf. Phlm 8). Scripture records a variety of divine punishments that were visited upon individuals and groups before the giving of the law, and God's condemnation of sin was obvious in that period because "death reigned from Adam to Moses." But when the law was given, God's people were made aware of the debt they owed to him because of sin. Before that, human beings collectively could be described as "those who did not sin in the likeness of Adam's transgression" (τοὺς μὴ ἁμαρτήσαντας ἐπὶ τῷ ὁμοιώματι τῆς παραβάσεως Ἀδὰμ). Yet, even without disobeying an explicit command as Adam did, people continued to sin, and so death reigned.[19] Death is later paired with "condemnation" (vv. 16, 18) and contrasted with "eternal life" (v. 21). As well as being the end of physical existence, there are penal and spiritual dimensions to this "enemy" (1 Cor 15:26). Three uses of the aorist verb ἐβασίλευσεν ("reigned") in vv. 14, 17, 21 point to the controlling power of sin and death in human life. But the future tense of the same verb is used in v. 17 with reference to believers' reigning "in life through the one man, Jesus Christ" (βασιλεύσουσιν), and the aorist subjunctive in v. 21 is used to convey the expectation that grace might "reign through righteousness, resulting in eternal life through Jesus Christ

[18] Jewett (*Romans*, 377) points to several Jewish traditions that Paul may have been opposing. In particular, the idea of the eternality of the law "meant that sin was defined exclusively as legal violation."

[19] Comparing 2:12, Schreiner (*Romans*, 278) says that if people "perish without the law, they are still held accountable for sin without possessing the law." This remains the position of those who have no knowledge of God's revealed will.

our Lord" (βασιλεύσῃ).[20] In this way the work of Christ is presented as the victory of one dominion over another.

One final observation about Adam prefaces the series of contrasts with Christ that emerge in vv. 15–17 before the comparison in vv. 18–19 is made. Adam is described as "a type of the Coming One" (τύπος τοῦ μέλλοντος). The word τύπος denotes a mark made by striking (the cognate verb τύπτειν means "strike") or by some other means so that it becomes a mold to shape something else. Hence it came to be used for a model, pattern, copy, or image.[21] Paul employs the term elsewhere with reference to OT events that become "examples for us" (τύποι ἡμῶν, 1 Cor 10:6). Certain things happened to the Israelites "typically" (τυπικῶς), and they were recorded "for our instruction, on whom the ends of the ages have come" (10:11). In the present passage Adam is a model or "type" of Christ in the sense that he prefigures or corresponds to him in a limited way. In an earlier letter Paul contrasted "the first man Adam" with "the last Adam" (1 Cor 15:45), who is also described as "the second man" or "the man of heaven" (15:47–49).[22]

5:15. The differences between Adam and Christ are outlined in vv. 15–17 before the formal comparison is made that shows their likeness (vv. 18–19). Paul's opening statement is abrupt and elliptical (Ἀλλ' οὐχ ὡς τὸ παράπτωμα, οὕτως καὶ τὸ χάρισμα, [lit.] "but not as the trespass, so also the gift"), which CSB renders, "But the gift is not like the trespass."[23] The word παράπτωμα ("trespass") signifies a

---

[20] The third-person singular imperative βασιλευέτω is used in 6:12 to introduce an exhortation flowing from this teaching about the two dominions ("do not let sin reign"). In 6:14 Paul uses the parallel verb κυριεύσει in the assertion that "sin will not rule over you, because you are not under the law but under grace."

[21] Cf. BDAG; Leonhard Goppelt, "τύπος κτλ.," *TDNT* 8:246–59. Cf. Rom 6:17 (τύπον διδαχῆς, "pattern of teaching"); 1 Thess 1:7; 2 Thess 3:9; Phil 3:17.

[22] Dunn (*Romans 1–8*, 277–79) discusses various theories regarding Paul's source for his Adam/Christ parallels.

[23] Jewett (*Romans*, 379, 381) follows Chrys C. Caragounis ("Rom 5:15–16 in the Context of 5:12–21: Contrast or Comparison?" *NTS* 31 [1985]: 142–45) and Stanley E. Porter ("The Argument of Romans 5: Can a Rhetorical Question Make a Difference?" *JBL* 110 [1991]: 673–74) in reading rhetorical questions in vv. 15a, 16a ("But is not the grace-gift just like the trespass?" and "Is not the gift like the one's sinning?"). They argue that these questions were posed by opponents, and the clauses that follow indicate Paul's answer. But this is not the easiest way to read the syntax of these verses, especially since γάρ ("for") would normally introduce a causal clause rather than the answer to a question.

"false step" or "offense" in relation to God. It is used throughout this passage as a synonym for sin (ἁμαρτία) and has a broader meaning than "transgression" (παράβασις).[24] Contrasted with Adam's trespass, the "gift" (χάρισμα) most naturally refers to what is later called Christ's "righteous act" (v. 18), or his "obedience" (v. 19). "Here the act of Christ is characterized as an embodiment of grace."[25]

The superiority of the gift over the trespass is expressed in terms of a "how much more" argument (cf. πολλῷ μᾶλλον in vv. 9, 10, 17). "By the one man's trespass the many died" (τῷ τοῦ ἑνὸς παραπτώματι οἱ πολλοὶ ἀπέθανον), meaning "all people" (vv. 12, 18, πάντας ἀνθρώπους). Paul contrasts this with the effect of "the grace of God and the gift" (ἡ χάρις τοῦ θεοῦ καὶ ἡ δωρεά). The noun δωρεά ("gift") is a synonym for χάρισμα here. "The grace of God" is paired with this gift to indicate its ultimate source, but the following clause also indicates that the gift is (lit.) "by the grace of the one man, Jesus Christ" (ἐν χάριτι τῇ τοῦ ἑνὸς ἀνθρώπου Ἰησοῦ Χριστοῦ). In other words, the gracious act of Christ is paired with the grace of God in sending him to be the solution to the problem of sin and death. The precise nature of the gift and its effect is revealed in what follows, but Paul's immediate aim is to stress the extremely rich provision of God. These gifts have "overflowed to the many" (εἰς τοὺς πολλοὺς ἐπερίσσευσεν), meaning that they are for all who are subject to the reign of sin and death. Paul only addresses the question of who might actually benefit from this gracious provision in v. 17.

5:16. A second contrast between Adam and Christ begins with an even more abbreviated statement than the one in v. 15 (καὶ οὐχ ὡς δι᾽ ἑνὸς ἁμαρτήσαντος τὸ δώρημα, [lit.] "and not as through one man's having sinned is the gift"). CSB renders this "and the gift is not like the one man's sin." As in v. 15, the causal clause that follows is linked to the preceding statement by the connective γάρ ("because"). The reason the gift of Christ cannot simply be compared with Adam's sin is explained in two ways. First, "from one sin came the *judgment*" (τὸ μὲν γὰρ κρίμα ἐξ ἑνός), "but from many trespasses came the *gift*" (τὸ δὲ χάρισμα ἐκ πολλῶν παραπτωμάτων). The judicial verdict passed on Adam (τὸ μὲν γὰρ κρίμα) was a simple consequence

---

[24] Cf. BDAG; Wilhelm Michaelis, "πίπτω, κτλ.," *TDNT* 6:170–72.

[25] Dunn, *Romans 1–8*, 279. Cranfield (*Romans*, 1:284) argues that the gift is more likely to refer to "the gracious gift of a status of righteousness before God," but surely the gift of righteousness is the result of Christ's prior gift of himself in death.

of his disobedience, but God's gracious provision in Christ was in response to "all the accumulated sins of the centuries."[26] Second, the outcome of Adam's sin and the verdict pronounced on him was "condemnation" or "punishment" (εἰς κατάκριμα), but the outcome of Christ's self-giving in death for sinners was "justification" (εἰς δικαίωμα). The noun κατάκριμα refers to more than the pronouncement of guilt (τὸ κρίμα) and covers the penalty involved (BDAG, cf. 5:18; 8:1). Doubtless, this picks up the teaching of Gen 3:22–24 that death involves alienation from God and not being able to live forever in his presence. Although δικαίωμα normally means "righteous requirement" (1:32; 2:26; 8:4), or "righteous act" (5:18), the noun functions here as a substitute for δικαίωσις (4:25; 5:18, "justification"). Paul appears to have chosen this word so it would function as a rhetorical counterpart to κατάκριμα (see §2.4).[27]

5:17. This verse is linked to the previous one by γάρ ("for" [not translated by CSB]). Continuing the contrasts outlined in vv. 15–16, Paul focuses again on the reign of death (v. 14) but introduces the alternative possibility of reigning in life through Christ. The sentence begins as a simple condition of fact: "Since by the one man's trespass, death reigned through that one man" (εἰ γὰρ τῷ τοῦ ἑνὸς παραπτώματι ὁ θάνατος ἐβασίλευσεν διὰ τοῦ ἑνός). This recapitulates the argument so far about the punishment of death spreading to all people. The sentence continues with an elaborate "how much more" argument (πολλῷ μᾶλλον as in vv. 9. 10, 15). As in v. 15, the deliverance made possible "through the one man, Jesus Christ" is contrasted with the condemnation that spread to all because of "the one man's trespass." The new idea in v. 17, however, is that those who receive "the overflow of grace" (τὴν περισσείαν τῆς χάριτος; cf. v. 15, ἐπερίσσευσεν) and "the gift of righteousness" (τῆς

[26] Cranfield, *Romans*, 1:286. Robert H. Gundry ("A Breaking of Expectations: The Rhetoric of Surprise in Paul's Letter to the Romans," in *Romans and the People of God*, 259) suggests that ἐκ πολλῶν παραπτωμάτων could also more literally mean "through (many transgressions), by way of them, out of them." Although ἐξ ἑνός could refer to Adam, in contrast with ἐκ πολλῶν παραπτωμάτων ("many trespasses"), it is more likely a reference to Adam's sin.

[27] Cf. BDAG. Jewett (*Romans*, 382) suggests that δικαίωμα contrasted with κατάκριμα could be translated "righteous decree," which of course refers to justification. Less likely is J. R. Daniel Kirk's view ("Reconsidering *Dikaiōma* in Rom 5:16," *JBL* 126 [2007]: 787–92) that δικαίωμα here denotes "the reparation demanded by God in the face of transgression," specifically the righteous requirement of death.

δωρεᾶς τῆς δικαιοσύνης) made possible by the Messiah's sacrificial death will "reign in life through the one man, Jesus Christ" (ἐν ζωῇ βασιλεύσουσιν διὰ τοῦ ἑνὸς Ἰησοῦ Χριστοῦ).[28]

The expression "those who receive" (οἱ λαμβάνοντες; cf. v. 11, ἐλάβομεν) limits the extent to which Christ's victory is enjoyed by "the many" (εἰς τοὺς πολλούς, v. 15). The universalism of the passage is qualified here, though the necessity of faith for justification has been clearly established in the letter so far.[29] The future tense of the verb "reign" points to an eschatological event, fulfilling the biblical hope of restored dominion for believers in the kingdom of God. As in 4:23–25; 5:9–10, the death and resurrection of Jesus are the implied means by which the gifts of righteousness and eternal life are offered. In view of what is said in 6:4–14, however, the expression "reign in life" implies that believers even now begin to reign over sin and death in anticipation of final victory through resurrection with Christ (cf. Col 3:1; Eph 2:6).[30] This verse forms a triumphant climax to vv. 15–17, offering hope to all who are captive to the rule of sin and death but trust in Jesus and his saving work.

5:18. The formal comparison Paul began to make between Adam and Christ in v. 12 is completed here, using a highly condensed style with no verbs. The introductory words (Ἄρα οὖν, "so then") indicate a conclusion to what has gone before. The first part of the comparison ("as through one trespass there is condemnation for everyone" [ὡς δι' ἑνὸς παραπτώματος εἰς πάντας ἀνθρώπους εἰς κατάκριμα]) summarizes what has been repeatedly said about the profound effect of Adam's sin. Jews have not escaped the consequences by having the law of God. The second part of the comparison ("so also through one righteous act there is justification leading to life for everyone" [οὕτως καὶ δι' ἑνὸς δικαιώματος εἰς πάντας ἀνθρώπους εἰς δικαίωσιν

---

[28] Paul uses the rare word περισσεία ("surplus, abundance") to convey the sense that more than enough grace has been shown. The idea that the saints will share in the rule of the messianic era can be found in texts such as Dan 7:22, 26–27; Wis 3:8; 5:15–16; 1QM 12:14–15; 1QpHab 5:4–5; Matt 19:28; Rev 20:4, 6.

[29] Compare also 10:9–11, where the universal offer of salvation to Jews and Gentiles is on the condition that individuals confess Jesus as Lord and believe in their heart that God raised him from the dead. Cf. Moo, *Romans*, 340.

[30] Cf. Ardel B. Caneday, "Already Reigning in Life through One Man: Recovery of Adam's Abandoned Dominion (Romans 5:12–21)," in *Studies in the Pauline Epistles: Essays in Honor of Douglas J. Moo*, ed. Matthew S. Harmon and Jay E. Smith (Grand Rapids: Zondervan, 2014): 27–43.

ζωῆς]) summarizes what has been said about the overwhelming superiority of Christ's action, here defined as "one righteous act" (δι' ἑνὸς δικαιώματος).[31] This term, together with the parallel "obedience" (v. 19, τῆς ὑπακοῆς), points to the righteous submission of the Son to the Father's will in death (cf. Phil 2:8). Jesus's whole life was devoted to obeying the Father, making his sacrifice a pure and perfect self-offering (cf. Heb 5:8–9; 9:14; 10:14), but Paul's focus here is on the single action by which Jesus overturned the disastrous effect of Adam's single action. As in 4:25, δικαίωσις is used with reference to justification, which makes entrance into eternal life possible. A genitive of result (ζωῆς, "for life") is translated by CSB as "leading to life." By repeating the expression εἰς πάντας ἀνθρώπους ([lit.] "for all people," cf. v. 12), Paul emphasizes again the universality of God's provision for all who are impacted by Adam's sin and its consequences, Jews and Gentiles together.[32]

5:19. The conjunction γάρ ("for") indicates that what follows is a further explanation of what has just been argued. Adam's "disobedience" (παρακοῆς) is compared with Christ's "obedience" (ὑπακοῆς). The effect of Adam's disobedience to the revealed will of God was that "the many were made sinners" (ἁμαρτωλοὶ κατεστάθησαν οἱ πολλοί). People do not simply sin in imitation of Adam, but they have been "made sinners" because of Adam's primal sin.[33] The effect of Christ's obedience to the righteous requirement of his Father is that "the many will be made righteous" (οὕτως καὶ . . . δίκαιοι κατασταθήσονται οἱ πολλοί). Paul employs the verb καθίστημι in the passive here ("made, constituted") with possibly two levels of meaning. Although the forensic sense of being reckoned as sinners in Adam could be the primary meaning, "the many" actually "became" sinners as a result of Adam's trespass. Similarly,

---

[31] Cranfield (*Romans*, 1:289) suggests that ἑνός, which is used twice in this verse, should be understood as masculine, meaning "one man's misdeed" in the first instance and "one man's righteous conduct" in the second (so also NRSV). But ESV, NIV, and CSB understand ἑνός as agreeing with παραπτώματος and δικαιώματος.

[32] Cranfield (*Romans*, 1:290) observes that the first occurrence of this expression in v. 18 does not mean that "all" is an "eternally unalterable quantity" since Christ is already delivering many from the state of condemnation. Likewise, the second "all" does not foreclose the question whether all will actually come to share in the proffered gift. Cf. Moo (*Romans*, 342–44); Mark Rapinchuk, "Universal Sin and Salvation in Romans 5:12–21," *JETS* 42 (1999): 433–41.

[33] Schreiner (*Romans*, 288–93) considers the theological implications.

when Paul says that "the many will be made righteous," the primary meaning is forensic,[34] but justification enables believers to offer every part of themselves to God "as weapons for righteousness" (6:12–13), to become "enslaved to righteousness" (6:17–19). The future tense could refer to final justification (as in 2:13), though the emphasis in vv. 1, 9, 17, 18 is on the present. The potential or logical outcome of Christ's obedience for all who believe is both justification and transformation.

5:20. The fact that Paul deals with the subject of law at the beginning and end of this passage shows how important it is for his argument. Even though an article is not used before νόμος, it is clear from the context that the law given by God to Israel is specifically in view.[35] As he unfolds God's solution to the problem of sin and death, he indicates that the law was not given as the means of deliverance from these oppressive powers. Indeed, God's purpose was "to make Israel more conscious of its solidarity in sin with the rest of Adam's offspring."[36] Previously Paul argued that God's law exposes the character of sin as transgression and makes people aware of the debt they owe him (vv. 13–14). Now he claims, "The law came along to multiply the trespass" (νόμος δὲ παρεισῆλθεν, ἵνα πλεονάσῃ τὸ παράπτωμα).[37] God's law was actually responsible for the multiplication of trespasses like Adam's! As Paul later argues, this happened because "the sinful passions aroused through the law were working in us to bear fruit for death" (7:5). Although positive things are said about the law in 7:7, 10, 12, 14, Paul insists that the commandment meant for life resulted in death because sin increases when confronted by God's commandments (7:7–13). Despite this outcome, it is nevertheless possible to see God's merciful purpose in

[34] Cf. Albrecht Oepke, "καθίστημι, κτλ.," *TDNT* 3:444–46.

[35] The conjunction δέ at the beginning of this verse signals a new development in the argument ("now"), returning to the theme of law raised in v. 13. The second use of δέ in v. 20 is adversative ("but").

[36] Dunn, *Romans 1–8*, 286. Paul's argument in 3:9–20 establishes that Scripture itself reveals this. Cf. Moo, *Romans*, 348; Biblical and Theological Themes §1.4.

[37] The verb παρεισῆλθεν literally means "come in beside" and does not in itself "say anything about the worth of the law depreciatory or otherwise" (Cranfield, *Romans*, 1:292). Contrast Dunn (*Romans 1–8*, 286) and Jewett (*Romans*, 387), who take the verb here and in Gal 2:4 to mean "slipped in, encroached." But Gal 3:19 (προσετέθη, "added") is more likely to be parallel in sense. Cf. Schreiner, *Romans*, 295.

giving the law because "where sin multiplied, grace multiplied even more" (οὗ δὲ ἐπλεόνασεν ἡ ἁμαρτία, ὑπερεπερίσσευσεν ἡ χάρις).[38]

Sin multiplied in Israel to the point that God's own people refused to accept their Messiah and handed him over to the Gentiles to be crucified, yet in this very act of rebellion, "grace multiplied even more." Salvation for the opponents of Jesus was provided in the death and resurrection of Jesus "according to God's determined plan and foreknowledge" (Acts 2:23; cf. 4:10–12; 5:30–31). In God's gracious purpose, this salvation was also then offered to people in every nation (Acts 20:21; 26:17–18). So the fundamental division in humanity is not between those who have the law and those who do not but between those who are in Adam and those who are in Christ.

5:21. The greater purpose of God in salvation history is revealed in this concluding comparison (ὥσπερ ["just as"], οὕτως καί ["so also"], as in v. 19). The rule of sin and death initiated by Adam is first recalled (ἐβασίλευσεν ἡ ἁμαρτία ἐν τῷ θανάτῳ, "sin reigned in death"). Two previous references have drawn attention to the reign of death (vv. 14, 17), but the expression here highlights the fact that sin is the cause of death, which is the divine penalty for sin (v. 12; cf. Gen 2:17). The rule of sin in the sphere of death is compared with the opposing and more powerful rule of grace, which is personified here as in v. 20. The main thrust of Paul's purpose clause is "so that grace might reign" (ἵνα . . . ἡ χάρις βασιλεύσῃ [aorist subjunctive]). Summarizing the argument of the previous verses, Paul celebrates that grace will reign "through righteousness, resulting in eternal life through Jesus Christ our Lord." "Righteousness" in this context (δικαιοσύνης) will be the equivalent of "the gift of righteousness" (v. 17), or "justification" (vv. 16, 18). "Eternal life" clarifies the meaning of "life" in vv. 17, 18. The passage ends with the recognition that the reign of grace has been achieved by Jesus Christ, who is acknowledged by those who "reign in life" through him (v. 17) as "our Lord" (cf. 5:1, 11).

[38] The rare verb ὑπερπερισσεύω is used intransitively here (BDAG, "be present in greater abundance") to form a climax to the series of terms expressing abundance in vv. 15, 17, 20. Cf. 2 Cor 7:4.

Bridge

Whereas much of Paul's teaching about sin in the early chapters of Romans points to individual responsibility before God, a corporate or collective view is presented here. "No one sins 'apart from' Adam, no one sins entirely alone, and no one sins without in some sense adding to the collective sin-burden of the race."[39] Paul does not explain in detail here how the legacy of sin was passed on, but Adam's sin unleashed a tyrant power that controls everyone who is born into this world. Death is a related power, reigning over human life because of sin (cf. 1 Cor 15:25–26, 54–56; Heb 2:14–18). Death is not simply the natural end of human life, as many people suppose, and it will not be defeated by medical science, as some vainly hope! Reflecting the viewpoint of Gen 2–3, Paul indicates that death is the penalty imposed by God for the primal sin, which was an expression of rebellion against God and his good purpose for humanity. But when Christ drew the "sting" of death by dying for sinners, the penalty of endless separation from God was removed (cf. 1 Cor 15:56–57). There are now two fundamental identities in humanity: those who are in Adam and those who are in Christ. No other identity has the same significance, and so Christians need to live as those who decidedly belong to Christ. The power of sin and death has been broken for us, and we "reign in life through the one man, Jesus Christ" (v. 17). "The age to come" has been inaugurated by the death and resurrection of Israel's Messiah. So those who belong to him begin to enjoy the benefits of his kingly rule in the present. Although born as the offspring of Adam, we become part of the new humanity through faith in Christ and what he has done for us.

[39] Byrne, *Romans*, 176.

VIII. Dying and Rising with Christ: Freed from Sin's Penalty to Be Slaves to God and to Righteousness (6:1–23)

This new section of the letter explores the implications of being "joined" with Christ in his death and resurrection. Returning to the style of 5:1–11 but applying the teaching of 5:12–21, Paul wants his readers to consider where they are in relation to Adam and Christ. "Do they still live under the reign of sin and death or do they live under the reign of grace and righteousness?"[1] Indicative statements become the basis for imperatives to live consistently with their new standing in Christ. In this respect Rom 6 has a pivotal role in the recursive structure of the letter as a whole (cf. Introduction II.C.4). Paul moves from the justification and salvation of sinners by the death of Jesus to the inherent obligation laid on believers to offer their justified and resurrected selves to God. As the concluding chapters show, this movement facilitates the restoration of true worship and righteousness among the nations (12:1–15:13).

> [1]What should we say then? Should we continue in sin so
> that grace may multiply? [2]Absolutely not! How can we who died
> to sin still live in it? [3]Or are you unaware that all of us who were
> baptized into Christ Jesus were baptized into his death? [4]There-
> fore we were buried with him by baptism into death, in order that,
> just as Christ was raised from the dead by the glory of the Father,
> so we too may walk in newness of life. [5]For if we have been
> united with him in the likeness of his death, we will certainly also
> be in the likeness of his resurrection. [6]For we know that our old
> self was crucified with him so that the body ruled by sin might be
> rendered powerless so that we may no longer be enslaved to sin,
> [7]since a person who has died is freed from sin. [8]Now if we died
> with Christ, we believe that we will also live with him, [9]because
> we know that Christ, having been raised from the dead, will not
> die again. Death no longer rules over him. [10]For the death he died,
> he died to sin once for all time; but the life he lives, he lives to
> God. [11]So, you too consider yourselves dead to sin and alive to
> God in Christ Jesus.
>
> [12]Therefore do not let sin reign in your mortal body, so that
> you obey its desires. [13]And do not offer any parts of it to sin as

[1] Wright, "Romans," 533. Paul's style changes from third person (5:12–21) to the more involving first-person plural (6:1–11, as in 5:1–11), with second-person forms of address emerging in 6:3, 11–14, 16–22.

weapons for unrighteousness. But as those who are alive from
the dead, offer yourselves to God, and all the parts of yourselves
to God as weapons for righteousness. [14]For sin will not rule over
you, because you are not under the law but under grace.

[15]What then? Should we sin because we are not under the
law but under grace? Absolutely not! [16]Don't you know that if you
offer yourselves to someone as obedient slaves, you are slaves of
that one you obey—either of sin leading to death or of obedience
leading to righteousness? [17]But thank God that, although you
used to be slaves of sin, you obeyed from the heart that pattern of
teaching to which you were handed over, [18]and having been set
free from sin, you became enslaved to righteousness. [19]I am using
a human analogy because of the weakness of your flesh. For just
as you offered the parts of yourselves as slaves to impurity, and
to greater and greater lawlessness, so now offer them as slaves
to righteousness, which results in sanctification. [20]For when you
were slaves of sin, you were free with regard to righteousness.
[21]So what fruit was produced then from the things you are now
ashamed of? The outcome of those things is death. [22]But now,
since you have been set free from sin and have become enslaved
to God, you have your fruit, which results in sanctification—and
the outcome is eternal life! [23]For the wages of sin is death, but the
gift of God is eternal life in Christ Jesus our Lord.

Context

The opening questions suggest a false inference from 5:20b–21 about the relationship between grace and sin. Paul responds by arguing that Christ has broken the power of sin and death by his own death and resurrection. Those who have been "buried with him by baptism into death" (v. 4) should live as those who have been brought by Christ from death to life (vv. 11, 12–14). Paul's claim that "sin will not rule over you, because you are not under the law but under grace" leads to a new stage of the argument, with two questions again drawing the wrong conclusion from what has been stated (v. 15). A series of contrasting options highlights the need for believers to present themselves to righteousness rather than to sin. The fruit of this new "slavery" is holiness or sanctification, and the result is eternal life (v. 22). Paul's return to the death-life contrast in v. 23 bridges to the development of that theme with respect to the law in 7:1–6 (see §§2.4, 2.6).

Structure

The opening questions ("What should we say then? Should we continue in sin so that grace may multiply?") are answered by a further question ("How can we who died to sin still live in it?"). Dying to sin is explained in terms of being "baptized into" Christ's death (v. 3) so that we might "walk in newness of life" (v. 4). Paul expands on what it means to die with Christ and enjoy new life in the present as we await physical resurrection with Christ (vv. 5–10) before challenging his readers to "consider yourselves dead to sin and alive to God in Christ Jesus" (v. 11).

The central paragraph (vv. 12–14) outlines the practical implications of this challenge, with a chiastic structure focusing attention on the central exhortation:

A Therefore do not let sin reign in your mortal body, so that you obey its desires.
  B And do not offer any parts of it to sin as weapons for unrighteousness.
    C But as those who are alive from the dead, offer yourselves to God,
  B´ and all the parts of yourselves to God as weapons for righteousness.
A´ For sin will not rule over you, because you are not under law but under grace.

A third section of the chapter (vv. 15–23) begins with questions implying that the claim in v. 14 is an encouragement to sin ("What then? Should we sin because we are not under law but under grace?").[2] Paul responds by contrasting different forms of spiritual slavery and their outcomes. Slavery to sin leads to death, but slavery to obedience leads to righteousness (v. 16). Slavery to sin is equated with slavery to moral impurity and lawlessness, with lawlessness the result. Slavery to righteousness results in holiness, and its end is eternal life (vv. 17–22). An exhortation about offering "the parts of yourselves" as "slaves to righteousness" (v. 19) echoes the challenge

[2] Dunn (*Romans 1–8*, 335–36) views vv. 12–23 as an hortatory unit with a sustained sequence of antitheses. But, if a twofold division is to be made, vv. 12–14 belong with vv. 1–11, and a new beginning is signaled by the questions in v. 15. Cf. Moo, *Romans*, 351.

in v. 13. A final warning restates the eternal consequences of offering yourselves to sin or to God (v. 23).

Outline:

1. From death to life (vv. 1–11)
2. Present yourselves to God (vv. 12–14)
3. From sin to righteousness (vv. 15–23)

6:1. As in 3:5; 7:7; 9:14, Paul's first question ("What shall we say then?") introduces a false inference that could be drawn from the preceding argument. His second question conveys the actual point: "Should we continue in sin so that grace may multiply?" (*ἐπιμένωμεν τῇ ἁμαρτίᾳ, ἵνα ἡ χάρις πλεονάσῃ;*).[3] Given the misrepresentation of his teaching mentioned in 3:8 ("Let us do what is evil so that good may come"), this question could represent the challenge of Jewish opponents. Since he did not require converts to keep the law of Moses, the charge could have arisen that his gospel promoted sin. But the precise way the challenge echoes 5:20b–21 suggests a logical progression in the argument and a broader concern "to counter the danger of antinomianism in the church."[4] Paul uses a similar rhetorical pattern in 6:15 to advance to the next stage of the argument.

6:2. Paul's emphatic response is "Absolutely not!" (*μὴ γένοιτο*, as in 3:4, 6, 31; 6:15; 7:7, 13; 9:14; 11:1, 11). This is followed by a further question, indicating the direction his argument will take: Christians are those who "died (in relation) to sin" (*οἵτινες ἀπεθάνομεν τῇ ἁμαρτίᾳ*). Before he explains what this means, Paul asks the logical question: "How can we still live in it?" (*πῶς ἔτι ζήσομεν ἐν αὐτῇ;*).[5] This does not mean Christians can be sinless,

[3] CSB translates ἐπιμένωμεν as a deliberative subjunctive (cf. Wallace, *Greek Grammar*, 467). But it could be hortatory ("Let us continue in sin"), which would make the inference from 5:20b even more insidious. Jewett (*Romans*, 395n25) refers to this as "a technique of ridicule."

[4] Cranfield, *Romans*, 1:297n1. Cranfield (1:295) argues that Paul's positive intention was "to insist that justification has inescapable moral implications." Dunn (*Romans 1–8*, 305) says Paul has modified the diatribe style to engage with his Christian audience, but he also explores the Jewish dimension to the question (326). See also Schreiner, *Romans*, 303–4.

[5] A dative of respect (τῇ ἁμαρτίᾳ) is followed by a dative of place (ἐν αὐτῇ), both expressions suggesting that sin is a power that rules over human life. Wallace (*Greek Grammar*, 570) describes ζήσομεν as a deliberative future, questioning the rightness of the proposal.

or unresponsive to sin, as his exhortations in vv. 12–14, 19 reveal. His question highlights the spiritual and moral *incongruity* of continuing in sin. In effect he goes on to expound the implications of the claim in 5:17 that "those who receive the overflow of grace and the gift of righteousness [will] reign in life through the one man, Jesus Christ."

There are four different ways the present passage indicates that Christians die to sin and are raised up. First, there is the *juridical sense* in which God treats believers as having died to sin when Christ died (6:6a, "crucified with him" [συνεσταυρώθη]; cf. 2 Cor 5:14–15; Gal 2:19; Col 3:3–4).[6] Christ's death was not a punishment for his own sin, but he suffered the penalty for sin that was due to us (5:12–21). Second, there is the *baptismal sense*, in which God's decision to regard Christ's death for our sins as our death is proclaimed and appropriated personally by faith (6:3–4a; cf. Col 2:12).[7] Third, there is the *moral sense*, in which believers express their identity as those who have died and been raised with Christ by ongoing faith and repentance, seeking to obey God in everyday life (6:4b–c, 5b, 6b–c; cf. 8:5–13; Col 3:5–14). Fourth, there is the *eschatological sense* in which believers die to sin finally and irreversibly through bodily death and resurrection to eternal life with Christ (6:8–10; cf. 1 Cor 15:20–26).

6:3. The expression ἢ ἀγνοεῖτε ("Or are you unaware") is a way of reminding the Romans about what they should have known already but needed to consider more carefully (cf. 7:1; 1 Cor 6:2, 9, 16, 19).[8] Being "baptized into Christ Jesus" involves being "baptized into his death." Calling upon the name of the Lord Jesus in baptism enables those who turn to him in faith to share in the bene-

[6] My approach broadly follows Cranfield (*Romans*, 1:299–300), who considers that the first sense is reflected in the simple claim that Christians are those who "died to sin" (v. 2). Moo (*Romans*, 391–95) provides a helpful excursus on Paul's "with Christ" conception. Schreiner (*Romans*, 305–6) simply takes v. 2 to refer to baptism.

[7] Cf. Cranfield, *Romans*, 1.299; Moo, *Romans*, 357–58. Baptism is an occasion for proclaiming what Christ has achieved for us and expressing repentance and faith in the risen Lord. Baptism signifies that those who respond in this way participate in the benefits of his sacrifice and are committed to living for him.

[8] Cf. Dunn, *Romans 1–8*, 308. Jewett (*Romans*, 396) argues from the use of the verb ἀγνοέω by classical rhetoricians that the material Paul is about to present on baptism must have been new to the Romans. But the context suggests he is building on an understanding they already have. Col 2:12 makes a similar assumption.

fits of his death (cf. 10:9–13; Acts 2:38; 22:16). In practice, baptism may be separated in time from the moment of conversion, but it provides "a focus and occasion for the divine-human encounter," serving as "a metaphor for the divine initiative in that encounter."[9] The link between baptism and death probably goes back to Jesus himself, who used baptism as a figure for his expected overwhelming by death (Mark 10:38–39; Luke 12:50).[10] Paul gives the familiar action of being baptized with water a profound theological significance by means of the expression "baptized into his death."[11] He uses the verb βαπτίζω elsewhere with reference to water baptism (1 Cor 1:14–16) but also uses it metaphorically with reference to Israel's being "baptized into Moses in the cloud and in the sea" (1 Cor 10:2) and Christians' being "baptized by one Spirit into one body" (1 Cor 12:13; cf. Matt 3:11; Acts 1:5; 11:16). The most natural way to read the present verse is to conclude that he moves from the literal meaning of baptism to highlight what it represents theologically in relation to Christ's death.

6:4. Linked by the connective οὖν ("therefore"), a restatement of v. 3 follows (συνετάφημεν αὐτῷ διὰ τοῦ βαπτίσματος εἰς τὸν θάνατον, "We were buried with him by baptism into death"). The sequence "died, buried, raised" recalls Paul's summary of the gospel in 1 Cor 15:3–4, which begins by affirming that "Christ died for our sins according to the Scriptures." A similar sequence is applied to *believers* in the present context, using verbs with the preposition σύν (v. 6, συνεσταυρώθη ["crucified with him"]; v. 4, συνετάφημεν αὐτῷ ["buried with him"]; v. 8, συζήσομεν αὐτῷ ["live with him"]).[12] Christians

[9] Dunn, *Romans 1–8*, 312. See Kruse, *Romans*, 270–79, on baptism in Paul's letters.

[10] Albrecht Oepke ("βάπτω, βαπτίζω κτλ.," *TDNT* 1:529–36) argues that βαπτίζω only occasionally means "bathe" or "wash" in Hellenistic usage. The idea of going under, being overwhelmed, or perishing is nearer the general sense. BDAG contends that the primary sense in the NT period and beyond is "wash ceremonially for purpose of purification" and that the metaphorical sense ("cause someone to have an extraordinary experience akin to an initiatory water-rite") is secondary. However, metaphorical use of this verb in the NT begins with John the Baptist and Jesus.

[11] Cf. Dunn, *Romans 1–8*, 308–13, 327–29. Donald W. B. Robinson ("Towards a Definition of Baptism," *RTR* 34 [1975]: 1–15) limits both noun and verb to a metaphorical sense in Rom 6:3–4; Col 2:12; Gal 3:27 but does not explain why the literal use was abandoned by Paul or how it was related to the metaphorical use.

[12] Moo (*Romans*, 393) contends that ideas of correspondence and causality are present when Paul uses this "with Christ" language, but "the idea of *participation* or

share together in the benefits Jesus obtained for them in his death, burial, and resurrection. Literally, the verb συνθάπτω means "bury together with" (BDAG). Burial signifies that a death has taken place. At one level baptism is like a funeral, proclaiming that the candidate died to sin when Christ himself was crucified (cf. v. 6 comment).[13] The expression διὰ τοῦ βαπτίσματος ("through baptism") is instrumental but does not mean baptism is an automatic or mechanical way of conveying the benefits of Christ's death.[14] Previous chapters have shown that faith is the means by which the promises of the gospel are appropriated. Baptism holds forth the possibility of cleansing from sin and new life in Christ. At the same time, it provides the opportunity to express faith in the crucified Messiah and to repent (cf. Acts 2:38; 11:15–18; 20:21): "God's kindness is intended to lead you to repentance" (Rom 2:4).

The broader purpose of baptism into Christ's death is expressed with a comparison: "Just as (ὥσπερ) Christ was raised from the dead by the glory of the Father, so we too (οὕτως καὶ ἡμεῖς) may walk in newness of life." Moral and spiritual renewal depends on a faith-union with Christ in his bodily resurrection from death. Variations of the formula ἠγέρθη ἐκ νεκρῶν ("raised from the dead") are found in 4:24; 8:11; 10: 9 (cf. 1:4, ἐξ ἀναστάσεως νεκρῶν, "the resurrection from the dead"). The phrase διὰ τῆς δόξης τοῦ πατρός ("by the glory of the Father") means that Jesus was raised by "the power of God gloriously exercised."[15] Similarly, the "newness of life" (καινότητι ζωῆς) that we experience by turning to Christ is a manifestation of the glory to come. God's glory was seen in the person and work of Jesus and supremely in his resurrection. It will be fully experienced by believers when we are raised from physical death (cf. 5:2; 8:18–30; Phil 3:12–21; Col 3:1–4). Set free from the condemnation for sin, we can serve God now "in the newness of the Spirit" (7:6,

---

association does seem to be basic to the expressions" (his emphasis).

[13] Burial was not often under the surface of the earth in Paul's day, but people were buried in tombs, as Jesus was, and in caves. Dunn (*Romans 1–8*, 314) therefore warns about tying the imagery of baptism and burial too closely to immersion in water.

[14] Wallace (*Greek Grammar*, 219) points out that the article in the expression διὰ τοῦ βαπτίσματος is anaphoric, pointing back to the previous reference to baptism by the use of the verb in v. 3. Moo (*Romans*, 361–66) discusses different explanations of the significance of baptism in Paul's argument.

[15] Cranfield (*Romans*, 1:304) notes the connection between glory and power in some texts (e.g., Exod 15:6; 1 Chr 16:28; Col 1:11; 1 Pet 4:11; Rev 1:6; 4:11; 5:12–13).

καινότητι πνεύματος), who facilitates the process of glorification (2 Cor 3:18). We become part of God's "new creation" in Christ (2 Cor 5:17; Gal 6:15, καινὴ κτίσις). Walking (περιπατήσωμεν) is a biblical metaphor for a pattern of life or moral conduct (e.g., Exod 16:4; Deut 8:6; Prov 6:12). This term is used again in 8:4, where the charge is not to "walk according to the flesh but according to the Spirit" (cf. 13:13; 14:15; Gal 5:16).[16]

6:5. A condition of fact, expressed by εἰ ("if, since") with two indicative verbs, brings Paul back to his basic theme of dying and rising with Christ. With a clear link to the preceding verse (γάρ, "for"), he argues, "If we have been united with him in the likeness of his death, we will certainly also be in the likeness of his resurrection." The adjective σύμφυτοι could be rendered "planted together" or "grafted together," though the term is used in a number of ways beyond the horticultural realm.[17] The dative expression τῷ ὁμοιώματι τοῦ θανάτου αὐτοῦ (lit., "by the likeness of his death") follows σύμφυτοι γεγόναμεν ("we are united") and is directly dependent on σύμφυτοι.[18] So the sense is simply, "We are joined together by the likeness of his death." Most translations, however, assume that the pronoun αὐτῷ should be understood and so include the words "with him." This indicates a personal union with Christ "in the likeness of his death." Various interpretations of τῷ ὁμοιώματι τοῦ θανάτου αὐτοῦ have been suggested, including the possibility that it refers back to baptism as the means by which Christ's death is appropriated by believers.[19] However, Paul's underlying idea is that

---

[16] See also 1 Cor 3:3; 7:17; 2 Cor 4:2; 5:7; 10:2–3; 12:18; Eph 2:2, 10; 4:1, 17; 5:2, 8, 15; Phil 3:17, 18; Col 1:10; 2:6; 3:7; 4:5; 1 Thess 2:12; 4:1, 12; 2 Thess 3:6, 11.

[17] In addition to horticultural applications, Jewett (*Romans*, 400) notes "biological references to knitting together the edges of a wound or the ends of broken bones, and social references to citizens clustering around their leader or sharing a particular ethos." He takes σύμφυτοι to mean "joined together" and understands Paul to mean that believers share "an indivisible, organic unity with Christ."

[18] The perfect indicative γεγόναμεν is normally rendered, "We have become," implying the inauguration of a relationship with Christ in the past with ongoing effect. However, if the aspectual value of the perfect tense is imperfectivity, this could be an emphatic way of describing the present state of believers.

[19] Cf. Barrett, *Romans*, 123–24. Dunn (*Romans 1–8*, 317–18) offers a good critique of this position and relates Paul's expression to 5:14, arguing that the believer has been united to Christ's death "to the extent that it can be experienced and is effective within the still enduring epoch of Adam." Schreiner (*Romans*, 313–15) and Jewett (*Romans*, 400–401) assess alternative understandings of Paul's expression.

believers died to sin when Christ died on the cross. "The likeness of his death" is thus a reference to our death to sin, which was made possible by Christ's death to sin (vv. 10–11). Baptism is a proclamation of what God has done for us in Christ and a means of embracing the implications for ourselves.

Paul's style becomes more abbreviated in the second part of this verse, which forms the conclusion to his conditional sentence. Assuming the repetition of key terms from the previous clause, the meaning is "we will be joined in the likeness of his resurrection." CSB appropriately renders the strong adversative ἀλλά as "certainly" in this sequence. The tense of the verb ἐσόμεθα could point to our resurrection from physical death as a future event, but surrounding references to walking in newness of life (v. 4) and no longer serving sin (v. 6) suggest a logical usage of the future tense. "The likeness of his resurrection" is the present experience of walking in newness of life.

6:6. Without a connective, τοῦτο γινώσκοντες ὅτι ("for we know that") introduces a deduction from what has just been stated.[20] Paul adds to the understanding of his readers with what follows. The expression ὁ παλαιὸς ἡμῶν ἄνθρωπος ("our old self") refers to "the whole self in its fallenness" rather than to a part of our selves, such as "our old nature."[21] Use of the word ἄνθρωπος ("man, human being") recalls Paul's contrast between Adam and Christ and the prospect of sharing the new life made possible by the one man Jesus Christ (5:12–21; cf. 1 Cor 15:45–49). So the reference is to "our common humanness worn out by its bondage to sin and death."[22] This humanity was (lit.) "crucified together with (Christ)" (συνεσταυρώθη, cf. Gal 2:19, Χριστῷ συνεσταύρωμαι ["I have been crucified with Christ"]). The pronoun αὐτῷ ("him") should be understood after the verb, as in v. 5. Paul combines forensic and "participationist" notions here,

---

[20] Wallace (*Greek Grammar*, 631–32) discusses the causal use of participles.

[21] Cranfield, *Romans*, 1:309. Moo (*Romans*, 373–74) rightly takes issue with those who simply identify "our old self" with "our old nature."

[22] Dunn, *Romans 1–8*, 318. Dunn argues, "The societal and salvation-history dimension here should not be reduced to the pietistic experience of the individual; but the reference is to Christians ('*our* old man') for whom the domination of sin has been broken by their identification with Christ's death." Cf. Jewett, *Romans*, 402–3.

with the passive verb describing God's action, not something believers do (cf. 8:13 comment).[23]

The apostle goes on to indicate God's purpose in this gracious Verdict: "So that the body ruled by sin might be rendered powerless." CSB provides an appropriate rendering of τὸ σῶμα τῆς ἁμαρτίας (lit., "the body of sin"), if the parallel with "our old self" is noted. The reference is generic, not simply individual. Paul uses the noun σῶμα with the attributive genitive τῆς ἁμαρτίας to stress the fact that sinful humanity is embodied.[24] The verb καταργηθῇ has a range of applications from "render ineffective, powerless" (cf. 3:3; 4:14) to "abolish, wipe out, set aside" (BDAG; cf. 3:31; 1 Cor 6:13; 15:24, 26; 2 Thess 2:8). The stronger sense may be intended here, where God's eschatological purpose is in view (the aorist verb is timeless).[25] Resurrected bodies will be free from sin's control. A second purpose clause with a present infinitive indicates what should follow from this: "So that we may no longer be enslaved to sin" (τοῦ μηκέτι δουλεύειν ἡμᾶς τῇ ἁμαρτίᾳ). A challenge is implicit in this statement, which vv. 12–23 develop extensively. Both the assurance that "our old self" was crucified with Christ and the promise of ultimate, bodily deliverance from sin's power are the motivation and empowerment for resisting sin in the present (cf. Phil 3:7–21; 1 John 3:2–3). If God's intention is that we should be free from sin, this should be *our* goal and earnest desire.

6:7. With a clear link to the preceding argument (γάρ, "for, since"), the reason for not serving sin is now expressed differently. Paul declares that (lit.) "the one who has died (ὁ ἀποθανών) is declared free from sin [δεδικαίωται ἀπὸ τῆς ἁμαρτίας]." This is the person who has been joined with Christ in the likeness of his death.[26] Buried with him by baptism into death, the believer has

---

[23] Moo, *Romans*, 395.

[24] Cf. Wallace, *Greek Grammar*, 87. Cranfield (*Romans*, 1:309) renders the expression "the whole man as controlled by sin," but Moo (*Romans*, 376) thinks this obscures the role of the body in our interactions with God and the world.

[25] Cranfield (*Romans*, 1:310) takes this as a reference to what takes place in baptism ("Our sinful self was hanged on the cross with Christ, in order that it might die"). But Paul's language is so decisive and absolute that a statement of God's ultimate purpose in allowing "our old self" to be crucified with Christ seems more to the point.

[26] Schreiner (*Romans*, 318–19) and Jewett (*Romans*, 404) discuss the possibility that this is an adaptation of certain rabbinic sayings or a reference to Jesus as the one who has died. But the reference to believers is more natural in the context.

come to acknowledge God's verdict that "our old self was crucified with him." In terms reminiscent of his teaching about God's justification of the ungodly (4:5), Paul uses an expression found nowhere else in his writings (δεδικαίωται ἀπὸ τῆς ἁμαρτίας, [lit.] "justified from sin"). "Freed from sin" (CSB) should be understood to mean "declared free from (responsibility in relation to) sin."[27] The declaratory sense of this verb is significant, with the perfect tense stressing the present reality of what is declared. In view of v. 6, we may conclude that freedom from the penalty for sin through justification by faith enables resistance to the power of sin.

6:8. A further conditional sentence bases the belief that "we will live with him" (συζήσομεν αὐτῷ) on the fact that "we have died with Christ" (ἀπεθάνομεν σὺν Χριστῷ). Certainty about the future is based on the conviction that we are the beneficiaries of his death.[28] Commentators are divided about whether συζήσομεν is a logical future, referring to life with Christ as a present experience, or a reference to resurrection with Christ on the last day. There is a sense in which believers are already "alive to God in Christ Jesus" (v. 11, cf. Eph 2:4–6; Col 2:13, συνεζωοποίησεν τῷ Χριστῷ ὑμᾶς σῦν αὐτῷ ["made you alive with him"]). But the new life we experience now is an anticipation of the life to come, made possible by our faith-union with Christ in his death and resurrection. References to being saved by his life in 5:11, 17, 21 are distinctly eschatological, suggesting that this is the locus of Paul's thinking here, even as he explores the present implications.[29]

6:9–10. A further reflection on Christ's experience is introduced by εἰδότες ὅτι ("because we know that," cf. 5:3). Unlike the opening words of v. 6, this introduces something that would have been obvious to the readers. Death as a power (5:14, 17) no longer

---

[27] Dunn, *Romans 1–8*, 320. According to BDAG, this construction with an active verb means "to cause someone to be released from personal or institutional claims that are no longer to be considered pertinent or valid, make free/pure." Passive forms of the verb are used with ἀπό in Sir 26:29; *T. Sim.* 6:1; Acts 13:38. Byrne (*Romans*, 197) suggests the translation "legally free from sin."

[28] The expression πιστεύομεν ὅτι ("we believe that") occurs also in 1 Thess 4:14. In Rom 10:8–9, Paul uses similar words to link public confession of Christ with belief in the heart that God raised him from the dead.

[29] A case for the logical future is made by Cranfield (*Romans*, 1:313) and Jewett (*Romans*, 406). But Dunn (*Romans 1–8*, 322) and Moo (*Romans*, 377) take it as a reference to the future life (cf. 2 Tim 2:11).

rules over Christ (θάνατος αὐτοῦ οὐκέτι κυριεύει) because he was decisively raised from the dead (ἐγερθεὶς ἐκ νεκρῶν) and no longer dies (οὐκέτι ἀποθνῄσκει). Jesus's resurrection was permanent, marking the beginning of a new era in salvation history. The connective γάρ ("for") introduces a supportive argument (v. 10), which prepares for Paul's application in v. 11. "The death he died, he died to sin once for all" (ὃ γὰρ ἀπέθανεν, τῇ ἁμαρτίᾳ ἀπέθανεν ἐφάπαξ). Like other human beings, Jesus experienced temptation, though he was personally innocent of sin (cf. 8:3; 2 Cor 5:21; Heb 4:15; 9:14). His undeserved death removed him from the sphere of sin and had a redemptive consequence for others (cf. 3:24–25; 8:3; 1 Cor 15:3; Gal 1:14).[30] The adverb ἐφάπαξ ("once for all," as in Heb 7:27; 9:12, 26–28 [ἅπαξ]; 10:10; 1 Pet 3:18 [ἅπαξ]) highlights the power of his achievement and its epoch-changing effect. His death was a completed event, but (lit.) "the life he lives, he lives to God" (ὃ δὲ ζῇ, ζῇ τῷ θεῷ). Double use of the present tense stresses that his resurrection life has no end. Paul later clarifies that Christ continues to reign in life to provide in every way for those who rely on him (8:31–39; cf. Heb 7:25).

6:11. What is claimed about Christ in v. 9–10 becomes the basis for a comparison that is introduced by οὕτως καί ὑμεῖς ("so you too," cf. v. 4). The present imperative λογίζεσθε ("consider, reckon") with the reflexive pronoun ἑαυτούς ("yourselves") calls for continuing reflection by believers on what it means to be united with Christ in his death and resurrection (cf. λογίζομαι in 3:28; 8:18; 14:14).[31] Paul does not mean "pretend" but "accept God's evaluation of yourself." We are to regard ourselves as (lit.) "dead with reference to sin and alive with reference to God" (νεκροὺς μὲν τῇ ἁμαρτίᾳ ζῶντας

---

[30] Both Dunn (*Romans 1–8*, 323) and Jewett (*Romans*, 407) deny any allusion to Christ's atonement for sin here, simply viewing this as a statement about his share in our subordination to the power of sin in death. But this makes Christ's death to sin simply representative rather than atoning. Cf. Kruse, *Romans*, 265–66.

[31] As noted in connection with 3:28, the verb λογίζομαι can mean "consider as a result of evaluating or calculating" (BDAG; cf. 8:36; 9:8). Jewett (*Romans*, 390) reads the indicative rather than imperative here. But this is inappropriate because Paul has been introducing the Romans to new perspectives on their relationship with God. The absence of εἶναι ("to be") from some manuscripts "produces an effective ellipse, and as the smoother reading, ought to be rejected" (Jewett, 390–91).

δὲ τῷ θεῷ).[32] "In union with Christ we *have been made* dead to sin and alive to God: it remains for us to appropriate (v. 11), and apply (vv. 12–13), what God has done for us."[33] Paul's simple formula indicates a dramatic reversal of the situation described in 1:18–3:20, where human beings are portrayed as being alive to *sin* and dead to *God*. Refusing to know God, humanity experiences the penalty and controlling power of sin. But the situation is transformed for those who, by God's grace, are "in Christ Jesus" (ἐν Χριστῷ Ἰησοῦ, cf. 8:1; 12:5; 16:3, 7, 9, 10).[34] Following on from 5:12–21, being "in Christ" means being part of the new humanity he has instituted by his death and resurrection. In terms of 6:2–10, "We are in Christ inasmuch as God accepts Christ's death as having been died for us and his risen life as being lived for us; for this means that in God's sight we died in his death, that is, we died in him, and were raised up in his resurrection, that is, in him, and now live in him."[35]

6:12. The central section of the chapter begins here, linked to the preceding one by the inferential conjunction οὖν ("therefore"). Paul explains the practical implications of the imperative in v. 11. As outlined in my comments on structure, a chiasm in vv. 12–14 highlights the importance of the central exhortation (v. 13 "offer yourselves to God"). Two warnings in the present tense prepare for this. The first uses a third-person imperative: "Do not let sin reign in your mortal body" (μὴ οὖν βασιλευέτω ἡ ἁμαρτία ἐν τῷ θνητῷ

[32] This is "the mind of faith," which embraces God's truth "as opposed to suppressing that truth with false ideologies" (Keener, *The Mind of the Spirit*, 44). See Wallace (*Greek Grammar*, 146, 154) on datives of reference. Byrne (*Romans*, 192) says "alive to God" essentially describes "the life of the new age," where, "set free from other 'lordships' (sin, death [law; cf. Gal 2:19]), one lives in total openness and surrender to God, acknowledging the sole claim and sovereignty of God."

[33] Moo, *Romans*, 380 (his emphasis). Keener (*The Mind of the Spirit*, 50) says, "For Paul, 'reckoning' offers the link between the justified new identity and the expected new, righteous behavior."

[34] Some manuscripts add τῷ κυρίῳ ἡμῶν ("our Lord") at the end of 6:11 (cf. v. 23). Metzger (*Textual Commentary*, 454) argues that, if this was original, there is no good reason it should have been deleted from a range of weighty early manuscripts. Hence, the shorter reading is to be preferred.

[35] Cranfield, *Romans*, 1:316. He opposes the view that "in Christ" is a matter of locality, mystical union, or sacramental realism, though he takes the sacraments to be "pledges of that reality." Moo (*Romans*, 380n150) takes the term to mean that we "belong to Christ as our representative, so that the decisions applied to him apply also to us." Cf. Campbell, *Paul and Union with Christ*, 333–43, 369–87.

ὑμῶν σώματι). Christians cannot be complacent: sin's rule needs to be resisted continually. The encouragement to do this is found in the promise of v. 14, where the parallel term κυριεύσει ("rule over") is used. "In your mortal body" refers to the whole person as fallen and subject to death (cf. v. 6, τὸ σῶμα τῆς ἁμαρτίας ["the body of sin"]). "So it is in the whole field of our life as the fallen human beings that we are called to resist sin's dominion."[36] The result clause εἰς τὸ ὑπακούειν ταῖς ἐπιθυμίαις αὐτοῦ ("so that you obey its desires") makes clear that failure to resist sin makes one captive to its desires (cf. v. 6c). Here, as in 1:24; 7:8; Gal 5:16, ἐπιθυμία may refer to more than physical lusts.[37]

6:13. The second warning is (lit.) "Do not offer the parts of yourself to sin as weapons for unrighteousness" (μηδὲ παριστάνετε τὰ μέλη ὑμῶν ὅπλα ἀδικίας τῇ ἁμαρτίᾳ). Paul employs the verb παρίστημι (lit., "place at the disposal") twice in this verse, where the notion of serving God, rather than sin, is the dominant idea (cf. vv. 16, 19 [twice]; 12:1).[38] A second-person present imperative shows that ongoing resistance involves withholding every part of ourselves from sin's control. Different parts of the body, including limbs and organs, are meant by the expression τὰ μέλη ὑμῶν ("your members," cf. 7:23; 1 Cor 12:14–26). The general sense may be "Do not give sin control of what you are or do,"[39] but Paul's use of body imagery shows that the battle with sin is physical as well as intellectual and spiritual. We use our bodies as a means of relating to God, to the world, and to other people. The parts of our bodies can either be "weapons for unrighteousness" or a means of serving

[36] Cranfield, *Romans*, 1:317. Jewett (*Romans*, 409) takes ἐν τῷ θνητῷ ὑμῶν σώματι to refer to "sin's death-dealing dominance over bodily relations, which results in the wrath described in 1:18–32 and the curse of Adam's death in 5:18–21."

[37] The variant αὐτῇ ("it") in 𝔓[46] and some Western witnesses is an attempt to improve on ταῖς ἐπιθυμίαις αὐτοῦ ("its desires"). TR follows later manuscripts in combining these two readings. Cf. Jewett, *Romans*, 391.

[38] Cf. Bo Reicke and Georg Bertram, "παρίστημι, παριστάνω," *TDNT* 5:837–41. This verb is used with reference to the service offered to a ruler or the service of slaves to their masters (see n. 48 below). The latter emerges as the dominant image in the passage.

[39] Dunn, *Romans 1–8*, 334, 337. Dunn (337–38) points out that there is no middle ground or neutral position here: "Man's desired independence of God is nothing other than a yielding submission and service on the side of sin in the warfare between unrighteousness and righteousness."

and pleasing God. Sin, rather than the devil, is the enemy in this portrayal of spiritual warfare (cf. 13:12; 16:20; 1 Thess 5:8; Eph 6:13–17). To place ourselves at the disposal of sin would be "to participate willingly in the war against God and to deny the redemption experienced in Christ."[40] "Those natural capacities and abilities that God has given us are weapons that must no longer be put in the service of the master from whom we have been freed."[41]

Paul's positive exhortation begins with the strong adversative ἀλλά ("but"). An aorist imperative using the same verb functions in a timeless fashion (παραστήσατε ἑαυτοὺς τῷ θεῷ, "Offer yourselves to God"), though the aorist may signal a more specific instruction than the present imperatives that precede it.[42] The empowerment for this is expressed in a clause recalling v. 11 (ὡσεὶ ἐκ νεκρῶν ζῶντας, "as those who are alive from the dead"). "The decisive event of Christ's resurrection has happened, making possible an actual change of the attitude and motivation from which ethical conduct derives for those identified with Christ in his death and resurrection: they can live as being sharers in Christ's resurrection life."[43] The concluding part of this exhortation also picks up language from the first part of the verse and relates it to God (καὶ τὰ μέλη ὑμῶν ὅπλα δικαιοσύνης τῷ θεῷ, "and [all] the parts of yourselves to God as weapons for righteousness"). Paul will soon show that being "enslaved to righteousness" (vv. 17–19) is equivalent to being "enslaved to God" (v. 22). If righteousness is to be operative in our lives in a practical way, we must personally submit every part of ourselves to God's control.

6:14. The reason for heeding the preceding exhortation (γάρ, "for") is the assurance that "sin will not rule over you, because you are not under the law but under grace." Sin will not be "lord of" (οὐ κυριεύσει) those who offer themselves to God in Christ and are justified by faith, since grace is the power that can "break the mastery

[40] Jewett, *Romans*, 410. The genitive ἀδικίας signifies purpose here ("for unrighteousness").

[41] Moo, *Romans*, 384–85.

[42] Moo (ibid., 382, 385) argues that no contrast is intended. However, Campbell (*Verbal Aspect and Non-Indicative Verbs: Further Soundings in the Greek New Testament* [New York: Peter Lang, 2008], 79–100) shows that, from an aspectual point of view, present imperatives are often used to convey more general instructions.

[43] Dunn, *Romans 1–8*, 338. However, Dunn points out that ὡσεί ("as if, as though") prevents us from concluding that we have completely experienced what it means to be resurrected with Christ. Cf. Byrne, *Romans*, 198.

of sin."[44] The rule of sin has in fact been broken by Christ's sacrificial death so that "those who receive the overflow of grace and the gift of righteousness reign in life through the one man, Jesus Christ" (5:17). Reigning in life through Christ is a present possibility, though complete freedom from sin will only be experienced with the resurrection of our bodies. Paul's promise is confirmed by the explanatory clause, "because you are not under the law but under grace." Rather than being the solution to the problem of sin and death, "the law came along to multiply the trespass" (5:20a; cf. 4:15; 7:5, 7–11). But "where sin multiplied, grace multiplied even more" (5:20b), meaning that grace triumphed over sin in the death and resurrection of Jesus. Grace now reigns through righteousness in the lives of those who are united with Christ in his death and resurrection (5:21). Paul is making a salvation-historical contrast here, with law and grace representing different realms or eras.[45] Although "under law" (ὑπὸ νόμον) is often a way of characterizing Jews (cf. 1 Cor 9:20; Gal 3:23; 4:4–5, 21), Paul links the law with sin, death, and the old epoch of Adam in 5:12–21. Since the law belongs to that pre-Christ era, it is not the way for Jews or Gentiles to experience deliverance from the rule of sin. More will be said about this in the next chapter (see also §1.4).

6:15. The third section of the chapter begins like the first, using Τί οὖν ("What then?") to introduce a critical question: "Should we sin because we are not under the law but under grace?"[46] This draws a false conclusion from the law-grace contrast in v. 14, implying that sin does not matter anymore because the gospel of grace proclaims our justification by faith. The temptation identified here is not sinning in order to experience more grace, but "sinning *because of* grace."[47] As in v. 2, a strong denial (μὴ γένοιτο, "Absolutely not!") introduces the question that provides a definitive answer.

---

[44] Dunn, *Romans 1–8*, 351 (emphasis removed). Dunn suggests that the future tense of κυριεύσει ("will rule") is both "a statement of fact and a promise."

[45] Cf. Moo, *Romans*, 389–90 (with important caveats); Schreiner, *Romans*, 326–27; David G. Peterson, *Possessed by God: A New Testament Theology of Sanctification and Holiness*, NSBT 1 (Downers Grove: InterVarsity, 1995), 143–49.

[46] The deliberative subjunctive ἁμαρτήσωμεν ("should we sin") is aorist and therefore timeless. Sin is viewed in a summary way as a lifestyle.

[47] Moo, *Romans*, 398.

6:16. Paul's challenge (οὐκ οἴδατε ὅτι, "don't you know that") is to acknowledge something that is familiar from everyday life. Habitually "presenting" yourself to someone makes you that person's slave: "If you offer yourselves to someone as obedient slaves, you are slaves of that one you obey." As in v. 13, two forms of self-offering (παριστάνετε ἑαυτούς) are possible, though the choice here is between "sin" and "obedience" as masters.[48] Obedience has just been described as the means by which either form of slavery is expressed (δούλους εἰς ὑπακοήν, [lit.] "slaves for obedience," and ᾧ ὑπακούετε, "whom you obey"). Since Paul's aim is to encourage obedience to God (vv. 13, 22), and such obedience is the way to experience practical righteousness (εἰς δικαιοσύνην, [lit.] "for righteousness"), he personifies this obedience as the desirable alternative. "Final justification" could be the meaning of "righteousness" in contrast with "death" here,[49] but righteousness has just been contrasted with unrighteousness as the present outcome of serving God rather than sin (vv. 12–13). "Righteousness" replaces "obedience" as the power to serve in vv. 18, 19, and 20, and "sanctification" is the outcome. When God's righteousness takes us captive through belief in the gospel and union with Christ, righteous behavior and right relationships are made possible.[50] The alternative is death (εἰς θάνατον), viewed as alienation from God.

6:17. Paul suddenly adopts a thanksgiving formula (χάρις δὲ τῷ θεῷ ὅτι, "but thank God that"; cf. 7:25a; 1 Cor 15:57; 2 Cor 2:14; 8:16; 9:15), highlighting how God's grace and righteousness have impacted the lives of his readers. Their former condition, like the

[48] S. Scott Bartchy (*First-Century Slavery and the Interpretation of 1 Corinthians 7:21*, SBLDS 11 [Missoula: Scholars Press, 1973], 37–120) and Dale B. Martin (*Slavery as Salvation: The Metaphor of Slavery in Pauline Christianity* [New Haven: Yale University Press, 1990], 1–49) describe how some people in the ancient world sold themselves into slavery for economic and social reasons.

[49] Cf. Cranfield, *Romans*, 1:322. Schreiner (*Romans*, 332) also takes this to refer to eschatological vindication but insists that obedience is a requirement for this.

[50] Compare the prophetic vision of God's enabling righteousness to dwell among his people so they become righteous in all their ways (Isa 32:15–17; 60:21; 61:3; cf. Jub. 16:26; 36:6; 1 En. 10:16; CD 1:7–8). Moo (*Romans*, 403) limits righteousness in Rom 6:16, 18–21 to right conduct, "conceived as a 'power' that exercises authority over the believer." Contrast Wright, "Romans," 545.

rest of humanity, was to be "slaves of sin."[51] Transformation came about when "you obeyed from the heart that pattern of teaching to which you were handed over." As previously, "heart" is used to refer to the control center of human personalities, involving thinking, feeling, and willing (1:21, 24; 2:5, 15, 29; 5:5; 9:2; 10:1). Servile or superficial obedience will not do. Since God "searches our hearts" (8:27), the law and circumcision must affect the heart (2:15, 29), and obedience and belief must be "from the heart" (6:17; 10:9–10). The fulfilment of new covenant expectations by the Spirit of God is implied by such heart language in 2:15, 29; 5:5; 6:17 (cf. Jer 31:33–34; Ezek 36:26–27). Change is brought about by the Spirit through the preaching of the gospel (cf. Rom 15:16, 18–19; 2 Cor 3).[52] The "pattern of teaching" (τύπον διδαχῆς) that moves hearts and molds people in God's way is the gospel, not some extra form of instruction (cf. Col 2:6–7).[53] The passive verb in the clause, "to which you were handed over" (εἰς ὃν παρεδόθητε), points to God's action in bringing believers under his authority through the gospel. Christian obedience is thus "the outgrowth of God's action in 'handing us over' to that teaching when we were converted."[54]

6:18. The transfer of allegiance just described is now portrayed in terms of freedom from one master in order to serve another: "Having been set free from sin, you became enslaved to righteousness" (ἐλευθερωθέντες δὲ ἀπὸ τῆς ἁμαρτίας ἐδουλώθητε τῇ δικαιοσύνῃ). This picks up the notion of freedom from v. 7, where it is differently expressed. Paul is not speaking about the freedom of

---

[51] Cranfield (*Romans*, 1:323) points out that ἦτε δοῦλοι τῆς ἁμαρτίας is effectively a concessive clause ("although you used to be slaves of sin") because it is subordinate to the next clause, which expresses the change for which Paul gives thanks.

[52] Schreiner (*Romans*, 334) rightly observes, "God must be the one who causes obedience to rise in human hearts because all human beings are 'slaves of sin.'" Cf. Robert A. J. Gagnon, "Heart of Wax and a Teaching that Stamps: Τύπος Διδαχῆς (Rom. 6:17b) Once More," *JBL* 112 (1993): 667–87; Peterson, *Transformed by God*, 105–55.

[53] See my comments on τύπος in 5:14. Francis W. Beare ("On the Interpretation of Romans VI.17," *NTS* 5 [1958–59]: 209–10) argues that this term indicates that the teaching is "a mold which gives to the new life its appropriate shape or pattern." Kruse (*Romans*, 281–82) agrees that the teaching on view here is the gospel.

[54] Moo, *Romans*, 401. Although Moo thinks Paul may be contrasting the form of Christian teaching with the form of Jewish teaching, he agrees that τύπος may also have been used to suggest that Christian teaching "molds" and "forms" those who have been handed over to it (402).

"autonomous self-direction, but of deliverance from those enslaving powers that would prevent the human being from becoming what God intended."[55] Freedom to serve God arises from justification by faith (cf. vv. 6–7). The liberation we experience in putting our trust in Christ's saving death puts us in a position to go on resisting sin and serving righteousness (vv. 12–13, 22). Righteousness is here personified as the power to resist sin and to bring about righteous behavior. As in v. 17, these passive verbs point to the intervention of God in our lives through the gospel. The theme of freedom is resumed in 8:2, but the notion of being freed to be enslaved again is unique to this passage. Serving God is actually the way to experience perfect freedom!

6:19. Paul acknowledges that slavery to righteousness is a limited way of speaking about the new life in Christ (ἀνθρώπινον λέγω, [lit.] "I speak humanly" [CSB: "I am using a human analogy"]). Similar apologies in 3:5; 1 Cor 9:8; and Gal 3:1 occur without a grammatical connection to the preceding clause. The words here, together with διὰ τὴν ἀσθένειαν τῆς σαρκὸς ὑμῶν ("because of the weakness of your flesh"), form the conclusion to v. 18. A new phase of the argument begins with ὥσπερ γάρ ("for just as"). Slavery in the Greco-Roman world was a harsh and demeaning institution. Elsewhere Paul pictures the Christian life in terms of freedom from slavery and adoption as children of God (8:12, 14–15; Gal 4:1–11; 4:21–5:1; 5:13). Here he talks about transfer from one form of slavery to another, "because of the weakness of your flesh," meaning that weak human nature needs to be stirred by such imagery (cf. Mark 14:38). Slavery expresses "the total belongingness, the total obligation, the total commitment and the total accountability, which characterizes the life under grace."[56]

Paul expands on the image with terms drawn from v. 13: "For just as you offered the parts of yourselves as slaves to impurity, and to greater and greater lawlessness, so now offer them as slaves to righteousness, which results in sanctification." Here the master they once served is called "impurity" (ἀκαθαρσία, cf. 1:24 comment) and

[55] Ibid., 402.

[56] Cranfield, *Romans*, 1:326. Moo (*Romans*, 404) understands ὥσπερ ("just as") here to signify that Christians should serve righteousness "with all the single-minded dedication that characterized their pre-Christian service of such 'idols' as self, money, lust, pleasure and power."

"lawlessness" (ἀνομίᾳ, cf. 4:7) to express different aspects of the life under sin. The expression τῇ ἀνομίᾳ εἰς τὴν ἀνομίαν should be translated literally ("to lawlessness for lawlessness") because the parallel expression τῇ δικαιοσύνῃ εἰς ἁγιασμόν ("to righteousness for sanctification") indicates that the goal or outcome of being slaves to righteousness is holiness. There has been debate about whether the noun ἁγιασμός here and in v. 22 describes a process of moral renewal or a state of holiness resulting from consecration to God and his service.[57] Paul uses the term in 1 Cor 1:30 with reference to the sanctification or "consecration" already experienced by those who call on Jesus Christ as Lord (1 Cor 1:2; 6:11; cf. 2 Thess 2:13). In 1 Thess 4:3–7 sanctification is contrasted with uncleanness and lawlessness as a condition to be maintained and preserved. So also here the most likely meaning is that sanctification is a dedicated state arising from being set free from the penalty for sin and becoming slaves to righteousness. But consecration to God and his service requires practical, everyday expression in holy living, as Paul will outline in Romans 12–15.

6:20–21. Paul's final appeal involves a challenge to reconsider the outcome of the two forms of slavery he has just outlined. First, he claims, "When you were slaves of sin, you were free with regard to righteousness."[58] Allegiance to one master prevented service to another (cf. Matt 6:24). Second, he asks, "What fruit was produced then from the things you are now ashamed of?"[59] A genuine change of heart is indicated when shame is expressed for practices once regarded as normal and desirable. The "end" or "outcome" (τέλος) of those things is death, viewed as the penalty for sin and forfeiture of eternal life (v. 23; cf. 5:12–21; 1 Cor 6:9–10).

6:22–23. Building on his assumption that they have now been "set free from sin and become enslaved to God [δουλωθέντες δὲ τῷ θεῷ]," Paul declares that they have the "fruit," which "results in

[57] Cranfield (*Romans*, 1:327–329) opts for the former, whereas Dunn (*Romans 1–8*, 346–49) argues that "consecration" or "a dedicated state" is more consistent with the biblical use of this term. Cf. Peterson, *Possessed by God*, 139–42. See §2.6.

[58] The dative τῇ δικαιοσύνῃ means "with respect to (or with reference to) righteousness." Cf. n. 32 above.

[59] Runge (*Discourse Grammar*, 371) notes that the use of the "far demonstrative" ἐκείνων (lit., "those things") signals that Paul's interest is not in the old fruit but in the new fruit he mentions in v. 22.

sanctification" (εἰς ἁγιασμόν, see v. 19 comment). Christian holiness is expressed in attitudes and behavior that flow from commitment to God in Christ. The ultimate "end" of this new slavery is eternal life. So, slavery to "obedience" (v. 16) or "righteousness" (vv. 18–20) is more than commitment to an ideal or ethic, for it involves a personal devotion to the God who brings believers to new life in Christ. This new life is one of dedication to God and the doing of his will. A summary-conclusion, introduced by γάρ (v. 23, "for"), recalls earlier claims: "The wages of sin is death, but the gift of God is eternal life in Christ Jesus our Lord." Sin is personified as the slave owner who pays his slaves "wages" (ὀψώνια),[60] but instead of bringing life, sin causes death. Contrasted with "eternal life," death means being eternally separated from God. Death is earned and deserved, but eternal life is "the gift of God" (τὸ χάρισμα τοῦ θεοῦ). By implication, "even if Christians managed to lead an entirely sanctified life, this would not oblige God to reward them with eternal life, for they will have done no more than what was required of them."[61] As in 5:11, 21, a significant climax in the argument is marked by the proclamation that "Christ Jesus our Lord" is the source of this salvation.

Bridge

This passage provokes important ethical questions. Can the gospel of justification by faith transform attitudes and behavior, or does it encourage complacency and sin? What are the moral implications of being baptized into Christ? Since Christians are "not under the law but under grace," where can we find the direction for godly living? Paul argues that the death and resurrection of Jesus inaugurated a new stage in God's dealing with humanity (cf. 5:18–21). Sharing by faith in the benefits of his redemptive work means being united with Christ in his death and resurrection. Indeed, "only those who make themselves one with his death can hope to experience the life

[60] Hans W. Heidland ("ὀψώνιον," *TDNT* 5: 591–92) points out that this word literally means "what is appointed for buying food" and then mostly "allowance (for maintenance)" in a military context (Luke 3:14; cf. 1 Cor 9:7). Paul uses it more generally for the "support" given to him by the churches (2 Cor 11:8).

[61] Witherington, *Romans*, 174. Note that this return to the theme of grace forms an inclusion with v. 14.

which is his life in the new age beyond."[62] Baptism into Christ is a means of confessing the significance of Christ's death and resurrection and choosing to live as those who have died with Christ and have been raised with him to newness of life. The rule of grace promotes and enables obedience as we reckon ourselves to be "dead to sin, but alive to God in Christ Jesus." God empowers us to resist sin when we present ourselves to him for obedience and the pursuit of holiness. Put differently, we are released from being "slaves of sin" by becoming obedient from the heart to the gospel teaching we have received. The gospel draws us into a pattern of Christlike service to God. As a result, we can be "slaves of righteousness" and "enslaved to God." Such slavery brings genuine freedom in holy living. Those who are truly grounded in the gospel experience the transforming power of grace and "draw their vital energies and motivations from God in Christ Jesus."[63] The Spirit's role in this process is highlighted in 7:6; 8:1–17.

[62] Dunn, *Romans 1–8*, 329. Keener notes, "Paul argues for a new identity in Christ, one defined historically in relation to Christ's death and resurrection and eschatologically in relation to believers' ultimate and completed destiny" (Keener, *The Mind of the Spirit*, 53).

[63] Dunn, *Romans 1–8*, 333.

IX. Released from the Law to Serve God in the New Way of the Spirit (7:1–25)

This chapter is not merely an aside, as has sometimes been argued. It is a further unpacking of 5:20 ("The law came along to multiply the trespass. But where sin multiplied, grace multiplied even more"). It also develops the claim that "you are not under the law but under grace" (6:14). Being "under grace" involves being liberated from sin's penalty and controlling power (6:15–23). Christians have been set free from slavery to sin to become obedient slaves of righteousness. Similar terms are used in 7:4–6 to describe what it means to be "released from the law" so as to "serve in the newness of the Spirit." But the full exposition of this Spirit-directed life is delayed until the next chapter. Paul first addresses the question of God's purpose in giving the law, highlighting its goodness, but also the power of sin and the flesh to bring death through the law (7:7–25). Progressive comments in the letter so far have pointed to the need for a full exposition of this theme (cf. 2:12–29; 3:19–20, 27–31; 4:13–15; 5:13, 20–21; 6:14). Paul's purpose is apologetic, answering objections that his gospel denigrates the law, and continuing his pattern of dealing with Jewish issues as they arise in the course of his argument.[1] But his overall aim in chapters 6–8 is to persuade his readers to live as the beneficiaries of the new covenant, which was inaugurated by the Messiah's death and resurrection (see §§1.4, 2.6).[2]

> [1]Since I am speaking to those who know the law, brothers and sisters, don't you know that the law rules over someone as long as he lives? [2]For example, a married woman is legally bound to her husband while he lives. But if her husband dies, she is released from the law regarding the husband. [3]So then, if she is married to another man while her husband is living, she will be called an adulteress. But if her husband dies, she is free from

[1] Whether such objections came from Jewish Christians or from Jewish opponents more broadly, they needed to be answered if the Roman Christians were to have an adequate understanding of the relationship between law and gospel and support Paul in his proposed mission to Spain. Cf. Seifrid, *Justification by Faith*, 226–27; Schreiner, *Romans*, 359.

[2] Wright ("Romans," 549) describes 7:1–8:11 as the "working heart" of chapters 5–8, "setting out *how God has renewed the covenant in Christ and by the Spirit*" (emphasis in original).

that law. Then, if she is married to another man, she is not an adulteress.

[4]Therefore, my brothers and sisters, you also were put to death in relation to the law through the body of Christ so that you may belong to another. You belong to him who was raised from the dead in order that we may bear fruit for God. [5]For when we were in the flesh, the sinful passions aroused through the law were working in us to bear fruit for death. [6]But now we have been released from the law, since we have died to what held us, so that we may serve in the newness of the Spirit and not in the old letter of the law.

[7]What should we say then? Is the law sin? Absolutely not! On the contrary, I would not have known sin if it were not for the law. For example, I would not have known what it is to covet if the law had not said, **Do not covet.** [8]And sin, seizing an opportunity through the commandment, produced in me coveting of every kind. For apart from the law sin is dead. [9]Once I was alive apart from the law, but when the commandment came, sin sprang to life again [10]and I died. The commandment that was meant for life resulted in death for me. [11]For sin, seizing an opportunity through the commandment, deceived me, and through it killed me. [12]So then, the law is holy, and the commandment is holy and just and good. [13]Therefore, did what is good become death to me? Absolutely not! On the contrary, sin, in order to be recognized as sin, was producing death in me through what is good, so that through the commandment, sin might become sinful beyond measure.

[14]For we know that the law is spiritual, but I am of the flesh, sold as a slave to sin. [15]For I do not understand what I am doing, because I do not practice what I want to do, but I do what I hate. [16]Now if I do what I do not want to do, I agree with the law that it is good. [17]So now I am no longer the one doing it, but it is sin living in me. [18]For I know that nothing good lives in me, that is, in my flesh. For the desire to do what is good is with me, but there is no ability to do it. [19]For I do not do the good that I want to do, but I practice the evil that I do not want to do. [20]Now if I do what I do not want, I am no longer the one that does it, but it is the sin that lives in me. [21]So I discover this law: When I want to do what is good, evil is present with me. [22]For in my inner self I delight in God's law, [23]but I see a different law in the parts of my body, waging war against the law of my mind and taking me prisoner to the law of sin in the parts of my body. [24]What a wretched man I am! Who will rescue me from this body of death? [25]Thanks be to

God through Jesus Christ our Lord! So then, with my mind I myself am serving the law of God, but with my flesh, the law of sin.

Context

Continuity with the previous chapter is signalled by the opening question with its reference to the law's authority (v. 1; cf. 6:14). Beginning with an illustration from marriage (vv. 2–3), Paul explains what it means to be "put to death in relation to the law," so as to "belong to another" (v. 4, recalling 6:1–11).[3] The absolute contrast between life "in the flesh" and serving God "in the newness of the Spirit" (vv. 5–6) anticipates 8:1–14. But in vv. 7–12, while upholding the goodness of God's holy law, Paul explains how "the sinful passions aroused through the law were working in us to produce death" (v. 6). In vv. 13–25 he describes the ongoing power of sin and the flesh, which prevents people from doing the will of God. The way to "bear fruit" for God is not through adherence to the law but by walking "according to the Spirit" (8:4), as explained in the next chapter.

Structure

In the opening paragraph (vv. 1–6) Paul continues the sort of dialogical exchange evidenced in Rom 6. A rhetorical question introduces the principle that "the law rules over someone as long as he lives" (v. 1). This principle is illustrated with reference to marriage (vv. 2–3) before it is applied to believers (v. 4). Claiming that his readers have been "put to death in relation to the law through the body of Christ," Paul indicates that God's intention for them is that they should belong to the risen Lord and "bear fruit for God." Their former life "in the flesh" is contrasted with "the newness of the Spirit" (vv. 5–6), and this change is related to having been "released from the law, since we have died to what held us."

The second paragraph (vv. 7–12) advances the argument by presenting a false inference from v. 5 in the form of a question ("Is the law sin?"). This is followed by an emphatic rejection ("Absolutely

[3] Echoes of the previous chapter in 7:4–6 include "put to death" (ἐθανατώθητε) and "died" (ἀποθανόντες, cf. 6:2, 6, 7, 8); "bear fruit" (καρποφορῆσαι, cf. 6:21, 22); "the sinful passions" (τὰ παθήματα τῶν ἁμαρτιῶν, cf. 6:19); "in your members" (ἐν τοῖς μέλεσιν ἡμῶν, cf. 6:13 ["all the parts of yourselves"]); "released" (κατηργήθημεν, cf. 6:6 ["abolished"]); "serve" (δουλεύειν, cf. 6:18, 22).

not!") and an explanation that "I would not have known sin if it were not for the law." Paul's first-person-singular narrative style continues with reference to the commandment about coveting.[4] Sin seized an opportunity through the commandment to deceive and bring death (vv. 8–11). Despite this negative outcome, he concludes that "the law is holy, and the commandment is holy and just and good" (v. 12).

The third paragraph (vv. 13–25) begins with a question expressing a false inference from vv. 11–12 ("Did what is good become death to me?"). An emphatic rejection ("Absolutely not!") is followed by an expanded version of Paul's argument about the law so far: "Sin, in order to be recognized as sin, was producing death in me through what is good, so that through the commandment, sin might become sinful beyond measure." He changes from the past tense to the present in the remaining verses to describe the conflict between the "mind" or "inner self" that joyfully agrees with God's law (vv. 16, 22) and the "flesh" or the "parts of my body" that are "waging war against the law of my mind and taking me prisoner to the law of sin in the parts of my body" (v. 23). "The result, then, is that the law of God, which aroused sin, is impotent to break the power of sin."[5] But Paul's cry for deliverance is followed by a thanksgiving for what God has made possible through Christ and a summary statement about the conflict he has articulated (vv. 24–25).

Outline:

1. Dead to the law (vv. 1–6)
2. The law's fatal effect (vv. 7–12)
3. The ongoing power of sin and the flesh (vv. 13–25)

7:1. The opening question in the Greek text (Ἢ ἀγνοεῖτε, "Or don't you know?" [cf. 6:3; 1 Cor 6:2, 9, 16, 19]) suggests a continuation of the preceding argument. It presumes the readers will agree with his proposition but need to consider the implications more carefully. CSB changes the order of the clauses, placing this

---

[4] Paul's reason for using the first-person singular in vv. 7–25 is discussed in my comments on vv. 7, 14.

[5] Moo, *Romans*, 424. Moo (450–51) takes the shift from past- to present-tense verbs to depict the continuing status of those who were involved in the past events narrated in vv. 7–11. In other words, he takes vv. 13–25 to describe Paul's pre-Christian situation from his present Christian perspective. But see my comment on v. 14.

question after Paul's identification of the readers as those who "know the law." "Brothers and sisters" occurs for the first time since 1:13, highlighting the familial relationship Paul shares with his readers collectively and strengthening the appeal to take his message seriously.[6] Contextually, his description of them as "those who know the law" (*γινώσκουσιν γὰρ νόμον*) must refer to the law of God. The proposition that "the law rules over someone as long as he lives" is true of any law or legal system, but the verb *κυριεύει* specifically recalls 6:14 ("sin will not rule over you [*κυριεύει*], because you are not under the law but under grace"). Having explored what it means to be "under grace" (6:15–23), Paul now wishes to justify and explain his claim that Christians are not "under the law." There is no reason to limit this address to Jewish Christians since Gentile believers could have gained knowledge of God's law from previous associations with Judaism and would rightly question the role of that law in their relationship with Christ. Indeed, this has been an ongoing issue for thoughtful Christians throughout the centuries. Paul has already insisted that Gentiles stand condemned with Israel by the law of God (3:19–20), but the question of the law's ongoing, directive function remains to be unpacked.

7:2–3. CSB's "for example" translates the connective *γάρ* ("for"). Paul illustrates his proposition with reference to marriage: "A married woman is bound by the law (CSB: 'legally bound') to her husband while he lives." The nature of that law is identified in the conditional clause that follows: if her husband dies, she is "released from the law regarding the husband" (*κατήργηται ἀπὸ τοῦ νόμου τοῦ ἀνδρός*, cf. 1 Cor 7:39).[7] Paul reflects Jewish, rather than

---

[6] Runge (*Discourse Grammar*, 122) calls this a redundant address, "accentuating a break in the discourse by making it more pronounced." Ἀδελφοί is used this way at key points in the letter (7:4; 8:12; 10:1; 11:25; 12:1; 15:14, 30; 16:17) and more generally to describe the familial relationship Christians have to one another in Christ (8:29; 14:10, 13, 15, 21; 16:14, 23). Only once does Paul refer to fellow Jews as brothers (9:3), but he qualifies this with *τῶν συγγενῶν μου κατὰ σάρκα* (lit., "my natural kin").

[7] Cranfield (*Romans*, 1:333–34) discusses different ways *τοῦ νόμου τοῦ ἀνδρός* has been understood and concludes that the most likely meaning is "the law in so far as it binds her to her husband." There are two intensive uses of the perfect tense in a gnomic sense in v. 2 (*δέδεται*, "is bound"; *κατήργηται*, "is released"). Cf. Wallace, *Greek Grammar*, 580–81. Note that *κατήργηται ἀπὸ τοῦ νόμου* ("released from the law") is used in anticipation of a similar expression in v. 6.

Roman, marital law in this connection and goes on to echo some of the language of Deut 24:2 LXX (γένηται ἀνδρὶ ἑτέρῳ, "belongs to another man"). Roman law did not release a wife from obligations to her husband immediately upon his death.[8] The logic of Paul's illustration is pressed home with a further conditional clause, beginning with ἄρα οὖν ("so then"): "If she is married to another man while her husband is living, she will be called an adulteress."[9] A third conditional clause uses terms that prepare for the application of the illustration in v. 4. If the woman's husband dies, "she is free from that law," meaning free from the law regarding her husband.[10] A result clause explains that "if she is married to another man, she is not an adulteress" (τοῦ μὴ εἶναι αὐτὴν μοιχαλίδα γενομένην ἀνδρὶ ἑτέρῳ).[11]

7:4. Paul's use of the inferential ὥστε ("therefore"), rather than a word expressing similarity or correspondence such as οὕτως, suggests that he is "drawing his conclusion from the principle stated in v. 1 as clarified by vv. 2 and 3; he is not treating his illustration as an allegory to be interpreted."[12] The redundant vocative ἀδελφοί μου ("my brothers and sisters") helps signal the transition to application by creating a break.[13] Paul immediately shows that he is adapting the marriage illustration when he declares, "You also were put to death in relation to the law" (καὶ ὑμεῖς ἐθανατώθητε τῷ νόμῳ). An active form of the same verb was used in relation to sin in 6:2 (ἀπεθάνομεν τῇ ἁμαρτίᾳ, "we died to sin"), but the passive here highlights the divine initiative. The qualifying phrase "through the body of Christ" (διὰ τοῦ σώματος τοῦ Χριστοῦ) parallels the notion of being crucified with Christ (6:6; cf. Gal 2:19; Col 1:22). When the Messiah offered

[8] Cf. Dunn, *Romans 1–8*, 360. Jewett (*Romans*, 431) also points out that Paul's description of male rights matches the Jewish, rather than the Roman, divorce law.

[9] The expression ἐὰν γένηται ἀνδρὶ ἑτέρῳ with a possessive dative literally means "if she becomes possessed by another man" (Wallace, *Greek Grammar*, 150). The gnomic future χρηματίσει ("she will be called") indicates that this is true of any time (Wallace, *Greek Grammar*, 571).

[10] The article before νόμου is anaphoric, pointing back to the previous reference to law, and so the expression is rightly translated "that law" (CSB). The wife is not free from law in general.

[11] The aorist participle γενομένην is used conditionally in the parallelism of this verse (lit., "if she becomes"). Cf. Wallace, *Greek Grammar*, 632–33.

[12] Cranfield, *Romans*, 1:335. However, Moo (*Romans*, 413–14) notes how features of the illustration in vv. 2–3 prepare for the theological conclusion in v. 4.

[13] Cf. Runge, *Discourse Grammar*, 119. See also n. 6 above.

his body as a sacrifice for sin, he delivered his people from the condemnation and curse of the law (cf. 8:1–3; Gal 3:10–14).

But, as the passage goes on to imply, the law's role in directing and sustaining the holiness of God's people is also brought to an end. As in 6:14, the law is "a 'power' of the 'old age' to which the person apart from Christ is bound."[14] Jewish and Gentile believers are delivered from the law's dominion through union with Christ in his death, "so that you may belong to another." Specifically, Christians belong to "him who was raised from the dead" (cf. 6:8–11). The language of belonging to another (γενέσθαι ὑμᾶς ἑτέρῳ) reflects the preceding illustration about being free to marry another but may also have been influenced by portrayals of the relationship between God and Israel in marital terms (e.g., Isa 54:5–6; 62:4–5; Jer 2:2; Ezek 16:7–8; Hos 2:19–20; cf. 2 Cor 11:2).[15] Belonging to the Messiah who was raised from the dead secures an eternal future with God but also makes possible a new way of life in the present (cf. 6:4). A second purpose clause (ἵνα καρποφορήσωμεν τῷ θεῷ, "in order that we may bear fruit for God") picks up the language of 6:22, indicating that commitment to the living Lord Jesus is the way to bear fruit. According to Col 1:9, this happens as we are "filled with the knowledge of his will in all wisdom and spiritual understanding." Galatians 5:22–23 highlights the Spirit's role in producing the fruit.[16]

7:5. The connective γάρ ("for") indicates that this verse and the next elucidate the claims of v. 4. A temporal contrast is first made with the expressions "when we were in the flesh" (ὅτε γὰρ ἦμεν ἐν τῇ σαρκί) and "now we have been released from the law" (νυνὶ δὲ κατηργήθημεν ἀπὸ τοῦ νόμου). Paul also changes to the first-person plural to include himself in the statement. This is important in view of the argument to come in vv. 7–13. The expression "in

---

[14] Moo, *Romans*, 415. This deliverance from the "power sphere" of the law does not mean believers can simply disregard the revelation of the character and will of God in the law. Moo (416) draws attention to 8:4; 13:8–10 and the way Paul speaks in Gal 6:2; 1 Cor 7:19; 9:20–22. Cf. Schreiner, *Romans*, 350–51; and n. 22 below.

[15] The first of two purpose clauses is introduced by εἰς τό with the infinitive γενέσθαι. Jewett's description of a "psychosexual unity between Christians and Christ" (*Romans*, 434) involves a misreading of 1 Cor 6:13–20, and it is inappropriate in the present context.

[16] Cranfield (*Romans*, 1:336–37) rejects the notion that bearing fruit for God means "bearing offspring to God," but Dunn (*Romans 1–8*, 363) and Jewett (*Romans*, 435) contend that there could be a missional dimension to this metaphor.

the flesh" can be used in a fairly neutral way to describe life in this world (2 Cor 10:3; Gal 2:20; Phil 1:22, 24; Phlm 16). But here and in 8:8, 9 Paul uses the expression negatively to refer to the condition of being determined and controlled by the flesh. The term itself "denotes physicality seen on the one hand as corruptible and on the other as rebellious; it is another way of saying 'in Adam,' of demarcating that humanity that is characterized by sin and consequently by death."[17] In that preconversion situation, when the flesh ruled our lives, "the sinful passions aroused through the law were working in us to bear fruit for death." The genitive in the expression τὰ παθήματα τῶν ἁμαρτιῶν is understood by CSB to be qualitative, defining those passions as sinful, but it could be objective, meaning "passions that lead to sins."[18] Such passions were (lit.) "working through the law in our members" (τὰ διὰ τοῦ νόμου ἐνηργεῖτο ἐν τοῖς μέλεσιν ἡμῶν). CSB ("aroused through the law") anticipates 7:8–11. Paul's mention of "our members" recalls the warning of 6:13 about not offering "any parts" of ourselves to sin. His shocking conclusion is that the law works in partnership with sin "to bear fruit for death" (εἰς τὸ καρποφορῆσαι τῷ θανάτῳ [cf. 6:21; 1 Cor 15:56]). As vv. 7–11 explain, "the law, in setting forth God's standard, arouses sins by stimulating human beings' innate rebelliousness against God."[19]

7:6. Picking up the language of the marriage illustration again (v. 2), Paul says, "But now we have been released from the law." This discharge (κατηργήθημεν) is articulated in terms of (lit.)

[17] Wright, "Romans," 560. The flesh is more than "the sinful nature." Moo describes it more broadly as "a 'power sphere' in which a person lives," which is clearly related to our physicality in a fallen world. Cf. Fee, *God's Empowering Presence*, 816–22; Dunn, *Theology of Paul*, 62–70.

[18] The only other use of τὰ παθήματα in Romans is with reference to "the sufferings of this present time" (8:18). Elsewhere Paul talks about sharing in the sufferings of Christ (2 Cor 1:5–7; Phil 3:10; Col 1:24; cf. 2 Tim 3:11). Only in Gal 5:24 does he use the term again with reference to bad affections or passions that lead to sin.

[19] Moo, *Romans*, 420. Moo argues against the view that the passions in view in v. 5 are the desires of people to establish their own righteousness. He contends that they are "the desires to disobey God and his law that are paradoxically, exacerbated by the law itself." But wrongly directed religious passion must surely be included in the scope of Paul's language here.

"having died to what held us" (ἀποθανόντες ἐν ᾧ κατειχόμεθα).[20] In the light of v. 4, death to the law is achieved through union with Christ in his death. A new pattern of service (ὥστε δουλεύειν ἡμᾶς, "so that we may serve") replaces captivity to the law, recalling the exchange of ownership argument in 6:17–22. Although CSB translates this as a purpose clause, it is more likely to express consequence ("with the result that we serve").[21] Following on from v. 4, the apostle explains how belonging to the resurrected Messiah enables us to "bear fruit for God." This new form of service is (lit.) "in the newness of the Spirit and not in the oldness of the letter" (ἐν καινότητι πνεύματος καὶ οὐ παλαιότητι γράμματος).[22] "Newness" opposed to "oldness" implies a new era in God's dealing with humanity (cf. 6:4, 6; 2 Cor 3:6, 14; Eph 4:22–24; Col 3:9–10). This era is characterized by the gift of the Holy Spirit, as Paul intimates in 5:5 and explains more fully in 8:1–27. As in 2:27–29, the letter-Spirit contrast is a salvation-historical one. The law given to Israel on tablets of stone is contrasted with the inward working of the Holy Spirit under the new covenant, writing the law on the hearts of believers (cf. 2 Cor 3:3–11). As a preface to vv. 7–12, where "law" occurs six times and "commandments" five times, "Paul uses 'letter' as a way of referring to the law as a set of commandments to be obeyed, as a written 'legal code.'"[23] The Trinity (God, the Messiah, and the Spirit) is involved in the establishment and maintenance of the new way set forth in vv. 4–6 (cf. 8:1–30; Gal 4:4–6; §2.3).

7:7. Paul's claim that the law works in partnership with sin "to bear fruit for death" provokes the questions: "What should we say

[20] The verb καταργέω is used in both verses in the passive with the meaning "be discharged or released" (BDAG).

[21] Cranfield (*Romans*, 1:339) argues that ὥστε δουλεύειν expresses an actual, rather than potential, result here.

[22] Cranfield (ibid., 1:339) says these are probably genitives of apposition: "in newness, that is, in the Spirit (cf. ἐν πνεύματι in 8:9 and κατὰ πνεῦμα in 8:4) and not in oldness, that is, according to the letter." Cranfield denies that Paul is opposing the law as such to the Spirit: "letter" is what "the legalist is left with as a result of his misunderstanding and misuse of the law" (1.340). But this fails to convey the radical contrast Paul is presenting in 7:4–6. Cf. Moo, *Romans*, 420–22.

[23] Rosner, *Paul and the Law*, 100. The written law continues to reveal the character and will of God and to expose sin. To read the law in this way is different from being "under the law" as an integrated code of obligation.

then? Is the law sin?" The first is a rhetorical way of highlighting the importance of the second. As in 6:2, 15, a strong denial follows a false inference (μὴ γένοιτο, "Absolutely not!"). Nevertheless, Paul concedes a link between sin and the law when he writes, (lit.) "But I would not have known sin if not through the law" (ἀλλὰ τὴν ἁμαρτίαν οὐκ ἔγνων εἰ μὴ διὰ νόμου).[24] A specific example of this knowledge is then given, using different tense forms: (lit.) "For indeed I should not know covetousness if the law had not said, You shall not covet" (τήν τε γὰρ ἐπιθυμίαν οὐκ ᾔδειν εἰ μὴ ὁ νόμος ἔλεγεν· οὐκ ἐπιθυμήσεις).[25] Both verbs "to know" in this context refer to experiential knowledge rather than simply factual knowledge. People sinned before the law was given, but they did not experience covetousness as a deliberate disobeying of God's revealed will (3:20; 5:13). Paul's choice of the tenth commandment as his example is significant. Without the extra details found in Exod 20:17 and Deut 5:21, this becomes a general command not to desire anything contrary to the will of God (cf. Rom 13:9). As such, "it directs attention to the inward root of man's outward wrong-doing."[26] Covetousness was an aspect of the primal sin in Gen 3 and then of Israel's rebellion in Exod 32:1–6, immediately after receiving the law at Sinai.

Paul adopts the first-person singular in a way that continues to provoke much discussion and disagreement. It is used with past-tense verbs in vv. 7–11 and with present-tense verbs in vv. 14–25. The "I" in vv. 14–25 will be considered in my comment on v. 14. Elsewhere in his letters Paul uses the first-person singular in three different ways: for uniquely personal experiences (e.g., 1 Cor 15:8), for typical or representative statements (e.g., Gal 2:20), or with a

[24] CSB's "on the contrary" implies that this sentence is a complete rejection of the link between the law and sin, but is this so? The aorist οὐκ ἔγνων ("I would not have known") together with εἰ μή ("if not") forms an abbreviated past contrary-to-fact condition. Cf. Wallace, *Greek Grammar*, 695; Moo, *Romans*, 433n29; Runge, *Discourse Grammar*, 89–90.

[25] The future tense ἐπιθυμήσεις ("You shall not covet") is a literal translation of the Hebrew, and its force is emphatic (Wallace, *Greek Grammar*, 452–53).

[26] Cranfield, *Romans*, 1:349. Byrne (*Romans*, 219) observes that Paul has already depicted "desire" as something typical of fallen humanity (1:24 [ἐπιθυμία]; 1:26–27). In Stoic and Hellenistic Jewish circles, desire was considered the root of all evil (cf. Byrne, 222, and n. 31 below). The terminology cannot be restricted to sexual lust. Cf. Keener, *The Mind of the Spirit*, 76–90.

hypothetical reference (e.g., 1 Cor 10:29–30).[27] Some contend that he simply speaks autobiographically here, but it is difficult to reconcile such views with the claim of vv. 9–10 ("Once I was alive apart from the law, but when the commandment came, sin sprang to life again and I died"), or with the insistence that prior to encountering Christ he was blameless with respect to "the righteousness that is in the law" (Phil 3:6).[28] Others have argued that the apostle employs the technique of "impersonation" or "speech-in-character" found in ancient Greco-Roman literature. This observation, however, leaves open the question of the character he portrays. Paul does not follow the procedural criteria by which an author would signal his adoption of this technique and identify the character.[29]

Echoes of Gen 2–3 suggest that Paul is either speaking in the name of Adam or as a representative of humanity in Adam. But he also seems to link Israel's reception of the law at Sinai with the disobedience of Adam and Eve, which brought sin and death into the world.[30] In this way the apostle develops the claims he made in 4:15; 5:13–14, 20 about the negative impact of the law on the human situation. The coming of the law to Israel turned sin into transgression,

---

[27] Cf. Gerd Theissen, *Psychological Aspects of Pauline Theology*, trans. J. P. Galvin (Philadelphia: Fortress, 1987), 191. Thiessen (201) concludes that the "I" in Romans 7 combines personal and typical traits and cannot be merely fictive or hypothetical.

[28] Moo (*Romans*, 425) summarizes and critiques strictly autobiographical approaches. Cf. Brian Dodd, *Paul's Paradigmatic "I": Personal Example as Literary Strategy*, JSNTSup 177 (Sheffield: Sheffield Academic, 1999), 222–24; Kruse, *Romans*, 314–21. However, Jan Lambrecht (*The Wretched "I" and Its Liberation: Paul in Romans 7 and 8*, LTPM 14 [Grand Rapids: Eerdmans, 1992], 74–91) responds well to these criticisms.

[29] Stanley K. Stowers ("Romans 7.7–25 as Speech in Character [προσωποπεία]," in *Paul in His Hellenistic Context*, ed. T. Engberg-Pedersen [Minneapolis: Fortress, 1995], 180–202) contends that the character in view is Gentiles who try to live by works of the law (Cf. Stowers, *Rereading of Romans*, 273). Jewett (*Romans*, 443–44) lists alternatives and argues that Paul's character is "artificially constructed in the light of his pre-conversion experience as a zealot, but with an eye to the current situation in the Roman churches." Cf. Will N. Timmins, "Romans 7 and Speech-in-Character: A Critical Evaluation of Stowers' Hypothesis," *ZNW* 107 (2016): 94–115.

[30] Cranfield (*Romans*, 1.342–44) emphasizes the Adamic link. Moo (*Romans*, 429–30) acknowledges that vv. 9–10 speak most directly to the situation of Adam but argues that they can also be explained with reference to the coming of the law to Israel. Cf. Thiessen, *Psychological Aspects*, 202–11; Keener, *The Mind of the Spirit*, 69–74. Contrast Schreiner, *Romans*, 362–63.

increased the trespass, and produced wrath.[31] This composite biblical perspective is expressed in the first-person singular not just for rhetorical vividness but because of Paul's "deep sense of personal involvement, his consciousness that in drawing out the general truth he is disclosing the truth about himself."[32] The introduction (v. 7) and the argument that flows from it suggest that his use of "I" is "an adaptation of the common diatribal style, to clarify the argument in a striking, persuasive and memorable way."[33] Sin and the law are personified along with "I" as actors in the drama he unfolds. Paul's overall aim in vv. 7–25 is to defend the goodness of the law of God while warning his readers about the impossibility of bearing fruit for God by attempting to keep the written code. This approach highlights the need for the new way of the Spirit announced in vv. 4–6 and expounded in 8:1–14.

7:8. Here and in v. 11 sin is described as (lit.) "having seized an opportunity through the commandment" (ἀφορμὴν δὲ λαβοῦσα ἡ ἁμαρτία διὰ τῆς ἐντολῆς). A military term (ἀφορμή) meaning "base of operations" (BDAG) points to the oppressive nature of sin.[34] Sin is a powerful enemy that uses God's "holy and just and good" commandment (v. 12) to achieve its destructive purpose. So the commandment that prohibits covetousness actually "produced in me coveting of every kind" (κατειργάσατο ἐν ἐμοὶ πᾶσαν ἐπιθυμίαν [cf. v. 5, ἐνηργεῖτο]). Paul does not explain the psychological process he has in mind here, but the allusion to Gen 2:16–17 in the following expression (χωρὶς γὰρ νόμου ἁμαρτία νεκρά, "for apart from the law sin is dead") is instructive. The serpent was only able to attack

[31] Cf. Moo, *Romans*, 428–31. Wright ("Romans," 563) similarly contends that "what happened on Sinai recapitulated what had happened in Eden." He notes the link between covetousness and the sin of Adam in Jewish literature (b. Sanh. 38b; 102a; Exod. Rab. 21:1; 30:7; 32:1, 7, 11). Cf. Dunn, *Romans 1–8*, 379.

[32] Cranfield, *Romans*, 1:344. Cranfield (1:342) thinks Paul is speaking "in a generalizing way without intending a specific reference to any particular individual or clearly defined group," but his comment about the significance of the first-person singular is applicable to the Adam-Israel view. Cf. Don B. Garlington, "Romans 7:14–25 and the Creation Theology of Paul," *TJ* ns 11 (1990): 200–202.

[33] Dodd, *Paul's Paradigmatic "I,"* 230. Dodd (229) compares 3:7–8 and Gal 2:17–18 in context and concludes that, "one element of the diatribal style is to personify the abstract as part of the argument."

[34] CSB translates in a more generalized way ("opportunity"), as in 2 Cor 5:12; 11:12; Gal 5:13; 1 Tim 5:14. But the military sense is applicable in this context.

because the commandment had been given. God's law was not the originator of sin, but it awoke in Adam, and later in Israel, "a latent human propensity to chafe and rebel at creaturely dependence on the Creator."[35] Sin was first expressed in Adam's disobedience, and so death came into the world because of sin. Human life was characterized by sin before the law was given to Israel, and "death reigned from Adam to Moses, even over those who did not sin in the likeness of Adam's transgression" (5:13–14). But Paul implies that sin was aroused in a new way when God's law was given at Sinai. It brought death to the people who were meant to experience life and blessing through the law (cf. Exod 32; Deut 28:15–68). They responded like Adam!

7:9–10. As noted previously, these verses most obviously speak about the situation of humanity in Eden, where life was once lived in intimate fellowship with God ("once I was alive apart from the law," ἐγὼ δὲ ἔζων χωρὶς νόμου ποτέ). "But when the commandment came" (ἐλθούσης δὲ τῆς ἐντολῆς), "sin sprang to life (again) and I died" (ἡ ἁμαρτία ἀνέζησεν ἐγὼ δὲ ἀπέθανον).[36] In the flow of Paul's argument, this was recapitulated when Israel was confronted with the law of God at Sinai. But expressions such as "I was alive" and "sin sprang to life" must be understood in a relative fashion when applied to that event. Israel was not sinless before the law was given, but "the coming of the commandment gave sin greater power and destructiveness than ever before," and it brought "a 'radicalizing' of the sentence of condemnation."[37] The basis for understanding Israel's response to the law in terms of the fall narrative is suggested by the following words: "The commandment that was meant for life resulted in death for me" (καὶ εὑρέθη μοι ἡ ἐντολὴ ἡ εἰς ζωήν, αὕτη εἰς θάνατον). If Adam had obeyed the command given to him in Gen 2:16–17, he would not have been prevented from accessing the tree of life (Gen

[35] Byrne, *Romans*, 219. Reflecting on Gen 3:1–7, Cranfield (*Romans*, 1:350) speaks of the commandment intended to preserve humanity's true freedom and dignity being misrepresented as a taking away of freedom and dignity and so becoming "an occasion of resentment and rebellion against the divine Creator, man's true Lord."

[36] It is debatable whether the preposition ἀνά ("again") in the compound verb ἀνέζησεν should be given its full force. BDAG suggests "sin became alive."

[37] Moo, *Romans*, 430, 432. Moo (430–31) considers why Paul expresses his own involvement in Israel's history in such vivid and personal terms, pointing to precedents for this in Jer 10:19–22; Lam 1:9–22; 2:20–22; Mic 7:7–10; Pss. Sol. 1:1–2, 6.

3:21). But Moses also taught the generation about to enter the promised land that the commandments were meant "for life" (Lev 18:5; Deut 4:1; 6:24; 8:1). Indeed, Israel was challenged to choose "life and prosperity" by obeying God's commands, instead of "death and adversity" (Deut 30:15). Life was associated with God's blessing in the land they were about to possess, and death with God's curse and exclusion from the land (30:16–20; cf. 28:1–68). Biblical history shows how successive generations chose to disobey God's law and experienced the predicted judgment.

7:11. Paul speaks representatively about this experience of sin and death by saying that sin seized an opportunity through the commandment and "deceived me" (ἐξηπάτησέν με). He repeats the opening words of v. 8 to make clear that sin, rather than the commandment, is the enemy, and echoes Gen 3:13 ("the serpent deceived me").[38] The serpent deceived the woman by distorting God's commandment and misrepresenting his intentions in giving it. When the woman disobeyed and involved her husband in the rebellion, "sin" (represented by the serpent) achieved its goal and brought death. As a person in Adam, therefore, Paul can say, "and through it killed [me]" (καὶ δι' αὐτῆς ἀπέκτεινεν). As an Israelite, he can also affirm that the giving of the law at Sinai resulted in a repetition of that experience for all the covenant people. God's good purpose was to bring life through the giving of the law and offer hope to the world. But the promised life only came when the destructive power of sin was fully realized and defeated in the death of God's Son (cf. Gal 3:6–26). The confrontation between law and sin was thus an essential preparation for the messianic salvation.

7:12. The conclusion to this section begins with the conjunction ὥστε ("so then").[39] Despite the law's role in sin's destructive purpose, it cannot be identified with sin, as the question in v. 7 implied. The law itself is holy, meaning that it comes from the one who is holy and manifests his holiness. Specific commandments in the law are holy for the same reason. They demonstrate God's character as just (Deut 4:8; Ps 119:7) and good (Pss 19:7–11; 119:39). Although

[38] The same compound verb is used to describe Eve's deception in 2 Cor 11:3; 1 Tim 2:14, but Gen 3:13 LXX uses the simple ἠπάτησεν.

[39] Paul uses the particle μέν ("on the one hand") without a balancing δέ ("on the other hand"). This may be because he is making an implicit contrast between the law in v. 12 and sin in the preceding verses.

Paul warns his readers about relying on the law for justification (3:19–20, 28) and identifies a new way to pursue righteousness and holiness (6:11–23; 7:4–6), he also warns them about denigrating the law as if it were unjust, evil, or not from God.

7:13. The word "good" is picked up from v. 12, and the idea of death from vv. 10–11, as Paul asks, "Therefore, did what is good become death to me?" (Τὸ οὖν ἀγαθὸν ἐμοὶ ἐγένετο θάνατος;). Following the pattern in 6:1–2, 15–16; 7:7, a new section of the argument begins with a false inference, which is then denied (μὴ γένοιτο, "Absolutely not!"). Nevertheless, a link between the law and death is acknowledged in the proposition that follows.[40] In the first of two purpose clauses, Paul declares that "sin, in order to be recognized as sin, was producing death in me through what is good" (ἡ ἁμαρτία, ἵνα φανῇ ἁμαρτία, διὰ τοῦ ἀγαθοῦ μοι κατεργαζομένη θάνατον). This summarizes vv. 7–11. Sin made use of God's good command in Eden to bring death into the world, and sin used the law given to Israel to bring condemnation and death instead of life to the covenant people. A second purpose clause expresses the further idea "so that through the commandment, sin might become sinful beyond measure" (ἵνα γένηται καθ' ὑπερβολὴν ἁμαρτωλὸς ἡ ἁμαρτία διὰ τῆς ἐντολῆς).[41] Sin's sinfulness was actually enhanced by its use of God's law, which revealed sin's true colors. Paul's broader argument suggests that

> sin's deceptive tactic of harnessing the law to be its instrument in bringing death was in fact encompassed within a wider divine purpose. God gave the law (to Israel) precisely to bring sin to a point of maximum concentration so that right there (Israel) "where sin increased, grace might abound" (5:20b), for the benefit of the entire world, in the person of Israel's Messiah (cf. 8:3–4).[42]

---

[40] As in v. 7, ἀλλά should be translated "but." CSB ("on the contrary") implies a total rejection of the link.

[41] The adverbial expression καθ' ὑπερβολήν means "to an extraordinary degree, beyond measure, utterly" (BDAG; cf. 1 Cor 12:31; 2 Cor 1:8; 4:17; Gal 1:13). It qualifies ἁμαρτωλός, which is used as an adjective here (BDAG, "sinful").

[42] Byrne, *Romans*, 221. This salvation-historical perspective fits with Paul's argument in 9:30–11:24 and Gal 3:19–26. Paul's complex sentence requires that ἐγένετο should be understood before κατεργαζομένη to provide the sense "was producing."

7:14. The connective *γάρ* ("for") links a confessional statement in the first-person plural (*οἴδαμεν ὅτι*, "we know that") with what has gone before.[43] Paul draws his readers into the argument, expecting them to affirm that "the law is spiritual" (*ὁ νόμος πνευματικός ἐστιν*), meaning that it comes from God and has a spiritual purpose. Given the letter-Spirit contrast in v. 6, he may also be suggesting that only those who have the Spirit may properly understand and respond to God's law (cf. 8:2–4).[44] Following this stylistic indicator of a transition, Paul returns to first-person singular forms but begins to speak in the present tense. The "I" continues to speak as a representative of humanity in Adam/Israel, acknowledging, (lit.) "But I am of the flesh" (*ἐγὼ δὲ σάρκινός εἰμι*)[45] and "sold under sin" (*πεπραμένος ὑπὸ τὴν ἁμαρτίαν*).[46] This last term recalls the charge that Jews and Gentiles are all "under sin" (3:9, *ὑφ' ἁμαρτίαν*). The present tense is used to provide an inside rather than an outside perspective on this situation, allowing Paul to give an existential account of what it means to delight in God's law but not be able to keep it. The problem is indwelling sin (vv. 17, 20) and the flesh (vv. 18, 25). The first-person singular is a vivid way of expressing his own personal involvement in the struggle he describes. But does Paul expect his Christian readers to see this conflict as their own?[47]

---

[43] The variant *οἶδα μέν* ("I know") is poorly attested and is unlikely to be the original. Paul's argument at this point calls for the sort of general assent he seeks to elicit with *οἴδαμεν γάρ* (8:22; 2 Cor 5:1) or *οἴδαμεν δέ* (2:2; 3:19; 8:28; 1 Tim 1:8).

[44] Jewett (*Romans*, 460–61) argues, "Paul intends to imply that the Torah was created, activated and authorized by the Spirit."

[45] The same adjective is used positively in 2 Cor 3:3 to describe human hearts in contrast with stone tablets. But contrasted with *πνευματικός* ("spiritual," 1 Cor 3:1), the term identifies those who are disappointingly "fleshly" or immature Christians. The parallel term in 1 Cor 3:3 (*σαρκικός*) defines the readers as "fleshly" in the sense of exhibiting envy and strife and "living like ordinary people." Cf. Heb 7:16.

[46] The perfect passive participle *πεπραμένος* encodes stativity and imperfectivity, expressing a continuing condition ("being sold"). Cf. Campbell, *Verbal Aspect and Non-Indicative Verbs*, 26–28. Compare the present tense participles in 7:23 ("waging war" and "taking me prisoner to the law of sin."

[47] Cranfield (*Romans*, 1:344) defends this view against various alternatives. So also James D. G. Dunn, "Romans 7:14–25 in the Theology of Paul," *TZ* 31 (1975), 257–73; Dunn, *Romans 1–8*, 387–89, 404–12; James I. Packer, "The 'Wretched Man' in Romans 7," in *Studia Evangelica II*, ed. F. Cross (Berlin: Acadamie, 1964), 621–27; Packer, "The 'Wretched Man' Revisited: Another Look at Romans 7:14–25," in *Romans and the People of God*," 76–81.

A problem for this view is that vv. 14, 23 seem to be incompatible with what is said about the believer's liberation from captivity to sin in 6:6, 14, 17–18, 22; 8:2. Moreover, there is no explicit mention of the Holy Spirit in 7:14–25. So most of the early church fathers thought Paul was describing an unregenerate person. Some modern commentaries argue that Paul is simply "looking back, from his Christian understanding, to the situation of himself, and other Jews like him, living under the law of Moses."[48] But is it reasonable to imagine that Paul uses the present tense to express with Christian hindsight "the existential anguish of the pious Jew—which as a pious Jew he did not actually experience (Phil 3:4–6), and which as a Christian he still does not experience"?[49] In 2:1–13, 17–29; 3:1–20; 27–28, he condemns his fellow Jews for their hypocrisy, disobedience, and false confidence in relation to the law. Later he contends that being "in the flesh" (7:5, ἐν τῇ σαρκί) involves a mindset that is "hostile to God because it does not submit to God's law. Indeed it is unable to do so" (8:7). The attitude reflected in 7:14–25 is different: Paul gives indications of the work of God's Spirit when he talks about delighting in God's law "in my inner self" (v. 22) and serving the law of God "with my mind" (v. 25).[50] He speaks as one who belongs to the new era of Christ and the Spirit but knows that he is still "of the flesh, sold under sin" (v. 14 ESV).[51] In this situation of being caught in the overlap of the ages, the self is divided.[52] Paul does not argue this way to commend obedience to the law to Christians. His purpose is to dramatize the need for the radical death to the law outlined in 7:4–6 before moving on to expound the "new

[48] Moo, *Romans*, 448. Cf. Byrne, *Romans*, 226; Wright, "Romans," 551–57.

[49] Dunn, *Romans 1–8*, 394. I have made Dunn's statement a question.

[50] Cranfield (*Romans*, 1:346) argues that the struggle portrayed here can only take place "where the Spirit of God is present and active (cf. Gal 5:17)." Garlington ("Romans 7:14–15," 212–28) similarly contends that the Christian is flesh and Spirit at the same time.

[51] CSB ("sold as a slave to sin") adds words that are not in the Greek ("as a slave"), forcing the reader to conclude that this describes an unregenerate person. But Paul's language is more subtle and differs from 6:16–18 in rhetorical purpose.

[52] Schreiner (*Romans*, 379–92) gives a helpful summary of arguments on both sides of this debate and concludes, "The arguments are so finely balanced because Paul does not intend to distinguish believers from unbelievers" (cf. Seifrid, *Justification by Faith*, 226–44). But this compromise will not work if "the overlap of the ages" is being portrayed in 7:14–25, since only Christians are caught in that situation.

way of the Spirit." Even those who delight in God's law and desire to keep it find that they cannot adequately obey the law and please God because of the ongoing power of sin and the flesh.

7:15. The first γάρ ("for") in this verse links what follows to the claim that "I am of the flesh, sold under sin." Paul declares that he does not "understand" what he does (ὃ κατεργάζομαι οὐ γινώσκω), meaning that he does not approve or condone it. The second γάρ introduces what he does not approve: "Because I do not practice what I want to do, but I do what I hate" (οὐ γὰρ ὃ θέλω τοῦτο πράσσω, ἀλλ' ὃ μισῶ τοῦτο ποιῶ). The disowning is much sharper than the willing here: "He wholly detests and abhors what he does as one 'sold under sin' (v. 14)."[53] Illustrations of frustrated moral impotence have been found in ancient pagan literature (e.g., Ovid, *Metamorphoses*, 7.20–21; Epictetus, *Diatr.* 2.26.4) and are common in human experience. But the difference here is that the struggle is to do the revealed will of God, moved by a mind that wants to submit to God's law (v. 25; contrast 8:7). Paul is confronted by an eschatological tension that is "rendered all the sharper and more poignant by the fact that the individual (believer) has already begun to experience the possibilities and promise of a wholly Spirit-directed life."[54]

7:16–17. A simple condition of fact leads Paul back to the view of the law expressed in v. 12: "Now if I do what I do not want to do, I agree with the law that it is good" (εἰ δὲ ὃ οὐ θέλω τοῦτο ποιῶ, σύμφημι τῷ νόμῳ ὅτι καλός). Without making excuses for himself, he points to the logical conclusion (νυνὶ δέ, "so now"): "I am no longer the one doing it, but it is sin living in me" (οὐκέτι ἐγὼ κατεργάζομαι αὐτὸ ἀλλὰ ἡ οἰκοῦσα ἐν ἐμοὶ ἁμαρτία). In other words, a failure to do what God requires, even while approving the goodness of God's command, is an indication of the power of indwelling sin. This is a new idea, introduced for the first time in Paul's writings but critical for understanding the situation of believers caught in the overlap of the ages. Sin and the flesh remain as active powers to be resisted (cf. 6:12–14; 8:12–13). Yet, "the fact that there is real conflict and

---

[53] Dunn, *Romans 1–8*, 389. Dunn (407) observes that the anguish of v. 15 must "express or at least include Paul's experience as one who has already been accepted by and through Christ and already received the Spirit."

[54] Dunn, *Romans 1–8*, 389. A similar sense of eschatological tension and frustration can be found in 1QS 11 and 1QH. Keener (*The Mind of the Spirit*, 90–97) outlines ancient beliefs about internal conflict.

tension is a sign of hope."[55] Paul will go on to talk about the way the law's essential requirement is fulfilled in those who "walk . . . according to the Spirit" in 8:4 (cf. 13:8–10).

7:18–19. The linking expression οἶδα γὰρ ὅτι ("For I know that") takes the argument of the previous verse a step further. Leaving the law out of the picture for the moment, Paul concentrates on the "I" and its relation to sin and the flesh, confessing that "nothing good lives in me, that is, in my flesh." As in v. 5, "the flesh" denotes "physicality seen on the one hand as corruptible and on the other as rebellious."[56] But Paul is not speaking in v. 18 about being wholly determined and controlled by the flesh because he goes on to say, "For the desire to do what is good is with me" (τὸ γὰρ θέλειν παράκειταί μοι [τὸ καλὸν]). This desire is later explained in terms of "the law of my mind" (v. 23), which approves of God's law and wants to serve it (v. 25). But "there is no ability to do the good" (τὸ δὲ κατεργάζεσθαι τὸ καλὸν οὔ).[57] This inability is then explained in terms reflecting v. 15b: "For I do not do the good that I want to do, but I practice the evil that I do not want to do." Paul does not distance the "I" from the flesh but expresses the fact that he is still a man of flesh and in that respect still part of the old era in Adam. Only physical death will sever this attachment. Meanwhile, for the Christian, flesh and Spirit are opposed to each other, "so that you don't do what you want" (Gal 5:17).[58]

7:20–21. Another condition of fact is used to repeat the substance of vv. 16a, 17: "Now if I do what I do not want, I am no longer the one that does it, but it is the sin that lives in me."[59] Then Paul introduces a new way of describing the conflict, using ἄρα ("so") to link this with the preceding verse. He also uses νόμος in a new way,

[55] Cranfield, *Romans*, 1:360. Cf. Gal 5:16–26.

[56] Wright, "Romans," 560.

[57] The conclusion of this sentence with οὔ ("not") in the best manuscripts prompted some copyists to add supplementary words, which are clearly secondary (cf. Metzger, *Textual Commentary*, 454–55). No subtle distinction between the different verbs "to do" or "to practice" should be understood in these verses.

[58] Dunn (*Romans 1–8*, 408) makes the important point that "sin cannot touch me in my belongingness to Christ, but sin still holds sway over the world to which 'I' still belong as a man of flesh."

[59] The first ἐγώ ("I") in v. 20 is only included in some manuscripts (cf. Metzger, *Textual Commentary*, 455). But it makes no difference to the sense of the verse if this is included or not.

contrasting another "law" with the law of God. Various attempts have been made to explain "this law" in terms of the "two-sidedness" of the law of God, but these seem forced.[60] What Paul finds from his own experience (εὑρίσκω, "I discover") is the presence of another ruling power other than the law of God. This "law" is that "when I want to do what is good, evil is present with me" (τῷ θέλοντι ἐμοὶ ποιεῖν τὸ καλόν, ὅτι ἐμοὶ τὸ κακὸν παράκειται). What is "present and ready for some purpose or action" (παράκειται, BDAG) is both "the desire to do what is good" (v. 18) and "evil" (v. 21). This claim about the lurking presence of evil echoes Gen 4:7.

7:22. The connective γάρ ("for") indicates that what is said here and in v. 23 explains the situation described in v. 21. The verb συνήδομαι means "delight in" (BDAG) and is a stronger expression of approval than σύμφημι ("agree with," v. 16).[61] Paul's delight in the law of God takes place in his "inner self." As the broader context suggests, he presents

> a salvation-history dualism or tension, not an anthropological dualism: the "I" is split not as a result of creation (or the fall), but primarily as the result of redemption; the "I" is split because the "I" of the believer belongs to, is stretched between the old epoch of sin and death (and law) and the new epoch of grace and life (and Spirit).[62]

The expression "in the inner self" (κατὰ τὸν ἔσω ἄνθρωπον) should be compared with 2 Cor 4:16, which highlights the daily renewal of "our inner person" (ὁ ἔσω ἡμῶν), and Eph 3:16, which speaks about being strengthened with power through God's Spirit "in the inner man" (τὸν ἔσω ἄνθρωπον). It is also likely that "the law of my mind"

[60] Dunn (*Romans 1–8*, 392) argues that Paul's teaching about the two-sidedness of the law "reinforces and interacts with the 'I' in its own two-sidedness." Cf. Wright, "Romans," 570; Schreiner, *Romans*, 375–77. Note the critique of such views by Cranfield, *Romans*, 1:361–62; Kruse, *Romans*, 309–10, and my comment on 8:2.

[61] Compare Ps 19:8, where the precepts of the Lord make the heart glad, and Ps 119, where the writer rejoices (v. 14), delights (vv. 16, 24, 47, 70), and takes pleasure (v. 35) in God's law. Against Jewett (*Romans*, 469), the social dimension ("rejoice together with others") does not seem to be present here.

[62] Dunn, *Romans 1–8*, 394. Dunn acknowledges that the concept of an inner man can be found in classical Greek philosophy and in Gnostic thought but highlights the difference in Paul's thinking. Cf. Garlington, "Romans 7:14–25," 221–23.

(v. 23, τῷ νόμῳ τοῦ νοός μου) and "with my mind" (v. 25, τῷ νοι) are parallel expressions that describe the renewed mind that enables believers to discern "what is the good, pleasing, and perfect will of God" (12:2). So the mind that delights in God's law is "the mind which is being renewed by God's Spirit; and the inner man of which Paul speaks is the working of God's Spirit within the Christian."[63]

7:23. With this inward delight in the law of God, Paul also perceives (βλέπω ["I see"]) "a different law in the parts of my body" (ἕτερον νόμον ἐν τοῖς μέλεσίν μου). This is the law that "when I want to do what is good, evil is present with me" (v. 21).[64] It is also described as "the law of sin in the parts of my body" (τῷ νόμῳ τῆς ἁμαρτίας τῷ ὄντι ἐν τοῖς μέλεσίν μου). Use of the word "law" in this last expression implies that "sin's exercising such authority over us is a hideous usurpation of the prerogative of God's law."[65] "In my members" (ἐν τοῖς μέλεσίν μου) may refer to more than "the parts of my body" (cf. 6:13 comment), though the body is the focus of Paul's cry in v. 24. With two vivid present participles, he talks about the ongoing reality of sin "waging war against the law of my mind" (ἀντιστρατευόμενον τῷ νόμῳ τοῦ νοός μου) and "taking me prisoner" (αἰχμαλωτίζοντά με). These military terms recall vv. 8, 11 (ἀφορμή, "base of operations"; cf. Gal 5:17; 1 Pet 2:11). "Paul feels that he is caught up in a warfare with sin, a continuing warfare in which his experience ('I') is typical of believers generally (6:13; 8:13), notwithstanding the aorists of 6:2–4 and 8:2."[66] The notion of being captive to sin also recalls his claim to be "sold under sin" (v. 14). But the extremeness of these statements should not be taken to mean that Paul is speaking about total and unremitting failure. The interpretive framework must be his exhortations in 6:12–23 and 8:12–13, which offer the hope of resisting sin and the flesh as believers yield every part of themselves to God and put to death "the deeds of the body" by the Spirit's leading and enabling.

---

[63] Cranfield, *Romans*, 1.363. Keener (*The Mind of the Spirit*, 98) denies that the inner self here is the new person in Christ and equates the law active in Paul's mind with the mind of the flesh (109, 116). But this is not a satisfactory way of relating 7:22–25 to 8:6–8. Although almost all manuscripts have τοῦ θεοῦ ("of God") in v. 22, codex B has copied τοῦ νοός ("of the mind") from v. 23.

[64] Wright ("Romans," 570–71) argues unconvincingly that "a different law" is really the law of God become the base of operation for sin (vv. 8, 11).

[65] Cranfield, *Romans*, 1:364.

[66] Dunn, *Romans 1–8*, 395.

7:24–25. Paul's exclamation ("What a wretched man I am!" Ταλαίπωρος ἐγὼ ἄνθρωπος) is followed by a rhetorical question ("Who will rescue me from this body of death?"). The last expression (τοῦ σώματος τοῦ θανάτου τούτου) is another way of describing "your mortal body" (6:12; cf. 8:11). "Death" refers to the death brought about by sin (7:10–13). Some would argue that Paul expresses here the position of the unconverted or of those whom sin and the law have brought to despair. The word ἄνθρωπος ("man") certainly suggests that he sees himself as a representative of fallen humanity. But his exclamation is a cry of anguish, not despair, and his question expresses a longing for the rescue he knows is surely coming (cf. 8:23). The tension he expresses is eschatological, not simply anthropological.[67] Coupled with his thanksgiving ("Thanks be to God through Jesus Christ our Lord!" χάρις δὲ τῷ θεῷ διὰ Ἰησοῦ Χριστοῦ τοῦ κυρίου ἡμῶν), this is surely the cry of a Christian who is confident of final release through resurrection from death (cf. 6:17).[68] Although "through Jesus Christ our Lord" could refer to Christ as the mediator of Paul's thanksgiving, it more likely refers to him as the agent of eschatological deliverance. In 1 Cor 15:56–57, a cry of victory through Christ is coupled with the acknowledgment that "the sting of death is sin, and the power of sin is the law." These verses parallel in content what is confessed in Rom 7:7–25.[69]

So Paul's exclamation, question, and thanksgiving are parenthetical, and "there is nothing surprising, awkward, or unnatural in the fact that Paul goes straight on to summarize what he has been saying from verses 14 to 23 about the way things are now."[70] The

[67] So Dunn (*Romans 1–8*, 396) argues, contrasting the anthropological reflection of Epictetus 1.3.3–6. That this can be the cry of one who has the Holy Spirit is clear from 8:23; 2 Cor 4:16–5:5; Phil 3:20–21. Schreiner (*Romans*, 382–84) notes that 8:10–13 "seems to confirm that 7:24 refers to a future redemption of the body, and that believers currently fight against a sinful body." Cf. Garlington, "Romans 7:14–15," 228–35.

[68] There are several versions of the opening words of v. 25, including ἡ χάρις τοῦ θεοῦ ("the grace of God") and εὐχαριστῶ τῷ θεῷ ("I thank God"). But the one that seems best to account for the rise of the others is χάρις δὲ τῷ θεῷ ("thanks be to God") in א[1] C[2] Ψ 33 81 88 etc. Cf. Metzger, *Textual Commentary*, 455.

[69] Cf. Robert J. Banks, "Romans 7:25a: An Eschatological Thanksgiving?," *ABR* 26 (1978): 38–39.

[70] Packer, "The 'Wretched Man' Revisited," 76. Any theory that v. 25b is a gloss should be rejected because there is no manuscript evidence for this.

words Ἄρα οὖν ("so then") link back to that argument, introducing two linked observations: "with my mind I myself am serving the law of God, but with my flesh, the law of sin." The emphatic αὐτός with the pronoun ἐγώ ("I myself") does not simply mean "I left to myself" (without Christ and the Spirit). The "I" who speaks is both the fleshly person of v. 14 and the "inner self" of v. 22, both claims being linked together by the μέν . . . δέ construction.

Bridge

Paul's declaration that "you also were put to death in relation to the law" may seem strange to modern readers. We do not think of ourselves as having been under the law before becoming Christians. But the apostle has already argued that the whole world is held accountable to God by his law (3:20). Here he asserts that, just as we died to sin's penalty and dominion through union with Christ in his death (6:1–11), so also we died to the law's condemnation and control "through the body of Christ" (7:4). Paul's testimony is that the written law cannot deliver us from sin and produce the obedience that pleases God because of the ongoing power of sin and the flesh (7:7–25). So what is the way to "bear fruit for God"? We must be "wedded" to Christ as the one who was raised from the dead (7:4) and serve God "in the newness of the Spirit, and not in the old letter of the law" (7:6). There is ongoing debate about whether Paul speaks about Christian experience in 7:14–25, but we can all identify with what he says about the conflict between "what I want to do" and "what I hate." Conversion "does not bring a complete release from the flesh, or an immediate and lasting victory over the power of sin."[71] Simply agreeing with God's law and desiring to keep it is not the way forward for the Christian. Moreover, "Paul is clear that the divided person is not the ideal and that the law, far from unifying the person, in fact divides this person."[72] Thankful for what Jesus has accomplished for us and confident about ultimate deliverance from "this body of death," we need to seek the direction and empowerment of God's Spirit to live in a way that pleases him (cf. 8:1–17).

---

[71] Dunn, *Romans 1–8*, 411–12.

[72] Keener, *The Mind of the Spirit*, 107.

X. The New Way of the Spirit: Life and Adoption, Perseverance and Hope (8:1–39)

The word πνεῦμα ("spirit") occurs more frequently in this chapter than in any other Pauline letter, mostly with reference to the Holy Spirit. God's Spirit is mentioned fifteen times in vv. 1–17 and four times in vv. 18–39. In the first section the Spirit is the agent of spiritual life and adoption. In the second section the Spirit enables believers to persevere in suffering and wait patiently for their God-given hope to be fulfilled. However, although the Spirit's work is a dominant theme in this chapter, the overall emphasis is on living in the light of the various forms of assurance God gives to his children about their status and destiny in Christ.[1] In vv. 1–30 Paul resumes the didactic and proclamatory style of 5:1–11. In vv. 31–39 he returns to the diatribe style of questions and answers familiar to us from the apologetic sections of the letter but adapted here to persuade readers about God's enduring love for them.

A. Life and Adoption through the Spirit (8:1–17)

> [1]Therefore, there is now no condemnation for those in Christ
> Jesus, [2]because the law of the Spirit of life in Christ Jesus has set
> you free from the law of sin and death. [3]What the law could not do
> since it was weakened by the flesh, God did. He condemned sin in
> the flesh by sending his own Son in the likeness of sinful flesh as
> a sin offering, [4]in order that the law's requirement would be ful-
> filled in us who do not walk according to the flesh but according
> to the Spirit. [5]For those who live according to the flesh have their
> minds set on the things of the flesh, but those who live according
> to the Spirit have their minds set on the things of the Spirit. [6]Now
> the mind-set of the flesh is death, but the mind-set of the Spirit
> is life and peace. [7]The mind-set of the flesh is hostile to God be-
> cause it does not submit to God's law. Indeed, it is unable to do
> so. [8]Those who are in the flesh cannot please God. [9]You, however,
> are not in the flesh, but in the Spirit, if indeed the Spirit of God
> lives in you. If anyone does not have the Spirit of Christ, he does

[1] Moo (*Romans*, 468) notes the movement from "no condemnation" (v. 1) to "no separation" (v. 39) and says, "Paul passes in review those gifts and graces that together assure the Christian that his relationship with God is secure and settled." Moo sees four divisions in the chapter (vv. 1–13, 14–17, 18–30, 31–39).

not belong to him. [10]Now if Christ is in you, the body is dead because of sin, but the Spirit gives life because of righteousness. [11]And if the Spirit of him who raised Jesus from the dead lives in you, then he who raised Christ from the dead will also bring your mortal bodies to life through his Spirit who lives in you.

[12]So then, brothers and sisters, we are not obligated to the flesh to live according to the flesh, [13]because if you live according to the flesh, you are going to die. But if by the Spirit you put to death the deeds of the body, you will live. [14]For all those led by God's Spirit are God's sons. [15]You did not receive a spirit of slavery to fall back into fear. Instead, you received the Spirit of adoption, by whom we cry out, "*Abba*, Father!" [16]The Spirit himself testifies together with our spirit that we are God's children, [17]and if children, also heirs—heirs of God and coheirs with Christ—if indeed we suffer with him so that we may also be glorified with him.

Context

Although there are indications of the Spirit's renewing work in 7:22–25, Paul now turns to express more fully what he means by "the newness of the Spirit" (7:6). The category of "flesh" also appeared in the preceding chapter (7:5, 18, 25) but is used extensively in 8:1–16 to describe the opposing power. Now, "it is the Spirit who can be described as determinative for Christian belonging and sonship (vv. 9, 14)."[2] The mention of suffering in order to be glorified with Christ (v. 17) introduces the next main subject of the chapter, which highlights the Spirit's enabling in the midst of suffering (vv. 23, 26–27).

Structure

The opening verses introduce the theme of release from condemnation (v. 1) and freedom from "the law of sin and death" (v. 2). Freedom from condemnation results from the provision of God's Son as a sin offering (v. 3). God's Spirit sets people free from "the law of sin and death" by convincing them about Christ's redemptive work and making it possible for "the law's requirement" to be fulfilled in those who "do not walk according to the flesh but according

[2] Dunn, *Romans 1–8*, 415. Dunn observes that in chapters 6–7 grace, righteousness, and Spirit episodically are the forces to defeat sin and death.

to the Spirit" (v. 4). The next section (vv. 5–8) develops this Spirit/flesh antithesis, highlighting two different mind-sets and the outcome of each: "death" on the one hand and "life and peace" on the other. With the insistence that Christians are not "in the flesh, but in the Spirit," Paul explains the life-giving work of the Spirit now and in the future (vv. 9–11). On this basis he appeals to his readers not to live according to the flesh but by the Spirit to "put to death the deeds of the body" (vv. 12–13). The concluding paragraph (vv. 14–17) contrasts the fear that spiritual slavery brings with the confidence that the Holy Spirit gives to those who have been adopted as God's children and can relate to him as Father.[3]

Outline:

1. The Spirit of life (vv. 1–13)
2. The Spirit of adoption (vv. 14–17)

8:1. A strong connective (ἄρα, "therefore") links the opening sentence to what has gone before, though not merely with 7:25. Paul's claim that "there is now no condemnation for those in Christ Jesus" draws out the significance of 7:4–6a, which asserts that believers were "put to death in relation to the law through the body of Christ." As in 7:6a (νῦνι), the adverb νῦν ("now") refers to the era of the new covenant, which was inaugurated by the gospel events (3:21, 26; 5:9, 11; 6:19, 21, 22; 7:17; 8:18, 22; 11:5, 30–31; 13:11; 16:26). But Paul's use of κατάκριμα ("condemnation") also points back to 5:16, 18, where it refers to the penalty arising from God's pronouncement of Adam's guilt. The related verb is used in v. 3 to indicate that God condemned human sin in the flesh of his own Son (cf. 2 Cor 5:21; Gal 3:13).[4] The adjective οὐδέν ("not one") is emphatic: no punishment at all will fall on "those who are in Christ Jesus," namely on those who are in a faith relationship with the

---

[3] Wright ("Romans," 574) observes that we are still watching the unfolding of the Adam-Christ contrast of 5:12–21 in this passage. The golden thread running through 8:1–11 is life: "The gift of God that the law wanted to give but could not, the gift that comes because God's Son has dealt with sin and death and God's life-giving Spirit has replaced sin as the indwelling power within God's people."

[4] Cf. BDAG ("death-sentence"); Jewett, *Romans*, 479–80 ("punishment"). There is no contradiction between this claim and Paul's teaching about judgment according to works (2:6–16) because the latter exposes the presence or absence of saving faith.

crucified Messiah.[5] This is a particularly significant claim in view of the ongoing struggle with sin and acknowledgment of personal failure in 7:14–25. So important is the assurance of freedom from condemnation that Paul expands on it in v. 34.

8:2. Linked to the preceding claim by γάρ ("because"), Paul asserts that there is no condemnation because the Spirit of God has set believers free from "the law of sin and death." Since the next verse clarifies that God condemned sin in the sacrificial death of his Son, the work of the Spirit is to give life though faith in Christ and what he achieved for us (cf. 3:25; 5:15–21; 8:10). "Life" involves freedom from "the law of sin and death." The epexegetical genitive τοῦ πνεύματος gives ὁ νόμος a figurative sense ("the 'law' of the Spirit"), while the objective genitive τῆς ζωῆς identifies the Spirit's essential role ("who confers life") and the dative ἐν Χριστῷ Ἰησοῦ points to the sphere in which the Spirit is experienced ("in Christ Jesus").[6] The Spirit of God has been given to all who belong to Christ (5:5; 8:9) and is "the divine antidote" to the "the law of sin and death."[7] Paul uses the second-person singular to apply his claim of liberation to each one individually (ἠλευθέρωσέν σε, "has set you free").[8] He later clarifies that the complete enjoyment of this freedom will only come with the redemption of our bodies (vv. 21–23).

---

[5] The extra words μὴ κατὰ σάρκα περιπατοῦσιν ("not walking according to the flesh") are found in A D[1] Ψ and other Greek manuscripts and are reflected in some ancient versions and early Christian writings. These words together with ἀλλὰ κατὰ πνεῦμα ("but according to the Spirit") are found in א[2] D[2] and some other Greek manuscripts and are reflected in a few versions. The longest reading is found in KJV, via the TR. But the shortest text, which makes no qualification, is strongly supported by early representatives of the Alexandrian and Western textual tradition (א* B C[2] D* G). The additions were interpolated from v. 4, where they are more appropriate to the argument.

[6] Against Dunn (*Romans 1–8*, 418), it is less likely that ἐν Χριστῷ Ἰησοῦ should be read with the following verb ("in Christ Jesus has set you free"). Cf. Jewett, *Romans*, 481.

[7] Cf. Fee, *God's Empowering Presence*, 522.

[8] The second-person singular σε ("you") is a well-attested reading (א B F G, some other manuscripts, versions, and fathers). The alternative με ("me") is more widely attested (A D and many manuscripts, versions and fathers) and conforms to the first person usage in 7:7–25, but it is likely to have been chosen to replace the more difficult σε (cf. Metzger, *Textual Commentary*, 456). The reading ἡμᾶς ("us") in Ψ and a few versions and fathers is clearly secondary.

"The law of sin and death" parallels "the law of sin" in 7:23, 25, where νόμος is used to describe a ruling force other than the law of God. "Death" is added in 8:2 as the divine punishment for sin (5:12; 6:23; 7:9–11). God's Spirit is the greater power, delivering Christians from the authority and control of sin and death. Some have argued that "the law of the Spirit of life" refers to "the law rightly understood and responded to" ("the eschatological law" fulfilled in those who walk by the Spirit, v. 4), while "the law of sin and death" refers to "the law caught in the nexus of sin and death."[9] Paul is said to have established the "two-sidedness" of the law of God in 7:21–23, 25. But his salvation-historical statements in 7:4, 6 make it difficult to see how he could conceive of that law, "not just as undergoing a transformation in the new era, but as the very *agent* of the liberation."[10] Indeed, he goes on to affirm that the law could not bring about the necessary deliverance, "since it was weakened by the flesh" (v. 3). Led by the Spirit, however,

> the believer is no longer an unresisting, or only ineffectually resisting, slave, nor is he one who fondly imagines that his bondage is emancipation. In him a constraint even stronger than sin is already at work, which both gives him an inner freedom (cf. 7:22, 25b [τῷ μὲν νοῒ δουλεύω νόμῳ θεοῦ]), and also enables him to revolt against the usurper sin with a real measure of effectiveness.[11]

8:3. This verse and the next comprise one complex sentence in Greek, linked to the preceding argument by γάρ ("for," not translated

[9] Cf. Dunn, *Romans 1–8*, 416–18; Wright, "Romans," 576–77; Jewett, *Romans*, 481. Dunn parallels "the law of the Spirit of life in Christ Jesus" with "the law of my mind" (7:23) and views "the law of sin and death" (8:2) and "the law of sin" (7:23, 25) as parallel references. But "law" in these expressions is deliberately used in the sense of a ruling power other than the law of God.

[10] Byrne, *Romans*, 242 (emphasis in original). Byrne (235) identifies "the law of the Spirit of life in Christ Jesus" as "not a law in the strict sense of a moral code but the Spirit itself in so far as, in the new age, it constitutes a new norm and possibility of life." Cf. Fee, *God's Empowering Presence*, 522–27; Moo, *Romans*, 473–77.

[11] Cranfield, *Romans*, 1:378. Although Moo (*Romans*, 477) takes a different view of 7:13–25, he is right to conclude that 8:2 significantly advances the discussion of chapters 5–7 by making explicit that the Spirit is "a key agent of liberation from the old realm of sin and death." Byrne (*Romans*, 235) takes "the law of the Spirit of life" to refer to the Spirit as "a new norm and possibility of life."

by CSB). Paul first explains how God has delivered us from condemnation and then in v. 4 outlines how the Spirit has freed us to serve God and do his will. The abbreviated expression τὸ ἀδύνατον τοῦ νόμου ἐν ᾧ ἠσθένει διὰ τῆς σαρκός (lit., "what was impossible for the law, because it was weak through the flesh") establishes the context for what follows.[12] The law could not bring about the necessary deliverance from sin and death because of the power of the flesh, so God sent "his own Son" (τὸν ἑαυτοῦ υἱόν, as in v. 32) to rescue us. CSB has added the words "God did" and understands the aorist participle πέμψας in a modal sense ("by sending"), putting this after the principal clause ("he condemned sin in the flesh"). God's sending of his Son "in the likeness of sinful flesh" (ἐν ὁμοιώματι σαρκὸς ἁμαρτίας) implies the incarnation of the preexistent Son of God (cf. 1:3–4 comment; Gal 4:4; Col 1:15–20).[13] In 1:23; 5:14; 6:5, ὁμοίωμα ("likeness") can be used in the sense of close similarity, but full identity is implied in Phil 2:7, when Paul speaks about Christ's being born "in the likeness of men" (ἐν ὁμοιώματι ἀνθρώπων). The Son truly assumed human nature while still existing "in the form of God" (ἐν μορφῇ θεοῦ ὑπάρχων, Phil 2:6). So in the present context, the implication is that "the Son of God assumed the selfsame fallen human nature that is ours, but that in his case that fallen human nature was never the whole of him—he never ceased to be the eternal Son of God."[14] The expression "in the likeness of sinful flesh" seeks to avoid the implication that Christ actually sinned. Paul affirms the sinlessness of Christ in 2 Cor 5:21 (cf. John 7:18; 8:46;

[12] Stanley E. Porter (*Idioms of the Greek New Testament,* 2nd ed. [Sheffield: Sheffield Academic, 1994], 91) describes τὸ ἀδύνατον τοῦ νόμου as an appositional accusative preceding the item it defines.

[13] Byrne (*Romans*, 243) points also to 2 Cor 8:9 and 1 Cor 8:6; 10:4; Gal 2:20 as supporting the view that the preexistence of the Son is implied in Rom 8:3. Cf. Brendan Byrne, *"Sons of God—Seed of Abraham": A Study of the Idea of the Sonship of God of All Christians in Paul Against the Jewish Background*, AnBib 83 (Rome: Pontifical Biblical Institute, 1979), 180–81, 198–205. Against Dunn's uncertainty (*Romans 1–8*, 420–21), see Fee, *God's Empowering Presence*, 530–31.

[14] Cranfield, *Romans*, 1:382. Cranfield points out that it was *fallen* human nature that needed to be redeemed. Byrne (*Romans*, 236) similarly says that Paul's language stresses "the depth of divine identification with the human condition." Cf. Peter T. O'Brien, *Commentary on Philippians*, NIGTC (Grand Rapids: Eerdmans, 1991), 224–26. As a human being Jesus was capable of sinning but did not yield to sin and the power of the flesh.

Heb 4:15; 7:27; 9:14; 1 Pet 2:22) and contrasts his perfect obedience with Adam's disobedience (5:19; Phil 2:8).

The words καὶ περὶ ἁμαρτίας ([lit.] "and for sin") belong to the participial clause and express the primary purpose of his being sent. In the LXX the expression περὶ ἁμαρτίας sometimes functions as a technical term for the particular sacrifice known as the "sin offering" (Heb לְחַטָּאת; e.g., Lev 5:7; 9:2; 14:31; Ps 39:7 [ET 40:6]; cf. Heb 10:6, 8; 13:11). It appears in a novel way in Isa 53:10 (rendering Heb אָשָׁם, "guilt offering") with reference to the death of the Suffering Servant. But Paul most likely uses the term in the former sense to identify the death of Jesus as "the sin offering" of the new covenant.[15] By this means God "condemned sin in the flesh" (κατέκρινεν τὴν ἁμαρτίαν ἐν τῇ σαρκί), namely in the person of his perfectly obedient Son. When he offered himself as a sacrifice for sin, he made it possible for sinful human beings to be rescued from the condemnation due to them (v. 1). So the sacrificial and substitutionary dimension to Christ's death is expressed by περὶ ἁμαρτίας, and the penal dimension is indicated by saying God condemned sin in his sinless humanity.[16]

8:4. God's purpose in condemning sin in the person of his Son is indicated now, as Paul explains how the Spirit enables believers to do God's will. Previously, δικαίωμα was used to express "justification" (5:16) and the "righteous act" of Christ in his saving death (5:18). But the expression τὸ δικαίωμα τοῦ νόμου means "the law's requirement" (note the plural δικαιώματα in 2:26). The singular noun suggests that "the law's requirements are essentially a unity, the plurality of commandments being not a confused and confusing conglomeration but a recognizable and intelligible whole, the fatherly will of God for his children."[17] A passive expression (πληρωθῇ ἐν

[15] Dunn (*Romans 1–8*, 422) says, "Such a sacrificial allusion would be wholly natural and unremarkable in a first-century context." Cf. Byrne, *Romans*, 243. Cranfield (*Romans*, 1:382) strangely denies that Paul makes a sacrificial reference here.

[16] Cranfield (*Romans*, 1:382) rightly observes that κατέκρινεν must denote punishment and not simply the sentence of condemnation. Cf. Moo, *Romans* 480–81; Kruse, *Romans*, 327–28. God's justice had to be satisfied to make justification or the definitive forgiveness of sins possible (cf. 3:25–26; 4:4–7).

[17] Cranfield, *Romans*, 1:384. Cf. Gottlob Schrenk, "δικαίωμα," *TDNT* 2:219–23; Jewett, *Romans*, 487. Paul echoes the teaching of Jesus in Mark 12:28–34 and parallels, where Deut 6:4–5 and Lev 19:18 are drawn together to describe the essential demand of the law. Wright ("Romans," 577) takes Paul to mean the "verdict" of life

ἡμῖν) implies that the law's righteous requirement is fulfilled "in us" by God's agency. The promise of the new covenant was that in the coming era God would place his law "within" his people and write it "on their hearts" (Jer 31:33). They would know God's will and be moved to do it. Such renewal would flow from the definitive forgiveness of their sins (Jer 31:34). In a parallel passage God promised to place his Spirit within his people to enable them to keep his law (Ezek 36:26–27).[18] Paul proclaims the fulfillment of these promises in those "who do not walk according to the flesh but according to the Spirit" (τοῖς μὴ κατὰ σάρκα περιπατοῦσιν ἀλλὰ κατὰ πνεῦμα). These words do not establish a condition for the law's requirement to be fulfilled in us but describe a pattern of life directed by God's Spirit, demonstrating his transforming presence.[19] As believers are directed by the Spirit rather than the flesh, the law is written on the heart, and the fruit God desires is produced in their lives (cf. 2:14–15, 26–29 comments; 13:8–10; Gal 5:6, 13–14).[20]

8:5. The γάρ ("for") that links this verse to the preceding one introduces a lengthy reflection on what causes people to walk either according to the flesh or according to the Spirit (v. 4). Those whose state or condition can be described as "according to the flesh" (οἱ κατὰ σάρκα ὄντες) characteristically "think about the things of the flesh" (τὰ τῆς σαρκὸς φρονοῦσιν) or "have their minds set on the things of the flesh."[21] But those who live "according to the Spirit" (οἱ δὲ κατὰ πνεῦμα) set their minds on "the things of the Spirit" (τὰ τοῦ πνεύματος). Paul's aim is "to highlight the radical differences

that the law announces "rather than the behaviour which it requires," but this breaks the link with 2:26 and the parallel with 2:15 ("the work of the law").

[18] Cf. Peterson, *Transformed by God*, 29–43, 136–55.

[19] The verb "walk" is used extensively in the NT, as the Hebrew verb הָלַךְ is in the OT, with the figurative meaning "conduct one's life" (6:4 comment). Opposing norms of conduct are indicated by the prepositional phrases beginning with κατά here.

[20] Moo (*Romans*, 482–85) argues that the law's just demand is perfectly fulfilled in Christ. It is fulfilled in Christians "not though their own acts of obedience but through their incorporation into Christ." Nevertheless, he concludes that Christian behavior, empowered by the Spirit, is "the necessary mark of those in whom this fulfillment takes place." Schreiner (*Romans*, 404–8) opposes a purely forensic view of the law's fulfillment in believers, as does Fee, *God's Empowering Presence*, 534–38.

[21] Cranfield (*Romans*, 1:386) and Dunn (*Romans 1–8*, 425–26) understand the verb φρονεῖν to mean "take someone's side, espouse someone's cause," and argue that the cognate noun in v. 6 describes the "mind" that brings about that commitment. But Moo (*Romans*, 487n81) rightly contends that this is an artificial distinction.

between the flesh and the Spirit as a means of showing why only those who 'walk/think/are' after the Spirit can have eschatological life."[22] People "think" a lot about what they value and desire, and this governs the way they behave (cf. 12:2; Gal 5:16–25; §2.6).

8:6–8. With the connective *γάρ* ("for" [CSB "now"]) and the cognate noun *φρόνημα* ("way of thinking, mind-set"), Paul continues the argument of the previous verse. Mind-set is the key to action, "not, however, just the process of ideas through the brain, but in the stronger sense of the settled and focused activity and concentration that characterizes the one state or the other."[23] The different attitudes and aspirations of the two different realms ("of the flesh" and "of the Spirit") are characterized in terms of their different outcomes ("death" or "life and peace"). Death and life were highlighted as alternatives in 5:17, 21; 6:11, 21–23; 7:9–11; 8:2, and peace was mentioned as the gift of God in 1:7; 2:10; 5:1.[24] The mind of the flesh is set on death (*διότι*, "for, because" [not translated by CSB]) because it is characterized by "hostility to God" (*ἔχθρα εἰς θεόν*; cf. *ἐχθροί* [5:10; 11:28, "enemies"]). Those who have a this-worldly attitude and commitment have no place for God in their thinking. They actually live in a state of enmity toward God, though they may claim to be wise and may even be religious (cf. 1:18–25; 5:10; Eph 2:14, 16). Their hostility is explained by a series of linked clauses: "because (the mindset of the flesh) does not submit to God's law, for it is unable (to do so)" (*τῷ γὰρ νόμῳ τοῦ θεοῦ οὐχ ὑποτάσσεται, οὐδὲ γὰρ δύναται*).[25] This flashback to the position outlined in 7:5, 7–11 should be contrasted with the positive attitude to the law of God portrayed in 7:15–24. There the joyful agreement of the "inner self" with the law of God cannot simply be a description of life in the flesh. Yet apart from the enabling of the Holy Spirit, there is

---

[22] Moo, *Romans*, 486. Compare Dunn, *Romans 1–8*, 425, 428.

[23] Wright, "Romans," 582. Cf. Keener, *The Mind of the Spirit*, 114–15, 127–28. Contrast 1:22, 28 with 12:2, and note Phil 2:5.

[24] These references show that "death" can be a present experience for those outside of Christ and "life and peace" a present experience for Christians. But Paul also envisages an ultimate experience of these realities arising from the eschatological judgment of God (2:6–11 comment).

[25] With Jewett (*Romans*, 488), we may read the middle voice of *ὑποτάσσεται* reflexively to mean "does not submit itself." CSB renders the second *γάρ* "indeed."

ability to do the will of God.[26] Indeed, Paul concludes, "Those who are in the flesh (ἐν σαρκί) cannot please God" (compare 7:5, ἐν τῇ σαρκί). Pleasing God (θεῷ ἀρέσαι) is the goal of those who genuinely belong to Christ (12:1–2; 14:18; cf. 1 Thess 2:4, 15; 4:1; 1 Cor 7:32–34).

8:9. With the simple adversative δέ ("but" [CSB "however"]) and the emphatic pronoun ὑμεῖς ("you"), Paul turns from considering the state of those who are simply "in the flesh" (ἐν σαρκί) to focus on his readers, whom he describes as being "in the Spirit" (ἐν πνεύματι). These are positional statements: flesh and Spirit are realms to which people belong. The result of being "in" one realm or the other is "conditioned patterns of thinking and acting—the one determined by belongingness to the world, the other by belongingness to God."[27] The conjunction εἴπερ expresses some caution ("if indeed"): "Paul summons the readers to consider whether the Spirit indwells them, wanting them to draw the conclusion he does."[28] God's dwelling (οἰκεῖ) in the midst of his people was central to the covenant he established through Moses, and it came to be linked with the sanctuary and its ritual (e.g., Exod 29:43–46; Lev 26:11–12; Ezek 37:26–28). Under the new covenant, however, God promises to place his Spirit within his people (Ezek 36:27) and to dwell among them in a more intimate and permanent way to transform them (2 Cor 3). So the body of each believer can be called "a temple of the Holy Spirit who is in you" (1 Cor 6:19), and a congregation of believers can likewise be called "God's temple" (1 Cor 3:16–17) because the Spirit of God lives in them (cf. Eph 2:18–22). Paul reinforces his point by putting the negative case: "[But] if anyone does not have the Spirit of Christ, he does not belong to him" (CSB does not translate δέ ["but"]). Christians are actually indwelt and possessed by the Spirit of Christ (πνεῦμα Χριστοῦ, cf. Acts 16:7; Gal

[26] Fee (*God's Empowering Presence*, 542) considers that v. 7 clinches his argument that 7:14–25 has nothing to do with a struggle that goes on in the life of the believer. But this conclusion arises from a failure to acknowledge the different attitudes to the law evidenced in these texts.

[27] Dunn, *Romans 1–8*, 428. "In the flesh" cannot be understood in a merely locative sense: Christians are not literally taken out of the flesh until their bodies are redeemed.

[28] Schreiner, *Romans*, 413. Wallace (*Greek Grammar*, 692–94) similarly highlights the rhetorical function of εἴπερ in a conditional sentence.

4:6; Phil 1:19; 1 Pet 1:11). The idea of belonging to Christ (ἔστιν αὐτοῦ) is similarly expressed with the genitive case in 1 Cor 3:23 (ὑμεῖς . . . Χριστοῦ); 15:23; Gal 5:24 (οἱ . . . τοῦ Χριστοῦ). By implication the Spirit of Christ manifests the character of Christ, and only those whose lives demonstrate by character and conduct that the Spirit of Christ is directing them "can claim to be under Christ's lordship."[29]

8:10. Paul advances his argument with a simple condition of fact, beginning with the assumption "now if Christ is in you" (εἰ δὲ Χριστὸς ἐν ὑμῖν). Just as those who are "in the Spirit" are indwelt by the Spirit, so also those who are "in Christ Jesus" (v. 1) have Christ living in them (cf. 2 Cor 13:5; Gal 2:20; Col 1:27). It is clear from vv. 8–9 that Christ is present through the Spirit and that "Christ and the Spirit are perceived in experience as one—Christ known only in and through the Spirit, the Spirit known only as (the Spirit of) Christ."[30] Two consequences follow in Paul's conditional sentence: "The body is dead because of sin, but the Spirit gives life because of righteousness" (τὸ μὲν σῶμα νεκρὸν διὰ ἁμαρτίαν τὸ δὲ πνεῦμα ζωὴ διὰ δικαιοσύνην). The body mentioned here is the body bound for death (7:24, τοῦ σώματος τοῦ θανάτου τούτου ["this body of death"]). Since Christians share this human condition,[31] the clause should be understood concessively in relation to what follows ("although the body is dead because of sin"). Rather than τὸ πνεῦμα referring to the human spirit, the following verse indicates that Paul has in mind the life-giving Spirit of God (cf. v. 2, "the Spirit of life"). The Spirit is given as the source of new life in the present and ultimately brings "life from the dead" (11:15). This is so "because of righteousness" (διὰ δικαιοσύνην), meaning God's righteousness in providing justification through the death of Jesus (cf. 5:17–21). Paul's conclusion here reflects the sequence of his argument in 8:1–4. The Spirit is

[29] Dunn, *Romans 1–8*, 429. Schreiner (*Romans*, 413) points out, "Paul is not addressing what believers claim but what they are, and thus the text emphasizes that all believers have the Spirit." But Dunn makes the further point that the Spirit of Christ will be manifested in Christlikeness.

[30] Dunn, *Romans 1–8*, 431. However, Paul is not saying the Spirit and Christ are identical, only that "they are inseparable in terms of the saving benefits conveyed to believers" (Schreiner, *Romans*, 414). See §2.3.

[31] Cranfield (*Romans*, 1:389) and Dunn (*Romans 1–8*, 431) both oppose the view that the reference is to the death of conversion/baptism. Compare v. 11 (τὰ θνητὰ σώματα, "mortal bodies") and Phil 3:21 ("the body of our humble condition").

given because of the gracious work of God that "inaugurated the new epoch and continues to sustain those in it."[32]

8:11. The climax of this section is a specific promise about physical resurrection. Another condition of fact is used to assure believers about the future consequence of being indwelt by God's Spirit. Picking up the language of v. 9, the first part of Paul's conditional sentence is, "If the Spirit of him who raised Jesus from the dead lives in you." As in other contexts the resurrection of believers from death is closely linked with the resurrection of Jesus (cf. 1 Cor 6:14; 15:20, 23; 2 Cor 4:14; Phil 3:21; 1 Thess 4:14). A shorter version of the same expression is repeated in the next clause, with the change to Χριστόν possibly designed to emphasize that Jesus was raised as the messianic head of his people (ὁ ἐγείρας Χριστὸν ἐκ νεκρῶν, "He who raised Christ from the dead"; cf. Col 1:18). In view of what was said in connection with v. 10 ("the body is dead because of sin"), the promise that God "will also bring your mortal bodies to life" (ζῳοποιήσει καὶ τὰ θνητὰ σώματα ὑμῶν) must refer to final resurrection (cf. 1 Cor 15:22), not to spiritual regeneration in the present. Some ancient manuscripts read διὰ τὸ ἐνοικοῦν αὐτοῦ πνεύμα ἐν ὑμῖν ("because of the Spirit who dwells within you"), but the best attested reading is διὰ τοῦ ἐνοικοῦντος αὐτοῦ πνεύματος ἐν ὑμῖν ("through his Spirit who lives in you").[33] The Spirit's role in creation is highlighted in Gen 1:2; Job 33:4; Ps 104:30, and he is appropriately mentioned here as God's agent in bringing believers to share in the new creation through bodily resurrection. "The Spirit's life-giving power is not circumscribed by the mortality of the body, but overcomes and transforms that mortality into the immortality of eternal life in a resurrected body."[34]

---

[32] Dunn, *Romans 1–8*, 432. Cf. Schreiner, *Romans*, 415; Kruse, *Romans*, 333–34; Keener, *The Mind of the Spirit*, 132–35.

[33] The accusative reading is found in B D F G Ψ and numerous minuscule and fathers, while the genitive reading is found in א A C P^c numerous minuscule and fathers. The versions are fairly evenly divided. Metzger (*Textual Commentary*, 456) points out that the weight of B when associated with D G (as here) is considerably lessened. The combination of text-types favors the genitive reading. Cranfield (*Romans*, 1.391–92) explains why the genitive may have been altered to the accusative by copyists, but Fee (*God's Empowering Presence*, 543n205) argues for the primacy of the accusative.

[34] Moo, *Romans*, 493. Fee (*God's Empowering Presence*, 553) doubts that the Spirit is ever the agent of the resurrection, but Schreiner (*Romans*, 416n8) points to

8:12–13. Paul introduces an ethical challenge, using the inferential "so then" (Ἄρα οὖν) and addressing his Roman readers as "brothers and sisters" again.[35] He pointedly includes himself in the claim that "we are not obligated to the flesh to live according to the flesh" (ὀφειλέται ἐσμὲν οὐ τῇ σαρκὶ τοῦ κατὰ σάρκα ζῆν). Nevertheless, he uses the first of two conditional clauses to imply that Christians can still be influenced and led by the flesh. Applying v. 6a to his readers with a second-person plural verb, he warns, "Because if you live according to the flesh, you are going to die" (εἰ γὰρ κατὰ σάρκα ζῆτε, μέλλετε ἀποθνήσκειν). The present tense (ζῆτε) implies continuing in the way of the flesh, for example, giving yourself to a life of material or sensual indulgence. Instead of a simple future tense, the verb μέλλετε is used with the infinitive ("you are about to die") to emphasize the certainty of eternal death as the punishment for that way of life. A second conditional clause shows that God's Spirit is the means of putting to death "the deeds of the body" (πράξεις τοῦ σώματος).[36] The instrumental dative πνεύματι ("by the Spirit") indicates that the Holy Spirit enables this rejection rather than being "a tool in the hands of Christians, wielded and managed by them."[37]

In v. 14 the Spirit leads the believer in opposing sin, while v. 13 emphasizes the Spirit's empowerment for that task. "Body" and "flesh" are clearly linked: "the mindset of the flesh" is the cause of the body's misdeeds. These include relational failures, not merely physical acts (cf. 1:28–32; Col 3:9).[38] The present indicative θανατοῦτε ("put to death") signifies continuous activity and functions like an imperative. Paul uses parallel terms elsewhere (Gal 5:24, ἐσταύρωσαν ["have crucified"]; Col 3:5, νεκρώσατε ["put to death']

Ezek 37:5–6, 9–10, 14 as a precedent and notes that 1 Cor 6:14 hints at the Spirit's work when speaking about resurrection by God's power. Cf. 1:4 comment.

[35] As in 5:18; 7:3, 25; 9:16, 18; 14:12, 19, the words Ἄρα οὖν introduce an important transition in the argument. As in 1:13; 7:1, 4, adding the redundant form of address ἀδελφοί ("brothers and sisters") "helps ensure that the reader slows down and pays close attention" (Runge, *Discourse Grammar*, 120).

[36] The parallel syntax with different content has the effect of sharpening the contrast (ibid., 230).

[37] Cranfield, *Romans*, 1:394 (noting that the reference to being "led by the Spirit" in v. 14 is a safeguard against such a manipulative view). Moo (*Romans*, 494–96) comments on the interplay of divine sovereignty and human responsibility in this process.

[38] Cf. Jewett, *Romans*, 495. Fee (*God's Empowering Presence*, 558–59) makes an artificial distinction between body and flesh here. Cf. Kruse, *Romans*, 335–36.

to convey the same idea. Radical rejection of the demands of the flesh in favor of the demands of the Spirit is required. "Mortification of the flesh" as traditionally understood involves self-inflicted bodily pain in order to gain control over the body. But Paul is talking about something different: drawing on the Spirit's power to reject everything we know to be sinful and positively walking in the way of the Spirit (cf. Gal 5:16, 25–26). This too can be painful, but it produces the fruit God desires. The challenge to choose "life" (ζήσεσθε) instead of "death" echoes Moses's words in Deut 30:15–20. But the difference under the new covenant is that we have the Spirit to keep us in the way of life, and the consequence of our choice is eternal.[39]

8:14. Another connective (γάρ, "for") links what follows to v. 13b. Being "led by God's Spirit" (πνεύματι θεοῦ ἄγονται) is a way of describing what it means to "put to death the deeds of the body" by the Spirit.[40] Paul's focus here is on the moral life of believers (cf. Gal 5:18), not on the giving of some new revelation or insight. The Spirit's leading will influence practical, everyday decisions about relationships and how to spend time, money, resources, and talents. At a personal level, "the daily, hourly putting to death of the schemings and enterprises of the sinful flesh by means of the Spirit is a matter of being led, directed, impelled, controlled by the Spirit."[41] The new idea here is that those who are led by the Spirit show themselves to be true "sons of God" (οὗτοι υἱοὶ θεοῦ εἰσιν). Israel was sometimes identified in Scripture as God's "son" or "sons" (e.g., Exod 4:22–23; Deut 14:1; Isa 1:2; 43:6; Jer 3:19; 31:9; Hos 1:10; 11:1). This designation embraced both males and females. In the wilderness they were led by his powerful presence (Exod 13:21–22; 14:19; 40:38). God's purpose was to humble and test them, to know what was in their heart, whether they would keep his commands (Deut 8:2). Paul's claim is that the sons of God in the gospel era are

[39] Thomas J. Deidun (*New Covenant Morality in Paul*, AnBib 89 [Rome: Pontifical Biblical Institute, 1981], 80) concludes that "the Spirit of holiness" (1:4) has taken possession of Christians, demanding our continuing yes to "God's liberating and vivifying activity in past, present, and future." Cf. Peterson, *Possessed by God*, 112–14.

[40] The pronoun ὅσοι can be understood in an inclusive or an exclusive sense. But Schreiner (*Romans*, 422) argues that "both can be considered true from different angles."

[41] Cranfield, *Romans*, 1:395. Cf. Fee, *God's Empowering Presence*, 563–64; Schreiner, *Romans*, 496.

identified by the indwelling presence and direction of the Holy Spirit (vv. 9–13). Sonship is redefined, and believing Jews and Gentiles belong together to this company (cf. 2 Cor 6:18–7:1; Gal 3:26–4:7).

8:15. Once again the connective γάρ ("for"; not translated by CSB) suggests a clarification of what has gone before. Paul explains that the Spirit they received is not "a spirit of slavery to fall back into fear" (οὐ . . . ἐλάβετε πνεῦμα δουλείας πάλιν εἰς φόβον). A similar pattern of speech can be found in 1 Cor 2:12; 2 Tim 1:7, where a negative statement highlights the significance of the positive. The fear they experienced, either in paganism or Judaism, indicated the spiritual bondage in which they once lived (cf. Gal 4:7–11, 15: 5:1). Paul does not imply that there is "a spirit of slavery" but simply asserts that God's Spirit has delivered his people from slavery and fear.[42]

Turning to Christ makes it possible to receive "the Spirit of adoption, by whom we cry out, '*Abba*, Father!'" The term πνεῦμα υἱοθεσίας indicates that the Spirit brings about "adoption as a son" or "sonship," testifying to the relationship with God made possible by the sending of "his own Son" (v. 3; cf. Gal 4:4–5; Eph 1:5). Adoption was not common in Israel but was practiced in the Greco-Roman world, where it was normally designated by other terms.[43] The notion of "adoption" may be implicit in what Paul says here, but "sonship" is a better translation because it maintains a verbal and theological link with v. 14 ("God's sons"). When Paul uses the word υἱοθεσία with reference to Israel (9:4), he doubtless has in mind the status and privileges of "sonship" attributed to God's people in various OT contexts (cf. v. 14 comment). Those who relate to God through his Son the Messiah and receive his Spirit are God's "sons" under the new covenant. This raises questions about the status of unbelieving Jews that must be answered in chapters 9–11.

---

[42] The genitive δουλείας expresses direction or purpose: God's Spirit was not given to bring about slavery (Fee, *God's Empowering Presence*, 565; Jewett, *Romans*, 497). Moo (*Romans*, 500) rightly critiques the view that πνεῦμα δουλείας refers to the work of the Spirit in the old age under the law.

[43] Cf. W. v. Martitz, "υἱοθεσία," *TDNT* 8:397–98. The word υἱοθεσία first appears in the second century BC but does not occur at all in the LXX. James M. Scott, (*Adoption as Sons of God: An Exegetical Investigation into the Background of* Υἱοθεσία *in the Pauline Corpus*, WUNT 2/48. [Tübingen: Mohr, 1992], 3–114) discusses the Jewish background, but Byrne (*Romans*, 252) disputes his conclusions, arguing that "sonship" rather than "adoption" is the best translation.

A critical role for the Spirit is indicated by the expression ἐν ᾧ κράζομεν· αββα ὁ πατήρ ("by whom we cry out, '*Abba*, Father!'" [cf. Gal 4:6]).[44] Paul expected his Gentile readers to know the Aramaic term "Abba," which was used by Jesus in his Gethsemane prayer (Mark 14:36) and doubtless lay behind his other addresses to God as "Father" (e.g., Matt 11:25; John 17:1). When he taught his disciples to pray as he did (Matt 6:9; Luke 11:2), he invited them to share to some extent in the intimacy of his relationship with the Father.[45] Significantly, Paul identifies the Spirit of *Christ* (v. 9) as making this possible. The verb κράζειν has a range of meanings, such as "cry out, scream, shriek" (BDAG). In the LXX it is often used to translate different Hebrew words for crying aloud or calling upon God (e.g., Pss 3:4 [LXX 3:5]; 4:3 [LXX 4:4]; 18:6 [LXX 17:7]; 34:6 [33:7]). Here it can be understood generally to refer to any kind of urgent prayer, with the first-person plural signifying a crying out together. The Spirit bestows and confirms the "sonship" of believers, enabling them to express dependence on God as Father, particularly in times of testing.[46]

8:16–17. Without a specific connection to the preceding verse, the first sentence here functions as a solemn and emphatic statement about the Spirit's work: "The Spirit himself testifies together with our spirit that we are God's children." CSB has rightly translated the neuter expression αὐτὸ τὸ πνεῦμα "the Spirit *himself*": the grammar does not mean the Spirit is an impersonal force. Paul's previous association of the Spirit with the indwelling Christ (vv. 9–11) implies that the Spirit is personal. Most likely, συμμαρτυρεῖ τῷ πνεύματι ἡμῶν means the Holy Spirit and our own human spirit are linked together as two witnesses to the fact that we are children of

[44] Cranfield (*Romans*, 1.398) argues convincingly against reading a full stop after υἱοθεσία and beginning the next sentence with ἐν ᾧ κράζομεν αββα ὁ πατήρ (NRSV).

[45] Cf. Joachim Jeremias, *The Prayers of Jesus* (London: SCM, 1967), 57–65. Fee (*God's Empowering Presence*, 410–12) assesses the scholarly response to the arguments of Jeremias. "Abba" was the regular Aramaic word for a male parent used by both adults and children. A rendering such as "Daddy" does not capture the respectful sense of the term. Paul adds ὁ πατήρ ("Father") to clarify the meaning of the Aramaic.

[46] Moo (*Romans*, 501–2) compares Gal 4:5–6 and the Spirit's bestowal and confirmation of sonship. Moo further observes that we miss the connotations of the verb κράζειν if we neglect its allusion to the emotions. Cf. Jewett, *Romans*, 498–99.

God ("testifies together with our spirit").[47] The human spirit is also mentioned in 1:9; 1 Cor 2:11; 5:3–5; 7:34; 14:14; 16:18; 1 Thess 5:23. We become children of God by the Spirit's enabling, and the certainty of that adoption is given as the Spirit prompts us to call upon God as Father. The more inclusive term "children of God" (τέκνα θεοῦ) replaces "sons" as Paul's focus turns toward the topic of inheritance (εἰ δὲ τέκνα, καὶ κληρονόμοι, "and if children, also heirs").

In the ancient world exclusive shares of an inheritance were often given to eldest or favored sons, but "now each member of the new community of faith, whether male or female, Gentile or Jew, Greek or barbarian, slave or free, child or adult, shares equally in the patrimony."[48] The promise to Abraham and his offspring to inherit "the world" (4:13 comment) is here explained in terms of being "heirs of God and coheirs with Christ" (κληρονόμοι μὲν θεοῦ, συγκληρονόμοι δὲ Χριστοῦ).[49] Paul's first expression implies that believers come to share in the life and glory of God himself, while the second indicates that they do so in company with the Messiah, who has already entered into that inheritance (v. 34).[50] An important challenge is introduced with the conjunction εἴπερ ("if indeed"). Paul is describing "a real condition that must be met for believers to enjoy the inheritance."[51] As in 6:4–6, 8, compound verbs are used to highlight the union of believers with Christ on the way to glory. If indeed we "suffer with him" (συμπάσχομεν), it is for a purpose: "so that we may also be glorified with him" (ἵνα καὶ συνδοξασθῶμεν). "For the glory of the kingdom of God is attained only through

[47] Compare the use of this compound verb in 2:15; 9:1. Cranfield (*Romans*, 1:403) argues that the prefix loses its force here and the dative means the Spirit testifies "to our spirit" (so also Wallace, *Greek Grammar*, 160–61). Contrast Fee, *God's Empowering Presence*, 568–69; Schreiner, *Romans*, 426.

[48] Jewett, *Romans*, 502. Nigel M. Watson ("'And If Children, Then Heirs' [Rom 8:17]—Why Not Sons?" *ABR* 49 [2001], 53–56) points to evidence for the Roman practice of leaving estates to daughters and not just sons.

[49] Cranfield (*Romans*, 1:405–7) discusses the differences between Paul's teaching about inheritance in Rom 4:13–14; 8:17; and Gal 4:7. In later Judaism the inheritance of God's people is not so much linked to a physical space but more generally describes life in God's presence (e.g., Pss. Sol. 14:10; 1 En. 40:9; 4 Macc 18:3). Cf. Werner Foerster, "κληρονόμος," *TDNT* 3:776–81.

[50] Cf. Schreiner, *Romans*, 427–28; Wallace, *Greek Grammar*, 129.

[51] Schreiner, *Romans*, 428. Cf. Dunn, *Romans 1–8*, 456 and my comment on 8:9.

participation in Christ, and belonging to Christ cannot but bring our participation in the sufferings of Christ."[52]

Bridge

Paul resumes the theme of assurance from 5:1–11 and develops it in the light of his intervening argument. Those who doubt their relationship with God because of sin need to know that "there is now no condemnation for those in Christ Jesus." This is another way of affirming justification and peace with God through the atoning death of Jesus (cf. 5:1, 9–11). Those who doubt their ability to persevere in the face of temptation and various forms of testing need to have the assurance of the Spirit's direction and power. Having spoken about the struggle involved in belonging to the eras of Adam and Christ at one and the same time (7:14–25), Paul now affirms that belonging to Christ is the more decisive reality, "since Christ is the man who has already conquered sin and death."[53] God condemned sin in the person of his Son and gave his Spirit to make it possible for the just requirement of his law to be fulfilled in his new covenant people. The sharp contrast between "the mind-set of the flesh" and "the mind-set of the Spirit" exposes two radically different life orientations and their consequences. Believers need to be assured about their present and future relationship with God as those who are "in the Spirit." But there is an important challenge in vv. 12–14 about living consistently in this relationship. Being directed and empowered by the Spirit, we can "put to death the deeds of the body" and live in a way that is pleasing to God. The Spirit also makes it possible for us to cry to God as Father in whatever circumstances we find ourselves, thus reassuring us that we are his children. As the Spirit produces in us a Christlikeness of attitude and behavior, he enables us to suffer with Christ and convinces us that we will be resurrected with him to share in his glory.

---

[52] Moo, *Romans*, 506. Cf. Phil 1:29; 3:10; 2 Cor 1:5. Wallace (*Greek Grammar*, 473–74) describes the ἵνα clause in 8:17 as expressing both purpose and result.

[53] Dunn, *Romans 1–8*, 435. Despite his unconvincing argument about the two-sidedness of the law, Dunn has much to say about the relationship between Rom 7 and 8 that is helpful. James I. Packer (*Knowing God* [London: Hodder and Stoughton, 1973], 186) contends that adoption is "the highest privilege that the gospel offers: higher even than justification."

B. Perseverance and Hope (8:18–39)

18 For I consider that the sufferings of this present time are
not worth comparing with the glory that is going to be revealed
to us. 19 For the creation eagerly waits with anticipation for God's
sons to be revealed. 20 For the creation was subjected to futility—
not willingly, but because of him who subjected it—in the hope
21 that the creation itself will also be set free from the bondage to
decay into the glorious freedom of God's children. 22 For we know
that the whole creation has been groaning together with labor
pains until now. 23 Not only that, but we ourselves who have the
Spirit as the firstfruits—we also groan within ourselves, eagerly
waiting for adoption, the redemption of our bodies. 24 Now in this
hope we were saved, but hope that is seen is not hope, because
who hopes for what he sees? 25 Now if we hope for what we do not
see, we eagerly wait for it with patience.

26 In the same way the Spirit also helps us in our weakness,
because we do not know what to pray for as we should, but the
Spirit himself intercedes for us with unspoken groanings. 27 And
he who searches our hearts knows the mind of the Spirit, because
he intercedes for the saints according to the will of God.

28 We know that all things work together for the good of those
who love God, who are called according to his purpose. 29 For
those he foreknew he also predestined to be conformed to the
image of his Son, so that he would be the firstborn among many
brothers and sisters. 30 And those he predestined, he also called;
and those he called, he also justified; and those he justified, he
also glorified.

31 What then are we to say about these things? If God is for
us, who is against us? 32 He did not even spare his own Son but
offered him up for us all. How will he not also with him grant us
everything? 33 Who can bring an accusation against God's elect?
God is the one who justifies. 34 Who is the one who condemns?
Christ Jesus is the one who died, but even more, has been raised;
he also is at the right hand of God and intercedes for us. 35 Who
can separate us from the love of Christ? Can affliction or distress
or persecution or famine or nakedness or danger or sword? 36 As
it is written:

> **Because of you**
> **we are being put to death all day long;**
> **we are counted as sheep to be slaughtered.**

[37]No, in all these things we are more than conquerors through him who loved us. [38]For I am persuaded that neither death nor life, nor angels nor rulers, nor things present nor things to come, nor powers, [39]nor height nor depth, nor any other created thing will be able to separate us from the love of God that is in Christ Jesus our Lord.

Context

This passage develops the notion that we suffer with Christ so that we may also be glorified with him (v. 17). It resumes the theme announced in 5:1–5, that the Spirit confirms "the hope of the glory of God" in the face of suffering by infusing our hearts with God's love. Suffering is first presented in a broad, creational context (vv. 18–25). Christians groan with the rest of creation, awaiting final redemption but living in hope because the Spirit has been given as the "firstfruits" of God's final harvest. Moreover, the Spirit groans with believers as he intercedes on their behalf (vv. 26–27). Reflecting on God's overall plan of salvation, Paul particularly focuses on the trials Christians face (vv. 28–39). Drawing these various threads together, he concludes a major division of the argument that began in 5:1–11, creating a "ring composition" or chiasm.[54] However, this section recalls various themes presented in 3:21–8:30, and it brings to a climax the exposition of the gospel in the letter so far.[55]

Structure

The problem of suffering is first addressed in relation to "the glory that is going to be revealed to us" (vv. 18–21). Glorification is associated with the revelation of "God's sons," which is linked to the hope that "the creation itself will also be set free from the bondage to decay into the glorious freedom of God's children." In a groaning creation Christians groan because they have the Spirit as a pledge that their adoption will be consummated in bodily redemption

[54] Cf. Moo, *Romans*, 293–94; Wright, "Romans," 508–14. Dunn (*Romans 1–8*, 467) argues that Paul is speaking about the fulfillment of Israel's hopes in 8:18–30 and is preparing for chapters 9–11 by raising questions about Israel's future.

[55] Dunn (*Romans 1–8*, 467) contends that 8:18–30, with its "glory" motif serving as a bracket for the whole section, actually climaxes the argument that began in 1:18: "Paul presents this cosmic outworking of salvation in strong Adam terms, as the final reversal of man's failure and climax of his restoration."

(vv. 22–23). The Spirit's intercessory work keeps us in this hope (vv. 24–27). God's overarching plan for his children—from foreknowledge to glorification—involves being "conformed to the image of his Son" (vv. 28–30). This gives a positive, transformative perspective to our suffering. The final section of the chapter underlines the certainty of the Christian hope (vv. 31–39). A crescendo of questions and answers highlights the themes of God's providential care (vv. 31–32), the eternal security of believers (vv. 33–34), and ultimate victory through suffering (vv. 35–37), before Paul utters his climactic words about the enduring and sustaining love of God (vv. 38–39).

Outline:

1. Suffering and glory (vv. 18–30)
2. The enduring love of God (vv. 31–39)

8:18. As in 3:28; 6:11, λογίζομαι ("I consider") indicates a firm conviction, which in Paul's case has been reached by "rational thought on the basis of the gospel."[56] Those who share his eschatological conviction live in hope even as they suffer. A clear link with the preceding verse is provided by γάρ ("for"), but Paul does not develop the causal connection between suffering and glory suggested by v. 17 until vv. 28–30. Indeed he sets the specific issue of suffering with Christ in the wider context of suffering in a fallen world. This could include sickness, disability, physical and mental pain, poverty, isolation, and bereavement. Paul's simple proposition is that "the sufferings of this present time" (τὰ παθήματα τοῦ νῦν καιροῦ) "are not worth comparing with" (οὐκ ἄξια . . . πρός) "the glory that is going to be revealed to us" (τὴν μέλλουσαν δόξαν ἀποκαλυφθῆναι εἰς ἡμᾶς).[57] As in 3:26; 11:5, "this present time" refers to the era of fulfillment in which God is bringing his new creation into being (8:22–23). Glory is frequently mentioned as the goal of God's saving purpose (e.g., 2:7, 10; 5:2; 8:21; 9:23; 1 Cor 2:7; 15:43). There is a sense in which God's glory is already experienced by believers

[56] Cranfield, *Romans*, 1:408.

[57] Byrne (*Romans*, 259) suggests that "a small price to pay" is a good way of bringing out the sense of calculation implied by οὐκ ἄξια (as in Prov 3:15; 8:11 LXX). Cf. 2 Cor 4:17.

through Christ and the Spirit,[58] but Paul mostly highlights the vast difference between the present and the future. In Jewish tradition, when Adam sinned, he lost the glory that was his as one created in the image and likeness of God (Gen 1:26–27; Ps 8:5; cf. Wis 2:23–24).[59] Paul indicates that "Christ alone has fulfilled the divine purpose in making man, and man is brought to that divine goal by sharing in or being conformed to Christ's glory."[60] The revelation that will literally come "toward us" (εἰς ἡμᾶς) will be utterly transforming. God's children will escape from "the bondage of decay" (v. 21), enjoy bodily redemption (v. 23), and be changed into the likeness of his Son (v. 29).

8:19. As he begins to elucidate the claim of v. 18 (γάρ, "for"), Paul personifies the created order as eagerly anticipating something. The noun ἀποκαραδοκία (BDAG, "eager expectation") only appears in Christian writings (cf. Phil 1:20), conveying the image of craning the neck to see what is coming. Literally, Paul says "the eager expectation of the creation waits for [ἀπεκδέχεται] the revelation of God's sons." The creation personified here (ἡ κτίσις) includes "the sum total of sub-human nature both animate and inanimate."[61] Believers are excluded from this reference since they are the subject of the revelation. Unbelievers by definition do not have this expectation. Angels are also excluded because they are not subject to physical "decay" (v. 21), though angels are included in Paul's broader use of the term "creation" in v. 39. As in v. 18, "the revelation" (τὴν . . . ἀποκάλυψιν) is an approaching eschatological event (cf. 2:5; 1 Cor 1:7; 2 Thess 1:7). Various tests for identifying the sons of God were provided in vv. 14–15, but the ultimate revelation is associated with the redemption of their bodies (v. 23). The created order has a "hope" of being liberated from "the bondage to decay" and sharing (lit.) "the freedom of the glory of God's children" (v. 21).

---

[58] Cf. Cranfield, *Romans*, 1:409–10. Compare 2 Cor 3:18 (ἀπὸ δόξης εἰς δόξαν, "from glory to glory"); 4:4, 6.

[59] Cf. Apoc. Mos. 20:2–3; 21.6; 3 Bar. 4.16; Gen. Rab. 12:6; 1QS 4:22–23; CD 3:19–20; 4QpPs[a] 3:1–2. Jewett (*Romans*, 510–11) summarizes the way OT writers speak about divine glory and its eschatological manifestation.

[60] Dunn, *Romans 1–8*, 457. Cf. 2 Cor 4:4, 6; Phil 3:21; Col 3:4; 2 Thess 2:14.

[61] Cranfield, *Romans*, 1.411–12. Cranfield discusses a range of alternative interpretations. Nature is personified as shouting and singing together for joy in Ps 65:12–13 and mourning in Isa 24:4; Jer 4:28; 12:4. Cf. Wis 16:24; 19:6.

8:20. Once again the conjunction γάρ ("for") shows the continuity of Paul's argument. The creation eagerly awaits transformation because it was "subjected to futility" (τῇ ματαιότητι ἡ κτίσις ὑπετάγη). Most likely this alludes to Gen 3:17–19, where God placed a curse on the ground because of humanity's rebellion against him (cf. 4 Ezra 7:11–12; 9:19–20). "Futility" means "the sub-human creation has been subjected to the frustration of not being able properly to fulfill the purpose of its existence, God having appointed that without man it should not be made perfect."[62] Futility is also a characteristic of human thinking in this fallen world (1:21, ἐματαιώθησαν ["became futile"]). A futility about the created order makes it a suitable environment for those who refuse to honor God as God. Subjection to futility was not something over which the creation had any control (οὐχ ἑκοῦσα, "not willingly"), but it happened "because of him who subjected it" (διὰ τὸν ὑποτάξαντα), as God's judicial decision.[63] With the strong adversative ἀλλά ("but"), Paul returns to the theme of hope, asserting that God subjected the creation to futility "in hope" (ἐφ' ἑλπίδι). This may allude to the promise of Gen 3:15 (as reflected in Rom 16:20).

8:21. The content of creation's hope is introduced by the conjunction ὅτι ("that").[64] In association with the resurrection of believers, "the creation itself will also be set free from the bondage to decay." This hope was variously expressed in Jewish writings (e.g., Isa 11:6–9; 65:17, 25; 66:22; Ezek 34:25–31; Jub. 1:29; 23:26–29; 1 En. 24–25). "The bondage to decay" (τῆς δουλείας τῆς φθορᾶς) involves being captive to corruption and death. But creation will be

[62] Cranfield, *Romans*, 1:413–14. The word ματαιότης occurs thirty-nine times in Ecclesiastes with reference to the disorder and frustration of life in this fallen world. Cf. Jewett, *Romans*, 513–14.

[63] The passive ὑπετάγη suggests that God is the agent of this subjection, and the participial expression τὸν ὑποτάξαντα ("the one who subjected") confirms this. Byrne (*Romans*, 258, 260–61) takes Adam "the subduer" to be the implied subject, but this view is critiqued by Moo, *Romans*, 515–16.

[64] Most of the oldest and best witnesses read ὅτι (𝔓[46] A B C D[2] 33 81 etc.), but a few read διότι (א D* F G etc.), which probably results from dittography, repeating the last syllable of ἐλπίδι (so Metzger, *Textual Commentary*, 456). Cranfield (*Romans*, 1:415) argues that διότι ("because, for") as the harder reading is more likely to be the original, introducing an explanation of why the creation was subjected in hope.

brought into (lit.) "the freedom of the glory of God's children."[65] Bondage will be replaced by freedom and decay by glory. Paul elsewhere indicates that this will take place when the Lord Jesus Christ transforms "the body of our humble condition into the likeness of his glorious body, by the power that enables him to subject everything to himself" (Phil 3:20–21; cf. 1 Cor 15:20–28). "The entire material universe will share the destiny of Christ's people—harmony with the divine will through re-creation—just as it shared in the consequences of human sin. So it is that the 'new heavens and new earth' correspond to man's new, resurrection body."[66]

8:22. The argument in vv. 19–21 is now expressed in a more dramatic way, with the introductory formula suggesting that Paul's readers share his perspective (*οἴδαμεν γὰρ ὅτι*, "for we know that"; cf. 2:2; 3:19; 7:14; 8:28). What believers know is that "the whole creation has been groaning together with labor pains until now." It is easy to observe how the natural world suffers from human neglect and abuse, but only from biblical teaching do we learn about the subjection of the whole created order to "groaning" as an expression of God's wrath against humanity's rebellion (v. 20). Moreover, only from Scripture do we learn that the creation has a hope of liberation and transformation (v. 21). Two verbs with the prefix *σύν* ("with") express the suffering of different parts of the creation in company with one another (*συστενάζει καὶ συνωδίνει*).[67] The image of a woman in labor particularly conveys the sense of suffering with the hope of new birth. "All creation waits together for the rebirth, the new birth of the world, which entails the coming into being of a new heaven

[65] CSB has understood *τῆς δόξης* in the expression *εἰς τὴν ἐλευθερίαν τῆς δόξης* adjectivally ("glorious"), but the parallel with *ἀπὸ τῆς δουλείας τῆς φθορᾶς* suggests it should be translated "the freedom of the glory" (NRSV, ESV). Contrast Wallace, *Greek Grammar*, 87–88.

[66] Murray J. Harris, *Raised Immortal: Resurrection and Immortality in the New Testament* (Basingstoke: Marshall, Morgan & Scott, 1983), 170. Cf. Isa 65:17–25; 2 Pet 3:13; Rev 21:1. Jewett (*Romans*, 514–15) shows how these hopes were developed in later Jewish texts. He concludes that "Paul's premise is that humans and the creation are inter-dependent and that human fulfillment is contextual and cosmic."

[67] This is not merely an intensive use of the preposition. The verb *στενάζω* ("sigh, groan") and the cognate noun occur frequently in the LXX. Cf. Johannes Schneider, "*στενάζω, στεναγμός, συστενάζω*," *TDNT* 7:600–603. The earth languishes and mourns because of its inhabitants (Isa 24:4–7; Hos 4:1–3; 4 Ezra 7.1–4). It may even cry out and its furrows weep together because of human sin (Job 31:38–40).

and a new earth."[68] The concluding "until now" (ἄχρι τοῦ νῦν) should be given its full eschatological force: this is "the 'now' of eschatological salvation in which the process of salvation is being worked out (cf. 3:21; 7:6; 8:1)."[69] Even though Jesus has done everything necessary to bring about "the restoration of all things" (Acts 3:21), we must still live in a creation "groaning" for redemption.

8:23. With a comparative expression (οὐ μόνον δέ, ἀλλὰ καί, [lit] "not only so, but also"], cf. 5:3), Paul points to the way believers share in the groaning of creation. "We ourselves who have the Spirit as the firstfruits" (αὐτοὶ τὴν ἀπαρχὴν τοῦ πνεύματος ἔχοντες) have the divine pledge of a greater gift to come. The word ἀπαρχή was widely used for the firstfruits of fields or flocks offered to God (e.g., Deut 18:4; 26:2, 10; Num 18:8–12), but here it is employed with reference to God's gift of the Spirit to his people. The Spirit himself is that gift (genitive of apposition), elsewhere described as "a down payment" or "pledge" of what is to come (2 Cor 1:22; 5:5; Eph 1:14, ἀρραβών).[70] "Firstfruits" evokes the image of God's final harvest, which is already underway, as the Spirit brings people to faith in Christ. Nevertheless, with an emphatic "we also" (ἡμεῖς καὶ αὐτοί), Paul asserts that Christians groan within themselves (ἐν ἑαυτοῖς στενάζομεν). We groan because we are still in a body subject to futility, sin, and decay (cf. 7:24; 2 Cor 5:2, 4) and are part of a groaning creation. The Spirit does not free us from this but "actually creates or at least heightens the tension and brings it to more anguished

---

[68] Georg Bertram, "ὠδίν, ὠδίνω," *TDNT* 9:673. Bertram discusses NT use of such terminology (without the prefix) in the light of LXX usage (e.g., Isa 26:17; 66:8; Jer 4:31; Hos 13:13; Mic 4:9–10). It was especially used in rabbinic literature in relation to the "birthpangs" of the Messiah. Cf. Matt 24:8; Mark 13:8; John 16:20b–22. Dunn (*Romans 1–8*, 472–73) points to biblical precedents for this concept.

[69] Dunn, *Romans 1–8*, 473. Cf. 3:26 (ἐν τῷ νῦν καιρῷ, "at the present time"). Dunn (489) concludes that Paul's thought "cherishes as much the certain hope of that deliverance as of its nearness."

[70] Gerhard Delling ("ἀπαρχή," *TDNT* 1:484–86) discusses different metaphorical uses of the term, including Rom 11:16; 1 Cor 16:15; Rev 14:4. In 1 Cor 15:20, 23 the resurrected Christ is "the firstfruits of those who have fallen asleep." Judith M. Gundry Volf (*Paul and Perseverance: Staying in and Falling Away* [Louisville: Westminster John Knox, 1990], 28–33) compares the notion of the Spirit as the divine "seal" (2 Cor 1:22; Eph 1:13; 4:30), providing both authentication of ownership and protection.

expression."[71] This is not the groaning of complaint but the groaning of frustrated longing and hope. We share the "futility" and "the bondage to decay" that characterize life in this world but do so as those who know the love of God and are confident about ultimate deliverance. So "the Spirit of adoption" (v. 15) enables us to "wait eagerly" (ἀπεκδεχόμενοι, as in v. 19) for the final manifestation and full enjoyment of our "sonship" (υἱοθεσίαν).[72] This is defined in terms of (lit.) "the redemption of our body" (τὴν ἀπολύτρωσιν τοῦ σώματος ἡμῶν), meaning the liberation of our bodies from futility and corruption by physical resurrection (cf. 1 Cor 15:42–44, 50). Paul is not talking about the release of souls from bodies but about new bodies for God's renewed people, fit for living in his new creation.

8:24–25. In the next linked clause (τῇ γὰρ ἐλπίδι ἐσώθημεν, "now in this hope we were saved"), the definite article is translated "this" because it refers back to the hope of bodily redemption mentioned at the end of v. 23.[73] Paul uses the aorist tense in a summary way (cf. vv. 29–30 comment). The passive voice identifies salvation as something accomplished by God (cf. Eph 2:5, 8; 2 Tim 1:9; Titus 3:5). The qualifying phrase "in hope" makes clear that the final effect of salvation is still to be experienced (cf. 5:9–10). The next sentence compares hope and sight, emphasizing the future orientation of hope ("but hope that is seen is not hope"). Once something hoped for is seen, it can no longer be a hope, "because who hopes for what he sees?" (ὃ γὰρ βλέπει τίς ἐλπίζει;).[74] So Paul expresses his main point with a simple condition of fact: "Now if we hope for what we do not

[71] Dunn, *Romans 1–8*, 474. Byrne (*Romans*, 263) says, "The Spirit engenders within believers a certain 'restlessness' with their lot at the present time when the new age 'overlaps' with the old (cf. v. 18)."

[72] Several witnesses, chiefly Western (𝔓[46vid] D G 614 it[dg] and others), omit υἱοθεσίαν here, probably because copyists saw a contradiction with v. 15. However, as the harder and best attested reading, it should be retained and explained with reference to the following phrase. See my comment on the translation of υἱοθεσία in v. 15.

[73] Wallace (*Greek Grammar*, 217–20) discusses the anaphoric (previous reference) use of the definite article. Contextually, the dative τῇ ἐλπίδι appears to parallel ἐφ' ἐλπίδι (v. 20, "in hope") and is locative rather than instrumental, pointing to the "sphere" in which salvation occurs (cf. Wallace, 140).

[74] The simple interrogative τίς ("who?") is well attested (𝔓[27vid] 𝔓[46] B* etc.) and appears to have given rise to several variants. Although ὑπομένει ("awaits," א* A 1739 etc) might be preferred as a more difficult reading than ἐλπίζει ("hopes," 𝔓[46] א[2] B C D F G etc.), the latter makes better sense in the flow of the argument. Cf. Metzger, *Textual Commentary*, 457.

see, we eagerly wait for it with patience." The verb "eagerly await" is used again (ἀπεκδεχόμεθα, cf. vv. 19, 23) but with an emphasis on waiting "with patience" (δι' ὑπομονῆς, cf. 2:7; 5:3–4; Heb 12:1). Patient, hopeful endurance, rather than resignation or complaint, is the challenge of this passage.

8:26. The adverb ὡσαύτως ("in the same way") is "a marker of similarity that approximates identity" (BDAG; cf. 1 Cor 11:25; 1 Tim 2:9; 3:8, 11; 5:25; Titus 2:3, 6), but the similarity is not made clear until the end of the verse. There is a chiastic structure to the argument, in which the outer elements explain the Spirit's work and the inner elements explain the situation of believers. So (lit.) "the Spirit also joins to help" (καὶ τὸ πνεῦμα συναντιλαμβάνεται) is amplified by "the Spirit himself intercedes with unspoken groanings" (αὐτὸ τὸ πνεῦμα ὑπερεντυγχάνει στεναγμοῖς ἀλαλήτοις),[75] and "in our weakness" (τῇ ἀσθενείᾳ ἡμῶν) is amplified by "because we do not know what to pray for as we should" (τὸ γὰρ τί προσευξώμεθα καθὸ δεῖ οὐκ οἴδαμεν). Although the compound verb συναντιλαμβάνεται could simply mean "helps" (BDAG; NRSV, ESV, NIV), the prefix σύν ("with") has been used with some significance in vv. 16, 17, 22, and so "joins to help" may be the meaning here. "The image of the Spirit shouldering the burden which our weakness imposes on us is quite a vivid one (cf. Ps 89:21 [LXX 88:22])."[76]

The particular weakness Paul has in mind is not knowing what to pray for in the context of suffering and groaning. The singular indefinite pronoun τί most likely refers to the thing prayed for rather than the actual words to use. The expression καθὸ δεῖ ("as we should") is explained by κατὰ θεόν ("according to [the will of] God") in v. 27. "Because of our finiteness and fallibility we cannot perceive fully what God would desire."[77] But the Spirit "joins to help" with this weakness by interceding for us (lit.) "with inarticulate groanings" (στεναγμοῖς ἀλαλήτοις). CSB's "unspoken" could be taken to mean "silent," but the adjective signifies "what cannot

[75] As in v. 16, the neuter expression αὐτὸ τὸ πνεῦμα is rightly translated "the Spirit *himself*." ℵ^{c} C K P etc. make explicit what is implicit in the compound verb ὑπερεντυγχάνει ("intercedes for") by adding ὑπὲρ ἡμῶν ("for us"). But the shorter reading is generally to be preferred and is better attested here (ℵ* A B D F G etc.).

[76] Cf. Dunn, *Romans 1–8*, 477, comparing LXX Exod 18:22; Num 11:17; and Luke 10:40.

[77] Schreiner, *Romans*, 443.

be expressed in words" (Louw and Nida; cf. 1 Pet 1:8 ["inexpressible"]). There is a long tradition of interpretation going back to Origen and Chrysostom that regards this as a reference to tongues speaking.[78] But tongues are associated with blessing and thanksgiving in 1 Cor 14:15–17, not groaning. Moreover, tongues in that context involved speech that required interpretation (contrast Acts 2:4–11). Only some of the Corinthians spoke in tongues (1 Cor 12:30; 14:5), whereas the Spirit's ministry of intercession is available to *all* who experience the limitation outlined here. The Spirit's groans are distinguished from the groans of Christians themselves (v. 23). They are "the Spirit's own 'language of prayer,' a ministry of intercession that takes place in our hearts (cf. v. 27) in a manner imperceptible to us."[79] Paul is not talking about believers praying silently but about the Spirit's mediation of our needs to the Father for us.

8:27. The conjunction δέ ("and") joins this conclusion to the preceding argument. God is often identified in Scripture as "he who searches our hearts" (e.g., 1 Sam 16:7; 1 Kgs 8:39; Pss 44:21; 139:1–2, 23; Prov 15:11; Jer 17:10). As such, he "knows the mind of the Spirit" (οἶδεν τί τὸ φρόνημα τοῦ πνεύματος, cf. v. 6), meaning in this context the intention behind the inarticulate groanings of the Spirit (cf. 1 Cor 2:11). CSB has taken ὅτι to mean "because," but it could also mean "that," indicating *what* God knows. The Spirit's "mind" is that "he intercedes for the saints according to the will of God" (κατὰ θεὸν ἐντυγχάνει ὑπὲρ ἁγίων). The "saints" are the sanctified community of the new covenant (cf. 1:7 comment). "Since these intercessory groanings of the Holy Spirit coincide completely with the will of God, then the requests are always granted."[80] Taking into account what is said in v. 34, we may conclude that the glorified Christ intercedes for believers "at the right hand of God" (cf. Heb

[78] Käsemann (*Romans*, 240–42) and Fee (*God's Empowering Presence*, 575–86) are two more recent examples. Note the lengthy response of Schreiner, *Romans*, 444–45.

[79] Moo, *Romans*, 525–26. Cf. Cranfield, *Romans*, 1:423; Dunn, *Romans 1–8*, 478–79; E. A. Obeng, "The Spirit Intercessor Motif in Paul," *ExpTim* 95 (1984): 360–64. After examining biblical and Jewish references to intercession, Obeng ("The Origins of the Spirit Intercession Motif in Romans 8:26," *NTS* 32 [1986]: 630) concludes that Paul is "the first to speak clearly of the Spirit as an intercessor."

[80] Peter T. O'Brien, "Romans 8:26, 27. A Revolutionary Approach to Prayer," *RTR* 46 (1987): 71.

7:25), responding to the needs laid bare by the Spirit, who is "hidden in the heart of man's creaturely inability and known only to God."[81] Thus, God as Trinity acts to sustain his people even when words fail to express their deepest anguish (cf. §2.3).

8:28. As in 2:2; 3:19, Paul uses the expression *οἴδαμεν δέ* ("we know"; cf. 7:14; 8:22, *οἴδαμεν γάρ*) to introduce a view he believes he shares with his readers. In the order of the Greek sentence, "the saints" (v. 27) are first defined as "those who love God" (*τοῖς ἀγαπῶσιν τὸν θεόν*). Many biblical texts highlight love as an essential aspect of a relationship with God (e.g., Exod 20:6; Deut 5:10; 6:5; 7:9; Josh 22:5; Matt 22:37; Mark 12:30), and Paul speaks about this again in 1 Cor 2:9; 8:3 (cf. Eph 6:24, "love for our Lord Jesus Christ"). The expression in 8:28 is significant because God's love for us is once more coming into focus (vv. 31–32, 35, 39; cf. 1:7; 5:5). Those who love God do so because he first loved them. Paul does not make love for God a condition for the fulfillment of his promise, but with the description "who are called according to his purpose," our love for God is taken as a sign of his effectual calling (cf. vv. 29–30, 37).[82]

Much debate has taken place about the way to understand *πάντα συνεργεῖ*. Although the apostle nowhere else uses *πάντα* as the subject of an active verb (though see Col 1:17), the context allows for that possibility (KJV, NRSV, ESV, CSB, "all things work together"). Alternatively, the subject could be an undefined "he" and *πάντα* could be an accusative of specification or respect ("in all things"). There is a textual variant that makes God the explicit subject, and this is reflected in NIV ("in all things God works"), though the literal sequence "for those who love God, God works" is awkward.[83]

---

[81] Dunn, *Romans 1–8*, 479. Dunn (493) argues that "it is precisely the *believer's* expression of agonized frustration and impotence which is also, at one and the same time, the *Spirit's* intercession on their behalf" (emphasis in original). Cf. vv. 15–16.

[82] Cf. Gundry Volf, *Paul and Perseverance*, 60. Runge (*Discourse Grammar*, 330–31) argues that this clause implies that "loving God necessitates trusting in his calling and purpose."

[83] Cf. Moo, *Romans*, 528n113. The shorter reading is broadly attested (א C D F G Ψ etc.), but ὁ θεός ("God") is found in some significant early witnesses (𝔓[46] A B etc.). It would be natural for an editor to add ὁ θεός, but it is hard to imagine why this might have been excluded if it were original. Cranfield (*Romans*, 1:425–28) considers eight possible ways of understanding the text and concludes that the shorter reading should be taken with *πάντα* as the subject of the verb.

Some have suggested that the Holy Spirit should be understood as the implied subject from vv. 26–27, but this option necessitates a change of subject in v. 29, where God must be in view with reference to "his Son."[84] It is more natural to see τὸν θεόν at the beginning of v. 28 as implying a change of referent, even though πάντα ("all things") is the grammatical subject of the new sentence. Moreover, the Spirit's work has been located *within* believers (vv. 14–16, 23, 26–27), whereas Paul is now describing God's control over every aspect of our lives. As in vv. 17, 22, 26, the verbal prefix σύν should be recognized in translation, so that συνεργεῖ is rightly rendered "work together." Paul is not describing an "evolutionary optimism" here or a divine-human synergism.[85] God in his sovereignty superintends all things, including the sufferings mentioned in v. 18. He can make all things work together "for good" (εἰς ἀγαθόν), meaning for the good purpose he had when he called us, not for our comfort, convenience, or material advantage.[86]

The concluding clause (τοῖς κατὰ πρόθεσιν κλητοῖς οὖσιν) modifies the opening clause, so that the whole sequence literally reads, "For those who love God, all things work together for good, for those who are called according to his purpose." This last clause recalls 1:6–7, where the readers are described as "called by Jesus Christ" and "loved by God, called as saints" (ἀγαπητοῖς θεοῦ, κλητοῖς ἁγίοις; cf. 1 Cor 1:1, 2, 24). God's purpose (πρόθεσις) in calling them is defined in the next two verses in terms of his overarching plan for his people (cf. Isa 46:10; Rom 9:11), where being "conformed to the image of his Son" is highlighted.[87]

8:29–30. The conjunction ὅτι ("for") introduces a string of verbs in the aorist tense, explaining how God's purpose (πρόθεσις) is worked out. This tense encodes a perfective aspect in the indicative mood, giving a summary perspective on the specified action. Each verb in the sequence is being used to make a general or gnomic

[84] Cf. Fee, *God's Empowering Presence*, 588–90. Jewett (*Romans*, 527) argues similarly and thinks "the content and rhetoric of vv. 29–30 will make it sufficiently clear that God, rather than the Spirit, must now become the subject."

[85] Cf. Dodd, *Romans*, 152–53; Jewett, *Romans*, 527.

[86] Cf. Moo, *Romans*, 529–30.

[87] Against the view that πρόθεσις refers to the choice of believers to place themselves in the service of God, Cranfield (*Romans*, 1:429) points to contextual reasons for seeing this as *God's* purpose. So also Jewett, *Romans*, 528.

statement (cf. 1:21–28; 3:23).[88] So it is possible to translate "foreknows . . . predestines . . . calls . . . justifies . . . glorifies." God is the subject in each case, grounding the Christian's certainty in the continuity of *his* actions. The additive marker καί ("also") signals the need to look for some correspondence between these different acts of God.[89] The objects of God's gracious activity are the same throughout the sequence, as indicated by the construction οὕς . . . τούτους καί ([lit.] "whom . . . these also"). Foreknowledge comes first (οὓς προέγνω, "whom he foreknows"). This does not simply mean knowledge in advance of what will happen (as in Acts 26:5; 2 Pet 3:17) or knowledge about who will believe. Paul reflects a use of the Hebrew verb "know" (יָדַע) to mean "choose" in the sense of establishing a relationship with someone (e.g., Gen 18:19; Exod 33:12; Jer 1:5; Amos 3:2 [Israel]).[90] The corresponding Greek verb with the prefix προ ("before") describes God's gracious initiative in electing or choosing his people (11:2; 1 Pet 1:2; cf. Acts 2:23; 1 Pet 1:20 [where Christ is the one chosen]). But the focus in this context is on God's engagement with individuals, not simply on his dealing with his people collectively.[91] God's unmerited choice took place "before the foundation of the world" (Eph 1:4 [ἐξελέξατο]; cf. 2 Tim 1:9, "before time began"). Another verb with the prefix προ ("before") continues the sequence (καὶ προώρισεν, "he also predestines").[92] Predestination relates to the purpose of election. God "decided beforehand" that those he chose would be "conformed to the image of his Son" (συμμόρφους τῆς εἰκόνος τοῦ υἱοῦ αὐτοῦ).[93] This

[88] Each action is viewed from an external vantage point: the aorist does not necessarily point to a moment in time. Cf. Campbell, *Verbal Aspect, the Indicative Mood*, 103–7. A consistent reading of the verbs in 8:29–30 is thus possible. Traditionally, the last one has been taken to point to a future reality, while the others point to the past. Contrast Gundry Volf, *Paul and Perseverance*, 11–12.

[89] Cf. Runge, *Discourse Grammar*, 339–40. The repeated pronoun οὕς ("whom") ensures that the reader "properly tracks the rapid changes" (p. 302).

[90] Terence E. Fretheim ("ידע," *NIDOTTE* 2:410) says, "The fundamentally relational character of knowing (over against a narrow intellectual sense) can be discerned, not least in that both God and human beings can be subject and object of the vb."

[91] Cf. Moo, *Romans*, 533; Gundry Volf, *Paul and Perseverance*, 14.

[92] Although the OT speaks about God's determining events in advance (e.g., 2 Kgs 19:25), the verb προορίζω is not used in the LXX. It is found in Acts 4:28; 1 Cor 2:7; Eph 1:5,11.

[93] The adjective σύμμορφος (BDAG, "similar in form") only occurs elsewhere in the NT at Phil 3:21, though the cognate verb is used in Phil 3:10. The related

recalls the language of Gen 1:27, which declares that human beings were made "in the image of God" (κατ' εἰκόνα θεοῦ). However, since all sin and "fall short of the glory of God" (Rom 3:23), we only attain our destiny as human beings when we are conformed to the image of the one who is himself the true image of God (2 Cor 4:4; Col 1:15 [εἰκὼν τοῦ θεοῦ]).

God's ultimate purpose is that his Son might be "the firstborn among many brothers and sisters" (εἰς τὸ εἶναι αὐτὸν πρωτότοκον ἐν πολλοῖς ἀδελφοῖς). As in Col 1:15, 18, πρωτότοκος ("firstborn") expresses "both the unique pre-eminence of Christ and also the fact that he shares his privileges with his brethren."[94] Conformity to the image of God's Son will take place when we are finally glorified with Christ (v. 17; cf. 1 Cor 15:49; Phil 3:21; 1 John 3:1–2), but Paul's teaching about enduring suffering in the present (vv. 18–27) suggests that a process of being conformed to the likeness of Christ is already underway (cf. Phil 3:10; Col 3:9–10).[95] The historical outworking of God's plan for those he chooses and predestines begins when he calls them (τούτους καὶ ἐκάλεσεν, [lit.] "these he also calls"). This picks up the cognate term κλητοῖς ("called") from v. 28. An effective calling is implied by the sequence of verbs here, since Paul goes straight on to say "these he also justifies" (τούτους καὶ ἐδικαίωσεν).[96] Justification on the basis of Christ's saving work is only secured by genuine faith (3:25, 28; 4:5; 5:1), and so the implication is that God's calling elicits that faith. Like the other verbs in the sequence, the final one is in the aorist tense (τούτους καὶ ἐδόξασεν, "these also he glorifies"). Although "the glory of God" remains a hope (5:2) and is yet to be revealed to us (8:18), Christ has

---

verb μεταμορφόω is used in a passive form in Rom 12:2; 2 Cor 3:18 ("be changed, transformed").

[94] Cranfield, *Romans*, 1:432. Cf. Dunn, *Romans 1–8*, 484–85; Wilhelm Michaelis, "πρωτότοκος," *TDNT* 6:877; Ps 89:27; Heb 1:6; 2:6–10; Rev 1:5.

[95] Dunn (*Romans 1–8*, 483) argues, "Paul has in view the *risen* Christ, the exalted Christ of the last age, not Jesus as he was on earth." So also Gundry Volf, *Paul and Perseverance*, 9–11. But Phil 3:10 also embraces "the fellowship of his sufferings, being conformed to his death."

[96] Paul's grammatical link between the verbs in this chain emphasizes an unbreakable connection between the events to which they refer. Cf. Gundry Volf, *Paul and Perseverance*, 12–14. Schreiner (*Romans*, 450–51) discusses the effectual call of God more extensively.

already been glorified by resurrection-ascension, and the glorification of believers is secured in him.[97]

8:31–32. A moving conclusion to what has just been claimed is introduced with a simple question ("What then [οὖν] are we to say about these things?" cf. 4:1; 6:1; 7:7). A series of further questions highlights three related themes: God's providential care (vv. 31–32), the eternal security of believers (vv. 33–34), and ultimate victory through suffering (vv. 35–37). Within this rhetorical framework, Paul has created "a remarkable web of biblical allusions and echoes."[98] Returning to the diatribe pattern used earlier in the letter, but employing the more inclusive first-person plural, Paul the pastor seeks to assure his readers about their relationship with God. The climax comes with a first-person singular confession in vv. 38–39.[99] The first theme is signaled by the question "If God is for us, who is against us?" Paul's readers may have been aware of many powerful opponents, but his point is, when God acts on your behalf, no one can truly succeed against you (cf. Pss 23:4; 56:9, 11; Isa 50:9). The words ὑπὲρ ἡμῶν ("for us") recall what is said about the death of Jesus in 5:6–8. This link is made more explicit in the first part of the second question ([lit.] "who did not even spare his own Son, but delivered him up for us all").[100]

An allusion to Gen 22:16 may be discerned in the expression "did not spare his own Son" (τοῦ ἰδίου υἱοῦ οὐκ ἐφείσατο). Abraham was blessed by God because he did not spare his only son (οὐκ ἐφείσω τοῦ υἱοῦ σου τοῦ ἀγαπητοῦ). Other LXX passages employ the

[97] Cranfield (*Romans*, 1:433) notes the absence of sanctification from the sequence in vv. 29–30 and suggests that Paul "may perhaps have felt that ἐδόξασεν covered sanctification as well as glorification." But such a view does not take account of the positional way Paul uses the terminology of sanctification (e.g., 1 Cor 1:2, 30; 2:11; 2 Thess 2:13–14). Cf. Peterson, *Possessed by God*, 136–37; §2.6.

[98] Cf. Wright "Romans," 610–11. Another way of dividing the passage is to see vv. 31–34 having a judicial emphasis and vv. 35–39 having a focus on God's love.

[99] Jewett (*Romans*, 532–35) discusses in some detail the elevated rhetorical style and structure of this passage, showing from the subject matter that it is "a peroration of the entire second proof (of the letter) that begins in 5:1–11."

[100] The relative pronoun ὅς ("who"), as in the hymnic passages Phil 2:6–11; Col 1:15–20, with the expression ὑπὲρ ἡμῶν πάντων παρέδωκεν αὐτόν ("delivered him up for us all"), has suggested to some commentators that Paul is using a preexisting formula. But Jewett (*Romans*, 536) points out that the language is typically Pauline and the particle γε ("even") is argumentative in style, drawing attention to the special significance of what is claimed.

same verb (e.g., 2 Sam 18:5; 21:7, 9), but none in connection with a beloved son.[101] Nothing could express the love of God for his people more convincingly than the fact that he "delivered him up for us all."[102] As noted in connection with 4:25, when the verb παρέδωκεν ("delivered up") is applied to the death of Jesus, an echo of Isa 53:6, 12 is probably intended. Paul includes himself and all his readers among the beneficiaries of the Servant's sacrificial death (ὑπὲρ ἡμῶν πάντων, "for us all"). Contextually, this inclusivism relates to those "who are called according to his purpose" (v. 28), whose destiny has just been outlined (vv. 29–30). In view of 3:29–4:25, "all" must include believing Jews and Gentiles.

The final part of the second question points to the practical consequences of being certain about the love of God for his people ("How will he not also with him grant us everything?"). The verb χαρίσεται ("freely grant") expresses the grace character of God's providence. "Since the incredible gift of Jesus's atoning death has already been granted, it is all the more certain that God will grant believers everything."[103] However, τὰ πάντα ("everything") cannot be taken to include every desire or whim we may have. In view of the preceding verses, the apostle means everything we need to wait with patience through suffering for the glory to be revealed to us and to be conformed to the image of God's Son.[104]

8:33–34. A second series of rhetorical questions focuses on the eternal security of believers. The first question (τίς ἐγκαλέσει κατὰ ἐκλεκτῶν θεοῦ; "Who can bring an accusation against God's elect?") is followed by a simple affirmation (θεὸς ὁ δικαιῶν, "God is the One

[101] Jewett (*Romans*, 537) draws attention to the use of this verb in Greco-Roman texts and concludes that the vocabulary is ordinary, but "the event to which Paul alludes is extraordinary and arresting." Jewett dismisses attempts to view the binding of Isaac in Jewish tradition as a precedent for understanding the atoning death of Jesus.

[102] CSB's "offered him up" gives an explicitly sacrificial sense to παρέδωκεν αὐτόν, whereas the verb normally means "hand over, give (over), deliver" (BDAG) and is translated that way in 4:25.

[103] Jewett, *Romans*, 538. He notes that the interrogative particle πῶς ("how") with a negative produces the sense of "surely, most certainly" (BDAG). Cf. 2 Cor 3:8. The verb χαρίζομαι (BDAG, "give freely as a favor, give graciously") is also used in Acts 3:14; 1 Cor 2:12; Phil 1:29; Phlm 22.

[104] Schreiner (*Romans*, 461) insists that "the good experienced is ultimately eschatological, but all things experienced in this age—including sufferings per the emphasis from 8:17–18—are for the benefit of believers." Cf. 1 Cor 3:21–23.

who justifies"). Paul uses the legal term ἐγκαλέσει (BDAG, "bring charges against, accuse"), which is also found in Acts 19:38, 40; 23:29; 26:2, 7. Human courts could bring unjust charges against Christians, but the apostle is speaking about the heavenly court and eschatological judgment.[105] God's elect (ἐκλεκτοὶ θεοῦ) are those "who are called according to his purpose" (v. 28, κλητοῖς), and Paul has already insisted that "those he calls he also justifies" (v. 30).[106] Justification is a divine verdict that cannot be reversed or abandoned. Some commentators read four questions in these verses, with the second being "God—who justifies us?," the third being "Who shall condemn us?," and the fourth being "Christ Jesus—who died, or rather was raised, who is at the right hand of God, who actually is interceding on our behalf?"[107] The point of the second and fourth questions would be to express an absurdity that moves the readers to respond with an emphatic denial. But the sequence "God is the One who justifies. Who is the one who condemns?" recalls Isa 50:8 and forms a natural antithesis. As understood by CSB, there is a double pattern of question and answer.

The second question (τίς ὁ κατακρινῶν; "Who is the one who condemns?") recalls the claim that "there is now no condemnation for those in Christ Jesus" (8:1). Condemnation is the opposite of justification. As previously emphasized, "Christ Jesus is the one who died," and on that basis justification was secured for God's elect (5:9). But "even more" (μᾶλλον δέ), Christ "has been raised; he also is at the right hand of God and intercedes for us." This affirms the great gospel events in chronological order but also in terms of their

[105] Cf. Dunn, *Romans 1–8*, 502. Jewett (*Romans*, 539–40) compares the adverse experiences listed in vv. 35, 38 and says the reference is to human courts, not the heavenly court. But this fails to take seriously the reference to divine justification and Christ's heavenly intercession in the immediate context.

[106] Paul nowhere else employs the plural term "the elect" (though see 16:13, "elect in the Lord"). The cognate verb ἐκλέγομαι ("choose [for oneself]") is used in 1 Cor 1:27, 28; Eph 1:4). A related term in 8:29 (προέγνω, "foreknew") also expresses the idea of divine choice.

[107] So Jewett, *Romans*, 540, following Barrett, *Romans,* 172–73, who notes that vv. 31, 32, 35 consist entirely of questions. Cranfield (*Romans*, 1:437–38) acknowledges that there is ancient support for this punctuation but concludes that it is unnecessary and unnatural. Cf. Wright, "Romans," 612–13.

ascending theological significance for Paul's argument.[108] Since Christ has been raised, we too will be raised and glorified with him (6:8; 8:11, 17). The claim that "he also is at the right [hand] of God" (ὅς καί ἐστιν ἐν δεξιᾷ τοῦ θεοῦ) reflects Ps 110:1. This text, which was used by Jesus in relation to the heavenly rule of the Messiah (e.g., Mark 12:35–37), is also echoed in Eph 1:20; Col 3:1; Heb 1:3; 8:1; 10:12; 12:2; 1 Pet 3:22. The psalmist portrays the ultimate victory of the Son of David over all his enemies, giving the hope of deliverance from every opposing power to those who belong to him. The claim that "he also intercedes for us" (ὅς καὶ ἐντυγχάνει ὑπὲρ ἡμῶν) is without parallel in Paul's writings. But in Heb 7:25 Christ's heavenly intercession is proclaimed at a climactic point in the argument as a guarantee that "he is able to save completely those who come to God through him."[109] Both Hebrews and Romans stress the finished nature of Christ's atoning work, and so the image of the heavenly intercessor stresses his ability to go on applying the benefits of his sacrifice to those who approach God through him (cf. Heb 4:14–16; 10:19–22; 1 John 2:1–2). Christ's presence "at the right hand of God" and his intercessory role guarantee that all God's elect will continue to find acceptance at the divine seat of judgment and be glorified with him.

8:35–37. A third set of rhetorical questions introduces the next topic: victory through suffering. The leading question is (lit.) "What can separate us from the love of Christ?"[110] In an emphatic position at the beginning of this sentence, the word ἡμᾶς ("us") draws Paul and his readers together. The verb χωρίζω is used with reference to

---

[108] The reading Χριστὸς Ἰησοῦς ("Christ Jesus") is widely attested (א A C etc.), with 𝔓[46] apparently adding the explicatory words ἅμα δέ. But the shorter reading Χριστός is well enough attested (B D etc.) and could be the original. The combination μᾶλλον δέ means "to a greater or higher degree" or "rather, all the more" (BDAG).

[109] Cf. David G. Peterson, *Hebrews and Perfection: An Examination of the Concept of Perfection in the "Epistle to the Hebrews,"* SNTSMS 47 (Cambridge: Cambridge University, 1982), 113–15. Together with Ps 110:1, Isa 53:12 may be a source of Paul's thinking about the intercessory role of the glorified Messiah. Heb 7:25 is clearly influenced by Ps 110:4. The verb ἐντυγχάνειν means "to approach with a complaint" in Acts 25:24; Rom 11:2, but "to intercede as a representative" in Rom 8:26, 27, 34; Heb 7:25.

[110] The interrogative pronoun τίς is used again as in vv. 33a, 34a but should be rendered "what?" here (CSB "who?") because seven forms of adversity follow and there is no indication that Paul is personifying these.

marital separation in 1 Cor 7:10, 11, 15 and implies complete severance or divorce from the love of Christ here.[111] What might cause such a separation? Six of the seven possibilities Paul mentions can be found elsewhere in his letters, describing his own experiences: θλῖψις ("affliction," 2 Cor 6:4); στενοχωρία ("distress," 2 Cor 6:5); διωγμός ("persecution," 1 Cor 4:12; 2 Cor 4:9; 2 Cor 12:10; Gal 5:11); λιμός ("famine, hunger," 1 Cor 4:11; 2 Cor 11:27); γυμνότης ("nakedness," 1 Cor 4:11; 2 Cor 11:27); κίνδυνος ("danger," 1 Cor 15:30; 2 Cor 11:26); μάχαιρα ("sword," no strict parallel, though Paul faced deadly dangers [Phil 1:20–21; 1 Cor 15:32; 2 Cor 11:32]).[112] Even taking these extreme experiences into account, the apostle can affirm that none "will be able to separate us from the love of God that is in Christ Jesus our Lord" (v. 39).

A citation from Ps 44:22 (43:23 LXX) is introduced with the familiar καθὼς γέγραπται ("as it is written"; cf. 1:17; 2:24; 3:4, 10; 4:17). This shows that "being put to death all day long" has always been the lot of God's people. But there is a difference for the Christian, for whom the expression "because of you" (ἕνεκεν σοῦ) specifically means "because of Christ" (cf. 1 Cor 15:30–31; 2 Cor 4:11). The claim that "we are counted as sheep to be slaughtered" explains the metaphor "being put to death all day long." The Servant of the Lord was "like a lamb led to the slaughter" (Isa 53:7) for the salvation of his people. So his suffering established a pattern for those he came to save (cf. v. 17; Phil 1:29–30; 3:10; 1 Pet 2:21–25). "Christ died for their sake, and they die for his. No one can therefore claim that their suffering divorces them from Christ and his cross."[113]

[111] The reading Χριστοῦ is strongly supported (A C D G K Ψ etc.) and binds together vv. 34 and 35 (cf. "the love of Christ" in 2 Cor 5:14; Eph 3:19). Two alternative readings appear to be scribal harmonizations with v. 39: θεοῦ τῆς ἐν Χριστῷ Ἰησοῦ (B etc., "the love of God that is in Christ Jesus") and θεοῦ (א 326 330 etc., "the love of God").

[112] Jewett (*Romans*, 544–48) provides an extensive discussion of these terms in the light of biblical and extrabiblical usage. He contends, "These seven forms of hardship could have provided the basis for critics within the early church to delegitimize sufferers, a possibility that Paul wished to counter."

[113] Jewett, *Romans*, 548. Jewett's thesis is that others were saying that such suffering disqualified the Roman Christians from being genuine disciples. But this finds no support in the text and is unnecessary. When people suffer for the sake of Christ, it is easy for them to doubt his continuing love for them.

The strong adversative ἀλλά ("but") at the beginning of v. 37 is appropriately rendered "no" by CSB. "In all these things" (ἐν τούτοις πᾶσιν) refers to the various trying circumstances listed in vv. 35–36. It points to victory, not by evading them or being spared them "but meeting them steadfastly, in the very experiencing of them."[114] The prefix on the verb ὑπερνικῶμεν has an intensive force (CSB: "we are more than conquerors").[115] This victory is "through him who loved us" (διὰ τοῦ ἀγαπήσαντος ἡμᾶς). The primary reference in this passage has been to Christ's death (cf. Gal 2:20), though Paul has also shown how his resurrection and ascension secure for us the hope of glory, and his continuing intercession sustains us in the benefits of his once-for-all sacrifice.

8:38–39. Linked to the preceding claim by γάρ ("for"), Paul's exultant conclusion is in the form of a personal confession of faith (πέπεισμαι, "I am persuaded"; cf. 14:14; 15:14; 2 Tim 1:5, 12). Nine possible hindrances to the continuation of believers in the love of God are listed ("neither death nor life, nor angels nor rulers, nor things present nor things to come, nor powers, nor height, nor depth") before the comprehensive claim "nor any other created thing" completes the sequence. "Death" is mentioned first because it featured in the biblical citation in v. 36. Contextually, "life" will include the various experiences mentioned in v. 35. Coupled with "angels," the word ἀρχαί ("rulers") most likely refers to heavenly authorities (cf. 1 Cor 15:24; Eph 1:21; 3:10; 6:12; Col 1:16; 2:10, 15).[116] Although δυνάμεις ("powers") is separated from this word pair, it is probably another way of describing spiritual beings or cosmic forces, in this case malevolent (cf. 1 Cor 15:24; Eph 1:21; 1 Pet 3:22). Elsewhere Paul affirms that Christ has defeated every opposing supernatural power (Col 2:15; cf. Eph 1:21, 22), "so that their effectiveness has been drastically curtailed and their final subjection

---

[114] Cranfield, *Romans*, 1:441.

[115] Cf. 5:20 (ὑπερεπερίσσευσεν ἡ χάρις, "grace multiplied even more"). Jewett (*Romans*, 548–49) illustrates from Greco-Roman literature how the verb ὑπερνικάω could be used for total victory in a military sense. But it could also refer to a decisive victory in athletic and philosophical contexts.

[116] According to 2 Cor 11:14, some angels are fallen and pose a threat to believers, hence their association with opposing forces here. Although angels are associated with the coming of the Lord Jesus in judgment (2 Thess 1:7–8), Paul says believers are to judge angels (1 Cor 6:3), presumably meaning those who have fallen.

assured."[117] "Things present" and "things to come" could include the natural and supernatural events predicted by Jesus as signs of the approaching end (e.g., Mark 13:5–27). Paul uses a similar expression in 1 Cor 3:22 when assuring his readers about God's grace toward them. "Height" and "depth" have been variously explained, but these spatial terms probably signify the entire universe: "either those things above the heavens and beneath the earth, heaven and earth itself, or, perhaps most likely, heaven and hell."[118] None of these powers or realms are able to separate us "from the love of God that is in Christ Jesus our Lord."

Paul relativizes all the potential forces opposing Christians—earthly and heavenly—by classifying them as part of God's creation (κτίσις is used more comprehensively here than in vv. 19–22). Christ, on the other hand, is lord of all. Responding to his own question in v. 35a, Paul enhances the language he previously used, declaring that nothing "will be able to separate us" (δυνήσεται ἡμᾶς χωρίσαι) from God's love.[119] Although only explicitly mentioned in 5:5, 8; 8:35, 37, 39, the prevailing power of God's love has been the apostle's theme in chapters 5–8. Supremely manifested in the sacrifice of Christ (5:8), God's love has been "poured out in our hearts through the Holy Spirit who was given to us" (5:5). It continues to be experienced in the enjoyment of every blessing that flows from the death, resurrection, and glorification of God's Son (8:31–39).[120] These saving events together give us the hope of sharing in his glory. Appropriately, the full name and title of "Christ Jesus our Lord" once more mark off a significant stage in the development of Paul's argument (cf. 5:1, 11, 21; 6:23; 7:25; 8:39).

---

[117] Cranfield, *Romans*, 1:442. Cranfield rightly opposes the view that all the items in Paul's list should be understood as spiritual powers of one kind or another. So also Jewett (*Romans*, 550) comments, "It is wise to interpret them as far as possible within the framework of Paul's theology and prior usage."

[118] Moo, *Romans*, 546. Cf. Schreiner, *Romans*, 465.

[119] In view of what is said in vv. 28–20, Schreiner (*Romans*, 466) rightly opposes the view that genuine believers can choose to depart from God and thereby fall outside the scope of the saving love of Christ. But this assurance does not exempt us from heeding the warnings of Scripture, persevering in faith, and expressing faith in obedience. In this way we confirm our calling and election (2 Pet 1:10). Cf. 2:7 comment.

[120] Cf. Wright, "Romans," 609, 617–18.

Bridge

Suffering is a universal experience for human beings and the whole created order, but Christians endure particular forms of suffering because of their commitment to Christ and the gospel. As Paul deals with the groaning of creation (vv. 18–22), the groaning of believers (vv. 23–25), and then the groaning of the Spirit (vv. 26–27), he makes each stage of his argument a reason for persisting in hope. Setting the whole process within the framework of God's eternal plan (vv. 28–30), he presses his readers to acknowledge that nothing can separate us from the love of God that is in Christ Jesus our Lord (vv. 31–39). Even the futility of life in this world and our experience of decay point to the greater reality God has in store for his people. Just as the future glory of our resurrection bodies is God's gift, so also the transformation of creation will be by God's enabling. Although we have a mandate to watch over and care for God's creation as we find it (Gen 1:28–30; 2:15), we cannot bring about its release from futility. The natural world has no future apart from the liberation that will come with the bodily resurrection of the children of God. All the effects of human rebellion against God will be reversed when his children experience the fullness of his glory. This will happen when we are resurrected with Christ and share together in God's new creation. Meanwhile, the Spirit contributes to our groaning by making us long for the redemption of our bodies. But the Spirit also helps us in this situation of weakness by interceding for us with groans too deep for words. Hope and weakness belong together for the Christian. God as "the searcher of hearts" recognizes the Spirit's groaning below the level of human consciousness and responds appropriately. So "all things," including "the sufferings of this present time," work together for the good of those who love God and are called according to his purpose. God's purpose is that we might be "conformed to the image of his Son," and that process is consummated when we are glorified with him. Everyday experiences of suffering are to be viewed in the context of God's prevailing love and his ultimate purpose for his people. Christians will emerge from the struggles of this life not simply as wounded warriors but as victors who reign triumphantly with Christ and who share his likeness.

XI. The Way of Salvation for Jews and Gentiles: The Righteousness that Comes from Faith in Christ (9:1–11:36)

These chapters are integral to Paul's exposition of the gospel as "the power of God for salvation to everyone who believes, first to the Jew, and also to the Greek" (1:16). Up to this point the apostle has demonstrated in various ways how God's promises to Israel about eschatological salvation have been fulfilled in the Messiah Jesus. Since many Israelites have failed to believe the gospel and experience the anticipated blessings, Paul sets out to explore the double issue of "the gospel's apparent failure with respect to Israel *and* its paradoxical success with respect to the Gentiles."[1] More fundamentally, he seeks to establish God's faithfulness to his ancient covenantal promises. Biblical quotations comprise more than 30 percent of the argument and play a critical role in addressing this issue. But there are also important self-references—as in the letter's introduction (1:1–15) and conclusion (15:14–16:27)—allowing Paul to identify his own distinctive role in the outworking of God's plan (9:1–3; 10:1–2; 11:1, 11, 13–14, 25).

Paul's personal anguish for fellow Israelites (9:1–5) leads him to focus on how Scripture sets forth God's electing grace (9:6–29) before addressing the specific issue of Israel's failure to pursue righteousness by faith (9:30–33). Expressing his concern for their salvation (10:1–2), he develops the contrast between righteousness from the law and righteousness from faith (10:2–13) and further explores the reasons for Israel's failure to respond to the gospel (10:14–21). His answer to the question about whether God has rejected his people is to present himself as a representative of the remnant according to grace anticipated in Scripture, who fulfills Israel's divine vocation (11:1–10). A further question about whether Israel has stumbled irrevocably is answered in terms of his own ministry as apostle to the Gentiles, which is designed to make Israel jealous (11:11–24). Paul reveals the final mystery concerning the future of Israel (11:25–32)

[1] Byrne, *Romans*, 282. Moo (*Romans*, 547–54) provides a lengthy introduction to these chapters. As in the previous apologetic sections of the letter, Paul uses rhetorical questions to advance his argument (9:14, 30; 10:8, 14–15a, 18, 19; 11:1, 7, 11), and in 9:19–23 he engages in a dialogue with an imagined opponent. See also Schreiner, *Romans*, 469–75; Wright, "Romans," 620–26.

before concluding his carefully woven argument with a hymn of praise to God (11:33–36).

Chapters 9–11 will be expounded under these headings:

A. Israel's Failure and God's Electing Grace (9:1–29)

B. Israel's Failure to Pursue Righteousness by Faith (9:30–10:4)

C. Israel's Failure to Understand the Law and the Prophets (10:5–21)

D. Hope in the Face of Judgment (11:1–10)

E. Hope in the Conversion of the Nations (11:11–24)

F. Hope in the Mercy of God (11:25–36)

A. Israel's Failure and God's Electing Grace (9:1–29)

[1]I speak the truth in Christ—I am not lying; my conscience testifies to me through the Holy Spirit— [2]that I have great sorrow and unceasing anguish in my heart. [3]For I could wish that I myself were cursed and cut off from Christ for the benefit of my brothers and sisters, my own flesh and blood. [4]They are Israelites, and to them belong the adoption, the glory, the covenants, the giving of the law, the temple service, and the promises. [5]The ancestors are theirs, and from them, by physical descent, came the Christ, who is God over all, praised forever. Amen.

[6]Now it is not as though the word of God has failed, because not all who are descended from Israel are Israel. [7]Neither are all of Abraham's children his descendants. On the contrary, **your offspring will be traced through Isaac.** [8]That is, it is not the children by physical descent who are God's children, but the children of the promise are considered to be the offspring. [9]For this is the statement of the promise: **At this time I will come, and Sarah will have a son.** [10]And not only that, but Rebekah conceived children through one man, our father Isaac. [11]For though her sons had not been born yet or done anything good or bad, so that God's purpose according to election might stand—[12]not from works but from the one who calls—she was told, **The older will serve the younger.** [13]As it is written: **I have loved Jacob, but I have hated Esau.**

[14]What should we say then? Is there injustice with God? Absolutely not! [15]For he tells Moses, **I will show mercy to whom I will show mercy, and I will have compassion on whom I will**

have compassion. 16 So then, it does not depend on human will
or effort but on God who shows mercy. 17 For the Scripture tells
Pharaoh, **I raised you up for this reason so that I may display
my power in you and that my name may be proclaimed in the
whole earth.** 18 So then, he has mercy on whom he wants to have
mercy and he hardens whom he wants to harden.

19 You will say to me, therefore, "Why then does he still find
fault? For who can resist his will?" 20 But who are you, a mere
man, to talk back to God? Will what is formed say to the one who
formed it, "Why did you make me like this?" 21 Or has the potter
no right over the clay, to make from the same lump one piece of
pottery for honor and another for dishonor? 22 And what if God,
wanting to display his wrath and to make his power known, endured with much patience objects of wrath prepared for destruction? 23 And what if he did this to make known the riches of his
glory on objects of mercy that he prepared beforehand for glory
— 24 on us, the ones he also called, not only from the Jews but also
from the Gentiles? 25 As it also says in Hosea,

> **I will call Not my People, my People,**
> **and she who is Unloved, Beloved.**
> 26 **And it will be in the place where they were told,**
> **you are not my people,**
> **there they will be called sons of the living God.**

27 But Isaiah cries out concerning Israel,

> **Though the number of Israelites**
> **is like the sand of the sea,**
> **only the remnant will be saved;**
> 28 **since the Lord will execute his sentence**
> **completely and decisively on the earth.**

29 And just as Isaiah predicted:

> **If the Lord of Hosts had not left us offspring,**
> **we would have become like Sodom,**
> **and we would have been made like Gomorrah.**

Context

Paul's teaching in the previous chapter about Christian identity and the hope of the gospel raises the question of Israel's ongoing role and significance. What is the future of ethnic Israel, if "the nations have begun to experience the grace and faithfulness of God which was once Israel's special privilege"?[2] There are pastoral as well as theological questions to be answered in this connection, "since the very reliability of God's purpose as the ground of Christian hope is called into question by the exclusion of the majority of Jews."[3] If God's purpose for Israel has been frustrated, this raises questions about the certainty of the Christian hope. Moreover, if God's love for Israel's has ceased, how can Christians rely on the assurances about God's love in 8:38–39? A number of themes from earlier chapters are picked up and developed in relation to this issue, including the identity and calling of Israel (9:4–13; cf. 2:17–3:2), and the justice and mercy of God (9:14–29; cf. 3:3–20). Paul goes on to identify Israel's pursuit of "works" for righteousness as the reason there is only a remnant enjoying the messianic salvation (9:30–10:4). His focus on God's mercy in 9:15–16, 23 prepares for the climactic development of that theme in 11:30–32.[4]

Structure

Paul's passionate concern for his fellow Israelites is first stated (vv. 1–5). Although the nature of the problem is only hinted at here, vv. 30–33 make clear that the issue has been their failure to believe the gospel and experience the messianic salvation. The intervening verses begin a defense of the proposition that is foundational to Rom 9–11: "It is not as though the word of God has failed" (v. 6a). The first supporting argument (v. 6b, "because not all who are descended from Israel are Israel") is established by the use of key biblical texts relating to the patriarchal era (vv. 7–13). Paul's teaching about election within the covenant people raises a question about the righteousness of God in showing mercy to some and hardening others. A further series of biblical texts, covering the period from exodus to exile, highlight God's intention to display his power and make his "name" known in all the earth (vv. 14–29). A chiastic structure can

[2] James D. G. Dunn, *Romans 9–16*, WBC 38B (Dallas: Word, 1988), 530.

[3] Charles E. B. Cranfield, *Introduction and Commentary on Romans IX–XVI and Essays*, vol. 2 of *A Critical and Exegetical Commentary on the Epistle to the Romans*, ICC (Edinburgh: T&T Clark, 1979), 2:447.

[4] On the structure, purpose, and argument of these chapters, see E. Elizabeth Johnson, "Romans 9–11: The Faithfulness and Impartiality of God," and Douglas Moo, "The Theology of Romans 9–11: A Response to E. Elizabeth Johnson," in Hay and Johnson, eds., *Pauline Theology, Volume III: Romans*, 211–58.

be discerned in vv. 6–29, with the outer elements focusing on God's love in choosing a people for himself and the central elements highlighting God's justice and mercy in saving some:[5]

A God's choice of seed for Abraham (vv. 6–9)
  B God's love for his chosen (vv. 10–13)
    C God's justice and mercy revealed (vv. 14–18)
    C´ God's justice and mercy revealed (vv. 19–24)
  B´ God's love for his chosen (vv. 25–26)
A´ God's choice of seed within Israel (vv. 27–29)

Outline (incorporating three main elements of the structure above):

1. Paul's concern for Israel (vv. 1–5)
2. God's love in choosing a people for himself (vv. 6–13)
3. God's justice and mercy in saving some (vv. 14–24)
4. God's love in rescuing a remnant (vv. 25–29)

9:1–2. There is no conjunction linking what follows with what has gone before, though Paul proceeds to address issues arising from his previous teaching (cf. above under "Context").[6] He begins with an abrupt assertion of his honesty, put positively ("I speak the truth in Christ") and negatively ("I am not lying"). The expression "in Christ" identifies the apostle as one who is "conscious of his dependence on the living Christ and on his authorization and approval."[7] A genitive absolute clause in the present tense (συμμαρτυρούσης μοι τῆς συνειδήσεώς μου, "my conscience testifies to me") points to the ongoing role of his conscience in confirming the truthfulness of his claim (cf. 2:15 comment). Conscience for Paul appears to be "the irrepressible knowledge one has 'with oneself' that an action is consistent or inconsistent with one's ethical norms."[8] If the testimony of

[5] This is a modification of Schreiner's outline (*Romans*, 472), who follows Jean-Noël Aletti, "L'argumentation paulinienne en Rm 9," *Biblica* 68 (1987): 41–56.

[6] Moo (*Romans*, 555n2) lists verbal and theological links between chs. 8 and 9.

[7] Dunn, *Romans 9–16*, 523. Cf. 2 Cor 2:17; 12:19. Dunn points out that being "in Christ" and "in the Holy Spirit" are two related aspects of "the basic condition of the believer for Paul."

[8] Jewett, *Romans*, 558–59. He contends that conscience functions as "an autonomous witness to the consistency of behavior and internalized norm." Cf. Robert Jewett, *Paul's Anthropological Terms: A Study of Their Use in Conflict Situations*,

Paul's conscience is (lit.) "in the Holy Spirit" (ἐν πνεύματι ἁγίῳ), he means that the Spirit is leading him (cf. 8:14 comment) and assuring him that he is not deceiving himself. Presumably this elaborate assertion of his honesty was necessary because some questioned it (cf. 2 Cor 11:31; Gal 1:20; 1 Tim 2:7). He wants his readers to believe his sorrow is great (λύπη μοί ἐστιν μεγάλη) and the anguish in his heart is unceasing (ἀδιάλειπτος ὀδύνη τῇ καρδίᾳ μου). But only as the argument unfolds does the reason for this grief become clear. The sudden change in his emotional tone from 8:31–39 is remarkable and arresting.[9]

9:3. The intensity of Paul's feeling is further indicated by a linked claim (γάρ, "for"). He expresses an extraordinary wish or prayer, using the imperfect tense in a potential way (ηὐχόμην, "I could wish").[10] The content of his wish is "that I myself were cursed and cut off from Christ for the benefit of my brothers and sisters." Having previously addressed the Roman Christians as "brothers and sisters" (1:13; 7:1, 4; 8:12), he clarifies that he now refers to brothers who are (lit.) "my countrymen by physical descent" (CSB: "my own flesh and blood") or "my natural kin" (τῶν συγγενῶν μου κατὰ σάρκα).[11] His willingness to suffer the curse of being cut off from the Messiah and his salvation (ἀνάθεμα . . . ἀπὸ τοῦ Χριστοῦ) for the sake of his fellow Israelites implies that "those on behalf of whom he offers himself stand under that curse themselves."[12] A parallel with

---

AGJU 10 (Leiden: Brill, 1971), 445–46. According to 1 Cor 8:7, 10, 12; 1 Tim 4:2; Titus 1:15, conscience is fallible, and so the Spirit's confirming role is significant here.

[9] Paul's concern for Israel's enjoyment of the messianic salvation is obvious in chs. 9–11. But it is also possible that Israel's vocational failure "threatens Paul's apostolic mission at its deepest level and gives him reason for such grief and anguish" (Windsor, *Vocation*, 203).

[10] Cranfield (*Romans*, 2:454–57) examines different ways the verb could be understood here and concludes that it is equivalent to the classical imperfect indicative with ἄν, used where a prayer or wish is recognized as unattainable or impermissible (see also n. 14 below). Wallace (*Greek Grammar*, 551–52) describes this as a tendential use of the imperfect.

[11] Paul uses συγγενεῖς ("fellow countrymen") without κατὰ σάρκα in 16:7, 21, and the singular συγγενῆ likewise in 16:11, to describe Jewish Christians in the Roman congregations with whom he has more than a natural connection.

[12] Moo, *Romans*, 558. Ἀνάθεμα is mostly used in Scripture in a negative way, meaning "something devoted to God to be destroyed," and hence "accursed" (cf. BDAG; Johannes Behm, "ἀνατίθημι κτλ.," *TDNT* 1:354; Lev 27:28–29; Deut 7:26; 13:15 [LXX 13:16]; Josh 6:17–18; 1 Cor 12:3; 16:22; Gal 1:8–9).

Moses's words to God in Exod 32:32 has been suggested, involving "an oath of extraordinary commitment."[13] Moses asked that he might be excluded from God's "book" if Israel could be forgiven and continue with him into their inheritance. But Paul could hardly be suggesting that his willingness to be separated from Christ might bring salvation to unbelieving Israel. Moreover, not even Paul's passionate concern for his natural kin could separate him from "the love of God that is in Christ Jesus our Lord" (8:39). So he must be expressing a hypothetical wish.[14] In 10:1 he speaks positively about his prayer for their salvation.

9:4. To highlight the reasons for his concern, Paul lists the blessings given by God to Israel, concluding with an extraordinary claim about their Messiah (v. 5). Foundationally, "they are Israelites," the chosen people of God, who continue to benefit from the promises made to Abraham, Isaac, and Jacob (v. 5, "the ancestors"). "Israel" was the covenant name given to Jacob, from whom the twelve tribes sprang (Gen 32:28; 35:10–12). Paul only uses the term "Israelite" once more in Romans, when he applies it to himself (11:1), but he uses "Israel" in 9:6 (twice), 27 (twice), 31; 10:19, 21; 11:2, 7, 25, 26. As in previous chapters, "Jews" is used when a contrast with Gentiles is made (9:24; 10:12).[15] Six terms then follow the relative pronoun ὧν ("whose"), identifying significant blessings granted by God to his people. These overlapping privileges were mostly first experienced in connection with the exodus redemption.

"Adoption" or "sonship" (υἱοθεσία) recalls the way their relationship with God is described in passages such as Exod 4:22–23; Deut 14:1; Jer 31:9; Hos 1:10; 11:1. But Paul's use of this term for Jewish and Gentile believers in Christ (8:15, 23 [comments]) raises the question of its ongoing significance for Israel. "The glory" (ἡ δόξα) refers to the manifestation of God's presence with his people

[13] Windsor, *Vocation*, 204. He argues that the most common meaning of the verb in the LXX is "swear an oath" (e.g., Gen 28:20; 31:13; Lev 27:2, 8; Deut 12:11, 17) and follows Jewett (*Romans*, 560) in reading the imperfect as indicating a real past action.

[14] Heinrich Greeven ("εὔχομαι, κτλ.," *TDNT* 2:778) argues for "wish" rather than "pray" or "vow" here. He concludes, "Paul is simply using a strong expression to show how much he suffers from the disobedience of his own people." Cf. Schreiner, *Romans*, 480.

[15] Richard H. Bell (*The Irrevocable Call of God: An Inquiry into Paul's Theology of Israel*, WUNT 2.184 [Tübingen: Mohr Siebeck, 2005], 199–200) argues that Paul's use of Israel/Israelites implies that the Jews are still the chosen people of God.

throughout the exodus (e.g., Exod 16:7, 10; 24:16–17; 40:34–35). God's glory was also revealed at the temple in Jerusalem (e.g., 1 Kgs 8:10–13; Ezek 10:3–5, 18–19) and was predicted to be ultimately manifest when God came among his people to fulfill his saving plan (e.g., Isa 60:1–3; Ezek 43:1–5; cf. Rom 5:2; 8:18). So the implied question is, "Where does Israel stand now in relation to the glory of God?" "The covenants" (αἱ διαθῆκαι) are the various expressions of God's commitment to Israel given throughout her history (e.g., Gen 15:18; 17:1–14; Exod 19:5; 24:7–8; 34:27; Deut 29:1; 2 Sam 23:5), climaxing with the promise of a new covenant (Jer 31:31–24).[16] "The giving of the law" (ἡ νομοθεσία) was intimately linked to the Sinai covenant.[17] "The service" (ἡ λατρεία) is the pattern of worship prescribed in the law for tabernacle and temple (e.g., Exod 12:25–26; Josh 22:27; 1 Chr 28:13), which was clearly meant to promote devotion to God in every sphere of life (e.g., Deut 6:13; Jer 7:1–11). "The promises" (αἱ ἐπαγγελίαι) include those originally made to the patriarchs, but later also through the prophets, concerning the future of Israel and the nations. When Paul identifies with his natural kin in this way, he implies that their privileges are ongoing and not merely a feature of Israel's past. But his argument in the following chapters is that many fellow Israelites are not experiencing the fulfillment of these blessings in the Messiah Jesus.

9:5. The relative pronoun ὧν ("whose") reappears twice, introducing οἱ πατέρες ("the fathers" [CSB: "the ancestors"]) as the foundational gift of God to Israel and the Messiah as the ultimate blessing. Building on the argument in Rom 4, Paul is about to show how God's dealings with Abraham, Isaac, and Jacob demonstrate his electing grace (9:7–13). In due course he asserts that "regarding

[16] Hellenistic and Rabbinic Jewish texts similarly refer to covenants in the plural (e.g., Wis 18:22; Sir 44:12, 18; 2 Macc 8:15; 4 Ezra 3:22; Str-B 3:262). The singular ἡ διαθήκη is well attested (𝔓46 B D G etc.) but is likely to be a scribal correction because the plural reading (א C K Ψ 33 81 etc.) is more unusual. Cf. Metzger, *Textual Commentary*, 459. Paul R. Williamson (*Sealed with an Oath: Covenant in God's Unfolding Purpose*, NSBT 23 [Downers Grove: InterVarsity, 2007]) examines the various biblical covenants and how they relate together in God's unfolding purpose for Israel.

[17] Cranfield (*Romans*, 2:462–63) argues from various parallels (e.g., 2 Macc 6:23; 4 Macc 5:35; 17:16; Let. Aris. 15; Philo, *Abr.*, 5; *Cher.*, 87) that the active sense of νομοθεσία adopted by CSB has better lexical support and fits the context well (cf. NRSV, ESV). Contrast Moo, *Romans*, 564.

election, they are loved because of the patriarchs" (11:28). With a change of syntax, the supreme privilege of Israel is clearly identified: the Israelites are those (lit.) "from whom the Messiah (came) by physical descent" (ἐξ ὧν ὁ Χριστὸς τὸ κατὰ σάρκα). The neuter article before κατὰ σάρκα gives this expression a technical, delimited meaning ("insofar as the flesh is concerned").[18] It is a feature of Paul's gospel that Jesus was "a descendant of David according to the flesh" (1:3) and that God "condemned sin in the flesh by sending his own Son in the likeness of sinful flesh as a sin offering" (8:3).

CSB has understood the following words to be an ascription of divinity to the Messiah: "who is God over all, praised forever. Amen" (ὁ ὢν ἐπὶ πάντων θεὸς εὐλογητὸς εἰς τοὺς αἰῶνας, ἀμήν). This is a natural rendering of the Greek, argued by numerous commentators and reflected in other versions such as NIV and ESV. However, since the earliest manuscripts did not have systematic punctuation, editors and translators have read the text in different ways. For example, a colon or full stop after σάρκα creates an independent clause ("God who is over all be blessed for ever!").[19] A comma after σάρκα and a full stop or comma after πάντων give the meaning "the Messiah, who is over all. God (be) blessed forever" (cf. KJV, NRSV, NASB). But an unattached doxology to God the Father is awkward here and inconsistent with the syntactical pattern Paul uses elsewhere (cf. 1:25; 11:36; 2 Cor 11:31; Gal 1:5; 2 Tim 4:18).[20]

The critical question is whether Paul would explicitly identify Christ as God. In support of this reading, Phil 2:6 should be considered (ἐν μορφῇ θεοῦ, "in the form of God"; ἴσα θεῷ, "equality with God"). See also Titus 2:13 ("our great God and Savior, Jesus Christ"). Moreover, in the next chapter Paul identifies Christ with "the Lord" of Joel 2:32, upon whom everyone must call for salvation (Rom 10:9–13).[21] In favor of the CSB rendering, a doxology

[18] Cf. BDF §266 (2); Cranfield, *Romans*, 2:464; Dunn, *Romans 9–16*, 528.

[19] Dunn (*Romans 9–16*, 528–29) argues for this on stylistic and theological grounds. It is the reading of RSV, NEB, TEV.

[20] Cf. Metzger, *Textual Commentary*, 460–61; Cranfield (*Romans*, 2:465–70) considers five punctuation options and a conjectural emendation. He concludes that the best reading is "the Messiah who is over all, God blessed forever, Amen." Moo (*Romans*, 565–68) counts eight variations with two punctuation options and adopts Cranfield's translation.

[21] Dunn (*Theology of Paul*, 234–60) argues that Jesus's lordship is "a status granted by God, a sharing in his authority" (254) but does not consider that Paul equates

to Christ as God is relevant to Paul's argument at this point. It provides an antithesis to the preceding phrase ("from them, by physical descent, came the Christ"), and implies that his fellow Israelites have rejected the one who is "the very embodiment of their sovereign Lord, their covenant God."[22]

9:6. Paul uses δέ ("now") with the unusual exclamation οὐχ οἷον ὅτι ("it is not as though") to introduce a new idea, qualifying what he has just said.[23] The failure of many Jews to believe the gospel is the cause of his grief and his willingness to be cut off from the Messiah for their salvation (vv. 2–3, cf. 10:1). But his rhetoric does not mean that "the word of God has failed" (ἐκπέπτωκεν ὁ λόγος τοῦ θεοῦ).[24] As in 3:4; 9:9, 28; 13:9, "the word of God" refers to a decree or promise recorded in Scripture (cf. 3:2, τὰ λόγια τοῦ θεοῦ ["the very words of God"]). "This is the reality that establishes or is embodied in each of the preceding privileges or benefits."[25] As Scripture itself teaches, God "does not go back on what he says" (Isa 31:2; cf. Num 23:19). God's word "remains forever" (Isa 40:8) and accomplishes what pleases him (Isa 55:11). The central issue in Rom 9–11 is the faithfulness of God to his promises. Paul's thesis statement in 9:6a "reaches all the way to 11:26 and thus anticipates the salvation of all Israel."[26]

Paul first defends this foundational belief by asserting that there has been a process of election *within* Israel: "because not all who are descended from Israel are Israel." The expression οἱ ἐξ Ἰσραήλ (lit., "those who are from Israel") relates to those who are physically

---

the exalted Christ with God in 9:5. Contrast Murray J. Harris, *Jesus as God: The New Testament Use of Theos in Reference to Jesus* (Grand Rapids: Baker, 1992), 154–65; Ben Witherington III, "Christ," *DPL* 98. See §2.3.

[22] Wright, "Romans," 631. Jewett (*Romans*, 568) says it also brings the passage into correlation with the confession in 1:3–4 (κατὰ σάρκα . . . κατὰ πνεῦμα ἁγιωσύνης) and avoids the syntactical difficulties involved in other readings of 9:5.

[23] Paul uses a mixture of two Greek idioms (οὐχ οἷον and οὐχ ὅτι), both of which have the same meaning. Cf. BDF §§304, 480 (5).

[24] The verb ἐκπίπτω literally means "fall off" (e.g., Acts 12:7 [chains]; Jas 1:11; 1 Pet 1:24 [flowers]), but it is used with a range of derived meanings (cf. BDAG). The idea that God's word does not fail is expressed in passages such as Josh 21:45; 23:14; 1 Sam 3:19; 2 Kgs 10:10.

[25] John Piper, *The Justification of God: An Exegetical and Theological Study of Romans 9:1–23,* 2nd ed. (Grand Rapids Baker, 1993), 49.

[26] John K. Goodrich, "The Word of God Has Not Failed: God's Faithfulness and Israel's Salvation in Tobit 14:3–7 and Romans 9–11," *TynBul* 67 (2016): 62.

descended from Israel/Jacob, while "Israel" on its own refers to a select group within that larger one (cf. 2:28–29). Such a distinction is reflected in some late Jewish texts (e.g., CD 4:2–12; 4QFlor 1:14–19; 1 En. 1:8–9) but not in the way Paul goes on to outline.[27] Believing Jews and Gentiles share in the eschatological blessings promised to Israel, but national Israel has "stumbled over the stumbling stone" of the Messiah (9:31–33). The issue Paul confronts in Rom 9–11 is whether the promises made to ethnic Israel will be fulfilled. The first step in his argument is to demonstrate from Scripture that God has narrowed "the apparent boundaries of election by choosing only some Jews to be saved (vv. 6–13, 27–29)."[28] To prove his point, the apostle uses a series of critical texts to give an overview of how God has historically dealt with his people. He begins with the patriarchs (vv. 7–13), moves on to Moses and the exodus (vv. 14–18), continues through the prophetic era until the exile of northern and southern kingdoms (vv. 19–29), and finally comes to the gospel period (vv. 30–33).

9:7–8. CSB renders the first claim, "Neither are all of Abraham's children his descendants" (cf. KJV, NIV, ESV). But Paul's Greek (οὐδ' ὅτι εἰσὶν σπέρμα Ἀβραὰμ πάντες τέκνα) is better understood in this way: "Neither is it the case that all of Abraham's children are his seed."[29] The noun σπέρμα ("seed, descendants, offspring") is the theologically significant term in vv. 7b, 8 and should be understood that way in v. 7a. This reading is consistent with the citation from Gen 21:12 that follows the strong adversative ἀλλά ("on the contrary"): (lit.) "in Isaac your seed will be called" (ἐν Ἰσαὰκ κληθήσεταί σοι σπέρμα). Paul shows that a process of election within the family of Abraham began with God's choice of Isaac, rather than Ishmael, to be the recipient of the covenant blessings. Physical descent was not the crucial qualification since both children had the same father.

[27] Dunn (*Romans 9–16*, 539–40) understands Paul's distinction here in terms of those who are "of the law" and those who are "of faith" (4:14, 16). Moo (*Romans*, 573–74) makes a broader distinction between ethnic Israel and a spiritual Israel but inappropriately includes Gentiles in the latter category. Cf. Jewett, *Romans*, 574–75.

[28] Moo, *Romans*, 569. Moo rightly argues that God is free "to 'expand' the dimensions of his people by choosing Gentiles (vv. 24–26)," though I would argue that the texts from Hosea in vv. 25–26 are not primarily used to establish this.

[29] So NRSV; Dunn, *Romans 9–16*, 540; Moo, *Romans*, 575n25; Schreiner, *Romans*, 495; and Jewett, *Romans*, 575–76. Contrast Cranfield, *Romans*, 2:473–76; Piper, *Justification of God*, 67–68; Byrne, *Romans*, 293.

The key terms "seed" and "called" are picked up in vv. 8, 12, 24, 25, 26, 29, indicating how foundational this text is for the argument to come.[30]

In the explanatory sentence that follows—introduced by τοῦτ' ἔστιν ("that is")—Abraham's children in the comprehensive sense are called τὰ τέκνα τῆς σαρκός ("the children by physical descent" [lit. "children of the flesh"]). But Abraham's children in the selective sense are simply called "God's children" (τέκνα τοῦ θεοῦ) or "children of the promise" (τὰ τέκνα τῆς ἐπαγγελίας). Of course, Isaac was a child of the flesh as Ishmael was, but Paul's point is that Isaac and his descendants were also "children of the promise" (cf. Gal 4:21–31). The latter are reckoned or considered "seed" (σπέρμα) in the narrower sense of being spiritual offspring. God is the implied subject of λογίζεται εἰς ("reckoned as, considered to be"), as in 2:26; 4:3–6, 8–11, 22–24. Use of the present tense here suggests that Paul is articulating "a principle according to which God acts in bestowing covenantal blessings."[31]

9:9. Paul indicates that he is about to explain the expression "children of promise" (v. 8) by placing the link word in an emphatic position at the beginning of the Greek sentence (ἐπαγγελίας γὰρ ὁ λόγος οὗτος, [lit.] "for this word is one of *promise*" [CSB: "for this is the statement of the promise"). A citation combining elements of Gen 18:10, 14 follows ("At this time I will come, and Sarah will have a son"). The catchword "son" in this supplementary text interprets the word "seed" in the previous one and prepares for the use of "sons" in later citations (vv. 26–27). Paul replaces the LXX verbal forms (ἐπαναστρέφων ἥξω, ἀναστρέψω, "I will [surely] return") with a simple future (ἐλεύσομαι, "I will come"), thus stressing God's presence and enabling in the conception of Isaac. The Lord's initiative in forming and saving his covenant people continues to be highlighted in vv. 13, 15, 17, 24.

---

[30] The future passive κληθήσεταί ("shall be called") could mean "shall be named" or simply "shall be" (BDAG, καλέω 1 a δ). However, what God "calls" people in vv. 25–26 is related to his calling of them into a relationship with himself (vv. 11, 24). The dative σοι is possessive in meaning here ("your").

[31] Moo, *Romans*, 577. The repeated word "promise" in this context recalls 4:13, 14, 16, 20, and "seed/descendants" recalls 4:13, 16, 18, showing the application of this principle to those who believe the gospel.

9:10. The expression οὐ μόνον δέ, ἀλλὰ καί ("not only [that], but also") signifies continuity as well as development of thought (cf. 5:3). It introduces a further argument to substantiate the claim that "not all who are descended from Israel are Israel" (v. 6). God's process of election within the family of Abraham continued to be worked out when "Rebekah conceived children through one man, our father Isaac." Paul alludes to Rebekah's twins, speaking about their conception "by one act of sexual intercourse" (ἐξ ἑνὸς κοίτην).[32] Isaac fathered Esau and Jacob together and became the spiritual forefather of the nation of Israel through the events described in Gen 25:21–34; 27:1–40.

9:11–13. The connective at the beginning of this long sentence (γάρ, "for") introduces a theological reflection on God's choice of Jacob over Esau, though the two sons are not named until v. 13. Paul phrases the first part of this sentence in negative terms, anticipating his argument about election being an expression of God's mercy and not a response to human merit (vv. 14–29). First, there is a circumstantial clause in the form of a genitive absolute (μήπω γεννηθέντων μηδὲ πραξάντων τι ἀγαθὸν ἢ φαῦλον, [lit.] "though they had not been born yet or done anything good or bad"). God's choice preceded the actions recorded in Gen 25:27–34; 27:1–40, when Esau sold his inheritance to Jacob and Jacob deceitfully secured Isaac's blessing. Second, a purpose clause explains the reason for the biblical citation that follows ("so that God's purpose according to election might stand"). The expression ἡ κατ' ἐκλογὴν πρόθεσις τοῦ θεοῦ means "God's purpose which is characterized by election."[33] "Stand" or "remain" (μένῃ) is the opposite of "fall" or "fail" (v. 6; cf. Isa 40:8). Third, the basis of God's elective activity is described (οὐκ ἐξ ἔργων ἀλλ' ἐκ τοῦ καλοῦντος, "not from works but from the one who calls"). Using a term familiar to us from earlier in the letter (ἐξ

[32] Dunn, *Romans 9–16*, 542. The primary meaning of κοίτη is "bed," but the word can also be used for the act of sexual intercourse (e.g., Wis 3:13, 16; Heb 13:4) and seminal emission (e.g., Num 5:20; cf. κοίτη σπέρματος in Lev 15:16–17, 32; 18:20; 22:4).

[33] Cranfield, *Romans*, 2:478. God's purpose (πρόθεσις) was mentioned in 8:28 and outlined in 8:29–30. Election (ἐκλογή) is mentioned here by name for the first time in Romans, though it was implied in 8:28–30; 9:4–8. Compare 11:5 (λεῖμμα κατ' ἐκλογὴν χάριτος, "a remnant chosen by grace"); 11:7, 28; 1 Thess 1:4. Although the term "election" does not appear in the LXX, the notion is expressed by the near cognate ἐκλεκτός (cf. Gottlob Schrenk, "ἐκλέγομαι," *TDNT* 4:182–83).

ἔργων, "from works"; 3:20, 27; 4:2), Paul insists that God's calling, which gives effect to his unmerited choice, is not based on human achievement. God's calling is an expression of his mercy and grace and is unrelated to what people have done or might do.[34] For this reason God's purpose according to election stands firm and secure (see §1.3).

The principal clause in this complex sentence includes a citation from the last line of Gen 25:23 (ἐρρέθη αὐτῇ ὅτι ὁ μείζων δουλεύσει τῷ ἐλάσσονι, [lit.] "it was said to her, 'The older will serve the younger'"). This revelation signaled a reversal of the normal pattern whereby leadership in the family passed to the older son, together with the father's inheritance. But the first two lines of Gen 25:23 make clear that God was concerned with Jacob and Esau as the progenitors of two nations ("two nations are in your womb; two peoples will come from you and be separated"), not simply as individuals.[35] So Paul adds a portion of Mal 1:2–3, putting the names of both Jacob and Esau before the respective verbs for emphasis (lit., "as it is written, '*Jacob* I have loved, but *Esau* I have hated'" [τὸν Ἰακὼβ ἠγάπησα, τὸν δὲ Ἠσαῦ ἐμίσησα]). The prophet is speaking about the historical outworking of God's purpose in relation to Israel and Edom (Mal 1:4–5). So "loved" denotes election to covenant blessing, and "hated" denotes exclusion from that role. The verbs refer to how God acted toward those two nations in pre-Christian history.[36] Paradoxically, however, in the gospel era believing Edomites as Gentiles may receive God's saving grace while many Israelites remain outside the sphere of eschatological blessing in the Messiah Jesus. Yet, just as the rejection of the Edomites was actually

[34] Moo (*Romans*, 582–83, 587–88) rightly excludes faith as a basis for election, even though the text does not explicitly state this. Piper (*Justification of God*, 51) describes God's choice of Jacob as an act of predestination or predetermination, not "pre-recognition." God's purpose is to be "free from all human influences in the election he performs" (53).

[35] But Moo (*Romans*, 571–72) rightly opposes those who see only salvation-historical roles, not the eternal destinies of individuals, as Paul's focus in this chapter. Cf. Piper, *Justification of God*, 56–73; Thomas R. Schreiner, "Does Romans 9 Teach Individual Election unto Salvation? Some Exegetical and Theological Reflections," *JETS* 36 (1993): 25–40.

[36] Cf. Moo, *Romans*, 587. Jewett's view (*Romans*, 580) that Edom represents for Paul the Israelites who have not responded to the gospel has no exegetical basis.

a temporary phenomenon, Paul goes on to argue that the rejection of a hardened portion of Israel is temporary also (11:2).

9:14–15. A new section of the argument is signaled by the connective οὖν ("then"), which also links what follows to what has gone before. As in 3:5–6; 6:1–2; 7:7, an attention-grabbing question ("What should we say then?") is followed by a topic question and then a strong denial ("Absolutely not!").[37] The particle μή in the topic question expects a negative answer (μὴ ἀδικία παρὰ τῷ θεῷ;). In effect, this means, "There is no injustice with God, is there?" Paul denies that God acts in a way that contradicts the truth of who he is.[38] To support this denial, he quotes from LXX Exod 33:19, in which God says to Moses, "I will show mercy to whom I will show mercy, and I will have compassion on whom I will have compassion" (ἐλεήσω ὃν ἂν ἐλεῶ, καὶ οἰκτιρήσω ὃν ἂν οἰκτίρω). God spoke these words after Israel rebelled against him at Sinai and made a golden calf (Exod 32:1–6). Moses destroyed the idolatrous objects and the tablets of the law, while the Lord acted in terrible judgment against his people (32:7–35). In response to Moses's pleas, however, the Lord promised that his presence would remain with Israel and that he would bring those whom he spared into the land he had sworn to give them (33:1–17). Moses asked to see God's glory, and the Lord proclaimed his *name* as gracious and compassionate (33:18–19).[39] God's *glory* was then revealed as he proclaimed himself "a compassionate and gracious God, slow to anger and abounding in faithful love and truth" (34:6).

The freedom of God to show mercy and compassion as he determines is essential to his name and his glory (cf. Exod 3:14, "I

---

[37] Cranfield (*Romans*, 2:482) contends that there is no need to imagine a particular objector here: Paul's reflective question is simply a way of advancing his argument. But he acknowledges that a real objector is in view in v. 19. Dunn (*Romans 9–16*, 551) argues that this is an in-house discussion arising from the Jewish conception of Israel's election. Cf. Johann D. Kim, *God, Israel, and the Gentiles: Rhetoric and Situation in Romans 9–11*, SBLDS 4 (Missoula: Scholars, 2000), 126.

[38] Piper (*Justification of God*, 94–96) argues on the basis of Paul's use of ἀδικία (especially in 1:18; 2:8; 3:3–5, 7; 1 Cor 13:6; 2 Thess 2:10, 12) that unrighteousness is the opposite of righteousness and truth. God is committed to displaying the truth of who he is in all his actions.

[39] Piper (*Justification of God*, 80) argues, "The request to see God's glory should be understood in this context as a desire to have God confirm his astonishing willingness to show his favor to a stiff-necked, idolatrous people (cf. 33:16f)."

am who I am"). God's words to Moses are significant beyond their particular historical context. God's mercy is a feature of how he continues to act with human beings (vv. 16, 18, 23; cf. 11:30–32). The first answer to the topic question in v. 15 is that "God is righteous because he is committed to proclaiming his name and advertising his glory by showing his goodness, grace, and mercy to people as he freely chooses."[40]

9:16. The continuing implication of the quote from Exod 33:19 is introduced by the inferential terms ἄρα οὖν ("so then"). Paul reasons that "it does not depend on human will or effort, but on God who shows mercy" (οὐ τοῦ θέλοντος οὐδὲ τοῦ τρέχοντος ἀλλὰ τοῦ ἐλεῶντος θεοῦ, [lit.] "not on the one who wills nor the one who runs, but on God who shows mercy").[41] An indicative verb with a subject must be supplied to make sense of these participial expressions, and so CSB understands "it depends" before the negated terms. God's mercy cannot be earned or deserved by what one desires or does; it simply flows from his unmerited decision to show mercy. This echoes the statement of unconditional election in vv. 11–12. Moreover, in answer to the question in v. 14, Paul asserts that God is acting righteously when he shows mercy.

9:17. The argument continues with another citation supporting the denial of the topic question in v. 14.[42] God cannot be charged with injustice even when he uses those who oppose him to fulfill his plan. The Lord spoke to Pharaoh through Moses in Exod 9:16, but here it is the Scripture that "speaks" (λέγει [present tense], cf. 4:3; 10:11; 11:2; Gal 4:30) to Pharaoh. God's address to the enemy of his people continues to reveal a vital aspect of his character and his way of operating in human history. Paul's interpretive translation differs from the LXX in certain important respects. The opening words (εἰς αὐτὸ τοῦτο, "for this reason") express a stronger sense of purpose than LXX (καὶ ἕνεκεν τούτου). Paul's use of ἐξήγειρά σε ("I raised

---

[40] Schreiner, *Romans*, 507. Cf. Piper, *Justification of God*, 88–89, 156–57.

[41] Dunn (*Romans 9–16*, 553) says that "willing" and "running" together sum up "the totality of man's capacity." He sees "running" as particularly relevant to "the lifestyle of the devout Jew in the intensity of his devotion." Cf. Sir 15:15, 17; Pss. Sol. 9:4–5.

[42] So Cranfield (*Romans*, 2:485) argues, noting that the same syntactical pattern can be found in vv. 15–16 and 17–18, with a scriptural citation linked back to v. 14 by γάρ ("for") and then an explanatory argument introduced by ἄρα οὖν ("so then").

you up"), rather than LXX διετηρήθης ("you have been preserved"), implies that God caused Pharaoh to appear on the stage of history for definite, positive reasons.[43]

Both purpose clauses are made to begin with ὅπως, linking God's two intentions closely together. First, God intended to display his power by delivering the Israelites from Pharaoh's oppressive control (ὅπως ἐνδείξωμαι ἐν σοὶ τὴν δύναμίν μου, "so that I may display my power in you [Pharaoh]"). Use of the word δύναμίς ("power"), rather than LXX ἰσχύς ("strength"), may be significant in the light of 1:16, where God's power to save is in view.[44] Despite Pharaoh's opposition, and even through it, the power of God for salvation came to Israel while judgment fell on Egypt. God's related intention was that his name might be "proclaimed in the whole earth" (καὶ ὅπως διαγγελῇ τὸ ὄνομά μου ἐν πάσῃ τῇ γῇ).[45] Israel's salvation was designed to disclose God's gracious character to the nations and so bless them in fulfilment of his promise to Abraham (Gen 12:3).

9:18. As in v. 16, the implications of the preceding citation are introduced by the inferential terms ἄρα οὖν ("so then"). God has mercy on some (ὃν θέλει ἐλεεῖ, [lit.] "he has mercy on whom he wills") in the sense that he brings them to know him, to trust him, and to benefit from his saving plan. But he hardens others (ὃν δὲ θέλει σκληρύνει, "he hardens whom he wills") so that they remain resistant to his warnings and reject his gracious overtures.[46] Hardening is the counterpart to showing mercy. God indicated that he would harden Pharaoh's heart, even as he sent Moses to address him, and promised to multiply his signs and wonders in the land of Egypt (Exod 4:21; 7:3). In due course we are told that "the LORD hardened Pharaoh's heart" (Exod 9:12; 10:20, 27; 11:10; 14:4, 8). Yet we also read that Pharaoh "hardened his heart" (Exod 8:15; cf. 7:22; 9:35; 13:15),

---

[43] Cf. Moo, *Romans*, 595–96. Cranfield (*Romans*, 2:485) discusses ways this verbal difference from the LXX has been understood.

[44] God's power to save is also the focus in 1 Cor 1:18, 24; 2:5; 6:14; 2 Cor 4:7; 6:7; 13:4; Eph 1:19; 3:7, 20; 2 Tim 1:8. God's power and his name overlap in meaning in this text (cf. Ps 54:1; Acts 4:7).

[45] According to Exod 33:19, a portion of which is cited in v. 15, God's "name" involves a propensity to show mercy and compassion on whomever he wills, without regard for human merit or effort.

[46] Moo (*Romans*, 596n47) observes the use of the verb σκληρύνω ("harden") in the LXX and NT to refer to "a spiritual condition that leads people to fail to revere God, obey his laws, and the like." Cf. Piper, *Justification of God*, 160–62.

suggesting that God's hardening took place as Pharaoh refused to acknowledge God's power and respond to his warnings. He was caught "in a hardening nexus from which he could not escape nor exercise any *totally independent* self-determining actions, since Yahweh was the ultimate cause of the hardening."[47]

In Exodus the issue is not Pharaoh's eternal salvation, but his role in the outworking of God's saving plan for Israel and the nations. But Paul goes on to use the biblical portrayal of Pharaoh as part of a developing argument about how individuals are saved eschatologically. From the beginning of the chapter, the apostle has expressed his concern for many Israelites who are not saved (9:1–5; cf. 10:1; 11:14). He is about to use eschatological terms contrasting "objects of wrath prepared for destruction" (v. 22) with "objects of mercy that he prepared beforehand for glory" (v. 23).[48] In this chapter he focuses on God's essential nature, not merely his actions in specific historical contexts.

9:19–21. An objection to the preceding claim is presented in a second-person singular form (Ἐρεῖς μοι οὖν, "You will say to me, therefore"; cf. 11:19). This recalls the diatribe style of 2:1–5, 17–29, though the opponent here need not be the same as in those earlier verses. Similar objections to Paul's teaching must have been encountered in a variety of contexts.[49] Two related questions are used to express the problem. The first is, "Why then does he still find fault?"

---

[47] Gregory K. Beale, "An Exegetical and Theological Consideration of the Hardening of Pharaoh's Heart in Exodus 4–14 and Romans 9," *TJ* 5 (1984): 149 (emphasis in original). Moo (*Romans*, 599) concludes that God's hardening does not "*cause* spiritual insensitivity to the things of God: it maintains people in the state of sin that already characterizes them" (emphasis in original). However, Piper (*Justification of God*, 160–78) notes that the hardening of Pharaoh's heart in Exod 4–14 was God's sovereign act to magnify his name, not a response to Pharaoh's stubbornness.

[48] Cranfield (*Romans*, 2:489) says we have no right to read the implications of v. 22 back into v. 18, but the progressive nature of the argument suggests that v. 18 is a preparation for the disclosures in vv. 22–24 about the eternal destinies of individuals. Pharaoh is a type of all other "objects of wrath." Cf. Beale, "Hardening," 129–54.

[49] Moo (*Romans*, 600n60) thinks the interlocutor here is likely to be "a Pharisaic Jew who criticizes Paul's doctrine for not leaving enough room for human free will." But Thomas H. Tobin (*Paul's Rhetoric in Its Contexts: the Argument of Romans* [Peabody: Hendricksen, 2004], 332) argues that the diatribe "serves only to raise the questions Paul wants to deal with." Cf. Jewett, *Romans*, 590–91.

(τί [οὖν] ἔτι μέμφεται;),[50] which is like the question raised in 3:7. The second is (lit.), "For who resists his will?" (τῷ γὰρ βουλήματι αὐτοῦ τίς ἀνθέστηκεν;). CSB inserts "can" into the translation, suggesting it is impossible for people to resist God's will. Literally, the Greek means that no one *does*, as a matter of fact, resist.[51] God's *effectual* will or decree is in view (v. 11, "God's purpose"). We all resist God's *moral* will in acts of disobedience.

If God hardens people like Pharaoh and they become unwitting agents of his saving plan, why does he still condemn them? Paul's answer so far has been that God acts this way to declare or show the glory of his name. In the present context he escalates the argument by drawing attention to the creaturely status of his challenger (v. 20, ὦ ἄνθρωπε, μενοῦνγε σὺ τίς εἶ, "But who are you, a mere man") and questioning the appropriateness of contending against God (ὁ ἀνταποκρινόμενος τῷ θεῷ, "who talks back to God").[52] Paul is not condemning people who honestly seek to understand God's ways but rather those who arrogantly challenge his justice and how he orders human affairs. The familiar biblical image of the potter and the clay makes the point: "Will what is formed say to the one who formed it, 'Why did you make me like this?'"[53] God's creative activity is signified by the verb πλάσσειν ("form") in certain contexts (e.g., Gen 2:7–8, 15; Job 10:8–9; Ps 33:15 [LXX 32:15]), but elsewhere it is used of God's electing activity (e.g., Deut 32:6; Isa 43:1, 7; 44:2, 21, 24). A further question (ἤ, "or") draws out the

---

[50] The οὖν that follows τί in 𝔓[46] B D G is probably a copyist's addition, following the pattern in 3:1, 9; 4:1; 6:1, 15; 7:7; 8:31; 9:14, 30; 11:7.

[51] Cf. Cranfield, *Romans*, 2:490. The perfect tense of ἀνθέστηκεν may be understood imperfectively or gnomically as conveying what is regularly true ("resists" rather than "has resisted"). The way God's sovereignty and human responsibility work together is discussed by Paul Helm, *The Providence of God* (Downers Grove: InterVarsity, 1994); and David M. Ciocchi, "Reconciling Divine Sovereignty and Human Responsibility," *JETS* 37 (1994): 395–412.

[52] The verb ἀνταποκρινόμαι means "answer in turn, reply, refute" (Job 32:12; Luke 14:6), but here it is used in the more negative sense of "answer back" (BDAG). Both Jewish and Gentile writings warned against such arrogance before God (cf. Jewett, *Romans*, 592). The particle combination μενοῦνγε (BDAG, "rather, on the contrary" [cf. 10:18; Phil 3:8]) is simply rendered "but" by CSB (but see 10:18).

[53] Some of LXX Isa 29:16 (μὴ ἐρεῖ τὸ πλάσμα τῷ πλάσαντι, "Will what is formed say to the one who formed it?") may be combined with elements of Isa 45:9; Wis 12:12 in the question τί με ἐποίησας οὕτως; ("Why did you make me like this?"). Cf. Job 10:9; Jer 18:1–12; Sir 33:18.

meaning for Paul's argument: "Has the potter no right over the clay, to make from the same lump one piece of pottery (σκεῦος ['vessel']) for honor and another for dishonor?" (cf. Wis 15:7).

Although vv. 6–18 concentrated on God's use of individuals and nations in the historical outworking of his plan, the subject of eternal salvation was implicitly introduced in vv. 1–5, and it is about to come into sharper focus in vv. 22–24. Paul's contrast between "honor" and "dishonor" matches his contrast between "glory" and "wrath," "mercy" and "destruction." God's sovereignty with regard to the ultimate salvation or condemnation of individuals cannot be divorced from the image of the potter and his clay in this verse.[54]

9:22. Using the connective δέ ("and, but") and picking up some of the language of the preceding verses, Paul begins to apply his argument to the situation of Jews and Gentiles faced with the gospel of Christ. A conditional sentence with an opening set of propositions (an extended protasis), but no conclusion (apodosis), effectively extends to v. 24.[55] CSB has made two questions out of these proposals, challenging the reader to consider the implications (so also NIV). This rendering simplifies the syntax and suggests that καί ("and") at the beginning of v. 23 introduces another dimension to God's actions in history.[56] The first question is, "And what if God, wanting to display his wrath and to make his power known, endured with much patience objects of wrath prepared for destruction?" Parallels with other verses are significant. "God . . . wanting to display his wrath and to make his power known" recalls v. 17, citing Exod 9:16 (cf. Jer 16:21).[57] God's power brings salvation to some

[54] Dunn (*Romans 9–16*, 557) contends, "The more natural sense of the metaphor is of vessels put to different uses within history" (as in v. 17; 2 Tim 2:20; cf. Jer 22:28; Hos 8:8; 1 Thess 4:14; 1 Pet 3:7). Cranfield (*Romans*, 2:492–95) also argues against applying these verses to the salvation of individuals. But contrast Piper, *Justification of God*, 202–4; Schreiner, *Romans*, 517–18.

[55] Cranfield (*Romans*, 2:492) points out that various attempts to construe an apodosis from vv. 23, 24, or 30 are unnecessary since incomplete conditional sentences are fairly common in classical Greek (cf. LSJM, "εἰ," B VII 1, 2) and occur several times in the NT (cf. Luke 19:42; John 6:62; Acts 23:9; Rom 2:17–23).

[56] This connective is missing from B and some other manuscripts, versions, and fathers but is attested by a wide range of reliable early witnesses.

[57] A causative reading of the participle θέλων ("because he wished") is favored by Moo, *Romans*, 605–6; Piper, *Justification of God*, 206–7; Schreiner, *Romans*, 519–20; Kruse, *Romans*, 386–87. A concessive reading ("although he wished") is

but judgment to others. God's enduring with much patience (ἤνεγκεν ἐν πολλῇ μακροθυμίᾳ) recalls 2:4, where his patience is an expression of his kindness (cf. Exod 34:6, "slow to anger" [μακρόθυμος]). "Objects of wrath" (σκεύη ὀργῆς, [lit.] "vessels of wrath") recalls v. 21, with its reference to "a piece of pottery" (σκεῦος, "vessel") made "for dishonor" (εἰς ἀτιμίαν).

Although God's patience with humanity involves restraining his judgment until the final display of his wrath and power, the context points to his patience with *individuals* who are offered the possibility of repentance and transformation but reject it (cf. 10:21; 1 Tim 1:16; 2 Pet 3:9). Although mercy is "the greater, overarching goal for which God does all things,"[58] the expression "prepared for destruction" (κατηρτισμένα εἰς ἀπώλειαν) implies that some are headed for final judgment (cf. 2:5, 8–9; Eph 2:3; Phil 3:19), and God's wrath is not yet fully expressed against them.[59]

9:23–24. A change of syntax (καὶ ἵνα γνωρίσῃ, "and in order to make known") is taken by CSB to introduce a second question ("And what if he did this to make known the riches of his glory on objects of mercy that he prepared beforehand for glory?"). Paul indicates that God's patience (v. 22) has "a very definite and positive purpose in view,"[60] which is to make known "the riches of his glory" (τὸν πλοῦτον τῆς δόξης αὐτοῦ). As in the foundational revelation in Exod 33:18–19, the revelation of the glory of God in Jesus Christ involves showing extraordinary mercy to stubborn sinners. This gives them the hope of being glorified with him, and sharing in his glorious inheritance (5:2; 8:17, 21, 30). In calling the beneficiaries "objects of mercy that he prepared beforehand for glory" (ἐπὶ σκεύη ἐλέους ἃ προητοίμασεν εἰς δόξαν), Paul emphasizes God's merciful

---

argued by Wright ("Romans," 641–42). However, the present tense points to what is always true of God and so the participle may function like a relative clause (Dunn, *Romans 9–16*, 558).

[58] Piper, *Justification of God*, 214. However, contrast what Piper (207–10) says about God's patience with "the vessels of wrath."

[59] Schreiner (*Romans*, 521–22) rightly takes the perfect passive participle κατηρτισμένα ("made ready") as indicative of God's agency but fails to note any difference in the use of the aorist active indicative προητοίμασεν (v. 23, "he prepared beforehand"). Contrast Piper, *Justification of God*, 211–14; Moo, *Romans*, 607.

[60] Dunn, *Romans 9–16*, 560. Cranfield (*Romans*, 2:496) suggests, "The ἵνα clause indicates the one ultimate gracious purpose of God, for the sake of which he also wills to show his wrath."

predetermination of their present status and future condition.[61] God has endured rebellious humanity with great patience in order to save the objects of his mercy (cf. Eph 2:7). This last expression is applied to the readers by the relative clause in v. 24 ("on us, the ones he also called, not only from the Jews but also from the Gentiles"). The call of Jews and Gentiles to receive his mercy in Christ Jesus was highlighted in 1:16; 3:29; 4:11–16 and comes back into focus in 10:11–13; 11:1–32. As in the case of Pharaoh, however, God's patience with those who oppose him will finally issue in judgment. This is confirmed by the biblical citations that follow.

9:25–26. Loosely connected to the preceding argument by ὡς καί ("as also"), two confirmatory quotations are offered together. God is the implied speaker in the book of Hosea (ἐν τῷ Ὡσηὲ λέγει, "in Hosea he says" [cf. Mark 1:2]), testifying to the divine inspiration of that prophetic work.[62] Paul first cites a portion of Hos 2:23 (LXX 2:25 adapted), with the order of the clauses reversed and with καλέσω ("I will call") replacing ἐρῶ τῷ ("I will say to").[63] "Called" in these verses means being "named" as God's people, but this is "an effectual naming, a naming which brings about a fundamental change in the object named."[64] Hosea addressed the northern kingdom of Israel just before the Assyrian invasions in the eighth century BC, which culminated in the exile of many Israelites from their homeland. With this judgment God treated them as "Not my People" (τὸν οὐ λαόν μου) and as "Unloved" (τὴν οὐκ ἠγαπημένην). But through the prophet he promises that he will again call them "my People" (λαόν μου) and "Beloved" (ἠγαπημένην). A citation from Hos 1:10 (LXX 2:1) confirms that God's focus is on the restoration of their relationship: "And it will be in the place where they

[61] The same verb is used in Eph 2:10 with reference to good works, "which God prepared ahead of time for us to do."

[62] CSB ("as it also says") does not acknowledge the fact that God is the speaker in the texts cited.

[63] LXX ἐλεήσω τὴν Οὐκ ἠλεημένην ("I will be merciful to no mercy") is changed to καλέσω . . . τὴν οὐκ ἠγαπημένην ἠγαπημένην ("I will call 'unloved,' 'beloved'"). Schreiner (*Romans*, 527) says it is likely that Paul had a text before him that read this way. Mercy is such a prominent theme in Paul's own argument that he is unlikely to have changed a text that expressed this so clearly.

[64] Cranfield, *Romans*, 2:500. This calling is another way of describing the calling to salvation mentioned in v. 24.

were told, you are not my people, there they will be called sons of the living God."[65]

Since Paul has just mentioned God's calling of Jews and Gentiles together (v. 24), some would argue that the Hosea texts predict the inclusion of many Gentiles in the people of God, while the Isaiah texts (vv. 27–28) predict the comparatively small number of Jews in the Christian community.[66] Gentiles are certainly now included among those whom God calls "my People," and they may be called "sons of the living God" (cf. 8:14–17). But that is not the original focus or intention of Hosea's message.[67] We must first ask how Hosea's predictions about the restoration of Israel have been fulfilled. Indeed, Paul's continuing concern in Rom 9–11 is to demonstrate how the word of God to *Israel* has not failed (9:6). So he juxtaposes Hosea's predictions about a comprehensive restoration of God's covenant people with Isaiah's prophecies about only a remnant being saved. This prepares for the claim that there is "at the present time a remnant chosen by grace" (11:5) and the prediction that "all Israel will be saved" (11:26). There is a tension in the prophetic literature that Paul applies to the situation of Israel as he observes it in the gospel era. Many Gentiles benefit from the messianic salvation, but it is misleading to imply that predictions about the restoration of Israel are fulfilled by the salvation of Gentiles. Gentile Christians become partners with believing Israelites in the church, but believing Gentiles do not simply become part of Israel or replace Israel.[68] Moreover, if Paul had wanted a biblical warrant

[65] Rather than being a topical reference, as Moo (*Romans*, 613–14) understands it, "in the place where it was said to them" (ἐν τῷ τόπῳ οὗ ἐρρέθη αὐτοῖς) is probably an attempt to convey the Hebrew idiom "instead of its being said" (Cranfield, *Romans*, 2:501, citing BDB, 880).

[66] E.g., Moo, *Romans*, 611–13; Schreiner, *Romans*, 527–28; Byrne, *Romans*, 304; Kruse, *Romans*, 388–89. Jewett (*Romans*, 600) takes "my people" to refer to "the mixed community of the church."

[67] Against Jewett (*Romans*, 599), Paul does not redefine Israel by including believing Gentiles here. There are echoes of Hosea's predictions in 1 Pet 2:10, where the context suggests that Gentile Christians are "re-enacting a chapter of Israel's history" by becoming the recipients of God's mercy and being named as God's people (J. Ramsey Michaels, *1 Peter*, WBC 49 [Waco: Word, 1988], 112–13). But Paul uses the Hosea texts more simply with reference to the fulfillment of God's purpose for Israel. See §2.5.

[68] Cf. §2.5; Donald W. B. Robinson, "The Salvation of Israel in Romans 9–11," in *Donald Robinson: Selected Works,* Volume 1: *Assembling God's People* (Sydney:

for the inclusion of Gentiles among the eschatological people of God at this point in his argument, there were more obvious texts he could have chosen (e.g., Isa 49:6; 60:3; Jer 3:17; Zech 8:22–23).

9:27–28. In contrast with Hosea's hopeful message, Paul introduces the first of two devastating citations from the book of Isaiah. These prophecies were delivered to the southern kingdom of Judah in the period 734–701 BC, when the threat of Assyrian invasion hung over the whole nation and the northern kingdom was finally destroyed. The first prediction is introduced with the dramatic words, "But Isaiah cries out concerning Israel." Citing an abbreviation of Isa 10:22–23, the apostle replaces LXX ὁ λαός ("the people") with ὁ ἀριθμὸς τῶν υἱῶν Ἰσραήλ ("the number of Israel's sons"), probably influenced by the wording of the previous quotation (CSB: "the number of Israelites"). This links the prophecies in vv. 25–29 together and confirms that they are all about the future of Israel. The prospect of becoming as numerous as "the sand of the sea" recalls the promise to Abraham in Gen 22:17 (cf. 32:12). But Isaiah sees that, despite that promise, "(only) the remnant will be saved" (τὸ ὑπόλειμμα σωθήσεται).[69] The reason given (γάρ, "for, since") is that "the Lord will execute his sentence completely and decisively on the earth."[70] Although the LXX differs from the Hebrew text here, it gives the general sense of destruction decreed by God and justice overflowing.[71]

9:29. A supporting quotation from Isa 1:9 is introduced with the words καὶ καθὼς προείρηκεν Ἠσαΐας ("and just as Isaiah predicted"). Parallel with the previous citation but using a conditional form of speech, it indicates again that God will preserve a remnant when he

Australian Church Record/Moore College, 2008), 55.

[69] LXX σωθήσεται ("shall be saved") is a rendering of יָשׁוּב ("shall return"). Paul substitutes ὑπόλειμμα for LXX κατάλειμμα ("remnant"), without any change of meaning (cf. 11:5, λεῖμμα).

[70] The best Greek texts (𝔓[46] ℵ* A B), early versions, and fathers have λόγον γὰρ συντελῶν καὶ συντέμνων ποιήσει κύριος ἐπὶ τῆς γῆς. TR, following ℵ[c] D G K P Ψ 33 88, etc., adds ἐν δικαιοσύνῃ, ὅτι λόγον συντετμημένον (KJV, "For he will finish the work, and cut *it* short in righteousness"). Early copyists appear to have added more of the wording of LXX Isa 10:22–23 here. Cf. Metzger, *Textual Commentary*, 462.

[71] Jewett (*Romans*, 603–4) argues that Paul's rendering of the text downplays the element of annihilating judgment, making λόγον a reference to the word of salvation, which the Lord will "execute with rigor and dispatch upon the earth." But this is not a natural reading of the text, even in the abbreviated form that Paul presents it.

acts in judgment (εἰ μὴ κύριος σαβαὼθ ἐγκατέλιπεν ἡμῖν σπέρμα, "if the Lord of Hosts had not left us offspring").[72] Comparing the annihilation of Sodom and Gomorrah in Gen 19:24–25, Isaiah foresees that without such a merciful provision, "we would have become like Sodom, and we would have been made like Gomorrah." Terrible judgment took place when the Babylonians invaded the southern kingdom and progressively exiled the people in 597, 587, and 582 BC. Then, in 538 BC, when the Persians had conquered Babylon, they allowed a remnant of the Jews to return to Jerusalem, to rebuild their city and temple. The word "offspring" (σπέρμα) forms an inclusion with the citation from Gen 21:12 in 9:7, suggesting that the true "seed" of Abraham is once more in view. But only in 11:7–32 does Paul explain how these prophecies are fulfilled eschatologically. The two citations from Isaiah offer further evidence that the word of God has not failed (v. 6). As Paul preaches the gospel to his fellow Israelites, the fact that *some* believe indicates that there is "at the present time a remnant chosen by grace" (11:5). "Even a remnant of believing Israelites at any given time certifies the continued presence of the Israel whom God foreknew, and, at the end, this Israel will be saved in full integrity."[73]

Bridge

Paul's passionate concern for his fellow Israelites is a reminder that grief, rather than anger, resentment, or resignation, is the proper response to unbelief in others. Moreover, his prayer for their salvation and his attempts to persuade them of their need for Christ are positive examples of how to cope with such grief. His list of the special blessings given to Israel highlights the particular pain of Jewish unbelief, but the teaching that follows has a wider application. The word of God has not failed: God is still at work in his world. Hope for the nations is grounded in the promises given to Israel and God's faithfulness in fulfilling them. The process of election outlined in biblical history, whether at a national or an individual level, is an expression of God's mercy and love. Election has

---

[72] The verb ἐγκατέλιπεν is cognate with λεῖμμα and ὑπόλειμμα ("remnant"). LXX σπέρμα ("seed") is different from the Hebrew שָׂרִיד כִּמְעָט ("a few survivors"), but Isa 6:13 does speak about the remnant as "the holy seed" (זֶרַע קֹדֶשׁ).

[73] Robinson, "The Salvation of Israel," 50.

never been a response to human merit or achievement but a free and gracious initiative on God's part—an expression of his unmerited favor. If people accuse God of injustice when he chooses some and not others, the charge cannot be upheld: justice demands punishment! Moreover, even though God hardens some, his patience and mercy offer hope that many may yet repent and be included in the final number of his people. So Paul's teaching about the sovereignty of God in saving a people for himself is meant to promote trust and encourage persistence in sharing the gospel of his grace with those who do not yet believe.

B. Israel's Failure to Pursue Righteousness by Faith (9:30–10:4)

30 What should we say then? Gentiles, who did not pursue
righteousness, have obtained righteousness—namely the righteousness that comes from faith.
31 But Israel, pursuing the law
of righteousness, has not achieved the righteousness of the law.
32 Why is that? Because they did not pursue it by faith, but as if it
were by works. They stumbled over the stumbling stone.
33 As it
is written,

> **Look, I am putting a stone in Zion to stumble over**
> **and a rock to trip over,**
> **and the one who believes on him**
> **will not be put to shame.**

1 Brothers and sisters, my heart's desire and prayer to God
concerning them is for their salvation.
2 I can testify about them
that they have zeal for God, but not according to knowledge.
3 Since they are ignorant of the righteousness of God and attempted to establish their own righteousness, they have not submitted
to God's righteousness.
4 For Christ is the end of the law for righteousness to everyone who believes,

Context

Paul brings his overview of God's relationship with Israel (9:6–29) to a climax by claiming that "they stumbled over the stumbling stone," who is their Messiah (9:32b–33). This happened because they pursued the law for righteousness as if it were by works rather than by faith (9:31–32a). At the same time, Paul celebrates the fact that "Gentiles, who did not pursue righteousness, have obtained righteousness—namely the righteousness that comes from faith" (9:30). These two approaches are highlighted again in 10:3, where the contrast is expressed in terms of "the righteousness of God" and "their own righteousness." In the following passage Paul relates these two approaches to different ways of understanding God's law and its purpose (10:5–8) and returns to the theme of Gentiles obtaining righteousness by faith as they call upon the risen Lord for salvation (10:9–13). In this way he continues to justify his fundamental assertion that the word of God has not failed (9:6)

Structure

In 9:30–31, Paul resumes his teaching about the righteousness that comes from faith, which is the outcome of God's justifying work in Christ (3:21–4:25). This has been "obtained" by Gentiles who did not pursue it, but not by Israel as a nation, because they pursued the law for righteousness, as if it were by works. A combination of Isa 28:16 and 8:14 is used to highlight Israel's stumbling over the "stone" of the Messiah rather than believing in him (9:32–33). In 10:1–2 Paul once more expresses his passionate concern for his fellow Israelites (cf. 9:1–5), acknowledging that they have a zeal for God "but not according to knowledge." This failure has prevented them from submitting to the righteousness of God that is received through faith and from seeing that "Christ is the end of the law for righteousness to everyone who believes" (10:3–4). Israel has failed to understand the significance of the Messiah whom God has sent to them.

Outline:

1. A misguided pursuit (9:30–33)
2. Zeal without knowledge (10:1–3)
3. Christ the end of the law for righteousness (10:4)

9:30–31. As in 6:1; 7:7; 8:31; 9:14, Paul begins a new stage in his argument with an attention-grabbing question ("What should we say then?"). This introduces a conclusion that could be drawn from the preceding context. Although 9:30–33 forms an introduction to 10:1–21, it also supplies a fitting conclusion to 9:1–29, identifying the failure of Israel that has caused Paul such intense sorrow and anguish of heart (9:1–2). A statement follows (ὅτι, "that" [not translated by CSB]), rather than another question.[74] The first part of the statement focuses on "Gentiles, who did not pursue righteousness." Without a definite article, ἔθνη is not a reference to "the Gentiles" generally but to "some Gentiles, namely, those who have believed."[75] These people are further defined as those "who did not pursue righteousness" (τὰ μὴ διώκοντα δικαιοσύνην). The verb used here and in the next verse suggests an energetic, zealous quest (cf. 12:13; 14:19; 1 Cor 14:1; Phil 3:12).[76] Paul does not mean that in their pagan life Gentile Christians had no concern to pursue moral righteousness. The rest of the sentence makes clear that a status of righteousness before God is intended, and the context relates this to the coming judgment of God.[77] What Gentile believers did not seek, they "obtained" (κατέλαβεν, cf. Phil 3:12), "namely the righteousness that comes from faith" (δικαιοσύνην δὲ τὴν ἐκ πίστεως). This recalls 4:11, 13 and Paul's teaching more generally about justification by faith, though the particular expression here is strictly only paralleled in 10:6 (ἡ δὲ ἐκ πίστεως δικαιοσύνη, "the righteousness that comes from faith"). Gentiles come to experience this by believing the gospel about the righteousness of God manifested in the saving work of Christ (cf. 1:17; 3:21–26). "Israel" in the rest of the sentence means unbelieving Israel, here literally defined as "pursuing the law of righteousness" (διώκων νόμον δικαιοσύνης). The context suggests that this last expression should be rendered "pursuing the law *for* righteousness" (see §2.4).[78]

[74] Dunn (*Romans 9–16*, 580) says that the statement could be read "with the suggestion of a question in the voice," meaning a question expecting an affirmative answer.

[75] Cranfield, *Romans*, 2:506. Cf. 2:14.

[76] The verbs διώκειν ("pursue") and καταλαμβάνειν ("obtain") are often used together to describe the attainment of goals (e.g., LXX Gen 31:23; Exod 15:9; Deut 19:6). Moo (*Romans*, 621n22) comments on the possible influence of Isa 51:1–7 on Paul's thought in 9:30–33.

[77] The term δικαιοσύνη is used with reference to moral righteousness in chs. 6–8. But here Paul returns to its use in chs. 1–4, concerning "the 'right' standing with God that is the product of God's justifying work in Christ" (Moo, *Romans*, 619). See §2.4; Byrne, *Romans*, 309–10; Schreiner, *Romans*, 535–36.

[78] Cf. Cranfield, *Romans*, 2:508n1; Schreiner, *Romans*, 537. Moo (*Romans*, 622–26) discusses alternative translations of νόμον δικαιοσύνης and ends up suggesting "the law that promises righteousness." Contrast Dunn, *Romans 9–16*, 581; Jewett, *Romans*, 610.

The law itself showed that righteousness is by faith (v. 32; cf. 10:6–8) and not simply by obedience to the commands of God. So Paul considers that unbelieving Israel "has not achieved the law" (εἰς νόμον οὐκ ἔφθασεν); they have not "attained" or "arrived at" (BDAG, cf. Phil 3:16) the position to which they were being directed by the law.[79] This aorist verb functions in a summary way, describing Israel's characteristic failure throughout the period from Moses to Christ and beyond (cf. v. 33; 10:4–5).

9:32–33. In response to another rhetorical question (διὰ τί; "Why is that?"), Paul explains the preceding claim. The brevity of the Greek (ὅτι οὐκ ἐκ πίστεως ἀλλ' ὡς ἐξ ἔργων) requires that we understand the verb "pursue" from the preceding sentence ("because they did not *pursue* it by faith, but as if it were by works").[80] Israel is not condemned for pursuing the law as such but for pursuing it as if it were a set of demands by which one could gain favor with God.[81] Paul's broader understanding of Torah is that it was meant to encourage faith in God for justification (cf. 3:2–3; 4:3–12; 10:6–8). A faith approach to the law might involve

> accepting, without evasion or resentment, the law's criticism of one's life, recognizing that one could never so adequately fulfill its righteous requirements as to put God in one's debt, accepting God's proffered mercy and forgiveness and in return giving oneself to him in love and gratitude and so beginning to be released from one's

[79] CSB adds "the righteousness of" to "the law" for clarification. Robert Badenas (*Christ the End of the Law: Romans 10:4 in Pauline Perspective*, JSNTSup 10 (Sheffield: JSOT, 1985], 104) maintains that ἔφθασεν should be rendered "come first," but with the preposition εἰς it always means "arrive at, attain" (cf. Gottfried Fitzer, "φθάνω, προφθάνω," *TDNT* 9:90–91).

[80] Although א[2] D Ψ 33 81and other manuscripts, versions, and fathers have ἔργων νόμου ("works of the law"), the shorter text is found in a range of more ancient witnesses (𝔓[46vid] א* A B F G and others) and is more likely to be the original. The longer text is presumably assimilated from 3:20, 28 (cf. Gal 2:16; 3:2, 5, 10).

[81] Dunn (*Romans 9–16*, 582) argues that ἐξ ἔργων should simply be understood in terms of the requirements of the law that mark off Jew from Gentile. However, this is not an adequate way to view the apostle's polemic here (cf. 3:20 comment). Jewett (*Romans*, 611) rightly observes that "this verse seeks to explain why Israel rejected the message about Christ rather than to discuss its attitude toward Gentiles." Cf. n. 94 below.

self-centeredness and turned in the direction of a humble obedience that is free from self-righteousness.[82]

Abruptly, without a grammatical link to the preceding sentence, Paul announces that "they stumbled over the stumbling stone" (προσέκοψαν τῷ λίθῳ τοῦ προσκόμματος), explaining the situation of unbelieving Israel in terms of the mixed biblical citation that follows. This is introduced with the familiar preface, "as it is written." Isaiah encouraged the people of Jerusalem to trust in the Lord and the "stone" he was putting in Zion (τίθημι, replacing LXX Isa 28:16, ἐμβαλῶ), which the prophet described as "a tested stone, a precious cornerstone, a sure foundation." But Paul substitutes words from an earlier passage in Isaiah's work: "a stone . . . to stumble over and a rock to trip over" (λίθον προσκόμματος καὶ πέτραν σκανδάλου). These words are adapted from LXX Isa 8:14 (ὡς λίθου προσκόμματι . . . ὡς πέτρας πτώματι), where God is described as a "sanctuary" for those who fear him but a stumbling stone "for the two houses of Israel."[83] Paul concludes with the promise of LXX Isa 28:16 ("and the one who believes on him will not be put to shame").[84] This contains the important words ἐπ' αὐτῷ ("on him"), which are not found in the Hebrew but allow for the development of a messianic interpretation.[85]

---

[82] Cranfield, *Romans*, 2:510. Psalm 119 is a good example of this approach. Against alternative views, Schreiner (*Romans*, 539–40) agrees that Israel is criticized here for a legalistic approach to the law.

[83] Christopher D. Stanley (*Paul and the Language of Scripture: Citation Technique in the Pauline Epistles and Contemporary Literature*, SNTSMS 74 [Cambridge: Cambridge University, 1992], 119–25) provides an extensive discussion of the way Paul handles the LXX and conflates these texts. Douglas A. Oss ("The Interpretation of the 'Stone' Passages by Peter and Paul: A Comparative Study," *JETS* 32 [1989]: 181–200) compares the way Peter and Paul use these texts. Cf. 14:13 comment.

[84] Paul's future indicative οὐ καταισχυνθήσεται ("will not be put to shame") replaces the subjunctive form in the LXX (οὐ μὴ καταισχυνθῇ). The Hebrew (לֹא יָחִישׁ) means "will not panic" or "will be unshakable." Some manuscripts (Ψ 6 33 etc.) contain the extra word πᾶς ("every"), but the shorter reading is better attested (א A B D G etc.).

[85] Cf. Wright, "Romans," 649–51. The messianic interpretation of the stone was common in Jewish literature (cf. Joachim Jeremias, "λίθος, λίθινος," *TDNT* 4:272–73). Jesus identified himself with the rejected "stone" of Ps 118:22–23 (LXX Ps 117:22–23) in Matt 21:42, 44 par., giving rise to a Christian exegetical tradition (cf. Acts 4:11; 1 Pet 2:4, 6–8). The linking of Isa 28:16; 8:14 by Peter and Paul suggests to some scholars that a collection of "stone" testimonies may already have

Combining these texts, the apostle draws together the positive and negative messages of Isaiah for Israel and provides a Christological conclusion to the chapter. Israel's failure to pursue the righteousness that comes by faith culminated in the rejection of the Messiah, who is the promised eschatological deliverer, soon to be described as "the end of the law for righteousness to everyone who believes" (10:4). Believing in Christ becomes the central theme in 10:9–16, where the last line of Isa 28:16 is repeated (10:11). The context makes clear that not being "put to shame" refers to the judgment of God and is another way of speaking about eschatological salvation. So, if it is *God* who has laid the messianic stone in Zion, there is a purpose in Israel's current stumbling that remains to be explained (10:1–21; 11:7–12, 25–32).

10:1. Abruptly, without a conjunction linking this new sentence to the preceding one, the readers are again intimately addressed as "brothers and sisters" (cf. 1:7; 7:1, 4; 8:12).[86] Paul resumes the first-person singular to persuade them of his ongoing concern for fellow Israelites, whom he previously described as (lit.) "my brothers, my countrymen by physical descent" (9:3).[87] In 9:2–3 he suggested that his intense sorrow and continuing anguish of heart could make him willing to be "cursed and cut off from Christ" if it could bring about their salvation. But here he expresses a more positive, heartfelt desire (ἡ μὲν εὐδοκία τῆς ἐμῆς καρδίας) and prayer to God (καὶ ἡ δέησις πρὸς τὸν θεόν) for their salvation.[88] Paul's intercession is "clear proof that he did not think of their present rejection as final

---

been circulating (e.g., Barnabas Lindars, *New Testament Apologetic: The Doctrinal Significance of Old Testament Quotations* [Philadelphia: Westminster, 1961], 175–79). Contrast Jewett, *Romans*, 612–13.

[86] The particle μέν would normally be followed by δέ in the next clause or sentence, creating a contrast. But here μέν on its own has the effect of putting the focus on Paul's prayer for the salvation of Israel as the singular issue.

[87] The external evidence favoring the reading ὑπὲρ αὐτῶν ("for them") is ancient and widespread ($\mathfrak{P}^{46}$ ℵ* A B D F G etc.). The alternative τοῦ Ἰσραήλ ἐστιν ("for Israel") is a later substitution, possibly made when this verse began a reading in church services (Metzger, *Textual Commentary*, 463).

[88] Although εὐδοκία is translated "desire" in most English versions, Jewett (*Romans*, 614–15) argues that it ordinarily means "good pleasure" and should be rendered that way here (compare Luke 10:21; Phil 2:13). Contrast Schreiner, *Romans*, 542.

and closed."[89] He prays for them to respond to the gospel with faith and acknowledge Jesus as Lord (10:9–13; 11:11–14).

10:2. The conjunction γάρ ("for"), which is not translated by CSB, indicates that Paul is about to explain why he continues to pray for the salvation of his fellow Israelites. In a formal and solemn way, he testifies to their zeal or jealousy for God.[90] Such zeal is commended in many biblical and later Jewish texts, sometimes specifically linked with the law or the tabernacle/temple (e.g., Num 25:11, 13; 1 Kgs 19:10, 14; 2 Kgs 10:16; Ps 69:9 [LXX 68:10]; Acts 21:20; cf. Sir 45:23; 1 Macc 2:26, 27; T. Ash. 4:5). But zeal for God could involve violence against those who opposed Israel's values and way of life, motivated by a passion to defend God's honor in the face of idolatry and godless behavior. Formerly, Paul expressed his zeal in devotion to the law and to the Pharisaic traditions, leading him to persecute the followers of Jesus (Acts 9:1–5; 22:3–5; 26:4–5; Gal 1:14; Phil 3:6). He now describes this sort of zeal as "not according to knowledge" (οὐ κατ' ἐπίγνωσιν).[91] Earlier in the letter he claimed that the law provided "the embodiment of knowledge and truth" (2:20), but Israel did not respond to this revelation in a way that honored God before the nations (2:21–24). Israel lacked "the knowledge of sin" the law was meant to provide (ἐπίγνωσις ἁμαρτίας, cf. 3:9–20) and resisted the message that "no one will be justified in [God's] sight by the works of the law" (3:20; cf. Ps 143:2). Consequently, they failed in their calling to be a light to the nations so that God's salvation might reach "to the ends of the earth" (Isa 49:6).

10:3. Linked to the preceding claim by the conjunction γάρ ("for, since"), this verse explains Israel's lack of knowledge as a failure to come to grips with God's righteousness and how it is bestowed. Two present participles are used in a causal relation to

---

[89] Cranfield, *Romans*, 2:513. He observes that εἰς σωτηρίαν ("for [their] salvation") is equivalent in sense to ἵνα σωθῶσιν ("that they may be saved").

[90] The verb μαρτυρέω is used with the dative of the person about whom the testimony is given and ὅτι followed by the content of the testimony in Matt 23:31; John 3:28; Gal 4:15; Col 4:13. The genitive in the expression ζῆλον θεοῦ is objective ("zeal for God").

[91] The change in Paul's theology of jealousy, when he turned to Christ, is aptly described by Richard H. Bell, *Provoked to Jealousy: The Origin and Purpose of the Jealousy Motif in Romans 9–11*, WUNT 2.63 (Tübingen: Mohr, 1994), 309–11. Cf. Albrecht Stumpff, "ζῆλος κτλ.," *TDNT* 2:877–82.

the indicative οὐχ ὑπετάγησαν ("have not submitted"). Israel's culpable ignorance of "the righteousness of God" is first highlighted by ἀγνοοῦντες ([lit.] "because they disregarded").[92] The expression τὴν τοῦ θεοῦ δικαιοσύνην ("the righteousness of God") could be a reference back to God's saving righteousness, as identified in 1:17; 3:21, 22 (δικαιοσύνη θεοῦ). Paul reverts to this more familiar way of describing God's righteousness at the end of 10:3 (τῇ δικαιοσύνῃ τοῦ θεοῦ). But the closest parallel to the expression at the beginning of the verse is in Phil 3:9, where Paul contrasts it with "a righteousness of my own from the law" (ἐμὴν δικαιοσύνην τὴν ἐκ νόμου). In the present context it could be recalling what he said in 4:1–25 about God's attributing righteousness to those who believe and be another way of speaking about justification by faith (cf. 4:25; 5:1). It could therefore be translated "the righteousness that comes from God" (NRSV). A second present participle (ζητοῦντες) is then used causally to indicate the coordinate problem: (lit.) "and because they were attempting to establish their own righteousness" (καὶ τὴν ἰδίαν [δικαιοσύνην] ζητοῦντες στῆσαι).[93]

Some have argued that the issue here is not the sin of self-righteousness but the way different first-century Jewish groups sought to validate their own righteousness over against one another and the Gentiles.[94] However, there is no indication in the immediate context that sectarian or nationalistic righteousness is Paul's essential concern. The contrast with God's righteousness suggests that the issue is anthropological: "to seek righteousness on the basis of fulfilling the 'works of the law' is to refuse to admit that one is part of

---

[92] Cf. BDAG; R. Bultmann, "ἀγνοέω, κτλ.," *TDNT* 1:116; Dunn, *Romans 9–16*, 587.

[93] The noun δικαιοσύνην ("righteousness") is included by some reliable witnesses (e.g., 𝔓[46] א[2] Ψ F G) but is omitted by others (e.g., א* A B D P 81 1739). The manuscript evidence favors omission, and shorter readings are generally taken to be the original. Scribes presumably added the word to clarify the meaning of τὴν ἰδίαν ("their own").

[94] E.g., E. P. Sanders, *Paul, the Law, and the Jewish People* (Philadelphia: Fortress, 1983), 36–39; Dunn, *Romans 9–16*, 587–88, 595–96; Jewett, *Romans*, 617–18. Wright ("Romans," 655) reduces the meaning of the expression to "establish a covenant membership that would be for Jews and Jews only." But such approaches do not fit with the challenges Paul presents in 2:17–29; 3:1–20 about the false confidence of fellow Israelites and their failure to live according to the knowledge of God and his will given to them in the law.

the sinful mass of humanity addressed by God's grace."[95] Since they pursued righteousness by their own efforts or "works" (cf. 9:32), "they have not submitted to God's righteousness" (τῇ δικαιοσύνῃ τοῦ θεοῦ οὐχ ὑπετάγησαν).[96] Paul's language here implies that "the righteousness of God is an active force to which one must humbly and obediently subordinate oneself."[97] Pride and self-confidence make submission to God's way impossible. In Paul's mind Israel's unwillingness to recognize and respond to Christ and the righteousness of God made known in the gospel was the tragic climax of a long-standing pattern of zeal for God that was "not according to knowledge."

10:4. Another γάρ ("for") links the argument that follows with the preceding sequence of ideas. The noun τέλος has a range of possible meanings but has mostly been translated "fulfillment," "goal," or "end" here. In salvation-historical terms, "Christ is the goal, the aim, the intention, the real meaning and substance of the law—apart from him it cannot be properly understood at all."[98] However, even though the idea of "goal" is applicable to the context, it is difficult to exclude the thought of "end" in the sense of "completion, conclusion, cessation."[99] The law has completed its task of revealing God's righteousness to everyone who believes, now that the Messiah has come. "Christ embodies that righteousness which the

---

[95] Byrne, *Romans*, 310. As Byrne acknowledges, this included making the law "a fence around a 'holy nation' set over against the unholy rest of humankind," though that is not Paul's primary accusation here.

[96] Modified by two present participles, the aorist indicative οὐχ ὑπετάγησαν should be understood in a summary fashion ("they have not submitted").

[97] Moo, *Romans*, 633. God's acting to put people right with himself through Christ cannot simply be ignored. Cf. Seifrid, *Justification by Faith*, 174–75; Schreiner (*Romans*, 543) speaks about God's saving righteousness "which includes his transforming work."

[98] Cranfield, *Romans*, 2:519, concluding a review of the three most popular interpretations. Badenas (*Christ the End of the Law*, 7–37) provides a more extensive history of interpretation and similarly opts for "goal" as the best rendering (38–80).

[99] Dunn (*Romans 9–16*, 589) argues that the English word "end" is the best rendering here because it can mean both "goal" and "termination" (NIV: "culmination"). "Outcome," "end result," or "termination" is the meaning in Rom 6:21, 22; 1 Cor 1:8; 10:11; 15:24; 2 Cor 11:5; Phil 3:19, but 2 Cor 3:13 could imply both "goal" and "end." In 1 Tim 1:5, τέλος clearly means "goal." Cf. Moo, *Romans*, 638–40; Schreiner, *Romans*, 545–46.

law promised."[100] This does not mean the law has lost its authority as a revelation from God or that the Christian life is completely law free (cf. Matt 5:17–48; Rom 13:8–10; 1 Cor 9:21). The problem was that Israel pursued the law for righteousness as if it were by "works" (9:31–32). But all along the law was pointing to the righteousness that comes from faith (10:6–8). This is now available for all through the preaching of Christ and the salvation he has made possible.[101] Paul is picturing the Mosaic law as "the center of an epoch in God's dealings with human beings that has now come to an end. The believer's relationship to God is mediated in and through Christ, and the Mosaic law is no longer basic to that relationship."[102] CSB has rightly taken *εἰς δικαιοσύνην παντὶ τῷ πιστεύοντι* as directly connected to *τέλος νόμου*, translating "the end of the law for righteousness to everyone who believes" (so also NASB, ESV). As well as the salvation-historical dimension to the argument here, Paul may be thinking experientially, noting that "those who trust in Christ cease using the law to establish their own righteousness."[103] The adjective *παντί* ("everyone") prepares for the universal claims in vv. 11–13 about the possibility of salvation for all—Jews and Gentiles alike—through faith in the resurrected Lord Jesus. "Christ, by ending the era of the law, during which God was dealing mainly with Israel, has made righteousness more readily available for Gentiles."[104]

---

[100] Badenas, *Christ the End of the Law*, 118. Moo (*Romans*, 641) concludes that Christ is the "end" of the law in the sense that he brings its era to a close, and its "goal" in the sense that "he is what the law anticipated and pointed towards." Cf. Wright, "Romans," 655–58.

[101] Dunn (*Romans 9–16*, 598) contends that what is brought to an end is "the law seen as a way of proving righteousness, of documenting God's special regard for Israel, of marking Israel out from the nations, the law understood in terms of works." However, this is not an adequate description of what Paul exposes and attacks in 2:17–3:20 or in 9:31–33.

[102] Moo, *Romans*, 642.

[103] Schreiner, *Romans*, 547. Moo (*Romans*, 637–38) argues that *εἰς δικαιοσύνην παντὶ τῷ πιστεύοντι* is more naturally a purpose or result clause (NRSV, NIV, "so that there may be righteousness for everyone who believes"). But Schreiner takes *εἰς* to be an adverbial preposition of general reference, so that *εἰς δικαιοσύνην* means "with reference to righteousness."

[104] Moo, *Romans*, 641–42. He observes that 10:4 is "the hinge on which the entire section 9:30–10:13 turns."

Bridge

Zeal for God without knowledge is a dangerous phenomenon. In Paul's case it drove him to persecute the followers of Jesus. Disregarding the righteousness of God and attempting to establish their own righteousness, Israelites like Paul failed to see their need for a right standing with God by faith. Long-term failure to submit to God's righteousness meant they did not recognize the significance of Christ's coming and their need for the benefits of his death and resurrection. Yet Paul rejoiced that many Gentiles had obtained the righteousness that comes by faith and were experiencing the blessings promised to Israel. Misguided zeal manifests itself in different patterns of religion in our world today and effectively keeps people from a right relationship with God. A common cause is the desire of many to establish their own righteousness by moral and religious achievement. Some even express their zeal by attacking Christians and undermining their influence. Nominal Christians may also imagine that they are right with God because they seek to live uprightly and show love to others, failing to understand things from God's perspective. Since we are "enemies" in need of reconciliation (5:10), God has acted to put people right with himself through the person and work of his Son. Only by faith in Christ and what he has accomplished for us can we be justified and escape the terrible consequences of the coming judgment of God. So we all need to submit to God's righteousness and abandon any attempt to establish our own righteousness (cf. 10:11–13).

C. Israel's Failure to Understand the Law and the Prophets (10:5–21)

[5]Since Moses writes about the righteousness that is from the
law: **The one who does these things will live by them.** [6]But the
righteousness that comes from faith speaks like this: **Do not say
in your heart, "Who will go up to heaven?"** that is, to bring
Christ down [7]or, **"Who will go down into the abyss?"** that is, to
bring Christ up from the dead. [8]On the contrary, what does it say?
The message is near you, in your mouth and in your heart.
This is the message of faith that we proclaim: [9]If you confess with
your mouth, "Jesus is Lord," and believe in your heart that God
raised him from the dead, you will be saved. [10]One believes with

the heart, resulting in righteousness, and one confesses with the
mouth, resulting in salvation. [11]For the Scripture says, **Everyone
who believes on him will not be put to shame,** [12]since there is
no distinction between Jew and Greek, because the same Lord of
all richly blesses all who call on him. [13]For **everyone who calls
on the name of the Lord will be saved.**

[14]How, then, can they call on him they have not believed in?
And how can they believe without hearing about him? And how
can they hear without a preacher? [15]And how can they preach
unless they are sent? As it is written: **How beautiful are the feet
of those who bring good news.** [16]But not all obeyed the gospel.
For Isaiah says, **Lord, who has believed our message?** [17]So faith
comes from what is heard, and what is heard comes through the
message about Christ. [18]But I ask, "Did they not hear?" Yes, they
did:

> **Their voice has gone out to the whole earth,**
> **and their words to the ends of the world.**

[19]But I ask, "Did Israel not understand?" First, Moses said,

> **I will make you jealous**
> **of those who are not a nation;**
> **I will make you angry by a nation**
> **that lacks understanding.**

[20]And Isaiah says boldly,

> **I was found**
> **by those who were not looking for me;**
> **I revealed myself**
> **to those who were not asking for me.**

[21]But to Israel he says, **All day long I have held out my hands to
a disobedient and defiant people.**

Context

Paul's proposition that "Christ is the end of the law for righteousness to everyone who believes" (v. 4) is confirmed in vv. 5–10 with a scriptural argument. Then, to back this up, Paul applies further texts to Jews and Gentiles who believe in Christ for righteousness (vv. 11–13). Although this inclusive note continues to v. 18, Paul is particularly concerned to explain how God has made it possible for Israel to hear the gospel and believe (vv. 19–21). This has happened through the apostle's own ministry to the nations (v. 18). With further citations he makes clear that it was always God's intention to make Israel jealous through the conversion of Gentiles. But for the moment Israel remains "a disobedient and defiant people" (v. 21). The argument in 10:18–21 prepares for the exposition of God's plan for Israel and the Gentiles in 11:1–32. Paul continues to establish the truth of his claim that the word of God has not failed (9:6).

Structure

Arising directly from 9:30–10:4, Paul indicates that there are two different ways of reading and responding to God's law (10:5–10). The first simply takes Lev 18:5 as the key. The second perceives the significance of Deut 30:12–14, understood in its context and in the light of its fulfilment in Christ. This passage points to the need for the righteousness that comes from faith, which is the message the apostle has been proclaiming in Romans. God's intention to save Jews and Gentiles through faith in the risen Lord Jesus is confirmed in 10:11–13 by citations from Isa 28:16 and Joel 2:32. As Paul outlines the process by which people come to call upon the Lord Jesus for salvation (vv. 14–17), he draws particular attention to Israel's unbelief and failure to obey the gospel, just as Isaiah predicted (v. 16; cf. Isa 53:1). The final paragraph (vv. 18–21) confirms that dispersed Israel has indeed heard the gospel because God's words have gone "to the ends of the world" (v. 18; cf. Ps 19:4). But Israel has failed to understand that even their unbelief is part of God's plan to enable many Gentiles to find him in Christ and to make his ancient people jealous (vv. 19–20; cf. Deut 32:2; Isa 65:1). God continues to hold out his hands to them through the preaching of the gospel, but they remain "a disobedient and defiant people" (v. 21; cf. Isa 65:2).

Outline:

1. Two ways of understanding God's law (vv. 5–10)
2. One way of salvation through faith in Christ (vv. 11–13)
3. No excuse for unbelieving Israel (vv. 14–21)

10:5. With a further connecting *γάρ* ("for, since"), Paul begins a complex defense of the proposition in v. 4. The biblical argument in vv. 5–14 is "a fusion between a classical 'speech-in-character' and a Hebrew *pesher*."[105] Two voices interact, "with Moses 'writing' in the initial text from Leviticus, and a personified 'righteousness by faith' 'speaking' the next five citations."[106] However, Paul is not pitting one passage against the other or suggesting that Moses is only the author of the first. In Lev 18:5 Moses writes about "the righteousness that is from the law" (τὴν δικαιοσύνην τὴν ἐκ [τοῦ] νόμου). This expression contrasts with "righteousness that comes from faith" (10:6, ἡ δὲ ἐκ πίστεως δικαιοσύνη [cf. 9:30, δικαιοσύνην τὴν ἐκ πίστεως]) and summarizes what Paul means by Israel's "pursuing the law of righteousness" (9:31; cf. Phil 3:9). The quotation is introduced by ὅτι ("that" [not translated by CSB]): "the one who does these things will live by them" (ὁ ποιήσας αὐτὰ ἄνθρωπος ζήσεται ἐν αὐτοῖς).[107] The aorist participle ποιήσας should be understood as timeless and generic, as in LXX Lev 18:5, where it is used conditionally (ἃ ποιήσας ἄνθρωπος ζήσεται ἐν αὐτοῖς, "a person will live if he does them"). This text is cited in a similar form in Gal 3:12 (without ἄνθρωπος), where doing what the law requires is contrasted with living by faith. Paul acknowledges that the commands of God were given to enable Israel to live in the land he gave them so that they might enjoy the blessings promised to them. Life in this world, rather than eternal life, is the focus of this text (cf. §1.4). Israel's failure to obey the law brought judgment in many ways, ultimately in the form of exile, just as Moses predicted (Lev 26:14–35; Deut 28:15–68). To ignore their historic failure and presume they could keep the law in their own strength was misguided and foolish.[108] Mercifully, this was not God's final word on the subject, as Paul goes on to show.

---

[105] Jewett, *Romans*, 622. He defines *pesher* as a short section of biblical text interspersed with explanatory comments. Cf. Tobin, *Paul's Rhetoric*, 343.

[106] Jewett, *Romans*, 622. The present tense of the verbs "writes" (v. 5) and "speaks" (v. 6) points to the continuing relevance of different "voices" in Scripture for Israel (Dunn, *Romans 9–16*, 602) and the readers.

[107] The positioning of ὅτι after γράφει ("writes") is textually well attested (א A D 33 81 etc.). But there is also strong and diverse support for its placement after νόμου ($\mathfrak{P}^{46}$ B D^2 G Ψ etc.) Cf. Moo, *Romans*, 643n1; 645n5.

[108] Paul's subsequent use of Deuteronomy implies that Lev 18:5 should not be read in isolation from the rest of the Torah. Cranfield (*Romans*, 2:521–22) applies the quotation to the perfect obedience of Christ in fulfilling the law. Against this view, see Dunn, *Romans 9–16*, 601; Moo, *Romans*, 646–47.

10:6–7. A contrast with the previous verse is indicated by the adversative use of δέ ("but"). Paul uses Deut 30:12–14 to show how Lev 18:5 had been wrongly interpreted by his fellow Israelites.[109] The character who now "speaks" (λέγει) is "the righteousness that comes from faith" (ἡ ἐκ πίστεως δικαιοσύνη). "This form of a 'speech-in-character,' in which a concept is made to speak as a person, is typical for ancient rhetoric and would have been readily understood by the audience."[110] The character speaks throughout Rom 10:6–8, not contradicting what Moses wrote in Lev 18:5, but drawing attention to complementary teaching in another part of the law.

The words "do not say in your heart" (μὴ εἴπῃς ἐν τῇ καρδίᾳ σου), which are found in LXX Deut 8:17; 9:4, are used by Paul to preface a reflection on Deut 30:12–14. God's people were warned not to think the land of Canaan and its wealth had been given to them because of their own power, ability, or righteousness. The further challenge to their thinking in Deut 30:1–10 was to recognize that they would inevitably fail to obey God and would experience his judgment, ultimately exile from the land. Nevertheless, even in that extreme situation God promised to restore his people by circumcising their hearts so they might truly love him and live before him in faithfulness. This promise was the basis for later predictions about a new covenant in Jer 24:6–7; 31:33; 32:39–41. From Paul's perspective God has made possible "the obedience of faith" that leads to eternal life (cf. Rom 1:5; 6:17; 15:17; 16:26).[111]

Moses's speech in Deut 30:11–14 develops with the assertion that the command he is giving them is "certainly not too difficult or beyond your reach." In fact, "it is not in heaven so that you have to ask, 'Who will go up to heaven, get it for us, and proclaim it to us so that we may follow it?'" (30:12). Israel did not need someone else to discover God's will and explain it to them since Moses was

[109] Cf. Dunn, *Romans 9–16*, 602. Moo (*Romans*, 645–46, 650) critiques those who take δέ to mean "and" here and see a complementary relationship between vv. 5 and 6. The former highlights doing; the latter highlights believing. Cf. Schreiner, *Romans*, 551–56.

[110] Jewett, *Romans*, 625. Tobin (*Paul's Rhetoric*, 343) provides examples.

[111] Cf. Wright, "Romans," 659. Wright seeks to understand the sequence of thought in 10:5–8 in the light of Second Temple eschatological readings of Deut 30. Paul explains how the Messiah's being "the goal of Torah" results in covenant renewal.

the definitive mediator and authorized interpreter of God's truth.[112] Moreover, Moses indicates that the enabling grace of God will accompany the message for those who choose "life and prosperity," rather than "death and adversity" (30:14–15).

Paul gives a Christological interpretation of Deut 30:12–14, introducing three explanatory comments with the words τοῦτ' ἔστιν ("that is"). This is reminiscent of the *pesher* (interpretive) method of explaining the contemporary significance of biblical texts found in some of the Qumran documents (e.g., 1 QS 8:14–15; 1 QpHab 7:4–5; 12:7–8), though Paul's approach is guided by his understanding of the movement of salvation history.[113] In the gospel era Moses's warning means that nothing needs to be done "to bring Christ down" (Χριστὸν καταγαγεῖν). The Messiah has come from heaven with divine authority (cf. 9:5 comment) and has brought the ultimate revelation of God's righteousness.[114] Deuteronomy 30:13 continues, "And it is not across the sea so that you have to ask, 'Who will cross the sea, get it for us, and proclaim it to us so that we may follow it?'" Paul modifies this text with a possible allusion to Ps 107:26 (LXX 106:26, καταβαίνουσιν ἕως τῶν ἀβύσσων, "they descend into the abyss"), giving the sense, "Who will go down into the abyss?" This modification is made because Deut 30:13 offers no direct point of contact with Christ's descent into death as going down "into the abyss" does.[115] In his case there is no need "to bring

[112] This passage was taken by contemporary Jewish writers to mean that the wisdom of God given to Moses was accessible in commands not too hard to keep (cf. Bar 3:29–4:1; Philo, *Post.* 84–85; *Mut.* 236–37; *Virt.* 183; *Praem.* 80; Tg. Neof. on Deut 30:11–14). Dunn (*Romans 9–16*, 603–5) shows how Paul's language and technique blend Jewish and Hellenistic interpretive styles.

[113] Cf. Moo, *Romans*, 655.

[114] Jewett (*Romans*, 626–27) follows Barrett (*Romans*, 199), taking this to mean that "the Messiah has appeared, and it is therefore impossible to hasten his coming (as some devout Jews thought to do) by perfect obedience to the law and penitence for its transgressions." But Paul's point is more likely to be that to pursue righteousness by works is to deny what God has already accomplished in Christ. Cf. Moo, *Romans*, 653–54. Wright ("Romans," 663) argues that is a reference to Christ's coming from God, "the incarnation of God's pre-existent Wisdom."

[115] Cf. Cranfield, *Romans*, 2:525. In Ps 107:26 (LXX 106:26) "the abyss" refers to the depths of the sea, and in Deut 8:7; 33:13 it denotes "deep water sources." But in texts like Ps 71:20 (LXX 70:20) it refers to the depths of the earth as the place of the dead. Moo (*Romans*, 655–56) disputes the allusion to Ps 107:26. Cf. Dunn, *Romans 9–16*, 606.

Christ up from the dead" (τοῦτ' ἔστιν Χριστὸν ἐκ νεκρῶν ἀναγαγεῖν, cf. Heb 13:20). The Messiah has been raised, and he is drawing people from every nation to experience the blessings of the new covenant (1:3–5; 4:23–24). God has acted definitively for the sake of his people and requires them to respond with faith to the message about what he has achieved. Indeed, "those who believe that Jesus is Lord, and that God raised him from the dead are the new-covenant people, the returned-from-exile people."[116]

10:8. Paul's adaptation of Deut 30:12–14 comes to a climax with the rhetorical challenge "on the contrary, what does it say?" (ἀλλὰ τί λέγει;). Having indicated what is *not* required (vv. 6–7), "the righteousness that comes from faith" speaks positively about how to respond to God's gracious initiative: "the message is near you, in your mouth and in your heart." With ἐγγύς ("near") transposed to the emphatic position at the beginning of the sentence and the adverb σφόδρα ("very") omitted, this is an exact citation from Deut 30:14. It shows "the consistency between the Christian proclamation and the original intent of the law."[117] "The word" (τὸ ῥῆμα) that Moses proclaimed was not simply a set of commandments, but a message about God's mercy and grace coupled with an invitation to choose between "life and prosperity, death and adversity" (Deut 30:15). God's word was "near" in the sense that it could be talked about, comprehended, and believed. The call to obey was facilitated by promises of God's enabling grace. As the second generation of Israelites stood on the borders of the promised land, they were being encouraged to express "the obedience of faith." Under the new covenant, Christ works through the gospel, by the power and leading of his Spirit, to enable saving faith and the obedience from the heart that Moses sought.

A third and final explanatory comment is also introduced with the words τοῦτ' ἔστιν ("that is"). This identifies the word that Moses

---

[116] Wright, "Romans," 660. Wright contends that "here, as in 2:25–29 and elsewhere, Paul's point is that those who share Christian faith are in fact 'doing the law' in the sense that Deuteronomy and Jeremiah intended."

[117] Jewett, *Romans*, 628. However, note the significant omission of LXX καὶ ἐν ταῖς χερσίν σου αὐτὸ ποιεῖν ("and in your hands to do it [i.e., the law]"). Dunn (*Romans 9–16*, 613) suggests that "the commandment is fulfilled in the word of faith (cf. 3:31), the word of faith we might say *is* the law of righteousness properly understood (9:31–32)."

proclaimed with the message of faith that Christians proclaim. "The message of faith" (τὸ ῥῆμα τῆς πίστεως) could be "the message about the need for faith" but more likely is "the message that elicits faith."[118] When the messengers of God proclaim the gospel, it comes "near" to people and makes belief possible. The plural subject of the verb κηρύσσομεν ("we proclaim") links Paul with others who preach this message. "For the first time, Paul's apostolic vocation becomes part of the actual argument of chaps. 9–11; this will grow through 10:14–18, and play a crucial role in 11:13–14."[119] The message of faith" brings salvation from the coming judgment of God and righteousness (10:9–10). The challenge, then, is to believe and "choose life" (Deut 30:19)!

10:9. The conjunction ὅτι (not translated by CSB) introduces the parallel explanation in vv. 9–10 of how "the message of faith" may be received and benefit people (mouth-heart-saved; heart-mouth-salvation) and should probably be translated "because."[120] Echoing the wording of Deut 30:14, Paul continues to show the link between his gospel and the teaching of Moses. Like the revelation of the law, the eschatological word of God is easily accessed, believed, and confessed. Paul indicates what will follow ("you will be saved") if certain conditions are met in the present ("if you confess with your mouth . . . and believe in your heart").[121] Confessing with the mouth is mentioned first because Paul is following the word order in Deut 30:14. But the pattern is reversed in v. 10, where believing with the heart comes first. It is clear from vv. 4, 11 that the critical response is to believe, suggesting that confession is the outward sign of genuine faith. Nevertheless, "the two formulations interpret each other, so that what is to be both believed and confessed is the more

[118] Cranfield (*Romans*, 2.526) opts for the first possibility, while Jewett (*Romans*, 629) opts for the second. Dunn (*Romans 9–16*, 606) suggests a combination of both possible meanings, noting the proximity of references to "in the mouth" and "in the heart" (so also Schreiner, *Romans*, 559).

[119] Wright, "Romans," 664. See §2.7.

[120] Cf. Cranfield, *Romans*, 2.526; Moo, *Romans*, 657; Jewett, *Romans*, 629 (as in NRSV, ESV). Schreiner (*Romans*, 559) defends the explicative reading of ὅτι implied by CSB.

[121] Moo (*Romans*, 658n61) rightly argues that this will be a logical future, "with its absolute time undetermined." In this verse, ἐν with the dative is used instrumentally and then spatially.

precisely defined."[122] "In your heart" implies "a deeply motivating belief" and not merely "a recitation of a creedal form."[123] But faith needs to be informed by the Word of God and articulated in ways that praise and honor God (cf. 15:7–13). Faith articulated strengthens the convictions of the heart.

"Jesus is Lord" (κύριον Ἰησοῦν) is an early Christian confession used in evangelism and the teaching associated with initiation (e.g., Acts 2:36; 1 Cor 8:6; 2 Cor 4:5; Col 2:6), as well as in congregational worship (e.g., Phil 2:11; 1 Cor 12:3; 16:22–23).[124] The divinity of Christ is implied by the claim that he is "the Lord" upon whom everyone must call for salvation in the coming judgment (vv. 12–13). Although Gentiles were aware of many "lords" (1 Cor 8:5), in Jewish circles the word κύριος was read in the LXX whenever the name of God was found in the Hebrew Bible (e.g., Joel 2:32, which is cited in v. 13). Paul's formulations imply that "Jesus as Lord shares in the one God's lordship."[125] Believing "that God raised him from the dead" is fundamental to this confession (e.g., 4:24; 8:11; Gal 1:1, 3; 1 Cor 6:14; 15:4–19).[126] The focus on Christ's resurrection here is a sequel to the question in v. 7, namely, who will "bring Christ up from the dead?" But belief in the redemptive nature of his death was previously highlighted as essential for salvation (e.g., 3:22–25; 5:1–2). Paul's gospel calls for a single response to the linked events of Jesus's death and resurrection and their outcome. Confessing Jesus as the resurrected Lord means acknowledging him as the one who was crucified for us and has been raised for our justification (cf. 4:24–25 comments). Believing and confessing in the way Paul outlines secures salvation from the judgment of God and new life in Christ, now and beyond death (6:1–11; 8:1–17).

---

[122] Cranfield, *Romans*, 2:527.

[123] Dunn, *Romans 9–16*, 609.

[124] Dunn (ibid., 607) points out that this "slogan of identification" was effectively a replacement for Israel's confession in Deut 6:4, as an expression of belonging to Jesus as Lord. Larry W. Hurtado (*Lord Jesus Christ: Devotion to Jesus in Earliest Christianity* [Grand Rapids: Eerdmans, 2003], 197–200) argues that this confession originated in Jewish Christian circles in Jerusalem. See §2.3.

[125] Dunn, *Romans 9–16*, 608.

[126] Cf. Vernon H. Neufeld, *The Earliest Christian Confessions*, NTTS 5 (Grand Rapids: Eerdmans, 1963), 43–47. Paul does not often use the language of "confession" (cf. 2 Cor 9:13; 1 Tim 6:12–13; Titus 1:16). The compound verb ἐξομολογέω is used in Rom 14:11; 15:9; Phil 2:11.

10:10. This verse provides a confirmation of the preceding one and a bridge to what follows. Linked by the connective γάρ ("for" [not translated by CSB]), it presents the same two responses to the apostolic message as v. 9 but in reverse order: (lit.) "with the heart one believes" (καρδίᾳ πιστεύεται) and "and with the mouth one confesses" (στόματι δὲ ὁμολογεῖται). In the rhetorical parallelism here, the outcome is described in two related ways: belief is (lit.) "for righteousness" (εἰς δικαιοσύνην), and confession is "for salvation" (εἰς σωτηρίαν). Bringing together these key terms, Paul returns to the theme statement of his letter in 1:16–17. Righteousness and salvation are different ways of explaining the benefits of believing with the heart and confessing with the mouth. Immediate and eternal results flow from accepting the apostolic message (cf. v. 9 comment).

10:11–13. In a series of linked clauses, each using the conjunction γάρ (CSB: "for," "since," "because," "for"), Paul cites two more biblical texts to confirm the necessity of faith in Christ for salvation. The first Scripture that "speaks" to the situation (λέγει ἡ γραφή) is Isa 28:16. In 9:33, a portion of this text was combined with words from Isa 8:14 and applied to Israelites who had "stumbled over the stumbling stone" God was putting in Zion. The messianic implications of Isa 28:16 are highlighted in both contexts by the LXX addition of the words ἐπ' αὐτῷ ("on him"). This expression gives to belief the sense of reliance on Christ. In the flow of the argument, not being "put to shame" is another way of speaking about being saved eschatologically.[127] Picking up on his claim about righteousness for "everyone who believes" (v. 4, παντὶ τῷ πιστεύοντι), the apostle begins to develop the universal implications of his gospel. He adds the word πᾶς ("every") to the citation from Isa 28:16 so that it reads, "Everyone who believes on him will not be put to shame." The legitimacy of this addition is argued in v. 12 and confirmed in v. 13, using a citation from Joel 2:32.[128]

[127] In both contexts Paul replaces the LXX emphatic negative future [using the aorist subjunctive] (οὐ μὴ καταισχυνθῇ) with a simple indicative future (οὐ καταισχυνθήσεται, "will not be put to shame"). This does not refer to psychological shame but to being exposed to the judgment of God.

[128] Paul may have been specifically influenced by the use of πᾶς in Joel 2:32 when he added this word to the citation from Isa 28:16.

The apostle concludes that there is "no distinction" between Jew and Greek in the need for saving faith (οὐ γάρ ἐστιν διαστολὴ Ἰουδαίου τε καὶ Ἕλληνος).[129] He uses a similar expression in 3:22 as a preface to his conclusion that "all have sinned and fall short of the glory of God" (3:23). In positive terms Jews and Gentiles are united in receiving the blessing of justification by faith (cf. Acts 15:9; Rom 4:9–12; Gal 3:6–9, 27–29; Eph 2:11–22). The Christological conclusion is that "the same Lord of all" (ὁ αὐτὸς κύριος πάντων, cf. Acts 10:36) "richly blesses all who call on him" (πλουτῶν εἰς πάντας τοὺς ἐπικαλουμένους αὐτόν).[130] "The universal lordship of Christ is the eschatological expression of the one God's sovereign purpose."[131] Elsewhere in Romans Paul uses the noun "riches" to emphasize the abundance of God's "kindness, restraint, and patience" (2:4), "the riches of his glory" (9:23), and "the riches of the wisdom and of the knowledge of God" (11:33). But here he uses the cognate verb to indicate that God makes his riches available to all through the person and work of his Son (cf. 1 Cor 1:5; 2 Cor 8:9; Eph 1:7; 2:4, 7; 3:8; Phil 4:19; Col 1:27).

Calling upon Jesus as Lord is the challenge of Joel 2:32 (LXX 3:5), which is cited as a climax to this section. "Joel 2 sits comfortably alongside Deuteronomy 30 as a powerful statement of how God will restore the fortunes of Israel after devastating judgment."[132] In its original context this passage was clearly a challenge for faithful Israelites to express their reliance on their covenant Lord for mercy and salvation in view of the approaching "day of the Lord."[133] Prior

[129] In this context "Greeks" appears to be a substitute for "Gentiles" since Paul is speaking about salvation being available for "all" who seek it in Christ. Jewett (*Romans*, 632) contends that "Greek" is a less discriminatory epithet than "Gentile."

[130] The expression ὁ αὐτὸς κύριος πάντων can also be translated "the same Lord is Lord of all" (NRSV, NIV, ESV). The participle πλουτῶν with εἰς means "being rich toward" (BDAG, πλουτέω).

[131] Dunn, *Romans 9–16*, 610. Paul argues in 3:39–30 that *God* rules both Jews and Gentiles and justifies all on the same basis. Contextually, however, the reference in 10:11 must be to *Christ* as "the same Lord of all," in whom all must believe for salvation (10:11). Cf. Moo, *Romans*, 659–60.

[132] Wright, "Romans," 665.

[133] The expression "call upon the Lord" or "call upon the name of the Lord" is widely used in the OT. Prayer is often meant, but more fundamentally, to call on the Lord is to identify as one of his covenant people. Christians expressed their continuity with Israel by using this terminology in a similar way while adapting it as a means of self-designation in relation to the risen Lord Jesus (cf. Acts 2:21; 9:14, 21;

to this challenge the prophet promised an eschatological outpouring of God's Spirit (Joel 2:28–29). In Paul's argument this citation is a means of tying together two important threads: salvation is available for "everyone who calls on the name of the Lord" (vv. 4, 11, 12), and Jesus is "the Lord" to confess and call upon for this deliverance (vv. 9–10, 12). By implication the gift of the Spirit is an immediate and continuing way in which the risen Lord "richly blesses all who call on him" (v. 12; cf. Acts 2:16–18, 33, 38–39).

10:14–15. The transitional conjunction οὖν ("then") carries the argument forward while introducing a new section. Paul returns to a diatribe method of argumentation, using a series of four rhetorical questions (vv. 14–15a) and two significant biblical citations (vv. 15b–16) before providing a summarizing conclusion in v. 17 to the logical argument developed in the section.[134] Each question begins with πῶς ("how") and takes up a motif from the preceding one. The first question picks up the word "call" from vv. 12–13 ("how can they call on him they have not believed in?").[135] The second question picks up the word "believe" and points to the need for people to "hear" the gospel if they are going to believe it. The third question identifies the need for someone to proclaim the gospel (cf. v. 8c) if it is to be heard and believed. "This is a clear reference to the decisive role of oral proclamation in the spread of the gospel in the early period before the publication of the gospels and the Pauline letters."[136] The fourth question insists that people can only preach if they are "sent" (ἀποσταλῶσιν), with the passive implying the agency of God. So the sequence in temporal terms is this: God sends preachers who proclaim the gospel so people may hear, believe, and call upon the Lord Jesus for salvation. Paul formulates a principle that is relevant to Jews and Gentiles alike, though he applies it particularly to Israel's failure in vv. 16, 18–21.

22:16; 1 Cor 1:2; 2 Tim 2:22; 1 Pet 1:17). Cf. Karl L. Schmidt, "καλέω, κτλ.," *TDNT* 3:499–500; Dunn, *Romans 9–16*, 610–11.

[134] Cf. Jewett, *Romans*, 635–36.

[135] The deliberative subjunctive in a question like this (πῶς ἐπικαλέσωνται, "How shall they call?") is in fact "a thinly disguised statement, though couched in such a way as to draw the listener into the text" (Wallace, *Greek Grammar*, 467). Jewett (*Romans*, 634) notes that there is stronger earlier textual evidence for the use of the subjunctive than for other variants in v. 14.

[136] Jewett, *Romans*, 638.

A text to support the fourth question is introduced with the familiar words "as it is written" (cf. 1:17; 2:24; 3:4, 10; 4:17; 8:36; 9:13, 33). Paul's citation from Isa 52:7 is closer to the Hebrew original than the LXX in certain respects (lit., "How beautiful are the feet of those who announce the gospel of good things"), though he departs from both textual traditions in using plural forms.[137] As in v. 8c (κηρύσσομεν, "We proclaim"), Paul identifies with others who "announce the gospel" (τῶν εὐαγγελιζομένων). This highly significant term is used in 1:15; 15:20 to describe his apostolic ministry. By implication many have been "sent" to proclaim "the good things" (τὰ ἀγαθά) identified by Isaiah: "peace," "salvation," and the reign of God that makes these eschatological gifts possible.[138] Paul was especially "called as an apostle (κλητὸς ἀπόστολος), and set apart for the gospel of God" (1:1). He received this "apostleship" (ἀποστολήν) from the risen Lord Jesus "to bring about the obedience of faith for the sake of his name among all the Gentiles" (1:5). The significance of this distinctive calling will become more obvious in the next chapter. Meanwhile, Paul uses the adjective ὡραῖοι ("timely" [BDAG], LXX ὡς ὥρα), which is rendered "beautiful," to describe "the feet" of those who bring the gospel to people.[139] "Feet" is a figure of speech called metonomy, which makes an attribute of those who bring the gospel stand for the preachers themselves (see §2.7).

10:16–17. Using the strong adversative ἀλλά ("but"), Paul returns to the subject of Israel's failure. The majority of his fellow Israelites have not welcomed the preachers of the gospel sent to them by God. Although the message has been offered to all without

---

[137] Jewett (*Romans*, 639) notes that Paul's translation comes closest to the Lucianic family of LXX versions. Paul omits ἐπὶ τῶν ὀρέων ("upon the mountains") and a specific reference to announcing "peace," though the words τῶν εὐαγγελιζομένων εἰρήνην ("those who preach peace") are found in some texts of Rom 10:15 (א^c D G K P Ψ 33 88 etc.). Cf. Metzger, *Textual Commentary*, 463.

[138] The eschatological significance of Isa 52:7 for Israel is confirmed by 11QMelch 11.2–19. Windsor (*Vocation*, 224) argues that Paul changes the singular of Isa 52:7 into the plural to identify the gospel preachers with the "we" of Isa 53:1, which is cited in the next verse. Paul presents his Gentile mission as "part of the fulfillment of the *plural* Israelites' role towards the nations."

[139] Dunn (*Romans 9–16*, 621–22) and Jewett (*Romans*, 640) argue for the appropriateness of translating ὡραῖοι "timely" or "opportune" here, but Schreiner (*Romans*, 568–69) contends that the Hebrew נָאווּ ("beautiful") should be our guide. The Greek adjective can certainly have the secondary sense of "attractive, beautiful" (BDAG).

distinction (vv. 11–13), "*all* did not obey the gospel" (οὐ πάντες ὑπήκουσαν τῷ εὐαγγελίῳ).[140] The word "obey" here has several echoes. It recalls Paul's commission to "bring about the obedience of faith" among the nations (1:5; cf. 15:18; 16:26) and the indication in 6:17 that conversion involves obeying from the heart "that pattern of teaching to which you were handed over." In the immediate context obeying the gospel means submitting to the righteousness of God it reveals (v. 3; cf. 1:17) and acknowledging the lordship of Christ (vv. 12–13). By implication obeying the gospel involves rejecting the pursuit of the law for righteousness (9:31) and the pattern of hypocrisy and disobedience set forth in 2:17–29.

Israel's failure to accept the gospel was anticipated by the prophet Isaiah, for he says, "Lord, who has believed our message?" So Israel's disobedience and unbelief are "two sides of the same coin."[141] Significantly, these words come from the so-called Fourth Servant Song (Isa 53:1), which goes on to speak about the Servant's substitutionary and atoning death for the salvation of God's people. CSB translates τῇ ἀκοῇ ἡμῶν "our message," but it would be better to render the expression "what was heard from us."[142] This recalls Paul's insistence that people need to "hear" about Christ (v. 14 [ἤκουσαν]), in order to believe and "obey" (ὑπήκουσαν) the gospel. Paul picks up Isaiah's term (ἐξ ἀκοῆς, "from what is heard"), as he completes the "syllogistic structure" of the argument in vv. 14–17:[143] "So faith comes from what is heard, and what is heard comes from the message about Christ."[144]

---

[140] This recalls the remnant theology in 9:6b, that "not all who are descended from Israel are Israel." Cf. 9:27.

[141] Moo, *Romans*, 665.

[142] Cf. Schreiner, *Romans*, 566–67. Although vv. 14–17 exclude the idea that salvation can be obtained apart from "hearing" the gospel, there are different ways in which people today can do this, including the reading of Scripture and Christian literature or encountering biblical teaching online.

[143] Jewett (*Romans*, 641–42) notes the importance of the inferential particle ἄρα ("so"), which introduces the summarizing conclusion to the argument begun in vv. 14–15a. Cranfield (*Romans*, 2.536–37) observes that v. 17 also effects the transition from the OT quotation in v. 16b to the subject of Israel's hearing.

[144] The reading ῥήματος Χριστοῦ ("the message about Christ") is strongly supported by early and diverse witnesses (e.g., 𝔓[46vid] ℵ* B C D*), but TR follows ℵ[c] A D[b, c] K P etc. in reading ῥήματος θεοῦ ("message about God" [KJV, "the word of God"]). This change appears to have been made because ῥήματος Χριστοῦ is not found elsewhere in the NT, whereas ῥῆμα θεοῦ occurs in Luke 3:2; John 3:34; Eph 6:17; Heb 6:5; 11:3.

10:18. As in v. 16, Paul uses the strong adversative ἀλλά ("but"), though here it introduces a new stage in his argument. Returning to the diatribal style of asking questions and answering them from Scripture (vv. 14–15), he applies the conclusion in v. 17 to Jewish and Gentile responses to the gospel (vv. 18–21). His first rhetorical question involves a double negative in Greek (μὴ οὐκ ἤκουσαν; "Did they not hear?), which expects a positive answer, as indicated by the particle combination μενοῦνγε ("indeed" [CSB: "Yes, they did"]; cf. 9:20). Without introduction the first two lines of Ps 19:4 (LXX 18:5) are cited to support this affirmation: "Their voice has gone out to the whole earth, and their words to the ends of the world." In its original context this describes the communication of knowledge about the Creator by different aspects of the creation (cf. Rom 1:19–20). But Paul applies the text analogously to "the words" (τὰ ῥήματα αὐτῶν) of the gospel preachers, which come from God himself (cf. vv. 8, 17). God makes himself known as Creator in the natural world and as Savior of the nations through the preaching of the gospel. "God's general revelation thus functions as a type and anticipation of the gospel message that extends to all peoples."[145]

In view of the fact that Paul was yet to go to Spain and that vast areas of "the inhabited world" (τῆς οἰκουμένης) remained untouched by the gospel, this claim appears to be "a hyperbolic vision of the full eschatological sweep of the gentile mission (cf. 1:8; 2 Cor 2:14; 3:2; Col 1:6, 23; 1 Thess 1:8)."[146] The extraordinary spread of the gospel in his own ministry "from Jerusalem all the way around to Illyricum" (15:19) was an indication of God's intention to make it known to all people, whether they hear or refuse to hear (cf. Acts 19:10; Col 1:23). But Paul's main point here is that Jews everywhere have had a chance to hear the gospel.

10:19. With the same introductory formula used in the previous verse (ἀλλὰ λέγω, "but I ask"), Paul poses another question. Once again a double negative in Greek implies the need for a positive answer (μὴ Ἰσραὴλ οὐκ ἔγνω; "Did Israel not understand?"). Here the verb "know" or "understand" brings a new dimension to the argument. Since Paul goes on to cite three biblical texts, the question most obviously means, "Did Israel not know what the Scriptures

[145] Schreiner, *Romans*, 572.

[146] Dunn, *Romans 9–16*, 624.

foretold about them?" This continues the thought of v. 2 that Israel's zeal for God is "not according to knowledge" (οὐ κατ' ἐπίγνωσιν). "Israel has ignored so many of its own scriptures which are now being fulfilled in Israel's rejection and the nations' acceptance of the word of faith."[147]

The first text cited comes from Moses ("First, Moses said").[148] Paul uses the present tense in this introductory formula and changes the pronouns in LXX Deut 32:21 from the third person to the second-person plural to emphasize that Moses continues to speak to Israel in this way. But it is actually God who speaks through Moses: "I will make you jealous of those who are not a nation; I will make you angry by a nation that lacks understanding." In its original context this verse is part of a prophetic denunciation of Israel's unfaithfulness to God.[149] In the first part of 32:21, God says, "They have provoked my jealousy with (their) so-called gods; they have enraged me with their worthless idols." The same verbs are employed in the second half of the verse to express God's judgment on his people: he will make *them* jealous and enrage *them*! When Paul uses the verb παραζηλόω again in 11:11,14, the context suggests the more positive sense of "provoke to emulation."[150] Paradoxically, this theme is foundational to Paul's explanation of why Israel's rejection by God is not final!

10:20–21. Two citations from Isaiah complete the sequence and continue Paul's answer to the rhetorical question posed in v. 19a. Isaiah speaks boldly (Ἠσαΐας δὲ ἀποτολμᾷ καὶ λέγει, [lit.] "and Isaiah is bold and says"), though it is God who once more addresses his people through his agent (cf. v. 19). Isaiah's boldness relates to the content of his message: that God would be found by those who were not looking for him and would reveal himself to those who were not

---

[147] Ibid., 631. Cf. Bell, *Provoked to Jealousy*, 97–104.

[148] A numerical sequence is not maintained with the introduction of the two texts from Isaiah in vv. 20–21, and so πρῶτος on its own may mean "from the outset" or "above all" (as in 1:8; 3:2). It is less likely that this adjective should be taken with the verb ἔγνω to mean, "Did not Israel know first?"

[149] "Those who are not a nation" and "a nation that lacks understanding" will be the various Gentile nations, "which God is using as his instruments in the course of history" (Cranfield, *Romans*, 2:539).

[150] Bell, *Provoked to Jealousy*, 39. Bell reveals the broad spectrum of meanings for the root קנא/ζηλ in the OT ("anger, jealousy, envy, emulation, zeal, and passionate love").

asking for him. Paul's first citation follows LXX A and Q versions of Isa 65:1. Paul understands this verse to be speaking about Gentiles entering into a relationship with the God of Israel. This reading is consistent with the last line of the Hebrew text, which says, "To a nation that did not call on my name" (אֶל־גּוֹי לֹא־קֹרָא בִשְׁמִי).[151] It also matches the promise in Isa 66:18–21 about nations who have not heard of God's fame or seen his glory being gathered to worship with his people in Jerusalem. The nations seek God because he first reveals himself to them, saying, "Here I am, here I am" (65:1). Paul envisages this being fulfilled in the propagation of the gospel to the Gentiles in his own time and particularly through his own ministry.

The second verse Paul cites follows LXX Isa 65:2 (with the words ὅλην τὴν ἡμέραν ["all day long"] transposed to the beginning for emphasis). This clearly speaks "to Israel" or "in reference to Israel" (πρὸς δὲ τὸν Ἰσραήλ).[152] To "hold out the hands" (ἐξεπέτασα τὰς χεῖράς μου) was normally a gesture of prayer to God (e.g., 1 Kgs 8:22, 38; Ps 143:6; Isa 1:15). So the image of the Lord's spreading out *his* hands to a "disobedient and defiant people" (πρὸς λαὸν ἀπειθοῦντα καὶ ἀντιλέγοντα) is surprising and shocking. But this imploring of his people is a sign of his continuing commitment to them and his desire to show mercy to them. Paul will explore this subject more thoroughly in the next chapter.

Bridge

This passage unfolds the way God works to bring people everywhere to himself by focusing on his dealings with Israel. The argument is especially relevant for Christians seeking to persuade Jews about their need for the gospel. The failure of many Israelites to understand and believe the gospel is rooted in their misreading of the law and the prophets. Obedience to God's law could never simply be the way to eternal life because of Israel's sin. But God promised to draw near to his people and put his word in their mouth and heart, enabling them to be saved by faith. This pattern of engagement has

---

[151] Cf. J. Alec Motyer, *The Prophecy of Isaiah* (Leicester: InterVarsity, 1993), 523–24. Against most commentators, Motyer argues that Isa 65:1 in the MT is speaking about Gentiles. Even the LXX version of the last line (τῷ ἔθνει οἳ οὐκ ἐκάλεσάν μου τὸ ὄνομα, "to a nation that did not call upon my name") can hardly refer to Israel, since there were always Israelites who did call upon the Lord as their covenant master.

[152] Cf. Dunn, *Romans 9–16*, 626; Jewett, *Romans*, 648.

been fulfilled in Christ and in the ministry of the gospel he makes possible to Jews and Gentiles alike. The obedience that brings eternal life is obedience to Christ and the gospel. From Paul's perspective Israel as a dispersed people has heard the message but has not believed and obeyed the call to trust in God's Son. Despite this resistance God continues to appeal to them through the preachers he sends to them. In fact, he desires to make them jealous by allowing many Gentiles to share in the blessings promised originally to Israel. Those who are sent by God proclaim the way of salvation and invite people everywhere to confess their need and call upon the risen Lord for deliverance. God uses this gracious message to move hearts to believe and mouths to confess so that people from every nation may obtain the righteousness that comes from faith. Although a ministry to Jews may involve special attention to the way in which God's ancient promises have been fulfilled, the challenge to respond to Christ and his saving work is the same for all people.

D. Hope in the Face of Judgment (11:1–10)

[1]I ask, then, has God rejected his people? Absolutely not!
For I too am an Israelite, a descendant of Abraham, from the tribe
of Benjamin. [2]God has not rejected his people whom he foreknew. Or don't you know what the Scripture says in the passage
about Elijah—how he pleads with God against Israel? [3]**Lord,
they have killed your prophets and torn down your altars. I
am the only one left, and they are trying to take my life!** [4]But
what was God's answer to him? **I have left seven thousand for
myself who have not bowed down to Baal.** [5]In the same way,
then, there is also at the present time a remnant chosen by grace.
[6]Now if by grace, then it is not by works; otherwise grace ceases
to be grace.

[7]What then? Israel did not find what it was looking for, but
the elect did find it. The rest were hardened, [8]as it is written,

> **God gave them a spirit of stupor,**
> **eyes that cannot see**
> **and ears that cannot hear,**
> **to this day**.

[9]And David says,

> **Let their table become a snare and a trap,**
> **a pitfall and a retribution to them.**

10 **Let their eyes be darkened so that they cannot see,**
and their backs be bent continually.

Context

As he does elsewhere in Romans, Paul begins a new stage of his argument with a rhetorical question ("I ask, then, has God rejected his people?"), which logically flows from what he has said in the preceding section (9:30–10:21). His question is answered with a strong denial ("Absolutely not!") and a biblically based proposition ("God has not rejected his people whom he foreknew"). Paul substantiates this proposition with a series of biblical arguments, reflecting some of the teaching in 9:6–29 and continuing to affirm that the word of God has not failed. In particular, "he divides Israel into two groups: a 'remnant,' enjoying the blessings of salvation and existing by virtue of God's gracious election (vv. 5–6; cf. 9:6b–13, 15–16, 18a, 22–23, 27–29), and 'the rest,' hardened by God in spiritual obduracy (vv. 7–10b; cf. 9:13b, 16–17, 18b, 22–23)."[153] As he considers Israel past and present, Paul lays the foundation for his prediction about Israel's future in 11:11–32.

Structure

There are two lines of argument in vv. 1–10, introduced by questions in vv. 1, 7. "Each question is followed by an answer in thesis form, supported with appropriate scriptural proofs in midrashic fashion."[154] Paul answers the first question ("has God rejected his people?") by pointing to himself as "an Israelite, a descendant of Abraham, from the tribe of Benjamin." He then cites a brief portion of Ps 94:14; 1 Sam 12:22, denying what the question proposes ("God has not rejected his people whom he foreknew"). This denial is supported by a reference to what Elijah says about Israel in 1 Kgs 19:10, 14 and God's response in 1 Kgs 19:18. Paul draws a conclusion from this in vv. 5–6 concerning election through grace alone. The second line of argument begins with the brief rhetorical question, "What then?" (v. 7). Paul's thesis is that Israel as a whole did

[153] Moo, *Romans*, 671–72. Moo observes that the concept of the remnant is used negatively in 9:27–29 but positively in 11:1–10 "as a pledge of God's continuing faithfulness to Israel and the promises he has made to her."

[154] Jewett, *Romans*, 651.

not find what it was looking for: the elect found it, but "the rest were hardened." This is supported by an adaptation of Deut 29:4, which speaks about a stupor being sent upon God's people, and a citation from Ps 69:22–23, which expands the portrayal of God's judgment on them.

Outline:

1. A remnant chosen by grace (vv. 1–6)
2. God's hardening of "the rest" (vv. 7–10)

11:1. The inferential conjunction οὖν ("then") links Paul's first rhetorical question to the preceding argument, where it was concluded that Israel is "a disobedient and defiant people" (10:21). Despite this he confidently suggests, (lit.) "God has not rejected his people, has he?"[155] Using the verb ἀπώσατο (BDAG, "push aside, reject, repudiate"), Paul apparently alludes to the promise in 1 Sam 12:22 and Ps 94:14 (LXX 93:14) that "the Lord will not abandon his people."[156] His question expecting a negative answer is followed by a strong denial (μὴ γένοιτο, "Absolutely not!"). The immediate justification for this denial is surprising: "For I too am an Israelite, a descendant of Abraham, from the tribe of Benjamin" (cf. 4:13–18; 9:4, 7–8). This self-introduction should be compared with how Paul describes himself in 2 Cor 11:22; Phil 3:4–5. Although many have argued that he simply puts himself forward as living proof of a Jewish-Christian remnant, the context suggests a broader meaning. In 10:8, 14–16 he includes himself among the preachers of the gospel sent to Israel, while in 11:13 he emphasizes that he is at the same time "apostle to the Gentiles." Paul is both a *saved* Israelite and a *preaching* Israelite: "Israel's future is guaranteed because Israel's

[155] As in 10:18, 19; 11:11, the verb λέγω ("I say, ask") alerts the reader to consider carefully what follows. Wright ("Romans," 675) suggests the meaning "so this is the question I must ask." The question that follows begins with μή ("not"), which implies a negative answer here, as in 3:3–4, 5–6; 9:14; 11:11.

[156] Hays (*Echoes*, 68–69) calls this a "contextual echo." Dunn (*Romans 9–16*, 634) observes that "the thought of God rejecting his people was entertained as a prospect, or question or conclusion" in a variety of OT texts (e.g., 2 Kgs 21:14; Jer 7:29), but the assurance that God has not or will not reject his people is less frequently found. Instead of τὸν λαὸν αὐτοῦ ("his people") in Rom 11:1, some witnesses (𝔓[46] G it[b, f, gx], Goth, Ambrosiaster, Ambrose, Pelagius) have τὴν κληρονομίαν αὐτοῦ ("his inheritance"), which appears to be a Western assimilation to LXX Ps 93:14.

divine vocation is in fact being fulfilled by an Israelite."[157] This chapter speaks against a "replacement" theology: God has not simply replaced the Jewish people with Gentile Christians (cf. §2.6).

11:2–3. Paul repeats the wording of the opening question in a propositional form ("God has not rejected his people"), adding the important qualification "whom he foreknew" (ὃν προέγνω [cf. Amos 3:2, ἔγνων, "known, chosen"]). This picks up the language of 8:29 but applies it to the nation of Israel, echoing the claim of 1 Sam 12:22 (ὅτι ἐπιεικέως κύριος προσελάβετο ὑμᾶς αὑτῷ εἰς λαόν, [lit.] "because the Lord graciously took you to himself as a people"). God's choice of Israel involved a decision to enter into a covenant relationship with that nation so as to fulfill his saving purpose for the world.[158] God's choice of individuals within that elect nation comes into focus in vv. 4–6, but another claim about Israel as a nation emerges in v. 28.[159] Paul's rhetorical appeal continues with the words, "Or don't you know what the Scripture says in the passage about Elijah?" The expression ἐν Ἠλίᾳ ([lit.] "in Elijah") is a way of referring to the portion of Scripture where Elijah is the main subject.[160] The context is more narrowly defined by the expression "how he pleads with God against Israel" (κατὰ τοῦ Ἰσραήλ). This accusation or complaint took place when Elijah fled from the threats of Jezebel and prayed that he might die (1 Kgs 19:1–5). He went to Horeb "the mountain of God," where he was challenged with the words, "What are you doing here, Elijah?" Elijah's response (19:10, 14) is reported in this way: "Lord, they have killed your prophets and torn down your altars. I am the only one left, and they are trying

---

[157] Windsor, *Vocation*, 232 (emphasis removed). Windsor (232–35) highlights the inadequacy of other interpretations of this verse. He goes on to note the significance of Paul's self-description as "a descendant of Abraham, from the tribe of Benjamin," and relates this to Israel's calling in Isa 41:8–9. Cf. Cranfield, *Romans*, 2.544.

[158] Schreiner (*Romans*, 580) notes that foreknowledge implies foreordination. This understanding is confirmed by the immediate context, "for προέγνω clearly functions as the antonym of ἀπώσατο." Cf. 2 Pet 1:20.

[159] Moo (*Romans*, 675) observes that God's choosing of the nation of Israel guarantees blessings and benefits to the people as a whole but does not guarantee salvation for every single Israelite. Cf. Dunn, *Romans 9–16*, 540.

[160] Cranfield (*Romans*, 2:545–46) notes examples of this citation method in Hebrew and Greek writings (cf. 9:25, "in Hosea"). The exact phrase "in Elijah" occurs in Midr. Cant. 1.6 (88[a]). Such methods were necessary before the chapter and verse system was established.

to take my life!" Although it has been argued that Paul modified these texts to suggest parallels with Jewish opposition in his own time (cf. 1 Thess 2:14–16) or with his own particular situation, the story of Elijah is more obviously retold to confirm God's ongoing commitment to his people.[161]

11:4. The apostle continues his pattern of rhetorical questioning by asking, "But what was God's answer to him?" A more literal rendering of the Greek (ἀλλὰ τί λέγει αὐτῷ ὁ χρηματισμός) would be, "But what does the oracle say to him?"[162] This expression implies that the prophet received a definitive answer from God concerning the extent of the remnant he was preserving in Israel: "I have left seven thousand for myself who have not bowed down to Baal" (cf. 1 Kgs 19:18). Elijah was not alone because God kept a sizable number of Israelites faithful to himself. There are several variations from the LXX (A and B text) in this citation. Most importantly, the second-person singular future (καταλείψεις, "you shall leave") is changed to the first-person aorist (κατέλιπον, "I have left"), which is closer to the Hebrew original.[163] The reflexive pronoun ἐμαυτῷ is added to highlight God's merciful action in preserving a people *for himself*. Given the significance attached to the number seven in Jewish thinking, "seven thousand" could be understood as "a symbol of completeness, perfection."[164] The fact that such people had not "bowed down to Baal" proved the genuineness of their relationship with God.[165] However, "it was God, by his own decision and for the accomplishment of his own purpose, who made the remnant to

---

[161] Cf. Jewett, *Romans*, 655–56; Moo, *Romans*, 676–78. Wright ("Romans," 676) thinks Paul is comparing himself with Elijah, but Schreiner (*Romans*, 581) argues against this, noting how God corrects Elijah's view that there is no remnant. It is likely that Paul translates freely from the Hebrew text of 1 Kings, perhaps from memory, because he does not follow any extant Greek version of the passage.

[162] Anthony T. Hanson, "The Oracle in Romans xi.4," *NTS* 19 (1972–73), 300. The term ὁ χρηματισμός (BDAG, "divine statement, answer") is without parallel in the NT but is found in 2 Macc 2:4. It seems to emphasize the divine origin and authority of the word that came to Elijah, though Moo (*Romans*, 676n27) disputes this.

[163] The Hebrew וְהִשְׁאַרְתִּי means "I shall leave," and this is reflected in the Lucianic Version of the LXX (καταλείψω). But Paul appears to have made his changes independently, for his own contextual reasons. Cf. Jewett, *Romans*, 657–58.

[164] Cranfield, *Romans*, 2:547. Cf. Karl H. Rengstorf, "ἑπτά κτλ.," *TDNT* 2: 628–30.

[165] The feminine τῇ βάαλ (unlike LXX τῷ) could reflect the Hebrew custom of reading בֹּשֶׁת (= αἰσχύνη, "shame"). Cf. Dunn, *Romans 9–16*, 638.

stand firm; and for this very reason its existence was full of promise for the rest of the nation."[166] Their continuing faithfulness was a demonstration of *God's* continuing faithfulness.

11:5. A conclusion to the preceding argument is drawn with the words οὕτως οὖν ("in the same way, then"). As in Elijah's day, "there is also at the present time a remnant chosen by grace" (The perfect tense of γέγονεν is rendered as present because it expresses a situation that still exists). The expression ἐν τῷ νῦν καιρῷ ("at the present time") recalls 3:26; 8:18, where it refers to the era of fulfillment. Paul brings out the eschatological significance of God's answer to the prophet (v. 4, κατέλιπον ἐμαυτῷ, "I have left for myself") by referring to the present reality of (lit.) "a remnant according to the election of grace" (λεῖμμα κατ' ἐκλογὴν χάριτος [CSB: "a remnant chosen by grace"]). The cognate term ὑπόλειμμα was used in 9:27 in a citation from Isa 10:22–23. Both nouns are related to the verb καταλείπω, which is used in 1 Kgs 19:18; Rom 11:4. The root idea of the remnant is that some will be "left" or "delivered" from disaster, especially from the judgment of exile (e.g., Isa 37:4; Jer 8:3; Mic 2:12).[167]

Various prophets promised that a remnant would be restored to a glorious Zion and experience the blessings of a renewed relationship with God (e.g., Isa 4:2–6; 10:20–23; 11:11; Jer 23:3–4; 31:7–14; Mic 4:6–8). Paul used κατ' ἐκλογήν in 9:11 to emphasize that God's purpose is characterized by election, without reference to the good or bad people might do. Here he uses the expression to indicate that the election of a remnant is "by grace" (χάριτος being a descriptive genitive). Grace signifies "divine benefaction in the form of unconditional access to God and specific benefits conveyed to the undeserving through Christ."[168]

[166] Cranfield, *Romans*, 2.547.

[167] Cf. Gottlob Schrenk and Volkmar M. Herntrich, "λεῖμμα κτλ.," *TDNT* 4:198–209; Ronald E. Clements, "'A Remnant Chosen by Grace' (Romans 11:5): The Old Testament Background and Origin of the Remnant Concept," in *Pauline Studies: Essays Presented to Professor F. F. Bruce on His 70th Birthday*, ed. Donald A. Hagner and Murray J. Harris (Grand Rapids: Eerdmans, 1980),106–21.

[168] Jewett, *Romans*, 659. Jewett reads too much into the perfect tense of γέγονεν, rendering it "has been born," whereas it simply functions in a stative way as a substitute for the present tense of the verb "to be" (cf. Stanley E. Porter, *Verbal Aspect in the Greek New Testament, with Reference to Tense and Mood,* 3rd ed., *Studies in Biblical Greek*, Book 1 [New York: Peter Lang Inc., 2003], 265).

11:6. When the apostle says, "Now if by grace, then it is not by works" (εἰ δὲ χάριτι, οὐκέτι ἐξ ἔργων), he returns to the argument specifically developed in 3:27–4:16; 9:30–10:4.[169] To underline the meaning of "not by works," Paul adds the words "otherwise grace ceases to be grace" (ἐπεὶ ἡ χάρις οὐκέτι γίνεται χάρις). Grace and works are contrasted in relation to divine election. God's choice has only ever been an expression of his grace, not a reward for human initiative or effort.[170] However, works proceeding from faith are the sign of a genuine relationship with God and are the basis for final judgment (2:6–11). The grace of God empowers believers to become obedient slaves of righteousness (6:12–23).

> The "remnant" that arises from the apostolic word is "chosen" by "grace" and remains fundamentally opposed to those who still understand the law according to "works" (Rom 11:6, cf. 9:32). The remnant thus continues to be opposed to "Israel," the "rest" who are still seeking to achieve righteousness by law (Rom 11:7, cf. 10:3, 20), failing to attain it (Rom 11:7, cf. 9:31), remain hardened by God himself (Rom 11:7–8, cf. 9:18), and in this way remain in opposition to God's Messiah, "stumbling" (Rom 11:9, cf. 9:32–33).[171]

11:7. As in 3:9; 6:15, a further stage in the argument begins with a transitional question (Τί οὖν; "What then?"). Paul's first proposition ("Israel did not find what it was looking for") echoes in different words what was said in 9:31. The tense in the expression ὅ

[169] The dative χάριτι signifies the manner by which membership of the elect remnant is achieved. Although οὐκέτι can have a temporal sense ("no longer"), it is a "marker of inference in a logical process here" (BDAG; cf. 7:17, 20; 14:15), since Paul does not envisage that election was at any time "by works." Cf. Dunn, *Romans 9–16*, 639.

[170] Some manuscripts, notably ℵ[2] B Ψ 33, add variations of the clause ἐπεὶ τὸ ἔργον οὐκέτι ἐστὶν ἔργον ("otherwise work is no more work"). This found its way into the KJV via the TR. But the existence of several forms of the addition throws doubt on the originality of any of them, and there is no reason the words should have been deleted if the longer reading was the original. Cf. Metzger, *Textual Commentary*, 464.

[171] Windsor, *Vocation*, 240. But, Windsor continues, "the apostolic word *against* Israel is only the beginning of the apostle's solution to Israel's 'hardening.'"

ἐπιζητεῖ is understood by CSB to be historical present.[172] However, to bring out the sense of an ongoing problem, which is relevant to the context, the present could retain its temporal reference ("what it looks for"), and the aorist οὐκ ἐπέτυχεν could be rendered "has not found."[173] Paul's next expression relates this to the teaching about an elect remnant in Israel, as indicated in 11:4–6 ("but the elect did find it," ἡ δὲ ἐκλογὴ ἐπέτυχεν). In the wider context of his argument, the elect includes believing Gentiles, but here the focus is on Israel. What the elect obtained by God's grace was the righteousness that comes from faith in their Messiah (9:30–10:4). But "the rest were hardened" (οἱ δὲ λοιποὶ ἐπωρώθησαν).[174] The passive verb here signifies God's action, which is clarified by the citations in vv. 8–10. Israel's culpability has already been outlined: "They have zeal for God, but not according to knowledge" (10:2); they have heard the gospel but not understood their need for its promises (10:18–19); while God continues to hold out his hands to them, they remain "a disobedient and defiant people" (10:21). Yet through all this God has been sovereign; Israel's hardening has not fallen outside his control or frustrated his purpose.

11:8. The first text Paul cites to support the claim that God has hardened "the rest" of Israel is introduced with the familiar "as it is written" (cf. 1:17; 2:24; 3:4, 10; 4:17; 8:36; 9:13, 33). Deuteronomy 29:4 (LXX 29:3) is modified to bring out the sense that Israel's spiritual insensibility is the result of divine hardening. Moses lamented that his people had seen with their own eyes everything the Lord did for them in Egypt, "yet to this day the Lord has not given you a mind to understand, eyes to see, or ears to hear." Paul implies that

---

[172] Cf. Wallace, *Greek Grammar*, 527–28. The present tense is replaced by the imperfect ἐπεζήτει ("was looking for") in F G 104 1836 to express the idea of continuous seeking in the past.

[173] The verb ἐπέτυχεν means "be successful in achieving or gaining what one seeks, obtain, attain to, reach" (BDAG). Cf. Heb 6:5; 11:33; Jas 4:2. It replaces the verb ἔφθασεν ("achieved"), which was used in 9:31. There Israel is described as "pursuing the law of righteousness," but it "has not achieved the righteousness of the law."

[174] The verb ἐπωρώθησαν basically means "petrify" (πῶρος is a kind of marble). The metaphorical application ("harden") occurs five times in the NT (Mark 6:52; 8:17; John 12:40; Rom 11:7; 2 Cor 3:14). Other verbs are also used to convey the same notion. Cf. Karl L. and Martin A. Schmidt, "παχύνω, πωρόω κτλ., *TDNT* 5:1025–28. If the aorist οὐκ ἐπέτυχεν is translated "has not found," the rest of the verse should be rendered, "The elect have found it, but the rest have been hardened."

the obtuseness of Israel in the wilderness continued to characterize the people's response to God's actions and words. To make his point, he changes the syntax of the verse and adds the words πνεῦμα κατανύξεως ("spirit of stupor") from Isa 29:10. Moses spoke about what God had *not* given them, whereas Isaiah portrayed a deliberate act of divine judgment, pouring out on them "a spirit" that would make them insensitive and unresponsive.[175] Observing the failure of many Israelites to understand and believe the gospel, Paul uses the prophet's words to highlight God's role in this situation: "God gave them a spirit of stupor, eyes that cannot see and ears that cannot hear, to this day." Israel's culpability was stressed in 10:2–3, 16–21, but God's involvement in the process is now indicated by the active verb ἔδωκεν ("gave") with πνεῦμα κατανύξεως ("spirit of stupor") as its object. God's immediate plan was for them to have ὀφθαλμοὺς τοῦ μὴ βλέπειν καὶ ὦτα τοῦ μὴ ἀκούειν ([lit.] "eyes so as not to see and ears so as not to hear").[176] This should be compared with the Lord's commission to Isaiah (Isa 6:9–10), which Jesus cited in connection with his own ministry (Matt 14:13–15; Mark 4:11–12; Luke 8:10). According to Acts 28:25–27, Paul applied Isa 6:9–10 to the rejection of his message by many Jews when he arrived in Rome. From the apostle's standpoint, ἕως τῆς σήμερον ἡμέρας ("to this day") meant that a pattern of obduracy had been evident in Israel from the time of Moses until the gospel era (cf. Acts 7:51–53).[177] The positive consequences of God's hardening of "the rest" are outlined in 11:11–12, 25–32, where it is made clear that such hardening may be a temporary condition for some.

[175] The rare word κατάνυξις (BDAG, "stupefaction") only occurs elsewhere in LXX Ps 59:5 (ET 60:3). In 2 Cor 3:14–16 Paul talks about the hardening of Israelite hearts in terms of the "veil" that covers them. The attributive genitive κατανύξεως defines the nature of "the spirit."

[176] Deuteronomy 29:4 (LXX 29:3) makes a negative statement ("the Lord has not given you"), whereas Paul makes a positive statement and changes the pronoun from the second to the third person ("God has given *them*"). Paul also inserts negative infinitival phrases ("so as not to see," "so as not to hear"). Wallace (*Greek Grammar*, 592–93) notes that articular infinitives more regularly convey purpose than result. CSB has weakened the sense by translating "eyes that cannot see and ears that cannot hear."

[177] Paul uses τῆς σήμερον ἡμέρας in 2 Cor 3:14 in a similar argument. The expression literally means "the today day," and hence "the present day." LXX Deut 29:3 has ἕως τῆς ἡμέρας ταύτης ("to this day"), which could be understood in a more limited way as referring only to the time of Moses.

11:9–10. A second supportive citation is introduced by the words, "And David says" (cf. 4:6). Psalm 69:22–23 (LXX 68:23–24) is an imprecation or prayer for judgment on David's enemies. In effect, to make his point, Paul uses all three sections of the Hebrew canon: the Law (Deut 29:4), the Prophets (Isa 29:10), and the Writings (Ps 69:22–23). Understood in relation to Christ, the eschatological Son of David, the psalm text applies to his opponents, who hate and insult him and end up persecuting his messengers as well. "Those who have mocked and tormented the sufferer have these judgments invoked on them."[178] The final two lines of the citation correspond exactly with the LXX ("Let their eyes be darkened so they cannot see, and their backs be bent continually"). This forms a direct link with the quote from Deut 29:4 in the previous verse, where God's judgment is expressed in terms of eyes that do not see and ears that do not hear. The opening lines of the citation are modified so that there is a call for "their feasting" (ἡ τράπεζα αὐτῶν, [lit. "their table"]) to become their downfall in two ways: "a snare and a trap, a pitfall and a retribution to them."[179] The words "a snare and a trap" are found together in Pss 34:8; 123:6–7; Prov 11:8–9; Hos 5:1–2. Paul apparently uses this pair to match the second pair of words already contained in LXX Ps 68:23, where they occur in reverse order ("for retribution and a pitfall"). It is unwise to press the details of the citation in relation to the situation Paul addresses other than to suggest that for him "their table" could represent "their table-fellowship: the unity and interrelatedness created by the law and so highly valued in Judaism."[180] This keeps them from "seeing" what God is offering them in the gospel.

---

[178] Wright, "Romans," 677. Note the various uses of this psalm in relation to Christ in Matt 27:34, 48 and par.; John 2:17; 15:25; 19:28–29; Acts 1:20; Rom 15:3; Heb 11:26; 12:2.

[179] Accusative nouns with εἰς ("for") substitute for predicate nominatives here due to Semitic influence (cf. Wallace, *Greek Grammar*, 47).

[180] Barrett, *Romans*, 211. Jewett (*Romans*, 664) takes "their table" as a reference to the cultic meal found in Greco-Roman religious texts (cf. Luke 22:30; 1 Cor 10:21) and relates Paul's reworking of LXX Ps 68:23 to the conflicts over eating mentioned in Rom 14. But this is irrelevant to the present context where the issue continues to be God's judgment on obdurate and unbelieving Israelites. Cf. Dunn, *Romans 9–16*, 642–43, 650.

Bridge

A careful reading of Scripture shows that the problem of Israel's unbelief is long-standing. Paul draws particular attention to the time of Elijah and quotes texts from other periods of Israel's history to make this point. Nevertheless, even though some were hardened and judgment came to his people collectively, God preserved a faithful remnant. So also in the gospel era, "God has not rejected his people whom he foreknew." Paul points to himself as an Israelite who has been brought to faith in the Messiah and in whose ministry Israel's calling to be a light to the nations is being fulfilled. The remnant of Jewish believers in the Messiah remains for Paul "a sign and pledge of the continuing fidelity of God."[181] But how can God be faithful to his promises and allow a hardening of "the rest" of Israel to occur? Human stubbornness is emphasized, but God is portrayed as the ultimate cause. God's hardening is with a view to revealing his power and glory (cf. 9:17–24). Israel's temporary "stupor" is designed to allow God's grace to shine more brightly when he enables the full number of his elect to believe. These principles can be applied to gospel ministry more generally. Salvation is always by God's gracious initiative, not by works (e.g., Eph 1:3–10; 2:1–10; 2 Thess 2:13–14; Titus 2:11–14; 3:4–7). Resistance and unbelief should never be treated as final and irreparable because God continues to call his elect from among the nations. The stupor we meet in some may only be temporary. Our prayer should be that the light of Christ would shine in the hearts of any who are hardened so that God's power and glory might be displayed.

E. Hope in the Conversion of the Nations (11:11–24)

> [11]I ask, then, have they stumbled so as to fall? Absolutely not! On the contrary, by their transgression, salvation has come to the Gentiles to make Israel jealous. [12]Now if their transgression brings riches for the world, and their failure riches for the Gentiles, how much more will their fullness bring!

[181] Byrne, *Romans*, 330. Byrne rightly observes that the operation of God's grace in the face of human failure and sin in the past is the basis of hope for the salvation of the remainder of Israel.

[13]Now I am speaking to you Gentiles. Insofar as I am an
apostle to the Gentiles, I magnify my ministry, [14]if I might somehow make my own people jealous and save some of them. [15]For if
their rejection brings reconciliation to the world, what will their
acceptance mean but life from the dead? [16]Now if the firstfruits
are holy, so is the whole batch. And if the root is holy, so are the
branches.

[17]Now if some of the branches were broken off, and you,
though a wild olive branch, were grafted in among them and
have come to share in the rich root of the cultivated olive tree,
[18]do not boast that you are better than those branches. But if you
do boast—you do not sustain the root, but the root sustains you.
[19]Then you will say, "Branches were broken off so that I might
be grafted in." [20]True enough; they were broken off because of
unbelief, but you stand by faith. Do not be arrogant, but beware,
[21]because if God did not spare the natural branches, he will not
spare you either. [22]Therefore, consider God's kindness and severity: severity toward those who have fallen but God's kindness toward you—if you remain in his kindness. Otherwise you too will
be cut off. [23]And even they, if they do not remain in unbelief, will
be grafted in, because God has the power to graft them in again.
[24]For if you were cut off from your native wild olive tree and
against nature were grafted into a cultivated olive tree, how much
more will these—the natural branches—be grafted into their own
olive tree?

Context

With his biblical argument about God's hardening a portion of Israel established (vv. 7–10), Paul returns to an earlier claim that they have "stumbled" (v. 11; cf. 9:32–33). But his question about whether they have stumbled "so as to fall" leads to an analysis of how their "full number" might be brought to salvation through faith in Christ (v. 12). This notion is critical for his climactic revelation about the future of Israel in vv. 25–32. As anticipated in 10:19 (citing Deut 32:21), God's intention is to make Israel jealous by bringing salvation to the Gentiles, especially through Paul's apostolic ministry (vv. 11, 13–14). Returning to the theme of "the elect" and "the rest" (v. 7), he uses the imagery of "the firstfruits" sanctifying "the whole batch" and "the root" sanctifying "the branches" (v. 16) to justify his hope for the salvation of many more Israelites. The figure of the root and the branches is developed in vv. 17–24 to explain what God has done in history, excluding some in Israel while grafting many Gentiles into his "cultivated olive tree." Paul uses this allegory to warn Gentile Christians about unbelief and arrogance.[182] At the same time, he uses it to highlight the possibility that God might graft many "natural branches" from Israel back into "their own olive tree." With this argument Paul continues to insist that the word of God has not failed (9:6).

Structure

This literary unit is introduced in the same way as the previous one, with a rhetorical link to what has gone before ("I ask, then") followed by a question expecting a negative answer ("Have they stumbled so as to fall?"), which is answered by an emphatic denial ("Absolutely not!"). The thesis of the unit is stated in the rest of v. 11 ("On the contrary, by their transgression, salvation has come to the Gentiles to make Israel jealous"). A "how much more" argument in v. 12 describes the outcome of Israel's present failure in terms of "riches for the world" and "riches for the Gentiles" and contemplates the blessing that the conversion of "their full number" might bring. Paul develops the notion that Israel may be made jealous in connection with his apostolic ministry to the Gentiles (vv. 13–14). Then he returns to the "how much more" argument of v. 12, using a series of conditional clauses in vv. 15–16.[183] The first indicates that Israel's "acceptance" will mean "life from the dead." The second offers hope of that acceptance in terms of the sanctification of "the whole batch" by "the firstfruits." The third expresses the same hope in terms of "the branches" being holy because "the root" is holy. This last proposition is expounded in the figure of the root and the branches in vv. 17–24, which Paul applies both to his Gentile readers and to unconverted Israelites. This pause for exhortation resumes

---

[182] Jewett (*Romans*, 693) describes this passage as "a brilliant fusion of allegory and diatribe that would have functioned effectively with Paul's audience in Rome, drawing them in the direction of supporting his audacious mission to Spain that would provide a truly inclusive reconciliation of the world."

[183] Jewett (*Romans*, 670) sees a chiasm in vv. 12–15, but this misses the close link between v. 15 and v. 16 syntactically.

the diatribe style of earlier passages, using repeated-second person singular address (vv. 17, 18, 20, 21, 22, 24).[184]

Outline:

1. God's plan for unbelieving Israel (vv. 11–12)
2. Paul's role in the outworking of God's plan (vv. 13–16)
3. God's kindness and severity to Jews and Gentiles (vv. 17–24)

11:11. Paul's introduction to this new section parallels his approach in v. 1. An obvious link with the preceding argument is indicated by λέγω οὖν ("I ask then") and is confirmed by a question expecting a negative answer (μὴ ἔπταισαν ἵνα πέσωσιν; [lit.] "they have not stumbled so as to fall, have they?").[185] This question is answered by the emphatic denial μὴ γένοιτο ("Absolutely not!"). The verb πταίω ("stumble") is only used here in the Pauline letters, though it occurs in Jas 2:10; 3:2; 2 Pet 1:10. Parallel terms can be found in 9:32–33 (προσκόπτω, πρόσκομμα, σκάνδαλον). More commonly Paul employs πίπτω ("fall"; cf. 11:22; 14:4; 1 Cor 10:8, 12; 13:8). Although there is a semantic overlap between these two verbs, the sequence here suggests the possibility of progressing from stumbling to falling, implying complete failure ("fall to rise no more").[186] But the stumbling of Israel is not permanent: "On the contrary, by their transgression, salvation has come to the Gentiles to make Israel jealous." Israel's stumbling is literally "their transgression" (τῷ αὐτῶν παραπτώματι). This term highlights the deliberate and intentional nature of their rejection of the gospel and recalls 4:25; 5:15, 17, 18, 20, where the same noun is rendered "trespass."[187] Salvation is literally "for the Gentiles" (τοῖς ἔθνεσιν) because of Israel's failure.

[184] Dunn (*Romans 9–16*, 652) observes that this warning to Gentile believers about presumptuous boasting echoes earlier rebukes concerning Jewish presumption (2:1–3:20). It also anticipates the more general warnings in 12:3, 16 about arrogance with regard to other believers.

[185] Cranfield (*Romans*, 2:554) argues that ἵνα with the subjunctive here is best understood as expressing result ("so as to"). Cf. Wallace, *Greek Grammar*, 473.

[186] Dunn, *Romans 9–16*, 653. Cf. Karl L. Schmidt, "πταίω," *TDNT* 6:883–84. Wilhelm Michaelis ("πίπτω κτλ.," *TDNT* 6:164–66) discusses the figurative use of πίπτω in terms of final judgment. In 11:22, however, this verb is used to describe Israel's present failure.

[187] Wright ("Romans," 681) argues that Israel has recapitulated the sin of Adam: "But, whereas the trespass of Adam brought sin and death to the world, the 'trespass'

As indicated previously, salvation means final deliverance from the consequences of sin (e.g., 5:9–10; 10:10–13), but there are immediate benefits for those who believe, notably the hope of the glory of God (e.g., 5:1–5; 8:1–39). Salvation comes to people in the present when they receive the gospel with faith. A purpose clause (εἰς τὸ παραζηλῶσαι αὐτούς, "to make them jealous") outlines how the reception of salvation by Gentiles may benefit unbelieving Israel.

In the narrative of Acts, rejection of the gospel by Jews in different contexts leads Paul to turn to the Gentiles. Isaiah 49:6 is cited as the theological justification for this initiative in Acts 13:45–48. Here, however, the divinely ordained sequence of events in Deut 32:21 is specifically the basis for the apostle's thinking.[188] Moses predicted that Israel would be rebellious and provoke God's jealous anger toward his people (Deut 32:5–21). God's judgment would be expressed in provoking *Israel* to jealousy, using those who were "not a nation" to achieve this. Paul sees the eschatological fulfillment of this sequence in Israel's rejection of the gospel, the consequent blessing of the nations through the conversion of many Gentiles to Christ and the subsequent provoking of Israel to jealousy. Many people today identify jealousy with envy and regard it as a base motivation, but the focus on salvation in this context suggests that παραζηλῶσαι has a more positive sense.[189] Paul means that certain Jews will recognize in the faith of Gentile Christians the eschatological blessings promised to Israel and be zealous to secure those blessings for themselves (cf. v. 13 comment). The conclusion to the Song of Moses in Deut 32:43 is cited with other texts in 15:9–12 to show that God always intended the nations to rejoice with Israel in the salvation of his people.

11:12. A "how much more" argument (as in 5:9, 10, 15, 17) picks up the notion of Israel's trespass from the previous verse (τὸ

---

of Israel has brought salvation and 'riches' to the world!" Bell (*Provoked to Jealousy*, 108–10) also argues in favor of the rendering "trespass."

[188] Cf. Bell, *Provoked to Jealousy*, 110–13. Cranfield's contention (*Romans*, 2:556) that Paul is taking about the Jews rejecting Jesus himself and handing him over to the Gentiles does not really fit the context.

[189] Bell (*Provoked to Jealousy*, 39–43) suggests the translation "provoke to emulation." Bell (168–99) argues that Israel's privileges have been extended to "the Church of Jews and Gentiles" and that in various ways the roles of Israel and Gentiles have been reversed. Contrast Jewett, *Romans*, 674.

παράπτωμα αὐτῶν, "their transgression") and celebrates the outcome as "riches for the world." A parallel clause describes "their failure" (τὸ ἥττημα αὐτῶν) as bringing "riches for the Gentiles."[190] Given the twofold reference to "riches" in the premise of this sentence, Paul implies that "their fullness" (τὸ πλήρωμα αὐτῶν) will bring unimaginable spiritual wealth (cf. 10:12). The noun πλήρωμα in this context means "that which is brought to fullness or completion" (BDAG). Use of the same noun in the expression τὸ πλήρωμα τῶν ἐθνῶν (v. 25, "the fullness of the Gentiles") suggests that the reference in v. 12 is to the full number of Israelites: "the predestined number of the saved."[191] Although he goes on to talk about "all Israel" being saved (v. 26), his use of πλήρωμα in relation to both the Gentiles and Israel signifies that he means the elect in both categories.

11:13–14. With the pronoun ὑμῖν ("you") in an emphatic position, Paul directly addresses his Gentile readers and introduces a new section of the argument, which continues to v. 32. Although the point is debated, most scholars consider that this letter is directed to a situation where Gentile Christians are in the majority, yet Jewish Christians are present in their community. Judaism still flourishes in the wider context of their city (cf. Introduction III.A).[192] Paul's argument indicates that he expected some resistance to his teaching about the future of Israel. Given the growth of Gentile Christianity and Paul's focus on ministry to Gentiles, it would have been easy for many to conclude that God and his apostle had given up on the Jews. His argument is introduced in an elaborate fashion (ἐφ' ὅσον μὲν οὖν,

[190] This conditional sentence is in the form of an ellipse without verbs, to be supplied by the reader (cf. BDF §481). "Loss" is a good translation of ἥττημα here because the paradoxical outcome is riches (BDAG). But Cranfield (*Romans*, 2:557) and Bell (*Provoked to Jealousy*, 114) argue for "defeat," because Deut 32 portrays Israel's disobedience leading to defeat by Gentiles (cf. ἥττημα in LXX Isa 31:8; 1 Cor 6:7).

[191] Jewett, *Romans*, 678. Cf. 4 Ezra 4:35–37; 2 Bar. 23:4–5. Moo (*Romans*, 689–90) proposes that a qualitative understanding of πλήρωμα could be combined with a quantitative one: "'fullness' is attained through a numerical process."

[192] Some have speculated that Paul is addressing Gentile Christians in Rome who are part of a community that is still predominantly Jewish-Christian in character (e.g., Donald W. B. Robinson, "Not Boasting over the Natural Branches: Gentile Circumspection in the Divine Economy," in *The Gospel to the Nations: Perspectives on Paul's Mission*, ed. Peter G. Bolt and Mark D. Thompson [Downers Grove: InterVarsity, 2000], 166–68). But this does not adequately account for the rhetoric in 11:1–32.

"inasmuch as then, insofar as").[193] Recalling what he says in 1:1, 5 about his divine commission (cf. Gal 1:15–16), Paul asserts (lit.), "I myself am apostle to the Gentiles" (εἰμι ἐγὼ ἐθνῶν ἀπόστολος).[194] As such, he continues, "I magnify my ministry" (τὴν διακονίαν μου δοξάζω), using a verb that he employs elsewhere to describe the obligation of humans everywhere to "glorify" God (1:21; 15:6, 9). In Paul's mind, "honoring the agency of apostolic service was a logical extension of this obligation."[195] In practical terms it meant devoting himself to winning the Gentiles and establishing them as disciples of Christ (cf. 1:8–15; 15:14–32), assured that this would ultimately serve the cause of Jewish conversion.

Consistent with his argument in v. 11 which is based on his understanding of Deut 32:21 (cf. 10:19), he concludes, "If I might somehow make my own people jealous and save some of them."[196] The particle πώς is "a marker of undesignated means or manner" (BDAG), signifying Paul's caution about the way this divine purpose may be achieved (cf. 1:10; Phil 3:11). As in 9:3, he identifies fellow Israelites as his own "flesh" (μου τὴν σάρκα [CSB: "my own people"]), and contemplates saving an indeterminate number of them (cf. 1 Cor 9:22, τινὰς σώσω, "that I may save some").[197] It is clear from 10:10–17 that salvation is only possible for Jews and Gentiles through faith in Christ. It also follows from 11:7–10 that those who are hardened against the gospel will only believe when God removes the "spirit of stupor." God himself must provoke Israel to jealousy and save them through faith in Christ. But Paul anticipates that this will happen as he pursues his evangelistic ministry to the nations with full vigor. "It is the magnificence of Paul's vision

[193] Cranfield (*Romans*, 2:559) argues that μὲν οὖν here means "contrary to what you may be inclined to think." However, Schreiner (*Romans*, 595) says, "This interpretation would be more convincing if μενοῦνγε were used, as in 9:20 and 10:18."

[194] Jewett (*Romans*, 678) argues that the anarthrous expression ἐθνῶν ἀπόστολος is not a title and should be rendered "an apostle to the Gentiles." But Paul surely does not mean that his service to the Jewish mission is "a generic obligation of every Gentile apostle." The phrase should be translated "apostle to the Gentiles" to indicate the distinctive nature of Paul's calling. Cf. Moo, *Romans*, 691n40.

[195] Jewett, *Romans*, 679. Dunn (*Romans 9–16*, 669–70) relates the magnification of Paul's ministry to Gentiles to his insistence on a law-free gospel.

[196] See my comment on παραζηλῶσαι ("make jealous") in 11:11.

[197] For the past, present, and future dimensions of salvation in Paul's teaching, see 1:16; 5:9–10; 8:24; 9:27; 10:1, 9–10, 13; 11:11, 14, 26; 13:11.

that he could see himself as called to such a crucial role in thus uniting Jew and Gentile under grace as the climax of God's purpose for creation" (see §2.7).[198]

11:15. The conjunction γάρ ("for") links a series of concluding claims to the argument in vv. 11–14. As in v. 12, the premise of a conditional clause ("If their rejection [brings] reconciliation to the world") is followed by a rhetorical question ("What will their acceptance mean but life from the dead?"). Since Paul insists that God has *not* rejected his people irrevocably (vv. 1–2), the expression ἡ ἀποβολὴ αὐτῶν must refer to their temporary casting away (cf. v. 17 comment) and the antonym ἡ πρόσλημψις to their final acceptance.[199] Meanwhile, "the reconciliation of the world" (καταλλαγὴ κόσμου) is the extraordinary outcome of Israel's present casting away. Paul is not a universalist in the sense of teaching that everyone will ultimately be saved whether they believe the gospel or not. According to 5:10–11, reconciliation involves the ending of hostility between God and his enemies, which Christ achieved by shedding his blood. As his ambassadors proclaim the message of reconciliation, people in every nation are experiencing the benefits of Christ's reconciling work (cf. 2 Cor 5:18–21). Moreover, as Jews and Gentiles turn to God in Christ, they are reconciled to each other and can praise God together for his mercy (15:7–12; cf. Eph 2:11–22). So the effect of Christ's reconciling work is being experienced everywhere. Paul's "how much more" argument ends with the claim that Israel's reception of the gospel will mean "life from the dead" (ζωὴ ἐκ νεκρῶν). Given the perspective of vv. 25–32, it is likely that this means the general resurrection at the end of time. The salvation of "all Israel" will be followed by the resurrection of the dead.[200]

11:16. Continuing the "how much more" argument that began in v. 12, Paul uses an abbreviated conditional clause to draw attention

---

[198] Dunn, *Romans 9–16*, 671.

[199] Cf. Cranfield, *Romans*, 2:562. Fitzmyer (*Romans*, 612) takes αὐτῶν in 11:15 to be a subjective genitive and understands Paul to be talking about Israel's rejection of God (so also Jewett, *Romans*, 680–81). However, see Schreiner, *Romans*, 597. The verb προσλαμβάνω, which is the cognate of πρόσλημψις, is used in 14:1, 3; 15:7 as Paul develops the implications of being accepted by God.

[200] Cf. Cranfield, *Romans*, 2:562–63; Dunn, *Romans 9–16*, 658; Moo, *Romans*, 694–96; Byrne, *Romans*, 339; Schreiner, *Romans*, 599; Jewett, *Romans*, 681. But see v. 27 comment.

to a principle of sanctification he deduces from Num 15:17–21. Israel was commanded to offer to the Lord a loaf from the first batch of dough, thus effectively consecrating the whole batch ("if the first-fruits are holy, so is the whole batch"). Elsewhere the noun ἀπαρχή signifies an initial work of God that is a pledge of more to come (8:23; 16:5; 1 Cor 15:20, 23; 16:15). In the flow of Paul's argument, this suggests that God's setting apart a portion of Israel through faith in the Messiah guarantees the consecration of "the rest" whom he intends to save.[201] A second conditional clause restates this principle, using the common OT link between branches and roots (e.g., Job 18:16; Jer 17:8; Hos 9:1): "And if the root is holy, so are the branches." This parallels the preceding claim in form but anticipates the argument to come in meaning where the patriarchs are most likely "the root" (vv. 17–18; cf. 9:5; 11:28, "forefathers" ESV).[202] So the second half of v. 16 is best viewed as a transitional expression, maintaining that "the unbelieving majority of the Jews are hallowed by their relationship to the patriarchs."[203]

11:17–18. Paul expands on his image of the root and branches (v. 16b), comparing the people of God to an olive tree that has both wild and natural branches. This figure is first used to explain how Jews and Gentiles can be one people, united in Jesus the Messiah and fulfilling God's covenant promises to the patriarchs. Although the apostle has been criticized for suggesting patterns of arboriculture that are unnatural or impossible here, he actually stretches his

[201] Cf. Cranfield, *Romans*, 2:563–64; Wright, "Romans," 683. The notion of being "sanctified by the Holy Spirit" through belief in the gospel is highlighted in Rom 15:16. This definitive act of God is associated with justification and redemption in other contexts (e.g., 1 Cor 1:2, 30; 6:11). But the idea that the rest of Israel is sanctified by those who believe is closer to 1 Cor 7:14, where Paul says the unbelieving marriage partner is "sanctified" by the believing one. Cf. Peterson, *Possessed by God*, 27–68, 87.

[202] Abraham and the patriarchs are described this way in Jewish texts such as 1 En. 93:5, 8; Philo, *Her.* 279; Jub. 21:24.

[203] Cranfield, *Romans*, 2:565. Dunn (*Romans 9–16*, 659) argues that Paul probably wanted to bring two ideas together here (early converts as promise of a complete harvest and God's promise to the patriarchs as assurance of his continuing faithfulness to Israel). But Schreiner (*Romans*, 600) dismisses this as "unnecessarily complicated," arguing that both images relate to the consecration of "all Israel" to God by his choice of the patriarchs. Kruse (*Romans*, 433–34) surveys a range of views and concludes that both images relate to the consecration of true Jews by the faith of Abraham (cf. 4:12).

metaphor to reflect the extraordinary course of salvation history.[204] Two conditional clauses introduce his argument. The first contains a lengthy protasis to identify the key elements in his allegory: "Now if some of the branches were broken off, and you, though a wild olive branch, were grafted in among them and have come to share in the rich root of the cultivated olive tree." The breaking off of some of the branches refers to the hardening of unbelieving Israel (vv. 7–10), which Paul also described as "their rejection" (v. 15). The passive verbs ἐξεκλάσθησαν ("broken off") and ἐνεκεντρίσθης ("grafted in") imply divine action. With the second-person singular pronoun σύ ("you") used for rhetorical emphasis, Gentile readers are now addressed individually.[205]

Israel is portrayed as God's "olive tree" in Jer 11:16; Hos 14:6, and as God's "planting" in later Jewish literature (e.g., 2 Macc 1:29; Jub 1:16; 1 En. 10:16; 26:1). However, the olive tree here is more broadly "the people of God, which is composed of both Jews and Gentiles."[206] CSB adds the adjective "cultivated" to signify God's nurturing and sustaining of this people. Every Gentile who has been grafted in among the believing remnant of Israel (ἐνεκεντρίσθης ἐν αὐτοῖς) is identified as being "a wild olive (branch)" (the adjective ἀγριέλαιος is used as a substantive). God's grafting makes it possible for each one to "become" (ἐγένου), literally, "a sharer together with" (συγκοινωνός) believing Israelites in (lit.) "the fatness of the root of the olive tree" (τῆς ῥίζης τῆς πιότητος τῆς ἐλαίας).[207] CSB has understood the second genitive to be one of quality and hence adjectival

[204] Cf. Cranfield, *Romans*, 2:565–66. Jewett (*Romans*, 684–85) discusses the way Paul's allegory differs from some Greco-Roman writers on the subject of grafting. Kruse (*Romans*, 439–41) surveys a variety of scholarly articles on Paul's olive tree analogy.

[205] Jewett (*Romans*, 683–84) follows Tobin (*Paul's Rhetoric*, 363), arguing that Paul's rhetoric is not directly addressing Gentile members of the Roman community here. But such passionate rhetoric must have had the recipients in mind, even if ostensibly directed to "an imaginary interlocutor."

[206] Schreiner, *Romans*, 605. In effect, Paul returns to the argument in 4:9–12, 23–25, where the promises to Abraham are applied to all who share his faith.

[207] These genitives occur in sequence in ℵ* B C Ψ and other manuscripts. This is likely to be the original reading since καί ("and") is found between the first two nouns in ℵ[2] A D[2] and other manuscripts, and the words τῆς ἐλαίας ἐγένου ("of the olive tree") are missing from 𝔓[46] D* F G and other manuscripts. These modifications were doubtless made because of the difficulty of the original. Cf. Metzger, *Textual Commentary*, 464.

("the rich root"). This follows BDAG, which takes πιότητος to refer to "the root with its oily richness" (ESV: "the nourishing root of the olive tree"). God's purpose was that, in company with believing Israelites, "the blessing of Abraham would come to the Gentiles by Christ Jesus, so that we could receive the promised Spirit through faith" (Gal 3:14).

Paul's first conditional clause concludes with an exhortation: "Do not boast that you are better than those branches" (μὴ κατακαυχῶ τῶν κλάδων). The compound of the verb καυχάομαι "brings out strongly the element of comparative superiority expressed in boasting."[208] This warning to Gentile Christians echoes earlier warnings to Jews about boasting (2:17, 23; 3:27–4:5). A second conditional clause identifies the misunderstanding that is implicit in such boasting: "But if you do boast—you do not sustain the root, but the root sustains you." Where CSB has put a dash, we should understand Paul to mean something like "remember" (ESV). A triumphant putting down of unbelieving Jews by Gentile Christians would be a denial of the truth that "the root" "carries" or "sustains" (βαστάζεις, cf. 15:1; Gal 6:2) the branches of the olive tree, both natural and grafted. "The root" is probably a reference to the patriarchs, who received the covenanted promises of God that initiated the people of God.[209] Paul seems to be addressing a particular situation that he knows to exist among the Roman Christians. Implicitly, he warns, "A church which is not drawing upon the sustenance of its Jewish inheritance (including the OT, but not only the OT), would be a contradiction in terms."[210] Positively speaking, he wants his readers to share his concern for the salvation of "the rest" of Israel.

---

[208] Rudolph Bultmann, "κατακαυχάομαι κτλ.," *TDNT* 3:653. Cf. BDAG; Jas 2:13 ("triumphs over"); 3:14 ("boast").

[209] Wright ("Romans," 684) thinks it is easier to see the root that bears both Gentile and Jewish Christians as the Messiah. But Paul's focus on Abraham and the promises made to him (4:1–25), combined with his argument in 9:6–12, suggests that he is thinking of the way God's plan for Israel and the nations was first articulated and came into effect through his engagement with the patriarchs. Cf. Dunn, *Romans 9–16*, 659–60.

[210] Dunn, *Romans 9–16*, 662. Moo (*Romans*, 703–4) argues on the basis of 14:1–15:13 that Paul is also concerned to address the dismissive attitude of Gentile Christians to Jewish believers as well as to unbelieving Jews. Moo (708–10) makes some helpful comments in this context about the continuity and discontinuity between Israel and the church.

11:19–20. Paul's diatribe continues as he puts into the mouth of an imaginary Gentile opponent a response to the preceding argument: "Then you will say, 'Branches were broken off so that I might be grafted in.'" With this argument, "the interlocutor throws Paul's words back in his face by employing precisely the same terms that Paul had used in v. 17."[211] A simple reply (*καλῶς*, "true enough") leads the apostle back to the issue of unbelief and faith: "They were broken off because of unbelief (*τῇ ἀπιστίᾳ*), but you stand by faith (*τῇ πίστει*)." The perfect tense (*ἕστηκας*, "you stand") highlights the present state of those who have obtained access to God by faith (as in 5:2). Boasting is excluded by acknowledging one's continuing dependence on God's grace (v. 22; cf. 3:27). So the warning is "Do not be arrogant, but beware." The expression *μὴ ὑψηλὰ φρόνει* literally means, "Do not think lofty things" (cf. 12:16; 1 Tim 6:17). The alternative is to cultivate a genuine fear (*ἀλλὰ φοβοῦ*). In biblical terms, this regularly means respect or reverence for God (NRSV, "stand in awe") based on the revelation of his character to his people.[212] However, the context suggests the possibility of rendering the imperative more negatively ("beware").

11:21. The conjunction *γάρ* ("for, because") indicates that what follows is the reason for Gentile Christians to "beware" (v. 20). Paul first focuses on the fact that "God did not spare the natural branches." In this context *κατὰ φύσιν* ("natural") refers to a "condition or circumstance as determined by birth" (BDAG; cf. 1:26; 2:14; 11:24). Those who were Jews by birth had the means of knowing and serving God (3:1–2; 9:4–5), but many failed to pursue the righteousness that comes from faith and were not prepared to receive their Messiah when he came (9:31–10:4). If these "natural branches" were removed because of unbelief, Paul affirms that God "will not spare you either" (*οὐδὲ σοῦ φείσεται*).[213] There is no continuing

---

[211] Jewett, *Romans*, 687.

[212] Jewett's view that this is "a fear concerning the loss of an allegedly superior status" (*Romans*, 688) is inconsistent with the theocentric argument that follows. Fear of God in the OT involved keeping his commandments, obeying his voice, walking in his ways, turning from evil, and serving him. Cf. Peterson, *Engaging with God*, 70–72.

[213] The typically Pauline expression *μή πως* ("lest") is found in some manuscripts (𝔓[46] D F G Ψ 33 etc.), which has the effect of softening the warning (KJV, "take heed lest"). Although Metzger (*Textual Commentary*, 464–65) argues that this is possibly

place among God's people for individuals who fail to believe his words and abandon their confidence in his grace (cf. 1 Cor 10:12). However, as in Hebrews, where there are several similar warnings (e.g., Heb 2:1–4; 3:1–4:13), accompanying messages provide the incentive for persevering in faith (e.g., Heb 4:14–5:10; 6:9–20).

11:22. A conclusion to the argument in vv. 17–21 begins with the challenge to (lit.) "take note then" (*ἴδε οὖν* [CSB: "therefore, consider"]). What Paul has been effectively highlighting is "God's kindness and severity" (*χρηστότητα καὶ ἀποτομίαν θεοῦ*). Nowhere else in Jewish writings are these two terms paired together to describe the way God acts in human history, suggesting that the apostle deliberately employed words "more typical of the Greco-Roman environment."[214] God's kindness was mentioned in 2:4 (cf. Eph 2:7; Titus 3:4 ["goodness" ESV]), and his wrath and righteous judgment were the focus in 1:18–2:16. But the word "severity" is only applied to God here in the NT (cf. Wis 5:20; 6:5; 11:10; 12:9; 18:15, where the adjective *ἀπότομος* ["severe, stern"] is used). The antithesis is developed with the contrasting terms *μέν* and *δέ*, highlighting first God's severity toward "those who have fallen" (*ἐπὶ τοὺς πεσόντας*). The same verb is used in v. 11 with reference to complete failure, but in this context it describes the hardening and unbelief of "the rest" of Israel. Paul considers this to be temporary (vv. 12–16, 24, 26–32). God's kindness to each and every one of his Gentile readers is emphasized by the use of a second-person singular pronoun (*ἐπὶ σέ* "toward you"), as in vv. 17, 18, 20. However, an unfulfilled conditional clause continues the warning from v. 21: "If you remain in (his) kindness" (*ἐὰν ἐπιμένῃς τῇ χρηστότητι*). This is another way of describing what it means to live by faith in the grace of God (contrast v. 23, "remain in unbelief"). "Those who do not cleave to God's goodness are threatened by 'the inflexible hardness and severity' of the Judge as the only alternative."[215]

---

what Paul wrote, the strong combination of א B C 81 1739 in support of the shorter text points in favor of the reading adopted by CSB. Cf. Jewett, *Romans*, 667.

[214] Jewett, *Romans*, 689–90. Paul uses absolute nominatives in reverse order for rhetorical effect in v. 22b (*ἀποτομία, χρηστότης*). Cf. 2:8–10; BDF §466.2–4.

[215] Helmut Koester, "*τέμνω κτλ.*," *TDNT* 8:108. In Col 1:23 Paul uses a condition of fact to make the same point. See also the warnings about persevering with a gospel-driven faith in 1 Cor 10:1–12; Gal 5:2–5; 1 Thess 3:1–5.

God's kindness to Gentiles has previously been described in terms of "riches for the world" (v. 12), reconciliation for the world (v. 15), and a grafting among believing Israelites so as to share in "the rich root of the cultivated olive tree" (v. 17). Paul's warning concludes with an "otherwise" clause (cf. v. 6; 1 Cor 5:10; Heb 9:26): "Otherwise you too will be cut off" (ἐπεὶ καὶ σὺ ἐκκοπήσῃ). Using the second-person singular once more, he confronts his Gentile readers with the prospect of sharing the fate of unbelieving Israelites. His warning is against "a false and unevangelical sense of security."[216] The antidote is to rely continually on the kindness of God revealed in the gospel as the basis of acceptance and continuance in the community of faith.

11:23–24. Paul expresses again his concern for the hardened portion of Israel and his confidence that God can bring in "their fullness" (v. 12). With the emphatic κἀκεῖνοι δέ ("And even they"), he affirms that "if they do not remain in unbelief, [they] will be grafted in." The same verb (ἐγκεντρισθήσονται) was used with reference to the grafting of Gentile believers into the "cultivated olive tree" of God's people (vv. 17, 19). It is used four times in vv. 23–24 to recall that argument and make a new claim. Given that unbelieving Israelites have been rejected by God (v. 15) and "broken off" (v. 17), their regrafting may seem impossible. But Paul asserts that, "God has the power (δυνατός) to graft them in again." The kindness and power of God are the basis for confidence that he can remove such hardening, enable belief, and restore those Israelites whom he chooses to save. God's power was mentioned in 1:4, 16, 20; 4:21; 9:17, 22 and will come into focus again in 14:4; 15:13, 19. "God is powerful enough to break through the resistance against grace, which is as formidable a barrier for Gentiles as for Jews."[217]

To reinforce this claim (γάρ, "for"), the apostle again addresses his Gentile readers individually, using the second-person singular (σύ). Gentiles who doubt the ability or intention of God to restore the hardened portion of Israel should remember the miracle of their

[216] Cranfield, *Romans*, 2:570. Dunn (*Romans 9–16*, 664) warns, "A doctrine of 'perseverance of the saints' which does not include the lessons of salvation-history has lost its biblical perspective." Moo (*Romans*, 707) notes that Paul echoes a consistent NT theme here: "Ultimate salvation is dependent on continuing faith; therefore, the person who ceases to believe forfeits any hope of salvation."

[217] Jewett, *Romans*, 692.

own conversion and incorporation into the people of God. Using a condition of fact, Paul reminds each one that "you were cut off from your native wild olive tree, and against nature were grafted into a cultivated olive tree." Here he uses the expression *κατὰ φύσιν* ("natural"; CSB: "native") to describe the "wild olive tree" (ἀγριελαίου) to which they naturally belonged. This is a way of speaking about the religious and cultural context into which they were born. The contrasting *παρὰ φύσιν* ("against nature") is employed to describe their grafting into the "cultivated olive tree" (*καλλιέλαιον*) to which they now belong. This believing community has its roots in the patriarchal era of biblical history and national Israel's relationship with God.[218] Using another "much more" argument (*πόσῳ μᾶλλον*), he affirms that "these—the natural branches—will be grafted into their own olive tree." "If the Gentile Christian can believe that God has actually grafted him into that holy stem to which he does not naturally belong, how much more readily ought he to believe that God is able and willing to do what is less wonderful—to restore to their own native stock the unbelieving Jews, when they repent and believe!"[219]

Bridge

When Paul writes about the stumbling and failure of Israel (11:11–16), he makes clear that God has not given up on his people. He has used the unbelief of many Israelites to bring the riches of the gospel to the nations and will use Gentile acceptance of the gospel to bring more Israelites to faith. All this demonstrates God's continuing faithfulness to his promises and to his ancient people. But what is to prevent Gentile Christians from stumbling to the point of being "cut off" (11:17–24)? Can genuine believers in Christ lose their salvation? Paul addresses this question by focusing on the kindness and severity of God. The kindness of God is ground for

[218] In v. 21 Paul uses *κατὰ φύσιν* with reference to Israelites as the "natural branches" of that "cultivated olive tree." Paul's Gentile mission "does not intend the creation of a separate Gentile church but rather a church of Jews and Gentiles, both of whom will have been enabled by the gospel of 'God's kindness and severity' to overcome their cultural prejudices" (Jewett, *Romans*, 693). Cf. §2.6; Moo, *Romans*, 708–10.

[219] Cranfield, *Romans* 2:572. Byrne (*Romans*, 343) observes, "Paul presents the inclusion of the Gentiles as both the hope-giving precedent and the paradigm for the 're-inclusion' of Israel."

believing that he will fulfill his promise to bring "the fullness" of his elect from every nation into his kingdom (cf. 1 Cor 1:8–9; Phil 1:6). Paul is convinced that his apostolic ministry is critical for this outcome, for both Jews and Gentiles. His warning is not to gloat over those who have been "broken off" by unbelief but to be warned by the severity of God and encouraged by his kindness to persist in faith. Remaining in the community of faith involves recognizing your dependence on the gracious promises of God. Genuine believers do not lose their salvation because they trust in the kindness and faithfulness of God and continue to be warned by his severity.

F. Hope in the Mercy of God (11:25–36)

25 I don't want you to be ignorant of this mystery, brothers
and sisters, so that you will not be conceited: A partial hardening
has come upon Israel until the fullness of the Gentiles has come
in. 26 And in this way all Israel will be saved, as it is written,

The Deliverer will come from Zion;
he will turn godlessness away from Jacob.
27 **And this will be my covenant with them**
when I take away their sins.

28 Regarding the gospel, they are enemies for your advantage,
but regarding election, they are loved because of the patriarchs,
29 since God's gracious gifts and calling are irrevocable. 30 As you
once disobeyed God but now have received mercy through their
disobedience, 31 so they too have now disobeyed, resulting in mercy to you, so that they also may now receive mercy. 32 For God has
imprisoned all in disobedience so that he may have mercy on all.

33 Oh, the depth of the riches
both of the wisdom and of the knowledge of God!
How unsearchable his judgments
and untraceable his ways!
34 **For who has known the mind of the Lord?**
Or who has been his counselor?
35 **And who has ever given to God,**
that he should be repaid?
36 For from him and through him
and to him are all things.
To him be the glory forever. Amen.

Context

The mercy of God was previously linked with his compassion and his desire to make known "the riches of his glory" (9:15, 16, 18, 23). Divine mercy comes to the fore again in 11:30–32 as Paul brings to a climax his argument about the salvation of Israel and the nations (see also 15:8–12).[220] In vv. 22–24 he considered the possibility that "the natural branches" discarded from the "olive tree" of God's people might be grafted in again because God has the power to do so. Now he explains how that will happen. Expanding on his claims in vv. 11–15, he reminds his Gentile readers that God's mercy has been shown to the whole world through the "stumbling" of Israel and the failure of many Israelites to believe the gospel. But God's plan is that their "fullness" will be released from hardness of heart and be saved by his mercy.

Structure

This passage has three distinct sections. In vv. 25–27 Paul outlines the final mystery of God's purpose for Israel and the Gentiles. The salvation of "all Israel" is linked to the coming in of "the fullness of the Gentiles." Israel's salvation is certified by a combination of divine promises from Isa 59:20–21 and 27:9. In the second section (vv. 28–32) Paul recalls previous arguments about the election of Israel and reiterates that the disobedience of Israel has resulted in mercy being shown to Gentiles. But God's ultimate intention is to have mercy on all. "The situation of Israel and the Gentiles is shown to be parallel in the reception of mercy despite the previous disobedience of each group."[221] In the third section (vv. 33–36) the apostle celebrates the depth of the riches and the wisdom and the knowledge of God, as indicated by the revelation and outworking of his saving plan. This hymn of praise includes a citation from Isa 40:13 and an allusion to Job 41:11 (MT; LXX 41:3) and concludes with a doxology.

---

[220] Dunn (*Romans 9–16*, 677) notes other verbal links between these chapters: election (9:11; 11:5, 7, 28) and calling (9:7, 12, 24–26; 11:29). He also notes links between 11:28–32 and 1:18–3:20 and 3:21–21.

[221] Jewett, *Romans*, 696. The universal scope of v. 32 reflects earlier arguments about sin (1:18–3:20) and salvation (3:21–5:21).

Outline:

1. The salvation of "all Israel" (vv. 25–27)
2. The overwhelming power of God's mercy (vv. 28–32)
3. The riches of the wisdom and knowledge of God (vv. 33–36)

11:25–26a. Paul sets out to support his claim that Israelites, who are "the natural branches," may be grafted again "into their own olive tree" (vv. 23–24). The conjunction *γάρ* ("for")—not translated by CSB—indicates this sequence. Using a distinctive formula found also in 1:13 (οὐ θέλω ὑμᾶς ἀγνοεῖν, "I don't want you to be ignorant"; cf. 1 Cor 10:1; 12:1; 2 Cor 1:8; 1 Thess 4:13), he draws attention to the importance of what he is about to say.[222] He wants them to know "this mystery" (τὸ μυστήριον τοῦτο), the content of which is then disclosed. But first he indicates that his purpose in making the mystery known is "so that you will not be conceited" (ἵνα μὴ ἦτε [παρ'] ἑαυτοῖς φρόνιμοι).[223] This is an abbreviated version or echo of the warning in Prov 3:7 LXX (μὴ ἴσθι φρόνιμος παρὰ σεαυτῷ, "Do not be wise in your own estimation"), with the singular changed to the plural (cf. 12:16). Paul continues to warn about arrogance in relation to unbelieving Israel. In vv. 17–24 he addresses Gentile readers individually, describing each one as "a wild olive branch." Here he turns to address the whole community again, using the term ἀδελφοί ("brothers and sisters"; cf. 1:13; 7:1, 4; 8:12, 29; 10:1; 12:1; 15:14, 30; 16:17).[224] Nevertheless, he must have the Gentile majority in view when he claims that unbelieving Israelites are enemies regarding the gospel "for your advantage" (v. 28), alluding to the argument in 11:11–12.

---

[222] Runge (*Discourse Grammar*, 105–7) discusses the significance of this sort of "metacomment" in Paul's writings.

[223] The simple dative ἑαυτοῖς ("to yourselves"), which is found in 𝔓[46] F G Ψ and other manuscripts, is most likely to be the original. The preposition παρ' ("among, with") in א C D and other manuscripts may be an assimilation to either LXX Prov 3:7 or Rom 12:16 (φρόνιμοι παρ' ἑαυτοῖς). In A B and other manuscripts, ἐν ("in") was added instead (perhaps influenced by LXX Isa 5:21). Cf. Jewett, *Romans*, 694.

[224] Dunn (*Romans 9–16*, 690) says, "It is by no means impossible that he had the Jewish Christians in view as well, since they would readily assume what is not actually stated in the metaphor, that they were original branches of the olive tree which had *not* been broken off."

The word μυστήριον ("mystery") was widely used in Greco-Roman religions, apocalyptic Judaism, and early Christian sources, where it often signified a divine revelation to the initiated.[225] Paul deliberately opposes such insider bias in his use of the term. The secret of how God will fulfill his saving plan is *publicly* revealed to counteract conceit, promote a general confidence in the mercy of God, and encourage heartfelt, united praise (vv. 25–36; cf. 15:8–13). The term is used again in 16:25–26 to refer to "the mystery" of the gospel, which is "now revealed and made known through the prophetic Scriptures" (cf. 1 Cor 2:1, 7; 4:1; Eph 1:9; 3:3, 4, 9; 6:19; Col 1:26, 27; 2:2; 4:3; 1 Tim 3:9, 16). In 11:25 Paul describes one element of the divine purpose that is discernible in Scripture yet still mysterious in the sense of surpassing human wisdom (cf. 1 Cor 13:2; 14:2; 15:51; Eph 5:32; 2 Thess 2:7). Although it is possible that Paul is imparting a special revelation that was given to him in the recent past, it is more likely that "the contents of this mystery are to be discerned in the OT seen in the light of the gospel events."[226] See 16:25–27 comments.

There are three elements to the mystery. First, "a partial hardening has come upon Israel" (ὅτι πώρωσις ἀπὸ μέρους τῷ Ἰσραὴλ γέγονεν).[227] Israel's fault was emphasized in 9:31–10:4; 10:16, 19–21; 11:11–12, but the judgment of divine hardening was highlighted as a simultaneous factor in 11:7–10, supported by two biblical texts. Second, it is now revealed that this hardening will continue "until the fullness of the Gentiles has come in" (ἄχρι οὗ τὸ πλήρωμα τῶν

[225] Cf. Günther Bornkamm, "μυστήριον, μυέω," *TDNT* 4:802–28. Evidence for its use in Jewish circles can be found in LXX Dan 2:18–19, 27–30, 47; 1QS 4:6, 18; 1QpHab 7:5, 8, 14; 1 En. 38:3; 51:3; 103:2; 104:10; 4 Ezra 12:37–38; 14:5–6, 26, 45–47; 2 Bar. 20:3; 48:3.

[226] Cranfield, *Romans*, 2:574. Cf. Dunn, *Romans 9–16*, 678–79, 690. Jewett (*Romans*, 698–99) critiques the view of Seeyoon Kim ("The 'Mystery' of Rom 11:25–26 Once More," *NTS* 43 [1997], 417–18) that this mystery was disclosed to Paul at the time of his conversion. Byrne (*Romans*, 349) notes that Paul gathers together under the heading "this mystery" what he has already taught about the salvation of Israel, but Moo (*Romans*, 716–17) argues that the new element is specifically the disclosure in v. 26a.

[227] The expression ἀπὸ μέρους is best understood adverbially (as in 15:15 ["on some points"], 24 ["for a while"]; 2 Cor 1:14; 2:5) to mean, "a hardening has come partially upon Israel" (Moo, *Romans*, 717n28). Wright ("Romans," 688) suggests that it could be translated "for a while" because the hardening is temporary rather than partial. The perfect indicative γέγονεν highlights the present reality of this hardening.

ἐθνῶν εἰσέλθῃ). Paul envisages an ongoing harvest of Gentile believers as the gospel goes out to the nations. Their "fullness" implies a foreordained number of converts (cf. 11:12 comment), though no indication of the size of this multitude is given. Their "coming in" could mean coming into the kingdom of heaven/God (e.g., Matt 5:20; 7:21; 18:3; 19:23, 24; 21:31) or coming into eternal life (e.g., Matt 18:8, 9; 19:17).[228] This revelation challenges Jewish expectations about how Gentiles come to share in Israel's salvation (e.g., Isa 2:2–3; 56:6–8; 60:1–16; Zech 14:16–17; Pss. Sol. 17:31, 34; 2 Bar. 68:5). The open secret now is that God's mission to the nations *precedes* the salvation of "all Israel." Paradoxically, a massive movement among the Gentiles becomes the means God uses to save the hardened portion of Israel (11:11–14). The third element in Paul's unfolding of the mystery clarifies this perspective. "And in this way" (καὶ οὕτως) means "in the circumstances which are indicated by the first two parts of the statement."[229] A temporal reading of καὶ οὕτως would mean "and then all Israel will be saved," but a modal reading ("and in this way all Israel will be saved") is more likely in the context.[230]

The means by which "all Israel will be saved" is more precisely explained by the biblical citation that follows. Given the argument in 9:6–33, Paul does not imply that every Israelite without exception will be saved. But various aspects of the argument in 11:11–24 indicate that national Israel "would one day experience a spiritual rejuvenation that would extend far beyond the present bounds of the remnant."[231] Some have identified "all Israel" as the community of Jews and Gentiles who believe in Jesus Christ, effectively equating Israel with the church.[232] However, since Paul is at pains to describe the outcome for Israel as the historic, covenant people of God, the salvation of "all Israel" cannot simply equate with, or include the

[228] Dunn (*Romans 9–16*, 680) thinks it is likely that Paul is drawing here "on pre-Pauline tradition which stems from Jesus."

[229] Cranfield, *Romans*, 2:576. However, it is going beyond the precise wording of the text to conclude that this only happens "*after* the full number of Gentiles have entered into the people of God" (Schreiner, *Romans*, 619; my emphasis).

[230] Cf. Jewett, *Romans*, 701; Kruse, *Romans*, 443n222.

[231] Moo, *Romans*, 718. See also Kruse, *Romans*, 448–56.

[232] Cf. Wright, "Romans," 689–90. Kruse (*Romans*, 450) notes that this was the view of Augustine and other early church fathers. Moo (*Romans*, 720n45) records that Calvin took this view, as did other sixteenth- and seventeenth-century theologians.

coming in of, the full number of Gentiles. The Israel that is partially hardened is national Israel. "All Israel" must mean "Israel as a whole, as a people, whose corporate identity and wholeness could not be lost even if in the event there were some (or indeed many) individual exceptions."[233] The issue of how and when this takes place is discussed below (see §2.5).

11:26b–27. As in 1:17; 2:24; 3:10; 4:17; 8:36; 9:33; 15:3, 9, 21, the formula "as it is written" introduces a biblical citation that confirms or develops the preceding argument. The perfect tense (γέγραπται) highlights the ongoing authority and relevance of what was written. Isaiah 59:20–21a is slightly modified, and words from Isa 27:9 are added (ὅταν ἀφέλωμαι τὰς ἁμαρτίας αὐτῶν, "when I take away their sins"), to make the point that Israel's deliverance can only take place by "acceptance of the gospel message about the forgiveness of sins in Jesus Christ."[234] God is portrayed as Israel's "Deliverer" (ὁ ῥυόμενος), though in Paul's argument the Son specifically fulfills this role (1:3–4; 5:10; 8:3, 32; cf. 9:5). The covenantal reference ("and this will be my covenant with them") comes from Isa 59:21, which goes on to speak about God's putting his Spirit upon them and placing his words in their mouth (cf. Ezek 36:27; Joel 2:28–29).

The Hebrew original of Isa 59:20 has the redeemer coming "to Zion" (לְצִיּוֹן), while the LXX reads "for the sake of Zion" (ἕνεκεν Σιων), but Paul has "from Zion" (ἐκ Σιὼν). Many commentators suggest that this change points to the final deliverance of Israel that will be accomplished by Christ when he comes from the heavenly Jerusalem,[235] but this is questionable. Paul follows the LXX (ἀποστρέψει ἀσεβείας ἀπὸ Ἰακώβ, "he will turn godlessness away

[233] Dunn, *Romans 9–16*, 681. Cf. Cranfield, *Romans*, 2:576–77; Robinson, "The Salvation of Israel," 47–63; Moo, *Romans*, 723; Tobin, *Paul's Rhetoric*, 372. Jewett's insistence that "all" does not lend itself to the expression of exceptions (*Romans*, 702) leads him to a universalism that ignores Paul's teaching about election within Israel. Moo (722n55) shows how the expression "all Israel" can be used representatively in the OT. A post-Pauline Jewish text (m. Sanh. 10:1) similarly says, "All Israelites have a share in the world to come" but then enumerates a list of exceptions.

[234] Moo (*Romans*, 729). Moo (725–26) rightly critiques the view that Israel will be saved in a special way, particularly opposing suggestions of a different covenantal theology for Jews and Gentiles. So also representatively Byrne, *Romans*, 354–55; Kruse, *Romans*, 453–56.

[235] E.g., Cranfield, *Romans*, 2:577–78; Schreiner, 619–23; Moo, *Romans*, 728.

from Jacob"), rather than the Hebrew ("to those in Jacob who turn from transgression"), to highlight the gracious act of God in delivering his people from their unbelief and disobedience. Taking this text as a specific reference to the work of the *returning* Messiah is odd. Although the heavenly Jerusalem is mentioned in Gal 4:26 (cf. Heb 12:22; Rev 3:12; 21:2), "Zion" and "Jacob" are literary variants for the people of Israel in Isa 59:20 and should be understood that way in Rom 11:26. Paul modifies the text to read "from Zion" because he wants to stress that the Messiah arises from the midst of God's holy people.[236] The promises of the new covenant have already been fulfilled through the coming of Israel's Messiah (1:3; 9:5; 15:8), and the blessings are available for anyone who believes the gospel, Jew or Gentile (1:16–17; 3:21–31; 4:1–25). These benefits are spread abroad through Paul's own ministry (1:8–15; 15:15–33). So 11:26–27 is not talking about a sudden turning to Christ by Jews at the Second Coming but about a process that continues in the present and reaches its climax when Christ returns.[237]

Isaiah 59:20–21 reflects the expectation that God will fulfil his covenant with Abraham by overcoming the hardness of Israelite hearts and giving his Spirit to them. Addition of the words "when I take away their sins" brings Paul's citation more closely in line with the promise of Jer 31:34.[238] Paul adapts Isaiah's prediction to express more emphatically the sequence of thought in Jeremiah's oracle: God will "turn away godlessness from Jacob" when he takes away their sins. Since the death of Christ has achieved the promised redemption (Rom 3:21–26) and made possible a definitive

---

[236] Fitzmyer (*Romans*, 625) suggests that "from Zion" may refer to "Jesus' descent from David, or more generically, his origin from among the chosen Jewish people of old (cf. 9:5); or even to Jerusalem as the place of Christ's death and resurrection." There is no mention of the Second Coming elsewhere in Rom 9–11, and the verb "will come" (Isa 59:20) simply refers to the coming of the Messiah as a future event from the prophet's point in time.

[237] Cf. Andreas J. Köstenberger and Peter T. O'Brien, *Salvation to the Ends of the Earth: A Biblical Theology of Mission*, NSBT 11 (Downers Grove: InterVarsity, 2001), 190–91; Kruse, *Romans*, 443–44, 451; and my comment on the second "now" in v. 31. Robinson ("The Salvation of Israel," 60) observes that Paul could hardly have expected the ministry of Peter, James, and John to Israel to be unsuccessful until his own Gentile mission had been completed (Gal 2:7–9).

[238] So Cranfield, *Romans*, 2:578–79. Cf. Schreiner, *Romans*, 620n24, against Moo, *Romans*, 728.

forgiveness of sins (4:5–8), what is needed now is a softening of hearts by God's Spirit to enable Israel to believe this message, confess Jesus as Lord (10:8–13), and enjoy the benefits.

11:28. With a μέν and δέ construction, Paul contrasts the present situation of Israel ("regarding the gospel, they are enemies for your advantage") with their permanent status as the covenant people of God ("but regarding election, they are loved because of the patriarchs").[239] There is no conjunction linking this statement with v. 27, but each of the following verses is linked to the preceding one by a connective, thus forming a discrete paragraph. Paul makes a summary claim in v. 28 that is explained and justified in vv. 29–32. He uses the strong term "enemies" (ἐχθροί, as in 5:10) with probably a double meaning. As in 9:31–32; 10:3, 14–21; 11:11, 12, 20, 23, 30–31, they have acted as enemies *toward God*, disobeying the gospel and being stubbornly opposed to its progress (cf. Phil 3:6; 1 Thess 2:14–16).[240] As in 9:27–29; 11:7b–10, 15, 25, God has correspondingly treated *them* as enemies, hardening and rejecting many in Israel (the contrast with ἀγαπητοί ["loved"] particularly suggests this). In the mystery of the divine purpose, Israel has expressed the hostility to God that is "characteristic of humankind in this age"[241] and experienced the hostility of God that is its consequence (cf. Isa 63:10; Jer 30:14). This has happened for the advantage of the nations (δι' ὑμᾶς, [lit.] "for your sake"; cf. 11:11, 12, 15, 17). The Jews are "loved" in the sense that they remain God's chosen people (cf. 11:1–2) because of his promises to the patriarchs (διὰ τοὺς πατέρας, [lit.] "for the sake of the fathers"; cf. 9:5, 13).[242] All Jews are included in this category, but only those whom God chooses will come to confess that Jesus is Lord and call upon him for salvation

---

[239] Moo (*Romans*, 729) says the assertion of Israel's dual status here "succinctly summarizes the dilemma that drives the whole argument of these chapters (9–11)."

[240] The expression κατὰ τὸ εὐαγγέλιον ("regarding the gospel") defines the precise way in which Israel is at enmity with God, and κατὰ τὴν ἐκλογήν ("regarding election") defines the way they are loved by God.

[241] Dunn, *Romans 9–16*, 685.

[242] Dunn (ibid., 684) says the prepositions are chosen for rhetorical effect, not because they necessarily mean the same thing each time. The election of Israel is frequently mentioned in Scripture (e.g., Deut 4:37; 7:7; 10:15; 14:2; 1 Kgs 3:8; Isa 41:8–9; 42:1; 43:10, 20; 44:1–2; 49:7). God's love has "nothing to do with the peculiar virtues of Israel or the patriarchs, but is rather an expression of divine choice, pure and simple" (Jewett, *Romans*, 707–8).

(10:9–13). This is the only way for them to be the renewed Israel of biblical prophecy.

11:29. Paul now justifies the claim that "regarding election, they are loved because of the patriarchs," by saying "since (*γάρ*) God's gracious gifts and calling are irrevocable." "The gifts" (*τὰ χαρίσματα*) that God gave to Israel are doubtless the sort of privileges listed in 9:4–5. "The calling of God" (ἡ κλῆσις τοῦ θεοῦ) is another way of speaking about his "election" of this people (11:28, ἐκλογήν). The word order here has been taken to imply that election is "one of the most important of those gifts,"[243] but it is more natural to read *καί* in its normal, copulative sense: "God's gracious gifts *and* calling." The adjective ἀμεταμέλητα ("irrevocable") is in the emphatic position at the beginning of this clause to emphasize God's faithfulness (cf. 3:3). This rare word is only used again in 2 Cor 7:10, where it qualifies "repentance" and means "not to be regretted." God does not "take back" what he gives, nor does he turn his back on a relationship he initiates. "God has not rejected his people whom he foreknew" (v. 2).

11:30–31. Once more a link with the preceding verse is indicated by the conjunction *γάρ* ("for"), which is not translated by CSB. A comparison formula (*ὥσπερ* ["just as"] . . . *οὕτως καί* ["so also"]) relates the experience of Paul's Gentile readers to the story of Israel. He uses this formula to explain how "God's elective love of the Jews will be manifest."[244] First, he restates the proposition that unbelieving Israelites are "enemies for your advantage" (v. 28), saying, "You once disobeyed God but now have received mercy through their disobedience." Gentile disobedience was highlighted in 1:18–32, and Jewish hypocrisy in relation to God's law in 2:1–9. But Paul is particularly thinking about Israel's disobedience to the gospel here (cf. 10:16, 21). The "once"-"now" contrast relates to the salvation-historical movement from the old era to the new (cf. 3:21–31). Salvation is now available for all who believe, but there has been a significant movement of the gospel to the Gentiles because of Israel's disobedience (cf. 11:11–12, 15, 17).

---

[243] Moo, *Romans*, 732. Contrast Cranfield, *Romans*, 2:581.

[244] Moo, *Romans*, 732. Moo (737–39) explores the distinction between corporate and individual election. The same ὥσπερ/οὕτως formula is used in 5:12, 19, 21. Cf. Runge *Discourse Grammar*, 300.

Paul repeats this point because it is so significant for the argument ("so they too have now disobeyed, [resulting] in mercy to you"). CSB has understood τῷ ὑμετέρῳ ἐλέει (lit., "for the sake of mercy for you") to modify the preceding verb. Many commentators, however, argue that it modifies the verb at the end of the sentence, resulting in the translation "by the mercy shown to you, they too may now receive mercy" (NRSV, ESV, NIV ["as a result of God's mercy to you"]). There are difficulties with either proposal, but CSB follows the most natural reading of the Greek syntax.[245] Either way Paul uses a final clause to indicate that Israel will experience the mercy of God as Gentile Christians have, overcoming disobedience and enabling saving faith (ἵνα καὶ αὐτοὶ νῦν ἐλεηθῶσιν, "so that they also now may receive mercy"). Although there is some textual uncertainty about this second "now" (νῦν), it should be accepted as the most difficult of three possible readings.[246] Like the "now" in v. 30, it refers to the gospel era. Paul simply means that "Israel is 'now' in the position to experience again God's mercy."[247] He is not alluding to a definitive event at the second coming of Christ but to a process that climaxes when that happens (cf. vv. 26b–27 comment).

11:32. This verse is linked with the preceding one by the conjunction γάρ ("for"). It functions as a conclusion to the paragraph beginning at v. 28, which in turn concludes the argument in chapters 9–11 and summarizes earlier teaching. On the one hand, Paul has shown how "God has imprisoned all in disobedience" (συνέκλεισεν, "confined, enclosed" [BDAG]; cf. Gal 3:22, 23). This recalls his claim that God "delivered over" humanity to the consequences of

[245] Cranfield (*Romans*, 2:582–86) offers an extensive argument in favor of relating the phrase to ἐλεηθῶσιν ("receive mercy"), but Moo (*Romans*, 734–35) critiques this approach. Disputing that τῷ ὑμετέρῳ ἐλέει must be understood instrumentally as a strict parallel to τῇ τούτων ἀπειθείᾳ ("through their disobedience"), he argues that the former is a dative of advantage ("for the sake of mercy for you"). Cf. Dunn, *Romans 9–16*, 688; Schreiner, *Romans*, 627–28.

[246] The second νῦν in this verse is attested by ℵ B D^{*,3} and a few other witnesses, but is omitted by 𝔓^{46} A D^{2} and many more witnesses. The adverb ὕστερον ("later, finally") is poorly attested but was possibly added or substituted as a more appropriate alternative. So νῦν appears to be the most difficult reading, giving rise to the alternatives. Cf. Jewett, *Romans*, 694.

[247] Moo, *Romans*, 735. Jewett (*Romans*, 711) suggests that this reference to the eschatological present lends urgent emphasis to Paul's appeal for support in the next stage of his missionary work (15:23–32).

their sin (1:24, 26, 28) and that all are "under sin" (3:9). Indeed, "all have sinned and fall short of the glory of God" (3:23). God's punishment for disobedience is to "imprison" both Jews and Gentiles in that state. They have no possibility of escape unless God releases them. On the other hand, this imprisonment is for the ultimate purpose of showing mercy "to all" (ἵνα τοὺς πάντας ἐλεήσῃ). The gospel is God's power of salvation "to everyone who believes" (1:16) because it reveals God's righteousness through Jesus Christ "to all who believe" (3:22). This universal note has been sounded throughout Romans, where it regularly refers to Jews and Gentiles as distinctive groups within humanity. Paul expounds a "representative universalism."[248] His triumphant conclusion is the great mercy shown to Gentiles in rescuing them from disobedience will be shown to disobedient Israelites. He is not saying everyone will ultimately be saved, since that would be a denial of his argument about election (8:28–30) and it would falsify his teaching about the judgment facing the unrepentant (2:5–10). God's mercy is for people of every race, culture, and social class. In the Roman context, where mercy was reserved for the worthy among captives and vanquished enemies, this was a remarkable claim. "Nowhere in the ancient world, outside of this text, was mercy granted in so indiscriminate and impartial a manner to 'all.'"[249]

11:33. An outburst of praise concludes Rom 9–11. "Paul, having caught a glimpse of the measureless majesty of God's mercy, falls back in an awe and wonder which struggles to find expression."[250] Without any specific Christological reference, praise is offered to God the Creator (cf. Rev 4:11; 7:12; 15:3–4; 16:7). The particle Ὦ ("Oh") expresses wonder about what follows. The nominative βάθος ("depth") is used without a verb, as "emotion overrides syntax." [251] This noun highlights the profundity or "inexhaustible

---

[248] Johannes Munck, "Israel and the Gentiles in the New Testament," *JTS* 2 (1951): 9. The "fullness of the Gentiles" (11:25) and the salvation of "all Israel" are two different but related arms of the divine purpose (cf. 4:11–12; 15:8–9; Isa 49:6). Believing Gentiles become partners with believing Israelites in the new humanity God is creating in Christ (cf. Robinson, "The Salvation of Israel," 55–57).

[249] Jewett, *Romans*, 711.

[250] Dunn, *Romans 9–16*, 702. Byrne (*Romans*, 358, 360) argues that this hymnic section concludes the entire presentation of the gospel in 1:16–11:32.

[251] Wallace, *Greek Grammar*, 60. The nouns that follow are nominal genitives of content, indicating that Paul's emphasis falls here, rather than on the head noun βάθος

depths" of God's riches, wisdom, and knowledge (cf. 1 Cor 2:10).[252] God's "riches" include his "kindness, restraint, and patience" toward the unrepentant (2:4), his "glory" in showing mercy (9:23), and all the benefits of salvation for Jews and Gentiles who call upon Jesus as Lord (10:12; cf. 11:12; Eph 3:8–9). God's "wisdom" (σοφία) is not explicitly mentioned elsewhere in Romans, but the "mystery" expounded in 11:25–32 is likely to be the wisdom Paul has in mind (cf. 1 Cor 1:17–2:16; Eph 3:8–10; Col 1:25–28). Knowledge (γνῶσις) is often linked with wisdom in biblical thought (e.g., Prov 2:6; 30:3; Eccl 2:26; Col 1:9; 2:3). But God's relational knowledge or foreknowledge was the particular sense in 8:29–30; 11:2, and so Paul is possibly identifying "God's electing love and the loving concern and care it involves."[253]

A second exclamation begins with ὡς ("how"; cf. Pss 8:1, 9; 66:3; Rom 10:15). This celebrates the fact that God's judgments are "unsearchable" and his ways are "untraceable."[254] Apart from divine revelation, humans cannot comprehend such things. God's "judgments" (κρίματα) are his judicial decisions, or the actions by which he expresses his justice.[255] Paul stressed in 2:2–3 that God's judgment on human sin is "based on the truth" (cf. 3:8; 5:16). As judge, however, God is also the helper and savior of his people (cf. Gen 18:25; Deut 10:18; Ps 103:6; Judg 11:27; Isa 30:18; Rom 3:21–26). God's justice in relation to Israel and the nations was the concern in chapters 9–11 (especially 9:14–33). "Particularly unfathomable was the idea of a divinely imposed obtuseness of Israel that provided time for the Gentile mission, combined with the expectation that its

---

(cf. Wallace, 93–94). Abstract nouns such as these commonly occur without an article in Greek, even though they are definite in sense.

[252] Dunn, *Romans 9–16*, 699. With Schreiner (*Romans*, 632–33), CSB has taken πλούτου ("riches") as a modifier of καὶ σοφίας καὶ γνώσεως θεοῦ ("both of the wisdom and of the knowledge of God"). But this is not the most natural way to read the syntax and fails to acknowledge the way each one of these terms is given a particular significance in Paul's argument. Cf. Cranfield, *Romans*, 2:589; Jewett, *Romans*, 716; Kruse, *Romans*, 457; NRSV, ESV.

[253] Cranfield, *Romans*, 2:589–90. Cf. 1 Cor 8:3; Gal 4:9; 2 Tim 2:19.

[254] The adjective ἀνεξεραύνητα is rare (BGAD) and corresponds with the word "depth" in the first exclamation: God's judgments are "unfathomable." The adjective ἀνεξιχνίαστοι means literally "not to be tracked out, inscrutable " (BDAG).

[255] Cf. Friedrich Büchsel and Volkmar Herntrich, "κρίνω, κτλ.," *TDNT* 3:924–33, 942.

completion would provoke a transformation of Israel's rejection of the gospel (11:11–14, 25–26)."[256] God's "ways" will most likely be the deeds by which he puts his judgments into effect (cf. Deut 32:4; Job 26:14; Pss 10:5 [LXX 9:26]; 77:19 [LXX 76:20]; Isa 55:8–9; Rev 15:3).

11:34–35. Three questions, derived from two biblical contexts, relate to the claims made about God in v. 33. The first two questions are from LXX Isa 40:13 (cf. Jer 23:18): "For who has known the mind of the Lord? Or who has been his counselor?" (cf. 1 Cor 2:16). The prophet refers to "the transcendent wisdom and self-sufficiency of God."[257] The third question could be Paul's own rendering of the Hebrew text of Job 41:11a (LXX 41:3a), possibly influenced by LXX Job 35:7. Literally, this asks, "Or who has given to him in advance, and it will be repaid to him?"[258] This picks up the idea of God's riches toward undeserving humanity: "That one could provide a gift that would place God in one's debt, requiring God in accordance with the ancient laws of reciprocity to provide a healthy recompense, is preposterous within the framework of Jewish and Christian monotheism."[259]

11:36. A causal clause reveals the assumptions about God that undergird the preceding affirmations and questions: "For from him and through him and to him are all things." Commentators have noted parallel expressions in Greek philosophical writings, especially in connection with Stoic pantheism.[260] But Paul is reflecting the theology outlined in the letter so far, and the biblical foundations on which

[256] Jewett, *Romans*, 718. Jewett is unnecessarily cynical about Paul's ability to fathom God's judgments in this connection.

[257] Cranfield, *Romans*, 2:591. Jewett (*Romans*, 713–15) contends that Paul added the biblical citations to a preexisting hymn. The inclusion of scriptural passages in hymnic material appears to be unprecedented, but Dunn (*Romans 9–16*, 698) points to the use of triads and biblical assertions throughout, suggesting the careful composition of the passage by Paul.

[258] Paul's text (ἢ τίς προέδωκεν αὐτῷ, καὶ ἀνταποδοθήσεται αὐτῷ;) does not derive from LXX Job 41:3, though it could have been influenced by LXX Job 35:7 (τί δώσεις αὐτῷ; ἢ τί ἐκ χειρός σου λήμψεται; "What do you give him, or what does he receive from your hand?"). Jewett (*Romans*, 720) agrees with Cranfield (*Romans*, 2:591) and others that Paul is responsible for the rendering we have.

[259] Jewett, *Romans*, 720.

[260] Cf. Cranfield, *Romans*, 2:591; Jewett, *Romans*, 721–22. Jewett makes an unnecessary distinction between Paul's creation theology and his exposition of the mystery of salvation.

it is based. Fundamental to biblical teaching is the belief that there is one God, who is the source of all that exists (ἐξ αὐτοῦ, "from him"), the sustainer of all things (δι' αὐτοῦ, "through him"), and the goal of everything (εἰς αὐτόν, "for him"). He will ultimately bring every aspect of our disordered world into conformity with his own will and purpose. When similar terms are applied to Christ in 1 Cor 8:5–6 and Col 1:15–17, Paul reveals the unique relationship of the Son with the Father and his role in creation and redemption (see §§1.1; 2.3).

Paul's hymn of praise climaxes with a formal doxology: "To him be the glory forever. Amen" (cf. 16:27; Gal 1:5; Eph 3:21; Phil 4:20; 1 Tim 1:17; 2 Tim 4:18). This echoes the conclusion to many psalms and other Jewish writings (e.g., LXX Pss 41:13; 72:19; 89:52; 106:48; 4 Macc 18:24; 1 En. 63:3; cf. Phil 4:20). As in 1:25; 9:5; 16:27, readers are invited to concur with Paul's ascription of praise to God by echoing the "amen" (cf. 1 Cor 14:16). If we have followed Paul through chapters 9–11, this will mean expressing

> joyful confidence that the deep mystery which surrounds us is neither a nightmare mystery of meaninglessness nor a dark mystery of arbitrary impotence but the mystery which will never turn out to be anything other than the mystery of the altogether good and merciful and faithful God.[261]

Bridge

As Paul engaged in God's mission to the nations, he hoped his efforts would contribute indirectly to the salvation of "all Israel." At one level his concern for their "fullness" to come to faith in Christ flowed from being an Israelite and sharing their heritage (9:1–5). At another level he had experienced the blessings of the new covenant himself and grieved over their stubbornness and refusal to accept what was offered to them in the gospel (10:1–21). Most importantly, however, he was concerned to uphold the faithfulness of God to his covenant people and to express this in his ministry (11:1–32). Our churches mostly consist of believing Gentiles who forget that God is still committed to delivering Israelites from unbelief and

[261] Cranfield, *Romans*, 2:592. Byrne (*Romans*, 360) argues, "The entire kerygmatic portion of the letter (1:16–11:36) thus ends with an invitation to give to God the recognition ('glory') which it is the essence of sin to refuse (1:21–23)." See §2.6.

disobedience. This spiritual transformation will take place when Jesus the Messiah is acknowledged as the true liberator of his people, who alone can take away their sins. God's promises and his purpose in choosing Israel in the first place are the basis of this conviction (11:26–29). An extraordinary display of God's mercy to Israel is linked to the display of his mercy to Gentiles, which is taking place everywhere (11:30–32). As we engage in evangelism ourselves, we play our part in God's mission to the nations. Our involvement should be with a sense of awe about the depths of his riches, wisdom, and knowledge, and with a humble acknowledgment that his judgments are unsearchable and his ways untraceable (11:33–36). We may not have all our questions answered, but Scripture reveals enough of God's plan for us to trust him completely. Rather than being discouraged by unbelief, we should be motivated by an overwhelming sense of God's mercy.

XII. True and Proper Worship: Love and Obedience to God's Will (12:1–13:14)

Paul turns from exposition to exhortation, using 12:1–2 as an introduction to the next main section of the letter (12:3–15:7).[1] However, whereas 12:3–13:14 deals more generally with issues of everyday service to God and nonconformity with the present evil age, 14:1–15:7 addresses identity and relational issues that were particularly relevant to the Roman Christians.[2] The more defensive approach in 14:1–15:7 corresponds with 2:1–3:20 in the "ring" structure of the letter (cf. Introduction II.C).

Romans 12–13 will be expounded under these headings:

A. Living in the Light of God's Mercies (12:1–2)
B. Serving One Another with Gifts and Ministries (12:3–8)
C. Love toward Believers and Unbelievers (12:9–21)
D. Living as Responsible Citizens (13:1–7)
E. Love in the End-Time (13:8–14)

A. Living in the Light of God's Mercies (12:1–2)

> [1]Therefore, brothers and sisters, in view of the mercies of God, I urge you to present your bodies as a living sacrifice, holy and pleasing to God; this is your true worship. [2]Do not be conformed to this age, but be transformed by the renewing of your mind, so that you may discern what is the good, pleasing, and perfect will of God.

Context

An immediate link to the celebration of God's mercy in 11:25–32 is provided by "the mercies of God" in 12:1, though the term probably embraces every saving action of God mentioned in the letter so far. God's mercies are the basis for Paul's appeal to live in a way that is consistent with the gospel. The exhortation to "present your bodies as a living sacrifice, holy and pleasing to God" restates the pivotal challenge in 6:12–14, using the language of worship. A

---

[1] Commands are rare in earlier chapters (cf. 6:11–13, 19; 11:18, 20) but are a significant feature of 12:1–15:7. Moo (*Romans*, 745) argues that the transition at 12:1 is not from "theology" to "practice" but "from a focus more on the 'indicative' side of the gospel to a focus more on the 'imperative' side of the gospel."

[2] Cf. Wright, "Romans," 700–703; Tobin, *Paul's Rhetoric*, 384–85.

parallel exhortation about not being conformed to this age but being "transformed by the renewing of your mind" (v. 2) offers the possibility of discerning and doing the will of God. These two verses together proclaim a reversal of the downward spiral depicted in Romans 1:18–32:[3]

wrath	mercy
refusing to glorify or thank God	(thankful) sacrifice
dishonoring the body	offering the body
senseless, idolatrous worship	understanding service
worthless mind	renewed mind
rejecting God's just sentence	approving the will of God

Structure

The arresting address in v. 1 links the following hortatory section (12:1–15:7) to the exposition of the gospel in the preceding chapters (1:16–11:36). Paul's initial exhortation (12:1–2) contains three imperatives, the first of which is "present your bodies as a living sacrifice, holy and pleasing to God."[4] This action is defined as (lit.) "your understanding service." The second exhortation is expressed negatively ("do not be conformed to this age"). This is matched by a positive exhortation ("but be transformed by the renewing of your mind"), which explains how to avoid the former. The concluding clause indicates the result of that transformed thinking ("so that you may discern what is the good, pleasing, and perfect will of God").

Outline:

1. Bodies devoted to God's service (12:1)
2. Minds that discern what is pleasing to God (12:2)

12:1. A clear consequence of the preceding argument is indicated by the conjunction οὖν ("therefore") and the expression διὰ τῶν οἰκτιρμῶν τοῦ θεοῦ (lit., "by the mercies of God").[5] Paul's

[3] This is a modification of the chart provided by Michael Thompson, *Clothed with Christ: the Example and Teaching of Jesus in Romans 12.1–15.13*, JSNTSup 59 (Sheffield: Sheffield Academic, 1991), 82.

[4] See n. 8 below regarding the imperatival function of the infinitive παραστῆσαι.

[5] Διά with the genitive indicates that "the mercies of God" are the means by which Paul makes his appeal (cf. 12:3, διὰ τῆς χάριτος τῆς δοθείσης μοι ["by the grace given

introductory words draw attention to the importance of the command they introduce. Moreover, they distinguish his exhortation from mere moral appeal by reference to "the work of salvation as its presupposition and basis."[6] The mercy of God was celebrated in 11:30–32, using the verb ἐλεέω (9:15 [citing Exod 33:19], 16, 18; 12:8; 1 Cor 7:25; 2 Cor 4:1; Phil 2:27; 1 Tim 1:13, 16) and the noun ἔλεος (9:23; 11:31; 15:9). The plural noun οἰκτιρμοί in this verse has a different root and is typically employed in the LXX with reference to specific deeds of mercy (e.g., 2 Sam 24:14; Ps 24:6 [ET 25:6]; Isa 63:15).[7] Paul could have in mind every indication of God's kindness, grace, and love in the letter so far. The verb παρακαλῶ can mean "comfort, encourage" (e.g., 2 Cor 1:4, 6; 7:6, 13; Eph 6:22; Col 2:2; 4:8), "plead" (e.g., 2 Cor 12:8), or "exhort, appeal, urge" (e.g., 1 Cor 1:10; 4:16; 16:5 2 Cor 10:1; Eph 4:1; Phil 4:2; 1 Thess 4:1; 1 Tim 2:1). Here it is employed in the third sense, with a certain formality, as the apostle urges his readers to adopt patterns of thinking and behavior impelled by the gospel (15:30; 16:1). As "brothers and sisters" in Christ (cf. 1:13; 7:1, 4; 8:12, 29; 10:1; 11:25; 15:14, 30; 16:17), Christians are recipients together of the eschatological mercies of God, called to minister to one another (12:3–8) and love one another (12:9–13).

Paul's first challenge is "to present your bodies as a living sacrifice" (παραστῆσαι τὰ σώματα ὑμῶν θυσίαν ζῶσαν).[8] This recalls 6:12–14, where an aorist imperative of the same verb functions in a timeless fashion ("offer yourselves to God"). Although it never appears in the LXX, this verb is a standard Hellenistic term for the

---

to me"]; 15:30 "through the Lord Jesus Christ and through the love of the Spirit"). CSB ("in view of the mercies of God") could be understood in a causal way. Against Schreiner (*Romans*, 643), the accusative would have to be used to convey a causal sense. Cf. Dunn, *Romans 9–16*, 709.

[6] Otto Schmitz, "παρακαλέω, παράκλησις," *TDNT* 5:795. Cf. Runge, *Discourse Grammar*, 102, 108.

[7] This noun and the cognate verb express a sympathy that is ready to help. There is no palpable distinction between these terms and ἐλεέω/ἔλεος in the LXX. In Rom 9:15 the verbs are used in parallel. The noun οἰκτιρμός is also used in 2 Cor 1:3; Phil 2:1; Col 3:12; Heb 10:28. Cf. Rudolph Bultmann, "οἰκτίρω κτλ.," *TDNT* 5:159–61.

[8] The aorist infinitive in indirect discourse after παρακαλῶ ὑμᾶς ("I urge you") should be construed as a command. Cf. Wallace, *Greek Grammar*, 603–4.

offering of a sacrifice.[9] No animal sacrifices are required under the new covenant because of the redemptive and propitiatory death of Jesus (3:24–25; 8:3; cf. 2 Cor 5:21; Heb 10:1–18). Nevertheless, his unique sacrifice demands a response, which is "the personal offering of the body, of earthly life, inseparable from the existence of the one who offers."[10] As those brought from death to life through union with Christ in his death and resurrection (6:3–11), Christians are to offer every part of themselves to God "as weapons for righteousness" (6:13). The initial presentation of ourselves to God in Christ needs to be regularly renewed, not merely by inner consecration but in the dedication of our bodies to his service (cf. 1 Cor 6:19–20).[11] In biblical thought, what is offered to God is holy (ἁγίαν), meaning that it is set apart for God. As those called to be "saints" (1:7, ἅγιοι ["holy ones"]), believers must live out the sanctified relationship made possible by Christ's sacrifice and the faith that the Holy Spirit enables (1 Cor 1:30; 6:11; 2 Thess 2:13–14).[12] This sacrifice is "living" (ζῶσαν) because it is offered by those who have been made alive in Christ (6:4, 11, 13; 8:13).[13] It is "pleasing to God" (εὐάρεστον τῷ θεῷ) because it fulfills the ideal of sacrifice, which is obedient service to God (cf. Heb 10:5–10).[14]

The presentation of ourselves to God in Christ as a living, holy, and pleasing sacrifice is described as τὴν λογικὴν λατρείαν ὑμῶν. Most English versions translate this "your spiritual worship," but "spiritual" sounds like a purely inward response, whereas Paul has

[9] Cf. Bo Reicke and Georg Bertram, "παρίστημι, παριστάνω," *TDNT* 5:837–41. They note a certain analogy between religious service and court ceremonial in the use of this terminology.

[10] Raymond Corriveau, *The Liturgy of Life: A Study of the Ethical Thought of St. Paul in His Letters to the Early Christian Communities* (Bruxelles and Paris: Desclée de Brouwer; Montreal: Les Editions Bellarmin, 1970), 171.

[11] Dunn (*Romans 9–16*, 709) notes that "the body" in Paul's thought represents the whole person "in his corporality, in his concrete relationships with the world."

[12] Cf. §2.6 and 15:16 comment.

[13] The adjectival participle ζῶσαν should be read as a predicate accusative with the following adjectives so that the sense is "a sacrifice—*alive*, holy, (and) acceptable to God." Cf. Wallace, *Greek Grammar,* 618–19; Cranfield, *Romans*, 2:600; Jewett, *Romans*, 724.

[14] The adjective εὐάρεστος ("pleasing, acceptable") appears also in 12:2; 14:8 (cf. 2 Cor 5:9; Eph 5:10; Phil 4:18; Col 3:20; Titus 2:9; Heb 13:21). The adverb εὐαρέστως, "acceptably," occurs in Heb 12:28 in a similar call to serve God with lives that do his will (13:1–16). See also 1 Pet 2:5 (εὐπροσδέκτους, "acceptable").

been emphasizing the need to offer our embodied selves to God. The renewal of the mind is a key to this (v. 2). A better translation might be "your reasonable service" or "your understanding service."[15] In the LXX the noun λατρεία denotes the cultic service required of priests and people (e.g., Exod 12:25; Josh 22:27; cf. Rom 9:4; Heb 9:1, 6). The cognate verb is similarly used (e.g., Exod 3:12; 23:25; cf. Heb 8:5; 9:9; 10:2), sometimes more broadly describing the lifestyle of service to God that was required of Israel (e.g., Josh 24:14, 15; Deut 6:13; cf. Acts 24:14; 26:7).[16] The alternative is to serve false gods (e.g., Exod 20:5; cf. Rom 1:25). In 1:9 Paul employs the verb in a transformed way with reference to his own gospel ministry (cf. 2 Tim 1:3). In Phil 3:3 he uses it comprehensively to describe the Spirit-directed service of new covenant worshippers (cf. Heb 9:14; 12:28). The adjective λογικός was a favorite term of the Greek philosophers, especially the Stoics, for whom it meant "belonging to the sphere of the λόγος or reason," and hence "spiritual" in the sense of "suprasensual."[17] Since rationality is what distinguishes human beings from animals, traditional sacrifices were often repudiated by these writers, and various forms of "rational sacrifice" were advocated instead. The LXX does not employ λογικός, though the prophets clearly indicate that God is honored by a genuine spiritual and moral engagement with him (e.g., Isa 1:10–16; 29:13; Mic 6:6–8). In some later Jewish writings, there was a blending of Hellenistic and biblical thinking about the spiritualization of worship.[18] Paul's emphasis is not on the interiorizing or moralization of worship but on the fact that God is to be served by regularly presenting ourselves to him on the basis of his merciful provisions in the Lord

[15] CSB ("your true worship") is not an accurate translation, though it conveys something of the radical implication of the text as a whole. Cranfield (*Romans*, 2:595) translates "your understanding worship" and Jewett (*Romans*, 729–30) "your reasonable worship." Paul is talking about the service rendered by those who truly understand the gospel and its implications for everyday life. Compare Keener, *The Mind of the Spirit*, 150–52, and contrast Moo, *Romans,* 752–53. "Service" is a more literal rendering of λατρεία than "worship" (cf. 1:9, λατρεύω, "serve").

[16] Cf. Peterson, *Engaging with God*, 64–70.

[17] Cf. Gerhard Kittel, "λογικός," *TDNT* 4:142–43; Cranfield, *Romans*, 2:602–4.

[18] A thorough analysis of relevant texts from different religious and philosophical traditions is provided by Everett Ferguson, "Spiritual Sacrifice in Early Christianity and its Environment," in *Aufstieg und Niedergang der Römischen Welt*, II 23:2, ed. Wolfgang Haase (Berlin, New York: de Gruyter, 1979), 1152–89.

Jesus Christ. This is the service that is "consonant with the truth of the gospel."[19]

12:2. The link between this verse and the previous one (καί, "and") could suggest that a set of parallel exhortations follows. But v. 2 is more likely to be subordinate to v. 1 in sense. Paul's sweeping exhortation for believers to present themselves as "a living sacrifice, holy and pleasing to God" has two implications.[20] The first is "do not be conformed to this age" (μὴ συσχηματίζεσθε τῷ αἰῶνι τούτῳ). A negative passive imperative is used with a permissive sense ("do not allow yourselves to be conformed"), with the present tense conveying a general precept. Some have argued that this verb refers to the outward and visible life of believers while the next one refers to their inward life.[21] However, the distinction Paul makes is more subtle. First, he speaks about outward influences on the Christian. "This age" refers to the present world order (1 Cor 1:20; 2:6, 8; 2 Cor 4:4; Gal 1:4), which is distinct from "the coming age" to which Christians truly belong. Paul recognizes "the power of social groups, cultural norms, institutions, and traditions to mold the patterns of individual behavior."[22] The challenge to resist the insidious influence of the present world order is presented again in 13:11–14, using different terms.

A second present imperative conveys the positive alternative: "but be transformed by the renewing of your mind" (ἀλλὰ μεταμορφοῦσθε τῇ ἀνακαινώσει τοῦ νοός). Here Paul speaks of a change that works from the inside outwards. Once again the passive should be understood in a

[19] Cranfield, *Romans*, 2:605. Corriveau (*Liturgy of Life*, 177) observes, "Dying with Christ, being crucified with him in baptism, stamps the whole earthly life of the Christian, sanctified by his Spirit, with the cultic character of his death on the cross."

[20] Cf. Moo, *Romans*, 754, following Christopher F. Evans, "Rom 12:1–2: The True Worship," in *Dimensions de la vie chrétienne*, ed. Lorenzo de Lorenzi (Rome: Abbaye de S. Paul, 1979), 25.

[21] Cranfield (*Romans*, 2:605–8) rightly opposes this approach. Compare Dunn, *Romans 9–16*, 712–13, 14. Paul only uses συσχηματίζειν here, but μετασχηματίζειν with the meaning "disguise" in 2 Cor 11:13, 14, 15.

[22] Dunn, *Romans 9–16*, 712. Dunn notes that Paul does not use the antithetical term "the coming age" (though the plural "coming ages" is in Eph 2:7). The contrast between the ages was becoming clear in Jewish writings in the second half of the first century.

permissive sense ("let yourselves be transformed").[23] The verb is used with a similar meaning in 2 Cor 3:18 ("transformed into the same image from glory to glory"), followed by the assertion that this is "from the Lord who is the Spirit." Christians depend on God's Spirit for transformation, both now and at the resurrection (Rom 7:6; 8:4, 10–13). Transformation in this age takes place through "the renewing of your mind," which leads to a change of behavior (8:5–8; cf. Titus 3:5).[24] This contrasts with the effect of "a corrupt mind, so that they do what is not right" (1:28). "There is no mind/body dualism in Paul; 'renewal of the mind' is bound up with 'presenting of bodies' (v. 1)."[25] The continuing work of mind renewal is elsewhere described as heart renewal (5:5; 6:17; cf. 2 Cor 3:2–3), which echoes biblical predictions about the effect of the new covenant (Jer 31:33; Ezek 36:26–27). As we allow our thinking to be molded by God's Spirit, we exhibit the character and values of the order that has already been manifested in Jesus Christ our Lord (Col 3:1–4). As the following clause indicates, Paul is thinking about the mind as the faculty that enables us to test or prove what God's will is. Renewal of the mind makes it possible to discern God's will and obey him in the face of countless pressures to do otherwise.[26] CSB has taken the words *τὸ ἀγαθὸν καὶ εὐάρεστον καὶ τέλειον* as epithets qualifying *τὸ θέλημα τοῦ θεοῦ* ("so that you may discern what is the good, pleasing, and perfect will of God"). However, it is also possible that these substantives should be taken in apposition to *τὸ θέλημα τοῦ θεοῦ* (NRSV, ESV: "so that you may discern what is the will of God—what is good and acceptable and

[23] The basic meaning of this verb is "remodel" or "change into another form" (Johannes Behm. "*μεταμορφόω*," *TDNT* 4:755). Paul's usage is consistent with Jewish apocalyptic thinking about bodily resurrection (cf. Dan 12:3; 1 En. 104:6; 1 Cor 15:51–53; Phil 3:21), adapted to include the idea of a transformation already in progress (cf. 2 Cor 3:18; 4:16–5:5; Phil 3:10–11).

[24] This is the first use of the term *ἀνακαίνωσις* ("renewal") in Greek literature. The corresponding verb is used in 2 Cor 4:16; Col 3:10. The notion of renewal is also expressed by Paul with terms such as *καινότης* ("newness") in 6:4; 7:6 and *καινὴ κτίσις* ("new creation") in Gal 6:15; 2 Cor 5:17.

[25] Dunn, *Romans 9–16*, 714. "The spirit" is the Godward side of humanity rather than "the mind," though they sometimes overlap (1:9; 8:16; 1 Cor 14:15; Eph 4:23). The futility of human thinking apart from a genuine relationship with God is reflected in Eph 4:17; Col 2:18; 1 Tim 6:5; 2 Tim 3:8; Titus 1:1.

[26] The articular infinitive *εἰς τὸ δοκιμάζειν ὑμᾶς* most likely expresses result.

perfect").[27] Important perspectives on the will of God for his people are given in 12:3–15:7.

Bridge

Worship is never far from Paul's mind in Romans. Humanity's failure to glorify God or show gratitude to him has resulted in idolatry, corrupt thinking, distorted relationships, and unrighteous behavior (1:18–32). But God has acted decisively through the death and resurrection of his Son to bring about a reversal of this situation (3:24–25; 5:12–21; 8:1–17). Now it is possible for people everywhere to respond to God's merciful provisions in Christ and serve God acceptably with renewed minds and behavior that pleases him (12:1–2). The essence of Christian worship is the presentation of ourselves as "a living sacrifice, holy and pleasing to God," which involves not being conformed to this age but being transformed by the renewing of our mind. Paul also indicates that praising God and giving thanks are an essential aspect of our service to God (1:8–10, 25c; 6:17; 7:25a; 11:33–36; 15:8–12). But the extraordinary implication of 12:1–2 is that

> sacred times and sacred places are superseded by the eschatological public activity of those who at all times and in all places stand "before the face of Christ" and from this position before God make the everyday round of so-called secular life into the arena of the unlimited and unceasing glorification of the divine will. At this point the doctrines of worship and Christian "ethics" converge.[28]

B. Serving One Another with Gifts and Ministries (12:3–8)

[3]For by the grace given to me, I tell everyone among you not to think of himself more highly than he should think. Instead,

[27] Cf. Cranfield, *Romans*, 2:595, 610–11; Keener, *The Mind of the Spirit*, 158–65. "The good" has biblical roots and is picked up in vv. 9, 21; 13:3–4. But "acceptable" and "perfect" were Greco-Roman terms Paul sought to correlate with the Hebrew concept of "the will of God" (cf. Jewett, *Romans*, 734–35).

[28] Ernst Käsemann, "Worship in Everyday Life: A Note on Romans 12," in *New Testament Questions of Today* (London: SCM, 1969), 191. I offer an assessment of this essay in "Worship and Ethics in Romans 12," *TynBul* 44 (1993): 271–88.

think sensibly, as God has distributed a measure of faith to each one. [4]Now as we have many parts in one body, and all the parts do not have the same function, [5]in the same way we who are many are one body in Christ and individually members of one another. [6]According to the grace given to us, we have different gifts: If prophecy, use it according to the proportion of one's faith; [7]if service, use it in service; if teaching, in teaching; [8]if exhorting, in exhortation; giving, with generosity; leading, with diligence; showing mercy, with cheerfulness.

Context

If Christians need to be transformed by the renewal of their mind rather than being conformed to the standards and values of "this age" (v. 2), "an inflated sense of self-importance . . . is the first area of their thinking which needs transformation" (v. 3).[29] This challenge is foundational for Paul's teaching about the way members of the body of Christ should exercise their God-given gifts for the benefit of others (vv. 5–8). Implicitly, he begins to teach about the primacy of love in the process of edifying the church. Love becomes more explicitly the focus in vv. 9–21, where it is applied more broadly to relationships inside and outside the body of Christ.

Structure

Paul's introductory words ("for by the grace given to me") recall his self-presentation to the Roman Christians in 1:1–15 (cf. 15:15–16). His solemn challenge about right thinking is related to the fact that God has "distributed a measure of faith to each one." With an extended comparison (vv. 4–5, καθάπερ . . . οὕτως, [lit.] "just as . . . so also"), he likens the way the body of Christ should function to the working of the human body. Paul's application of this analogy begins with the claim that his readers are beneficiaries of God's grace as he is, with different gifts to share (v. 6a). Seven are listed, with a brief reference to how each should be used for the benefit of others in the body (vv. 6b–8).[30]

---

[29] Thompson, *Clothed with Christ*, 87. Moo (*Romans*, 759) argues that Paul writes as he does in vv. 3–8 "mainly because it was integral to his understanding of the way in which the gospel was to transform the lives of Christians."

[30] Dunn (*Romans 9–16*, 720) thinks the "rhythmic structure in vv. 3–5 (two sets of four lines) . . . probably indicates a pattern of parenesis worn smooth by regular use."

Outline:

1. The mind for effective ministry (12:3)
2. The pattern of effective ministry (12:4–8)

12:3. A clear link to the preceding verse is provided by the conjunction *γάρ* ("for"). As in v. 1, Paul addresses his readers with a certain formality, speaking here "by the grace given to me" (*διὰ τῆς χάριτος τῆς δοθείσης μοι*). Most likely this refers to the grace of his apostolic calling (1:1–15; 15:15–16; cf. 1 Cor 3:10; Gal 2:9). He uses a similar expression in v. 6 with reference to the gifts given to believers in general. Although he writes with unique authority as Christ's ambassador, he acknowledges the grace of God shown in the gifting of others (cf. 1:11–12). His challenge to "everyone among you" (*παντὶ τῷ ὄντι ἐν ὑμῖν* [cf. 1:7]) goes beyond his specific warning to Gentile Christians about arrogance in relation to Jewish unbelief in 11:13–32.[31]

The fourfold reference to thinking is emphatic (*μὴ ὑπερφρονεῖν παρ' ὃ δεῖ φρονεῖν ἀλλὰ φρονεῖν εἰς τὸ σωφρονεῖν*, [lit.] "not to think more highly than it is necessary to think, but to think with a view to sober thinking"). Right thinking is Paul's concern in 8:5; 11:20; 12:16; 14:6; 15:5.[32] Here the piling up of terms points to a fundamental way in which believers need to have their minds renewed (v. 2). Frequent examples of this sort of wordplay can be found in Greek literature, where sober mindedness is listed as one of the cardinal virtues.[33] High-mindedness is to be avoided because it goes "beyond what is necessary" (*παρ' ὃ δεῖ*), which contextually means beyond the will of God (v. 2).[34] Pride in one's gifts and abilities

---

The exhortation in vv. 6–8 becomes "increasingly telegraphic in style."

[31] Runge (*Discourse Grammar*, 109) notes that the "metacomments" Paul uses here and in v. 1 have the effect of "highlighting the propositions that they introduce and mitigating the harshness that a simple imperative would have conveyed."

[32] See also 1 Cor 13:11; 2 Cor 13:11; Gal 5:10; Phil 1:7; 2:2, 5; 3:15, 19; 4:2, 10; Col 3:2; 1 Tim 6:17. The related noun *φρόνημα* ("mind, mindset") is employed in Rom 8:6, 7, 27, and the adjective *φρόνιμος* ("conceited") in 11:25; 12:16. The compound *ὑπερφρονεῖν* is not used anywhere else in the NT, but *σωφρονεῖν* is found in 2 Cor 5:13; Titus 2:6 (cf. Mark 5:15; Luke 8:35; 1 Pet 4:7). Cf. Georg Bertram, "*φρήν κτλ.*," *TDNT* 9:232–34.

[33] Cf. Jewett, *Romans*, 739–41. Paul reflects the classical contrast between high-mindedness and sober mindedness.

[34] Walter Grundmann ("*δεῖ κτλ.*," *TDNT* 2:24) observes that *δεῖ* in the NT often denotes the will of God for human conduct.

comes naturally to fallen human beings but is challenged by the recognition that these are God given. Put another way, sensible thinking can be measured by the standard of faith. Various interpretations of the clause "as God has distributed a measure of faith to each one" have been suggested. Most likely the noun μέτρον is used metaphorically to mean "a standard or norm."[35] As elsewhere in Romans, "faith" means "faith in Christ" through belief in the gospel. The focus here is not on the quantity of faith or on particular gifts of faith (1 Cor 12:9) but on the fact that faith is given "to each one" (ἑκάστῳ is in an emphatic position at the beginning of the clause in Greek). When we acknowledge that the gift of faith puts us on an equal footing with other Christians, self-promotion and competitiveness should be dispelled.[36]

12:4–5. Another γάρ ("for") links these verses to the preceding one (CSB: "now" suggests also the beginning of a new train of thought). Those who measure themselves and others by the standard of faith God has provided will recognize that they are "one body in Christ and individually members of one another." The metaphor of the body is expressed in classical fashion with the comparative adverbs καθάπερ . . . οὕτως ("just as . . . in the same way"; cf. BDAG; 1 Cor 12:12). Paul begins by stating certain obvious facts about the human body and its operation: "We have many parts in one body, and all the parts do not have the same function." He develops a spiritual analogy by claiming that "we who are many are one body in Christ." Similar terms were used to express political and cosmic solidarity in the Greco-Roman world.[37] As in 1 Cor 10:16–17; 11:29; 12:12–27, however, Paul moves beyond the secular use of the metaphor to proclaim their unity in Christ and their interdependence as believers (cf. Eph 4:4, 12, 16; Col 2:19; 3:15). The second part

[35] The primary meaning of μέτρον is "an instrument for measuring, *measure*," and the secondary meaning is "the result of measuring, *quantity, number*" (BDAG). Cranfield (*Romans*, 2:613–16) and Moo (*Romans*, 761) read the first sense here. Dunn (*Romans 9–16*, 721–22) argues less convincingly for the second.

[36] Cranfield (*Romans*, 2:613–16) concludes that believers are not to estimate themselves according to fluctuating subjective feelings and personal opinions but according to their God-given relation to Christ. Schreiner (*Romans*, 653) defends the view that Paul means "the quantity of faith or trust that each believer possesses." Contrast Wright, "Romans," 709.

[37] Jewett, *Romans*, 743. Cf. Jewett, *Terms*, 201–50 ("The History of Research") and 288–304 ("The Doctrinal Developments in Romans").

of the similitude is that believers are "individually members of one another" (τὸ δὲ καθ' εἷς ἀλλήλων μέλη, cf. BDF §305). Their unity is not organic or mystical but "historical and confessional, shaped by the 'in Christ' relationship."[38]

12:6. The present participle ἔχοντες ("having") with the connective δέ ("and, but") signifies a continuation of the previous argument, though English versions mostly begin a new sentence here.[39] The whole clause is read as an indicative by CSB ("according to the grace given to us, we have different gifts"). Paul highlights the grace shown to each member of Christ's body, adapting the expression he used to describe the grace given to him (v. 3). Divine grace (χάρις) is experienced in the saving work of Christ (3:24; 5:2, 15) and in God's gifts (χαρίσματα) to those who believe the gospel. "Χάρισμα is the reality of χάρις coming to visible expression in the actual being and doing of members of the body one for another in their mutual interdependence."[40] A selection of gifts or ministries is listed, with indications as to how they should be exercised. "Out of the received gift arises the function, and therefore also out of the statement which indicates the gift arises the imperative which says how the function is rightly fulfilled."[41] Those who take the exhortation in v. 3 seriously will use their gifts in the service of God and other believers without thinking of themselves more highly than they ought to think.

Seven gifts are mentioned, beginning with prophecy (cf. 1 Cor 14:1–5). No hierarchy is suggested by the order, and Paul's list does not include some of the more spectacular gifts mentioned in 1 Cor 12:8–10, 28–30. It is unlikely that he writes with specific knowledge of the gifts being exercised in the Roman congregations. Speaking generally, he observes two categories (as in 1 Pet 4:11): verbal (prophecy, teaching, exhorting) and nonverbal (service, giving, leading, showing mercy). They are presented artfully: the first four are introduced by εἴτε ("whether, if") and conclude

---

[38] Jewett, *Romans*, 744. Jewett concludes, "Christ is the larger reality within which the various congregations and individual members are to find their unity." The unity of Christ's body is actually characterized by diversity!

[39] Jewett (*Romans*, 744) follows Dunn (*Romans 9–16*, 725) in taking the participial clause as a continuation of the body metaphor in vv. 4–5, which means that the list of gifts in vv. 6–8 is descriptive and exemplary. Contrast Moo, *Romans*, 763–64.

[40] Dunn, *Romans 9–16*, 726.

[41] Cranfield, *Romans*, 2:618, translating Adolph Schlatter.

with a qualifying phrase (κατά ["according to"] in v. 6 and ἐν ["in"] in vv. 7–8). The focus shifts to the person ministering the gift in vv. 7b–8a (ὁ διδάσκων, "the one who teaches"; ὁ παρακαλῶν, "the one who exhorts"). This pattern continues in the abbreviated reference to three final gifts in v. 8b (without εἴτε).[42]

In the OT, prophecy involved the reception and transmission of divine revelation. According to Acts 2:16–21, the gift of the Spirit at Pentecost marked the inauguration of "the last days," when all God's people would prophesy (Joel 2:28–32). In the narrative of Acts, prophesying embraces a variety of verbal ministries and does not mean that everyone spoke with the authority of a canonical prophet or an apostle.[43] But Paul uses the terminology more narrowly to describe a particular mode of Christian communication (1 Cor 11:4–5; 12:10; 14:1–40; 1 Thess 5:19–22). On occasions this may have involved the spontaneous sharing of spiritual insights or revelations, but Paul seems to envisage something more serious, sustained, and reflective: "the public proclamation of gospel truth as applied pastorally and contextually to the hearers."[44] Some were actually designated as prophets (1 Cor 12:28–29; Eph 4:11), but the apostle could also wish that all his readers might prophesy for the edification of the church (1 Cor 14:1–5, 39). There is, in fact, an overlap in the way he uses the verbs prophesy, teach, and exhort.[45] The expression κατὰ τὴν ἀναλογίαν τῆς πίστεως ("according to the proportion of [one's] faith") has been variously interpreted. The close correspondence between this phrase and the one in v. 3 (μέτρον πίστεως, "a measure of faith") suggests that, once again, "faith" means "faith in Christ." Those who prophesy should do so "in agreement with the standard which they possess in their apprehension of, and response to the grace of God in Jesus Christ—they are to be careful not to utter (under the impression that they are inspired) anything which

---

[42] Jewett (*Romans*, 746) takes the number seven to convey the sense of "exemplary universality," but this is probably reading too much into Paul's intention.

[43] Cf. Peterson, *Acts*, 60–65. Prophesying in Acts becomes the means of giving expression to that relational knowledge of God made possible by Jesus and the Spirit.

[44] Anthony C. Thiselton, *The First Epistle to the Corinthians: A Commentary on the Greek Text*, NIGTC (Grand Rapids: Eerdmans, 2000), 826.

[45] Cf. David G. Peterson, "'Enriched in Every Way': Gifts and Ministries in 1 Corinthians," in *The Wisdom of the Cross: Exploring 1 Corinthians*, ed. Brian S. Rosner (Nottingham: Apollos, 2011), 134–63.

is incompatible with their believing in Christ."[46] The word ἀναλογία means "a state of right relationship involving proportion" (BDAG).

12:7. Although the noun διακονία ("service") can be used with reference to the ministry of proclaiming the gospel (11:13; cf. Acts 20:24; 21:19; 2 Cor 4:1; 5:18), it is more likely here that Paul refers to the rendering of practical help to those in need (cf. 15:25–26; Acts 6:1, 2; 2 Cor 8:4). This could include giving, leading, and showing mercy (v. 8).[47] The qualification ἐν τῇ διακονίᾳ ("in service") suggests that the gift is to be used "in accordance with its true nature."[48] Those who delight in serving others should give themselves to exploring the potential of this gift and exercise it accordingly. Changing to a participial form (ὁ διδάσκων, [lit.] "the one who teaches"), Paul focuses on the person who has the gift. Some were officially recognized as "teachers" in the early churches (cf. διδάσκαλοι in Acts 13:1; 1 Cor 12:28–29; Eph 4:11; Jas 3:1), but Christians in general were encouraged to teach one another (e.g., 1 Cor 14:26; Col 3:15; Heb 5:12). The expression ἐν τῇ διδασκαλίᾳ ("in teaching") encourages those who can teach, whether formally or informally, to find ways of using their gift for the benefit of fellow believers.

12:8. As noted in connection with v. 1, the verb παρακαλῶ has a range of possible meanings, including "comfort, encourage, plead, exhort." While teaching involves instruction and explanation, exhortation involves application and appeal. But these ministries must overlap to a certain extent.[49] The term ὁ παρακαλῶν ("the one who exhorts") has no formal equivalent in NT gift lists. But in 1 Thess 2:3–4 Paul uses the cognate noun to describe his initial appeal to the Thessalonians with the gospel. In 1 Tim 4:13 he speaks of "exhortation" in association with the public reading of Scripture and of teaching as an essential feature of congregational leadership (1 Tim

[46] Cranfield, *Romans*, 2:621. Cf. Dunn, *Romans 9–16*, 727–28; Wright, "Romans," 711. Schreiner (*Romans*, 656) takes Paul to mean that prophecy should be exercised "in proportion to one's personal faith."

[47] Jewett (*Romans*, 748) narrows the meaning unnecessarily to the service involved in the common meals of the Roman congregations.

[48] Moo, *Romans*, 767.

[49] Cranfield (*Romans*, 2.624) describes exhortation as "the pastoral application of the gospel to a particular congregation, both to the congregation as a whole and also to the members of it severally." Jewett (*Romans*, 750–51) compares the pattern of exhortation encouraged in Greco-Roman writings with the pattern outlined in the NT.

6:2; 2 Tim 4:2; Titus 1:9; 2:6, 15). Christians generally can exhort, encourage, or comfort one another in a range of situations (e.g., 1 Cor 14:3, 31; 2 Cor 1:4; 7:7; Col 4:8; 1 Thess 4:18; 5:11; Heb 3:13: 10:25). So ἐν τῇ παρακλήσει ("in exhortation") suggests exercising this multifaceted ministry as appropriate to the context.

The remaining ministries involve practical care and support. "The one who gives" (ὁ μεταδιδούς) most likely distributes personal possessions or resources (LXX Job 31:17; Luke 3:11; Eph 4:28). The term Paul employs is paralleled by references to sharing with other believers in 12:13; 15:27 (1 Cor 9:10–11; 2 Cor 8:4; 9:13; Phil 4:15). Such giving is to be pursued "with generosity" (ἐν ἁπλότητι).[50] This noun has the sense of "simplicity" or purity of heart in 2 Cor 11:3; Eph 6:5; Col 3:22, which could also be implied here. A liberality "arises out of and expresses the simplicity and single-mindedness of the person of faith."[51] Paul elsewhere teaches that generous giving is stimulated by reflecting on the generosity of God (2 Cor 9:10–15).

"The one who leads" (ὁ προϊστάμενος) could be someone who officially presides over a congregation as an elder or overseer (cf. 1 Thess 5:12; 1 Tim 3:5; 5:17). The passive participle literally means "the one who is set before/over (others)." However, as with teaching, exhorting, and giving, the reference is probably general, allowing for different manifestations of Christian leadership.[52] This ministry is to be conducted "with diligence" (ἐν σπουδῇ), which could apply to any kind of activity on behalf of others (v. 11; cf. 2 Cor 8:7–8). "The one who shows mercy" (ὁ ἐλεῶν) could be someone with a special sympathy for the sick and needy or for those in any kind of distress (Luke 10:37).[53] The challenge is to express this "with

[50] Whereas the phrases ἐν τῇ διδασκαλίᾳ ("in teaching") and ἐν τῇ παρακλήσει ("in exhortation") signify the sphere in which these ministries are to be conducted, ἐν ἁπλότητι ("with generosity"), ἐν σπουδῇ ("with diligence"), and ἐν ἱλαρότητι ("with cheerfulness") indicate the spirit and manner in which the last three ministries are to be exercised. Cf. Cranfield, *Romans*, 2.645.

[51] Dunn, *Romans 9–16*, 730. So also Moo, *Romans*, 768.

[52] Cranfield (*Romans* 2:626–27) observes that the last three ministries listed in v. 8 belong together, so that the leader could be "the administrator in charge of the charitable work of the congregation," or the like. But the term need not be so limited.

[53] Rudolph Bultmann ("ἔλεος κτλ.," *TDNT* 2:481) illustrates the way this language was used in Judaism for practical expressions of "human kindness and pity."

cheerfulness" (ἐν ἱλαρότητι, cf. 2 Cor 9:7) rather than being bowed down or depressed by sharing in the struggles of others.[54]

Bridge

Paul's challenge about minds being renewed has a particular application to how Christians think about themselves and the gifts he has given them (vv. 3–8). Many evaluate church membership in terms of how it will benefit *them*, but Paul focuses on belonging to a church in order to give and to serve *others*. The standard God provides for evaluating ourselves and engaging in effective ministry is the faith he gives to each one through the preaching of the gospel. Every member should play a discerning and committed role in edifying or building up the body of Christ (cf. 1 Cor 14:1–5, 12, 26; Eph 4:12, 16). This may take place within the regular gatherings of a church or by grasping everyday opportunities to encourage and care for one another (cf. 15:1–2; 1 Cor 8:1, 10; 10:23; 1 Thess 5:11). God is pleased when we serve his people in this way. "While all ministry must be understood as a response to God's grace, and not in any sense a cultivation of his favor, ministry to others is an important aspect of our self-giving to God."[55]

C. Love toward Believers and Unbelievers (12:9–21)

9 Let love be without hypocrisy. Detest evil; cling to what is
good. 10 Love one another deeply as brothers and sisters. Outdo
one another in showing honor. 11 Do not lack diligence in zeal; be
fervent in the Spirit; serve the Lord. 12 Rejoice in hope; be patient
in affliction; be persistent in prayer. 13 Share with the saints in their
needs; pursue hospitality. 14 Bless those who persecute you; bless
and do not curse. 15 Rejoice with those who rejoice; weep with
those who weep. 16 Live in harmony with one another. Do not be
proud; instead, associate with the humble. Do not be wise in your
own estimation. 17 Do not repay anyone evil for evil. Give careful
thought to do what is honorable in everyone's eyes. 18 If possible,

[54] "A particularly cheerful and agreeable disposition may well be evidence of the special *charisma* that marks a person out for this particular service" (Cranfield, *Romans*, 2:627). The Greek expression could be literally rendered "with hilarity"!

[55] Peterson, *Engaging with God*, 178–79. Paul's teaching about edification is outlined on 206–15. Note how the teaching about ministry in the body of Christ (vv. 3–8) is an expression of the "understanding service" commended in vv. 1–2.

as far as it depends on you, live at peace with everyone. [19]Friends, do not avenge yourselves; instead, leave room for God's wrath, because it is written, **Vengeance belongs to me; I will repay,** says the Lord. [20]But

> **If your enemy is hungry, feed him.**
> **If he is thirsty, give him something to drink.**
> **For in so doing**
> **you will be heaping fiery coals on his head.**

[21]Do not be conquered by evil, but conquer evil with good.

Context

Far from being a series of loosely connected exhortations, this passage is "artfully constructed for rhetorical impact."[56] Introduction of the topic of love follows naturally from the teaching about having a proper regard for one's gifts and responsibilities within the body of Christ (vv. 3–8; cf. 1 Cor 12–13). Practical care for other believers is the focus in vv. 9–13, love in the context of opposition in vv. 14–16, and nonretaliation in vv. 17–21. A series of OT allusions "indicates a strong concern on the part of Paul to root this most demanding of ethical obligations in the tried and tested wisdom of Jewish scripture and experience."[57] But the echo of Jesus's teaching on love is strong in v. 14 (cf. Matt 5:44; Luke 6:27–28) and "is probably intended to set the keynote for the verses which follow (12:14–13:7), before being picked up again more explicitly in 13:8–10."[58]

Structure

With no conjunction linking this section to the preceding one, Paul makes an assertion about love in a verbless clause (v. 9a, [lit.] "love without pretense"). This is then amplified by two participial clauses in the present tense (lit., "detesting evil, clinging to good").

---

[56] Jewett, *Romans*, 756, arguing against Cranfield, *Romans*, 2:628. Moo (*Romans*, 771–74) considers a range of views about the structure and interconnection of the various exhortations in this passage.

[57] Dunn, *Romans 9–16*, 738. Dunn suggests allusions to Sir 7:34 in v. 15, Prov 3:7, Isa 5:21 in v. 16; Prov 3:4 in v. 17; Ps 34:14 (LXX 33:15) in v. 18; Lev 19:18, Deut 32:35 in v. 19; Prov 25:21–22 in v. 20, and T. Benj. 4:3 in v. 21. Cf. John Piper, *"Love Your Enemies": Jesus' Love Command in the Synoptic Gospels and the Early Christian Paraenesis*, SNTSMS 38 (Cambridge: Cambridge University, 1979), 112–14.

[58] Dunn, *Romans 9–16*, 738.

"The good" that Christians are to pursue in their relationships with one another is articulated in a series of carefully balanced clauses, mostly employing present participles (lit., "being affectionate towards one another with brotherly love, taking the lead in honoring one another, not flagging in diligence, being fervent in spirit, serving the Lord, rejoicing in hope, being patient in affliction, persisting in prayer, sharing with the saints in their needs, pursuing hospitality"). These could be understood as descriptive of genuine love rather than being strictly prescriptive.[59] A different syntactical pattern emerges in vv. 14–21 as the focus turns to demonstrating love in the face of opposition. Five imperatival forms introduce the section (vv. 14–15, "Bless those who persecute you; bless and do not curse. Rejoice with those who rejoice; weep with those who weep").[60] Then three present participles are used to explain what this involves (v. 16a–c, [lit.] "thinking the same thing toward another; not thinking arrogantly, but associating with the lowly"). Another imperative in v. 16d ("Do not be wise in your own estimation") is followed by four present participles in vv. 17–19a (lit., "not repaying anyone evil for evil; taking thought for what is good in the sight of all people; if possible on your part, living at peace with everyone; not taking revenge, beloved"). A final imperative (v. 19b, [lit.] "but give place to God's wrath") is supported by citations from Deut 32:35a and Prov 25:21–22 in vv. 19c–21, showing the importance of the command. A passive present imperative and its active counterpart form the conclusion (v. 21, "Do not be conquered by evil, but conquer evil with good").

Outline:

1. Love without pretense (12:9–13)
2. Love in the context of opposition (12:14–16)
3. Love instead of retaliation (12:17–21)

12:9. A simple maxim, without a grammatical link to the preceding argument, acts as a heading for what follows (ἡ ἀγάπη ἀνυπόκριτος, [lit.] "love [is] without pretense"; cf. 2 Cor 6:6; 1 Pet

[59] Cf. Kruse, *Romans*, 474–75. CSB with most versions translates a series of imperatives here. But this obscures subtleties in the text and gives the impression that each idea Paul expresses is of equal importance. Cf. Runge, *Discourse Grammar*, 264–65; Moo, *Romans*, 776nn27–28; Jewett, *Romans*, 755, 758–60.

[60] Two infinitives are used in v. 15 in an imperatival way (cf. Phil 3:16; BDF §389).

1:22). In a few Jewish sources the noun ἀγάπη occasionally denotes love for God (e.g., Jer 2:2; Wis 3:9; Let. Aris. 229), but mostly it refers to love between people (e.g., 2 Sam [LXX 2 Kgdms] 1:26; 13:15; Eccl 9:1).[61] Early Christian writers employed this little-used noun and its cognates in a novel way to describe their Trinitarian experience of divine love and its outworking in their lives. In 5:5 Paul stated that "God's love has been poured out in our hearts through the Holy Spirit who was given to us." The Spirit provides believers with personal assurance of the love of God, which was historically demonstrated in Christ's death for us (5:8; cf. 8:32, 35, 37, 39). By implication the Spirit also enables believers to love God (8:28) and express love for others (12:9; 13:10; 14:15; cf. Gal 5:22–26). Using the adjective ἀνυπόκριτος, which derives from ὑποκριτής ("actor"), Paul sets out to describe the characteristics of "love without pretense."[62] No playacting or insincerity is possible if human love is to reflect the love of God. Two participial clauses in v. 9 begin to articulate what this involves: "detesting evil" (ἀποστυγοῦντες τὸ πονηρόν) and "clinging to what is good" (κολλώμενοι τῷ ἀγαθῷ). These strong verbs suggest a passionate commitment to discern and do what is good in God's sight (cf. 12:2) while rejecting everything God hates (cf. Pss 34:14; 37:27; Amos 5:15; 1 Thess 5:21–22). "The good" with respect to Christian relationships is particularly outlined in vv. 10–16 and "the evil" in vv. 17–21.[63]

12:10. Love for other believers is indicated by Paul's twofold use of the term "one another" and his employment of the noun φιλαδελφία ("brotherly love"; cf. 1 Thess 4:9; Heb 13:1; 1 Pet 1:22; 2 Pet 1:7). This term normally expressed familial love but was occasionally applied to those in religious or political associations

[61] Cf. Moo, *Romans*, 775n24. Victor P. Furnish (*The Love Command in the New Testament* [Nashville: Abingdon, 1973], 220–22) identifies a more extensive use of the related verb.

[62] Cf. Ulrich Wilckens, "ὑπυκρίνομαι κτλ.," *TDNT* 8:559–71; Walter T. Wilson, *Love without Pretense: Romans 12.9–21 and Hellenistic-Jewish Wisdom Literature*, WUNT 46 (Tübingen: Mohr-Siebeck 1991), 152. Thompson (*Clothed with Christ*, 92–94) argues that Paul's use of this term is also rooted in the teaching of Jesus.

[63] Jewett, *Romans*, 759. The verb ἀποστυγέω ("hate") only occurs here in the NT, but κολλάω ("join closely together") is used with reference to marriage (Matt 19:5), union with a prostitute instead of being "joined" to the Lord (1 Cor 6:16–17), and other relationships (e.g., Luke 15:15; Acts 5:13; 9:26; 10:28; 17:34).

(e.g., 1 Macc 12:10, 17; 2 Macc 15:14).[64] Christians were doubtless moved to adopt such terminology by the fact that Jesus called his disciples "brothers" (Mark 3:33–35; Matt 25:40; 28:10; John 20:17) and encouraged them to treat one another accordingly (Matt 23:8; Luke 22:32). The adjective φιλόστοργοι, which is only found here in the NT, was widely used in Greek literature with reference to family affection.[65] The combination of these two terms for love is significant (CSB: "Love one another deeply as brothers and sisters"). Adoption into the family of God brings believers into a Spirit-directed relationship (8:14–17) where a certain type of affection is appropriate. One way of showing this is indicated in the next clause (τῇ τιμῇ ἀλλήλους προηγούμενοι). CSB ("Outdo one another in showing honor") introduces an unfortunate note of competition into the context. The verb literally means "go first and lead the way" (BDAG) and is best understood to have that meaning here (lit. "taking the lead in honoring one another"). The readers were to abandon "the heated Graeco-Roman competition for personal honour with its catastrophic repercussions of dishonour, choosing instead to associate with the lowly" (12:16).[66]

12:11. Continuing the pattern begun in v. 9b, three linked clauses outline the way genuine love is expressed. The first (τῇ σπουδῇ μὴ ὀκνηροί, [lit.] "not flagging in diligence") echoes the sort of warning against laziness or slackness found in Prov 6:6, 9; 20:4; 21:25; 22:13; 26:13–16; 31:2; Matt 25:26.[67] In a congregational context this might mean failing to fulfill your obligations or not playing your part as a member of the fellowship (e.g., v. 8, "leading, with diligence"). The second clause (τῷ πνεύματι ζέοντες, [lit.] "being fervent in the Spirit") highlights the way to overcome indolence in

---

[64] Cf. Hans F. von Soden, "ἀδελφός κτλ.," *TDNT* 1:144–46.

[65] Cf. Dunn, *Romans 9–16*, 740–41; Jewett, *Romans*, 761n46.

[66] J. R. Harrison, "The Erasure of Distinction: Paul and the Politics of Dishonour," *TynBul* 67 (2016): 85. Harrison notes that in 13:7b "this was to be done without omitting to honour the high status individuals at the apex of the social pyramid to whom honour was legitimately due."

[67] The adjective ὀκνηρός means "possessing ὄκνος (a state involving shrinking from something 'holding back, hesitation, reluctance'), *idle, lazy, indolent*" (BDAG). The noun σπουδή means "earnest commitment in discharge of an obligation or experience of a relationship, eagerness, earnestness, diligence, willingness, zeal" (BDAG). Cf. 2 Cor 7:11, 12; 8:7, 8, 16.

the Christian life.[68] In view of 8:15–16, it is likely that Paul envisages God's Spirit producing such fervor in the spirit of believers. The third clause (τῷ κυρίῳ δουλεύοντες, [lit.] "serving the Lord") is a reminder that the grace of justification and the gift of the Spirit is for the purpose of evoking obedient service (6:12–23; 7:6; 8:1–12; 12:1–2).[69] So diligence in serving others is encouraged by being fervent in spirit, which also enables devoted service to God.

12:12. Three participial clauses expand on the need for spiritual fervor and faithful service (lit., "rejoicing in hope, being patient in affliction, persisting in prayer").[70] These Godward and future-directed commitments are also linked at other points in the letter. In 5:2–5 rejoicing in hope is coupled with persevering in suffering, and the Spirit's enabling is highlighted. In 8:24–27 patient hope is linked with the Spirit's intercession when believers do not know what to pray for. Paul's wish-prayer in 15:13 is that his readers may "overflow with hope by the power of the Holy Spirit."

12:13. Two further participial clauses tease out the meaning of love without pretense (lit., "sharing with the saints in their needs; pursuing hospitality"). As in Gal 6:6; Phil 4:15, the verb κοινωνέω ("share") carries the sense of making financial or other material contributions.[71] Believers in Christ have been set apart to belong to God and to one another. As God's "holy ones" (οἱ ἁγίοι, cf. 1:7 ["saints"]), they have familial obligations that extend to such practical care (15:25–27; cf. Acts 2:44–47; 4:32–37). Hospitality (τὴν φιλοξενίαν) was "deeply rooted and highly regarded in ancient society."[72] Early Christian missionary activity was dependent on it

---

[68] Cf. Cranfield, *Romans*, 2:633–34. Apollos is similarly described as being "fervent in spirit" in Acts 18:25. The verb ζέω literally means "boil, seethe" but was used figuratively of emotions to mean "enthusiastic, excited, on fire" (BDAG).

[69] The reading τῷ κυρίῳ ("the Lord") is widely attested and is likely to be the original. The alternative τῷ καιρῷ ("the appointed time") is supported chiefly by Western witnesses and probably arose from a visual error in copying. Cf. Jewett, *Romans*, 755.

[70] The verb προσκαρτερέω in this context means "busy oneself with, be busily engaged in, be devoted to" (BDAG). It is used with reference to persistent prayer in Acts 1:14; 2:42; 6:4; Col 4:2.

[71] Jewett (*Romans*, 764–65) unduly narrows the application of this exhortation to the sharing of economic resources with those who returned to Rome after the deportation under Claudius.

[72] Dunn (*Romans 9–16*, 743–44) provides examples from pagan and Jewish sources. He also notes Jesus's dependence on hospitality (e.g., Mark 1:29–31; 14:3; Luke

(e.g., Mark 6:8–11; Acts 16:15, 34; 20:7–11; 21:7–8), and believers needed to be reminded of its strategic importance (cf. 1 Tim 3:2; Titus 1:8; Heb 13:2; 1 Pet 4:9). Paul himself was hoping to be cared for by the Roman Christians in the near future (15:28). Perhaps his use of the strong term διώκοντες ("pursuing") was related to the fact that the city had many visitors, some of whom would have been believers from other parts of the empire. Instead of growing weary in expressing such love, they were to be proactive in receiving strangers as guests.

12:14. A change of style signals a new direction in the passage. Now the focus is on responding to hostility from outsiders and caring for those who are impacted by such opposition. There is no evidence for specific persecution in Rome around the time Paul wrote, but sporadic opposition in different parts of the empire was common from the beginning of Christianity (cf. Acts; 1 Thess 2:14–15; Phil 1:29; 2 Tim 3:12). Three imperatives reflect the teaching of Jesus about loving enemies, combining elements of the tradition in Luke 6:27–28 and Matt 5:44 (cf. 1 Cor 4:12; 1 Pet 3:9; Did 1.3b): "Bless those who persecute you; bless and do not curse."[73] Paul adopts the blessing-curse contrast found in the words of Jesus and OT precedents. Blessing in a Jewish context implied calling on God to bestow protection, grace, peace, or some special favor (e.g., Gen 27:27–29; Num 6:24–26). Cursing someone meant calling on God to withhold his favor or to bring his judgment on people (e.g., 2 Sam 16:5–13; 2 Kgs 2:24).[74] Persecutors are (lit.) "those who pursue" (τοὺς διώκοντας, cf. v. 13) believers in ways that cause them harm.

12:15. Paul uses two infinitives to indicate how the preceding commands may be fulfilled. CSB has rendered these as imperatives ("rejoice with those who rejoice; weep with those who weep").[75] Since the focus has turned to relationships with opponents, such peo-

10:38–42) and his practice and commendation of it "as a model of divine generosity" (Mark 2:15–17; Matt 11:19; Luke 14:1–24). Cf. Kruse, *Romans*, 478–79.

[73] Cf. Dunn, *Romans 9–16*, 745; Piper, *Love Your Enemies*, 49–65; Thompson, *Clothed with Christ*, 96–105, Jewett, *Romans*, 765–66. The pronoun ὑμᾶς ("you") is strongly supported in the manuscript tradition (e.g., ℵ A D [in another position] Ψ), but the shorter reading in 𝔓[46] B and others is more likely to have been the original. The addition could have been made under the influence of Matt 5:44.

[74] Cf. Hermann W. Beyer, "εὐλογέω κτλ.," *TDNT* 2:754–65.

[75] See n. 60 above on the imperatival use of infinitives.

ple must be included within the scope of the exhortation: "Whether among fellow believers or outsiders, the person of faith is to sympathize and share in joys and sorrows."[76] Nevertheless, believers are more likely to have had opportunities for demonstrating such sympathy in the closeness of their everyday relationships (1 Cor 12:26; Phil 2:17–18).

12:16. Paul begins a complex exhortation with the maxim τὸ αὐτὸ εἰς ἀλλήλους φρονοῦντες (lit., "thinking the same toward one another"), which appears in a shortened form in 2 Cor 13:11; Phil 2:2; 4:2. This calls for a common care and consideration of others rather than a uniformity of thought on every issue. CSB ("Live in harmony with one another") does not adequately represent this. The maxim is amplified in what follows (μὴ τὰ ὑψηλὰ φρονοῦντες ἀλλὰ τοῖς ταπεινοῖς συναπαγόμενοι, [lit.] "not thinking lofty things, but associating with the lowly").[77] Paul echoes the concern of 11:20 (cf. 1 Cor 4:10), but his argument here has a broader application.[78] His use of three terms with the root φρόν ("think") recalls his emphasis on right thinking in v. 3. The climax of the sequence is an imperative (μὴ γίνεσθε φρόνιμοι παρ' ἑαυτοῖς, "Do not be wise in your own estimation"). This could relate to the situation exposed in 14:1–15:7, where a sense of superiority or competition between believers in Rome is treated as harmful and destructive (see especially 15:5). But Paul could also be challenging the way his readers dealt with opposition from a culture that "bred strife and jealousy both between and within different classes."[79] Genuine love is only possible when natural human differences are set aside.

12:17–18. Three present participles return the focus more obviously to relationships with outsiders. First, (lit.) "repaying no one evil for evil," which parallels 1 Thess 5:15; 1 Pet 3:9. Vengeance in v. 19 is a stronger expression of this. Paul's warning echoes the

---

[76] Jewett, *Romans*, 767. Jewett gives examples of similar exhortations from Jewish and pagan literature. Cf. Cranfield, *Romans*, 2:641–42; Dunn, *Romans 9–16*, 746.

[77] Cf. Wilson, *Love without Pretense*, 179. The adjective ταπεινοῖς is more likely to be masculine than neuter here. Cf. Cranfield, *Romans*, 2.644

[78] Thompson (*Clothed with Christ*, 106) suggests that Paul is pointing to the example of Jesus, "who did not draw back in self-righteous pride, but associated with the lowly." Proverbs 3:7 could also have influenced Paul's wording.

[79] Bruce W. Winter, "Roman Law and Society in Romans 12–15," in *Rome in the Bible and the Early Church*, ed. P. Oakes (Grand Rapids: Baker, 2002), 79. Cf. Dunn, *Romans 9–16*, 747; Jewett, *Romans*, 769–71.

sentiment of various Jewish and non-Jewish writings.[80] There are also similarities with the teaching of Jesus (e.g., Matt 5:38–42), though a definite allusion is debated. The word μηδενί ("no one") must include the most hostile opponents.

A second clause puts the positive alternative, which is (lit.) "considering what is good in the sight of all people" (προνοούμενοι καλὰ ἐνώπιον πάντων ἀνθρώπων [cf. Prov 3:4; 2 Cor 8:21]). The participle προνοούμενοι means "give careful thought to" (BDAG). Paul is calling for a recognition of what is valued by human beings generally (CSB: "what is honorable in everyone's eyes"). This does not mean accepting everything others espouse, but rather it means taking into account what is widely recognized to be good. Particularly in the first-century Roman context, "gaining some understanding of the motivations of the government and of pagan neighbors, involved in various forms of harassment from public to private, would be an appropriate expression of 'genuine love.'"[81]

The positive alternative to retaliation is stated with a third present participle (μετὰ πάντων ἀνθρώπων εἰρηνεύοντες [lit., "living at peace with all people"). Peace is to be sought with fellow believers (2 Cor 13:11; 1 Thess 5:13) *and* with unbelievers. This encouragement is preceded by a double qualification (εἰ δυνατὸν τὸ ἐξ ὑμῶν [lit., "if possible, so far as it depends on you"]).[82] Paul acknowledges that peace may not be possible in each and every circumstance, but Christians should make every effort to achieve and maintain it.

12:19. The final warning against retaliation is elaborate. Instead of avenging themselves, as those who know themselves to be loved by God, believers are literally to "give place to wrath" (δότε τόπον τῇ ὀργῇ). The biblical citation at the end of the verse makes clear that God's wrath is in view (CSB: "Leave room for God's wrath"). Retaliation involves "usurping God's place."[83] Between the

---

[80] Cf. Piper, *Love Your Enemies*, 19–48; Wilson, *Love without Pretense*, 187–88. Note especially Prov 17:13; 20:22; 24:29; Sir 27:22–28:26; Jos. Asen. 23:9; 28:4, 14; 29:3.

[81] Jewett, *Romans*, 773. Cranfield (*Romans*, 2:645–46) suggests that Christians are to display the good that the gospel makes possible "in the sight of all people." But this is not a natural way to read the verse (cf. Moo *Romans*, 785; Schreiner, *Romans*, 672).

[82] There may be an allusion to Ps 34:14 (LXX 33:15) here or to the teaching of Jesus reflected in Mark 9:50.

[83] Jewett, *Romans*, 776. Jewett suggests that "give place" means "give space" for God's wrath to be revealed. Although the actual phrase δότε τόπον ὀργῇ is paralleled

participial clause indicating what is to be avoided and the imperative giving the positive alternative, Paul addresses his readers as "beloved" (ἀγαπητοί, cf. 16:5, 8, 9, 12). CSB's "friends" is weak in view of 1:7, where the Roman believers are described as ἀγαπητοῖς θεοῦ ("loved by God"). Rejection by others is hurtful, "but the salve of God's love for us is the best healing for it."[84] According to 1:18–32, God's wrath may be manifested in the present, but 2:5–11 indicates that the ultimate revelation is yet to come (cf. 2 Thess 1:6–8). Patient trust in the justice of God is required (cf. 1 Pet 2:23). Moreover, this is a time for blessing, not cursing, opponents (v. 14). Paul's appeal to "leave room" for God's wrath is given a scriptural basis ("for it is written") with reference to Deut 32:35 ("vengeance belongs to me; I will repay").[85] The divine source of this claim is affirmed by addition of the words, "says the Lord."

12:20–21. A supporting citation from LXX Prov 25:21–22a is introduced with the conjunction ἀλλά ("but"). This gives practical guidance about how to bless opponents rather than curse them. In the context of persecution, feeding your enemy if he is hungry and giving him something to drink if he is thirsty would be a radical way of showing love and seeking peace with everyone (v. 18; cf. Luke 6:27–36). The enigmatic words "for in so doing you will be heaping fiery coals on his head" have been variously interpreted. Most obviously, such generosity toward enemies would compound their guilt unless they repented.[86] If this is Paul's meaning, he will not be encouraging Christians to act kindly toward their enemies for the purpose of making their judgment more severe but simply stating that good actions may have that outcome. However, many commentators think that such a negative tone is inconsistent with the context. They view the "fiery coals" as a metaphor for "the burning pangs of shame."[87] More specifically, it is suggested that Paul is holding

---

in Plutarch, *Cohib. ira* 14, Paul most probably derived the idiom from Jewish wisdom texts such as Wis 12:10, 20; Sir 4:5; 13:22; 16:14. Cf. Eph 4:26–27; Heb 12:17.

[84] Schreiner, *Romans*, 672.

[85] Paul's version of this text follows the Hebrew in putting the pronoun ἐμοί (לִי, "to me") in the emphatic position at the beginning of the clause. Since the same pattern is found in Heb 10:30, it may be that both writers were following another Greek version (both are actually closer to the Aramaic Targum than to the LXX or Hebrew).

[86] Cf. Piper, *Love Your Enemies*, 115–19; Schreiner, *Romans*, 674–76.

[87] Moo, *Romans*, 789. Cf. Jewett, *Romans*, 777; Byrne, *Romans*, 384; Kruse, *Romans*, 484–85.

out the possibility that the antagonist may be converted.[88] The problem with this line of argument is that the image of "fiery coals" in OT usage consistently signifies God's judgment.[89] Moreover, a reference to God's judgment here would parallel the promise of his vengeance in v. 19.

There is no mention of any special reward from God for those who act so graciously (cf. Prov 25:22b). Rather, Paul concludes with the second-person singular warning, "Do not be conquered by evil, but conquer evil with good" (*μὴ νικῶ ὑπὸ τοῦ κακοῦ ἀλλὰ νίκα ἐν τῷ ἀγαθῷ τὸ κακόν*). The present tense of these imperatives indicates the generality of the command and the need for persistence in such behavior. An inclusion with v. 9 is formed, reminding the reader that the whole passage has been about love without pretense. The motivation for doing good is ultimately "the mercies of God" (v. 1) and "the grace given to us" (v. 6). The way to conquer evil when it confronts you in any form of opposition is to demonstrate the love of God. "To retaliate is to be overcome both by the evil of one's enemy and also by the evil of one's own heart which responds to the other's evil."[90]

Bridge

Genuine love is more than a benevolent disposition toward others. It involves rejecting what is evil and clinging to what is good. Love for fellow believers should express family affection, recognizing the special relationship into which God has brought us. Practically, this means taking the lead in honoring one another, being diligent in fulfilling responsibilities, sharing with others in their needs, and pursuing hospitality. Spiritual fervor, issuing in such service to the Lord, is maintained by rejoicing in hope, being patient in affliction, and being persistent in prayer. Blessing rather than cursing is the keynote when dealing with opponents. Paul knew the pressure we feel to respond with anger and vengeance. Alluding to the teaching of Jesus and quoting Scripture, he insists

[88] Noting that an Egyptian ritual involving coals of fire in a dish on one's head was a sign of repentance, Dunn (*Romans*, 751) takes the metaphor to mean "you will win him" in a missionary sense.

[89] Cf. 2 Sam 22:9=Ps 18:8, 12; Job 41:20–21 (LXX 41:12–13); Ps 140:10; Prov 6:27–29; Ezek 24:11; 4 Ezra 16:53.

[90] Cranfield, *Romans*, 2:659.

that believers should leave vengeance to God and look for ways of showing love to enemies. Positive, outgoing goodness is advocated, not merely passive resistance. Within this context Paul indicates that relationships with believers and nonbelievers alike require sympathy, humility, and the pursuit of peace.

D. Living as Responsible Citizens (13:1–7)

[1]Let everyone submit to the governing authorities, since
there is no authority except from God, and the authorities that
exist are instituted by God. [2]So then, the one who resists the authority is opposing God's command, and those who oppose it will
bring judgment on themselves. [3]For rulers are not a terror to good
conduct, but to bad. Do you want to be unafraid of the authority?
Do what is good, and you will have its approval. [4]For it is God's
servant for your good. But if you do wrong, be afraid, because it
does not carry the sword for no reason. For it is God's servant, an
avenger that brings wrath on the one who does wrong. [5]Therefore,
you must submit, not only because of wrath but also because of
your conscience. [6]And for this reason you pay taxes, since the authorities are God's servants, continually attending to these tasks.
[7]Pay your obligations to everyone: taxes to those you owe taxes,
tolls to those you owe tolls, respect to those you owe respect, and
honor to those you owe honor.

Context

Some commentators have described this section as a parenthesis that fits awkwardly into the context. Consequently, they seek to establish the particular historical and political circumstances that made this insertion necessary.[91] But the passage continues the teaching of 12:14–21 about dealing with outsiders. In particular, Paul's exhortation to leave vengeance to God (12:19) prepares for his explanation of the way governing authorities may function as God's servants to bring wrath on those who do wrong (13:4). Indeed, the theme of "good" and "bad" runs through the whole context (12:2, 9, 17, 21; 13:3, 4, 10). The focus on what is owed to others (13:7) prepares for the opening challenge of the next section (13:8, "Do not

[91] Jewett (*Romans*, 785–86) considers the various historical scenarios that might have been addressed by Paul. Cf. Dunn, *Romans 9–16*, 768–70, 772–74; Byrne, *Romans*, 385–87; Kruse, *Romans*, 489–92.

owe anyone anything, except to love one another"). Against the possibility that his message in 12:2 implied freedom from the obligation to obey rulers who belong to this age, Paul shows that "submission to government is another aspect of that 'good' which the Christian, seeking to 'approve' the will of God, will exemplify."[92]

Structure

Without a formal link to the preceding passage, Paul announces a new theme in v. 1, using a third-person middle imperative ("Let everyone submit to the governing authorities"). This command is given a theological justification in a point-counterpoint form, introduced by the conjunction γάρ ("Since there is no authority except from God, and [the authorities] that exist are instituted by God"). A two-part consequential statement in v. 2 begins with ὥστε ("So then, the one who resists the authority is opposing God's command, and those who oppose it will bring judgment on themselves"). A justification for this warning is given in v. 3a in a brief statement introduced by γάρ ("For rulers are not a terror to good conduct, but to bad"). The argument proceeds in a diatribe form in vv. 3b–5, addressing an imaginary opponent in the second-person singular. A rhetorical question ("Do you want to be unafraid of the authority?") is followed by a command and a promise ("Do what is good, and you will have its approval"). A theological justification for this challenge is introduced by γάρ in v. 4a ("For it is God's servant for your good"). The alternative response is considered in a conditional clause with a warning ("But if you do wrong, be afraid"). The explanation for this warning is given in two linked causal clauses, each beginning with γάρ ("because it does not carry the sword for no reason. For it is God's servant, an avenger that brings wrath on the one who does wrong"). The conjunction διό ("therefore") introduces a formal conclusion in v. 5 ("Therefore, you must submit, not only because of wrath but also because of your conscience"). Paul addresses his readers more generally with second-person plural verbs in vv. 6–7 as he applies the teaching more broadly ("And for this reason you pay

[92] Moo, *Romans*, 792. Byrne (*Romans*, 386) views this passage as playing "a significant role in Paul's self-presentation to the Roman community." Cf. Philip H. Towner, "Romans 13:1–7 and Paul's Missiological Perspective: A Call to Political Quietism or Transformation?" in *Romans and the People of God*, ed. Soderlund and Wright, 149–69.

taxes, for [the authorities] are God's servants, continually attending to these tasks. Pay your obligations to everyone: taxes to those you owe taxes, tolls to those you owe tolls, respect to those you owe respect, and honor to those you owe honor").

Outline:

1. Submit to the governing authorities (13:1–5).
2. Pay your obligations to everyone (13:6–7).

13:1. Paul continues to focus on how Christians should relate to outsiders (cf. 12:14–21), introducing the idea of submission to governing authorities formally. *Πᾶσα ψυχή* ("every person") echoes the language of the LXX, often found in legal contexts (e.g., Lev 7:27 [Heb כָּל־נֶפֶשׁ]).[93] This formula allows for no exceptions. A third-person present imperative (ὑποτασσέσθω) has the middle sense of "submit oneself" (cf. Titus 3:1; 1 Pet 2:13), which implies recognizing a divinely established order in this context.[94] "The governing authorities" (ἐξουσίαις ὑπερεχούσαις) would include various imperial and local offices in the first-century Roman governmental system.[95] A theological rationale for Paul's exhortation is introduced with a causal clause (*γάρ*,"since"): no matter what rulers themselves may claim, "there is no authority except from God, and (the authorities) that exist are instituted by God" (cf. Prov 8:15–16; 21:1; Jer 27:5–7; Dan 2:21; 4:17, 25, 32; 5:21; Sir 10:4; Wis 6:3; John 19:11). For emphasis this biblical perspective is stated negatively and positively, with ὑπὸ θεοῦ (lit., "by God") being used in both clauses. The perfect participle *τεταγμέναι* ("instituted") highlights the present reality

---

[93] Adopting a less formal style, some textual witnesses (e.g., 𝔓[46] D* G) read *πάσαις ἐξουσίαις ὑπερεχούσαις ὑποτάσσεσθε* ("Be subject to all the governing authorities"). But this is clearly a secondary reading.

[94] Cf. Gerhard Delling, "*τάσσω κτλ.*," *TDNT* 8:39–46. Stanley E. Porter ("Romans 13:1–7 as Pauline Political Rhetoric," *FilN* 3 [1990], 121) demonstrates that the majority of instances of this verb in NT ethical contexts speak of voluntary submission, rather than simply obedience. Cf. Cranfield, *Romans*, 2.660–63.

[95] Jewett (*Romans*, 787–88) rightly opposes the view that this expression could relate to angelic powers behind political authorities. He argues that the somewhat redundant combination of the noun and participle here has a broad reference to "a range of officials placed in superior positions of political authority, duly appointed to their tasks, and currently exercising their power." Cf. Cranfield, *Romans*, 2:656–60; Dunn, *Romans*, 760.

of these divine appointments.[96] This assertion about the God and Father of Jesus Christ being responsible for the establishment of Roman governmental institutions challenged popular myths about a pantheon of deities being responsible for the foundation and maintenance of the city and its empire.[97] Submission to such a regime meant acknowledging the authority of its representatives to fulfill the roles ascribed to them (vv. 3–4, 6–7), not endorsing every policy or action they pursued.

13:2. The inferential conjunction ὥστε ("so then") introduces two consequences of the preceding claim: "The one who resists the authority is opposing God's command, and those who oppose it will bring judgment on themselves." Failure to submit to human rulers expresses resistance to God's will.[98] Paul's use of the cognate διαταγή (BDAG: "that which has been ordered or commanded") identifies "the actual basis of submission under governmental authority as an *order* willed by God even for Christians."[99] The perfect tense in the substantive expression οἱ δὲ ἀνθεστηκότες should be read as a present ("those who oppose"), corresponding with the singular present form in the first clause (ὁ ἀντιτασσόμενος, "the one who resists").[100] This second warning concludes with the assertion that (lit.) "they will receive judgment against themselves" (ἑαυτοῖς κρίμα λήμψονται, cf. Ezek 4:5; Job 9:19; Wis 12:12). The nature of that judgment is explained in vv. 3–5, where God's condemnation is linked with the penalties imposed by civic authorities.

13:3. Justification for the preceding warning is given in a brief statement introduced by γάρ ("For rulers are not a terror to good conduct, but to bad"). Paul returns to the general categories of good

---

[96] The verb τάσσω means "bring about an order of things by arranging, arrange, put in place" (BDAG). It is the root of ὑποτάσσω ("place under, subject") in v. 1, ἀντιτάσσω ("resist, oppose") and διαταγή ("order, command") in v. 2. Cf. n. 94 above.

[97] Jewett, *Romans*, 790.

[98] The verb ἀντιτάσσομαι ("resist, oppose") is used twice in the first clause but nowhere else in Paul's letters (see n. 95 above). The synonym ἀνθίστημι was used in 9:19, with reference to resisting God's will. Dunn (*Romans 9–16*, 762) points to uses of ἀντιτάσσομαι in the LXX for resistance to superior forces (e.g., Lev 26:37; Deut 7:24; Josh 1:5).

[99] Lorenz Oberlinner, "διατάσσω, διαταγή," *EDNT* 1:314 (emphasis in original).

[100] Against Jewett (*Romans*, 791), it is a misreading of the perfect tense in a participle to imply that Paul is addressing past problems of opposition with continuing implications. Cf. Dunn, *Romans 9–16*, 762.

and evil mentioned in 12:9, 21. While there were certainly unjust and malevolent officials in the Roman Empire, the focus here is on their ideal function. Rulers are not meant to be a cause of fear to those who do good (τῷ ἀγαθῷ ἔργῳ, [lit.] "to the good work") but to those who do evil. Paul himself experienced unjust treatment from Roman officials (e.g., Acts 16:22–24; 24:24–27; 2 Cor 11:25) but never encouraged civil disobedience or outlined a program for political subversion.[101] Adopting a diatribe form, he begins to address an imaginary opponent with second-person singular verbs ("Do you want to be unafraid of the authority?"). Given the difficulties experienced in the reign of Claudius (cf. Introduction III.A), Roman Christians may have had reason to fear mistreatment from the state. But Paul's fundamental solution is "Do what is good, and you will have its approval." CSB has followed NRSV in rendering ἔπαινον ἐξ αὐτῆς "its approval" (the feminine possessive pronoun agrees with τὴν ἐξουσίαν, "the authority"). This is more likely than ESV, which takes the latter to refer to "the one who is in authority," and reads the promise in a more personal fashion ("you will receive his approval"). Many inscriptions have been recovered from this era pointing to the official practice of giving praise (ἔπαινος) to public benefactors.[102] But Paul is speaking about informal approval for doing good in everyday social contexts.

13:4. Continuing his address to an imaginary opponent in the second-person singular, Paul gives a twofold explanation of the authority's role, using the surprising term "God's servant" (θεοῦ διάκονος).[103] Positively, the authority acts as God's servant "for your

[101] Throughout history there have been rulers who were a cause of fear to those who do good while rewarding those who do evil. For example, Nero, who was in power when Paul wrote this letter, severely mistreated Christians in Rome after fire broke out in 64 (Tacitus, *Ann.* 15.44). Such political contexts raise the question of submission in an acute form. Cf. Moo, *Romans*, 808–10. Kruse (*Romans*, 494–95) outlines the way some early Christian writers dealt with the issue of rulers abusing their God-given authority.

[102] Cf. Bruce W. Winter, "The Public Honouring of Christian Benefactors: Romans 13:3–4 and 1 Peter 2:14–14," *JSNT* 34 (1988): 91–94. Winter contends that there must have been Christians of considerable means who could be public benefactors and gain such recognition.

[103] The term "servant" (διάκονος) actually had a prestigious meaning in some Roman descriptions of those holding public office (cf. Jewett, *Romans*, 794). The term is used of Christ himself in 15:8.

good" (σοὶ εἰς τὸ ἀγαθόν). The use of a singular pronoun stresses the personal benefit to each reader. Some have related this to "the good" mentioned in 8:28, which is conformity to the image of God's Son.[104] In the present context, however, "the good" is more likely to be political and social rather than moral and spiritual. With a future conditional construction ("But if you do wrong, be afraid"), Paul begins to expand on the negative function of government. Symbolically, the authority carries the sword for judgment against wrongdoers. This could refer to capital punishment or, more generally, to the power to restrain evil and maintain peace.[105] The expression οὐ εἰκῇ (lit. "not in vain" [CSB: "for no reason"]) implies that the sword will definitely be used, where appropriate. The theological justification for this is given with the renewed claim that the authority is "God's servant," expanded now to include the idea that it is "an avenger that brings wrath on the one who does wrong" (cf. Isa 7:18–20; 8:7–8; 10:5–11). The noun ἔκδικος ("avenger") recalls the warning not to "avenge" yourselves in 12:19 (ἐκδικοῦντες). By implication, the governing authority is God's agent in bringing divine wrath against evildoers in the present era. Law enforcement agents may punish evildoers in a way that is forbidden to individual members of a community. This is God's provision for the maintenance of peace and order.

13:5. Using the inferential conjunction διό ("therefore"), Paul begins to draw the argument in vv. 1–4 to a close, restating the need to be subject (ἀνάγκη ὑποτάσσεσθαι). Here, the noun ἀνάγκη ("necessity") puts the matter beyond debate. Once again the importance of avoiding the wrath of the governing authorities is highlighted ("not only because of wrath"), while prominence is given to the notion of conscience ("but also because of [your] conscience"). Greek συνείδησις refers to the knowledge one has with oneself about something, particularly "the inward faculty of distinguishing right and wrong" (BDAG). Some would understand διὰ τὴν συνείδησιν narrowly to mean avoidance of "the painful 'conscience-pang.'"[106]

[104] E.g., Cranfield, *Romans*, 2:665–66.

[105] Jewett (*Romans*, 795) points out that the swords in question would not be ceremonial daggers but military swords, which were "the classical symbol for governmental coercion."

[106] Jewett, *Romans*, 797, following Cecil A. Pierce, *Conscience in the New Testament*, SBT 1/15 (London: SCM, 1955), 34–38. Jewett takes a wider view

But such a view is not demanded by the context. Paul simply implies that those who know God's will about subjecting themselves to governing authorities should behave accordingly. He is not speaking of conscience as an independent form of guidance but addressing those whose consciences have been informed by biblical teaching.[107]

13:6. The expression διὰ τοῦτο γάρ ("And for this reason") refers back to the twofold argument about avoiding wrath and responding to conscience in v. 5. Second-person plural verbs are used in vv. 6–7 to address the readers collectively. Paul first reminds them that they "also pay taxes" (καὶ φόρους τελεῖτε), with the noun here and in v. 7 specifically describing tribute to the Roman government.[108] Complaints about taxes and those who collected them were common in the early years of Nero's reign (cf. Suetonius, *Nero* 6.10 §1; Tacitus, *Ann.* 13.50–51). Paul gives a surprising dimension to this practice with the claim that tax collectors are (lit.) "God's ministers" (λειτουργοὶ θεοῦ) who have the specific responsibility of (lit.) "continually attending to this very thing" (εἰς αὐτὸ τοῦτο προσκαρτεροῦντες).[109] In 15:16 he uses λειτουργός with reference to himself as "a minister of Christ Jesus to the Gentiles," and in Phil 2:25 he describes Epaphroditus as "(your) minister to my need." But the sense here is that tax officials are "God's public servants" rather than servants of the gospel. They collect the taxes that make effective government possible for all.

13:7. Without a connective, the apostle's final appeal begins with this command: "Pay your obligations to everyone" (ἀπόδοτε πᾶσιν τὰς ὀφειλάς). An echo of Jesus's teaching may be heard here (Matt 22:21 par., "Give, then, to Caesar the things that are Caesar's, and to God the things that are God's"). But the verb ἀποδίδωμι was widely used with the meaning "pay back" what you owe, and so literary dependence on the Gospel texts is not proved by this verbal

---

of conscience in his interpretation of 2:15; 9:1, as indicated in my comments on these verses.

[107] Cf. Christian Maurer, "σύνοιδα, συνείδησις," *TDNT* 7:916; Moo, *Romans*, 803.

[108] Konrad Weiss ("φέρω κτλ." *TDNT* 9:78) notes that φόρος was mainly used for "tribute to be paid by subject people." Jewett (*Romans*, 798–99) refers to several recent studies suggesting that many of the Roman Christians must have been "emigrants and noncitizens, some of whom were apparently subject to the tribute tax." In this way they contributed to the cost of government in the city.

[109] Porter ("Romans 13:1–7," 135) takes εἰς αὐτὸ τοῦτο as the "completive" of the participle. Cf. Cranfield, *Romans*, 2:669.

parallel.[110] Since governmental authorities serve the community as God's ministers, "reciprocity is required by those receiving such benefits."[111] Paul's simple command is explained with four parallel phrases. "To everyone" (πᾶσιν) in this context will mean to every government official according to the responsibility and function of each one.[112] The first clause establishes the pattern for the sequence: (lit.) "to the one (owed) the tribute, the tribute" (τῷ τὸν φόρον τὸν φόρον). As in v. 6, τὸν φόρον refers to the tribute payable by noncitizens. The generic term τὸ τέλος ("tolls"), which is used in the next clause, covers "a wide range of import and use taxes levied by the government."[113] Thus, direct and indirect taxes are included in this verse. The next two terms express different forms of respect owed to civic officials. In vv. 3–4, φόβος and the cognate verb conveyed the sense of "terror": the punitive role of government should engender a legitimate fear of punishment for doing wrong. But the noun is used more positively here with the sense of "fear" or "respect" (cf. Prov 24:21).[114] "Honor" (τὴν τιμήν) was central to the Roman imperial system, where it was a crucial social obligation.[115] In view of 12:2, however, Paul would have expected his readers to be discerning about the way they showed respect and honor to those in public offices.

Bridge

Being subject to civic authorities involves recognizing God's sovereignty in the establishment of structures of government for the welfare of individuals and societies. The challenge for Christians

---

[110] Cf. Friedrich Büchsel, "δίδωμι κτλ." *TDNT* 2:167; Thompson, *Clothed with Christ*, 111–20.

[111] Jewett, *Romans*, 801. Cf. Friedrich Hauck, "ὀφείλω κτλ.," *TDNT* 5:560, 564.

[112] Cranfield (*Romans*, 2:670–73) argues that "fear" is characteristically due to God rather than civic officials and includes God as the third referent. But this is an awkward intrusion in a rhetorical formulation relating to different human authorities.

[113] Jewett, *Romans*, 802. Different tax farmers and civic officials were responsible for each type of tax.

[114] According to Jewett (*Romans*, 802), after AD 53 citizens were required to have the same fear for imperial administrators as for Caesar himself. Paul normally uses the language of fear in relation to God (3:18; 11:20; 2 Cor 5:11; 7:1, 11; Phil 2:12), but that meaning does not fit the immediate context here. See also n. 112 above.

[115] Cf. Richard Shaller, "Poverty, Honor, and Obligation in Imperial Rome," *Criterion* 37 (1998): 12–20; J. E. Lendon, *Empire of Honor: The Art of Government in the Roman World* (Oxford: Clarendon, 1997), 30–175.

is to uphold those offices and show proper respect for those who hold them. For Paul resistance to legitimate authority meant resisting God's rule and his intentions for human life. Putting it positively, honoring those in public office and paying your dues is a particular way of showing neighbor love (13:8–10). But the passage is not calling for blind obedience to the will of the state, since service to God with renewed minds is the Christian's primary calling. (12:1–2). Sometimes loyalty to God may require disobedience to the governing authorities (e.g., Acts 4:19–20; 5:29), though imprisonment or some other form of punishment may be the outcome. In a democratic society there are legitimate ways of removing unjust officials and seeking redress through different levels of the political and legal system. Mostly, however, the challenge is to participate in advancing the welfare of a society by engaging in public debates, voting with discernment, and holding elected representatives to their commitments and responsibilities.

E. Love in the End-Time (13:8–14)

> 8Do not owe anyone anything, except to love one another,
> for the one who loves another has fulfilled the law. 9The com-
> mandments, **Do not commit adultery; do not murder; do not**
> **steal; do not covet;** and any other commandment, are summed up
> by this commandment: **Love your neighbor as yourself.** 10Love
> does no wrong to a neighbor. Love, therefore, is the fulfillment
> of the law.
>
> 11Besides this, since you know the time, it is already the hour
> for you to wake up from sleep, because now our salvation is near-
> er than when we first believed. 12The night is nearly over, and the
> day is near; so let us discard the deeds of darkness and put on the
> armor of light. 13Let us walk with decency, as in the daytime: not
> in carousing and drunkenness; not in sexual impurity and promis-
> cuity; not in quarreling and jealousy. 14But put on the Lord Jesus
> Christ, and don't make plans to gratify the desires of the flesh.

Context

Paul returns to the theme of love via a negative injunction ("Do not owe anyone anything"), restating the positive command in v. 7a ("Pay your obligations to everyone") and adding, "except to love one another." An inclusion is formed between the explanatory clause in v. 8b ("For the one who loves another has fulfilled the law") and the conclusion in v. 10b ("Love, therefore, is the fulfillment of the law"). This note of fulfillment leads into a paragraph highlighting the urgency of living as those who know that "our salvation is nearer than when we first believed" (v. 11). This links with 12:2 and sets the exhortations in chapters 12–13 firmly within an eschatological framework. There are also echoes of 6:1–14 in this section, with its focus on walking in a way that demonstrates what it means to "put on" the Lord Jesus Christ (13:14).

Structure

The paragraph about love is clearly linked to the preceding one by repeating v. 7a in a negative form (v. 8a, "Do not owe anyone anything"). The new topic is introduced with the words "except to love one another." As noted above, an inclusion is formed between v. 8b ("for the one who loves another has fulfilled the law") and v. 10b ("Love, therefore, is the fulfillment of the law"). Four of the Ten Commandments are cited in v. 9, with the injunction about neighbor love from Lev 19:18 used to sum up these and any other such commands. The conclusion to v. 10 defines the relation of love to law.

The second paragraph provides an explicitly eschatological context for Paul's ethical challenge. Knowing the significance of "the time" and "the hour," believers are to "discard the deeds of darkness and put on the armor of light" (vv. 11–12). Paul explains these injunctions in reverse order. Putting on the armor of light means walking with decency, as in the daylight. Discarding the deeds of darkness means "not in carousing and drunkenness; not in sexual impurity and promiscuity; not in quarreling and jealousy" (v. 13). The positive injunction is restated in v. 14, with the exhortation to "put on the Lord Jesus Christ," echoing the command at the end of v. 12 to "put on the armor of light." The negative challenge to discard the deeds of darkness is restated as "don't make plans to gratify the desires of the flesh."

Outline:

1. Fulfill the law of love (13:8–10).
2. Walk in the light of Christ (13:11–14).

13:8. There is no grammatical link to the preceding verse, but a negative version of the command in v. 7a ("Pay your obligations to everyone") marks the transition ("Do not owe anyone anything"). Every debt is to be discharged except the debt of love, which can never be fully paid. Love for others should be expressed on a daily basis, recognizing that the need for love never ends. Given the emphatic command not to owe anyone anything, the word ἀλλήλους ("one another") should be understood in the broadest sense.[116] Paul has moved from considering the expression of love among believers (12:9–13) to the wider obligations of love in an unbelieving world (12:14–13:7). Here he uses the verb ἀγαπᾶν ("to love"), which is the cognate of ἀγάπη ("love") in 12:9 (see comment).

Paul introduces a theological reason for giving such prominence to neighbor love, using the connective γάρ ("for"). The command to "love your neighbor as yourself" (Lev 19:18, cited in Matt 5:43; 19:19; Mark 12:31 par.; Rom 13:9; Gal 5:14; Jas 2:8) is anticipated in the expression ὁ ἀγαπῶν τὸν ἕτερον (lit., "the one who loves the other"). "The other" is any person whom God presents "to affect for good or ill."[117] When Paul concludes that the person who loves in this way "has fulfilled the law" (νόμον πεπλήρωκεν), he means that the person has accomplished the original intent and purpose of the law given to Israel (cf. Matt 5:17–20; Gal 5:13–15). Especially in view of the present tense of ὁ ἀγαπῶν ("the one who loves"), it would be better to understand the perfect indicative πεπλήρωκεν as conveying a continuous sense ("fulfills").[118] It is the ongoing exercise of love that constitutes the eschatological fulfillment of the law, not obedience to each and every command of the law. This is now a possibility for those who walk "according to the Spirit" (8:4; cf. Gal 5:22–23; §1.4).[119]

---

[116] Cf. Cranfield, *Romans*, 2:674–75; Dunn, *Romans 9–16*, 776. Contrast Jewett (*Romans*, 807–15), who consistently limits ἀλλήλους to fellow Christians. Moo (*Romans*, 812) rightly observes that this command does not forbid a Christian from ever incurring a debt: "It rather demands that Christians repay any debts they do incur promptly and in accordance with the terms of the contract."

[117] Cranfield, *Romans*, 2:676. Cf. Luke 10:25–37.

[118] See my comment on the translation of the perfect tense in 3:21. Moo (*Romans*, 814n25) gives πεπλήρωκεν a stative meaning in 13:8, which comes close to recognizing the imperfective aspect of the verb in this context.

[119] Thompson (*Clothed with Christ*, 126–30) notes that the verb πληροῦν can convey the sense of "accomplish" without the exactitude implicit in ποιεῖν ("do" in 2:13; Gal 3:10, 12; 5:3) and φυλάσσειν ("keep" in 2:26; cf. Gal 6:13; Acts 7:53; 21:24). But it can also carry an eschatological connotation (as in Matt 5:17; Rom 8:4; Gal 5:14).

13:9. The claim about fulfilling the law is justified in the sentence that follows, though the link word γάρ ("for") is not translated by CSB. Paul refers collectively to the seventh, sixth, eighth, and tenth commandments ("Do not commit adultery; do not murder; do not steal; do not covet") as examples of what neighbor love will *not* do. As in the LXX, the future indicative is used imperatively, literally rendering the Hebrew. The unusual order of the commandments follows the LXX B version of Deut 5:17–18 and some other Jewish texts.[120] The argument is immediately broadened to include "any other commandment" of the Mosaic law. These are "summed up" (ἀνακεφαλαιοῦται) or essentially expressed by the positive command of Lev 19:18 ("Love your neighbor as yourself").[121] The expression ἐν τῷ λόγῳ τούτῳ ("in this word") identifies this command as a revealed word from God (cf. 9:6, 9, 28), like the "ten words" of the Decalogue (LXX Exod 34:28; Deut 10:4).[122] Since Jewish writers prior to Paul did not give special prominence to Lev 19:18, it is likely that the apostle was influenced by the tradition in which Jesus combined it with Deut 6:5 and declared that "all the Law and the Prophets depend on these two commands" (Matt 22:40; cf. Mark 12:31; Luke 10:26–28).[123] The context of Lev 19:18 gives both positive and negative examples of neighbor love, including provisions for the poor, the foreign resident, and the disabled (vv. 9–18, 33–34). Jesus drew out the implications of such commands in his teaching (e.g., Matt 5:43–48; Luke 10:29–37) and perfectly demonstrated such love in the course of his ministry. Leviticus 19:18 is sometimes understood to be calling for self-love or self-esteem as a prerequisite for loving others. But the appeal is simply for God's

---

[120] Cf. Moo, *Romans*, 815n31. The article τό treats these commandments as a unit (cf. Wallace, *Greek Grammar*, 238). Several manuscripts add the ninth commandment ("You shall not bear false witness") in v. 9, but this is clearly an attempt to conform to OT precedents. Cf. Metzger, *Textual Commentary*, 467.

[121] The verb ἀνακεφαλαιόω means "bring everything to a head" (it is an intensive form of κεφαλαιόω) and hence "sum up" in a literary or rhetorical sense (cf. BDAG; Dunn, *Romans 9–16*, 778). Its only other NT use is in Eph 1:10, where it describes God's plan to "bring everything together" in the Messiah.

[122] Cf. Dunn, *Romans 9–16*, 778.

[123] Thompson (*Clothed with Christ*, 121–40) explores the influence of Jesus's teaching on Paul's thinking in this regard. Note especially his comments on fulfilling "the law of Christ" (Gal 6:2).

people to show the sort of care and concern for others that they naturally have for themselves (cf. Matt 7:12).

13:10. Picking up the negative sense of the four commandments quoted from the Decalogue in v. 9, Paul abruptly declares, "Love does no wrong to a neighbor" and concludes, "Love, therefore, is the fulfillment of the law."[124] Love involves refraining from certain forms of behavior and positively seeking the welfare of others. The noun πλήρωμα in this context most likely expresses the sense of the cognate verb πεπλήρωκεν ("fulfills") at the end of v. 8. If love is the fulfillment of the law, the question is raised about the continuing relevance of the Ten Commandments. The teaching of Jesus and Paul's own exposition of the demands of love (12:9–21) suggest that "if love is cut free from any commandments, it easily dissolves into sentimentality, and virtually any course of action can be defended as 'loving.'"[125] The commandments given to Israel are a continuing guide to the dimensions and obligations of neighbor love, though Jesus and his apostles have much more to say about the practical expression of that love.[126]

13:11. Paul provides an eschatological challenge as a further motivation for godly living, returning to the emphasis of 12:2 on not being conformed to "this age." The expression καὶ τοῦτο εἰδότες τὸν καιρόν ("besides this, since you know the time") introduces additional information to heighten the force of what has just been said (cf. 5:3; 6:9; 1 Cor 15:58; 2 Cor 4:14; 5:6; Gal 2:16).[127] In other contexts, "the time" (τὸν καιρόν) clearly means the era that began with the coming of Christ and ends with his return (e.g., 3:26; 8:18; 11:5; 1 Cor 7:29; Eph 5:16; 1 Thess 5:1). Paul expected the Roman Christians to know that "the present time will eventually culminate in that future event, and that what happens in this age has significance

---

[124] When Jewett (*Romans*, 813–15) limits ἡ ἀγάπη to the hypothetical "love feast" shared by the Roman Christians, he shows that his reading of this passage has been too narrowly forced into an ecclesial context.

[125] Schreiner, *Romans*, 694.

[126] Cf. Cranfield, *Romans*, 2:679. Rosner (*Paul and the Law*, 159–205) shows how Paul treats the law as wisdom for our instruction (cf. Rom 15:4). See §1.4.

[127] Wallace (*Greek Grammar*, 631) notes that the participle here may function causatively ("since you know"). Jewett (*Romans*, 819) takes Paul to be referring to a hymn called "The Critical Time" that was known to the Romans. But this is highly speculative, especially when he relates it to "the Messiah's return in the eschatological love feast." Cf. Dunn, *Romans 9–16*, 793–94; Byrne, *Romans*, 398.

in the age to come."[128] But the clause beginning with ὅτι ("that" [not translated by CSB]) introduces an even more specific time reference, highlighting the urgency of the situation: "It is already the hour for you to wake up from sleep."[129] Sleep represents complacency and a lack of readiness for the approaching day (cf. Matt 25:5–13; Mark 13:33–37; 14:37–38; 1 Thess 5:3–7). So the person who is awake will be expectant, prayerful, morally alert, and prepared to meet the Lord. In the explanatory clause that follows, the temporal marker νῦν ("now") contributes to the sense of urgency: "because now our salvation is nearer than when we [first] believed."[130] Given the argument in 8:19–25, "our salvation" could be understood positively in terms of the bodily resurrection of believers in a renewed creation. But the negative aspect of deliverance from God's wrath should not be forgotten (2:5; 5:9; cf. 1 Thess 1:10). Paul does not give a specific time reference for these cosmic events and does not necessarily mean that Christ would return within the lifetime of his readers. His language simply suggests that, if the return of Christ is to happen at a particular point in time, "each hour that we live must bring us an hour nearer to it."[131]

13:12. An imminent end to the present age is further indicated by the assertion that "the night is nearly over" (προέκοψεν, "far advanced" [BDAG]) and (lit.) "the day draws near" (ἤγγικεν). This end expectation is variously reflected in the Gospels (e.g., Matt 24:33 = Mark 13:29; Luke 18:8a; John 16:16–33) and elsewhere

---

[128] Thompson, *Clothed with Christ*, 144. Thompson (141–60) argues for the influence of Jesus's teaching on Paul's argument in this passage, though the apostle is not "slavishly following dominical tradition." See §1.6.

[129] The reading ὑμᾶς ("you") is well attested and likely to be original. This was probably changed to ἡμᾶς ("us") in some manuscripts (𝔓[46vid] ℵ[c] D G Ψ etc.) to conform to ἡμῶν ("our") in the next clause. Some manuscripts omit the pronoun altogether (as does KJV). Cf. Metzger, *Textual Commentary*, 467.

[130] CSB ("when we first believed") reads the aorist ἐπιστεύσαμεν in an ingressive sense (cf. Wallace, *Greek Grammar*, 558–59). The pronoun ἡμῶν ("our") is more likely to go with ἡ σωτηρία ("salvation") than ἐγγύτερον (cf. NRSV, NASB, ESV, "nearer to us") because ἔγγυς in NT eschatological statements is never followed by a genitive object. Cf. Moo, *Romans*, 821n25.

[131] Cranfield, *Romans*, 2:682. However, Cranfield (ibid., 2:684) acknowledges that "in the first decades the natural tendency may perhaps have been to reckon more readily with a short, than with a long, interval." Putting it more strongly, we may say that if Paul had reckoned with a long interval he might have expressed himself differently. Cf. Dunn, *Romans 9–16*, 786–87.

in the NT (e.g., 1 Cor 7:29; 1 Thess 5:1–11; Heb 10:25; Jas 5:8–9; 1 Pet 4:7; 1 John 2:18; Rev 22:20).[132] The argument of Romans 1–11 is that Christ has done everything to defeat the powers of evil and bring his elect into the kingdom prepared for them. All that remains is for him to return to consummate God's plan of salvation (cf. 16:20). According to 2 Pet 3:9, the delay is an expression of God's patience since he does not want any to perish but "all to come to repentance." The logical consequence (οὖν, "therefore, so") is to "discard (ἀποθώμεθα) the deeds of darkness," and (lit.) "put on (ἐνδυσώμεθα) the weapons of light."[133] Christians should "dress" as those who belong to the coming day. We are to discard the "deeds" (ἔργα) that are characteristic of the present age (cf. 12:2) and put on the "weapons" (ὅπλα, as in 6:13) that God supplies so that we may stand and fight in his service (2 Cor 6:7; 10:3–5; Eph 6:11–17; 1 Thess 5:8).[134] These weapons belong to the light (possessive genitive) that comes from Christ himself (Eph 5:13–14). Put another way, the light of Christ is seen in this dark world when believers clothe themselves with his character and reflect that in their everyday resistance to evil (v. 14; cf. Matt 5:14–16).

13:13. Without a connective, this verse picks up and applies some of the imagery of the previous one. Paul exhorts his readers to "walk" (περιπατήσωμεν, as in 6:4) "as in the day" (ὡς ἐν ἡμέρᾳ). The metaphorical sense of "day" has already been established, and so the challenge is to live with reference to the coming age (cf. 1 Thess 5:4–8). Christians are to behave as those who belong already to God's new order, "whose lives are already illumined by the brightness of the coming day."[135] The adverb εὐσχημόνως means

---

[132] Moo (*Romans*, 821n20) observes the way Paul applies OT teaching about "the day of the Lord" to "the day of the Lord Jesus Christ."

[133] Instead of ἀποθώμεθα ("discard"), several witnesses read ἀποβαλώμεθα (e.g., 𝔓[46] D[*, 3] F G). The first verb is normal in formulas of renunciation in the NT (e.g., Eph 4:22, 25; Col 3:8) and so the harder reading rule should favor the second. Cf. Cranfield, *Romans*, 2:685n3; Jewett, *Romans*, 816. The difference in meaning is slight.

[134] Jewett (*Romans*, 823–34) compares the association of light with weapons in the War Scroll from Qumran. The expression "weapons of light" implies that believers should engage in the struggle between light and darkness, guided and empowered by the risen Lord. Albrecht Oepke ("ὅπλον κτλ., *TDNT* 5:292–94) shows that the plural ὅπλα is consistently used to represent weapons rather than armor.

[135] Cranfield, *Romans*, 2:687.

"decently" or "appropriately" (BDAG; cf. 1 Cor 14:40; 1 Thess 4:12). This word group was frequently used in Greek literature to describe conduct that conformed to publicly accepted standards.[136] For the Christian, however, appropriate conduct is measured with reference to Christ and the sort of teaching found in Rom 12–13. This means rejecting the way of life characteristic of the "night" or the present evil age. Three pairs of nouns give a summary picture of what Paul means: "Not in carousing and drunkenness; not in sexual impurity and promiscuity; not in quarreling and jealousy." The plurals in the first and second pairs (μὴ κώμοις καὶ μέθαις, μὴ κοίταις καὶ ἀσελγείαις) suggest frequent repetition.[137] Quarreling and jealousy can easily arise in Christian community life (1 Cor 3:3; 2 Cor 12:20; Gal 5:20), and Paul knew Christians could easily fall into various forms of licentiousness (1 Cor 5–6).

13:14. The strong adversative ἀλλά ("but") introduces a climactic restatement of the challenges in the preceding verses. "Put on the Lord Jesus Christ" (ἐνδύσασθε τὸν κύριον Ἰησοῦν Χριστόν) echoes the command at the end of v. 12 to "put on the armor of light" and explains how to "walk with decency" (v. 13). An indicative form of the same verb is used in Gal 3:27, where Paul claims that "as many of you as have been baptized into Christ have put on Christ." The imperative in the present context is a challenge to realize in everyday life the implications of that encounter: "to embrace again and again, in faith and confidence, in grateful loyalty and obedience, him to whom we already belong."[138] This means allowing our lives to be molded by his character and will. Significantly, the lordship of Jesus Christ is stressed here, as at other key points in the letter (1:3, 7; 4:24; 5:1, 11, 21; 6:23; 7:25; 8:39; 15:6, 30). The associated challenge to discard the deeds of darkness involves (lit.) making "no provision for the flesh for (the satisfaction of) its desires" (τῆς

---

[136] Cf. Jewett, *Romans*, 825.

[137] The plural κοίταις (lit., "beddings") implies multiple sexual encounters, while ἀσελγείαις means "sexual excesses" or "debaucheries" (cf. Otto Bauernfield, "ἀσέλγεια," *TDNT* 1:490). Winter ("Romans 12–15," 86–88) outlines the way Roman dinner parties commonly included all the behavior listed by Paul here.

[138] Cranfield, *Romans*, 2:688. Note the parallel with Paul's argument about dying and rising with Christ in 6:1–14. Dunn (*Romans 9–16*, 790) relates the concept of putting on Christ to Paul's Adam Christology. Cf. Schreiner, *Romans*, 700–701. We might also draw a link to the idea of obeying from the heart "that pattern of teaching to which you were handed over" (6:17).

σαρκὸς πρόνοιαν μὴ ποιεῖσθε εἰς ἐπιθυμίας).[139] As in 7:18, 25; 8:3–9, 12–13, "flesh" means human nature in rebellion against God (cf. Gal 5:16–26).

Bridge

Previous references to the Mosaic law raise questions about its role as "norm for personal and social ethics in the redefined people of God."[140] This passage indicates that Christians fulfill the law not by dutifully keeping its commands but by loving God and loving others. Nevertheless, the law gives both negative and positive guidelines about the practical expression of love. These are filled out and augmented in the teaching of Jesus and his apostles. Moreover, the command to "put on the Lord Jesus Christ" means acting as he did to demonstrate love to perfection (Eph 5:2). The related challenge is to "discard the deeds of darkness and put on the armor of light." Here the imminence of Christ's return and the expectation of living with him in his eternal kingdom is the motivation for living differently. So walking in love means adopting the pattern of life outlined in vv. 13–14, reflecting the character and will of the risen Lord Jesus. Paul's eschatological teaching means that believers have entered a new era of existence in which the conditions of the old age still hold sway, but the resources of the new age enable them to "live by its power."[141]

---

[139] CSB ("Don't make plans to gratify the desires of the flesh") does not allow for the possibility that πρόνοια may have the more comprehensive sense of "provision" (BDAG; NRSV; ESV). This would mean allowing no loopholes or opportunities for the flesh to satisfy its desires.

[140] Dunn, *Romans 9–16*, 775.

[141] Ibid., 792.

XIII. Judgment and Identity: Resolving Conflicts in the Christian Community (14:1–15:13)

A surprising array of interpretations has been offered to explain the conflict between the "weak" and the "strong" addressed in 14:1–15:7.[1] But the context offers important clues about the nature of Paul's argument. The previous chapter concludes with the challenge to fulfill the law by demonstrating love for others and to "put on the Lord Jesus Christ" (13:8–14). A celebration of Christ's ministry to unite "the circumcised" and "the Gentiles" in praise of God follows (15:8–13). In between these passages, Paul emphasizes the need for love rather than a judgmental attitude among believers (14:15) and reflects on what will promote peace and edification in the Roman situation (14:19). References to disputes about food and the observance of certain days in honor of the Lord suggest that some were concerned to keep aspects of the Jewish ceremonial law.

"The Jewish law was nowhere else more distinctive and determinative of social relationships than in the food laws and laws regarding sabbaths and festivals."[2] The use of clean-unclean language in 14:14–20 particularly points in this direction. A correspondence between 14:1–15:7 and 2:1–3:20 in the chiastic structure of the letter is also significant (cf. Introduction II.C.4). The theme of divine judgment and the identity of true believers is prominent in both sections. But Christ as Lord is now the key to everything (14:4, 6–8, 14, 15, 18; 15:3, 5, 6, 7). As in other defensive passages, biblical citations play a key role (14:11; 15:3, 9–12). An inclusion is formed between the opening challenge to welcome one another

[1] Cf. Cranfield, *Romans*, 2:690–97; Moo, *Romans*, 826–33; Schreiner, *Romans*, 703–10; Mark Reasoner, *The 'Strong' and the 'Weak': Romans 14:1–15:13 in Context*, SNTSMS 103 (Cambridge: Cambridge University, 1999), 5–22; William S. Campbell, "The Rule of Faith in Romans 12:1–15:13," and Mark Reasoner, "The Theology of Romans 12:1–15:13," in *Pauline Theology, Volume III: Romans*, 259–99. Kruse (*Romans*, 509–10) critiques the view of Kevin B. McCruden ("Judgment and Life for the Lord: Occasion and Theology of Romans 14:1–15:13," *Biblica* 86 [2005]: 229–44) that no actual conflict between the weak and the strong in Rome is envisaged in the text.

[2] Dunn, *Romans 9–16*, 795 (e.g., Let. Aris. 139, 142; Philo, *Mos.* 1.278). See more fully ibid., 799–802, 804–6, 810–12.

(14:1) and the charge to welcome one another "just as Christ also welcomed you, to the glory of God" (15:7).[3]

Romans 15:8–13 is a celebratory coda that forms an impressive conclusion to the exhortation in 14:1–15:7 while summarizing the argument about God's purpose for Jews and Gentiles outlined earlier in the letter. This coda also provides a transition to Paul's exposition of his role in God's plan for the nations in 15:14–21.[4] Romans 14:1–15:13 will be expounded under these headings:

A. Leaving Judgment to God (14:1–12)
B. Loving Those Who Think Differently (14:13–23)
C. Living to Glorify God (15:1–13)

A. Leaving Judgment to God (14:1–12)

[1]Accept anyone who is weak in faith, but don't argue about disputed matters. [2]One person believes he may eat anything, while one who is weak eats only vegetables. [3]One who eats must not look down on one who does not eat, and one who does not eat must not judge one who does, because God has accepted him. [4]Who are you to judge another's household servant? Before his own Lord he stands or falls. And he will stand, because the Lord is able to make him stand.

[5]One person judges one day to be more important than another day. Someone else judges every day to be the same. Let each one be fully convinced in his own mind. [6]Whoever observes the day, observes it for the honor of the Lord. Whoever eats, eats for the Lord, since he gives thanks to God; and whoever does not eat, it is for the Lord that he does not eat it, and he gives thanks to God. [7]For none of us lives for himself, and no one dies for himself. [8]If we live, we live for the Lord; and if we die, we die for the Lord. Therefore, whether we live or die, we belong to the Lord. [9]Christ died and returned to life for this: that he might be Lord over both the dead and the living. [10]But you, why do you judge your brother or sister? Or you, why do you despise your brother or sister? For we will all stand before the judgment seat of God. [11]For it is written,

[3] In my comment on 14:1, I explain why I think "welcome" is a better translation than "accept" in these verses.

[4] Cf. Schreiner, *Romans*, 703–4; and n. 61 below.

As I live, says the Lord,
every knee will bow to me,
and every tongue will give praise to God.

12 So then, each of us will give an account of himself to God.

Context

The challenge to "put on the Lord Jesus Christ" and fulfill the law by walking in love (13:8–14) is now applied to a particular problem in Rome. Although love is only explicitly mentioned in v. 15, the demands of love are set forth throughout the chapter. But the relationship of believers to Christ as Lord is shown to be the critical factor in their acceptance of one another as they struggle with issues of identity and judgment. As in 2:1–16, Paul's rebuke about judging others is followed by a reminder that all must face the judgment of God (14:3–4, 10–12). Both the "weak" and the "strong" are addressed in 14:1–12, but attention turns especially to the latter in 14:13–23.

Structure

A thematic exhortation introduces the new topic (v. 1, [lit.] "welcome the person who is weak in faith, but not for disputes over opinions"). The weak-strong distinction is first explained with reference to food, using a μέν . . . δέ contrast (v. 2, "One person believes he may eat anything, while one who is weak eats only vegetables"). Arguments about "disputed matters" are to be avoided because they provoke judgmental attitudes (v. 3a–b), but the fundamental reason for obeying the exhortation in v. 1 is (lit.) "because God has welcomed him" (v. 3c; cf. 15:7). This perspective is developed with the question, "Who are you to judge another's household servant?" (v. 4a).[5] The import of this question is explained with three affirmations about the relation of believers to their master (v. 4b–d).

The weak-strong distinction is further explained with reference to religious festivals, using another μέν . . . δέ contrast (v. 5a–b, [lit.] "One person judges one day to be more important than another day,

[5] Moo (*Romans*, 834–35) sees a "ring composition," with the first and third paragraphs (vv. 1–3, 10–12) stating in almost identical language Paul's main point and the middle paragraph (vv. 4–9) providing the theological foundation to his commands. However, the theological argument actually extends from v. 3c to v. 12.

but another judges every day [the same]"). The guiding principle emerges in a further exhortation (v. 5c, "Let each one be fully convinced in his own mind"). This is articulated by joining the matters of food and festivals together and explaining how both parties may act appropriately in relation to God (v. 6). The principle that (lit.) "none of us lives to himself, and no one dies to himself" (v. 7) is explained in relation to living and dying to the Lord and thus belonging to the Lord (v. 8). Christ's lordship over believers in life and death is said to be the purpose of his own death and resurrection (v. 9).

The rhetorical questions in v. 10 return to the challenge about judging or looking down on fellow believers (cf. vv. 3–4). The theological argument at this point is that "we will all stand before the judgment seat of God" (v. 10c). This is confirmed by a biblical citation in v. 11 and the conclusion that "each of us will give an account of himself to God" (v. 12).

Outline:

1. Avoid arguments about doubtful issues (vv. 1–4).
2. Act as those who truly belong to the Lord (vv. 5–12).

14:1. A progression in the argument from the last chapter is suggested by Paul's use of the conjunction δέ (not translated by CSB), which could mean "so" in this context.[6] The second-person plural imperative προσλαμβάνεσθε addresses the readers collectively, following ἐνδύσασθε (13:14, "put on"). Paul exhorts them to "extend a welcome to" (BDAG, NRSV, ESV), rather than simply "accept," (CSB, NIV) certain people. The meaning could be "welcome into your homes" or "welcome into the fellowship of the church in your homes" (cf. 16:5, 23).[7] A positive, hospitable attitude is encouraged toward those who think differently about the matters addressed here. Most likely, the singular expression τὸν ἀσθενοῦντα τῇ πίστει

[6] Runge (*Discourse Grammar*, 28–36) suggests the translation "so" where a moderate development in the narrative or argument is indicated. An adversative reading of δέ as "but" would be inappropriate here and in v. 10.

[7] Cf. Jewett, *Romans*, 835–36. Gerhard Delling (προσλαμβάνω κτλ.," *TDNT* 4:15) notes that this verb is only found in the middle in the NT, where it means "take to oneself" (Acts 17:5; 18:26 [people]; 27:33, 36 [food]) or "receive hospitably" (Acts 28:2; Phlm 17). The present tense of the imperative provides a general instruction rather than indicating something that must take place continuously.

(lit., "the one who is weak in faith") refers to a category of persons. This epithet was possibly "imposed on the subordinate group by an opposing group that was in a more dominant position."[8] However, since Paul identifies with the "strong" in 15:1, he tacitly approves of the distinction (see also 14:14, 20 comments). The behavior of "the weak in faith" is outlined essentially with reference to food and festivals (vv. 2–3, 5–6), suggesting that they were mainly Jewish Christians concerned to express their identity as the people of God by keeping aspects of OT ceremonial law. Wine may have been an issue because of its association with the libations of pagan sacrifice (cf. v. 21 comment). It is possible that some Gentile converts who were previously attached to Judaism shared the same concerns.[9]

In terms of the argument in vv. 13–23, "weak in faith" means weak with respect to what their faith in Christ will allow them to do.[10] A warning is attached to the positive imperative: (lit.) "(but) not for disputes about opinions" (μὴ εἰς διακρίσεις διαλογισμῶν).[11] Paul opposes welcoming people with the intention of arguing about the legitimacy of their convictions. The weak are not regarded by the apostle as a threat to the gospel or as destructive of Christian unity, though he does engage in "some further education toward greater maturity (vv. 14, 20)."[12] Judaizers sought to impose obedience to "the works of the law" as a matter of obligation (cf. Gal 2:11–16; 3:1–5; 5:1–11; 6:12–13). But for these believers it may have been

[8] Jewett, *Romans*, 834–35. Gustav Stählin ("ἀσθενής κτλ.," *TDNT* 1:490–93) shows that the terminology was used for physical illness, social or economic inferiority, and powerlessness of any kind. Jewett observes the way Horace (*Sat.* 1.9.67–72) also writes about an ethical-religious weakness as Paul does here.

[9] As noted previously, "the Jewish law was nowhere else more distinctive and determinative of social relationships than in the food laws and laws regarding sabbaths and festivals" (Dunn, *Romans 9–16*, 795). Cf. Let. Aris. 139, 142; Philo, *Mos.* 1.278; Tobin, *Paul's Rhetoric*, 25–44.

[10] Cranfield (*Romans*, 2:697–98) discusses different ways Paul uses the language of faith. He concludes that in 14:1–2, 22–23 the meaning is not "weakness in basic Christian faith but weakness in assurance that one's faith permits one to do certain things" (700). Dunn (*Romans 9–16*, 798) says "to be 'weak in faith' is to fail to trust God completely and without qualification," but the context supports Cranfield's more specific explanation. Cf. Moo, *Romans*, 836.

[11] Cranfield (*Romans*, 2:698, 701) argues that the expression means "not in order to pass judgments on his scruples." Moo (*Romans*, 837n45) discusses this possibility but concludes that the better alternative is "quarrels over disputed matters."

[12] Dunn, *Romans 9–16*, 799. Cf. Schreiner, *Romans*, 712–14.

simply a matter of conscience not to abandon practices that were personally significant for them. As vv. 2–3 indicate, they were also critical of others who did not have the same scruples.

14:2–3. Using a μέν . . . δέ contrast, Paul explains, "One person believes he may eat anything, while one who is weak eats only vegetables." The Jewish food laws did not require vegetarianism, but Jews in pagan contexts sometimes found that it was the simplest way to avoid eating meat that was not kosher (with the blood properly drained; cf. Lev 3:17; 7:26–27; 17:10–14; Acts 15:20, 29; 21:25) or that was tainted by association with idolatry.[13] Disputes over such practices could provoke judgmental attitudes and unhealthy divisions. So, "one who eats must not look down on one who does not eat, and one who does not eat must not judge one who does." The choice of verbs here is significant: the strong might "despise" or "look down on" the weak (μὴ ἐξουθενείτω) for their legalism, while the weak might "judge" the strong (μὴ κρινέτω) for their apparent laxity.[14] Paul's countercultural challenge reflects the radical teaching of Jesus about refusing to judge others (Matt 7:1–5; Luke 6:37; cf. Jas 4:11–12).

Greco-Roman education encouraged informed, critical judgments of issues and persons, and Jewish community life involved judging what was consistent with God's law. Paul allows for judgment in the process of church discipline (1 Cor 5:3–5, 12–13; cf. Matt 18:15–18) but opposes "censorious condemnation of others in day-to-day relations."[15] The fundamental reason for heeding his warning is (lit.) "for God has welcomed him" (προσελάβετο; cf. 14:1 comment; 15:7). This gospel perspective points to the danger of acting in a way that denies "the mercies of God" (12:1). God welcomes sinners into the fellowship of his people without regard for their

---

[13] Cf. Dunn, *Romans 9–16*, 801–2. Parallels with the situation addressed in 1 Cor 8 cannot be too closely drawn since there is no mention of meat offered to idols in Rom 14. See also my comments on vv. 20–21 below.

[14] Dunn (*Romans 9–16*, 802) notes that Paul's use of κρίνω ("judge") frequently has the sense of "condemn" (2:1, 3, 12, 27; 3:7; 14:3, 4, 10, 13, 22; 1 Cor 5:3, 12–13; 11:31; Col 2:16; 2 Thess 2:12).

[15] Thompson, *Clothed with Christ*, 167. Cf. Jewett, *Romans*, 839–41; 1 Cor 4:3–5; Jas 4:11–12. Jewett applies the teaching of this passage to "the Christian love feast," which he takes to be in Paul's mind here and in 12:13; 13:10. But there is no evidence that anything like the common meal in 1 Cor 11:17–34 took place in the Roman congregations or that they even met together in one place.

background, status, or performance. Believers should not treat one another in a way that denies this fellowship of grace.

14:4. Using the second-person singular to personalize his appeal (cf. 2:1–5, 17–27; 13:3–4), Paul specifically addresses anyone who is weak in faith and judges those who think and act differently (*σὺ τίς εἶ ὁ κρίνων*, "Who are you to judge?"). The one being criticized is pointedly described as "another's household servant" (*ἀλλότριον οἰκέτην*). The familial sense of this designation is an important aspect of the argument.[16] Applied to Christians, this means leaving the judgment of other believers to their Lord. The next clause (*τῷ ἰδίῳ κυρίῳ στήκει ἢ πίπτει* [lit., "before his own master he stands or falls"]) expresses a general principle about masters and servants that can be applied to the perseverance of believers in relation to their heavenly Lord (cf. 1 Cor 1:8; 10:12–13; 16:13; Phil 1:6; 1 Thess 3:8).[17] Paul's confident affirmation (*σταθήσεται δέ*, "And he will stand") is based on an assurance about God's power to do this: "Because the Lord is able to make him stand" (*δυνατεῖ γὰρ ὁ κύριος στῆσαι αὐτόν*). Here, as in vv. 6–12, "the Lord" is most likely the Lord Jesus (cf. v. 14), with parallel references to "God" pointing to his divinity. "By taking on themselves the role of judge the 'weak' are acting as if they are the ones who determine if the 'strong' are saved on the day of judgment."[18]

14:5. A further distinction between the weak and the strong is their attitude to religious festivals. This is explained with another contrast (*Ὃς μὲν [γὰρ] κρίνει ἡμέραν παρ' ἡμέραν, ὃς δὲ κρίνει πᾶσαν ἡμέραν*, [lit.], "for one person judges one day to be above another

---

[16] In a Roman context, *οἰκέτης* meant "member of the household" (BDAG), including everyone dependent on the master, such as children, slaves, freed persons, clients, and spouses. Cf. Jewett, *Romans*, 841–42. But the term could be used more narrowly for "house servant" or "domestic" (cf. Luke 16:13; Acts 10:7; 1 Pet 2:18).

[17] If *τῷ ἰδίῳ κυρίῳ* is understood as a dative of reference, the meaning is "it is in relation to his own master that he stands or falls." Cf. Dunn, *Romans 9–16*, 804; Jewett, *Romans*, 842. This phrase most naturally applies to the master-slave relationship here, but the secular meaning of *κύριος* gives way to the theological when the definite article is used ("the Lord"). Cf. Moo, *Romans*, 840–41.

[18] Schreiner, *Romans*, 718. Although *ὁ κύριος* ("the Lord") is well attested here (e.g. 𝔓[46] ℵ A B C), some manuscripts (e.g. D F G) read *ὁ θεός* ("God"), probably influenced by v. 3.

day, but another judges every day [the same]").[19] In this play on words, the judgment is not of people but of practices. Jewish festivals were probably uppermost in Paul's mind, but Roman feast days cannot be totally excluded.[20] Despite his generous attitude toward these differences, Paul's guiding principle challenges complacency (ἕκαστος ἐν τῷ ἰδίῳ νοῒ πληροφορείσθω, "Let each one be fully convinced in his own mind"). The same rare verb was used with reference to Abraham in 4:21 (cf. BDAG; Col 4:12). If minds are being renewed so that believers can discern God's will (12:2), both the weak and the strong must go on thinking about the issues that divide and become "fully convinced" about what is good and acceptable in the situation. The implications of this challenge are drawn out in vv. 13–23.

14:6. Three propositions explain how the weak and the strong may act appropriately in relation to God and one another. The first relates to festivals (ὁ φρονῶν τὴν ἡμέραν κυρίῳ φρονεῖ, [lit.] "the one setting his mind on the day sets his mind in relation to the Lord"). In 8:5–7 this verb and the cognate noun were used to describe mind-sets, and therefore patterns of life, determined by the flesh or the Spirit. Here the sense is simply "acknowledging the importance of" (BDAG), or "holding an opinion on" a particular day, because one has the mind-set of pleasing God (CSB: "Whoever observes the day, observes it for the honor of the Lord").[21] The second and third propositions return to the issue of eating or not eating in honor of the Lord. The common factor is giving thanks to God (εὐχαριστεῖ γὰρ τῷ θεῷ), which betrays the right mind-set (cf. 1:21 comment;

---

[19] The conjunction γάρ ("for") is found in א* A P and some minuscules, versions, and fathers, but it is missing from 𝔓[46] א[c] B D F G and other witnesses. The weight of this textual evidence suggests that it was a later addition. Syntactically, it is unnecessary in a sentence with the μέν . . . δέ construction. Cf. Cranfield, *Romans*, 2:704.

[20] Cf. Reasoner, *The 'Strong' and the 'Weak,'* 285. Jewett (*Romans*, 844) contends, "The argument is generic, incorporating a wide variety of possible viewpoints and practices in Paul's audience." But Dunn (*Romans 9–16*, 804–6) is much more convinced about a Jewish background to the dispute, especially concerning Sabbath keeping.

[21] Although there is no grammatical link between this clause and the preceding verse, the use of φρονῶν and φρονεῖ helps to explain what it means to be "fully convinced" about what is pleasing to God. The verb φρονέω can be used with the sense of developing an attitude based on careful thought (cf. Phil 2:5).

1 Cor 10:30; 1 Tim 4:3–5).[22] Eating with gratitude to God, whether vegetables alone or whatever is provided, expresses the belief that what you are doing is legitimate in his sight and honoring to him. The threefold use of *κυρίῳ* and the twofold use of *τῷ θεῷ* in this verse emphasize the Godward focus that is critical. If the weak and the strong can acknowledge the devotion of one another to the same Lord Jesus, "they will be able to share their meals with each other without insisting on uniformity."[23]

14:7–9. Paul grounds the preceding argument (*γάρ*, "for") in a principle: "None of us lives to himself, and no one dies to himself." The twofold use of *οὐδείς* ("no one") relates to Christians, not people in general, as the following conditional clauses show. Christians are those who live to please the Lord Jesus and die trusting in him. Therefore (*οὖν*), changing the grammatical construction, Paul concludes that in life and death "we belong to the Lord" (*τοῦ κυρίου ἐσμέν*). A further explanation (*γάρ*, "because" is not translated by CSB) takes us to the gospel basis for this claim. "For this" (*εἰς τοῦτο*), "Christ died and returned to life" (*Χριστὸς ἀπέθανεν καὶ ἔζησεν*), "that he might be Lord over both the dead and the living" (*ἵνα καὶ νεκρῶν καὶ ζώντων κυριεύσῃ*).[24] These decisive events established his saving lordship over believers. The unusual order of "the dead and the living" corresponds with the verbal sequence "died and came to life." So, if Christ rules over his people from life to death, "he certainly is the final arbiter in matters of calendar and diet."[25]

14:10. Paul draws this section of the chapter to a close with two second-person singular questions (cf. v. 4). As in v. 1, *δέ* ("but") could be translated "so" to mark a development in the argument. As in v. 3, Paul uses the verb *κρίνεις* ("judge") to define the attitude of

---

[22] Blessing God for food was a Jewish custom that Christians adopted (e.g., Acts 27:35; 1 Cor 10:16; 11:24; Did. 9.2–3; 10.1–4; Herm. Sim. 2.6; 5.1). Jewett (*Romans*, 846) also points to Greco-Roman practices in this regard.

[23] Jewett, *Romans*, 847.

[24] The aorist *ἔζησεν* has an ingressive sense here ("came to life"). The aorist *κυριεύσῃ* literally means "rule over." Against Cranfield (*Romans*, 2:708) and Moo (*Romans*, 845), no ingressive sense is required by the aorist subjunctive after *ἵνα*.

[25] Jewett, *Romans*, 849. The oldest and best-attested reading of v. 9a is *ἀπέθανεν καὶ ἔζησεν* (א* A B C etc.). Perhaps influenced by 1 Thess 4:14, some scribes sought to define more precisely the meaning of the unusual verb *ἔζησεν* by replacing it with the more usual *ἀνέστη* ("was raised," as in F G 629 vg etc.) or by different combinations of the three verbs. Cf. Metzger, *Textual Commentary*, 468; Jewett, *Romans*, 830.

the weak and ἐξουθενεῖς ("despise" [v. 3, "look down on"]) to define the attitude of the strong. The singular is used again for rhetorical impact, even though two groups are being addressed. At one level, the apostle wants them to reflect on their familial relationship (τὸν ἀδελφόν σου, "your brother or sister"; cf. v. 4). At another level he wants them to recall that, weak or strong, "we will all stand before the judgment seat of God" (cf. 2:5–16; 2 Cor 5:10 ["Christ"]).[26]

14:11–12. The final assertion in v. 10 is reinforced with a citation from Scripture ("for it is written"). The opening words ("As I live, says the Lord") are taken from Isa 49:18, but the bulk of the citation is from Isa 45:23 ("Every knee will bow to me, and every tongue will give praise to God"). The oath formula, "as I live," guarantees what is promised because the living God undertakes to make it happen (cf. Num 14:21, 28; Jer 22:24; Ezek 5:11). CSB has rightly taken ἐξομολογήσεται (BDAG, "confess, admit") to mean "praise," because that is the meaning of the verb in parallel with other terms in 15:8–11. As in Isa 45:23, bending the knee and giving public praise to God is an acknowledgment of his sovereignty. In Rom 10:9–13; Phil 2:11 this devotion is explicitly to the risen Lord Jesus. But it follows (ἄρα [οὖν], "so [then]") from the reference to "every knee" and "every tongue" that each believer (ἕκαστος ἡμῶν, "each of us") "will give an account of himself (to God)" (περὶ ἑαυτοῦ λόγον δώσει [τῷ θεῷ]).[27] As in 2:6–11, the genuineness of faith will be revealed in the lives of those who profess to know God. Since God in Christ is the judge of all (2:16), there is no room for believers to look down on or judge one another.

---

[26] The best attested reading is θεοῦ ("of God"), but a number of correctors, later manuscripts, and versions read Χριστοῦ ("of Christ"), which appears to be an assimilation to 2 Cor 5:10. A comparison of these texts shows that Paul saw no essential difference between the judgment of God and of Christ. Cf. Dunn, *Romans 9–16*, 809.

[27] There are two textual problems in this verse, and in both cases the shorter reading is likely to be the original. The external evidence for ἄρα ("so") is good (B D* F G P* etc.), but the evidence for ἄρα οὖν ("so then") is also strong (א A C D² L Pᶜ etc.). Although τῷ θεῷ ("to God") is well attested (א A C D L P etc.), it is omitted by B F G etc. Copyists may have added the phrase to clarify the reference of the verb. Cf. Metzger, *Textual* Commentary, 469; Jewett, *Romans*, 831.

Bridge

The challenge of this passage is to welcome into your fellowship those with different religious customs, but "not for disputes over opinions." Christians continue to differ about issues such as abstaining from meat or from wine and observing the Sabbath or other holy days. But the focus in contemporary debates often goes beyond matters related to the Mosaic law.[28] Paul's challenge is based on the fact that God has graciously welcomed a diversity of people into relationship with himself. This makes each believer a "household slave," individually responsible to the Lord Jesus for his or her convictions and practices. Everything must be for the honor and glory of God, expressing gratitude to him for his saving grace, and acknowledging ultimate accountability to the crucified and resurrected Lord. Moreover, our relationship with God makes us brothers and sisters (vv. 10, 13, 15) who should not judge or look down on one another but love and encourage one another in devotion to Christ. Further reflection on the gospel may challenge the legitimacy or continuing helpfulness of certain practices, but Paul warns about the way such challenges are expressed to one another. We are ultimately accountable to God as judge for the way we behave, not to one another.

B. Loving Those Who Think Differently (14:13–23)

> [13]Therefore, let us no longer judge one another. Instead decide never to put a stumbling block or pitfall in the way of your brother or sister. [14]I know and am persuaded in the Lord Jesus that nothing is unclean in itself. Still, to someone who considers a thing to be unclean, to that one it is unclean. [15]For if your brother or sister is hurt by what you eat, you are no longer walking according to love. Do not destroy, by what you eat, someone for whom Christ died. [16]Therefore, do not let your good be slandered, [17]for the kingdom of God is not eating and drinking, but righteousness,

[28] Contemporary Christians divide over patterns of devotion and corporate worship, liturgical texts, congregational music, leadership styles, engagement with social and political issues, and various lifestyle choices. Biblical warrants may be given, and positions may be strongly defended, but often these are matters of personal preference arising from past experiences or church tradition. Cf. Moo, *Romans*, 881–82.

peace, and joy in the Holy Spirit. [18]Whoever serves Christ in this
way is acceptable to God and receives human approval.
[19]So then, let us pursue what promotes peace and what builds
up one another. [20]Do not tear down God's work because of food.
Everything is clean, but it is wrong to make someone fall by what
he eats. [21]It is a good thing not to eat meat, or drink wine, or do
anything that makes your brother or sister stumble. [22]Whatever
you believe about these things, keep between yourself and God.
Blessed is the one who does not condemn himself by what he
approves. [23]But whoever doubts stands condemned if he eats, because his eating is not from faith, and everything that is not from
faith is sin.

Context

This passage continues the warnings of the previous one, as Paul tells both the weak and the strong not to judge one another but then focuses on the behavior of the latter. The challenge is not to put a stumbling block or pitfall in the way of a brother or sister who considers certain foods to be unclean. Walking in love may mean refraining from eating meat, or drinking wine, or doing "anything that makes your brother or sister stumble" (v. 21). When Paul talks about serving the Messiah in this way and building up one another (vv. 18–19), he addresses both parties again. But the final emphasis of the passage is on the behavior of the strong that may impact the weak (vv. 20–23). This prepares for the next section with its emphasis on pleasing others for their good and glorifying God with a united mind and voice (15:1–13).

Structure

With a clear link to the preceding passage (οὖν, "therefore"), Paul repeats his warning about judging fellow believers (v. 13a, "let us no longer judge one another"). Using the same verb, he asks the strong to "decide" (κρίνατε) never to put a stumbling block or pitfall in the way of the weak (v. 13b). This warning is supported by Paul's solemn declaration of confidence that "nothing is unclean in itself" (v. 14). Such a radical challenge to the Jewish way of thinking about food echoes the teaching of Jesus and effectively endorses the convictions of the strong. Yet Paul concedes that "to someone who considers a thing to be unclean, to that one it is unclean." This means that it is possible to hurt a fellow Christian by what you eat (v. 15), indicating that "you are no longer walking according to love." The seriousness of this situation is emphasized with the warning not to "destroy, by what you eat, someone for whom Christ died."

A second use of the conjunction οὖν ("therefore") introduces the further idea that such behavior may become a cause of slander from outsiders (v. 16). "For" (γάρ) eating and drinking without considering the impact on a fellow believer ignores the relational implications of the kingdom of God (v. 17). "For" (γάρ not translated by CSB) whoever serves the Messiah by displaying kingdom values is "acceptable to God and receives human approval" (v. 18).

A third use of οὖν in the emphatic formula ἄρα οὖν (v. 19, "so then") introduces the positive encouragement to both parties to pursue "what promotes peace" and "what builds up one another." Three verses in a row without connectives explain the implications of this exhortation for the strong. First, they are not to "tear down God's work because of food" (v. 20a). Paul repeats v. 14a in an abbreviated form (v. 20b, "everything is clean") but warns that "it is wrong to make someone fall by what he eats." Second, they are to acknowledge, "It is a good thing not to eat meat, or drink wine, or do anything that makes your brother or sister stumble" (v. 21). Third, they are urged to keep whatever they believe about these things between themselves and God (v. 22a–b). Paul concludes this sequence by pronouncing a blessing on the person "who does not condemn himself by what he approves" (v. 22c). But "whoever doubts stands condemned if he eats, because his eating is not from faith" (v. 23 a–b). The reason for this is that "everything that is not from faith is sin" (v. 23c).

Outline:[29]

1. Care for the weak (vv. 13–15).
2. Consider the impact on outsiders (vv. 16–18).
3. Promote peace and edification (vv. 19–23).

14:13. There are three balanced clauses in this warning, setting the agenda for what follows. The first is linked to the preceding exhortation by the conjunction οὖν ("therefore") and provides a succinct summary of vv. 10c–12. Previously, the warning against

[29] Following Dunn, *Romans 9–16*, 816, who points to the roughly chiastic structure of the paragraph. Cf. Thompson, *Clothed with Christ*, 200–207.

judging was associated with the "weak in faith" (vv. 3, 4, 10), but now it is applied to both parties since Paul includes himself in the exhortation (μηκέτι ἀλλήλους κρίνωμεν, "let us no longer judge one another"). The second clause begins with the strong adversative ἀλλά ("but") and uses the same verb with a different nuance (τοῦτο κρίνατε μᾶλλον [lit., "instead decide this"]; cf. v. 5; 1 Cor 2:2; 7:37; 2 Cor 2:1). Paul specifically addresses the strong in what follows.[30] The third clause indicates that they must decide "never to place a stumbling block or pitfall in the way of a brother" (τὸ μὴ τιθέναι πρόσκομμα τῷ ἀδελφῷ ἢ σκάνδαλον). This recalls the teaching of Jesus in the Synoptic Gospels, where the σκάνδαλον word group is found in warnings about hindering belief (Matt 18:6–7; Mark 9:42; Luke 17:1–2).[31] In 9:33 (citing LXX Isa 8:14) λίθον προσκόμματος ("a stone to stumble over") was used in parallel with πέτραν σκανδάλου ("a rock to trip over") to describe how many Israelites stumbled over the Messiah in their pursuit of the law for righteousness (cf. 11:9 [σκάνδαλον], citing LXX Ps 68:23–24). Both words are used together again in 14:13 to identify a danger facing those who have now turned to Christ.[32] If the strong put pressure on the weak to eat meat, the latter may falter or fail in their faith.

14:14. Without a connective Paul introduces a theological conviction he would like all his readers to share.[33] He does this emphatically, using two verbs in the perfect tense with present meanings (οἶδα καὶ πέπεισμαι, "I know and am persuaded"; cf. 8:38; 15:14). The phrase ἐν κυρίῳ Ἰησοῦ could refer to what Paul perceives to be generally

[30] Cf. Dunn, *Romans 9–16*, 817. Jewett (*Romans*, 856–57) argues that both the weak and the strong continue to be addressed here. But the focus in vv. 14–18 is clearly on the strong, and the call for mutual edification does not come until v. 19.

[31] Cf. Dunn, *Romans 9–16*, 818. The actual form of Paul's admonition may have been provided by LXX Lev 19:14 (cf. Thompson, *Clothed with Christ*, 174–84).

[32] According to BDAG, σκάνδαλον literally means "a device for catching something alive, a trap," and figuratively "an action or circumstance that leads one to act contrary to a proper course of action or set of beliefs, temptation to sin, enticement to apostasy, false belief." The noun πρόσκομμα can either refer to the act of stumbling or something that causes people to stumble. "Although the words related to stumbling were broadly used in Greco-Roman culture, the metaphorical sense of religious offense is distinctively Jewish" (Jewett, *Romans*, 857).

[33] Dunn (*Romans 9–16*, 818) suggests that Paul's rhetoric would have the double effect of "demonstrating his complete conviction about the cleanness of all foods to 'the weak' and of making 'the strong' more amenable to the teaching which follows."

true in the light of his relationship with the Lord Jesus ("in the Lord Jesus"; cf. Gal 5:10; Phil 2:24; 2 Thess 3:4). But ὅτι ("that") could be introducing a specific reference to the teaching of Jesus.[34] The content of his conviction is simply stated (οὐδὲν κοινὸν δι' ἑαυτοῦ, "nothing is unclean in itself"; cf. Mark 7:18–23; Matt 15:10–11, 15–20). In the context of his discussion about food, κοινός ("common") means "ritually unclean" (cf. 1 Macc 1:47, 62; Mark 7:2; Acts 10:14, 28; 11:8). The division between clean (edible) foods and unclean (inedible) foods set out in Lev 11 and Deut 14 "corresponded to the division between holy Israel and the Gentile world."[35] As Paul explains in 1 Cor 6:11, cleansing and sanctification may now be found in a relationship with God through Christ and the Spirit (2 Thess 2:13; Acts 15:9; Heb 9:13–14; 10:10; 13:12; 1 Pet 1:2, 22). However, a qualifying clause beginning with εἰ μή ("except" [CSB, "still"]) allows that "to someone who considers a thing to be unclean, to that one it is unclean" (τῷ λογιζομένῳ τι κοινὸν εἶναι, ἐκείνῳ κοινόν).[36] Such a person still thinks it is necessary to keep the ceremonial aspects of the law to identify as one of God's holy people.

14:15. This verse draws out the implications of the warning in v. 13c, using related terms and making clear that the problem is "what you eat" (διὰ βρῶμα, [lit.] "because of food"]). The issue is not what is consumed in private but what is eaten in the presence of "anyone who is weak in faith" (v. 1).[37] Paul personalizes the potential offense by using the second-person singular again (εἰ ὁ ἀδελφός σου λυπεῖται, "if your brother [or sister] is hurt"; cf. vv. 4, 10). He returns to the theme of love that dominated his argument in

---

[34] Cf. Cranfield, *Romans*, 2:712–13; Jewett, *Romans*, 859. Thompson (*Clothed with Christ*, 194–99) argues that Paul assumed knowledge of the dominical tradition by the strong in Rome, but he corrects its use "in order to lead his readers into the way of Christ—walking in love" (see v. 15).

[35] Gordon J. Wenham, "The Theology of Unclean Food," *EvQ* 53 (1981): 11. Cf. Dunn, *Romans 9–16*, 818–19. These laws were meant to aid Israel in maintaining her holy status and fulfilling God's covenant purpose (Exod 19:5–6). Dunn (ibid., 818–19) notes the importance of the purity laws for Second Temple Judaism.

[36] Jewett (*Romans*, 860) rightly observes that λογιζομένῳ implies an intellectually well-grounded belief (cf. 3:28; 8:18), not merely a "subjective reaction."

[37] Jewett (*Romans*, 860) restricts this to "the love-feast" he envisages being shared by the Roman Christians, but see n. 15 above. The conjunction γάρ ("for") links with v. 13c, not with v. 14, since Paul is now teasing out what it means to "put a stumbling block or pitfall in your brother's way."

12:9–21; 13:8–10 and is implicit in 14:3–4, 10 (οὐκέτι κατὰ ἀγάπην περιπατεῖς, "You are no longer walking according to love"). Jesus's teaching that "nothing is unclean in itself" must be applied in the light of his emphasis on the absolute priority of loving one another. Hurting a brother or sister in this context means more than causing grief or emotional pain. The warning that follows ("Do not destroy, by what you eat, someone for whom Christ died") implies bringing about his or her spiritual ruin (μὴ ἀπόλλυε, cf. 1 Cor 8:11).[38] As vv. 20–23 suggest, someone with the liberty to eat anything may put pressure on another to eat in a way that is "not from faith" and thus cause them to stand condemned before God.[39] The expression "for whom Christ died" (ὑπὲρ οὗ Χριστὸς ἀπέθανεν) "confers upon the brother or sister a preciousness that simply overwhelms all selfish considerations (2 Cor 5:14–17)."[40]

14:16. The inferential particle οὖν ("therefore") signals a development in the argument based on what has gone before. The new idea for the readers to consider is the impact that their actions may have on outsiders: "Do not let your good be slandered" (μὴ βλασφημείσθω ὑμῶν τὸ ἀγαθόν; cf. 1 Cor 10:30). Paul uses the same verb in 2:24 (citing Isa 52:5) to identify the way God's name was "blasphemed" among the nations because of Israel's behavior. In 3:8 he reports how opponents slanderously misrepresented his gospel teaching. In the present context, "your good" probably refers to the gospel and its implications, not just to the liberty of the strong (cf. 1 Tim 6:1; Titus 2:5).[41] The preceding mention of "someone for whom Christ died" (v. 15) points in this direction, as does the following verse.

---

[38] Schreiner (*Romans*, 733–35) notes that several words in the context point to eschatological judgment and ultimate ruin: "The very salvation of the 'weak' was at stake." Faith is destroyed if the moral norms regarded as consistent with faith are violated. Cf. Reasoner, *The 'Strong' and the 'Weak,'* 84.

[39] Cf. Cranfield, *Romans*, 2:714–15; Moo, *Romans*, 854–55. Like Moo, Jewett (*Romans*, 861–62) talks about the strong urging the weak to "violate their conscience," although that terminology is not used here. Against Moo and Jewett, the present tense of the imperative μὴ ἀπόλλυε provides a general instruction that is not necessarily continuous ("do not destroy"). Cf. Campbell, *Verbal Aspect and Non-Indicative Verbs*, 91–95.

[40] Byrne, *Romans*, 416. The strong are to display toward the weak "the same kind of self-sacrificing love which they, themselves once 'weak' (5:6), received from Christ."

[41] Cf. Cranfield, *Romans*, 2:715–17; Dunn, *Romans 9–16*, 821. Jewett (*Romans*, 862) limits "your good" to "the freedom of the strong" and argues that the slander

14:17. Paul supports the preceding warning (γάρ, "for") with a profound statement about the kingdom of God. Although Jesus often used this term, the apostle only occasionally employs it, mostly with a future reference (1 Cor 6:9, 10; 15:50; Gal 5:21; Eph 5:5; Col 4:11; 1 Thess 2:12; 2 Thess 1:5; cf. 1 Cor 15:24). Here, however, it denotes a present reality that he presumes his readers will know about (cf. 1 Cor 4:20). The evidence for God's rule in the lives of his people is "righteousness, peace, and joy in the Holy Spirit." Given the meaning of such terms earlier in the letter, it is likely that Paul refers to the right relationship with God that is established through faith in Christ, bringing peace with God, and the gift of the Holy Spirit (5:1–5). These are the essential blessings of life in the kingdom of God. The reality of this new relationship is demonstrated in the corporate life of believers (12:9–21; 15:13). Joy in Christian relationships is fostered by the Spirit (cf. Gal 5:22–26).[42]

14:18. Further support for the warning in v. 16 is given in this sentence. The conjunction γάρ ("for") is used again, as in v. 17, but is not translated by CSB. Serving the Messiah "in this way" or "in this matter" (ἐν τούτῳ) means reflecting the kingdom realities described in v. 17[43] and not allowing the good of the gospel to be slandered by anyone (v. 16). This service (δουλεύειν, cf. 1:1; 6:16; 7:6; 12:11) is another example of the "service" (12:1, λατρεία) that is "acceptable to God" (εὐάρεστος τῷ θεῷ), since it is determined by what God has done for us in Christ (cf. §2.6). Rather than bringing shame on the gospel, it is also the sort of behavior that may be (lit.) "approved by people" (καὶ δόκιμος τοῖς ἀνθρώποις [CSB, "receives human approval"]). The love of Christians toward one another will commend them and their Lord to unbelieving outsiders (cf. 12:17b ["Give careful thought to do what is honorable in everyone's eyes"]; John 13:35).

14:19. A new stage in the argument is signaled by the use of two conjunctions together (Ἄρα οὖν, "So then"). First, the encouragement

may come from those inside and outside the church (cf. Moo, *Romans*, 855–56).

[42] It is most likely that ἐν πνεύματι ἁγίῳ ("in the Holy Spirit") relates specifically to χαρά ("joy") rather than to all the preceding nouns (cf. 1 Thess 1:6; Gal 5:22). Paul is not thinking of righteousness as a moral quality here or peace as a state of mind made possible by the Spirit. Cf. Cranfield, *Romans*, 2:718–19.

[43] Cranfield (*Romans*, 2:719–20) argues that the singular expression here views the three items righteousness, peace, and joy in the Holy Spirit as forming a single whole.

to "pursue what promotes peace" (τὰ τῆς εἰρήνης διώκωμεν) builds on what was said in v. 17.[44] God's gift of peace through the gospel must impact how believers relate to one another and to outsiders (12:18; cf. Heb 12:14; 1 Pet 3:11). Edification is the new idea in this verse (καὶ τὰ τῆς οἰκοδομῆς τῆς εἰς ἀλλήλους, "and what builds up one another"), although the notion has been implicit in the argument so far (vv. 1–18). The noun οἰκοδομή is used again in 15:2 and the related verb in 15:20. The idea of God's "building" a new people for himself is foundational for understanding Paul's application of this terminology (e.g., Jer 24:6; 31:4; 33:7 [Gentiles are included in Jer 12:16]). Jesus affirms that he will build or establish this new community (Matt 16:18), and Paul sees himself as the Lord's agent continuing this work (15:15–21; cf. 1 Cor 3:9; 2 Cor 10:8; 12:19; 13:10). Building the church involves founding, maintaining, and maturing Christian congregations. Believers have an important part to play in the process as they minister God's truth to one another in love (1 Cor 14:3–5, 12, 17, 26; 1 Thess 5:11; Eph 4:12, 16). Even in matters of food and drink, they have the opportunity to "build up one another" and so "build" or strengthen the church (1 Cor 8:1, 10; 10:23). Love and edification belong together in Paul's thought.[45]

14:20. Three verses in a row without connectives explain the implications of the preceding exhortation for the strong. Paul first uses the forceful second-person singular to warn, "Do not tear down" (μὴ κατάλυε). This is the opposite of "build up" (v. 19; Gal 2:18; cf. 2 Cor 10:8; 13:10). "God's work" in this context could refer both to the spiritual life of individuals and to the believing community as a body.[46] Such destruction can even occur because of seemingly trivial matters such as food (ἕνεκεν βρώματος, "because of food"). So Paul

---

[44] Jewett (*Romans*, 853–54) argues in favor of reading the indicative διώκομεν ("we pursue"), which has better textual support (א A B G^{gr} P etc.) than the hortatory subjunctive διώκωμεν ("let us pursue"; C D Ψ 33 81 etc.). Elsewhere in Romans the phrase Ἄρα οὖν is always followed by the indicative (5:18; 7:3, 25; 8:12; 9:16, 18; cf. 14:12). However, Metzger (*Textual Commentary*, 469) argues that the context (with imperatives in vv. 13, 20) points to the hortatory subjunctive as the original, even though the indicative would be the harder reading in this sequence.

[45] Cf. David G. Peterson, *Encountering God Together* (Phillipsburg: P&R, 2013), 43–58. See §2.5.

[46] Cranfield (*Romans*, 2:722) rightly notes, "The building up of the Church and the building up of the individual members are two aspects of the same process." But he unnecessarily narrows the meaning of "God's work" to individuals in v. 20 (723).

repeats v. 14a in a modified form (πάντα μὲν καθαρά, "everything is clean").[47] Then he emphatically contrasts this positive statement with a warning (ἀλλὰ κακὸν τῷ ἀνθρώπῳ τῷ διὰ προσκόμματος ἐσθίοντι, "but it is wrong to make someone fall by what he eats"). The genitive expression διὰ προσκόμματος identifies attendant circumstances (cf. 2:27; 4:11), meaning that the person eats "in such a way as results in the presence of a stumbling-block."[48] The flow of the argument suggests that this refers to the strong Christian who eats nonkosher meat in a way that causes the weak Christian to eat and so stumble.[49]

14:21. The positive alternative is now presented. The word κάλος ("good") is in the emphatic position at the beginning of the sentence, making a contrast with κακός ("wrong") in v. 20. Paul says, "It is a good thing not to eat meat, or drink wine, or do anything that makes your brother or sister stumble."[50] Previous references to food are now specifically related to the eating of "meat" (κρέα). For the first time in this chapter Paul also mentions the drinking of wine. Since this precedes the more general "or do anything that makes your brother or sister stumble" (μηδὲ ἐν ᾧ ὁ ἀδελφός σου προσκόπτει), it is possible that he is speaking generally rather than identifying a specific problem he knows to exist in the Roman situation. Another possibility is that he alludes to a Jewish pattern of asceticism that involved abstinence from eating meat and drinking wine in Gentile contexts (cf. Dan 1:10–16; 10:3; T. Jud. 15:4; T. Reu. 1:9–10). Wine had a sacred significance in Greco-Roman culture, and so when

[47] The wording in v. 14 is οὐδὲν κοινὸν δι' ἑαυτοῦ ("nothing is unclean in itself"). The statement in v. 20 is closer to the comment at the end of Mark 7:19 (καθαρίζων πάντα τὰ βρώματα, [lit.] "making all foods clean"]) and Luke 11:41 (πάντα καθαρὰ ὑμῖν ἐστιν, "everything is clean for you"). Cf. LXX Gen 7:3, 8; Lev 11:47; 14:4.

[48] Cf. Cranfield, *Romans*, 2:699, 723–24. Dunn (*Romans 9–16*, 826) translates "eats with offense" and thinks the expression could also apply to the weak person stumbling by following the example of the strong. Cf. Byrne, *Romans*, 421–22.

[49] Winter ("Romans 12–15," 90–91) argues that the privilege of buying kosher meat may have been suspended with the banning of Jewish and Jewish-Christian agitators from Rome by Claudius in AD 49. This could have forced "the weak in faith" to eat only vegetables (v. 2).

[50] The reading προσκόπτει (א[1] A C etc.) is likely to be the original. Many manuscripts (א[2] B D F G etc.) add ἢ σκανδαλίζεται ἢ ἀσθενεῖ ("or scandalize or weaken"). These additions may have been influenced by 1 Cor 8:11–13. The original reading in א is λυπεῖται ("grieve"), which is picked up by P (λυπεῖται ἢ σκανδαλίζεται ἢ ἀσθενεῖ, "grieve or scandalize or weaken"). Cf. Jewett, *Romans*, 854.

Jews abstained, it may have been to avoid association with pagan ceremonies.[51] Whatever the historical context may have been, the principle Paul articulates is that those who have liberty in these matters should restrain themselves in the presence of those who have reservations.

14:22. Paul continues to address the strong, using a second-person singular form of address again (cf. vv. 4, 10, 15). This is the third verse in a row without a formal link to what precedes it. The rhetorical effect is to present each item in the sequence as an outworking of the exhortation in v. 19. Here is a further expression of what it means to pursue peace and edification. The statement *σὺ πίστιν [ἣν] ἔχεις* ("the faith that you have") is rendered, "Whatever you believe about these things" by CSB.[52] The imperative "keep between yourself before God" (*κατὰ σεαυτὸν ἔχε ἐνώπιον τοῦ θεοῦ*) is not a call to be secretive about what you believe. As in vv. 1–2, "faith" is used in the special sense of "confidence that one's faith allows one to do a particular thing."[53] So the meaning in context is "If a weak brother is going to be hurt by one's giving outward expression to one's freedom, then one should be content with the inward experience of it, of which God is the only witness."[54] A beatitude (*μακάριος*, cf. Matt 5:3–11; Rom 4:7–8) commends the blessedness of the person "who does not condemn himself by what he approves" (*ὁ μὴ κρίνων ἑαυτὸν ἐν ᾧ δοκιμάζει*). Contextually, Paul's

---

[51] Cf. Jewett, *Romans*, 868–69. Jewett draws attention to Lev 10:9; Ezek 44:21; Jer 35:6–7 as possible influences on Jewish thinking in this regard. He observes that there were Greco-Roman patterns of asceticism, but nowhere outside Jewish and Christian sources is abstention from eating meat linked with the *κοινός* ("unclean") issue, as in this passage. Drinking wine is not forbidden in the OT. It is regarded as a blessing from God in Deut 7:13; 11:14, and it became an established part of the Passover ritual (cf. Mark 14:23–25 par.).

[52] The relative *ἥν* ("that") is well attested (א A B C etc.), and its omission in the great mass of witnesses is explicable as an attempted stylistic improvement. Without the relative, a statement can be read ("You have faith"), or a question ("Do you have faith?"). Cf. Cranfield, *Romans*, 2:726; Jewett, *Romans*, 854.

[53] Cranfield, *Romans*, 2:726. Dunn (*Romans 9–16*, 827) opposes this view, arguing that the reference is simply to trust in God, which varies in strength from believer to believer. But see n. 56 below.

[54] Cranfield, *Romans*, 2:726. Moo (*Romans*, 862) says, "This will mean that the 'strong' are not to brag about their convictions before the 'weak' and, especially, that they are not to propagandize the 'weak.'" Schreiner (*Romans*, 732) takes it that the strong "should abstain from food and drink that grieves the 'weak' at public meals."

focus here is on the strong Christian who does not condemn himself "by allowing himself to insist on the outward exercise of his liberty, to the ruin of his weak fellow-Christian."[55]

14:23. Attention now turns to the weak Christian "who doubts" (ὁ δὲ διακρινόμενος, cf. 4:20). The expression "if he eats" (ἐὰν φάγῃ) narrows the meaning of doubt to the context, where the weak in faith do not believe that they can eat things that are unclean (vv. 2, 14, 22). If such a person does eat, he or she stands "condemned" (κατακέκριται) (lit.) "because it is not from faith" (ὅτι οὐκ ἐκ πίστεως). The phrase ἐκ πίστεως ("from faith") recalls Paul's characteristic way of defining a saving response to the gospel (1:17; 3:26, 30; 4:16; 5:1; 9:30, 32; 10:6). It is repeated in the general maxim that concludes this section of the argument (πᾶν δὲ ὃ οὐκ ἐκ πίστεως ἁμαρτία ἐστίν, "and everything that is not from faith is sin"). Although "faith" may be broadly defined as "creaturely dependence, which is man's proper attitude and response to God,"[56] Paul will be thinking more specifically about the response to God in Christ made possible through the preaching of the gospel. Every conviction and action that is inconsistent with an individual's professed faith is "sin" in that it is an expression of human presumption.[57]

The doxology found at 16:25–27 in a broad and ancient range of manuscripts (𝔓[61vid] ℵ B C D etc.) is also printed here in some texts (A P 5 33 104 arm). In other texts and versions (L Ψ *Byz* and elsewhere) the doxology only occurs here. This variation is apparently

[55] Cranfield, *Romans*, 2:727. Cf. Schreiner, *Romans*, 732–33. As in vv. 3,10, 13, the verb κρίνειν is used with the connotation "judge, condemn." As in 1:28; 2:18, δοκιμάζειν means "approve" or "judge to be good." Cranfield suggests that the person could be condemning himself in the sense of "bringing God's judgment on himself" (2:727).

[56] Dunn, *Romans 9–16*, 829. Dunn argues that Cranfield's reference to the "faith" issue articulated in the passage (*Romans*, 2:728–29) misses the point. In the final analysis, however, the maxim must be applicable to the context. Dunn also observes that interpretations in terms of "conscience" obscure what Paul is saying.

[57] Schreiner (*Romans*, 738–39) insists on the universality of Paul's concluding maxim and affirms that Augustine was right in claiming that any act done apart from faith is sin. However, Byrne (*Romans*, 419) warns that many mundane actions do not proceed from faith and are not sin. The universality of the maxim should be interpreted in terms of acting or not acting in accordance with one's faith.

the result of the letter being sent in different forms to different destinations.[58]

Bridge

Paul presents a remarkably open view of church here, "whose integrity can only be preserved when each group takes responsibility for the growth towards maturity of the other side."[59] The apostle had earlier insisted that Christians are "not under the law but under grace" (6:14). They are "released from the law" so as to serve "in the newness of the Spirit and not in the old letter of the law" (7:6). So he draws out the implications of that claim with regard to the ritual law: for those in Christ, "nothing is unclean in itself" (v. 14a) and "everything is clean" (v. 20b; cf. Acts 10:9–16; 15:9). But the "weak" may have contrary convictions (v. 14b). The new way of the Spirit essentially entails "walking according to love" (v. 15), which means taking the command of the law to love one's neighbor seriously and not putting a stumbling block or pitfall in another believer's way (v. 13). Positively speaking, when differences arise over religious practices, love demands the pursuit of what promotes peace and edification (vv. 19–22). An abuse of Christian liberty by the "strong" in any church situation may hurt the "weak" (even to the point of destroying their faith) and bring the cause of Christ into disrepute (vv. 15–18). "Only when liberty is liberty to deny oneself and not just liberty to enjoy all that God the creator has provided is it the liberty of the Spirit of Christ."[60]

C. Living to Glorify God (15:1–13)

[1]Now we who are strong have an obligation to bear the
weaknesses of those without strength, and not to please ourselves.
[2]Each one of us is to please his neighbor for his good, to build

[58] Other witnesses omit the doxology altogether, and 𝔓[46] has it after 15:33. Metzger (*Textual Commentary*, 470–73) discusses the evidence more fully. Jewett (*Romans*, 4–18) considers the question with reference to the different forms of Romans that have survived. Cf. 16:25–27 comment.

[59] Jewett, *Romans*, 866. Cf. Moo, *Romans*, 882–84.

[60] Dunn, *Romans 9–16*, 832. Dunn (834–35) argues that genuine liberty arises out of faith and must be conditioned by love. "Christian liberty must be defended against the condemnatory attitude of the weak as much as against the disdainful self-indulgence of the strong (v. 3)."

him up. [3]For even Christ did not please himself. On the contrary, as it is written, **The insults of those who insult you have fallen on me.** [4]For whatever was written in the past was written for our instruction, so that we may have hope through endurance and through the encouragement from the Scriptures. [5]Now may the God who gives endurance and encouragement grant you to live in harmony with one another, according to Christ Jesus, [6]so that you may glorify the God and Father of our Lord Jesus Christ with one mind and one voice.

[7]Therefore accept one another, just as Christ also accepted you, to the glory of God. [8]For I say that Christ became a servant of the circumcised on behalf of God's truth, to confirm the promises to the fathers, [9]and so that Gentiles may glorify God for his mercy. As it is written,

> **Therefore I will praise you among the Gentiles,**
> **and I will sing praise to your name.**

[10]Again it says, **Rejoice, you Gentiles, with his people!** [11]And again,

> **Praise the Lord, all you Gentiles;**
> **let all the peoples praise him!**

[12]And again, Isaiah says,

> **The root of Jesse will appear,**
> **the one who rises to rule the Gentiles;**
> **the Gentiles will hope in him.**

[13]Now may the God of hope fill you with all joy and peace as you believe so that you may overflow with hope by the power of the Holy Spirit.

Context

Paul addresses the strong again (cf. 14:21–22), identifying with them in a challenge "to bear the weaknesses of those without strength, and not to please ourselves." This picks up the theme of love from 14:15, expressed here in terms of pleasing one's neighbor "for his good, to build him up" (cf. 14:19–21). Paul's exhortation is backed up with a reflection on the way "even Christ did not please himself," citing Ps 69:9 as a scriptural basis for encouraging endurance and hope in this situation. A wish-prayer asks that the readers may be in agreement with one another, "according to Christ Jesus," so that they may glorify "the God and Father of our

Lord Jesus Christ with one mind and one voice." This prepares for the emphasis on Jews and Gentiles glorifying God together for his mercy in vv. 8–12. But before that theme is developed, Paul restates the need to "accept one another" (cf. 14:1 comment), just as the Messiah accepted them, "to the glory of God." God's purpose in sending the Messiah is then summed up in terms that recall 1:1–6, 13–17; 3:21–31; 4:1–25; 9:30–11:36. A wish-prayer to "the God of hope" concludes the section and expresses Paul's fundamental concern for his readers to overflow with hope.[61]

Structure

The conjunction δέ ("now") signals a development of the argument from the preceding passage, with the subject ἡμεῖς οἱ δυνατοὶ ("we who are strong") linking specifically with 14:21–22. Two infinitives in v. 1 outline the obligation that Paul lays on the strong: "to bear the weaknesses of those without strength" and "not to please ourselves." Without a connective Paul explains what this last point means, using terms that relate to the preceding argument: (lit.) "Let each of us please his neighbor for his good, for edification" (v. 2; cf. vv. 15, 19–21). A theological reason is given for this in v. 3 ("For even Christ did not please himself"), supported by a citation from Ps 69:9 (introduced by the strong adversative ἀλλά [on the contrary"] and καθὼς γέγραπται ["as it is written"]). A further explanatory clause (v. 4, "for") indicates that the Scriptures were written for our instruction and encouragement, to promote endurance and provide hope. A wish-prayer in vv. 5–6 is linked to the preceding claim by δέ ("now") and calls upon "the God who gives endurance and encouragement" to grant the Roman Christians "to live in harmony with one another, according to Christ Jesus." The purpose clause that follows ("so that you may glorify the God and Father of our Lord Jesus Christ with one mind and one voice") anticipates vv. 8–13. But before Paul develops that theme, he rounds off 14:1–15:6 with a challenge introduced by the inferential conjunction

[61] Richard J. Gibson ("Paul the Missionary, in Priestly Service of the Servant-Christ [Romans 15.16]," in *Paul as Missionary: Identity, Activity, Theology and Practice*, ed. T. J. Burke and Brian S. Rosner, LNTS [London: T&T Clark, 2011], 57–62) argues for 15:8–21 as a distinct literary unit with a chiastic structure. But the thematic links between 15:8–13 and 15:1–7 are sufficient to classify this as a conclusion to the latter and a transition to the next stage of the argument.

διό ("therefore"). Returning to the language of welcome (v. 7, [lit.] "welcome one another, just as the Messiah welcomed you"), he also repeats the idea of giving glory to God (cf. v. 6).

A forward-pointing expression (λέγω γάρ, "for I say") attracts attention to what Paul is about to say. A profound theological claim is made about Christ's having become "a servant of the circumcised on behalf of God's truth, to confirm the promises to the fathers, and so that Gentiles may glorify God for his mercy" (vv. 8–9a). Picking up some important emphases in the letter so far, Paul "sets the local conflict in Rome against the panorama of salvation history in order to stimulate them to obedience."[62] Four biblical texts predict that Gentiles will join with Jews in praising God for the appearance of the Messiah and his rule over the nations (vv. 9b–12). The Messiah has given the Gentiles "hope" (v. 12, citing Isa 11:10), and so Paul concludes this section with a wish-prayer addressed to "the God of hope" (v. 13). He asks that God might fill them "with all joy and peace as you believe, so that you may overflow with hope by the power of the Holy Spirit."

Outline:

1. Please others (vv. 1–7).
2. Praise God (vv. 8–12).
3. Overflow with hope (v. 13).

15:1. A development of the preceding argument is indicated by the connective δέ ("now"). For the first time Paul explicitly identifies himself with those he calls the "strong" (ἡμεῖς οἱ δυνατοὶ, "We who are strong"), though his assertions in 14:14, 20 were clearly pointing in this direction. "The weak (in faith)" (14:1–2) are now called "those without strength" (τῶν ἀδυνάτων) who have certain "weaknesses" (τὰ ἀσθενήματα). A moral obligation is laid on the strong, using the verb ὀφείλομεν ("we ought") in the emphatic position at the beginning of the sentence.[63] Two infinitives tease out the nature of that obligation. Positively, the challenge is "to bear (βαστάζειν) the weaknesses of those without strength," which is a call to help

---

[62] Moo, *Romans*, 874.

[63] The same verb is employed in 13:8; 15:27. Paul also uses the cognate nouns ὀφειλέτης ("debtor") in 1:14; 8:12; 15:27 and ὀφειλή ("debt, obligation") in 13:7.

the weak "carry their burden of scruples."[64] Negatively, the challenge is "not to please ourselves" (καὶ μὴ ἑαυτοῖς ἀρέσκειν). Both expressions should be understood in relation to the specific situation described in the previous chapter, though the principles may be applied to conflicts among Christians more widely (cf. 1 Cor 10:24; 10:33–11:1; 13:5; Phil 2:4, 21).

15:2. Without a connective, this verse qualifies the challenge at the end of v. 1. The exhortation is applied individually and positively now (ἕκαστος ἡμῶν τῷ πλησίον ἀρεσκέτω, [lit.] "Let each of us please his neighbor"). Use of the word "neighbor" recalls 13:9–10, with its reference to Lev 19:18. Here is another way of expressing the love command. Pleasing one's neighbor would clearly be an obligation for every believer, but the context indicates its special relevance to the strong in relation to "those without strength" (v. 1; cf. 14:15). Two expressions of purpose follow (εἰς τὸ ἀγαθὸν πρὸς οἰκοδομήν, [lit.] "for the good, for edification"), echoing the argument in 14:19–21.[65] Although it is valid to translate "for his good, to build him up" (CSB), Paul's concern is for the welfare of the church as a body and not simply for individual members (cf. 12:5).

15:3. A theological reason is given for the preceding exhortation: "for even the Messiah did not please himself" (καὶ γὰρ ὁ Χριστὸς οὐχ ἑαυτῷ ἤρεσεν).[66] The following context suggests that ὁ Χριστός should be translated "the Messiah" or "the Christ" here, since Paul gives a salvation-historical reason for his exhortations. He begins with a reference to the example of the Messiah (cf. 1 Cor 10:33–11:1; 2 Cor 8:8–9; Eph 5:1–2; Phil 2:5–11) emerging from the pattern of his unique, redemptive suffering. A citation from Ps 69:9 (LXX 68:10) highlights a particular aspect of that suffering: "The insults of those who insult you have fallen on me" (οἱ ὀνειδισμοὶ τῶν ὀνειδιζόντων σε ἐπέπεσαν ἐπ' ἐμέ). This is introduced with the familiar formula "as it is

---

[64] Thompson, *Clothed with Christ*, 209. The verb βαστάζω can be used literally, or figuratively with the sense of "bearing anything burdensome" (BDAG; cf. Luke 14:27; Acts 15:10; Gal 6:2, 17). Thompson notes the special significance of Isa 53:4, as cited in Matt 8:17 with reference to Jesus. Cf. Dunn, *Romans 9–16*, 837.

[65] There are wrong reasons for pleasing others (cf. Gal 1:10; 1 Thess 2:4; also Eph 6:6; Col 3:22), and so Paul gives positive goals for pleasing the weak. Cf. 1 Cor 10:33.

[66] The titular form (ὁ Χριστός) indicates a reference to the messianic role of Jesus (cf. 7:4; 8:35; 9:3, 5; 14:18; 15:7, 19; 16:16). The aorist ἤρεσεν could embrace the whole of his ministry, but supremely he suffered the hostility of humanity to God in his death, to which the citation points.

written" (cf. 1:17; 2:24; 3:4, 10; 4:17; 8:36; 9:13, 33; 10:15; 11:8, 26; 15:21). The strong adversative ἀλλά (CSB: "on the contrary") is used because Paul is stressing that, far from pleasing himself, the Messiah submitted himself to the insults of God's opponents. According to Mark 15:32; Matt 27:44, this happened to Jesus on the cross. Jesus's use of Ps 69:4 in John 15:25 suggests that he was responsible for developing a pattern of Christian reflection on the messianic implications of this psalm.[67] In his willingness to suffer insults and hatred for the salvation of his people, Jesus demonstrated what it means to serve others for their good (cf. Mark 10:43–45; 1 Pet 2:21–25). Paul's specific challenge seems to be that, if the strong seek to please the weak and accommodate to their scruples, they may expose themselves to the sort of reproaches and ridicule from opponents that Jesus himself experienced.[68]

15:4. Paul's broader reason for citing this Scripture is now articulated: (lit.) "For whatever was written before was written for our instruction" (ὅσα γὰρ προεγράφη, εἰς τὴν ἡμετέραν διδασκαλίαν ἐγράφη). Although he fundamentally uses Scripture to outline God's saving plan and point to the need for the Messiah's suffering and resurrection, the apostle discerns a wider didactic significance in the biblical record (cf. 1:2, 17; 4:22–24; 12:19–20; 13:8–10; 1 Cor 9:10; 10:11; §2.2). The purpose clause that follows could be translated, "so that through endurance and through the encouragement of the Scriptures we may have hope" (ἵνα διὰ τῆς ὑπομονῆς καὶ διὰ τῆς παρακλήσεως τῶν γραφῶν τὴν ἐλπίδα ἔχωμεν). It is possible that the article in διὰ τῆς ὑπομονῆς is anaphoric ("through that endurance"), pointing back to the endurance of the Messiah implied by Ps 69:9, which is the basis for our endurance.[69] Hope is a gift of God through

---

[67] See also Ps 69:9 in John 2:17. The psalm is cited for different reasons in Acts 1:20; Rom 11:9–10 and echoed in many other contexts (e.g., Matt 27:34, 48; Mark 3:21; 15:23, 36). Charles H. Dodd (*According to the Scriptures: The Sub-Structure of the New Testament* [London: Nisbet, 1952], 61–108) argues that it was one of the major texts used by the earliest Christians to reflect on the topic of "The Servant of the Lord and the Righteous Sufferer."

[68] Cf. Thompson, *Clothed with Christ*, 223.

[69] Cf. ibid., 225–28. Thompson (227–28) concludes that Paul's attitude to steadfastness in suffering involves more than an imitation of Christ (cf. 1 Thess 1:6): "It is an *extension* of Jesus' experience, and a necessary part of conformity to Christ in the present in order to be fit for ultimate conformity to the glory of the Son at the resurrection (Phil 3:10–11; Rom 8:18, 29)."

the gospel, which is realized and experienced in everyday life and relationships (5:2, 4–5; 18:17–30; 12:12; 13:11–14; 15:12–13). Paul's immediate point here is that "hope is generated through carefully reading, understanding, and obeying the OT."[70] As Paul goes on to show (vv. 8–12), the biblical hope is that Jews and Gentiles will be united in praise of God by the work of the Messiah. If the strong act in a Christlike way toward the weak, all will be encouraged to press on in hopeful service to their Lord (cf. 14:5–12).

15:5–6. An intercessory wish-prayer is linked to the preceding claim by δέ ("now"). The ascription to "the God of endurance and encouragement" (ὁ δὲ θεὸς τῆς ὑπομονῆς καὶ τῆς παρακλήσεως) picks up two key ideas from v. 4, identifying God as the ultimate source of these biblical blessings (CSB: "the God who gives endurance and encouragement").[71] Paul speaks of God in the third person (δῴη ὑμῖν, "may he give you" [the optative mood is required by this prayer form]). At the same time, he addresses the readers, articulating their fundamental need, which is (lit.) "to think the same among yourselves" (τὸ αὐτὸ φρονεῖν ἐν ἀλλήλοις [CSB: "to live in harmony with one another"). This recalls the exhortation in 12:16 (τὸ αὐτὸ εἰς ἀλλήλους φρονοῦντες, [lit.], "thinking the same toward one another"). But Paul's prayer indicates that such unity cannot be achieved apart from God's enabling. The phrase "according to Christ Jesus" (κατὰ Χριστὸν Ἰησοῦν) has a special significance in light of 15:3–4. From "the Messiah" or "the Christ" as a title (v. 3), he moves to the more personal address "Christ Jesus" (v. 5) and then to "our Lord Jesus Christ" (v. 6). The focus is not on "achieving unanimity in doctrine or practice but rather on bearing abuse for each other and pleasing each other as Christ did."[72] This wish-prayer serves to remind them

[70] Schreiner, *Romans*, 748. The present subjunctive ἔχωμεν ("we might have") provides a proverbial statement of God's purpose in giving us "the endurance" and "the encouragement of the Scriptures." Cf. Campbell, *Verbal Aspect and Non-Indicative Verbs*, 55.

[71] Cf. Gordon P. Wiles, *Paul's Intercessory Prayers: The Significance of the Intercessory Prayer Passages in the Letters of St. Paul*, SNTSMS 24 (Cambridge: Cambridge University, 1974), 22–44. Similar wish-prayers occur in 15:13; 1 Thess 3:11–13; 5:23–24 (cf. 2 Thess 2:16–17; 3:5, 16; 2 Tim 1:16, 18). But shorter introductory benedictions (such as in 1:7) and closing benedictions (such as in 15:33; 16:20) are variations of the same form.

[72] Jewett, *Romans*, 884. Cranfield (*Romans*, 2:737n4) takes the expression to relate to the will of Christ rather than to his example. But the context suggests conformity

of how they should relate to one another and to inform them about what they should be praying for one another.

The purpose clause that follows conveys Paul's ultimate concern ("so that you may glorify the God and Father of our Lord Jesus Christ with one mind and one voice"). To "glorify" God (δοξάζητε) means to praise him for who he is and what he has done (cf. 15:9; 2 Cor 9:13; Gal 1:24).[73] Human beings characteristically fail to do this (1:21 comment), but God has acted decisively in history to transform the situation (15:8–13). To glorify him as "the God and Father of our Lord Jesus Christ" (cf. 2 Cor 1:3; 11:31; Eph 1:3; 1 Pet 1:3) means honoring him as the one who has engaged with us in the person and work of his Son Jesus Christ (1:3–4). Glorifying God (lit.) "together with one voice" (ὁμοθυμαδὸν ἐν ἑνὶ στόματι [CSB: "with one mind and one voice"])[74] means being united in praise for what he has done for us in Christ. If the Roman Christians do this, it will be impossible for them to look down on one another or sit in judgment of one another (14:3–4, 10, 13). Paul's concern for the glory of God is expressed again in the next verse (cf. 4:20–21).

15:7. As in 1:24; 2:1; 4:22; 13:5; 15:22, Διό ("therefore") introduces a significant inference from the preceding paragraph, providing a formal conclusion to the argument that began in 14:1. But the imperative προσλαμβάνεσθε ("welcome, receive" [cf. 14:1 comment]) is here applied to the readers generally (ἀλλήλους, "one another"; cf. 14:13). "The hostility cannot be overcome if only one side participates in this breaking down of barriers."[75] The imperative in 14:3 was reinforced with the claim that *God* has welcomed

---

to the demonstrated character of Christ. Cf. Thompson, *Clothed with Christ*, 228–29.

[73] In the LXX δόξα is regularly used to translate Heb. כָּבוֹד ("glory"), as used in relation to the divine "splendor" (e.g., Ps 97:6 [LXX 96:6]; Exod 40:35; Isa 6:3; 40:5). Cf. Gerhard von Rad and Gerhard Kittel, "δοκέω, δόξα, δοξάζω κτλ.," *TDNT* 2:232–55. The verb is used differently in Rom 8:17 (συνδοξασθῶμεν), 30; 11:13; 1 Cor 6:20; 12:26; 2 Cor 3:10; 2 Thess 3:1.

[74] The adverb ὁμοθυμαδόν means "with one mind, purpose, impulse" (BDAG). Cf. Hans W. Heidland, "ὁμοθυμαδόν," *TDNT* 5:185–86. The term is used in Acts of Christians praying together (1:14; 2:1, 46; 4:24; 5:12), gathering for teaching (20:18; cf. 8:6), and agreeing in decision making (15:25). It is also used of those who are united in their opposition to Christians (7:57; 18:12; 19:29; cf. 12:20).

[75] Jewett, *Romans*, 888. If there were congregations of the "weak" and the "strong" in Rome, "both are called upon here to invite and welcome members of the other groups into their congregational meetings."

the person who is "weak in faith." Picking up the theological argument from 15:3–4, Paul now specifies, "just as *the Messiah* also welcomed you" (καθὼς καὶ ὁ Χριστὸς προσελάβετο ὑμᾶς).[76] As in v. 3, the titular form (ὁ Χριστός) points to Jesus as Messiah, who has welcomed sinners of every type to share in his eschatological banquet (Matt 8:10–12; Luke 14:15–24; 15:2; Acts 10:1–11:18; Rev 19:6–9). Consequently, they should welcome one another with the same grace. "The reception of sinners which began during Jesus's ministry was most clearly manifested on the cross, and continues in the present as Christ forgives and receives those who come to him in faith."[77] The concluding phrase (εἰς δόξαν τοῦ θεοῦ, "to/for the glory of God") links Paul's prayer (v. 6) with his exposition of how the Messiah enables Jews and Gentiles to glorify God together (vv. 8–13). Christ's reconciling work was for the glory of God, and a faithful response to his initiative will similarly glorify God. A generous welcome to fellow believers brings glory to God because God's character is reflected in such behavior.

15:8. As previously argued, a coda to the exhortation in 14:1–15:7 begins here, placing the challenge of those verses within the broader framework of God's purpose for Jews and Gentiles. The priority of Jews in God's plan of salvation was first articulated in 1:16–17 (cf. 2:9; 3:1–4; 9:4–5; 11:11–32).[78] The expression λέγω γάρ ("for I say") draws attention to the importance of what Paul is about to say. A profound theological claim is made about Christ's having become "a servant of the circumcised on behalf of God's truth."[79] As

---

[76] The pronoun ὑμᾶς ("you") is widely supported by a good range of ancient witnesses (א A C D² F G etc.). The alternative ἡμᾶς ("us"), which is found in B D* P etc., generalizes the application beyond the more pointed second-person plural references in vv. 5–6. Copyists are likely to have made this correction to embrace readers of the letter in other contexts.

[77] Thompson, *Clothed with Christ*, 232. CSB has taken καθώς in its strictly comparative sense ("just as"), but it could be understood in a causal way ("because"). Cf. Cranfield, *Romans*, 2:739. The comparative understanding puts the focus on the *manner* in which Christ welcomed them.

[78] It cannot simply be concluded that "most, if not all the weak will have been Jews, and a good many of the strong will have been Gentiles" (Cranfield, *Romans*, 2:742). But whatever the makeup of these two groups, the broader question of how Jews and Gentiles may worship God together is the critical issue (see §2.6).

[79] Dunn (*Romans 9–16*, 846) observes that "Christ" is a proper name here rather than a title: "to say that Jesus as 'the Messiah' acted for the Jews would seem to be unnecessarily tautologous."

in 3:30; 4:12, περιτομή ("circumcision") denotes the Jewish people. Christ became a servant (διάκονος) to bring the covenant people back to God (cf. Matt 15:24), thus enabling them to fulfill their calling to be a light to the nations (cf. Isa 49:5–6).[80] Jesus gave an indication of this when he talked about coming "to serve, and to give his life as a ransom for many" (Matt 20:28; Mark 10:45 [διακονῆσαι]). The expression "on behalf of God's truth" (ὑπὲρ ἀληθείας θεοῦ) recalls 3:4, 7, where the reference is to the faithfulness of God in fulfilling his "very words" (3:2). More specifically in 15:8, Paul has in view God's promises to the patriarchs: Christ came "to confirm the promises to the fathers" (cf. 4:16; 9:4; 11:28). "This careful description of Christ's relation to Israel not only clears away any possibility of justifiable hostility and competition between the ethnic groups in Rome, but also prepares the way for the completion of the global mission on the Spanish peninsula."[81]

15:9. A further infinitive expands on the purpose of Christ's becoming "a servant of the circumcised on behalf of God's truth." This happened "so that Gentiles may glorify (δοξάσαι) God for his mercy." Christ came "to confirm *both* phases of God's saving purpose: to Jew first and also to Gentile."[82] The mercy of God, which was highlighted in 9:15–18, 23; 11:30–32, is now the focus of praise for Jews and Gentiles together. The biblical citations that follow confirm this vision. With the introduction "as it is written," Paul provides a catena of texts from the three main sections of the Hebrew canon (Law, Prophets, and Writings). Several praise words are used in parallel here to explain what it means to glorify God verbally.

The first citation is from LXX Ps 17:50 (18:49), which is also found in 2 Sam 22:50: "Therefore I will praise you among the Gentiles, and I will sing praise to your name." In this passage, in view of God's mighty deliverance, David the faithful Jew promises

---

[80] The perfect infinitive γεγενῆσθαι ("became") could indicate that this is his continuing role: Christ remains the servant of the Jews. This reading is supported by א A C[2] D[1] L P etc. The aorist γένεσθαι is also well supported (B C* D* F G etc.) but is likely to be secondary because the perfect is the more difficult reading. Cf. Cranfield, *Romans*, 2:741; Jewett, *Romans*, 886.

[81] Jewett, *Romans*, 892. Cf. 15:23–32. Jewett overstates the case when he describes this mission as "the primary purpose of the letter."

[82] Dunn, *Romans 9–16*, 848. Moo (*Romans*, 876–78) discusses the awkward syntax in the Greek text and argues that v. 8b and v. 9a are two parallel purpose expressions dependent on v. 8a. See also Schreiner, *Romans*, 754–56.

to (lit.) "confess" (ἐξομολογήσομαί; cf. 14:11) God before the nations and "sing" (ψαλῶ) to his name. God's "name" represents his person and character and is a synonym for his "glory" (cf. Exod 33:18–23). Paul goes on to clarify how he has been fulfilling this role. As the Jewish apostle of the risen Lord Jesus, he has been commissioned to make God's salvation known among the Gentiles through the preaching of the gospel (15:15–21).[83]

15:10–12. Three more texts are successively linked to the one before by the words καὶ πάλιν ("and again"; cf. 1 Cor 3:20; Heb 1:5, 6). Although λέγει in v. 10 could mean "it says" (CSB), it is also possible that God could be the understood subject ("he says," NRSV). An exact quotation of part of LXX Deut 32:43 follows: "Rejoice (εὐφράνθητε), you Gentiles, with his people." This command concludes the Song of Moses, where the sequence is significant. In this prophetic vision, rebellious Israel is punished (Deut 32:19–35) and then vindicated by God (32:36–42), giving rise to the challenge for the nations to rejoice.[84] By implication, the messianic deliverance provides the ultimate vindication of God's covenant people and enables Gentiles to rejoice with believing Israelites and "glorify God for his mercy" (v. 9a).

The third citation (v. 11) is from LXX 116:1 (117:1) with slight verbal variation.[85] This text is also in the form of a command: "Praise (αἰνεῖτε) the Lord, all you Gentiles; let all the peoples praise (ἐπαινεσάτωσαν) him." Once again the original context is important for Paul's argument. The psalmist calls upon *all* the nations to praise God because his faithful love to his people is great and "the Lord's faithfulness endures forever." In terms of eschatological fulfillment, Gentiles are now coming in great numbers to join in praise with thankful Israelites because the messianic redemption has

---

[83] Jewett (*Romans*, 894) observes that a strictly Christological reading of this text would make Christ himself the one who praises God before the nations (cf. Heb 2:11–13). However, διὰ τοῦτο in this context points back to the truth expounded in v. 8 ("Christ became a servant of the circumcised"), making this a response by believers like Paul to God's saving actions in Christ. Contrast Moo, *Romans*, 878–79.

[84] The Hebrew text of Deut 32:43 (הַרְנִינוּ גוֹיִם עַמּוֹ) means, "You nations praise his people." The reason for this is that God will avenge the blood of his servants, take vengeance on his adversaries, and "will purify his land and his people."

[85] The LXX has τὸν κύριον after αἰνεῖτε, and the second verb is a second-person imperative (ἐπαινέσατε).

been accomplished and its benefits are being proclaimed to people everywhere.

The fourth citation (v. 12) is attributed to Isaiah and is in the form of a messianic prediction. LXX Isa 11:10 is abbreviated to read, "The root of Jesse will appear, the one who rises to rule the Gentiles; the Gentiles will hope in him."[86] Jesse was the father of David, making this is a prophecy about a son of David who will rule both Israel and the nations in such a way that the hope of the nations is fulfilled in him (cf. Rom 1:3–6; Jer 23:5 ["a righteous branch for David"]). Jesus provides that hope because he is the Messiah who "did not please himself" (vv. 3–4) but gave himself up to deliver believers in every nation from the rule of sin and death (5:15–21).

15:13. Paul picks up the theme of hope from the citation in v. 12 and addresses a wish-prayer to "the God of hope" (Ὁ δὲ θεὸς τῆς ἐλπίδος). The Messiah is the object of hope in Isa 11:10, but God the Father is likely viewed as the source of that hope in the present context.[87] Paul asks that his readers may be filled "with all joy and peace in *believing*" (ἐν τῷ πιστεύειν [CSB: "as you believe"]), implying that genuine joy and peace come from believing the gospel about the crucified and resurrected Messiah.[88] The purpose of this divine filling is "so that you may overflow with hope by the power of the Holy Spirit" (εἰς τὸ περισσεύειν ὑμᾶς ἐν τῇ ἐλπίδι ἐν δυνάμει πνεύματος ἁγίου). Hope is the gift of God through the gospel and is a major theme in this letter (4:18; 5:2, 4, 5; 8:20, 24–25; 12:12; 15:4, 12, 24). The hope of sharing in the glory of God has profound implications for everyday Christian discipleship. Paul wants this hope to be fully experienced by believers as they struggle with various afflictions or experience conflict in their midst. Both the weak and the strong may "overflow" with this transforming hope as the Holy Spirit enables them to express joy and peace in their relationships (cf. 1:7 com-

[86] Although ῥίζα can mean "root" (as in 11:16–18), the image here is of a "shoot" that springs up from the root (BDAG). "Shoot of David" is a messianic designation in Sir 47:22; 4QPat 3–4; 4QFlor 1:11; 4QpIsa 3:10ff.; 1QSb 5:26; Rev 5:5; 22:16.

[87] Cf. Cranfield, *Romans*, 2:747. The genitive τῆς ἐλπίδος expresses source, as in v. 5 (τῆς ὑπομονῆς, τῆς παρακλήσεως). The optative πληρώσαι is required by the wish-prayer form (cf. v. 5, δῴη).

[88] In place of πληρώσαι πάσης χαρᾶς καὶ εἰρήνης, which is widely attested, B F G read πληροφορῆσαι (ἐν) πάσῃ χαρᾷ καὶ εἰρήνῃ ("give you full assurance in all joy and peace"). This reading, which is undoubtedly secondary, appears to have arisen because of some theological discomfort with the original.

ment).[89] Paul's aim in this letter has been to show the Gentiles how their hope rests on Israel's Messiah, which means comprehending "what their relation is to the Jew, to Israel, and in particular to the Israelite Paul, by whom in God's design the benefits of salvation have been ministered to them."[90]

Bridge

The radical inclusivity of this passage is not based on a simple theory of tolerance or the need to value different points of view. Rather, it rests on "the welcoming action of Christ himself, as experienced in faith."[91] Jesus the Messiah welcomed sinners and ate with them in the course of his earthly ministry (Luke 15:2). The exalted Lord Jesus now welcomes people of every background into the fellowship of his people through the preaching of the gospel (Rom 10:9–13). God is glorified when Christians act like Christ in relation to one another and demonstrate his self-sacrificing concern to put the welfare of others first. In practical terms this means pleasing other believers for their good and for the edification of the church. "Only in the weakness of mutual interdependence as members of one body in Christ is there the full strength of grace."[92] God is glorified when Christians put aside their differences over religious practices and learn to support one another, praising him with a united mind and voice. The confession of a common hope in Christ as we rejoice together in what he has accomplished for us fulfills God's purpose for his people. Sharing together in the praise of God should have a profound impact on Christian relationships. As we acknowledge our common hope, we may be filled with the joy and peace that come from believing the gospel and show genuine love to one another in Christ (12:9–16; 13:8–10).

---

[89] Joy and peace are mentioned together in 14:17 as essential marks of the kingdom of God. Elsewhere, peace is mentioned in 1:7; 2:10; 3:17; 5:1; 8:6; 14:19; 15:33; 16:20, and joy in 15:32 (rejoicing in 12:12, 15; 16:19).

[90] Donald W. B. Robinson, "The Priesthood of Paul in the Gospel of Hope," in *Reconciliation and Hope*, ed. Robert J. Banks (Grand Rapids: Eerdmans, 1974), 232. Robinson argues that "Romans is both an exposition of the gospel of hope and at the same time Paul's *apologia* for his 'priesthood' in that gospel," as highlighted in 15:14–21.

[91] Jewett, *Romans*, 889.

[92] Dunn, *Romans 9–16*, 843.

XIV. Paul's Mission Plans and Final Messages (15:14–16:27)

A correspondence between the opening and closing sections of this letter is obvious, as Paul returns to the theme of his apostleship to the nations (15:14–21; cf. 1:1–7) and writes again about his longing to visit the Romans (15:22–33; cf. 1:8–15). The "epistolary frame" shows parallels with other Pauline letters in content and style, but the closing sections are longer than normal, pointing to specific circumstances surrounding the composition of this letter.[1] Paul wants the Roman Christians to understand that his ministry to them, with indications of his need for their support, is based on "his apostolic call to plant churches among the Gentiles."[2] The disclosure of his immediate travel plans is followed by a series of personal messages designed to strengthen their relationship with one another and with the apostle, preparing for his impending visit to them (16:1–27).

A. Three Significant Destinations (15:14–33)

[14]My brothers and sisters, I myself am convinced about you that you also are full of goodness, filled with all knowledge, and able to instruct one another. [15]Nevertheless, I have written to remind you more boldly on some points because of the grace given me by God [16]to be a minister of Christ Jesus to the Gentiles, serving as a priest of the gospel of God. My purpose is that the Gentiles may be an acceptable offering, sanctified by the Holy Spirit. [17]Therefore I have reason to boast in Christ Jesus regarding what pertains to God. [18]For I would not dare say anything except what Christ has accomplished through me by word and deed for the obedience of the Gentiles, [19]by the power of miraculous signs and wonders, and by the power of God's Spirit. As a result, I have fully proclaimed the gospel of Christ from Jerusalem all the way around to Illyricum. [20]My aim is to preach the gospel where

---

[1] Moo (*Romans*, 884) lists the following elements in the closing section of Romans that are paralleled elsewhere in his letters: travel plans (15:14–29); request for prayer (15:30–32); prayer-wish for peace (15:33); mention of associates (16:1–2); exhortation to greet one another (16:3–15); the "holy kiss" (16:16a); warning/exhortation (16:17–19); eschatological wish-promise (16:20a); concluding "grace" (16:20b); greetings from associates (16:16b, 21–23); doxology (16:25–27).

[2] Schreiner, *Romans*, 761. Schreiner rightly implies that Paul is not simply concerned with the conversion of individuals.

Christ has not been named, so that I will not build on someone
else's foundation, [21]but, as it is written,

> **Those who were not told about him will see,**
> **and those who have not heard will understand.**

[22]That is why I have been prevented many times from coming to you. [23]But now I no longer have any work to do in these
regions, and I have strongly desired for many years to come to
you [24]whenever I travel to Spain. For I hope to see you when
I pass through and to be assisted by you for my journey there,
once I have first enjoyed your company for a while. [25]Right now I
am traveling to Jerusalem to serve the saints, [26]because Macedonia and Achaia were pleased to make a contribution for the poor
among the saints in Jerusalem. [27]Yes, they were pleased, and indeed are indebted to them. For if the Gentiles have shared in their
spiritual benefits, then they are obligated to minister to them in
material needs. [28]So when I have finished this and safely delivered
the funds to them, I will visit you on the way to Spain. [29]I know
that when I come to you, I will come in the fullness of the blessing
of Christ.

[30]Now I appeal to you, brothers and sisters, through our Lord
Jesus Christ and through the love of the Spirit, to strive together
with me in fervent prayers to God on my behalf. [31]Pray that I may
be rescued from the unbelievers in Judea, that my ministry to Jerusalem may be acceptable to the saints, [32]and that, by God's will,
I may come to you with joy and be refreshed together with you.

[33]May the God of peace be with all of you. Amen.

Context

Paul has articulated God's great plan to bring Gentiles to hope in Israel's Messiah and rejoice with believing Israelites in the fulfillment of his promises (vv. 8–13). He begins to explains his own role in the divine plan by expressing confidence in the maturity and capability of the Roman Christians, while acknowledging that he has written to them boldly on some points because of his particular calling (vv. 14–16). His approach recalls 1:1–15, where he first links his desire to minister to them with his apostolic calling. The character of his ministry and his particular reason for wanting to visit Rome are further explained (vv. 17–29). In preparation for his proposed visits to Jerusalem, Rome, and Spain, Paul seeks the prayer support of his readers and prays for "the God of peace" to be with them all (vv. 30–33). Here, and in the concluding chapter, he seeks to draw the Romans "ever more deeply into his ambit and mission as minister of the gospel to the Gentiles."[3] Cf. §2.7.

Structure

This section begins with a personal address to the readers as "my brothers and sisters." Paul's diplomatic declaration of confidence in them is coupled with an acknowledgment that he has written to them boldly on some points because of the grace given to him by God (vv. 14–15). He then portrays his apostolic calling in terms of being (lit.) "a minister of Christ Jesus to the Gentiles, serving as a priest of the gospel of God, so that the offering of the Gentiles may be acceptable, sanctified by the Holy Spirit" (v. 16; cf. 12:1; 15:8–13).[4] The conjunction οὖν ("therefore") introduces a consequential statement: (lit.) "I have this boast in Christ Jesus regarding what pertains to God" (v. 17). This is backed up (γάρ, "for") with a disclaimer: (lit.) "I would not dare to say anything except what Christ has accomplished through me for the obedience of the Gentiles" (v. 18a–c). A series of linked phrases disclose how God has worked through Paul's ministry: (lit.) "by word and deed, by the power of signs and wonders, and by the power of God's Spirit" (18d–19b).[5] The result has been (ὥστε) that Paul has "fully proclaimed (πεπληρωκέναι) the gospel of Christ from Jerusalem all the way around to Illyricum" (v. 19c–d). What follows from all this (οὕτως δέ, "so now") is that he aims "to preach the gospel where Christ has not been named" (v. 20a). This is explained by a purpose clause (v. 20b, "so that I will not build on someone else's foundation"), which he supports with a citation from Isa 52:15 in v. 21.

A new stage of the argument begins with the inferential conjunction διό (v. 22, "therefore, for this reason"). Paul's preoccupation with fulfilling his gospel mission from Jerusalem to Illyricum has prevented him from visiting Rome. But now he declares that he no longer has any "place" (τόπον) in these regions and reminds them

[3] Byrne, *Romans*, 434.

[4] CSB takes the purpose clause to refer to Paul's purpose ("My purpose"), but the reference is more likely to God's purpose.

[5] CSB transposes λόγῳ καὶ ἔργῳ ("by word and deed") to earlier in the sentence, but it should be read as introducing a sequence explaining how God has worked through Paul's ministry.

that he has had a strong desire (ἐπιποθίαν) for many years to come to them (v. 23; cf. 1:9–15). Introducing the idea that he will visit them whenever he travels to Spain (v. 24), he makes clear that he wants to be "assisted by you for my journey there." But first he wants to enjoy their company for a while.

The next stage in the unveiling of Paul's plans is introduced by νυνὶ δέ (v. 25, "now however, right now"). He is going to Jerusalem, (lit.) "serving the saints." The explanation for this ministry (v. 26, γάρ, "for") is that "Macedonia and Achaia were pleased to make a contribution to the poor among the saints in Jerusalem." Paul repeats that "they were pleased" to do this (v. 27) before adding that "they are indebted to them." He explains this indebtedness in a conditional clause: "For if the Gentiles shared in their spiritual benefits, then they are obligated to minister to them in material needs." Paul ties the three proposed destinations together by saying, "When I have finished this and have safely delivered the funds to them, I will visit you on the way to Spain" (v. 28). He concludes this reflection on his travel plans by expressing his confidence that, when he comes to them, he will come "in the fullness of the blessing of Christ" (v. 29).

The final paragraph begins with a solemn request for prayer (v. 30, Παρακαλῶ δὲ ὑμᾶς, ἀδελφοί, "Now I appeal to you, brothers and sisters"). Paul appeals to them "through our Lord Jesus Christ and through the love of the Spirit," asking them to strive together with him in fervent prayers to God on his behalf. The first two prayer requests concern his trip to Jerusalem (v. 31, [lit.] "that I may be rescued from the disobedient in Judea, and my service to Jerusalem may be acceptable to the saints"). The third request concerns his trip to Rome (v. 32, "that, by God's will, I may come to you with joy and be refreshed together with you"). A wish-prayer for "the God of peace" to be with them all concludes the paragraph (v. 33; cf. 16:20).

Outline:

1. Paul's foundational ministry (vv. 14–21)
2. Sharing in the apostolic task (vv. 22–33)

15:14. CSB does not translate the conjunction δέ, which signals a new stage in the argument ("now"). A new topic is also indicated by Paul's directly personal address to the readers ("my brothers and sisters").[6] He writes emphatically to express his confidence in their maturity (πέπεισμαι καὶ αὐτὸς ἐγὼ περὶ ὑμῶν, [lit.] "I am convinced, even I myself, about you"). This is "Christian courtesy, not flattery,"[7] though there is an element of hyperbole in the language that follows. Literally, he declares that "you yourselves are also full of goodness" (καὶ αὐτοὶ μεστοί ἐστε ἀγαθωσύνης), "filled with all knowledge" (πεπληρωμένοι πάσης [τῆς] γνώσεως),[8] "able also to instruct one another" (δυνάμενοι καὶ ἀλλήλους νουθετεῖν).[9] The use of μεστοί and πεπληρωμένοι provides an antithesis to Paul's description of unredeemed humanity in 1:29 and highlights that he is addressing a radically changed group of people. Christians are filled with goodness when they are filled with the knowledge of God and his will in Jesus Christ (cf. 1 Cor 1:5; 2 Cor 4:6; 8:7; Col 2:3). Put another way, goodness is a fruit of the Spirit (Gal 5:22; cf. Eph 5:9), and God is able to fulfill "every desire to do good" that he puts within us (2 Thess 1:11).[10]

15:15. The conjunction δέ should be understood in an adversative way here ("but, nevertheless"). Paul's elaborate expression of confidence in the Roman Christians is designed to prevent any misunderstanding of his manner of writing to them (τολμηρότερον

---

[6] As in 1:13; 7:1, 4; 8:12, 29; 10:1; 11:25; 12:1; 14:10, 13, 15, 21, males and females are addressed with the term ἀδελφοί. Omission of μου ("my") in some manuscripts (𝔓[46] D* G 1739 etc.) is explicable in terms of the fact that Paul rarely uses this pronoun with the vocative ἀδελφοί. Cf. 1 Cor 1:11; 14:39 (where it is omitted by some manuscripts); Phil 3:1. Other terms of endearment are added in 1 Cor 15:58; Phil 4:1.

[7] Cranfield, *Romans*, 2:752. The verb πέπεισμαι is similarly used in 8:38; 14:14. Kruse (*Romans*, 536–37) points to various indications in Romans of the immaturity of the readers but thinks Paul was encouraging them to further progress by such positive affirmations.

[8] The article τῆς is omitted by 𝔓[46] A C D F etc. but is included by ℵ B P Ψ etc. If the shorter reading is favored, the meaning will be "with every kind of knowledge." Jewett (*Romans*, 900–901) considers other minor variants to the text of 15:14–16.

[9] The verb νουθετεῖν means "to have a corrective influence on someone" (Johannes Behm, "νουθετέω, νουθεσία," *TDNT* 4:1019). Here, the reference will be to "the reciprocal brotherly ministry of the members exercising pastoral oversight with a sense of congregational obligation" (ibid., 4:1022). Cf. Acts 20:31; 1 Cor 4:14; Col 1:28; 3:16; 1 Thess 5:12, 14; 2 Thess 3:15.

[10] The word ἀγαθωσύνη ("goodness") is not used elsewhere in Romans, but ἀγαθός ("good") is used with reference to the revealed will of God (e.g., 7:12, 13; 8:28; 12:2), and the sort of behavior that should flow from knowing God's goodness (e.g., 2:7, 10; 12:9, 21; 14:16; 16:19). The synonym καλός is used less frequently (7:16, 18, 21; 12:17; 14:21). "Goodness" is an important notion in this letter.

δὲ ἔγραψα ὑμῖν ἀπὸ μέρους, "more boldly in parts" [CSB: "more boldly on some points"]). Certain sections of this letter could be considered presumptuous since he had not founded or ever visited their gatherings.[11] What right did he have to warn and advise them as he did? In fact, he claims to have written this way to "remind" them (ὡς ἐπαναμιμνῄσκων ὑμᾶς), suggesting that much of his content would be familiar to them. Unusually, a double compound verb is used for emphasis here. Reminding Christians of gospel truths and their implications is always helpful (cf. 1 Cor 4:17; 2 Tim 1:6; 2 Pet 1:12). But Paul has written to the Romans because of the grace given to him by God (διὰ τὴν χάριν τὴν δοθεῖσάν μοι ὑπὸ τοῦ θεοῦ; cf. 1:5; 12:3, 6). The following verse makes clear that this is a reference to his divine calling to be Christ's apostle to the nations. Apart from ministering to their needs (1:11–15), he wants to involve them in the next stage of his gospel mission (15:22–32). In 16:25–27 he implies that the insights God has given to him will strengthen them and advance "the obedience of faith among all the Gentiles."

15:16. God's purpose for Paul is indicated by the expression εἰς τὸ εἶναί με λειτουργὸν Χριστοῦ Ἰησοῦ εἰς τὰ ἔθνη (lit., "that I might be a minister of Christ Jesus to the Gentiles"). The word λειτουργός ("servant, minister") was used in 13:6 with reference to civic authorities, but the context suggests a more sacral application here.[12] As in 1:9, Paul is a special agent of God whose role is to serve him (λατρεύω) "in the gospel of his Son." The modifying clause ἱερουργοῦντα τὸ εὐαγγέλιον τοῦ θεοῦ employs a sacrificial metaphor ("serving as a priest of the gospel of God").[13] The next clause explains the reason for this metaphor: "that the Gentiles may be an acceptable offering,

---

[11] The adverbial expression ἀπὸ μέρους ("in part") could modify "more boldly," or "I have written," or "to remind you." It is most natural to take it in relation to the verb that precedes it (ἔγραψα, "I have written"). Since Paul refers to earlier parts of the letter with this verb, it is an ordinary narrative aorist rather than an epistolary aorist.

[12] The political and public use of the noun and related verb in the Greco-Roman world is discussed by Hermann Strathmann and Rudolf Meyer, "λειτουργέω κτλ," *TDNT* 4:216–18. In the LXX, λειτουργός is used fourteen times, mostly with the sense of "servant," but with reference to ministering priests in Isa 61:6; Neh 10:40; Sir 7:30.

[13] Cf. Jewett, *Romans*, 907. The verb ἱερουργέω does not occur anywhere else in the Greek Bible, but Josephus and Philo use it with reference to various sacrificial ministries. By derivation it means "perform the work of a priest," but it is also used in in a broader sense ("present or offer sacrifices") without specifying whether a priest is responsible. Cf. Gottlob Schrenk, "ἱερός κτλ," *TDNT* 3:351–52.

sanctified by the Holy Spirit." CSB takes this to refer to Paul's goal, adding the words "my purpose," but the sequence suggests that *God's* purpose is still in view. The apostle is not a priestly mediator between his converts and God, and he has no material sacrifice to offer. Rather, he preaches the gospel so that Gentiles *themselves* can offer their praise (v. 9) and obedience (v. 18) to God (cf. 1:5; 16:26).

The expression ἡ προσφορὰ τῶν ἐθνῶν is often taken to mean "the offering consisting of the Gentiles" (appositional genitive), implying that Paul offers his converts to God like a priest. But the genitive is more likely subjective: Paul's gospel ministry enables the self-offering of people from every nation to God.[14] They present themselves "as a living sacrifice, holy and pleasing to God" (εὐάρεστον τῷ θεῷ), which is "the understanding service" of the new covenant (12:1 comment). The participial clause ἡγιασμένη ἐν πνεύματι ἁγίῳ (v. 16, "sanctified by the Holy Spirit") stands in apposition to εὐπρόσδεκτος ("acceptable"), suggesting that the work of the Spirit in drawing Gentiles into a faith relationship through Jesus Christ is what makes them acceptable to God (vv. 17–19; cf. 1 Cor 1:2; 6:11; 1 Thess 4:7–8; 2 Thess 2:13; 1 Pet 1:2).

> Although the primary reference is to Paul's evangelistic preaching, by which individuals are brought to Christ and churches are established, it is clear that the apostle sees his ongoing ministry to believers, even the writing of this letter, as a means of enabling Christians to live the consecrated life that is pleasing to God.[15]

15:17. The inferential conjunction οὖν ("therefore") links the next statement with what Paul has just said (lit., "I therefore have

[14] An appositional genitive is understood here by Cranfield (*Romans*, 2:756) and others. But Robinson ("The Priesthood of Paul," 231–32), Dunn (*Romans 9–16*, 860–61), and Moo (*Romans*, 890) consider that the genitive could be subjective. Paul is possibly alluding to the prophetic motif of the eschatological pilgrimage of the nations to Zion (cf. esp. Isa 66:20; also 45:14; 60:5–17; 61:6). Cf. Kruse, *Romans*, 538.

[15] Peterson, *Engaging with God*, 181. Dunn (*Romans 9–16*, 860–61) rightly observes that Paul's "priestly" ministry was radically different because it was conducted out in the world, rather than in some sacred space, and the offering it made possible breached "the fundamental cultic distinction between Jew and Gentile." The breaking down of the distinction between sacred and profane was part of the breaking down of the division between those two groups within humanity. See §§2.6, 2.7.

this boast"). The article before the noun καύχησιν is demonstrative in effect, pointing back to the claim in v. 16. Paul has previously mentioned legitimate boasting (5:2, 3, 11) and illegitimate boasting (3:37; 4:2). The boast he mentions here is legitimate because it is "in Christ Jesus" and concerns "what pertains to God" (τὰ πρὸς τὸν θεόν), that is, "what God has accomplished in Paul's mission" (cf. Col 1:28–29).[16]

15:18–19. Paul's boast is further explained: (lit.) "for (γάρ) I would not dare to say anything except what (ὧν οὐ) Christ has accomplished through me for the obedience of the Gentiles (εἰς ὑπακοὴν ἐθνῶν)." The obedience of Gentiles to the gospel contrasts with what is said about Jews (10:16, 21; 11:30–32; 15:31). Three linked phrases outline how this has come about through Paul's ministry (δι' ἐμοῦ, "through me"): (lit.) "by word and deed, by the power of signs and wonders, and by the power of God's Spirit."[17] The expression λόγῳ καὶ ἔργῳ, ("by word and deed") is chiastically explained by the next two phrases. The work of the Spirit is contextually related to the preaching of the gospel (v. 19b; cf. 1 Cor 2:4), and "deed" is amplified by v. 19a. Paul uses the combination σημείων καὶ τεράτων ("signs and wonders") as Luke does in Acts 4:30; 5:12; 14:3; 15:12 (cf. Heb 2:4).[18] Luke's testimony is that Paul was involved in healing the sick (Acts 14:8–10; 19:11–12; 28:8–9), raising the dead (20:9–12), delivering people from demonic possession (16:16–18), and acting in judgment against opponents (13:9–11).[19] As "signs," these supernatural activities pointed to the power and presence of God. As

[16] Jewett, *Romans*, 909. The article is found in B C[vid] D F G etc. but is missing from 𝔓[46] ℵ A L P Ψ etc. Jewett (901) agrees with Cranfield (*Romans*, 2:757) that the article provides a more difficult reading and is likely to be original.

[17] See n. 5 above regarding the CSB rendering of this sentence. Three adverbial phrases modify the verb κατειργάσατο ("accomplished"). The reading πνεύματος θεοῦ ("Spirit of God") is well attested (𝔓[46] ℵ D[1] Ψ etc.), but B only has πνεύματος, and other texts have πνεύματος ἁγίου (A D* F G etc.). Cranfield (*Romans*, 2.758n5) and Jewett (*Romans*, 901–2) favor the shortest reading, but Metzger (*Textual Commentary*, 473) argues in favor of the longer reading in the earliest witness (𝔓[46]).

[18] The word σημεῖον ("sign") is used in Rom 4:11; 1 Cor 1:22; 14:22; 2 Cor 12:12; 2 Thess 2:9; 3:17, and τέρας ("wonder") in 2 Cor 2:12; 2 Thess 2:9. "Wonders" and "signs" are mentioned separately in Acts 2:19, and in that order together in 2:22 (with "miracles" [δυνάμεσι]), 43; 6:8; 7:36. "Signs and great miracles" are recorded in Acts 8:13, and "signs" alone in 8:6.

[19] Cf. Peterson, *Acts*, 83–87. In continuity with the miracles of Jesus, signs and wonders in Acts validate the messengers and their message, demonstrating the

"wonders," they elicited awe and faith. The power of God's Spirit is a related, but different phenomenon in this context (implied by the twofold use of ἐν δυνάμει, "by the power"). Most likely the allusion is to what was highlighted in v. 16, namely, the drawing of Gentiles into a sanctified relationship with God through faith in Christ (cf. Acts 11:15–18; 15:8–9). Such demonstrations of the power of God authenticated Paul's role as an ambassador of Christ to the nations.[20]

The result has been (ὥστε) that Paul has (lit.) "fulfilled the gospel of Christ from Jerusalem all the way around to Illyricum."[21] The extent of his mission to the Gentiles is outlined in geographical and theological terms. Jerusalem was the starting point because it was the source of the "spiritual benefits" he shared with the nations (v. 27; cf. Gal 2:1–10). The expression καὶ κύκλῳ μέχρι τοῦ Ἰλλυρικοῦ (lit., "even around as far as Illyricum") suggests that he operated in a wide arc from Jerusalem to the Roman province of Illyricum. That region was on the Adriatic coast, stretching from the north of modern Albania to the south of Croatia. It could have been reached by road from Macedonia before Paul turned south to Achaia (Greece), where he stayed for three months and most likely wrote to the Romans (cf. Acts 20:1–3). He may only have preached "up to" (μέχρι) the border of Illyricum, but there was time for him to enter the region after meeting Titus in Macedonia (2 Cor 7:5–16).[22]

The expression πεπληρωκέναι τὸ εὐαγγέλιον τοῦ Χριστοῦ means more than preaching the whole message of the gospel. The context implies that he faithfully fulfilled his commission to proclaim and establish the gospel. As in 1:1, 9, τὸ εὐαγγέλιον is used

---

powerful presence of the kingdom of God and pointing forward to the blessings that will be experienced in the new creation.

[20] Jewett (*Romans*, 911) rightly argues that the Spirit is the means by which the risen Lord is present to his people but wrongly concludes that manifestations of miracle-working power were "routine features" in the Roman congregations. Paul is talking about the miracles associated with his apostolic ministry in other places.

[21] It is difficult to be certain about whether τοῦ Χριστοῦ should be translated "about the Messiah" or "of Christ." The genitive is certainly objective, and only here in Romans is εὐαγγέλιον qualified by τοῦ Χριστοῦ. It would be appropriate for Paul to emphasize that he proclaimed Israel's Messiah to the Gentiles (cf. vv. 8–12), but examples of this expression in other letters do not require this specificity (1 Cor 9:12; 2 Cor 2:12; 9:13; 10:14; Gal 1:7; Phil 1:27; 1 Thess 3:2; 2 Thess 1:8).

[22] Jewett (*Romans*, 913–14) argues that there were several months in the summer and fall of 56 when the province could have been visited.

in a dynamic sense ("the preaching of the gospel"), in parallel with εὐαγγελίζεσθαι (v. 20, "to evangelize"). The verb πεπληρωκέναι could simply mean that he executed "a commanded action."[23] However, with τὸ εὐαγγέλιον as object, it is likely that Paul meant fulfilling the demands of preaching the gospel by founding and nurturing churches, teaching believers, and grounding them firmly in the faith. This would be consistent with the description of his ambitions in 1:1–15; 15:14–16 (cf. Acts 13–20). A similar expression is used in Col 1:25 (πληρῶσαι τὸν λόγον τοῦ θεοῦ, [lit.] "to fulfill the word of God"). In that context the apostle describes his ministry goals even more comprehensively (Col 1:24–2:7).[24]

15:20–21. The adverb οὕτως ("so") with δέ ("now" [not translated by CSB]) points to what follows from the description of Paul's ministry so far. The participle φιλοτιμούμενον ("aspiring, aiming"),[25] in conjunction with the infinitive εὐαγγελίζεσθαι, expresses the apostle's goal of preaching the gospel where Christ has not yet been acknowledged.[26] This aspiration is further explained by a purpose clause: "so that I will not build on someone else's foundation" (ἵνα μὴ ἐπ' ἀλλότριον θεμέλιον οἰκοδομῶ). In 1 Cor 3:9–15 Paul describes himself as "a skilled master builder," laying the foundation of Jesus Christ for the church in Corinth, which is "God's building" (θεοῦ οἰκοδομή). But here he uses the metaphor differently: he will not build a church where someone else has already laid a foundation (cf. 2 Cor 10:15–16).[27] This strategy has nothing to do with personal rivalry but is driven by the expectation of Isa 52:15 that nations will be greatly amazed at the exaltation of the Suffering Servant and

[23] Cf. Gerhard Delling, "πλήρης κτλ.," *TDNT* 6:297; Jewett, *Romans*, 914. Paul claims to have completed "that trail-blazing, pioneer preaching of (the gospel) which he believed it was his own special apostolic mission to accomplish" (Cranfield, *Romans*, 2:762)

[24] Cf. David G. Peterson, "Maturity: The Goal of Mission," in *The Gospel to the Nations: Perspectives on Paul's Mission*, ed. Peter Bolt and Mark Thompson (Leicester: Apollos; Downers Grove: InterVarsity, 2000;) 185–204; Paul Bowers, "Fulfilling the Gospel: The Scope of the Pauline Mission," *JETS* 30 (1987): 185–98.

[25] The verb φιλοτιμέομαι was originally used for striving after civic honors but came to be used more generally for vocational goals, or "the willingness to carry out a task set by a superior" (Jewett, *Romans*, 915). Cf. 2 Cor 5:9; 1 Thess 4:11.

[26] The passive verb ὠνομάσθη may mean "be acknowledged, honored," but "named in worship" (Dunn, *Romans 9–16*, 865) may read too much into the context.

[27] See my comments on οἰκοδομή ("building") in 14:19.

kings will "shut their mouths" because of him. Introduced with the familiar "as it is written," the latter part of this text predicts that this will happen because "those who were not told about him will see, and those who have not heard will understand."[28] As a pioneer evangelist, Paul has so far brought that understanding to people in the region from Jerusalem to Illyricum. He keeps evangelizing where Christ has not been named, encouraged by the expectation that people everywhere will see and understand his message about the Lord Jesus Christ.

Some commentators suggest that Paul's nonintervention rule in v. 20 is contradicted by his desire to minister to the Romans (1:3–15; 15:14–16). But the following verses indicate that his main reason for wanting to visit them is to gain their support for the next stage of his mission, not to grow a new church in their midst (15:22–32). His exposition of the gospel and its implications in this letter are parts of that plan. He wants the Roman Christians to be united with him in understanding, living out, and propagating the gospel in a new region.

15:22–24. The inferential conjunction διό ("therefore, for this reason") signals the beginning of a new stage in the argument (CSB: "That is why"]. Paul's preoccupation with fulfilling his gospel mission from Jerusalem to Illyricum has "also" (καί) hindered him (ἐνεκοπτόμην, [lit.] "I was prevented") "many times" (τὰ πολλὰ) from visiting Rome (thus explaining 1:13).[29] But now he declares that he no longer has any "place" or "opportunity" in this region (cf. τόπον in 12:19; Eph 4:27; Heb 12:17), implying that "the pioneer work of evangelism which is his special task has already been accomplished."[30] "Fulfilling the gospel" (v. 19) clearly meant establishing viable mission centers in that territory, rather than personally

[28] It is significant that this text forms an introduction to the so-called Fourth Servant Song in Isa 52:13–53:12, announcing in advance the outcome of the Servant's unmerited suffering.

[29] The verb ἐγκόπτω ("cut down, impede, hinder") refers to hindrances in the way of the gospel in Gal 5:7; 1 Thess 2:18, and prayer in 1 Pet 3:7. Together with τὰ πολλά, the imperfect passive here suggests "a series of specific hindrances such as those mentioned in Paul's catalog of missional impedances and disasters in 2 Cor 11:24–29" (Jewett, *Romans*, 922).

[30] Cranfield, *Romans*, 2:766. Cranfield vigorously opposes the view that Paul had a limited view of what he must do before the imminent return of Christ. Dunn (*Romans 9–16*, 871) thinks Cranfield confuses "the issue of the geographical scope

evangelizing every village or town (cf. Acts 19:8–10). Paul adds a reminder that he has had a strong desire (ἐπιποθίαν) for many years to come to Rome (cf. 1:11, ἐπιποθῶ), before introducing the idea that he will visit his readers "whenever" he travels to Spain (ὡς ἂν πορεύωμαι εἰς τὴν Σπανίαν).[31] We cannot be certain why this was his goal, but apparently he wanted to begin another arc of gospel work, beginning from Rome and terminating in Spain.

Rome held territory in Spain from the end of the third century BC, though it was not until the time of Augustus that the whole peninsula was subjugated and three provinces were created.[32] Evidence of substantial Jewish settlement in Spain does not appear until the third and fourth centuries AD. So Paul could not count on using synagogues as bases of operation or rely on some knowledge of Jewish beliefs in the Spanish community.[33] Moreover, Spain was resistant to Greco-Roman culture and was regarded as "barbarian" (cf. 1:14 comment). According to 1 Clement 5:6–7, which was written from Rome in about AD 96, Paul eventually reached "the limit of the west" (τὸ τέρμα τῆς δύσεως), though scholars debate whether this refers to Spain.[34]

Paul's focus is on visiting Rome first ("for I hope to see you when I pass through," ἐλπίζω γὰρ διαπορευόμενος θεάσασθαι ὑμᾶς). But his ultimate aim is to be "assisted by you for my journey there" (καὶ ὑφ' ὑμῶν προπεμφθῆναι ἐκεῖ). The verb translated "assisted for my journey" could mean sending him on his way with food, money,

---

of Paul's vision with that of the near expectation of the Parousia." Cf. Schreiner, *Romans*, 775–76.

[31] Some manuscripts add ἐλεύσομαι πρὸς ὑμᾶς ("I will come to you") after Σπανίαν (א[2] 6 33 etc.) as a clarification of the awkward syntax in these verses, but the shorter reading is much better attested. Paul uses ὡς ἄν as an equivalent for ὅταν ("whenever") with the subjunctive (cf. BDF § 455 [2]; 1 Cor 11:34; Phil 2:23).

[32] Jewett (*Romans*, 77–79) provides details about the Roman colonization and administration of Spain. Spain would have presented Paul with formidable challenges linguistically and politically.

[33] Cf. Jewett, *Romans*, 75; W. Paul Bowers, "Jewish Communities in Spain in the Time of Paul the Apostle," *JTS* 26 (1975): 395–402.

[34] Frederick F. Bruce (*Paul: Apostle of the Heart Set Free* [Grand Rapids: Eerdmans, 1977], 447–48) points out that τὸ τέρμα τῆς δύσεως could refer to Rome as Paul's western goal, where, according to Clement, "He bore testimony before the rulers, and so departed from the world." If it refers to Spain, there are difficulties in reconstructing Paul's movements after the imprisonment mentioned in Acts 28. Cf. Peterson, *Acts*, 720–21, 723–25.

appropriate transport, travel companions, or letters of introduction (BDAG; cf. Acts 15:3; 20:38; 21:5; 1 Cor 16:6, 11; 2 Cor 1:16; Titus 3:13; 3 John 6). "By refraining at this point from making specific demands, Paul conveys his willingness to trust the hospitality of the Roman churches and to receive whatever they deemed appropriate."[35] To reinforce this cautious approach, Paul stresses that he *first* wants to enjoy their company for a while (ἐὰν ὑμῶν πρῶτον ἀπὸ μέρους ἐμπλησθῶ). This suggests that issues of support will not be raised until a personal relationship is established with them all.

15:25–26. Another surprise is introduced by the words νυνὶ δέ (v. 25, "now however" [CSB: "Right now"]). Paul is in the process of going (πορεύομαι) to Jerusalem, (lit.) "serving the saints" (διακονῶν τοῖς ἁγίοις).[36] As in 1:7; 8:27; 12:13; 15:31; 16:2, 15, the term ἁγίοι ("saints" or "holy ones") describes those set apart through faith in Christ to belong to God and to one another (cf. 1 Cor 1:2, 30; 6:11; 2 Thess 2:13), only here the reference is specifically to Christians in Jerusalem. The explanation for Paul's service in this case (γάρ, "for") is that "Macedonia and Achaia were pleased to make a contribution for the poor among the saints in Jerusalem." Two provinces previously evangelized by the apostle are singled out for special mention, the names signifying the Christians who lived there.[37] The verb εὐδόκησαν ("pleased") highlights the voluntary nature of their contribution. Literally, they were seeking to "establish a particular fellowship" (κοινωνίαν τινὰ ποιήσασθαι) with the poor believers in Jerusalem.[38] As in Acts 2:42, the noun κοινωνία

[35] Jewett, *Romans*, 926.

[36] It is likely that the present participle διακονῶν is used here to express purpose (CSB: "to serve"). Cf. 12:7 comment. The word group is mostly used by Paul with reference to the collection (15:31; 2 Cor 8:4, 19–20; 9:1, 12–13; cf. Acts 11:29; 12:25). This was a fulfillment of the promise he had made to go on remembering the poor in Jerusalem (Gal 2:10).

[37] The Galatian churches had already contributed to this collection (1 Cor 16:1–3). Perhaps Paul chose to limit his reference to Macedonia and Achaia because they were the most recent contributors and he was writing to the Romans during a winter stay in Achaia (Acts 20:1–3). Jewett (*Romans*, 919) notes that the singular form εὐδόκησεν is found in 𝔓[46] B and a few other manuscripts. He translates "Macedonia was pleased and also Achaia" and offers an explanation of why Paul may have written this way (Jewett, 927–28).

[38] Cf. Jewett, *Romans*, 928–29; Scott McKnight, "Collection for the Saints," *DPL* 143–47; Keith F. Nickle, *The Collection: A Study in Paul's Strategy*, SBT 48 (London: SCM, 1966).

("partnership, fellowship") is used with reference to the sharing of material resources.[39] Paul employs the term in a similar way in 2 Cor 9:13 when discussing this same collection (*ἁπλότητι τῆς κοινωνίας* [lit,] "the generosity of the partnership/contribution"). An earlier collection for Jerusalem Christians in a time of famine is recorded in Acts 11:27–30; 12:25. The later collection is only briefly mentioned in Acts 24:17, but Paul makes much of it in 1 Cor 16:1–4 and 2 Cor 8–9. The term "saints" in this context is particularly poignant. Israel as a nation was called to be God's holy people (Exod 19:5–6), yet Paul distinguishes Christian Jews from the rest by calling them "the saints." Their poverty may have been a result of their commitment to Christ and the social alienation they suffered as a consequence.[40]

15:27. Paul repeats the claim that Macedonia and Achaia were pleased to make a contribution for the poor among the saints in Jerusalem (*εὐδόκησαν γάρ*, CSB: "Yes, they were pleased") but then adds, "and indeed are indebted to them" (*καὶ ὀφειλέται εἰσὶν αὐτῶν*).[41] A sense of obligation can be a powerful motivation for freely chosen acts of grace (cf. 1:14; 8:12; 13:8; 15:1). A condition of fact explains the debt of the Gentile churches in these terms: "For if the Gentiles have shared in their spiritual benefits, then they are obligated to minister to them in material needs." Gentiles received a share (*ἐκοινώνησαν*) in the spiritual blessings promised to Israel (*τοῖς πνευματικοῖς αὐτῶν*, cf. 15:8–12) through the preaching of the gospel (cf. 1:11–12). This gift moved many to establish a particular fellowship (v. 26, *κοινωνίαν*

[39] Cf. Peterson, *Acts*, 16–61. Cf. Acts 2:44–45; 4:32 ("They held everything in common" [*ἅπαντα κοινά*.]). Yet this sharing of material things was clearly an expression of the new relationship experienced together through a common faith in Christ. Paul uses the cognate verb in Rom 12:13; Gal 6:6; Phil 4:15 with reference to financial or other material contributions. In 15:27 the reference is to the sharing of spiritual benefits.

[40] It has been suggested that "the poor" could be an honorific title equivalent to "the saints" (reading *τῶν ἁγίων* as an exegetical genitive), but Jewett (*Romans*, 929–30) rightly argues that the genitive is partitive and that Paul is concerned with "the poor among the saints." Dunn (*Romans 9–16*, 882) limits this poverty to Jewish Christians coming to Jerusalem from the Diaspora, but it could easily have been the experience of converts from Judaism who were resident in the city.

[41] Cranfield (*Romans*, 2:773n2) rightly takes *αὐτῶν* here to refer to the poor saints "as being representative of the whole Jerusalem church." It is clear from the next sentence that the Gentiles are spiritually indebted to Jerusalem believers collectively for the gospel. Dunn (*Romans 9–16*, 873–74) considers different reasons Paul may have promoted this particular collection. Cf. McKnight, "Collection," 143–47.

τινά) with the poor among the saints in Jerusalem.[42] Paul apparently encouraged the Gentile churches he had founded to express their debt of gratitude to Israel by serving Jewish believers with regard to their "material needs" (ἐν τοῖς σαρκικοῖς λειτουργῆσαι αὐτοῖς).[43] This was not meant to be a literal repayment for what the Gentiles had received but rather the response of grace to grace (2 Cor 9:7–15). The gift of the Gentile churches to Jerusalem was a significant consequence of Paul's "priestly" ministry of the gospel (v. 16 comment) and an outworking of their obedience to the gospel (v. 19).

15:28–29. Using the inferential conjunction οὖν ("so"), Paul concludes his reflection on the three proposed journeys. First, he refers to Jerusalem ("when I have finished this and safely delivered the funds to them"). Metaphorically, "this fruit" (τὸν καρπὸν τοῦτον) refers to the collection, which is the result of his ministry as a Jewish apostle to the nations. Two aorist participles describe this activity: ἐπιτελέσας ("completed"; cf. 2 Cor 8:6, 11; Phil 1:6) and σφραγισάμενος ("sealed"). The second verb was used in connection with the completion of a delivery, which in this case could mean "to guarantee its delivery against theft and embezzlement."[44] Then he mentions Rome and Spain together (ἀπελεύσομαι δι' ὑμῶν εἰς Σπανίαν, "I will visit you on the way to Spain"). He concludes by saying, (lit.) "and I know that when I come to you, I will come in the fullness of the blessing of Christ." This expresses confidence about the reception he will receive in Rome. His expression ἐν πληρώματι εὐλογίας Χριστοῦ ("in the fullness of the blessing of Christ") could embrace their hospitality and fellowship, opportunities for mutual ministry, and being sent on his way with their full support (cf. 1:11–12, 13; 15:24). Here is another implied compliment about

[42] The same verb is used in 12:13 with the sense of "sharing with the saints in their needs" (ταῖς χρείαις τῶν ἁγίων κοινωνοῦντες). Here "the saints" are Christians in general.

[43] The verb λειτουργεῖν denotes service to the Lord in prayer and ministry to one another in Acts 13:2 and is used of priestly service to God in Heb 10:11. The noun λειτουργός ("public servant, minister") is used in Rom 13:6; 15:16; Phil 2:25, and λειτουργία ("service, ministry") in 2 Cor 9:12; Phil 2:17, 30. The adjective σαρκικός ("fleshly") is not used polemically in the contrast with πνευματικός ("spiritual") here but simply as a reference to everyday needs.

[44] Jewett, *Romans*, 932 (BDAG, "when I have placed the sum that was collected safely [sealed] in their hands"). Cf. 2 Cor 8:20–23. But Cranfield (*Romans*, 2:775) suggests that the participle here could mean "confirm the collection's significance."

their spiritual maturity (v. 14), encouraging them to act accordingly. More broadly, the fullness of Christ's blessing could refer to "the expansive triumph of the gospel that Paul's letter and travel aim to advance."[45]

15:30. Paul's solemn charge to his readers is reminiscent of the opening words of 12:1 (παρακαλῶ δὲ ὑμᾶς, ἀδελφοί, "Now I appeal to you, brothers and sisters"). Two linked phrases indicate that this is more than a moral appeal.[46] The first (διὰ τοῦ κυρίου ἡμῶν Ἰησοῦ Χριστοῦ, "through our Lord Jesus Christ") draws attention to their common relationship with Christ and his authority over them (cf. 14:4–9). The second phrase (διὰ τῆς ἀγάπης τοῦ πνεύματος, "through the love of the Spirit") focuses on the love the Spirit makes possible (cf. 5:5; 12:9 comment). With a recognition of Christ's lordship and a loving concern for Paul and his welfare, they are exhorted (lit.) "to strive together with me in your prayers to God on my behalf" (συναγωνίσασθαί μοι ἐν ταῖς προσευχαῖς ὑπὲρ ἐμοῦ πρὸς τὸν θεόν). The compound συναγωνίζεσθαι only occurs here in the Greek Bible, but the root verb is similarly used in relation to prayer in Col 4:12 (ἀγωνιζόμενος). The compound means "join with someone in common effort" (BDAG). CSB adds the word "fervent" to emphasize the need for intensity and persistence in praying. Paul does not regard prayer as a struggle with God but as a means of appealing to him for help in the difficulties of gospel ministry, especially the spiritual battle against opponents.[47]

15:31–32. Specific prayer requests are indicated by two uses of ἵνα and three subjunctive verbs. First, Paul asks that "I may be rescued from the unbelievers in Judea" (ῥυσθῶ ἀπὸ τῶν ἀπειθούντων ἐν τῇ Ἰουδαίᾳ). Literally, he describes those who may be hostile to him as "the disobedient" (cf. 2:8; 10:16, 21; 11:30, 31), expecting serious

---

[45] Jewett, *Romans*, 934. The shorter reading εὐλογίας Χριστοῦ is well attested (𝔓[46] א* A B C D etc.), but this was expanded in later witnesses (א[c] Ψ 33 88 etc.) by the insertion of τοῦ εὐαγγελίου τοῦ ("the gospel of").

[46] Although ἀδελφοί ("brothers and sisters") is missing from 𝔓[46] B, it is widely supported (א A C D F G etc.). Jewett (*Romans*, 919) argues that 𝔓[46] B are susceptible to omission and that "in view of the stronger witness for inclusion, the word ἀδελφοί should be considered original." Cf. 15:14 comment.

[47] Cf. Dunn, *Romans 9–16*, 878. The verb συναγωνίζομαι was used in ancient Greek sources in military and athletic contexts. Cf. Victor C. Pfitzner, *Paul and the Agon Motif: Traditional Athletic Imagery in the Pauline Literature*, NovTSup 16 (Leiden: Brill, 1967), 120–25.

opposition from Jews who have rejected the gospel (cf. 1 Thess 2:14–16; 2 Thess 3:1–2). Acts 21:26–36 describes the immediate outcome of his visit to Jerusalem: Paul's prayer was answered but in a surprising way. Misrepresented as profaning the temple he was rescued by the Roman authorities from mob violence and later from assassination (Acts 23:12–24). Providentially, he was brought to Rome as a prisoner of the emperor (cf. Acts 28:11–16)!

Second, the apostle asks that "my ministry to Jerusalem may be acceptable to the saints." The noun διακονία ("service, ministry") picks up his reference to serving the saints in v. 25 (διακονῶν).[48] His prayer that the financial contribution from the Gentile churches might be "acceptable to the saints" (εὐπρόσδεκτος τοῖς ἁγίοις) signifies an awareness of some suspicion in Jerusalem about his work among the nations, especially in relation to his law-free gospel. Acts 21:20–25 bears witness to that disquiet and the attempt of James and the elders to forestall any attack on him. Paul's passing comment in Acts 24:17 suggests that the gift was understood and received in the right spirit.[49]

Third, he asks that, "by God's will, I may come to you with joy and be refreshed together with you."[50] His coming "with joy" (ἐν χαρᾷ) logically relates to the previous requests. Delivered from danger, he wants to visit Rome with the knowledge that the collection from the Gentiles was acceptable to the Jerusalem believers. His coming "by God's will" (διὰ θελήματος θεοῦ) signifies a reliance on God's sovereignty to bring this about, with openness to the possibility that his prayer could be answered in a number of ways (cf. 1:10 comment).[51] The expression that "I may . . . be refreshed together with you" (συναναπαύσωμαι ὑμῖν) recalls his hope that they might be

---

[48] Instead of διακονία ("service"), several witnesses, chiefly Western (B D* G^gr), read δωροφορία ("the bringing of a gift"), which Metzger (*Textual Commentary*, 474) describes as "an obvious gloss defining the purpose of Paul's journey."

[49] Cf. Stephan Joubert, *Paul as Benefactor: Reciprocity, Strategy, and Theological Reflection in Paul's Collection*, WUNT 124 (Tübingen: Mohr Siebeck, 2000), 207.

[50] Some commentators dispute that this is a third prayer request, viewing it as the ultimate goal of the two requests just mentioned (e.g., Moo, *Romans*, 911). However, since Paul himself has been praying assiduously about being able to come to them (1:9–11) and is aware of so many reasons he may be prevented from coming to them with joy, it seems likely that he would want the Romans to include this in their prayers for him.

[51] Different words qualify διὰ θελήματος ("by the will") in the manuscripts, but θεοῦ ("of God") is the best attested (𝔓^46 ℵ^2 A C D^2 etc.). Paul nowhere else speaks

"mutually encouraged" by each other's faith (1:12, συμπαρακληθῆναι ἐν ὑμῖν).[52] Other references to refreshment in Paul's letters use the root verb ἀναπαύω and involve the resolution of problems concerning the mission of the gospel (1 Cor 16:18; 2 Cor 7:13; Phlm 7, 20). So, in the context of mutual, spiritual encouragement, Paul may be alluding to the resolution of tensions in the Roman context that could play a part in "frustrating the plans for the Spanish mission."[53]

15:33. A third wish-prayer concludes a section of Paul's address to his readers in this chapter (cf. vv. 5–6; 13). In each case the content of the prayer relates to the immediately preceding argument (cf. 1 Thess 5:23; 2 Thess 3:16). Paul's desire for "the God of peace" to be with them is briefly expressed without a verb (Ὁ δὲ θεὸς τῆς εἰρήνης μετὰ πάντων ὑμῶν). God is the source of genuine peace, reconciling us to himself through the cross of Christ (5:1; 8:6), enabling personal relationships without strife by the operation of his Spirit (14:19; 15:13) and providing final victory over all the powers of evil (2:10; 16:20). The inclusive reference to "all" of the Romans echoes 1:6–7 and is unique to this letter. Paul reinforces his plea for all to act graciously and lovingly toward one another (12:3–18; 13:8–10), especially with regard to the matters discussed in 14:1–15:7. This concern is further expressed in the greetings that follow in 16:1–16. Paul's "amen" invites them to respond with an "amen" of their own (cf. 1:25; 16:27), thus affirming the need for God to bring his peace to bear on their situation.[54]

Bridge

As Paul highlights the distinctiveness of his own apostolic ministry, he gives several indications of the way others could share

---

of "the will of Jesus Christ" (ℵ*), or "of Christ Jesus" (D* F G), or "of our Lord Jesus" (B).

[52] The compound verb only occurs elsewhere in the Greek Bible in Isa 11:6 (with the meaning "sleep with"). It is strongly attested in the manuscripts of Rom 15:32 but is strangely missing from 𝔓[46] B. This omission may be a transcriptional error (cf. Metzger, Textual Commentary, 474) or an attempt to avoid a rare and ambiguous term (Jewett, 920). In a few Western witnesses it is replaced by ἀναψύξω ("I will be refreshed") or ἀναψύχω ("I am refreshed").

[53] Jewett, *Romans*, 938.

[54] Ἀμήν is attested by a variety of textual groups (ℵ B C D L P Ψ etc.) but is missing from 𝔓[46] because the doxology of 16:25–27 is placed here. Other manuscripts leave out the ἀμήν but do not include the doxology (e.g., A F G).

in his work. The churches in Macedonia and Achaia were able to contribute to Paul's collection for the saints in Jerusalem in order to express gratitude for receiving the blessings of the gospel from believing Israelites (vv. 25–27). The Roman Christians were encouraged to provide practical support for the next stage of his missionary outreach (vv. 24, 29) and to share in his struggles through prayer (vv. 30–32). Christians today can similarly share in the work of the gospel by supporting those who are engaged in pioneer evangelism and church planting and by taking opportunities to share the message themselves. Like Paul, some may even initiate ministry in places where Christ has not been previously named. Even so, there were aspects of Paul's calling that were unique. As apostle to the Gentiles, he took the lead in establishing the gospel in churches across the eastern half of the Roman Empire. A significant aspect of his apostolic ministry was the writing of letters that came to be recognized as having the authority of Scripture (2 Pet 3:16). In the providence of God, these provided an inspired exposition and application of the gospel that was valid for the edification and maturation of churches throughout the centuries. In his own time Paul also acted as a bridge builder between the Gentile churches he founded and Jewish Christianity. In particular, he used the collection for the saints in Jerusalem as a means of highlighting God's long-standing plan to unite Jews and Gentiles in praise of his victorious Son (cf. vv. 8–12). In this way he showed how the theology of grace, love, and service he articulated can radically impact converts from different cultures, to the glory of God.

B. Commendation, Greetings, Warnings, and Blessings (16:1–27)[55]

[1] I commend to you our sister Phoebe, who is a servant of the
church in Cenchreae. [2] So you should welcome her in the Lord in
a manner worthy of the saints and assist her in whatever matter

[55] The textual history of chapter 16, and issues related to the different placements of the doxology traditionally located in 16:25–27, are discussed by Metzger, *Textual Commentary*, 470–73. See also my Introduction (sec I) and n. 115 below. Peter Lampe ("The Roman Christians of Romans 16," in *The Romans Debate,* rev. ed., ed. Karl P. Donfried [Peabody: Hendrickson, 1991], 217–21) provides a helpful summary of the reasons the chapter should be considered as an original part of the letter.

she may require your help. For indeed she has been a benefactor of many—and of me also.

[3]Give my greetings to Prisca and Aquila, my coworkers in Christ Jesus, [4]who risked their own necks for my life. Not only do I thank them, but so do all the Gentile churches. [5]Greet also the church that meets in their home. Greet my dear friend Epaenetus, who is the first convert to Christ from Asia. [6]Greet Mary, who has worked very hard for you. [7]Greet Andronicus and Junia, my fellow Jews and fellow prisoners. They are noteworthy in the eyes of the apostles, and they were also in Christ before me. [8]Greet Ampliatus, my dear friend in the Lord. [9]Greet Urbanus, our coworker in Christ, and my dear friend Stachys. [10]Greet Apelles, who is approved in Christ. Greet those who belong to the household of Aristobulus. [11]Greet Herodion, my fellow Jew. Greet those who belong to the household of Narcissus who are in the Lord. [12]Greet Tryphaena and Tryphosa, who have worked hard in the Lord. Greet my dear friend Persis, who has worked very hard in the Lord. [13]Greet Rufus, chosen in the Lord; also his mother—and mine. [14]Greet Asyncritus, Phlegon, Hermes, Patrobas, Hermas, and the brothers and sisters who are with them. [15]Greet Philologus and Julia, Nereus and his sister, and Olympas, and all the saints who are with them. [16]Greet one another with a holy kiss. All the churches of Christ send you greetings.

[17]Now I urge you, brothers and sisters, to watch out for those who create divisions and obstacles contrary to the teaching that you learned. Avoid them, [18]because such people do not serve our Lord Christ but their own appetites. They deceive the hearts of the unsuspecting with smooth talk and flattering words.

[19]The report of your obedience has reached everyone. Therefore I rejoice over you, but I want you to be wise about what is good, and yet innocent about what is evil. [20]The God of peace will soon crush Satan under your feet. The grace of our Lord Jesus be with you.

[21]Timothy, my coworker, and Lucius, Jason, and Sosipater, my fellow countrymen, greet you.

[22]I Tertius, who wrote this letter, greet you in the Lord.

[23]Gaius, who is host to me and to the whole church, greets you. Erastus, the city treasurer, and our brother Quartus greet you.

[25]Now to him who is able to strengthen you according to my gospel and the proclamation about Jesus Christ, according to the revelation of the mystery kept silent for long ages [26]but now revealed and made known through the prophetic Scriptures,

according to the command of the eternal God to advance the obedience of faith among all the Gentiles—[27]to the only wise God, through Jesus Christ—to him be the glory forever! Amen.

Context

The conjunction δέ ("now"), which is not translated by CSB, suggests that there is a connection between the preceding section and the commendation of Phoebe in vv. 1–2. Her coming to Rome is linked to Paul's coming (cf. 15:23–24, 28–29), and she is to be given whatever help she needs to prepare for that. A series of greetings and commendations in vv. 3–16 reveal the large number of believers in Rome already known to Paul (a total of 26), many of whom had been coworkers. His call to express close and friendly bonds with other Christians in the city builds on his teaching about mutual care and respect for one another (12:1–15:13). At the same time, he seeks to enhance the personal relationship between himself and his readers in preparation for his visit. An unexpected warning about avoiding false teachers and their influence follows (vv. 17–20a), before the greetings of those who are with Paul in Corinth are conveyed (vv. 20b–23). The concluding doxology picks up important expressions from earlier in the letter, drawing attention to the power of the gospel to "advance the obedience of faith among all the Gentiles" and strengthen the readers in their service to God (vv. 25–27). This doxology subtly restates Paul's role in the plan of God for the nations and his purpose in writing this letter (cf. §2.7).

Structure

The commendation of Phoebe in vv. 1–2 broadly follows the pattern found in similar epistolary passages: introduction, credentials, and a desired action.[56] A series of second-person plural encouragements to greet other believers in their community follows (vv. 3–15, ἀσπάσασθε). Descriptions of those to be greeted vary from a complex expression of gratitude to Prisca and Aquila (vv. 3–4) to the mere listing of individuals and those who are with them (vv. 14–15). This segment concludes with a charge to "greet

[56] Cf. Chan-Hie Kim, *The Form and Structure of the Familiar Greek Letter of Recommendation*, SBLDS 4 (Missoula: Scholars Press, 1972), 7, 72, 126. Jewett (*Romans*, 942) notes the oddity of Paul's return to Phoebe's credentials in v. 2b.

one another with a holy kiss" and a declaration that "all the churches of Christ send you greetings" (v. 16).

A warning passage in vv. 17–19 begins with the solemn words Παρακαλῶ δὲ ὑμᾶς, ἀδελφοί ("Now I implore you, brothers and sisters"; cf. 12:1; 15:30). Paul instructs them to watch out for certain false teachers, basing his warning on a description of their motivation and their effect on the unsuspecting (v. 18, γάρ ["because"]). Acknowledging that the report of the obedience of the Roman Christians has "reached everyone," he rejoices over them but wants them to be "wise about what is good, and yet innocent about what is evil" (v. 19). The segment concludes in v. 20 with a promise ("The God of peace will soon crush Satan under your feet") and a brief wish-prayer ("The grace of our Lord Jesus be with you").

The greetings in vv. 21–23 are mostly in the third-person indicative (ἀσπάζεται) and come from Paul's coworkers and others who are with him. Tertius, who has actually penned the letter, sends a first-person greeting (v. 22, ἀσπάζομαι ὑμᾶς ἐγώ [lit., "I myself greet you"]). The chapter finishes with a complex doxology in vv. 25–27. This picks up some of the themes of the letter concerning the power of God to strengthen his people through the proclamation of the gospel of Christ, the scriptural basis of this gospel, and Paul's role in revealing "the mystery kept silent for long ages" so as "to advance the obedience of faith among all the Gentiles."

Outline:

1. Welcoming and assisting Phoebe (vv. 1–2)
2. Greeting Paul's coworkers and friends (vv. 3–16)
3. Watching out for false teachers and their effect (vv. 17–20)
4. Glorifying God with the apostle and his associates (vv. 21–27)

16:1. As noted above, the conjunction δέ ("now," not translated by CSB) suggests a link between the preceding section and what follows. By welcoming Phoebe appropriately, the Roman Christians will be preparing to receive Paul. The practice of sending letters of recommendation is noted in 1 Macc 12:4; 2 Macc 9:25; 2 Cor 3:1. Different patterns of commendation in the Pauline letters emerge in 1 Cor 16:15–18; Phil 4:2–3; 1 Thess 5:12–13a; Phlm, 10–17. Phoebe is first commended (Συνίστημι) as "our sister," meaning that, first and foremost, she is to be received as a fellow believer.[57] Her credentials are then announced: (οὖσαν [καὶ] διάκονον τῆς ἐκκλησίας τῆς ἐν Κεγχρεαῖς [lit.] "She is [also] a servant of the church in Cenchreae."[58] Although there were six towns with the name Cenchreae at that time, most probably Paul refers to the eastern port of Corinth (cf. Acts 18:18), which was about ten kilometers from where he is likely to have written to the Romans. Ancient epistolary practice would suggest that Paul's recommendation was "related to her task of conveying and interpreting the letter in Rome as well as in carrying out the business entailed in the letter."[59] Given the importance of its contents—both for the apostle's mission plans and for the readers—he was "undoubtedly investing a great deal in Phoebe when he entrusted the letter to her."[60]

Much discussion has focused on the significance of Phoebe's role as διάκονος. Paul mostly uses this term to refer to himself and his coworkers as "servants" or "ministers" of God (1 Cor 3:5; 2 Cor 6:4; Eph 6:21; Col 1:7; 4:7; 1 Tim 4:6) or of the gospel (2 Cor 3:6; Eph 3:7; Col 1:23). Only in Phil 1:1; 1 Tim 3:8, 12 does διάκονος denote an office in the local church (see also Ignatius, *Eph* 2:1; *Magn* 6.1), which could be the sense here ("a deacon of the church in Cenchreae"). However, it is difficult to be certain about what that ministry might have entailed. While the "overseer" (ἐπίσκοπος) in 1 Tim 3:1–7 was required to be "an able teacher," there is no such demand for the "deacon" in 1 Tim 3:8–13. Moreover, the assumption in both of these passages is that congregational leaders were

---

[57] The verb συνίστημι is used in 3:5; 5:8 with the sense "prove, demonstrate," but here it means "commend," as in 2 Macc 9:25; 2 Cor 3:1; 5:12; 6:4; 10:12, 18. Dunn (*Romans 9–16*, 886) observes that the designation ἀδελφή ("sister") "seems to have been particularly characteristic of Christianity (1 Cor 7:15; 9:5; Phlm 2; Jas 2:15; Ignatius, *Pol.* 5.1; 2 Clement 12:5; 19:1; 20:2; Herm. Vis. 2.2.3; 2.3.1)."

[58] The word καί ("and, also") is found in 𝔓[46] ℵ[2] B C* etc. but not in ℵ* A C[2] D F G etc. If this is the original reading, it could have been modified in copying because of the awkwardness of the syntax. It is likely to be original because it lends weight to Phoebe's qualifications. Cf. Jewett, *Romans*, 941.

[59] Jewett, *Romans*, 943. Cf. E. Randolph Richards, *Paul and First-Century Letter Writing: Secretaries, Composition, and Collection* (Downers Grove: InterVarsity, 2004), 188–209. Her task could have included having the letter copied for distribution among the churches of Rome, reading it aloud in different contexts, and answering questions about its meaning.

[60] Allan Chapple, "Getting *Romans* to the Right Romans: Phoebe and the Delivery of Paul's Letter," *TynBul* 62 (2011): 198.

men. In view of the way diaconal ministry developed in subsequent years, commentators often argue that Phoebe's ministry involved "visitation of the sick, poor relief, and perhaps financial oversight."[61] But this reads too much formality into the earliest period of church life, when the pattern of leadership was still fluid and more gift oriented (cf. 12:7 comment; 1 Cor 12:4–11, 27–30). If Paul's description of Phoebe as "benefactor of many—and of me also" (v. 2) is considered in relation to the term διάκονος, we may surmise that, at the very least, she served the church in Cenchreae by hosting gatherings in her home (cf. Lydia in Acts 16:14–15, 40) and by materially supporting ministries like Paul's.[62]

16:2. Based on his commendation of Phoebe, Paul wants the Romans to do two things (indicated by two subjunctive verbs after ἵνα ["that"]).[63] First, they should "welcome her in the Lord in a manner worthy of the saints." The verb προσδέχομαι here ("receive favorably, welcome," as in Luke 15:2; Phil 2:29) parallels προσλαμβάνω ("receive, welcome") in 14:1; 15:7. Hospitality worthy of a distinguished visitor from another church is indicated by the context, expressing full acceptance or her and unhindered fellowship in the Lord. Second, Paul wants them to "assist her in whatever matter she may require your help" (παραστῆτε αὐτῇ ἐν ᾧ ἂν ὑμῶν χρῄζῃ πράγματι).[64] The indefinite construction ἐν ᾧ ἂν could simply mean that they should care for her in every way. But there may have been particular matters for which Phoebe needed help, such as the

---

[61] Cranfield, *Romans*, 2:781; Moo, *Romans*, 914. Moo notes that διάκονος was used of female officeholders in this period (cf. *New Docs* 2:193–94; 4:239–41) and that the feminine term διακόνισσα ("deaconess") was a later way of identifying female deacons. Cf. Susan Mathew, *Women in the Greetings of Romans 16:1–16: A Study of Mutuality and Women's Ministry in the Letter to the Romans* (LNTS [JSNTS] 471; London/New York: Bloomsbury, 2013), 66–74.

[62] Cf. Dunn, *Romans 9–16*, 886–87. Jewett (*Romans*, 944–45) rightly critiques the view that Phoebe was being recommended as an official teacher and missionary of her home church. But he goes beyond the evidence in speculating that as host of the church in Cenchreae she may have "presided over the eucharistic celebrations and was responsible for the ordering of the congregation" (947). Cf. Mathew, *Women in the Greetings*, 74–81.

[63] The subjunctive after ἵνα normally expresses purpose, but the construction could be imperatival after συνίστημι ("I commend") in v. 1, which is effectively the way CSB reads the sequence ("so you should ").

[64] The verb παρίστημι has several meanings in the NT, but the context here suggests "help, assist" (BDAG). Cf. 2 Tim 4:17 ("stood with me").

propagation of Paul's letter in the churches of Rome, preparations for his visit, and arrangements for his mission to Spain.[65] A concluding explanatory clause beginning with καὶ γάρ ("for indeed," "for also") returns to the matter of her status or significance: "she has been a benefactor of many—and of me also" (αὐτὴ προστάτις πολλῶν ἐγενήθη καὶ ἐμοῦ αὐτοῦ). This suggests she was a person of relative wealth, status, and influence who supported itinerant evangelists like Paul and his companions and was able to pay for her own trip from Cenchreae to Rome with the letter. The term προστάτις cannot be construed to mean "congregational leader" because Paul is using it with reference to her broader ministry of generosity to various individuals and to himself.[66]

16:3–4. A series of second-person plural encouragements to greet others in their community follows (ἀσπάσασθε occurs fifteen times in vv. 3–15, followed by a general exhortation to "greet one another with a holy kiss" in v. 16). Since none of Paul's other letters carries so many greetings of this kind, we are bound to ask why Romans concludes like this. He may have simply been asking the Roman Christians "to convey his own greetings to the respective individuals and groups,"[67] but the context invites a more literal reading ("you greet"). Different house churches in the city were to acknowledge and express bonds of fellowship with one another and with the named individuals. Many are identified as the apostle's coworkers or as people he has come to know in other ways. The Romans will honor Paul and be ready to embrace him and his

[65] Jewett (*Romans*, 946–48) argues that the "matter" Paul had in mind was Phoebe's sponsorship of his mission to Spain. He thinks this is established by the concluding description of her as his benefactor, which begins with the words καὶ γὰρ αὐτή ("for she also"). But see Mathew, *Women in the Greetings*, 81–85.

[66] The feminine noun προστάτις only occurs here in biblical Greek, meaning "a woman in a supportive role, *patron, benefactor*" (BDAG). Dunn (*Romans 9–16*, 888–89) discusses the evidence for women as patrons, protectors, and benefactors in Greco-Roman and Jewish cultures. See n. 61 above.

[67] Moo, *Romans*, 919. Harry Y. Gamble Jr., (*The Textual History of the Letter to the Romans: A Study in Textual and Literary Criticism*, SD 42 [Grand Rapids: Eerdmans, 1977] 93) argues that "the imperative form of the greeting verb functions here as a surrogate for the first person indicative form, and so represents a direct personal greeting for the writer himself to the addressees."

mission if they first honor those in their midst whom he identifies as associates and friends.[68]

The first to be greeted are Prisca and Aquila, who worked with Paul in Corinth and Ephesus (cf. Acts 18:1–3, 18–21, 26).[69] Aquila was a Jew from Pontus in Asia Minor, but Acts gives no information about Prisca's background. Both apparently became Christians in Rome, moving to Corinth when Emperor Claudius ordered all the Jews to leave the capital in 49. There they met Paul and began to share in ministry with him. After the death of Claudius in 54, when the imperial edict lapsed, they would have been free to return to Rome. The mention of the wife's name first is sometimes taken to mean she had a higher social status in the Roman context.[70] But it is more likely that Prisca's name is given preference because of her prominence in the early Christian missionary movement.[71] As Paul's "coworkers in Christ Jesus" (τοὺς συνεργούς μου ἐν Χριστῷ Ἰησοῦ), they were not merely his helpers but colleagues who sometimes worked independently from him in evangelism, teaching, and nurturing churches.[72] When Paul adds "who risked their own necks for my life" (οἵτινες ὑπὲρ τῆς ψυχῆς μου τὸν ἑαυτῶν τράχηλον ὑπέθηκαν), he possibly refers to the Ephesian crisis mentioned in Acts 19:23–31 (cf. 1 Cor 15:32). In this threatening situation they may have been able to "intervene effectively with the authorities on Paul's behalf."[73]

[68] Cf. Kruse, *Romans*, 558; Mathew, *Women in the Greetings*, 38–42, 92–93. Jewett (*Romans*, 952–53) discusses the significance of such greetings in the honor-and-shame culture of ancient Rome. Particularly when extended across the barriers erected by previous conflicts, their greeting of one another could have helped unite them in support of Paul's mission to Spain.

[69] Cf. Peterson, *Acts*, 505–6. The diminutive form "Priscilla" is found in Acts 18:2, 18, 26, and some secondary manuscripts of Rom 16:3. "Aquila and Prisca" is the reading of the best manuscripts of 1 Cor 16:19, and "Prisca and Aquila" in 2 Tim 4:19. Chapple ("Getting *Romans* to the Right Romans," 207–9) argues that, together with Phoebe, they may have been responsible for having Paul's letter copied and read to the various groups in Rome.

[70] Cf. Jewett, *Romans*, 955–56.

[71] Cf. Mathew, *Women in the Greetings*, 87–88.

[72] The significant ministry of Priscilla and Aquila to Apollos in Ephesus (Acts 18:24–28) is a good example of this. Paul uses the term συνεργός similarly in Rom 16:9, 21, but variously in 1 Cor 3:9; 2 Cor 1:24; 8:23; Phil 2:25; 4:3; Col 4:11; 1 Thess 3:2; Phlm 1, 24. The only other NT use is in 3 John 8.

[73] Jewett, *Romans*, 957. Jewett understands risking their necks to be a colloquialism for a quick death by decapitation, which was normally the privilege of Roman

That would be reason enough for Paul to record his personal gratitude to them. But when he adds that "so do all the Gentile churches" give thanks for them, he implies that their total contribution to the Gentile mission was widely acknowledged. The Roman Christians were being asked to join this circle of gratitude by greeting Prisca and Aquila across whatever divisions existed between the gatherings in that city.

16:5. As well as greeting Prisca and Aquila, the Christians in Rome were to greet also "the church that meets in their home" (*τὴν κατ' οἶκον αὐτῶν ἐκκλησίαν*). The word *ἐκκλησία* ("gathering, assembly, church"), which is much used in Paul's other letters, can only be found in this final chapter of Romans, where it has three applications.[74] It is used theologically to describe the various gatherings that belong to Christ (v. 16), which are dispersed throughout the nations (v. 4). It is also used locally with reference to the Christian congregation in a particular town or city (v. 1 [Cenchreae]; v. 23 [Corinth]). More narrowly, it is applied to gatherings in the homes of believers (v. 5; cf. 1 Cor 16:19; Phlm 2; Col 4:15). It is also likely that house churches are indicated by different terminology in vv. 10, 11, 14, 15.[75] Prisca and Aquila were patrons or hosts of the church that met in their home. This gathering is likely to have included believers from other households (contrast vv. 10b, 11b). Their gifts and experience would have equipped them to act as spiritual leaders of this congregation.

Without a connective, Paul calls on his readers to "greet my dear friend Epaenetus" (*τὸν ἀγαπητόν μου*, [lit.] "my beloved"). This term of endearment is used again in vv. 8, 9, 12 (cf. 1:7; 11:28; 12:19), and elsewhere in his letters. It may simply be equivalent to

---

citizens. He takes their intervention with the authorities on Paul's behalf as a confirmation of their high social status. Cf. Dunn, *Romans 9–16*, 892.

[74] The ordinary secular use of *ἐκκλησία* can be seen in Acts 19:32, 41 with reference to the informal gathering of the citizens of Ephesus to accuse Paul and his companions, and in 19:39 with reference to "the regular assembly" where charges were properly brought. Cf. Karl L. Schmidt, "*ἐκκλησία*," *TDNT* 3:505, 513–14.

[75] Jewett (*Romans*, 53–55, 62–69) discusses what can be known about the housing situation in ancient Rome. Prisca and Aquila may have been wealthy enough to live in a private dwelling, whereas many Romans could only afford to rent apartments. Four of the five groups mentioned in chapter 16 lack patrons and could simply have met in crowded tenement buildings where the leadership pattern may have been more collective and egalitarian.

"brother" here, but Paul goes on to describe Epaenetus as (lit.) "the firstfruits of Asia for Christ" (ἀπαρχὴ τῆς Ἀσίας εἰς Χριστόν), indicating why he may have had a special affection for him. In 1 Cor 16:15 the household of Stephanas is similarly described as "the firstfruits of Achaia." Literally, ἀπαρχή is used with reference to the first part of a harvest, which is offered in sacrifice to God (8:23; 11:16; cf. Deut 18:4; 26:2, 10; Neh 10:37; Ezek 44:30). As the first convert in Asia, Epaenetus would have had a long-standing relationship with the apostle and with Prisca and Aquila. He may have moved from Ephesus to Rome with them and is likely to have been a member of their house church.

16:6. The earliest textual evidence is divided between reading Μαρία ("Mary") as the person to be greeted here (A B C P Ψ etc.) and Μαριάμ ("Miriam"), which is more strongly attested (𝔓[46] ℵ D F G L etc.). If, as seems likely, the latter is the original spelling,[76] this woman could have been of Jewish origin (cf. Exod 15:20). When Paul says that she "has worked very hard for you" (ἥτις πολλὰ ἐκοπίασεν εἰς ὑμᾶς), the implication is that she has labored in gospel ministry for some time, since Paul regularly uses the verb and the cognate noun in that connection (e.g., 16:12; 1 Cor 3:8; 15:58; Gal 4:11; Col 1:29; 1 Thess 5:12).[77] She may have been one of the earliest missionaries to visit Rome. Mary/Miriam is the third of nine women mentioned in Paul's greetings, most of whom are identified as gospel workers.

16:7. Andronicus is a Greek masculine name, here belonging to "a Hellenized Jew."[78] Much discussion has taken place about whether Ἰουνιαν should be accented with a circumflex and so be read as an abbreviated form of the common masculine name Junianus in the accusative (Ἰουνιᾶν). The earliest manuscripts were not accented, but when that process began, an acute accent was supplied (Ἰουνίαν), indicating that the accusative form of the feminine name Junia was understood.[79] The latter occurs more than 250 times in Greek and

[76] Jewett (*Romans*, 949) argues that the semiticized Μαριάμ is more likely to have been changed into the common Greek form Μαρία than vice versa.

[77] Cf. Friedrich Hauck, "κόπος, κοπιάω," *TDNT* 3:829–30.

[78] Dunn, *Romans 9–16*, 894, citing Josephus, *Ant.* 13.75, 78.

[79] Ἰουνιαν is unaccented in ℵ A B* C D* F G P but is given an acute accent in B^2 D^2 $Ψ^{vid}$ and numerous minuscules. Cf. Metzger, *Textual Commentary*, 475–76; Jewett, *Romans*, 950. The reading Ἰουλίαν ("Julia"), which occurs in 𝔓[46] and some

Latin inscriptions found in Rome alone, whereas the abbreviated male name Junias is unattested anywhere. Andronicus and Junia are likely to have been a married couple (alternatively, they could have been brother and sister). Like Prisca and Aquila in v. 3, they are warmly commended by Paul. Given the tensions highlighted in 14:1–15:7, the prominence given to these two Jewish Christian couples is significant.

Andronicus and Junia are first described as "my people" (τοὺς συγγενεῖς μου [CSB: "my fellow Jews"]), highlighting their common Jewish origin (cf. 9:3; 16:11, 21). Second, they are called "my fellow prisoners" (συναιχμαλώτους μου), though we have no way of knowing when or where they experienced imprisonment together for the sake of the gospel. Third, they are said to be "noteworthy among the apostles" (ἐπίσημοι ἐν τοῖς ἀποστόλοι). While some have argued that Paul means "outstanding in the eyes of the apostles," most commentators from patristic times have understood him to mean "outstanding in the group who may be designated apostles."[80] But in what sense could they have been "among the apostles"? A number of "apostles" other than the Twelve were witnesses of the risen Christ (cf. 1 Cor 15:7).[81] If Andronicus and Junia were part of that group, this would explain Paul's description of their being "in Christ before me." But it is also possible that they were later envoys of particular churches, as Paul and Barnabas were from Antioch (cf. Acts 13:1–4; 14:26–28). As such, they would have been involved in gospel proclamation rather than being merely agents of financial and practical support for others (cf. 2 Cor 8:23; Phil 2:25).[82] Whatever their precise calling, Paul had a high regard for them both. Fourth,

---

ancient versions, appears to have been influenced by v. 15. Cf. Mathew, *Women in the Greetings*, 97–101.

[80] Cranfield, *Romans*, 2:789. Karl H. Rengstorf ("ἐπίστημος," *TDNT* 7:267) points out that the adjective Paul uses marks out a person or thing in comparison with other representatives of the same class, in this case with other apostles. Mathew (*Women in the Greetings*, 101–5) evaluates arguments on both sides of this exegetical divide.

[81] The resurrection appearances in 1 Cor 15:5–8 are in chronological order. "Cephas" is mentioned with "the Twelve" in v. 5 (although there were eleven until Matthias replaced Judas). "James" (the Lord's brother, and not one of the Twelve) is then linked with a larger group of "all the apostles" in v. 7.

[82] Cf. Moo, *Romans*, 923–24; Schreiner, *Romans*, 796–97; Jewett, *Romans*, 963. Although Paul occasionally includes an even wider group of coworkers in the category of "apostles" (1 Cor 4:9; 9:5–6; Gal 1:19), Paul W. Barnett ("Apostle," *DPL* 48)

Andronicus and Junia are described as being "also in Christ before me" (καὶ πρὸ ἐμοῦ γέγοναν ἐν Χριστῷ), meaning that they became Christians before Paul did and that his association with them had been long-standing. Junia's actual role is not specified, but Paul's description of them as a couple shows that she was more than a wife accompanying her husband on his mission (1 Cor 9:5). "She has shared imprisonment with him because she was identified as a significant player herself in the Christian cause."[83]

16:8–10a. A series of shorter commendations follow. The Romans are to greet Ampliatus, whom Paul describes as "my dear friend in the Lord" (τὸν ἀγαπητόν μου ἐν κυρίῳ), cf. v. 5b). Ampliatus was a common Roman slave name. They are also to greet Urbanus, whom he calls "our coworker in Christ" (τὸν συνεργὸν ἡμῶν ἐν Χριστῷ. Like Prisca and Aquila (v. 3), he was a missionary colleague. Stachys too may have been a coworker, but he is only called "my dear friend" (τὸν ἀγαπητόν μου). Apelles gets the unusual designation "approved in Christ" (τὸν δόκιμον ἐν Χριστῷ). The term Paul uses means "genuine on the basis of testing" (BDAG). This suggests that Apelles had faithfully endured some trying situation for Christ that was well known to the readers.[84]

16:10b–11. A charge to greet "those who belong to the household of Aristobulus" (τοὺς ἐκ τῶν Ἀριστοβούλου) introduces a new category of persons. Since Aristobulus himself is not to be greeted, he may be dead or not a Christian. But there are members of his household who are believers, who gather together to express their faith in Christ as an informal house church. The name Aristobulus is rare in Roman records and inscriptions and is likely to belong to someone who was born elsewhere. It was much used in the Hasmonean dynasty and in the family of Herod the Great.[85] A link with that family is possibly strengthened by the encouragement to

---

argues that, as the "last of all" to whom the risen Lord appeared (1 Cor 15:8), Paul was the last who was strictly an apostle of Christ, called directly by the risen Lord.

[83] Bruce W. Winter, *Roman Wives, Roman Widows: The Appearance of New Women and the Pauline Communities* (Grand Rapids: Eerdmans, 1995), 203.

[84] Cranfield (*Romans*, 2:790–91) and Jewett (*Romans*, 964–66) discuss the significance of these names in the light of archaeological evidence.

[85] Cranfield (*Romans*, 2:791–92), Dunn (*Romans 9–16*, 896), and Jewett (*Romans*, 966) consider the possibility that this Aristobulus was the grandson of Herod the Great, who came to Rome as a hostage with his brother Herod Agrippa I and was educated with the future emperor Claudius. He died between AD 45 and 48.

greet Herodion, "my fellow Jew" (τὸν συγγενῆ μου, cf. v. 7). Perhaps he was a member of the same congregation. Paul returns to the pattern of v. 10b when he asks the Romans to greet "those who belong to the household of Narcissus who are in the Lord." Narcissus is not to be greeted, perhaps because he also is either dead or not a Christian. Only those members of his household who are "in the Lord" are to be acknowledged.[86]

16:12. Paul now calls upon the Roman believers to greet three women, "who have worked hard in the Lord." The verb κοπιάω ("labor") is used twice in this verse (cf. v. 6 comment). Since the names Tryphaena and Tryphosa are similar and they are joined together in Paul's commendation (τὰς κοπιώσας ἐν κυρίῳ), they may have been sisters who worked together in the Lord's service.[87] Persis is especially identified as "my dear friend" (τὴν ἀγαπητήν, cf. vv. 5, 8, 9). Whether she comes from a Gentile or Jewish background, she is to be honored by all for her intensive involvement in gospel ministry: she "worked very hard in the Lord" (πολλὰ ἐκοπίασεν ἐν κυρίῳ).

16:13. Rufus is described as "chosen in the Lord" (τὸν ἐκλεκτὸν ἐν κυρίῳ), which could be said of any believer (1:6–7; 8:33; 9:24). Although this designation could point to some special calling,[88] Paul may simply have applied different terminology to different people in this chapter for the sake of variety. The identification is not personal, but when Paul adds "also his mother—and mine" (καὶ τὴν μητέρα αὐτοῦ καὶ ἐμοῦ), the implication is that his mother had provided hospitality to Paul at some stage or cared for him in other ways. In other words, Paul's association with Rufus could have been personal and long-standing.

---

[86] Cranfield (*Romans*, 2:792–93), Dunn (*Romans 9–16*, 896), and Jewett (*Romans*, 967–68) argue that this Narcissus may have been the slave freed by Claudius whose wealth became proverbial and whose influence on Claudius was considerable. He was forced to commit suicide shortly after Nero's accession, only a year or two before Paul wrote to the Romans.

[87] Jewett (*Romans*, 968) observes that these are Greek names, but there is evidence for the use of Tryphaena in Jewish circles.

[88] Cranfield (*Romans*, 2:793–94), Dunn (*Romans 9–16*, 897), and Jewett (*Romans*, 969) consider the possibility that this might be the Rufus mentioned together with Alexander in Mark 15:21, whose father was Simon of Cyrene. If Mark's Gospel was written for the Christians in Rome, it is a reasonable assumption that Alexander and Rufus were well known there.

16:14–15. Two groups of people complete Paul's list. The first includes five men (Asyncritus, Phlegon, Hermes, Patrobas, Hermas) and "the brothers and sisters who are with them." Although the apostle may not have been personally acquainted with these individuals, he identifies them as key figures among a group of believers. They presumably met together as a house church, and those named may have been leaders.[89] The second group involves Philologus and Julia, who are likely to have been husband and wife since Nereus is linked with his unnamed sister (τὴν ἀδελφὴν αὐτοῦ). Like the other Greek names in this chapter, Olympas points to someone from outside of Rome, slave or free, who has come to live in the capital. Those associated with these five men and women are designated as "all the saints who are with them" (τοὺς σὺν αὐτοῖς πάντας ἁγίους). "The saints" echoes Paul's opening address to the Roman believers collectively (1:7), but here the apostle identifies the members of a particular house church.[90]

16:16. Paul's exhortation to "greet one another with a holy kiss" reinforces the idea that the preceding greetings are designed to express their unity in Christ and the familial relationships arising from their common faith. The same request is made in 1 Cor 16:20; 2 Cor 13:12; 1 Thess 5:26 (cf. 1 Pet 5:14, ἐν φιλήματι ἀγάπης ["with a kiss of love"]). In the Greco-Roman world and in Jewish custom, kisses were for relatives, rulers, and friends. Occasions of kissing included greeting, parting, honoring someone, or expressing reconciliation (e.g., Luke 7:38, 45; 15:20; 22:47–48; Acts 20:37–38).[91] Justin (*Apology* 1:65) gives early testimony to the practice of Christians kissing one another after praying together and before celebrating "the Eucharist" (cf. Tertullian, *De Oratione* 18 ["the kiss of peace"]). But it is a mistake to read

[89] Jewett (*Romans*, 970–71) discusses the significance of these names and concludes that all five are Greek, signifying people of low social status, either slave or former slave. His designation of their association as a "tenement church" differentiates them from the groups that met in larger houses owned by patrons.

[90] Although Paul speaks about "the saints in Jerusalem" (15:26) more narrowly as "the saints" (15:25; 1 Cor 16:1; 2 Cor 8:4; 9:1, 12), there is no reason to identify this house group in Rome as being specifically Jewish Christian. The names are certainly not Jewish.

[91] Gustav Stählin ("φιλέω κτλ.," *TDNT* 9:119) observes that in the literature "it is secondary that the kiss expresses erotic inclination." "A holy kiss" will express Christian fellowship, not sensual feelings or erotic attachment.

that degree of formality back into the situation Paul addresses. If the Christians in Rome were going to "greet one another with a holy kiss," it could have been in everyday contacts as well as in their gatherings together.[92]

The wider nature of Christian fellowship is stressed when Paul says, "All the churches of Christ send you greetings." The verb "greet" appears in the third-person plural here (ἀσπάζονται ὑμᾶς, [lit.] "they greet you"), whereas the singular third person is used when the greetings of Paul's companions are recorded (vv. 21–23). As in v. 4, he speaks on behalf of all the Gentile churches, here identified as "the churches [belonging to] Christ" (αἱ ἐκκλησίαι πᾶσαι τοῦ Χριστοῦ; cf. Gal 1:22, "the Judean churches that are in Christ"). This "all" may reflect the fact that he had a rendezvous in Corinth "with representatives of churches participating in the Jerusalem offering, which occurred at approximately the time of writing Romans (Acts 20:3–4)."[93] But Paul could simply be encouraging the Roman Christians to recognize a mutuality with the many churches that were in existence across the eastern half of the Empire.

16:17. Paul's sudden return to hortatory mode (Παρακαλῶ δὲ ὑμᾶς, ἀδελφοί, "Now I urge you, brothers and sisters"; cf. 12:1; 15:30) concerns the need "to watch out for those who create divisions and obstacles contrary to the teaching that you learned." This is so unexpected and different in character from the preceding section that some have viewed vv. 17–20a as a non-Pauline interpolation. In particular, the change of tone to denunciation and warning is said to produce "an egregious break in the flow and tone of Paul's series of greetings to honored leaders of the Roman churches."[94] But

[92] Cranfield (*Romans*, 2:796) presumes the liturgical kiss was already a part of their celebration of the Lord's Supper and imagines Paul's letter will be read out when they are all somehow "assembled for worship." Jewett (*Romans*, 974) more realistically imagines this to be a loving greeting "beyond the small circle of the house or tenement churches to the members of other groups." He notes that the exhortations in 1 Cor 16:20; 2 Cor 13:12; 1 Thess 5:26 are addressed to divided or conflicted congregations. Cf. Kruse, *Romans*, 573–74.

[93] Jewett, *Romans*, 976–77. Paul presents himself as having the backing of these churches in his approach to the Roman Christians for their support in the next stage of his gospel outreach.

[94] Jewett, *Romans*, 986. Jewett thinks the peace benediction in 16:20 contains a kind of curse, and that vv. 17–20 interrupt the series of greetings in vv. 1–16, 21–23.

the injunction to "greet one another with a holy kiss" (v. 16) surely allows for the exclusion of those whose doctrine causes dissensions and who "do not serve our Lord Christ but their own appetites." Indeed, Paul's mention of "all the churches of Christ" makes it natural for him "to remember the troubles which had afflicted them, and from which the Christian community in Rome was unlikely to be exempt."[95]

Although vv. 17–19 represent a sudden change of mood, they contain important verbal links to earlier sections of the letter and other Pauline letters.[96] There are unmistakable parallels to Phil 3:18–19 and 2 Cor 11:13–15 in the characterization of theses false teachers, but the warning is general enough to be classified as preventative. The verb *σκοπεῖν* ("watch out") has the sense of "look at critically" here.[97] Those to watch out for cause "dissensions" (BDAG; τὰς διχοστασίας, cf. Gal 5:20) and "obstacles" or "stumbling blocks" (τὰ σκάνδαλα, cf. 9:33; 11:9; 14:13) "contrary to the teaching that you learned" (παρὰ τὴν διδαχὴν ἣν ὑμεῖς ἐμάθετε). This last expression surely refers to the foundational teaching of the gospel and its implications (6:17; cf. 1 Cor 4:6; Eph 4:20; Phil 4:9; Col 1:7) rather than to some later doctrinal formulation.[98] The Roman Christians are to "avoid" (ἐκκλίνετε) those who compromise or obscure this fundamental teaching rather than welcome them uncritically.[99] Paul

---

He argues that the passage contains direct contradictions to the argument of Romans, that the rhetoric and vocabulary are non-Pauline, and that it sets a firm limit on those who should be greeted as legitimate members of the Christian family. But see n. 95 below.

[95] Cranfield, *Romans*, 2:798. Cranfield offers a detailed response to the arguments of Käsemann (*Romans*, 416–19). Jewett (*Romans*, 986–88) offers a more developed version of the arguments put forward by Käsemann and others.

[96] Dunn (*Romans 9–16*, 901) argues that there are too few grounds for regarding vv. 17–19 as an interpolation. He regards this as a postscript and compares Paul's practice of appending a final paragraph in his own hand (1 Cor 16:21–24; Gal 6:11–18; Col 4:18; 2 Thess 3:17), "in which he was by no means averse to a final polemical thrust (1 Cor 16:22; Gal 6:12–13)." Cf. Moo, *Romans*, 928–29; William J. Hassold, "'Avoid them': Another Look at Romans 16:17–20," *CurTM* 27 (2000): 196–208.

[97] Cf. Ernst Fuchs, "σκοπέω," *TDNT* 7: 414–15. The verb has a more positive nuance in 2 Cor 4:18; Gal 6:1; Phil 2:4; 3:17.

[98] Despite the echo of 6:17 here, Jewett (*Romans*, 990) concludes that, "the rhetoric in these verses stems from a time after Paul."

[99] In place of the present imperative ἐκκλίνετε (attested in ℵ* B C Ψ etc.), the aorist ἐκλίνατε is found in 𝔓[46] ℵ[2] A D F G etc. The present imperative is more likely

is not commending a pattern of formal church discipline here (cf. 1 Cor 5:9–13; 2 Thess 3:6) but alertness to any appearance of false teaching in their midst.

16:18. The reasons for avoiding false teaching are now developed (γάρ, "because"). "Such people" (οἱ τοιοῦτοι) cause dissensions and put obstacles in the way of Christian unity and faithful discipleship because they "do not serve our Lord Christ but their own appetites." Paul turns from the effect of their teaching to their motivation, which clearly contrasts with his own (1:8–15; 15:15–21; 1 Cor 2:1–4; Col 1:24–29). Since they serve their own pleasure or desires (τῇ ἑαυτῶν κοιλίᾳ, as in Phil 3:19),[100] they cannot be serving Christ and his gospel (cf. 12:11; 14:18; 2 Tim 3:1–5). Although Paul could have a libertine agenda in mind, he may also be reflecting on the broader reality that false teachers pander to the flesh in "religious" ways and seek to gratify their own ego by securing enthusiastic followers (e.g., Gal 4:8–17).[101] Their method is to "deceive the hearts of the unsuspecting with smooth talk and flattering words." The hendiadys διὰ τῆς χρηστολογίας καὶ εὐλογίας emphasizes that they misuse their rhetorical skills to deceive (ἐξαπατῶσιν, as in 7:11; 2 Cor 11:3; Eph 5:6; Titus 1:10). Their target is (lit.) "the hearts of the innocent" (τὰς καρδίας τῶν ἀκάκων).[102] Church history is sadly replete with examples of such deception.

16:19. The link with the previous verse is not obvious, and so CSB does not translate the connective γάρ ("for"). Paul echoes what he says in 1:8 about the faith of the Roman Christians being

---

to be original because it is the more difficult reading. "An alteration in the direction of greater definiteness is more likely than one in the opposite direction" (Cranfield, *Romans*, 2:708n4). Cf. Jewett, *Romans*, 985.

[100] Fundamentally, the noun κοιλία refers to the "cavity" of the body that stores such organs as the stomach, intestines, and womb, but it can also be used with reference to any one of those organs individually. It thus comes to represent the "seat of inward life, of feelings and desires" (BDAG).

[101] Cf. Cranfield, *Romans*, 2:799–800, 801–2. Paul may have had more than one group in mind, or "he may have been warning in a quite general way against a danger which he knew would always threaten the churches but could present itself in many different forms" (p. 802). Cf. Dunn, *Romans 9–16*, 904; Schreiner, *Romans*, 803.

[102] The adjective ἄκακος literally means "without evil" and so can refer to a person of integrity or innocence (e.g., Prov 2:21; Job 2:3; 8:20; Jer 11:19; Heb 7:26). In some contexts it means "inexperienced, or simple in relation to evil" (e.g., Prov 21:11), which is more the sense in Rom 16:18. Cf. Walter Grundmann, "κακός κτλ.," *TDNT* 3:482.

"reported in all the world" when he declares that "the report of your obedience has reached everyone" (ἡ ὑμῶν ὑπακοὴ εἰς πάντας ἀφίκετο). As in 1:5; 6:16; 10:16; 15:18; 16:26, "obedience" should be understood as the obedience that responds with faith in the gospel and seeks to live by it. Following the warning in vv. 17–18, the claim in v. 19a could mean that in resisting false teaching the Romans have "a reputation to live up to."[103] The report of their obedience has reached everyone; "therefore" (οὖν) Paul rejoices over them and wishes them "to be wise about what is good, and yet innocent about what is evil" (σοφοὺς εἶναι εἰς τὸ ἀγαθόν, ἀκεραίους δὲ εἰς τὸ κακόν). A contrast with the concluding challenge in v. 18 is clear from the ἀκάκων-κακόν wordplay ("without evil-evil"; cf. 12:21; 13:12–13; Matt 10:16).

16:20. Paul's wish-prayer in 15:33 was that "the God of peace" might be with all of the Roman Christians. In 15:13 the present enjoyment of the gift of peace was linked with joy and believing, "so that you may overflow with hope by the power of the Holy Spirit." Now a promise is given about the ultimate victory of "the God of peace" over all the powers of evil: he will "soon crush Satan under your feet" (συντρίψει τὸν σατανᾶν ὑπὸ τοὺς πόδας ὑμῶν ἐν τάχει). There is an echo of Gen 3:15 here, particularly as the hope of that passage is reflected in later biblical texts (e.g., Ps 91:13; Luke 10:18–20; cf. T. Sim. 6:6; T. Levi 18:12). This eschatological vision may be applied to the defeat of false teachers in their immediate situation because of the unusual wording (ὑπὸ τοὺς πόδας ὑμῶν, "under your feet"). But the complete end to Satan's power and the universal peace that will flow from that victory is the broader meaning of the imagery.[104] Paul's promise is followed by another wish-prayer: "the grace of our Lord Jesus be with you" (Ἡ χάρις τοῦ κυρίου ἡμῶν Ἰησοῦ μεθ' ὑμῶν). Until that final defeat of Satan and his influence

[103] Cranfield, *Romans*, 2:802.

[104] Cf. Cranfield, *Romans*, 2:803; Dunn, *Romans 9–16*, 905. Cranfield disputes the view that ἐν τάχει ("quickly, soon") should be taken as "a proof that Paul was sure that the Parousia would occur within, at the most, a few decades." Jewett (*Romans*, 994–95) argues that v. 20a speaks about the immediate victory of the churches over a "demonic heresy," if the advice of vv. 17–19 is followed. Cf. Kruse, *Romans*, 580–81.

in human affairs, Christians need to live in daily dependence on the grace of Christ and his enabling.[105]

16:21. This is the first of three verses with greetings to the Romans from those who were with Paul when he composed his letter. The third-person singular indicative (*ἀσπάζεται ὑμᾶς*, "he greets you") is similarly used in Col 4:10–14; Phlm 23–24, while plural verbs are used in 1 Cor 16:19–20; Phil 4:21b–22. Timothy, who is elsewhere identified as "my dearly loved and faithful child in the Lord" (1 Cor 4:17; cf. Acts 16:1–3; Phil 2:22) and as a brother in Christ (2 Cor 1:1; Col 1:1; Phlm 1), is here described more formally as Paul's "coworker" (*ὁ συνεργός μου*, cf. vv. 3, 9; 1 Thess 3:2 ["God's coworker"]). In Acts 20:4 Timothy is listed with those who accompanied Paul on his long journey from Corinth via Macedonia and Ephesus to Jerusalem. Lucius (*Λούκιος*) is otherwise not named as a Pauline companion, unless he is to be identified with Luke, "the beloved physician" (*Λουκᾶς* in Col 4:14; Phlm 24; 2 Tim 4:11).[106] The Jason mentioned here could have been a delegate from Thessalonica (cf. Acts 17:5–7, 9), though he is not mentioned as being with Paul in Acts 20:4. Sosipater is likely to be the "Sopater, son of Pyrrhus, from Berea" identified in that verse. These last two, or possibly Lucius, Jason, and Sosipater together, are called "my fellow countrymen" (*οἱ συγγενεῖς μου*, cf. 9:3; 16:7, 11). "By explicitly identifying these persons as his fellow Jews, he makes plain that although he identified himself with the 'strong' Gentile majority in Rome, he maintains respectful, collegial relationships with Jewish Christian leaders."[107]

---

[105] The shorter reading Ἡ *χάρις τοῦ κυρίου ἡμῶν Ἰησοῦ μεθ' ὑμῶν* is attested by the best Alexandrian witnesses (𝔓[46] ℵ B) and is likely to be original. A large group of witnesses add the title "Christ" (A C Ψ etc.). The omission of any form of this wish-prayer in D F G and other Western witnesses is apparently due to the fact that similar words are introduced in v. 24 in these manuscripts (v. 24 is not found in the earliest manuscripts). Cf. Metzger, *Textual Commentary*, 476; Cranfield, *Romans*, 2:803–4.

[106] Cranfield (*Romans*, 2:805) thinks this is a possibility because "Luke" has been identified as an affectionate or pet name for Lucius (BDAG, *Λουκᾶς*), and Luke could have been with Paul in Corinth. However, Luke only resumes his first-person plural account in Acts 20:7, suggesting that he joined Paul and his companions in Troas and did not visit Corinth. The Lucius mentioned in Acts 13:1 never appears again in connection with Paul.

[107] Jewett, *Romans*, 978. If Lucius is Luke, the Gentile companion of Paul, he cannot be included as one of Paul's "fellow countrymen."

16:22. A direct greeting to the believers in Rome is given by Tertius (ἀσπάζομαι ὑμᾶς ἐγὼ Τέρτιος, "*I* Tertius greet you"), who literally describes himself as the one "who wrote this letter in the Lord" (ὁ γράψας τὴν ἐπιστολὴν ἐν κυρίῳ). CSB has followed other English versions, viewing "in the Lord" as modifying "greet" ("I greet you in the Lord").[108] But it is equally possible that Tertius is saying he viewed his task as Paul's amanuensis as a service to the Lord. Such a personal greeting from the scribe to the recipients was unusual. Whether Tertius was an independent secretary or a slave, Paul honors him by allowing him to speak on his own behalf to the Romans.[109]

16:23. The Gaius whom Paul describes as "my host" (ὁ ξένος μου) also sends his greeting to the Roman Christians. He is likely the Gaius Paul baptized in Corinth (1 Cor 1:14). It is also possible that this was the first name of Titius Justus, whose house was next door to the synagogue in Corinth, where the earliest believers gathered when they were ejected from the synagogue (Acts 18:7).[110] When Paul describes Gaius as host "to the whole church" (καὶ ὅλης τῆς ἐκκλησίας), he probably means that Gaius had a particularly large home where it was possible for the different house groups in Corinth to meet together (cf. 1 Cor 11:18, 22; 14:23). "A typical well-to-do home of the time could accommodate meetings of 30–40, at best 50 . . . and there is no good reason to suppose that 'the whole church' in Corinth was by this time any larger."[111]

---

[108] Cranfield (*Romans*, 1.2–5) discusses the manner in which Tertius may have acted as Paul's amanuensis or scribe. Ian J. Elmer ("I Tertius: Secretary or Co-author of Romans," *ABR* 56 [2008]: 45–60) contends that Tertius would have been more than a secretary taking dictation, but there is no way of establishing this with any confidence.

[109] Jewett (*Romans*, 979–80) considers that the designation "in the Lord" introduces Tertius as "the appropriately informed, Christian scribe who could present Paul's message to the Roman congregations in a credible manner." Jewett speculates that Tertius was a slave supplied to Paul by Phoebe and due to accompany Phoebe to Rome for the presentation of the letter to the churches there.

[110] Cranfield (*Romans*, 2:807) mentions that Titius is a Roman "*gens* name," and argues that this person is likely to have had a first name like Gaius.

[111] Dunn, *Romans 9–16*, 910–11. Cf. Thiselton, *Corinthians*, 27–28; Roger W. Gehring, *House Church and Mission: The Importance of Household Structures in Early Christianity* (Peabody: Hendrickson, 2004), 139–40. Jewett (*Romans*, 980–81) disagrees, counting between six and ten groups of believers in Corinth, and concluding that "the whole church" could not have been accommodated in one home.

Erastus is a Latin name, which correlates with the fact that he holds the office of "city treasurer" (ὁ οἰκονόμος τῆς πόλεως) in Corinth. This title could mean that he was in charge of city works or was more broadly responsible for the management of the material resources of the city.[112] Another Erastus, one of Paul's coworkers, is mentioned in Acts 18:22 and 2 Tim 4:20. The Erastus who sends his greeting to the Roman Christians has been identified with a civic official by that name who is mentioned in a Latin inscription belonging to the first century. But there has been debate about how Paul's Greek term relates to the Latin term *aedelis*, which is found in the inscription.[113] Whatever the precise details of his office, Erastus was an important Corinthian official who was a Christian and a supporter of Paul's missionary endeavors.

The last person to send greetings from Corinth is (lit.) "Quartus the brother" (Κούαρτος ὁ ἀδελφός). CSB has translated this "our brother Quartus," but it is possible that Paul refers to Quartus as the brother of Erastus.[114]

16:24. The wish-prayer printed by CSB as a footnote ("The grace of our Lord Jesus Christ be with you all") is a Western reading found only in D (F G without Ἰησοῦ Χριστοῦ) Ψ and later manuscripts. It is not found in the earliest and most reliable manuscripts of Paul's letter, which have a form of this wish-prayer in v. 20. Another strand of later manuscripts includes the contents of v. 24 after v. 27. These variations are linked to another problem, namely, the placement of the doxology, which in many of the earliest manuscripts is

He thinks Paul refers to Gaius hosting Christian travelers from all over the Roman Empire passing through Corinth. However, it would be unusual for Paul to describe Christians everywhere as "the whole church."

[112] Cf. Gerd Theissen, *The Social Setting of Pauline Christianity: Essays on Corinth*, trans. J. H. Schültz (Philadelphia: Fortress, 1982), 76–83.

[113] Theissen (ibid., 82–83) argues that Paul's term (οἰκονόμος) probably refers to the office of *quaestor* that was normally held before appointment as *aidelis*. But Andrew D. Clarke ("Another Corinthian Erastus Inscription," *TynBul* 42 [1991]: 151) concludes that *quaestor* and *aidelis* may have been identical. Cf. Kruse, *Romans*, 585–87.

[114] Cf. Jewett, *Romans*, 983–84. Cranfield (*Romans*, 2:808) opposes this view and argues that the reference is simply to "brother Quartus." But this concludes the greetings in vv. 21–23 with something of an anticlimax, unless Quartus is well known to the Roman readers in another way.

found at 16:25–27 but which also occurs after 14:23 or 15:33. One group of texts lacks the doxology entirely.[115]

16:25–27. On the strength of impressive manuscript evidence (𝔓[61] א B C D 81 1739 and others), these verses should be regarded as part of the original form of the letter, though important questions remain about the placement of the doxology in different positions by different manuscript traditions.[116] The structure of the doxology is complex, with an overload of words and phrases recalling previous sections of the argument (particularly 1:1–7).[117] No other Pauline letter concludes with a doxology like this, though there are doxological elements in Rom 1:25; 9:5: 2 Cor 9:15; Gal 1:5; Phil 4:20, and a doxology concludes a major epistolary segment in Rom 11:33–36; Eph 3:20–21. The closest NT parallel would be Jude 24–25 (cf. Mart. Pol. 20:2).

The opening ascription (Τῷ δὲ δυναμένῳ ὑμᾶς στηρίξαι, "Now to him who is able to strengthen you") indicates that God is to be praised because he is able to establish, confirm, and support believers in whatever trials they may face (cf. 1 Thess 3:2:2–3, 13; 2 Thess 2:17; 3:3). Trials may be physical (8:35–37), relational (14:11–15:7), or theological (16:17–19). God's power was highlighted in 1:16, 20; 4:21; 9:17, 22; 11:23; 14:4; 15:13, 19 and was contrasted with other powers in 8:38–39. God's ability to strengthen believers is said to be "according to my gospel and the proclamation about Jesus Christ" (κατὰ τὸ εὐαγγέλιόν μου καὶ τὸ κήρυγμα Ἰησοῦ Χριστοῦ).[118]

[115] Cf. Metzger, *Textual Commentary*, 476–77; Moo, *Romans*, 936n2.

[116] Cranfield (*Romans*, 2:808–9) speculates that this doxology, either in its present or a briefer form, was added first to a short form of Romans ending with 14:23. Subsequently, in its present form it was added to the full form of the epistle and also to a form ending with 15:33. He concedes that Paul may have written the doxology but thinks it is more likely to be post-Pauline. Jewett (*Romans*, 998–1002) lists those who view it as post-Pauline and those who defend its authenticity as a Pauline creation. Jewett argues for it to be a post-Pauline interpolation based on a hypothetical Hellenistic Jewish doxology and contends that the final redaction contradicts the teaching of Romans 9–11. But his argument is remarkably obtuse with regard to the links between 16:25–27 and earlier parts of the letter. The authenticity of the doxology is argued by Moo, *Romans*, 936n2; Schreiner, *Romans*, 816–17; Kruse, *Romans*, 587–89; and others.

[117] Cf. Dunn, *Romans 9–16*, 913; I. Howard Marshall, "Romans 16:25–27—an Apt Conclusion," in Soderlund and Wright, eds., *Romans and the People of God*, 170–84.

[118] The καί here is probably explanatory (cf. BDF §442 [9]), giving the sense "my gospel, that is to say, the proclamation of Jesus Christ" (Cranfield, *Romans*,

The word "gospel" has been used numerous times in the letter (1:1, 9, 16: 2:16 ["my gospel"]; 10:16; 11:28; 15:16, 19), and its contents and implications have been the focus of Paul's attention throughout. The noun κήρυγμα ("preaching") was not used (cf. 1 Cor 1:21; 2:4; 15:14; 2 Tim 4:17; Titus 1:3), but the cognate verb describes the preaching about Jesus Christ in 10:8, 14, 15. The preposition κατά with the accusative means "according to, in accordance with, in conformity with, corresponding to" (BDAG). Paul means that his gospel preaching about Jesus Christ assures us of God's power to strengthen and sustain his people to the end (cf. 8:28–39) and is actually the means by which God achieves that goal.[119]

A second clause beginning with κατά further defines the gospel by which God is able to strengthen his people: (lit.) "according to the revelation of the mystery kept silent for long ages, but now manifested" (κατὰ ἀποκάλυψιν μυστηρίου χρόνοις αἰωνίοις σεσιγημένου, φανερωθέντος δὲ νῦν). Paul has not spoken previously in this letter about the gospel in these terms (though see 1 Cor 2:1, 6–10; 4:1; Eph 1:9; 3:3, 4, 9; 6:19; Col 1:26, 27; 2:2; 4:3). The noun μυστηρίον ("mystery") was used specifically in 11:25 with reference to God's intentions for Israel and the nations (see comment).[120] Paul's preference in Romans has been to talk about the righteousness of God being revealed in the preaching of the gospel about the saving work of God (1:17, ἀποκαλύπτεται; 3:21, πεφανέρωται).[121] The language of "mystery" is introduced again here as a preparation for restating his own role in the process of revelation.

2:810). The genitive Ἰησοῦ Χριστοῦ is surely objective ("the proclamation about Jesus Christ").

[119] Paul's desire to visit the Romans to impart "some spiritual gift" to strengthen them (1:11) is explained in terms of mutual encouragement "by each other's faith" (1:12) and his eagerness to "preach the gospel" to them (1:15). He wants to strengthen them by expounding the gospel and its implications to them.

[120] Peter T. O'Brien (*The Letter to the Ephesians*, PNTC [Grand Rapids: Eerdmans, 1999]) summarizes the use of μυστήριον in the Pauline letters and concludes, "There are not a number of 'mysteries' with limited applications, but one supreme 'mystery' with a number of applications." The essence of the mystery is the way God's plan of salvation is fulfilled in the Messiah.

[121] Elsewhere in Romans Paul uses the language of revelation with reference to God's wrath (1:18), God's invisible attributes being manifested through what he has made (1:19–20), the final judgment (2:5), and the glory to be revealed (8:18) when the "sons of God" are resurrected from the dead.

A new clause is then indicated by the syntax (*διά τε γραφῶν προφητικῶν . . . γνωρισθέντος*, "and made known through the prophetic Scriptures"). Paul has emphasized from the beginning of the letter that the gospel was "promised beforehand through his prophets in the Holy Scriptures" (1:2), and he has regularly explained the gospel and its implications from Scripture. The gospel fulfills what the prophets foretold, but there was an element of mystery about what was promised in the OT that needed to be disclosed and explained by Jesus and the apostolic writers. The gospel was both hidden and revealed in Scripture, and God gave Paul a distinctive role in understanding and unfolding the mystery.[122]

A phrase beginning with *κατά* points to God's sovereignty in this regard: "according to the command of the eternal God" (*κατ' ἐπιταγὴν τοῦ αἰωνίου θεοῦ*). The eternal God "has determined the juncture in which he, as the Lord of history, will reveal the mystery of the gospel to human beings."[123] The word *ἐπιταγή* ("command") has not previously been used, but it occurs in 1 Cor 7:6, 25; 2 Cor 8:8; 1 Tim 1:1; Titus 1:3; 2:15. Another phrase (*εἰς ὑπακοὴν πίστεως εἰς πάντα τὰ ἔθνη*, [lit.] "for the obedience of faith among all the nations") recalls what Paul says about his own role in the divine plan (1:5).[124] The revelation of "the mystery" is for the purpose of bringing people from every nation to faith in Israel's Messiah. In ministering the gospel to the Gentiles, Paul hoped he might somehow make the unbelieving portion of Israel jealous and thus save some of them too (11:14; see §2.7).

The identity of the one who has power to strengthen believers through the gospel is finally declared to be "the only wise God, through Jesus Christ" (*μόνῳ σοφῷ θεῷ, διὰ Ἰησοῦ Χριστοῦ*). God's wisdom was previously highlighted in a hymn of praise concluding Paul's exposition of the mystery of God's plan for Israel and the nations (11:33–36). God's wisdom was supremely revealed through the person and work of his Son Jesus Christ and is made known to the world through the preaching of the gospel (1:3; 15:6; cf. 1 Cor 1:24, 30). The

---

[122] Cf. Schreiner, *Romans*, 814–15.

[123] Ibid., 814.

[124] Jewett (*Romans*, 1009–10) insists that *εἰς πάντα τὰ ἔθνη* means "for all the Gentiles," while *ἐν πᾶσιν τοῖς ἔθνεσιν* (1:5, "among all the nations") allows for Jews to be included among the beneficiaries of the gospel. But this is special pleading to substantiate his argument that 16:25–27 is a non-Pauline interpolation. Cf. Cranfield, *Romans*, 2:812n5; Dunn, *Romans 9–16*, 916.

final ascription of the letter is "to him be the glory forever" (ᾧ ἡ δόξα εἰς τοὺς αἰῶνας). God is glorified when we acknowledge what he has revealed about himself and his purpose for us and respond with faith and obedience (1:21; 4:20; 15:6, 9; cf. 1 Cor 6:20; 10:31; 2 Cor 9:13; Gal 1:24). Paul's "amen" encourages readers to echo his praise to God for the great truths outlined in this doxology and throughout the letter.

Bridge

A list of names with indications of their personal links to Paul does not at first glance seem relevant to Christians in subsequent generations. The apostle was preparing the Romans to welcome him at a particular moment in time and to unite in supporting him for the next stage of his ministry. At the same time, he was challenging them to acknowledge the diversity of individuals and gatherings that constituted "the saints" in Rome. The names listed here represent people with different racial, social, and religious backgrounds.[125] In particular, many were gospel workers like Paul who had labored to propagate the faith, establish churches, and nurture believers. Greeting and honoring such people across the divides of race, social status, gender, culture, or even ways of expressing discipleship continue to be ways of acknowledging God's transforming grace and the work of the Holy Spirit in others. More broadly, this chapter provides a challenge to churches about working together to promote the gospel in a particular region. But acceptance of others who profess faith in Christ cannot be at any cost. Paul's warning to watch out for false teachers and avoid them is a reminder that Christians are to be discerning about such matters for their own sake and for the sake of the gospel (vv. 17–18; cf. Matt 7:15–23; Gal 1:1–15; Phil 3:2–3; Col 2:8–23). With the encouragement to be "wise about what is good, and yet innocent about what is evil" comes the promise of ultimate victory over Satan's power (vv. 19–20). With the example of those who have stood firm for Christ and the gospel (vv. 21–23), we are also given the encouragement that God is able to strengthen and sustain his people in every circumstance through the preaching of revealed truth (vv. 25–27) and enable them to share in the eternal worship, which is the ultimate aim of his saving work through Jesus Christ (cf. 15:8–13). To God be the glory forever! Amen.

[125] Cf. Lampe, "The Roman Christians," 216–30.

Select Bibliography

Commentaries on Romans

Barrett, Charles K. *A Commentary on the Epistle to the Romans*. BNTC. London: Black, 1971.

Byrne, Brendan. *Romans*. SP 6. Collegeville: The Liturgical Press, 1996.

Cranfield, Charles E. B. *A Critical and Exegetical Commentary on the Epistle to the Romans, Volume 1: Introduction and Commentary on Romans I–VIII*. ICC. Edinburgh: Clark, 1975.

——. *Volume 2: Commentary on Romans IX–XVI and Essays*. ICC. Edinburgh: Clark, 1979.

Dodd, Charles H. *The Epistle of Paul to the Romans*. London: Hodder & Stoughton, 1932. London: Fontana, 1959.

Dunn, James D. G. Word Biblical Commentary. Vol. 38A *Romans 1–8*. Dallas: Word, 1988.

——. Word Biblical Commentary. Vol. 38B *Romans 9–16*. Dallas: Word, 1988.

Fitzmyer, Joseph A. *Romans: A New Translation with Introduction and Commentary* AB 33. New York: Doubleday, 1993.

Jewett, Robert. *Romans: A Commentary*. Hermeneia. Minneapolis: Fortress, 2007.

Käsemann, Ernst. *Commentary on Romans*. ET by Geoffrey Bromiley. Grand Rapids: Eerdmans; London: SCM, 1980.

Kruse, Colin G. *Paul's Letter to the Romans*. PNTC. Grand Rapids: Eerdmans. Nottingham: Apollos, 2012.

Moo, Douglas J. *The Epistle to the Romans*. NICNT. Grand Rapids/ Cambridge: Eerdmans, 1996.

Schreiner, Thomas R. *Romans*. BECNT 6. Grand Rapids: Baker Academic, 1998.

Witherington, Ben, III, with Darlene Hyatt. *Paul's Letter to the Romans: A Socio-Rhetorical Commentary*. Grand Rapids: Eerdmans, 2004.

Wright, N. Thomas. "The Letter to the Romans: Introduction, Commentary, and Reflections." Pages 395–770 in volume 10 of *The New Interpreter's Bible*. Edited by L. E. Keck. 13 vols. Nashville: Abingdon, 1994–2004.

Other Books and Articles

Aune, David E. "Romans as a *Logos Protretpikos*." Pages 278–96 in *The Romans Debate*. Edited by Karl P. Donfried. Revised and expanded edition. Peabody: Hendrickson, 1991.

Badenas, Robert. *Christ the End of the Law: Romans 10:4 in Pauline Perspective*. JSNTSup 10. Sheffield: JSOT, 1985.

Bailey, Daniel P. "Jesus as the Mercy Seat: The Semantics and Theology of Paul's Use of *Hilasterion* in Romans 3:25." *TynBul* 51 (2000): 155–58.

Baker, Bruce A. "Romans 1:18–21 and Presuppositional Apologetics." *BSac* 155 (1998): 280–98.

Banks, Robert J. "Romans 7:25a: An Eschatological Thanksgiving?" *ABR* 26 (1978): 34–42.

Barrett, Matthew M., and Ardel B. Caneday, eds. *Four Views on the Historical Adam*. Grand Rapids: Zondervan, 2013.

Bartchy, S. Scott. *First-Century Slavery and the Interpretation of 1 Corinthians 7:21*. SBLDS 11. Missoula: Scholars Press, 1973.

Bassler, Jouette M. *Divine Impartiality: Paul and a Theological Axiom*. SBLDS 59. Chico: Scholars Press, 1982.

Beale, Greg K. "An Exegetical and Theological Consideration of the Hardening of Pharaoh's Heart in Exodus 4–14 and Romans 9." *TJ* 5 (1984): 129–54.

Beare, Francis W. "On the Interpretation of Romans VI.17." *NTS* 5 (1958–59): 206–10.

Bell, Richard H. *The Irrevocable Call of God: An Inquiry into Paul's Theology of Israel*. WUNT 2.184. Tübingen: Mohr Siebeck, 2005.

——. *Provoked to Jealousy: The Origin and Purpose of the Jealousy Motif in Romans 9–11*. WUNT 2.63. Tübingen: Mohr Siebeck, 1994.

Blocher, Henri *Original Sin: Illuminating the Riddle* NSBT 5. Leicester: Apollos. Downers Grove: InterVarsity, 1997.

Bowers, Paul. "Fulfilling the Gospel: The Scope of the Pauline Mission." *JETS* 30 (1987): 185–98.

Boyarin, Daniel. *A Radical Jew: Paul and the Politics of Identity*. Berkley: University of California Press, 1994.

Brown, Michael J. "Paul's Use of δοῦλος Χριστοῦ Ἰησοῦ in Romans 1:1." *JBL* 120 (2001): 723–37.

Byrne, Brendan. *"Sons of God—Seed of Abraham": A Study of the Idea of the Sonship of God of All Christians in Paul Against the Jewish Background*. AnBib 83. Rome: Pontifical Biblical Institute, 1979.

Calhoun, Robert M. *Paul's Definition of the Gospel in Romans 1*. WUNT 2.316. Tübingen: Mohr Siebeck, 2015.

Campbell, Constantine R. *Paul and Union with Christ: An Exegetical and Theological Study*. Grand Rapids: Zondervan, 2012.

—. *Verbal Aspect and Non-Indicative Verbs: Further Soundings in the Greek of the New Testament*. New York: Peter Lang, 2008.

—. *Verbal Aspect, the Indicative Mood, and Narrative: Soundings in the Greek of the New Testament*. New York: Peter Lang, 2007. Campbell, Douglas A. *The Rhetoric of Righteousness in Romans 3.21–26*. JSNTSup 65. Sheffield: Sheffield Academic, 1992.

Caragounis, Chris C. "Rom 5:15–16 in the Context of 5:12–21: Contrast or Comparison?" *NTS* 31 (1985): 142–45.

Carson, Donald A. "Atonement in Romans 3:21–26." Pages 119–36 in *The Glory of the Atonement: Biblical, Theological and Practical Perspectives in Honor of Roger Nicole*. Edited by Charles E. Hill and Frank A James. Downers Grove: InterVarsity, 2004.

—. "The Vindication of Imputation: On Fields of Discourse and Semantic Fields." Pages 46–78 in *Justification: What's at Stake in the Current Debates*. Edited by Mark Husbands and Daniel J. Treier. Downers Grove: InterVarsity. Leicester: Apollos, 2004.

Carson, Donald A., Peter T. O'Brien, and Mark A. Seifrid, eds. *Justification and Variegated Nomism*, Volume 1: *The Complexities of Second Temple Judaism*. WUNT 2.140. Mohr Siebeck: Tübingen. Grand Rapids: Baker, 2001.

—. *Justification and Variegated Nomism*, Volume 2: *The Paradoxes of Paul*. WUNT 2.181. Mohr Siebeck: Tübingen. Grand Rapids: Baker, 2004.

Chapple, Allan. "Getting *Romans* to the Right Romans: Phoebe and the Delivery of Paul's Letter." *TynBul* 62 (2011): 195–214.

Christoffersson, Olle. *The Earnest Expectation of the Creature*. Coniectanea Biblica, NT 23. Stockholm: Almqvist, 1990.

Ciocchi, David M. "Reconciling Divine Sovereignty and Human Responsibility." *JETS* 37 (1994): 39–412.

Clarke, Andrew D. "The Good and the Just in Romans 5:7." *TynBul* 41 (1990): 128–32.

—. "Rome and Italy." Pages 455–81 in *The Book of Acts in Its First Century Setting*. Vol. 2 *Graeco-Roman Setting*. Edited by David

W. J. Gill and Conrad Gempf. Grand Rapids: Eerdmans; Carlisle: Paternoster, 1994, 455–81.

Clements, Ronald E. "'A Remnant Chosen by Grace' (Romans 11:5): The Old Testament Background and Origin of the Remnant Concept." Pages 106–21 in *Pauline Studies: Essays Presented to Professor F. F. Bruce on His 70th Birthday*. Edited by Donald A. Hagner and Murray J. Harris. Exeter: Paternoster. Grand Rapids: Eerdmans, 1980.

Corrigan, G. M. "Paul's Shame for the Gospel." *BTB* 16 (1986): 23–27.

Corriveau, Raymond. *The Liturgy of Life: A Study of the Ethical Thought of St. Paul in His Letters to the Early Christian Communities*. Bruxelles and Paris: Desclée de Brouwer. Montreal: Les Editions Bellarmin, 1970.

Craigie, Peter C. *Psalms 1–50*. WBC 19. Waco: Word, 1983.

Das, A. Andrew. "The Gentile-Encoded Audience of Romans: The Church outside the Synagogue." Pages 29–46 in *Reading Paul's Letter to the Romans*. Edited by Jerry L. Sumney. SBL Resources for Biblical Study 73. Atlanta: SBL, 2012.

——. *Solving the Romans Debate*. Minneapolis: Fortress, 2007.

Davies, Glenn N. *Faith and Obedience in Romans: A Study of Romans 1–4*. JSNTSup 39. Sheffield: Sheffield Academic, 1990.

Deidun, Thomas J. *New Covenant Morality in Paul*. AnBib 89. Rome: Pontifical Biblical Institute, 1981.

Dodd, Brian. *Paul's Paradigmatic "I": Personal Example as Literary Strategy*. JSNTSup 177. Sheffield: Sheffield Academic, 1999.

Dodd, Charles H. *The Bible and the Greeks*. London: Hodder & Stoughton, 1935.

Donaldson, Terence L. "'Riches for the Gentiles' (Rom 11:12): Israel's Rejection and Paul's Gentile Mission." *JBL* 112 (1993): 92–98.

Donfried, Karl P., ed. *The Romans Debate*. Revised and expanded edition. Peabody: Hendrickson, 1991.

Dunn, James D. G. "'Baptized' as Metaphor." Pages 294–310 in *Baptism, the New Testament and the Church: Historical and Contemporary Studies in Honour of R. E. O. White*. Edited by Stanley E. Porter and Anthony R. Cross. JSNTSup 171. Sheffield: Sheffield Academic, 1999.

——. *Christology in the Making: A New Testament Inquiry into the Origin of the Doctrine of the Incarnation*. London: SCM. Philadelphia: Westminster, 1980.

——. "Once More, Πίστις Χριστοῦ." Pages 730–44 in *Society of Biblical Literature 1991 Seminar Papers*. Edited by E. H. Lovering Jr. Atlanta: Scholars Press, 1991.

——. "Romans 7:14–25 in the Theology of Paul." *TZ* 31 (1975): 257–73.
——. *The Theology of Paul the Apostle*. Grand Rapids: Eerdmans. Edinburgh: T&T Clark, 1998.
Evans, Christopher F. "Rom 12:1–2: The True Worship." Pages 7–33 in *Dimensions de la vie chrétienne*. Edited by Lorenzo de Lorenzi. Rome: Abbaye de S. Paul, 1979.
Fee, Gordon D. *God's Empowering Presence: The Holy Spirit in the Letters of Paul*. Peabody: Hendrickson, 1994.
Fitzmyer, Joseph A. "The Consecutive Meaning of ἐφ' ᾧ in Romans 5.12." *NTS* 39 (1993): 321–39.
Gagnon, Robert A. J. *The Bible and Homosexual Practice: Texts and Hermeneutics*. Nashville: Abingdon, 2001.
——. "Heart of Wax and a Teaching that Stamps: Τύπος Διδαχῆς (Rom. 6:17b) Once More." *JBL* 112 (1993): 667–87.
Gamble, Harry Y., Jr. *The Textual History of the Letter to the Romans*. SD 42. Grand Rapids: Eerdmans, 1977.
Garlington, Don B. *Faith, Obedience and Perseverance: Aspects of Paul's Letter to the Romans*. WUNT 79. Tübingen: Mohr-Siebeck, 1994.
——. "The Obedience of Faith in the Letter to the Romans Part 1: The Meaning of *hypakoē pisteōs* (Rom 1:5; 16:26)." *WTJ* 52 (1990): 201–24.
——. "Romans 7:14–25 and the Creation Theology of Paul." *TJ* 11 (1990): 197–235.
Garnet, Paul. "Atonement Constructions in the Old Testament and the Qumran Scrolls." *EvQ* 46 (1974): 131–63.
Gathercole, Simon J. *Defending Substitution: An Essay on Atonement in Paul*. Grand Rapids: Baker, 2015.
——. "Justified by Faith, Justified by His Blood: The Evidence of Romans 3:21–4:25." Pages 147–84 in volume 2 of Carson, O'Brien, and Seifrid, *Justification and Variegated Nomism*.
——. "A Law unto Themselves: The Gentiles in Romans 2:14–15 Revisited." *JSNT* 85 (2002): 27–49.
——. *Where Is Boasting? Early Jewish Soteriology and Paul's Response in Romans 1–5*. Grand Rapids: Eerdmans, 2001.
Gehring, Roger W. *House Church and Mission: The Importance of Household Structures in Early Christianity*. Peabody: Hendrickson, 2004.
Gibson, Richard J. "Paul the Missionary, in Priestly Service of the Servant-Christ (Romans 15.16)." Pages 51–62 in *Paul as Missionary: Identity, Activity, Theology and Practice*. Edited by Trevor J. Burke and B. S. Rosner. LNTS. London: T&T Clark, 2011.
Goldsworthy, Graeme. *Christ-Centered Biblical Theology: Hermeneutical Foundations and Principles*. Nottingham: Apollos, 2012.

Gundry, Robert H. "A Breaking of Expectations: The Rhetoric of Surprise in Paul's Letter to the Romans." Pages 254–70 in *Romans and the People of God: Essays in Honor of Gordon D. Fee on the Occasion of His 65th Birthday.* Edited by Sven K. Soderlund and N. T. Wright. Grand Rapids/Cambridge: Eerdmans, 1999.

Gundry Volf, J. M. *Paul and Perseverance: Staying in and Falling Away.* Tübingen: Mohr-Siebeck; Louisville: Westminster/John Knox, 1990.

Hanson, Anthony T. "The Oracle in Romans xi.4." *NTS* 19 (1972–73): 300–302.

Harmon, Matthew S., and Jay E. Smith, eds. *Studies in the Pauline Epistles: Essays in Honor of Douglas J. Moo.* Grand Rapids: Zondervan, 2014.

Harris, Murray J. *Jesus as God: The New Testament Use of* Theos *in Reference to Jesus.* Grand Rapids: Baker, 1992.

Harrison, James R. *Paul's Language of Grace in Its Graeco-Roman Context.* WUNT 172. Tübingen: Mohr Siebeck, 2003.

Harvey, John D. *Listening to the Text: Oral Patterning in Paul's Letters.* ETS. Grand Rapids: Baker, 1998.

Hay, David M., and E. Elizabeth Johnson, eds. *Pauline Theology III: Romans.* Minneapolis: Fortress, 1995.

Hays, Richard B. *Echoes of Scripture in the Letters of Paul.* New Haven: Yale University, 1989.

——. *The Faith of Jesus Christ: An Investigation of the Narrative Structure of Galatians 3:1–4:11.* 2nd ed. SBLDS 56. Grand Rapids: Eerdmans, 2001.

——. "'Have We Found Abraham to Be Our Forefather according to the Flesh?' A Reconsideration of Rom 4:1." *NovT* 27 (1985): 76–98.

Head, Peter M. "Jesus' Resurrection in Pauline Thought: A Study of Romans." Pages 58–80 in *Proclaiming the Resurrection.* Edited by Peter M. Head. Carlisle: Paternoster, 1998.

Helm, Paul. *The Providence of God.* Downers Grove: InterVarsity, 1994.

Hooker, Morna D. "Adam in Romans 1." *NTS* 6 (1960): 300–1.

——. *From Adam to Christ: Essays on Paul.* Cambridge: Cambridge University Press, 1990. Reprint. Eugene: Wipf and Stock, 2008.

Hultgren, Arland J. *Paul's Gospel and Mission: The Outlook from His Letter to the Romans.* Philadelphia: Fortress, 1985.

Hurtado, Larry W. *Lord Jesus Christ: Devotion to Jesus in Earliest Christianity.* Grand Rapids: Eerdmans, 2003.

Husbands, Mark, and Daniel J. Treier, eds. *Justification: What's at Stake in the Current Debates.* Downers Grove: InterVarsity: Leicester: Apollos, 2004.

Jeremias, Joachim. *The Prayers of Jesus.* London: SCM, 1967.

Jewett, Robert. *Paul's Anthropological Terms: A Study of Their Use in Conflict Situations*. AGJU 10. Leiden: Brill, 1971.

———. "Romans as an Ambassadorial Letter." *Int* 36 (1982): 5–20.

Johnson, E. Elizabeth. *The Function of Apocalyptic and Wisdom Traditions in Romans 9–11*. SBLDS 109. Atlanta: Scholars Press, 1989.

Johnson, Luke T. "Rom 3:21–26 and the Faith of Jesus." *CBQ* 44 (1982): 77–90.

Johnson, S. Lewis, Jr. "Romans 5:12—an Exercise in Exegesis and Theology." Pages 298–316 in *New Dimensions in New Testament Study*. Edited by Richard N. Longenecker and Merrill C. Tenney. Grand Rapids: Zondervan, 1974.

Judge, E. A., and G. S. R. Thomas. "The Origin of the Church at Rome: A New Solution." *RTR* 25 (1966): 81–93.

Karris, Robert J. "Romans 14:1–15:13 and the Occasion of Romans." Pages 65–84 in *The Romans Debate*. Edited by Karl P. Donfried. Revised and expanded edition. Peabody: Hendrickson, 1991.

Käsemann, Ernst. "Worship in Everyday Life: A Note on Romans 12." Pages 188–95 in *New Testament Questions of Today*. London: SCM, 1969.

Keener, Craig S. *The Mind of the Spirit: Paul's Approach to Transformed Thinking*. Grand Rapids: Baker Academic, 2016.

Kim, Chan-Hie. *The Form and Structure of the Familiar Greek Letter of Recommendation*. SBLDS 4. Missoula: Scholars Press, 1972.

Kim, Johann D. *God, Israel, and the Gentiles: Rhetoric and Situation in Romans 9–11*. SBLDS 4. Missoula: Scholars Press, 2000.

Kim, Seyoon. *The Origin of Paul's Gospel*. WUNT 2.4. Tübingen: Mohr Siebeck, 1981; Grand Rapids: Eerdmans, 1982.

Kinoshita, Junji. "Romans—Two Writings Combined: A New Interpretation of the Body of Romans." *NovT* 7 (1964): 258–77.

Kirk, J. R. Daniel. "Reconsidering *Dikaiōma* in Rom 5:16." *JBL* 126 (2007): 787–92.

Kruse, Colin G. *New Testament Models for Ministry: Jesus and Paul*. Nashville: Thomas Nelson, 1983.

Lambrecht, Jan. *The Wretched "I" and Its Liberation: Paul in Romans 7 and 8*. LTPM 14. Louvain: Peeters. Grand Rapids: Eerdmans, 1992.

Lampe, Peter. "The Roman Christians of Romans 16." Pages 217–21 in Donfried, *The Romans Debate Revised*.

Lincoln, Andrew T. "From Wrath to Justification: Tradition, Gospel, and Audience in the Theology of Romans 1:18–4:25." Pages 130–59 in volume 3 of Hay and Johnson, *Pauline Theology*.

Lindars, Barnabas. *New Testament Apologetic: The Doctrinal Significance of Old Testament Quotations*. Philadelphia: Westminster, 1961.

Longenecker, Richard N. *Biblical Exegesis in the Apostolic Period*. Grand Rapids: Eerdmans, 1975.

——. "The Focus of Romans: The Central Role of 5:1–8:39 in the Argument of the Letter." Pages 49–69 in Soderlund and Wright, *Romans and the People of God*.

——. *Introducing Romans: Critical Issues in Paul's Most Famous Letter*. Grand Rapids/Cambridge: Eerdmans, 2011.

Marshall, I. Howard. "The Development of the Concept of Redemption in the New Testament." Pages 153–69 in *Reconciliation and Hope: New Testament Essays on Atonement and Eschatology Presented to L. L. Morris on His 60th Birthday*. Edited by Robert Banks. Exeter: Paternoster; Grand Rapids: Eerdmans, 1974.

——. "The Meaning of 'Reconciliation.'" Pages 258–74 in *Jesus the Saviour: Studies in New Testament Theology*. London: SPCK, 1990.

——. "Salvation, Grace and Works in the Later Writings in the Pauline Corpus." *NTS* 42 (1996): 339–58.

Martin, Dale B. *Slavery as Salvation: The Metaphor of Slavery in Pauline Christianity*. New Haven: Yale University, 1990.

Martin, Ralph P. *Reconciliation: A Study of Paul's Theology*. Revised ed. Grand Rapids: Zondervan, 1989.

——. "Reconciliation: Romans 5:1–11." Pages 36–48 in *Romans and the People of God: Essays in Honor of Gordon D. Fee on the Occasion of His 65th Birthday.* Edited by Sven K. Soderlund and N. T. Wright. Grand Rapids/Cambridge: Eerdmans, 1999.

Mathew, Susan. *Women in the Greetings of Romans 16:1–16: A Study of Mutuality and Women's Ministry in the Letter to the Romans*. LNTS [JSNTSup] 471. London/New York: Bloomsbury, 2013.

McFadden, Kevin W. "Does ΠΙΣΤΙΣ Mean Faith(fulness) in Paul?" *TynBul* 66 (2015): 251–70.

Metzger, Bruce M. ed. *A Textual Commentary on the Greek New Testament*. 2nd ed. Stuttgart: German Bible Society; New York: American Bible Society, 1994.

Michaels, J. Ramsey. *1 Peter*. WBC 49. Waco: Word, 1988.

Milne, Douglas J. W. "Genesis 3 in the Letter to the Romans." *RTR* 39 (1980): 10–18.

Minear, Paul S. *The Obedience of Faith: The Purpose of Paul in the Epistle to the Romans*. SBT Second Series 19. London: SCM, 1971.

Moo, Douglas J. "Israel and the Law in Romans 5–11: Interaction with the New Perspective." Pages 185–216 in vol. 2 of Carson, O'Brien, and Seifrid, *Justification and Variegated Nomism*.

Morris, Leon L. *The Apostolic Preaching of the Cross*. Leicester: Inter-Varsity. Grand Rapids: Eerdmans, 1965.

——. "The Theme of Romans." Pages 249–63 in *Apostolic History and the Gospel: Biblical and Historical Essays Presented to F. F. Bruce on His 60th Birthday*. Edited by W. Ward Gasque and Ralph P. Martin. Exeter: Paternoster, 1970.

Motyer, J. Alec. *The Prophecy of Isaiah*. Leicester: InterVarsity, 1993.

Nanos, Mark D. "To the Churches within the Synagogues of Rome." Pages 11–28 in Sumney, *Reading Paul's Letter to the Romans*.

Neufeld, Vernon H. *The Earliest Christian Confessions*. NTTS 5. Grand Rapids: Eerdmans, 1963.

Nichols, Grant S., and Richard J. Gibson, "Four Keys to the Literary Structure of Romans." Unpublished.

Obeng, E. A. "The Origins of the Spirit Intercession Motif in Romans 8:26." *NTS* 32 (1986): 621–32.

——. "The Spirit Intercessor Motif in Paul." *ExpTim* 95 (1984): 360–64.

O'Brien, Peter T. *Commentary on Philippians*. NIGTC. Grand Rapids: Eerdmans, 1991.

——. *Introductory Thanksgivings in the Letters of Paul*. NovTSup 49. Leiden: Brill, 1977.

——. *The Letter to the Ephesians*. PNTC. Grand Rapids: Eerdmans. Leicester: Apollos, 1999.

——. *The Letter to the Hebrews*. PNTC Grand Rapids: Eerdmans. Nottingham: Apollos, 2010.

——. "Romans 8:26, 27. A Revolutionary Approach to Prayer." *RTR* 46 (1987): 65–77.

Ortlund, Raymond C., Jr. *God's Unfaithful Wife: A Biblical Theology of Spiritual Adultery*. NSBT 2. Downers Grove: InterVarsity. Leicester: Apollos, 2003.

Oss, Douglas A. "The Interpretation of the 'Stone' Passages by Peter and Paul: A Comparative Study." *JETS* 32 (1989): 181–200.

Packer, James I. "The 'Wretched Man' in Romans 7." Pages 621–27 *Studia Evangelica* II. Edited by F. Cross. Berlin: Acadamie, 1964.

——. "The 'Wretched Man' Revisited: Another Look at Romans 7:14–25." Pages 70–81 in *Romans and the People of God: Essays in Honor of Gordon D. Fee on the Occasion of His 65th Birthday.* Edited by Sven K. Soderlund and N. T. Wright. Grand Rapids/Cambridge: Eerdmans, 1999.

Pao, David W. *Thanksgiving: An Investigation of a Pauline Theme*. NSBT 13. Downers Grove: InterVarsity. Leicester: Apollos, 2002.

Peterson, David G. *The Acts of the Apostles*. PNTC. Grand Rapids: Eerdmans. Nottingham: Apollos, 2009.

——. *Encountering God Together*. Nottingham: InterVarsity, 2013. Phillipsburg: P & R, 2013.

——. *Engaging with God: A Biblical Theology of Worship*. Downers Grove: InterVarsity, 1992.

——. "'Enriched in Every Way': Gifts and Ministries in 1 Corinthians." Pages 134–63 in *The Wisdom of the Cross: Exploring 1 Corinthians*. Edited by Brian S. Rosner. Nottingham: Apollos, 2011.

——. *Hebrews and Perfection: An Examination of the Concept of Perfection in the 'Epistle to the Hebrews.'* SNTSMS 47. Cambridge: Cambridge University, 1982.

——. "Maturity: The Goal of Mission," Pages 185–204 in *The Gospel to the Nations: Perspectives on Paul's Mission*. Edited by Peter Bolt and Mark Thompson. Leicester: Apollos. Downers Grove: InterVarsity, 2000.

——. *Possessed by God: A New Testament Theology of Sanctification and Holiness*. NSBT 1. Downers Grove: InterVarsity. Leicester: Apollos, 1995.

——. *Transformed by God: New Covenant Life and Ministry*. Nottingham: InterVarsity. Downers Grove: InterVarsity, 2012.

——. "Worship and Ethics in Romans 12." *TynBul* 44 (1993): 271–88.

Pfitzner, Victor C. *Paul and the Agon Motif: Traditional Athletic Imagery in the Pauline Literature*. NovTSup 16. Leiden: Brill, 1967.

Piper, John. "The Demonstration of the Righteousness of God in Rom 3:25, 26." Pages 183–91 in *The Pauline Writings*. Edited by Stanley E. Porter and Craig A. Evans. Biblical Seminar 34. Sheffield: Sheffield Academic, 1995.

——. *The Future of Justification: A Response to N. T. Wright*. Wheaton: Crossway, 2007.

——. *The Justification of God: An Exegetical and Theological Study of Romans 9:1–23*. 2nd ed. Grand Rapids: Baker, 1993.

——. *"Love Your Enemies": Jesus' Love Command in the Synoptic Gospels and the Early Christian Paraenesis*. SNTSMS 38. Cambridge: Cambridge University, 1979. Wheaton: Crossway, 2012.

Porter, Stanley E. "The Argument of Romans 5: Can a Rhetorical Question Make a Difference?" *JBL* 110, (1991): 655–77.

——. *Idioms of the Greek New Testament*. 2nd ed. Sheffield: Sheffield Academic, 1994.

——. *Verbal Aspect in the Greek New Testament, with Reference to Tense and Mood,* 3rd ed., *Studies in Biblical Greek*, Book 1. New York: Peter Lang Inc., 2003.

Powers, Daniel G. *Salvation through Participation: An Examination of the Notion of Believers' Corporate Unity with Christ in Early Christian Soteriology*. CBET 29. Leuven: Peeters, 2001.

Pryor, John W. "Paul's Use of Ἰησοῦς—a Clue for the Translation of Romans 3:26?" *Colloquium* 16.1 (1983): 31–45.

Rapinchuk, Mark. "Universal Sin and Salvation in Romans 5:12–21." *JETS* 42 (1999): 427–41.

Rapske, Brian. *The Book of Acts in Its First Century Setting*. Vol. 3: *The Book of Acts and Paul in Roman Custody*. Grand Rapids: Eerdmans. Carlisle: Paternoster, 1944.

Richards, E. Randolph. *Paul and First-Century Letter Writing: Secretaries, Composition, and Collection*. Downers Grove: InterVarsity, 2004.

Reasoner, Mark. *The Strong and the Weak: Romans 14:1–15:13 in Context*. SNTSMS 103. Cambridge: Cambridge University, 1999.

Robinson, Donald W. B. "'Faith of Jesus Christ'—a New Testament Debate." *RTR* 29 (1970): 71–81.

—. "Not Boasting over the Natural Branches: Gentile Circumspection in the Divine Economy." Pages 161–73 in *The Gospel to the Nations: Perspectives on Paul's Mission*. Edited by Peter G. Bolt and Mark Thompson. Leicester: Apollos; Downers Grove: InterVarsity, 2000.

—. "The Priesthood of Paul in the Gospel of Hope." Pages 231–45 in *Reconciliation and Hope. New Testament Essays on Atonement and Eschatology Presented to L. L. Morris on His 60th Birthday*. Edited by Robert J. Banks. Exeter: Paternoster; Grand Rapids: Eerdmans, 1974.

—. "The Salvation of Israel in Romans 9–11," Pages 47–63 in *Donald Robinson Selected Works*. Volume 1: *Assembling God's People*. Edited by Peter G. Bolt and Mark D. Thompson. Sydney: Australian Church Record/Moore College, 2008. Originally published in *RTR* 26 1967: 81–96.

—. "Towards a Definition of Baptism." *RTR* 34 (1975): 1–15.

Rosner, Brian S. *Paul and the Law: Keeping the Commandments of God*. NSBT 31. Nottingham: Apollos; Downers Grove: InterVarsity, 2013.

Runge, Steven E. *Discourse Grammar of the Greek New Testament: A Practical Introduction for Teaching and Exegesis*. Peabody: Hendrickson, 2010.

Sanders, Ed P. *Paul and Palestinian Judaism: A Comparison of Patterns of Religion*. Philadelphia: Fortress, 1977.

—. *Paul, the Law, and the Jewish People*. Philadelphia: Fortress, 1983.

Sandnes, Karl O. *Paul—One of the Prophets? A Contribution to the Apostle's Self-Understanding*. WUNT 2/43. Tübingen: Mohr, 1991.

Schreiner, Thomas R. "Does Romans 9 Teach Individual Election unto Salvation? Some Exegetical and Theological Reflections." *JETS* 36 (1993): 25–40.

——. "Israel's Failure to Attain Righteousness in Romans 9:30–10:3." *TJ* 12 (1991): 209–20.

——. *The Law and Its Fulfillment: A Pauline Theology of Law*. Grand Rapids: Baker, 1993.

Scott, James M. *Adoption as Sons of God: An Exegetical Investigation into the Background of* Υἱοθεσία *in the Pauline Corpus*. WUNT 2/48. Tübingen: Mohr, 1992.

Seifrid, Mark A. *Christ Our Righteousness: Paul's Theology of Justification*. NSBT 9. Downers Grove: InterVarsity. Leicester: Apollos, 2000.

——. *Justification by Faith: The Origin and Development of a Central Pauline Theme*. NovTSup 68. Leiden: Brill, 1992.

——. "Paul's Use of Righteousness Language against Its Hellenistic Background." Pages 39–74 in *Justification and Variegated Nomism, Volume 2: The Paradoxes of Paul.* Edited by Donald A. Carson, Peter T. O'Brien, and Mark A. Seifrid. WUNT 2.181. Mohr Siebeck: Tübingen. Grand Rapids: Baker, 2004.

——. "Righteousness Language in the Hebrew Scriptures and Early Judaism." Pages 415–42 in *Justification and Variegated Nomism,* Volume 1: *The Complexities of Second Temple Judaism.* Edited by Donald A. Carson, Peter T. O'Brien, and Mark A. Seifrid. WUNT 2.140. Mohr Siebeck: Tübingen. Grand Rapids: Baker, 2001.

——. "The Subject of Romans 7:14–25," *NovT* 34 (1992): 313–33.

——. "Unrighteous by Faith: Apostolic Proclamation in Romans 1:18–3:20." Pages 105–45 in *Justification and Variegated Nomism,* Volume 2: *The Paradoxes of Paul.* Edited by Donald A. Carson, Peter T. O'Brien, and Mark A. Seifrid. WUNT 2.181. Mohr Siebeck: Tübingen. Grand Rapids: Baker, 2004.

Soderlund, Sven K., and N. T. Wright, eds. *Romans and the People of God: Essays in Honor of Gordon D. Fee on the Occasion of His 65th Birthday.* Grand Rapids/Cambridge: Eerdmans, 1999.

Stanley, Christopher D. *Paul and the Language of Scripture: Citation Technique in the Pauline Epistles and Contemporary Literature*. SNTSMS 74. Cambridge: Cambridge University, 1992.

Stowers, Stanley K. *The Diatribe and Paul's Letter to the Romans*. SBLDS 57. Chico: Scholars Press, 1981.

——. "Paul's Dialogue with a Fellow Jew in Romans 2:1–9." *CBQ* 46 (1984): 707–22.

——. *A Rereading of Romans: Justice, Jews and Gentiles*. New Haven: Yale University, 1994.

——. "Romans 7.7–25 as Speech in Character (προσωποπεία)." Pages 180–202 in Troels Engberg-Pedersen, *Paul in His Hellenistic Context*. Minneapolis: Fortress, 1995.

Sumney, Jerry L., ed. *Reading Paul's Letter to the Romans*. SBL Resources for Biblical Study 73. Atlanta: SBL, 2012.

Tajra, Harry W. *The Martyrdom of St. Paul: Historical and Judicial Contexts, Traditions and Legends*. WUNT 2.67. Tübingen: Mohr, 1994.

Tate, Marvin E. *Psalms 51–100*. WBC 20 Dallas: Word, 1990.

Theissen, Gerd. *Psychological Aspects of Pauline Theology*. Translated by J. P. Galvin. Philadelphia: Fortress, 1987.

——. *The Social Setting of Pauline Christianity: Essays on Corinth*. Translated by J. H. Schültz. Philadelphia: Fortress, 1982.

Thiselton, Anthony C. *The First Epistle to the Corinthians: A Commentary on the Greek Text*. NIGTC. Grand Rapids: Eerdmans; Carlisle: Paternoster, 2000.

Thompson, Michael. *Clothed with Christ: The Example and Teaching of Jesus in Romans 12:1–15:13*. JSNTSup 59. Sheffield: Sheffield Academic, 1991.

Thompson, Richard W. "The Alleged Rabbinic Background of Rom 3:31." *ETL* 63 (1987): 136–48.

Timmins, Will N. *Romans 7 and Christian Identity: A Study of the 'I' in Its Literary Context.* SNTSMS 168 Cambridge: Cambridge University Press, 2017.

——. "Romans 7 and Speech-in-Character: A Critical Evaluation of Stowers' Hypothesis," ZNW 107 (2016): 94–115.

Tobin, Thomas H. "The Jewish Context of Rom 5:12–14." *Studia Philonica Annual* 13 (2001): 159–75.

——. *Paul's Rhetoric in Its Contexts: The Argument of Romans*. Peabody: Hendricksen, 2004.

VanDoodewaard, William. *The Quest for the Historical Adam: Genesis, Hermeneutics, and Human Origins*. Grand Rapids: RHB, 2015.

Wagner, J. Ross. *Heralds of the Good News: Paul and Isaiah "in Concert" in the Letter to the Romans*. NovTSup 101. Leiden: Brill, 2002.

Wallace, Daniel B. *Greek Grammar Beyond the Basics*. Grand Rapids: Zondervan, 1996.

Waters, Guy P. *Justification and the New Perspectives on Paul: A Review and Response*. Phillipsburg: P & R, 2004.

Watson, Francis "Two Roman Congregations." Pages 203–15 in Donfried, *The Romans Debate,* 1991.

Watson, Nigel M. "'And If Children, Then Heirs' (Rom 8:17)—Why Not Sons?" *ABR* 49 (2001): 53–56.

Wedderburn, Alexander J. M. *The Reasons for Romans*. Edinburgh: T&T Clark, 1988.

Wiefel, Wolfgang. "The Jewish Community in Ancient Rome and the Origins of Roman Christianity." Pages 85–101 in Donfried, *The Romans Debate* 1991.

Williams, Sam K. "Again Pistis Christou." *CBQ* 49 (1987): 431–47.

—. "The 'Righteousness of God' in Romans." *JBL* 99 (1980): 241–90.

Williamson, Paul R. *Sealed with an Oath: Covenant in God's Unfolding Purpose*. NSBT 23. Nottingham: Apollos; Downers Grove: InterVarsity, 2007.

Windsor, Lionel J. *Paul and the Vocation of Israel: How Paul's Jewish Identity Informs His Apostolic Ministry, with Special Reference to Romans*. BZNW 205. Berlin/Boston: de Gruyter, 2014.

Winninge, M. *Sinners and the Righteous: A Comparative Study of the Psalms of Solomon and Paul's Letters*. Stockholm: Almqvist & Wiksell, 1995.

Witherington, Ben, III. *The Acts of the Apostles: A Socio-Rhetorical Commentary*. Grand Rapids: Eerdmans. Carlisle: Paternoster, 1998.

Wright, N. T. *Justification: God's Plan and Vision*. London: SPCK, 2009.

—. "The Law in Romans 2." Pages 131–50 in *Paul and the Mosaic Law*. Edited by James D. G. Dunn. WUNT 89. Tübingen: Mohr, 1996; Grand Rapids: Eerdmans, 2000.

Zeisler, John A. *The Meaning of Righteousness in Paul: A Linguistic and Theological Investigation*. SNTSMS 20. Cambridge: Cambridge University Press, 1972.

Name Index

Subject Index

L

M

N

P

R

S

T

U

W

Scripture Index

1 Kings

2 Kings

1 Chronicles

2 Chronicles

Nehemiah

Esther

Job

Psalms

Romans

1 Corinthians

2 Corinthians

Galatians

1 Thessalonians

2 Thessalonians

1 Timothy

Extrabiblical Sources Index